T0355525

Rover 45 & MG ZS Series
Owners workshop Manual

Peter T. Gill

Models covered

(4384 - 400 - 2AM1)

Rover 45 and MG ZS Hatchback and Saloon models, including special/limited editions

Petrol engines: 1.4 litre (1396 cc), 1.6 litre (1588 cc), 1.8 litre (1796 cc), 2.0 litre (1997 cc) & 2.5 litre (2497 cc)
Turbo-diesel engines: 2.0 litre (1994 cc)

Does NOT cover 6-speed CVT automatic transmission fitted to 1.8 litre models

© Haynes Group Limited 2008

A book in the **Haynes Service and Repair Manual Series**

ISBN: **978 1 78521 487 5**

British Library Cataloguing in Publication Data
A catalogue record for this book is available from the British Library.

**Haynes Group Limited
Haynes North America, Inc**

www.haynes.com

Contents

LIVING WITH YOUR ROVER/MG

Safety first!	Page	0•5
Introduction	Page	0•6

Roadside Repairs

Introduction	Page	0•7
If your car won't start	Page	0•7
Jump starting	Page	0•8
Wheel changing	Page	0•9
Identifying leaks	Page	0•10
Towing	Page	0•10

Weekly Checks

Introduction	Page	0•11
Underbonnet check points	Page	0•11
Engine oil level	Page	0•12
Power steering fluid level	Page	0•12
Brake fluid level	Page	0•13
Coolant level	Page	0•13
Tyre condition and pressure	Page	0•14
Washer fluid level	Page	0•15
Wiper blades	Page	0•15
Battery	Page	0•16
Electrical systems	Page	0•17
Lubricants and fluids	Page	0•18
Tyre pressures	Page	0•18

MAINTENANCE

Routine Maintenance and Servicing

Petrol models	Page	1A•1
Maintenance specifications	Page	1A•2
Maintenance schedule	Page	1A•3
Maintenance procedures	Page	1A•6
Diesel models	Page	1B•1
Maintenance specifications	Page	1B•2
Maintenance schedule	Page	1B•3
Maintenance procedures	Page	1B•5

Contents

REPAIRS & OVERHAUL

Engine and Associated Systems

4-cylinder petrol engine in-car repair procedures	Page	2A•1
V6 petrol engine in-car repair procedures	Page	2B•1
Diesel engine in-car repair procedures	Page	2C•1
Petrol engine removal and overhaul procedures	Page	2D•1
Diesel engine removal and overhaul procedures	Page	2E•1
Cooling, heating and ventilation systems	Page	3•1
Fuel and exhaust systems – 4-cylinder petrol engines	Page	4A•1
Fuel and exhaust systems – V6 petrol engines	Page	4B•1
Fuel and exhaust systems – diesel engines	Page	4C•1
Emission control systems	Page	4D•1
Starting and charging systems	Page	5A•1
Ignition system – petrol engines	Page	5B•1
Preheating system – diesel engines	Page	5C•1

Transmission

Clutch	Page	6•1
Manual transmission	Page	7A•1
Automatic transmission	Page	7B•1
Driveshafts	Page	8•1

Brakes and Suspension

Braking system	Page	9•1
Suspension and steering	Page	10•1

Body Equipment

Bodywork and fittings	Page	11•1
Body electrical systems	Page	12•1

Wiring Diagrams

	Page	12•21

REFERENCE

Dimensions and weights	Page	REF•1
Conversion factors	Page	REF•2
Buying spare parts	Page	REF•3
Vehicle identification	Page	REF•4
General repair procedures	Page	REF•5
Jacking and vehicle support	Page	REF•6
Radio/cassette anti-theft system	Page	REF•7
Tools and working facilities	Page	REF•8
MOT test checks	Page	REF•10
Fault finding	Page	REF•14

Index

	Page	REF•27

Advanced driving

Many people see the words 'advanced driving' and believe that it won't interest them or that it is a style of driving beyond their own abilities. Nothing could be further from the truth. Advanced driving is straightforward safe, sensible driving - the sort of driving we should all do every time we get behind the wheel.

An average of 10 people are killed every day on UK roads and 870 more are injured, some seriously. Lives are ruined daily, usually because somebody did something stupid. Something like 95% of all accidents are due to human error, mostly driver failure. Sometimes we make genuine mistakes - everyone does. Sometimes we have lapses of concentration. Sometimes we deliberately take risks.

For many people, the process of 'learning to drive' doesn't go much further than learning how to pass the driving test because of a common belief that good drivers are made by 'experience'.

Learning to drive by 'experience' teaches three driving skills:

- ☐ Quick reactions. (Whoops, that was close!)
- ☐ Good handling skills. (Horn, swerve, brake, horn).
- ☐ Reliance on vehicle technology. (Great stuff this ABS, stop in no distance even in the wet...)

Drivers whose skills are 'experience based' generally have a lot of near misses and the odd accident. The results can be seen every day in our courts and our hospital casualty departments.

Advanced drivers have learnt to control the risks by controlling the position and speed of their vehicle. They avoid accidents and near misses, even if the drivers around them make mistakes.

The key skills of advanced driving are **concentration,** effective all-round **observation, anticipation** and **planning.** When **good vehicle handling** is added to these skills, all driving situations can be approached and negotiated in a safe, methodical way, leaving nothing to chance.

Concentration means applying your mind to safe driving, completely excluding anything that's not relevant. Driving is usually the most dangerous activity that most of us undertake in our daily routines. It deserves our full attention.

Observation means not just looking, but seeing and seeking out the information found in the driving environment.

Anticipation means asking yourself what is happening, what you can reasonably expect to happen and what could happen unexpectedly. (One of the commonest words used in compiling accident reports is 'suddenly'.)

Planning is the link between seeing something and taking the appropriate action. For many drivers, planning is the missing link.

If you want to become a safer and more skilful driver and you want to enjoy your driving more, contact the Institute of Advanced Motorists at www.iam.org.uk, phone 0208 996 9600, or write to IAM House, 510 Chiswick High Road, London W4 5RG for an information pack.

Working on your car can be dangerous. This page shows just some of the potential risks and hazards, with the aim of creating a safety-conscious attitude.

General hazards

Scalding

• Don't remove the radiator or expansion tank cap while the engine is hot.
• Engine oil, automatic transmission fluid or power steering fluid may also be dangerously hot if the engine has recently been running.

Burning

• Beware of burns from the exhaust system and from any part of the engine. Brake discs and drums can also be extremely hot immediately after use.

Crushing

• When working under or near a raised vehicle, always supplement the jack with axle stands, or use drive-on ramps. *Never venture under a car which is only supported by a jack.*
• Take care if loosening or tightening high-torque nuts when the vehicle is on stands. Initial loosening and final tightening should be done with the wheels on the ground.

Fire

• Fuel is highly flammable; fuel vapour is explosive.
• Don't let fuel spill onto a hot engine.
• Do not smoke or allow naked lights (including pilot lights) anywhere near a vehicle being worked on. Also beware of creating sparks (electrically or by use of tools).
• Fuel vapour is heavier than air, so don't work on the fuel system with the vehicle over an inspection pit.
• Another cause of fire is an electrical overload or short-circuit. Take care when repairing or modifying the vehicle wiring.
• Keep a fire extinguisher handy, of a type suitable for use on fuel and electrical fires.

Electric shock

• Ignition HT voltage can be dangerous, especially to people with heart problems or a pacemaker. Don't work on or near the ignition system with the engine running or the ignition switched on.

• Mains voltage is also dangerous. Make sure that any mains-operated equipment is correctly earthed. Mains power points should be protected by a residual current device (RCD) circuit breaker.

Fume or gas intoxication

• Exhaust fumes are poisonous; they often contain carbon monoxide, which is rapidly fatal if inhaled. Never run the engine in a confined space such as a garage with the doors shut.
• Fuel vapour is also poisonous, as are the vapours from some cleaning solvents and paint thinners.

Poisonous or irritant substances

• Avoid skin contact with battery acid and with any fuel, fluid or lubricant, especially antifreeze, brake hydraulic fluid and Diesel fuel. Don't syphon them by mouth. If such a substance is swallowed or gets into the eyes, seek medical advice.
• Prolonged contact with used engine oil can cause skin cancer. Wear gloves or use a barrier cream if necessary. Change out of oil-soaked clothes and do not keep oily rags in your pocket.
• Air conditioning refrigerant forms a poisonous gas if exposed to a naked flame (including a cigarette). It can also cause skin burns on contact.

Asbestos

• Asbestos dust can cause cancer if inhaled or swallowed. Asbestos may be found in gaskets and in brake and clutch linings. When dealing with such components it is safest to assume that they contain asbestos.

Special hazards

Hydrofluoric acid

• This extremely corrosive acid is formed when certain types of synthetic rubber, found in some O-rings, oil seals, fuel hoses etc, are exposed to temperatures above 400°C. The rubber changes into a charred or sticky substance containing the acid. *Once formed, the acid remains dangerous for years. If it gets onto the skin, it may be necessary to amputate the limb concerned.*
• When dealing with a vehicle which has suffered a fire, or with components salvaged from such a vehicle, wear protective gloves and discard them after use.

The battery

• Batteries contain sulphuric acid, which attacks clothing, eyes and skin. Take care when topping-up or carrying the battery.
• The hydrogen gas given off by the battery is highly explosive. Never cause a spark or allow a naked light nearby. Be careful when connecting and disconnecting battery chargers or jump leads.

Air bags

• Air bags can cause injury if they go off accidentally. Take care when removing the steering wheel and/or facia. Special storage instructions may apply.

Diesel injection equipment

• Diesel injection pumps supply fuel at very high pressure. Take care when working on the fuel injectors and fuel pipes.

⚠️ *Warning: Never expose the hands, face or any other part of the body to injector spray; the fuel can penetrate the skin with potentially fatal results.*

Remember...

DO

• Do use eye protection when using power tools, and when working under the vehicle.

• Do wear gloves or use barrier cream to protect your hands when necessary.

• Do get someone to check periodically that all is well when working alone on the vehicle.

• Do keep loose clothing and long hair well out of the way of moving mechanical parts.

• Do remove rings, wristwatch etc, before working on the vehicle – especially the electrical system.

• Do ensure that any lifting or jacking equipment has a safe working load rating adequate for the job.

DON'T

• Don't attempt to lift a heavy component which may be beyond your capability – get assistance.

• Don't rush to finish a job, or take unverified short cuts.

• Don't use ill-fitting tools which may slip and cause injury.

• Don't leave tools or parts lying around where someone can trip over them. Mop up oil and fuel spills at once.

• Don't allow children or pets to play in or near a vehicle being worked on.

MG ZS Saloon

Launched in November 1999, the Rover 45 and MG ZS models covered by this manual are a further development based on the Rover 400 four- and five-door Saloon and Hatchback series.

The engine/transmission unit is mounted trans-versely across the front of the car. It is available with a 1.4, 1.6 and 1.8 litre 4-cylinder petrol engines, 2.0 and 2.5 litre V6 petrol engines and also 2.0 litre turbo-diesel engines.

Petrol engine operation, including fuelling and ignition, is electronically controlled by a Modular Engine Management System (MEMS) version 3 on 4-cylinder engines and a Siemens EMS2000 on V6 engines. Engine emissions are controlled by a comprehensive range of features, including: an exhaust gas catalytic converter with oxygen sensors, crankcase gas recirculation, and fuel evaporation control.

Diesel engine operation, including fuel injection timing and quantity, is controlled by an Electronic Diesel Control (EDC) system. The high pressure rotary fuel injection pump is electronically controlled by the EDC, and has no mechanical connection to the throttle pedal. Engine emissions are controlled by a comprehensive range of features, including: an exhaust gas catalytic converter, crankcase gas recirculation, and exhaust gas recirculation (EGR).

The transmission and differential are an integral unit in a common housing attached to the left-hand side of the engine. Drive from the differential to the front wheels is via unequal-length solid driveshafts, with constant velocity joints and dynamic dampers.

Your Rover Manual

The aim of this manual is to help you get the best value from your vehicle. It can do so in several ways. It can help you decide what work must be done (even should you choose to get it done by a garage), provide information on routine maintenance and servicing, and give a logical course of action and diagnosis when random faults occur. However, it is hoped that you will use the manual by tackling the work yourself. On simpler jobs, it may even be quicker than booking the car into a garage and going there twice, to leave and collect it. Perhaps most important, a lot of money can be saved by avoiding the costs a garage must charge to cover its labour and overheads.

References to the 'left' or 'right' of the vehicle are in the sense of a person in the driver's seat facing forward.

Acknowledgements

Thanks are due to Draper Tools Limited, who supplied some of the workshop tools, and to all those people at Sparkford who helped in the production of this Manual.

We take great pride in the accuracy of information given in this manual, but vehicle manufacturers make alterations and design changes during the production run of a particular vehicle of which they do not inform us. No liability can be accepted by the authors or publishers for loss, damage or injury caused by any errors in, or omissions from the information given.

Project vehicles

The main vehicle used in the preparation of this manual, and which appears in many of the photographic sequences, was a Rover 45, 5-door Hatchback. Also used was the MG ZS 180 4-door Saloon, which has the 2.5 litre V6 engine fitted.

Rover 45 Saloon

The following pages are intended to help in dealing with common roadside emergencies and breakdowns. You will find more detailed fault finding information at the back of the manual, and repair information in the main chapters.

If your car won't start and the starter motor doesn't turn

☐ If it's a model with automatic transmission, make sure the selector is in P or N.
☐ Open the bonnet and make sure that the battery terminals are clean and tight.
☐ Switch on the headlights and try to start the engine. If the headlights go very dim when you're trying to start, the battery is probably flat. Get out of trouble by jump starting (see next page) using a friend's car.

If your car won't start even though the starter motor turns as normal

☐ Is there fuel in the tank?
☐ Has the engine immobiliser been deactivated?
☐ Is there moisture on electrical components under the bonnet? Switch off the ignition, then wipe off any obvious dampness with a dry cloth. Spray a water-repellent aerosol product (WD-40 or equivalent) on ignition and fuel system electrical connectors like those shown in the photos. (Note that diesel engines don't usually suffer from damp).

A A poor earth connection can cause intermittent faults in more than one circuit.

B Check the security and condition of the battery connections.

C Visually check engine harness connections/multiplugs, including the alternator connectors.

D Check the main fuse links, fuse and relays in the engine compartment fusebox.

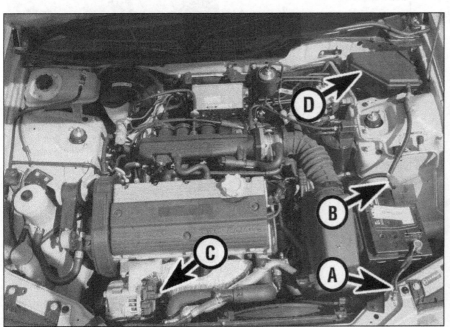

Check that electrical connections are secure (with the ignition switched off) and spray them with a water-dispersant spray like WD-40 if you suspect a problem due to damp

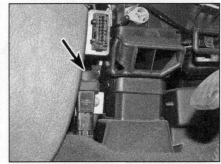

E If the automatic fuel cut-off switch has been triggered, reset it by pressing the rubber disc on top of the switch. Located inside the vehicle, to the left of the clutch pedal.

Jump starting

When jump-starting a car using a booster battery, observe the following precautions:

✔ Before connecting the booster battery, make sure that the ignition is switched off.

✔ Ensure that all electrical equipment (lights, heater, wipers, etc) is switched off.

✔ Take note of any special precautions printed on the battery case.

✔ Make sure that the booster battery is the same voltage as the discharged one in the vehicle.

✔ If the battery is being jump-started from the battery in another vehicle, the two vehicles MUST NOT TOUCH each other.

✔ Make sure that the transmission is in neutral (or PARK, in the case of automatic transmission).

 HAYNES HINT *Jump starting will get you out of trouble, but you must correct whatever made the battery go flat in the first place. There are three possibilities:*

1 *The battery has been drained by repeated attempts to start, or by leaving the lights on.*

2 *The charging system is not working properly (alternator drivebelt slack or broken, alternator wiring fault or alternator itself faulty).*

3 *The battery itself is at fault (electrolyte low, or battery worn out).*

1 Connect one end of the red jump lead to the positive (+) terminal of the flat battery

2 Connect the other end of the red lead to the positive (+) terminal of the booster battery.

3 Connect one end of the black jump lead to the negative (-) terminal of the booster battery

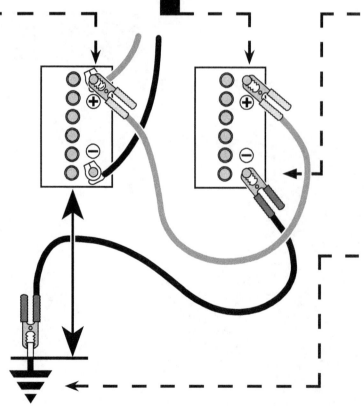

4 Connect the other end of the black jump lead to a bolt or bracket on the engine block, well away from the battery, on the vehicle to be started.

5 Make sure that the jump leads will not come into contact with the fan, drive-belts or other moving parts of the engine.

6 Start the engine using the booster battery and run it at idle speed. Switch on the lights, rear window demister and heater blower motor, then disconnect the jump leads in the reverse order of connection. Turn off the lights etc.

Wheel changing

 Warning: Do not change a wheel in a situation where you risk being hit by other traffic. On busy roads, try to stop in a lay-by or a gateway. Be wary of passing traffic while changing the wheel – it is easy to become distracted by the job in hand.

Some of the details shown here will vary according to model. For instance, the location of the spare wheel and jack may not be the same on all cars. However, the basic principles apply to all vehicles.

Preparation

- [ ] When a puncture occurs, stop as soon as it is safe to do so.
- [ ] Park on firm level ground, if possible, and well out of the way of other traffic.
- [ ] Use hazard warning lights if necessary.

- [ ] If you have one, use a warning triangle to alert other drivers of your presence.
- [ ] Apply the handbrake and engage first or reverse gear (or Park on models with automatic transmission).

- [ ] Chock the wheel diagonally opposite the one being removed – a couple of large stones will do for this.
- [ ] If the ground is soft, use a flat piece of wood to spread the load under the jack.

Changing the wheel

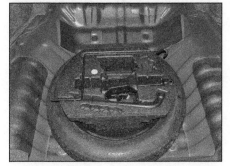

1 Lift up the floor carpet in the boot space and remove the wheel changing toolkit from inside the spare wheel. Unscrew the spare wheel retaining cap.

2 On steel wheels, use the end of the wheel brace to lever off the wheel trim. On alloy wheels, remove the locking wheel nut cover with the special tool provided.

3 Slacken each of the wheel nuts by half a turn, using the special adaptor on the locking wheel nut.

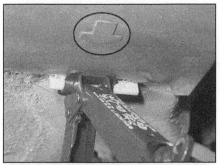

4 Locate the jack head under the correct jacking point – this is the area between the two protrusions on the sill. This may be indicated by an arrow pressed in the sill.

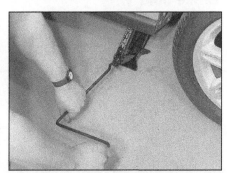

5 Turn the jack handle until the wheel is clear of the ground. If the tyre is flat make sure that the vehicle is raised sufficiently to allow the spare wheel to be fitted.

6 Remove the flat wheel and slide it under the sill near the jack; this is a safety measure in case the jack collapses.

Finally . . .

- [ ] Remove the wheel chocks.
- [ ] Stow the jack and tools in the correct location.
- [ ] Some spare wheels are for temporary use only, if so, drive with extra care, especially when cornering – limit yourself to a maximum of 50 mph, and to the shortest possible journeys, while it is fitted.
- [ ] Check the tyre pressure on the wheel just fitted. If it is low, or if you don't have a pressure gauge with you, drive slowly to the nearest garage and inflate the tyre to the correct pressure.
- [ ] Have the damaged tyre or wheel repaired as soon as possible, or another puncture will leave you stranded.

7 Fit the spare wheel into position and tighten the nuts moderately with the wheelbrace.

8 Lower the car to the ground and tighten the wheel nuts in a diagonal sequence. Where applicable refit the wheel trim.

Identifying leaks

Puddles on the garage floor or drive, or obvious wetness under the bonnet or underneath the car, suggest a leak that needs investigating. It can sometimes be difficult to decide where the leak is coming from, especially if the engine bay is very dirty already. Leaking oil or fluid can also be blown rearwards by the passage of air under the car, giving a false impression of where the problem lies.

 Warning: Most automotive oils and fluids are poisonous. Wash them off skin, and change out of contaminated clothing, without delay.

 The smell of a fluid leaking from the car may provide a clue to what's leaking. Some fluids are distinctively coloured. It may help to clean the car carefully and to park it over some clean paper overnight as an aid to locating the source of the leak. Remember that some leaks may only occur while the engine is running.

Sump oil

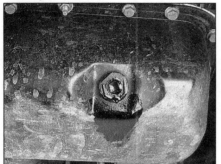

Engine oil may leak from the drain plug...

Oil from filter

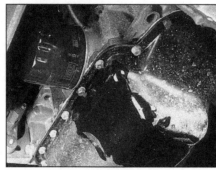

...or from the base of the oil filter.

Gearbox oil

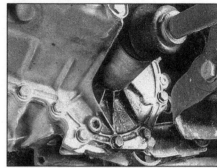

Gearbox oil can leak from the seals at the inboard ends of the driveshafts.

Antifreeze

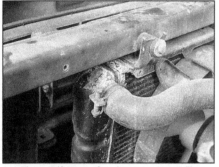

Leaking antifreeze often leaves a crystalline deposit like this.

Brake fluid

A leak occurring at a wheel is almost certainly brake fluid.

Power steering fluid

Power steering fluid may leak from the pipe connectors on the steering rack.

Towing

☐ The Rover 45/MG ZS is not fitted with towing eyelets. The lashing eyelets fitted to the front and rear of the car are intended for use by emergency services during vehicle recovery and should not be used for any other purpose.

Introduction

There are some very simple checks which need only take a few minutes to carry out, but which could save you a lot of inconvenience and expense.

These *Weekly checks* require no great skill or special tools, and the small amount of time they take to perform could prove to be very well spent, for example:

☐ Keeping an eye on tyre condition and pressures, will not only help to stop them wearing out prematurely, but could also save your life.

☐ Many breakdowns are caused by electrical problems. Battery-related faults are particularly common, and a quick check on a regular basis will often prevent the majority of these.

☐ If your car develops a brake fluid leak, the first time you might know about it is when your brakes don't work properly. Checking the level regularly will give advance warning of this kind of problem.

☐ If the oil or coolant levels run low, the cost of repairing any engine damage will be far greater than fixing the leak, for example.

Underbonnet check points

◀ 4-cylinder petrol engine

A *Engine oil level dipstick*

B *Engine oil filler cap*

C *Coolant expansion tank*

D *Brake fluid reservoir*

E *Windscreen washer fluid reservoir filler cap*

F *Battery*

G *Power steering fluid reservoir*

◀ Diesel engine

A *Engine oil level dipstick*

B *Engine oil filler cap*

C *Coolant expansion tank*

D *Brake fluid reservoir*

E *Windscreen washer fluid reservoir filler cap*

F *Battery*

G *Power steering fluid reservoir*

Engine oil level

Before you start

✔ Make sure that the car is on level ground.
✔ Check the oil level before the car is driven, or at least 5 minutes after the engine has been switched off.

 HAYNES HiNT *If the oil is checked immediately after driving the vehicle, some of the oil will remain in the upper engine components, resulting in an inaccurate reading on the dipstick.*

The correct oil

Modern engines place great demands on their oil. It is very important that the correct oil for your car is used (see *Lubricants and fluids*).

Car care

● If you have to add oil frequently, you should check whether you have any oil leaks. Place some clean paper under the car overnight, and check for stains in the morning. If there are no leaks, then the engine may be burning oil.
● Always maintain the level between the upper and lower dipstick marks (see photo 3). If the level is too low, severe engine damage may occur. Oil seal failure may result if the engine is overfilled by adding too much oil.

1 The dipstick is located at the right-hand end of the engine, at the rear of the engine on 4-cylinder petrol models, and at the front of the engine on 6-cylinder petrol and diesel models (see *Underbonnet check points*). Withdraw the dipstick.

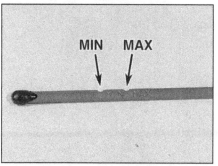

3 Note the oil level on the end of the dipstick, which should be between the upper MAX mark and the lower MIN mark (on some models, the dipstick has HI and LO markings). Approximately 1.0 litre of oil will raise the level from the lower mark to the upper mark.

2 Using a clean rag or paper towel, wipe all the oil from the dipstick. Insert the clean dipstick into the tube as far as it will go, then withdraw it again.

4 Oil is added through the filler cap. Rotate the cap through a quarter-turn anti-clockwise and withdraw it. Top-up the level. A funnel may help to reduce spillage. Add the oil slowly, checking the level on the dipstick often. Do not overfill.

Power steering fluid level

Before you start

✔ Park the vehicle on level ground.
✔ Set the front roadwheels in the straight-ahead position.
✔ The engine should be turned off and the system cold.

✔ Do not operate the steering once the engine is stopped.

Safety first!

● If the reservoir requires repeated topping-up, there is a fluid leak somewhere in the system which should be investigated immediately.
● If a leak is suspected, the car should not be driven until the power steering system has been checked.

1 The power steering fluid reservoir is located on the right-hand side of the engine compartment. UPPER and LOWER level marks are indicated on the side of the reservoir and the fluid level should be maintained between these marks at all times.

2 If topping-up is necessary, first wipe the area around the filler cap with a clean rag before removing the cap.

3 When adding fluid, pour it carefully into the reservoir to avoid spillage – be sure to use only the specified fluid. After filling the reservoir to the correct level, make sure that the cap is refitted securely to avoid leaks and the entry of foreign matter into the reservoir.

Brake fluid level

 Warning: Brake fluid can harm your eyes and damage painted surfaces, so use extreme caution when handling and pouring it. Do not use fluid which has been standing open for some time, as it absorbs moisture from the air, which can cause a dangerous loss of braking effectiveness.

Before you start

✔ Make sure that your car is on level ground.

✔ Cleanliness is of great importance when dealing with the braking system, so take care to clean around the reservoir cap before topping-up. Use only clean brake fluid from a container which has stood for at least 24 hours (to allow air bubbles to separate out).

Safety first!

● If the reservoir requires repeated topping-up, this is an indication of a fluid leak somewhere in the system, which should be investigated immediately.

● If a leak is suspected, the car should not be driven until the braking system has been checked. Never take any risks where brakes are concerned.

 The fluid level in the reservoir will drop slightly as the brake pads wear down, but the fluid level must never be allowed to drop below the MIN mark.

1 The brake master cylinder and fluid reservoir is located at the rear right-hand end of the engine compartment. The MAX and MIN level marks are indicated on the side of the reservoir and the fluid level should be maintained between these marks at all times.

2 If topping-up is necessary, wipe the area around the filler cap with a clean rag before removing the cap. Before topping-up, it is a good idea to inspect the reservoir. The system should be drained and refilled (see Chapter 9) if deposits, dirt particles or contamination are seen in the fluid. Pour fluid carefully into the reservoir to avoid spilling it on surrounding painted surfaces.

3 Be sure to use only the specified brake fluid since mixing different types of fluid can cause damage to the system and/or a loss of braking effectiveness. After filling the reservoir to the correct level, make sure that the cap is refitted securely to avoid leaks and the entry of foreign matter. Wipe off any spilt fluid.

Coolant level

 Warning: DO NOT attempt to remove the expansion tank pressure cap when the engine is hot, as there is a very great risk of scalding. Do not leave open containers of coolant about, as it is poisonous.

Car Care

● With a sealed-type cooling system, adding coolant should not be necessary on a regular basis. If frequent topping-up is required, it is likely there is a leak. Check the radiator, all hoses and joint faces for signs of staining or wetness, and rectify as necessary.

● It is important that antifreeze is used in the cooling system all year round, not just during the winter months. Don't top up with water alone, as the antifreeze will become diluted.

1 The coolant level varies with the temperature of the engine. When the engine is cold, the coolant level should be on the MAX marking on the side of the reservoir. When the engine is hot, the level may rise slightly.

2 If topping-up is necessary, wait until the engine is cold, then cover the expansion tank cap with a rag and unscrew the filler cap anti-clockwise. Wait until the hissing ceases, indicating that all pressure is released, then unscrew and remove the filler cap.

3 Add coolant (a mixture of water and antifreeze) through the expansion tank filler neck, until the coolant is up to the MAX level. Refit the cap; turning it clockwise as far as it will go until it is secure.

Tyre condition and pressure

It is very important that tyres are in good condition, and at the correct pressure - having a tyre failure at any speed is highly dangerous. Tyre wear is influenced by driving style - harsh braking and acceleration, or fast cornering, will all produce more rapid tyre wear. As a general rule, the front tyres wear out faster than the rears. Interchanging the tyres from front to rear ("rotating" the tyres) may result in more even wear. However, if this is completely effective, you may have the expense of replacing all four tyres at once! Remove any nails or stones embedded in the tread before they penetrate the tyre to cause deflation. If removal of a nail does reveal that the tyre has been punctured, refit the nail so that its point of penetration is marked. Then immediately change the wheel, and have the tyre repaired by a tyre dealer.

Regularly check the tyres for damage in the form of cuts or bulges, especially in the sidewalls. Periodically remove the wheels, and clean any dirt or mud from the inside and outside surfaces. Examine the wheel rims for signs of rusting, corrosion or other damage. Light alloy wheels are easily damaged by "kerbing" whilst parking; steel wheels may also become dented or buckled. A new wheel is very often the only way to overcome severe damage.

New tyres should be balanced when they are fitted, but it may become necessary to re-balance them as they wear, or if the balance weights fitted to the wheel rim should fall off. Unbalanced tyres will wear more quickly, as will the steering and suspension components. Wheel imbalance is normally signified by vibration, particularly at a certain speed (typically around 50 mph). If this vibration is felt only through the steering, then it is likely that just the front wheels need balancing. If, however, the vibration is felt through the whole car, the rear wheels could be out of balance. Wheel balancing should be carried out by a tyre dealer or garage.

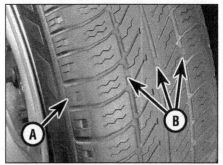

1 Tread Depth - visual check
The original tyres have tread wear safety bands (B), which will appear when the tread depth reaches approximately 1.6 mm. The band positions are indicated by a triangular mark on the tyre sidewall (A).

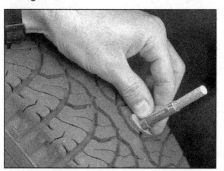

2 Tread Depth - manual check
Alternatively, tread wear can be monitored with a simple, inexpensive device known as a tread depth indicator gauge.

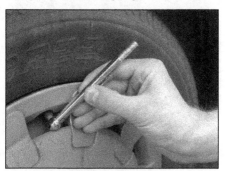

3 Tyre Pressure Check
Check the tyre pressures regularly with the tyres cold. Do not adjust the tyre pressures immediately after the vehicle has been used, or an inaccurate setting will result.

Tyre tread wear patterns

Shoulder Wear

Underinflation (wear on both sides)
Under-inflation will cause overheating of the tyre, because the tyre will flex too much, and the tread will not sit correctly on the road surface. This will cause a loss of grip and excessive wear, not to mention the danger of sudden tyre failure due to heat build-up.
Check and adjust pressures
Incorrect wheel camber (wear on one side)
Repair or renew suspension parts
Hard cornering
Reduce speed!

Centre Wear

Overinflation
Over-inflation will cause rapid wear of the centre part of the tyre tread, coupled with reduced grip, harsher ride, and the danger of shock damage occurring in the tyre casing.
Check and adjust pressures

If you sometimes have to inflate your car's tyres to the higher pressures specified for maximum load or sustained high speed, don't forget to reduce the pressures to normal afterwards.

Uneven Wear

Front tyres may wear unevenly as a result of wheel misalignment. Most tyre dealers and garages can check and adjust the wheel alignment (or "tracking") for a modest charge.
Incorrect camber or castor
Repair or renew suspension parts
Malfunctioning suspension
Repair or renew suspension parts
Unbalanced wheel
Balance tyres
Incorrect toe setting
Adjust front wheel alignment
Note: *The feathered edge of the tread which typifies toe wear is best checked by feel.*

Washer fluid level

● Screenwash additives not only keep the windscreen clean during bad weather, they also prevent the washer system freezing in cold weather – which is when you are likely to need it most. Don't top-up using plain water, as the screenwash will become diluted, and will freeze in cold weather.

● Check the operation of the windscreen and rear window washers. Adjust the nozzles using a pin if necessary, aiming the spray to a point slightly above the centre of the swept area.

 Warning: On no account use engine coolant antifreeze in the screen washer system – this may damage the paintwork.

1 The reservoir for the windscreen and (where applicable) rear window washer systems is located at the front right-hand side of the engine compartment.

2 When topping-up the reservoir, a screenwash additive should be added in the quantities recommended on the bottle.

Wiper blades

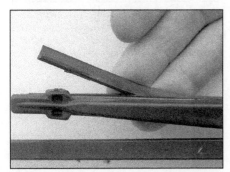

1 Check the condition of the wiper blades. If they are cracked or show any signs of deterioration, or if the glass swept area is smeared, renew them. For maximum clarity of vision, wiper blades should be renewed annually, as a matter of course.

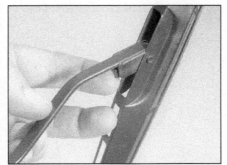

2 To remove a wiper blade, pull the arm fully away from the glass until it locks. Swivel the blade through 90°, press the locking tab with a finger nail and slide the blade out of the arm's hooked end. On refitting, ensure that the blade locks securely into the arm.

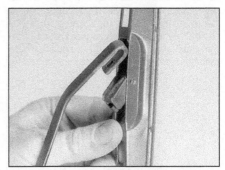

3 On Hatchback models, don't forget to check the tailgate wiper blade as well. Swivelling the blade through 90°, then depressing the retaining clips and sliding the blade from the arm will remove the blade.

Battery

Caution: Before carrying out any work on the vehicle battery, read the precautions given in 'Safety first!' at the start of this manual.

✔ Make sure that the battery tray is in good condition, and that the clamp is tight.

Corrosion on the tray, retaining clamp and the battery itself can be removed with a solution of water and baking soda. Thoroughly rinse all cleaned areas with water. Any metal parts damaged by corrosion should be covered with a zinc-based primer, then painted.

✔ Periodically (approximately every three months), check the charge condition of the battery as described in Chapter 5A.

✔ If the battery is flat, and you need to jump start your vehicle, see *Jump starting*.

1 The battery is located on the left-hand side front of the engine compartment. The exterior of the battery should be inspected periodically for damage such as a cracked case or cover.

2 Check the tightness of the battery cable clamps to ensure good electrical connections. You should not be able to move them. Also check each cable for cracks and frayed conductors.

3 If corrosion (white, fluffy deposits) is evident, remove the cables from the battery terminals, clean them with a small wire brush, then refit them. Automotive stores sell a tool for cleaning the battery post . . .

4 . . . as well as the battery cable clamps.

HAYNES
HINT

Battery corrosion can be kept to a minimum by applying a layer of petroleum jelly to the clamps and terminals after they are reconnected.

Electrical systems

✔ Check all external lights and the horn. Refer to the appropriate Sections of Chapter 12 for details if any of the circuits are found to be inoperative, and renew the fuse if necessary. Fit a new fuse of the same rating. If a second fuse blows, it is important that you find the reason – do not use a fuse with a higher rating.

✔ Visually check all accessible wiring connectors, harnesses and retaining clips for security, and for signs of chafing or damage.

HAYNES HiNT *If you need to check your brake lights and indicators unaided, back up to a wall or garage door and operate the lights. The reflected light should show if they are working properly.*

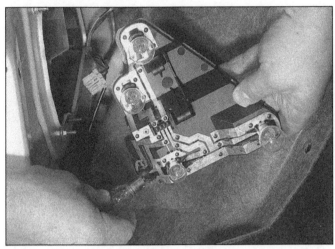

1 If a single indicator light, stop-light, sidelight or headlight has failed, it is likely that a bulb has blown, and will need to be renewed. Refer to Chapter 12 for details. If both stop-lights have failed, it is possible that the switch has failed (see Chapter 9).

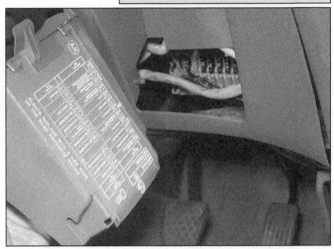

2 If more than one indicator or tail light has failed, it is likely that either a fuse has blown or that there is a fault in the circuit (see Chapter 12). The main fusebox is located behind the driver's storage compartment located in the facia beneath the steering wheel. Pull the compartment outwards away from the facia; the fusebox can be viewed behind the facia.

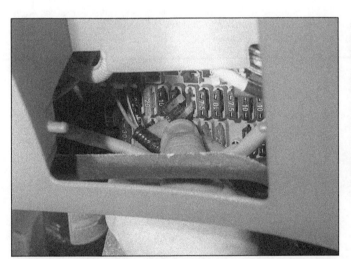

3 To renew a fuse, pull it out directly from the fusebox. Always fit a new fuse of the same rating, available from car accessory shops. It is important that you find the reason why the fuse failed – see *Electrical fault finding* in Chapter 12.

4 Additional fuses and relays are located in the fusebox at the left-hand side rear of the engine compartment.

Lubricants and fluids

Engine:

Petrol....................................	Multigrade engine oil, viscosity SAE 10W/40 to ACEA A2 or A3
Diesel	Multigrade engine oil, viscosity SAE 10W/40 to ACEA A3 and ACEA B3
Cooling system...................................	Havoline Antifreeze Coolant (Havoline AFC) mixed with the appropriate amount of water to protect the cooling system (mixture of 50% will provide protection to -48 degrees C). The antifreeze must be ethylene glycol based (no methanol or phosphate) with corrosion inhibitors, which meet the BS6580 and BS5117 specifications
Manual transmission:	
R65 transmission	Gear oil viscosity SAE 70W-80W. Esso BV, Shell SF5288, Mobil Mobilube 1 SHC or Unipart BV
PG1 transmission	Transmission is filled for life with Texaco MTF 94 (Unipart MTF 94). To refill or top-up use 10W/40 viscosity oil, Texaco MTF 94, Unipart MTF 94 or Caltex MTF 94
Automatic transmission...........................	Texaco N402 fluid or equivalent
Braking system...................................	AP New Premium Super DOT 4 or Castrol Universal DOT 4 fluid
Power steering system	Automatic transmission fluid (ATF) to Dexron II D or III specification
General greasing	Multi-purpose lithium-based grease to NLGI consistency No 2

Tyre pressures (cold)

Note: *This is a selection of typical tyre pressures – refer to your handbook, service station wallchart or dealer for greater detail. Pressures apply only to original equipment tyres and may vary if any other makes or type is fitted. Check with the tyre manufacturer or supplier for correct pressures if necessary. Pressures also vary for increased loads or towing – refer to your car's handbook or dealer.*

Petrol models	Bar	lbf/in^2
185/65 R14:		
Front & rear..	1.9	28
195/55 R15 (except 2.0 litre model):		
Front & rear..	2.1	30
195/55 R15 (2.0 litre model):		
Front	2.2	32
Rear..	2.1	30
205/45 R16:		
Front	2.3	33
Rear..	2.1	30
205/50 R16 and 205/45 R17 (except 2.5 litre model):		
Front & rear..	2.1	30
205/45 R17 (2.5 litre model):		
Front	2.3	33
Rear..	2.1	30
Spare (Space saver wheel with T125/80 R15 tyre fitted)*	4.2	61
Diesel models		
185/65 R14:		
Front & rear..	2.1	30
195/55 R15:		
Front	2.2	32
Rear..	2.1	30
205/45 R16, 205/50 R16 and 205/45 R17:		
Front	2.3	33
Rear..	2.1	30
Spare (Space saver wheel with T125/80 R15 tyre fitted)*	4.2	61

* Note: *The space saver spare wheel is for temporary use only and has a maximum road speed limit of 50 mph.*

Chapter 1 Part A:
Routine maintenance and servicing – petrol models

Contents

	Section number			Section number
Air cleaner filter element renewal	25		Introduction	1
Air conditioning system check	11		Lock and hinge lubrication	19
Alarm remote keypad battery renewal	6		Maintenance	2
Auxiliary drivebelt tension and condition check	12		Rear brake check	15
Bodywork corrosion check	5		Road test	23
Brake fluid renewal	24		Seat belt check	21
Camshaft timing belt renewal	29		Spark plug renewal	26
Coolant renewal	27		SRS system component check	22
Coolant specific gravity check	7		SRS system component renewal	31
Driveshaft and gaiter check	16		Suspension and steering check	17
Engine oil and filter renewal	3		Transmission oil/fluid level check	8
Exhaust system check	13		Transmission oil/fluid renewal	30
Front brake check	14		Underbonnet and underbody hose and pipe condition check	10
Fuel filter renewal	28		Vacuum hose condition check	9
Handbrake check and adjustment	18		Windscreen and number plate condition check	20
Heater/ventilation air intake filter renewal	4			

Degrees of difficulty

| Easy, suitable for novice with little experience | | Fairly easy, suitable for beginner with some experience | | Fairly difficult, suitable for competent DIY mechanic | | Difficult, suitable for experienced DIY mechanic | | Very difficult, suitable for expert DIY or professional | |

Lubricants and fluids................................ Refer to *Weekly Checks* on page 0•18

Capacities

Engine oil refill and filter change
K16 petrol engines .... 4.5 litres
KV6 petrol engines .... 5.2 litres
Cooling system.. 5.5 litres (from dry)

Manual transmission
R65 .... 2.0 litres (from dry)/1.8 litres (drain and refill)
PG1 .... 2.2 litres (from dry)/2.0 litres (drain and refill)

Automatic transmission................................ 4.0 litres (drain and refill)

Power steering reservoir .... 0.35 litres

Fuel tank .... 55 litres

Washer system reservoir .... 6.0 litres

Cooling system
Antifreeze mixture:
   50% antifreeze .... Protection down to – 48°C

Fuel system
Idle speed:
   4-cylinder engines .... 825 ± 50 rpm (controlled by ECM)
   6-cylinder engines .... 750 ± 50 rpm (controlled by ECM)
Idle mixture (CO content) – engine at operating temperature .... Less than 0.5 %
Recommended fuel .... Minimum octane rating of 95 RON (premium unleaded)

Ignition system
Firing order:
   4-cylinder engines .... 1-3-4-2 (No 1 cylinder at timing belt end of engine)
   6-cylinder engines .... 1-6-5-4-3-2 (No 1 cylinder at timing belt end of engine)
Crankshaft rotation....................................... Clockwise (viewed from timing belt end of engine)
Ignition timing... Controlled by engine management system – no adjustment possible
Spark plugs:

	Type	Electrode gap
All engines	Unipart GSP 66527	1.0 mm
	Unipart GSP 6662	1.0 mm

Braking system
Front and rear brake pad friction material minimum thickness .... 3.0 mm
Rear brake shoe friction material minimum thickness .... 2.0 mm
Handbrake lever travel .... 7 to 11 clicks

Tyre pressures .... Refer to the end of *Weekly checks* on page 0•18

Torque wrench settings

	Nm	lbf ft
Alternator-to-mounting bracket nuts/bolts:		
With air conditioning................................	25	18
Without air conditioning	45	33
Automatic transmission:		
Drain plug...	45	33
Level plug...	14	10
Auxiliary drivebelt tensioner bolt:		
M8..	25	18
M10...	45	33
Brake caliper bleed screws	10	7
Brake caliper guide pin bolts	27	20
Brake drum retaining screws	7	5
Engine oil drain plug:		
4-cylinder engines	28	21
6-cylinder engines	25	18
Fuel pipe-to-filter unions	30	22
Manual transmission filler/level plug:		
R65-type transmission	28	21
PG1-type transmission............................	40	30
Plug top coils to camshaft cover	9	7
Roadwheel nuts	110	81
Spark plug/coil cover to camshaft cover	9	7
Spark plugs		
4-cylinder engines	27	20
6- cylinder engines	25	18
Wheel cylinder bleed screws	7	5

The maintenance intervals in this manual are provided with the assumption that you will be carrying out the work yourself. These are based on the minimum maintenance intervals recommended by the manufacturer for vehicles driven daily. If you wish to keep your vehicle in peak condition at all times, you may wish to perform some of these procedures more often. We encourage frequent maintenance because it enhances the efficiency, performance and resale value of your vehicle.

If the vehicle is driven in dusty areas, used to tow a trailer, or driven frequently at slow speeds (idling in traffic) or on short journeys, more frequent maintenance intervals are recommended.

When the vehicle is new, it should be serviced by a factory-authorised dealer service department, in order to preserve the factory warranty.

Every 250 miles or weekly

☐ Refer to Weekly checks

Every 7500 miles or 6 months – whichever comes first

☐ Engine oil and filter – renew (Section 3)

Note: *Frequent oil and filter changes are good for the engine. We recommend renewing the oil and filter at these intervals, or at least twice a year.*

Every 12 000 miles or 12 months – whichever comes first

☐ Heater/ventilation air intake filter – renew (Section 4)

Every 15 000 miles or 12 months – whichever comes first

☐ Bodywork corrosion check (Section 5)
☐ Alarm remote keypad batteries – renew (Section 6)
☐ Coolant specific gravity – check (Section 7)
☐ Transmission – check oil/fluid level (Section 8)
☐ Vacuum hose – check condition (Section 9)
☐ Underbonnet and underbody hoses and pipes – check condition (Section 10)
☐ Air conditioning system check (Section 11)
☐ Auxiliary drivebelt – check condition and tension (Section 12)
☐ Exhaust system check (Section 13)
☐ Front brake check (Section 14)
☐ Rear brake check (Section 15)
☐ Driveshaft and gaiter check (Section 16)
☐ Suspension and steering check (Section 17)
☐ Handbrake check (Section 18)
☐ Lock and hinge lubrication (Section 19)
☐ Windscreen and number plate check (Section 20)
☐ Seat belt check (Section 21)
☐ SRS system component check (Section 22)
☐ Road test (Section 23)

Every 30 000 miles or 2 years – whichever comes first

☐ Brake fluid – renew (Section 24)

Every 45 000 miles or 3 years – whichever comes first

☐ Air filter element – renew (Section 25)

Every 60 000 miles or 4 years – whichever comes first

☐ Spark plugs – renew (Section 26)
☐ Coolant – renew (Section 27)
☐ Fuel filter – renew (Section 28)
☐ Camshaft drivebelt – renew (Section 29)*
☐ Transmission oil/fluid – renew (Section 30)

* Note: *Although the normal interval for the camshaft drivebelt renewal is 90 000 miles, it is strongly recommended that the drivebelt is changed at 60 000 miles on vehicles which are subjected to intensive use, ie, mainly short journeys or a lot of stop-start driving. The actual belt renewal interval is therefore very much up to the individual owner, but bear in mind that severe engine damage may result if the belt breaks.*

Every 15 years, regardless of mileage

☐ SRS components – renew (Section 31)

Underbonnet view of a 4-cylinder petrol engine model

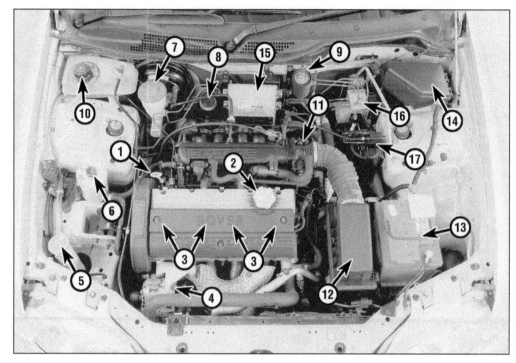

1 Engine oil dipstick
2 Engine oil filler cap
3 Spark plugs
4 Alternator
5 Washer fluid reservoir cap
6 Power steering fluid
   reservoir cap
7 Brake fluid reservoir/
   master cylinder
8 Clutch fluid reservoir/
   master cylinder
9 Fuel filter
10 Coolant expansion tank
11 Throttle body
12 Air filter housing
13 Battery
14 Engine compartment
   fusebox
15 Engine management ECU
16 ABS unit
17 Charcoal canister (fuel
   evaporative system)

Underbonnet view of a V6 petrol engine model

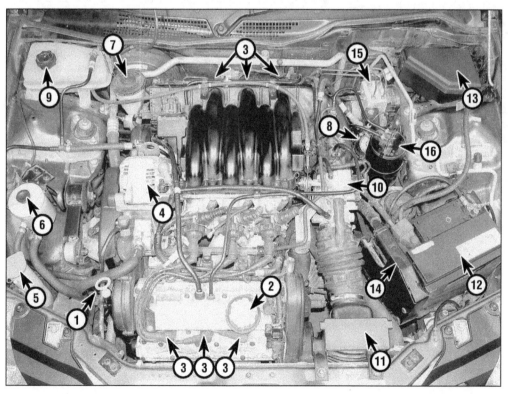

1 Engine oil dipstick
2 Engine oil filler cap
3 Spark plugs
4 Alternator
5 Washer fluid reservoir cap
6 Power steering fluid
   reservoir cap
7 Brake fluid reservoir/
   master cylinder
8 Fuel filter
9 Coolant expansion tank
10 Throttle body
11 Air filter housing
12 Battery
13 Engine compartment
   fusebox
14 Engine management ECU
15 ABS unit
16 Charcoal canister (fuel
   evaporative system)

Front underbody view of a V6 petrol engine model

1   Brake caliper
2   Anti-roll bar
3   Suspension lower arm
4   Track rod
5   Power steering rack
6   Manual transmission
7   Exhaust system front pipe
8   Gearchange rod
9   Oil cooler
10 Engine oil filter
11 Sump drain plug
12 Driveshaft
13 Engine lower steady bar

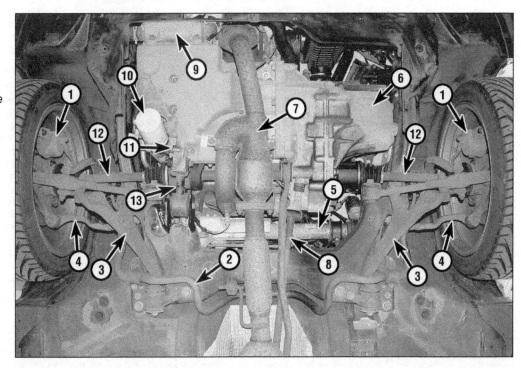

Rear underbody view of a a V6 petrol engine model

1   Handbrake cables
2   Rear trailing arm
3   Suspension coil/strut
4   Fuel tank
5   Suspension lower arm
6   Exhaust system tailbox
7   Trailing arm front
    compensator link
8   Anti-roll bar

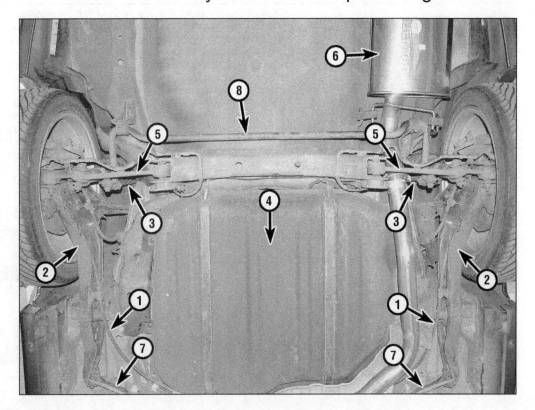

1 Introduction

This Chapter is designed to help the home mechanic maintain his/her vehicle for safety, economy, long life and peak performance.

The Chapter contains a master maintenance schedule, referring to Sections dealing specifically with each task in the schedule, or other Chapters. Visual checks, adjustments, component renewal and other helpful items are included. Refer to the accompanying illustrations of the engine compartment and the underside of the vehicle for the locations of the various components.

Servicing your vehicle in accordance with the mileage/time maintenance schedule and the following Sections will provide a planned maintenance programme, which should result in a long and reliable service life. This is a comprehensive plan, so maintaining some items but not others at the specified service intervals will not produce the same results.

As you service your vehicle, you will discover that many of the procedures can be grouped together, because of the particular procedure being performed, or because of the close proximity of two otherwise-unrelated components to one another. For example, if the vehicle is raised for any reason, the exhaust can be inspected at the same time as the suspension and steering components.

The first step in this maintenance programme is to prepare yourself before the actual work begins. Read through all the Sections relevant to the work to be carried out, then make a list and gather together all the parts and tools required. If a problem is encountered, seek advice from a parts specialist, or a dealer service department.

2 Maintenance

1 If, from the time the vehicle is new, the routine maintenance schedule is followed closely and frequent checks are made of fluid levels and high-wear items, as suggested throughout this Manual, the engine will be kept in relatively good running condition and the need for additional work will be minimised.
2 It is possible that there will be times when the engine is running poorly due to the lack of regular maintenance. This is even more likely if a used vehicle, which has not received regular and frequent maintenance checks, is purchased. In such cases, additional work may need to be carried out, outside of the regular maintenance intervals.
3 If engine wear is suspected, a compression test will provide valuable information regarding the overall performance of the main internal components. Such a test can be used as a basis to decide on the extent of the work to be carried out. If, for example, a compression

test indicates serious internal engine wear, conventional maintenance as described in this Chapter will not greatly improve the performance of the engine, and may prove a waste of time and money unless extensive overhaul work is carried out first.
4 The following series of operations are those most often required to improve the perform- ance of a generally poor-running engine:

Primary operations

a) Clean, inspect and test the battery (See 'Weekly checks').
b) Check all the engine-related fluids (See 'Weekly checks').
c) Check the condition and tension of the auxiliary drivebelt(s).
d) Renew the spark plugs.
e) Inspect the twin coils and HT leads (under spark plug cover).
f) Check the condition of the air cleaner filter element, and renew if necessary.
g) Renew the fuel filter (where fitted).
h) Check the condition of all hoses, and check for fluid leaks.

5 If the above operations do not prove fully effective, carry out the following operations:

Secondary operations

a) Check the charging system (see relevant Part of Chapter 5A).
b) Check the ignition system (see relevant Part of Chapter 5B).
c) Check the fuel system (see relevant Part of Chapter 4A or 4B).

Every 7500 miles or 6 months

3 Engine oil and filter renewal

Note: An oil filter removal tool and a new oil drain plug sealing washer will be required for this operation.
1 Frequent oil and filter changes are the most important preventative maintenance procedures, which can be undertaken by the DIY owner. As engine oil ages, it becomes diluted and contaminated, which leads to premature engine wear.
2 Before starting this procedure, gather together

all the necessary tools and materials. Also make sure that you have plenty of clean rags and newspapers handy, to mop-up any spills. Ideally, the engine oil should be warm, as it will drain more easily, and more built-up sludge will be removed with it. Take care not to touch the exhaust or any other hot parts of the engine when working under the vehicle. To avoid any possibility of scalding, and to protect yourself from possible skin irritants and other harmful contaminants in used engine oils, it is advisable to wear gloves when carrying out this work.
3 Access to the underside of the vehicle will be greatly improved if it can be raised on a lift, driven onto ramps, or jacked up and

supported on axle stands (see *Jacking and vehicle support*). Whichever method is chosen, make sure that the vehicle remains level, or if it is at an angle, that the drain plug is at the lowest point. Where applicable, remove the engine/transmission undershield for access to the drain plug **(see illustration)**. The drain plug is located at the front of the sump on 4-cylinder engines, and at the rear of the sump on 6-cylinder engines.
4 Remove the oil filler cap from the cylinder head cover.
5 Using a spanner, or preferably a suitable socket and bar, slacken the drain plug about half a turn **(see illustrations)**. Position the

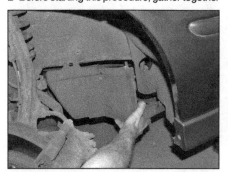

3.3 Remove the right-hand inner wing panel

3.5a Slackening the engine oil drain plug – 4-cylinder engines

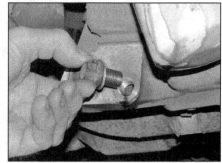

3.5b Oil drain plug – 6-cylinder engines

3.7 Fit new washer (arrowed) to the drain plug

3.8a Oil filter location – 4-cylinder engines

3.8b Oil filter location – 6-cylinder engines

draining container under the drain plug, and then remove the plug completely. If possible, try to keep the plug pressed into the sump while unscrewing it by hand the last couple of turns.

 HAYNES HINT *As the plug releases from the threads, move it away sharply, so that the stream of oil from the sump runs into the container, not up your sleeve.*

6 Allow some time for the oil to drain, noting that it may be necessary to reposition the container as the oil flow slows to a trickle.
7 After all the oil has drained; wipe the drain plug and the sealing washer with a clean rag. The sealing washer should be renewed as a matter of course **(see illustration)**. Clean the area around the drain plug opening, and refit the plug, complete with the new sealing washer. Tighten the plug securely, preferably to the specified torque, using a torque wrench.
8 The oil filter is located at the right-hand front corner of the engine on 4-cylinder engines, and at the rear of the sump on 6-cylinder engines. Access is most easily obtained by jacking up the front of the vehicle (see *Jacking and vehicle support*) **(see illustrations)**.
9 Move the container into position under the oil filter.
10 Use an oil filter removal tool to slacken the filter initially, then unscrew it by hand the

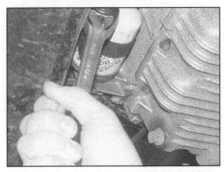

3.10 Slackening the filter using an oil filter removal tool

rest of the way **(see illustration)**. Empty the oil from the old filter into the container.
11 Use a clean rag to remove all oil, dirt and sludge from the filter sealing area on the engine. Check the old filter to make sure that the filter's rubber sealing ring has not stuck to the engine. If it has, carefully remove it.
12 Apply a light coating of clean engine oil to the sealing ring on the new filter **(see illustration)**, then screw the filter into position on the engine. Tighten the filter firmly by hand only – **do not** use any tools.
13 Remove the old oil and all tools from under the vehicle then, if applicable, lower the vehicle to the ground.
14 Fill the engine through the filler hole in the cylinder head cover, using the correct grade and type of oil (see *Lubricants and fluids*). Pour in half the specified quantity of oil first, and then wait a few minutes for the oil to drain into

3.12 Apply clean oil to the seal on the oil filter

the sump. Continue to add oil, a small quantity at a time, until the level is up to the lower mark on the dipstick. Adding approximately 1.0 litre will bring the level up to the upper mark on the dipstick.
15 Start the engine and run it for a few minutes, while checking for leaks around the oil filter seal and the sump drain plug. Note that there may be a delay of a few seconds before the low oil pressure warning light goes out when the engine is first started, as the oil circulates through the new oil filter and the engine oil galleries before the pressure builds-up.
16 Stop the engine, and wait a few minutes for the oil to settle in the sump once more. With the new oil circulated and the filter now completely full, recheck the level on the dipstick, and add more oil as necessary.
17 Dispose of the used engine oil safely.

Every 12 000 miles or 12 months

4 Heater/ventilation air intake filter renewal

Models with conventional heater

1 Release the fixings and remove the lower cover panel from the passenger's side of the facia.
2 Release the two securing clips and remove the cover from the heater unit housing.

3 Withdraw the filter element from the heater unit and discard it.
4 Clean the inside of the filter housing and cover, then fit a new filter using the reversal of the removal procedure.

Models with air conditioning

5 Release the fixings and remove the lower cover panel from the passenger's side of the facia.
6 Undo the two securing bolts and withdraw the glovebox from the facia panel.

7 Undo the four screws securing the glovebox lower rail and withdraw it from the facia panel.
8 Release the two securing clips and remove the cover from the evaporator/heater unit housing.
9 Withdraw the filter element from the heater unit and discard it, noting the airflow direction arrow for refitting.
10 Clean inside the filter housing and cover, then fit a new filter (noting direction arrow) using the reversal of the removal procedure.

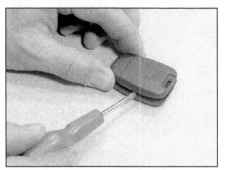

6.1a Using a flat-bladed screwdriver, carefully prise the two halves of the keypad apart . . .

6.1b . . . to expose the battery

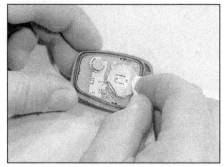

6.3 Fit the new battery, handling it with a piece of tissue paper to avoid touching the battery contact surfaces

Every 15 000 miles or 12 months

5 Bodywork corrosion check

1 Start at the front of the car and work along each body panel in turn, looking for any signs of paintwork damage. It may be possible to repair small scratches with a touch-up pen. These should be purchased from a Rover dealer, to get an accurate colour match.

2 Larger scratches that have penetrated the primer or exposed the bare metal beneath should be repaired professionally. The Rover 45 has an extensive Anti-Corrosion Warranty, the terms of which specify how bodywork repairs must be carried out; failure to adhere to the guidelines may invalidate the warranty. Have the damage assessed by a Rover Dealer or automotive bodywork specialist at the earliest opportunity.

3 Check each body panel for evidence of corrosion, such as raised blisters behind the paintwork and rust-coloured staining. Pay particular attention to vulnerable areas, including the wheel arches, the front edge of the bonnet, the front valence (under the front bumper) and the lower edges of the doors. Corrosion can quickly destroy bodywork, so have any dubious-looking areas examined by a professional.

7.3 Using a hydrometer to measure the specific gravity of the coolant

4 Jack up the front/rear car and support it securely on axle stands (see *Jacking and vehicle support*).

5 Examine the underside of the car for signs of corrosion. Look for cracking or flaking of the metal floorpan. Pay particular attention to the areas around the suspension and steering components mountings. Look for damage that may have been caused by attempting to jack up the car at incorrect jacking points.

6 Check for corrosion along the length of the side sills, which run between the front and rear wheel arches.

7 The underside of the vehicle is coated with a protective sealant, which helps to prevent corrosion. If this coating has been scraped off at any point, due to an impact or repair work, it must be re-applied as soon as possible, to protect the bodywork beneath.

6 Alarm remote keypad battery renewal

1 Place the keypad on a work surface and, using a flat-bladed screwdriver, carefully prise the two halves of the keypad apart **(see illustrations)**. Take care to avoid damaging the rubber seal and internal components with the screwdriver blade.

2 Remove the battery from the terminal clips, noting which way up it is. Press each keypad button in turn and hold it down for a few seconds, to fully discharge the electronic components inside.

3 Obtain a new battery of the correct type and insert it between the terminal clips, ensuring that it is fitted the correct way around (the positive '+' side faces upwards). Avoid touching the contact surfaces of the battery as you do this, by handling it with a piece of tissue paper; moisture from fingertips can cause the battery surfaces to corrode **(see illustration)**.

4 Press the two halves of the keypad back together, ensuring that the rubber seal is correctly located, then check the operation of the keypad.

7 Coolant specific gravity check

1 Ensure that the engine has cooled completely before starting work.

2 Slowly unscrew the coolant expansion tank cap by about half a turn, allowing any residual pressure in the cooling system to reduce gradually – use a cloth to protect your hands from any escaping steam.

3 Insert a hydrometer into the expansion tank filler neck and measure the specific gravity of the coolant **(see illustration)**.

4 The hydrometer shown in the photo incorporates an integral syringe, which allows a 'sample' of the coolant to be collected. The coloured indicator balls inside the hydrometer float or sink in the coolant sample, depending on the specific gravity.

5 If the specific gravity is too low, do not try to correct it by adding neat antifreeze, as it may not mix completely with the existing coolant and could lead to 'hot spots' in the cooling system. With reference to Section 27, partially drain the cooling system, then refill it with antifreeze and water mixed in the correct proportions.

6 If the specific gravity is too high, refer to Section 27 and partially drain the cooling system, then top-up with clean water.

8 Transmission oil/fluid level check

Manual transmission

1 Ensure that the vehicle is parked on level ground then, where applicable, remove the engine/transmission undershield to gain access to the transmission filler/level plug.

2 Remove all traces of dirt from around the filler/level plug, which is located on the left-hand side of the transmission, behind the driveshaft inboard joint. Place a suitable container beneath the plug to catch any

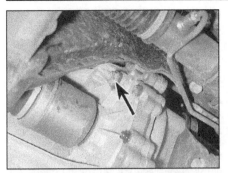

8.2a Transmission filler/level plug (arrowed) – R65-type transmission

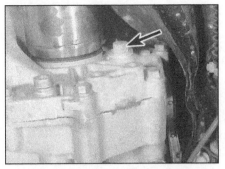

8.2b Transmission filler/level plug (arrowed) – PG1-type transmission

8.5 Topping-up the transmission oil level – PG1-type transmission

escaping oil, then unscrew the plug and recover the sealing washer **(see illustrations)**.

3 Check that the oil is level with the bottom of the filler/level plug hole. **Note:** *Oil which has collected behind the filler/level plug will probably trickle out when the plug is removed, this can give a false impression that the level is correct.*

4 If necessary, top-up using the specified type of oil (see *Lubricants and fluids*). Refilling the transmission is an awkward operation. Allow plenty of time for the oil level to settle properly before checking it. Note that the car must be parked on flat level ground when checking the oil level.

5 Using a tube inserted through the filler/level plug hole, slowly top up the level until the oil reaches the bottom of the filler/level plug hole **(see illustration)**. Allow plenty of time for the level to stabilise.

6 When the level is correct, refit the filler/level plug, using a new sealing washer, and tighten it to the specified torque.

Automatic transmission

 Warning: The transmission fluid may be extremely hot.

7 Remove the engine undertray, which is secured by a number of quick-release screw fasteners.

8 The fluid level is checked with the transmission at operating temperature, and with the engine running. Starting at P, and with the footbrake firmly pressed, move the selector lever through each position. Pause in each position for a few seconds, then return to position P.

9 Clean the area around the level plug, which is located directly below the selector cable – it may even be necessary to detach the cable for better access.

10 Using a 5 mm Allen key, unscrew the filler/level plug, which will probably be very tight. Recover the sealing ring – a new one will be needed when refitting.

11 The level must be just below the bottom edge of the level plug hole (use a cranked tool such as an Allen key to check the level). With the engine running, allow any excess fluid to drain.

12 If the level is correct, refit the plug using

a new sealing washer, and tighten it to the specified torque. Switch off the engine.

13 If topping-up is required, switch off the engine and remove the air cleaner as described in Chapter 4A or 4B.

14 Clean around the filler pipe on top of the transmission – it is vital that no dirt enters the transmission at any stage. Pull out the filler plug.

15 Start the engine, then slowly add clean fluid of the specified type (see *Lubricants and fluids*). Add small amounts at a time, until fluid starts to flow from the level plug hole, then refit the filler plug firmly into its pipe. Refit the air cleaner as described in Chapter 4A or 4B.

16 Move the selector lever through all positions as described in paragraph 8, and allow any excess fluid to run out.

17 When the level stabilises, stop the engine. Refit and tighten the level plug (with a new sealing washer) to the specified torque.

18 Refit the engine undertray on completion.

9 Vacuum hose condition check

1 Open the bonnet and check the condition of the vacuum hose that connects the brake servo to the inlet manifold **(see illustration)**. Look for damage in the form of chafing, melting or cracking. Check that the union nuts and T-joints (where applicable) are secure. Also examine the vacuum hoses serving the evaporative loss emission control and fuel pressure regulation systems.

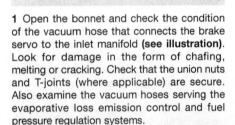

9.1 Check the condition of the brake servo vacuum hose

2 A leak in a vacuum hose means that air is being drawn into the hose (rather than escaping from it) and this makes leakage very difficult to detect. If you suspect that a vacuum hose may be leaking, the following method may help you to pinpoint it. Start the engine and allow it to idle. Hold one end of a length of narrow bore tubing close to your ear, and then run the other end along the vacuum hose. If a leak exists, you should be able to hear a hissing noise through the tubing as the air 'escapes' into the hose at the suspected leak.

10 Underbonnet and underbody hose and pipe condition check

 Warning: Refer to the safety information given in 'Safety first!' and Chapter 3, before disturbing any of the following systems components.

Coolant

1 Carefully check the radiator and heater coolant hoses along their entire length. Renew any hose that is cracked, swollen or which shows signs of deterioration. Cracks will show up better if the hose is squeezed **(see illustration)**. Pay close attention to the clips that secure the hoses to the cooling system components. Hose clips that have been overtightened can pinch and puncture hoses, resulting in leakage.

2 Inspect all the cooling system components (hoses, joint faces, etc) for leaks. Where any

10.1 Checking the condition of a coolant hose

HAYNES HINT

Leaks in the cooling system will usually show up as white or antifreeze-coloured deposits around the point of leakage.

problems of this nature are found on system components, renew the component or gasket with reference to Chapter 3.

3 A leak from the cooling system will usually show up as white or rust-coloured deposits, on the area surrounding the leak **(see Haynes Hint)**.

Fuel

4 Petrol leaks are difficult to pinpoint, unless the leakage is significant and hence easily visible. Fuel tends to evaporate quickly once it comes into contact with air, especially in a hot engine bay. Small drips can disappear before you get a chance to identify the point of leakage. If you suspect that there is a fuel leak from the area of the engine bay, leave the vehicle overnight then start the engine from cold, with the bonnet open. Metal components tend to shrink when they are cold, and rubber seals and hoses tend to harden, so any leaks may be more apparent whilst the engine is warming-up from a cold start.

5 Check all fuel lines at their connections to the fuel rail, fuel pressure regulator and fuel filter **(see illustration)**. Examine each rubber fuel hose along its length for splits or cracks. Check for leakage from the crimped joints between rubber and metal fuel lines. Examine the unions between the metal fuel lines and the fuel filter housing. Also check the area around the fuel injectors for signs of O-ring leakage.

6 To identify fuel leaks between the fuel tank and the engine bay, the vehicle should be raised and securely supported on axle stands (see *Jacking and vehicle support*). Inspect the

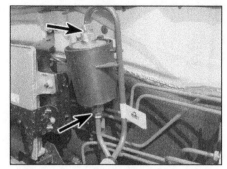

10.5 Check for fuel leaks at the fuel filter unions (arrowed)

petrol tank and filler neck for punctures, cracks and other damage. The connection between the filler neck and tank is especially critical. Sometimes a rubber filler neck or connecting hose will leak due to loose retaining clamps or deteriorated rubber.

7 Carefully check all rubber hoses and metal fuel lines leading away from the petrol tank. Check for loose connections, deteriorated hoses, kinked lines, and other damage. Pay particular attention to the vent pipes and hoses, which often loop up around the filler neck and can become blocked or kinked, making tank filling difficult. Follow the fuel supply and return lines to the front of the vehicle, carefully inspecting them all the way for signs of damage or corrosion. Renew damaged sections as necessary.

Engine oil

8 On 6-cylinder engines, check the hoses leading to the engine oil cooler at the front of the engine bay for leakage **(see illustration)**. Look for deterioration caused by corrosion and damage from grounding, or debris thrown up from the road surface.

Power-assisted steering fluid

9 Examine the hose running between the fluid reservoir and the power steering pump, and the return hose running from the steering rack to the fluid reservoir. Also examine the high-pressure supply hose between the pump and the steering rack **(see illustration)**.

10 Where applicable, check the hoses leading to the PAS fluid cooler at the front of the engine bay. Look for deterioration caused

by corrosion and damage from grounding, or debris thrown up from the road surface.

11 Pay particular attention to crimped unions, and the area surrounding the hoses that are secured with adjustable worm drive clips. PAS fluid is thin oil and usually red in colour.

Air conditioning refrigerant

12 The air conditioning system is filled with a liquid refrigerant, which is retained under high pressure. If the air conditioning system is opened and depressurised without the aid of specialised equipment the refrigerant will immediately turn into gas and escape into the atmosphere. If the liquid comes into contact with your skin, it can cause severe frostbite. In addition, the refrigerant may contain substances that are environmentally damaging; for this reason, it should not be allowed to escape into the atmosphere.

13 Any suspected air conditioning system leaks should be immediately referred to a Rover dealer or air conditioning specialist. Leakage will be shown up as a steady drop in the level of refrigerant in the system – refer to Section 11 for details.

14 Note that water may drip from the condenser drain pipe, underneath the car, immediately after the air conditioning system has been in use. This is normal, and should not be cause for concern.

Brake fluid

15 With reference to Chapter 9, examine the following items and their connections for signs of fluid leaks – master cylinder, proportioning valve, ABS hydraulic unit, and fluid reservoir **(see illustration)**. Brake fluid is an effective paint stripper, so if cracked or bubbling paintwork on or around any of the braking system components is found, suspect fluid leakage.

16 If fluid loss is evident, but the leak cannot be pinpointed in the engine bay, the brake calipers and underbody brake lines should be carefully checked with the vehicle raised and supported on axle stands (see *Jacking and vehicle support*). Leakage of fluid from the braking system is a serious fault that must be rectified immediately.

17 Brake hydraulic fluid is toxic with a watery consistency. New fluid is almost colourless, but it becomes darker with age and use.

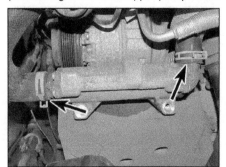

10.8 Check for leaks at the oil cooler hose connections (arrowed)

10.9 Check the power steering fluid hose (arrowed) for damage

10.15 Check the brake pipe unions on the ABS unit for leakage

12.4 Slackening the power steering pump belt tensioner

Unidentified fluid leaks

18 If there are signs that a fluid of some description is leaking from the vehicle, but you cannot identify the type of fluid or its exact origin, park the vehicle overnight and slide a large piece of card underneath it. Providing that the card is positioned in roughly in the right location, even the smallest leak will show up on the card. Not only will this help you to pinpoint the exact location of the leak, it should be easier to identify the fluid from its colour. Bear in mind, though, that the leak may only be occurring when the engine is running!

Vacuum hoses

19 Refer to Section 9.

11 Air conditioning system check

A Rover dealer or air conditioning specialist must check the air conditioning system using dedicated test equipment.

12 Auxiliary drivebelt tension and condition check

General information

1 The auxiliary drivebelt(s) is located at the right-hand side of the engine
2 Due to their function and material makeup, drivebelts are prone to failure after a period of time and should therefore be inspected.
3 Since the drivebelt is located very close to the right-hand side of the engine compartment, it is possible to gain better access by raising the front of the vehicle (see *Jacking and vehicle support*) and removing the right-hand wheel, then removing the splash shield from inside the wheel arch.
4 On 4-cylinder engines there are two drivebelts fitted; both are driven from the crankshaft pulley.
a) *The outer belt drives the power steering pump, and is automatically tensioned by a spring-loaded roller* **(see illustration)**.
b) *On vehicles without air conditioning, the inner belt drives the alternator, and has*

12.14a Slacken the alternator upper pivot mounting bolts (arrowed) . . .

a manual tensioner at the base of the alternator. When air conditioning is fitted, this belt also drives the refrigerant compressor. In this configuration, a spring-loaded roller automatically controls belt tension.

5 On 6-cylinder engines there is only one drivebelt fitted, a spring-loaded tensioner is fitted to automatically maintain the correct tension on the belt. The belt drives:
a) *The power steering pump.*
b) *The alternator.*
c) *The air conditioning compressor.*

Checking condition

6 Apply the handbrake, chock the rear roadwheels, then jack up the front of the car and support it on axle stands (see *Jacking and vehicle support*). Remove the right hand roadwheel and the splash shield from inside the wheel arch.
7 With the engine switched off, inspect the full length of the drivebelt(s) for cracks and separation of the belt plies. It will be necessary to turn the crankshaft (using a socket or spanner on the crankshaft pulley bolt) in order to move the belt from the pulleys so that the full length of the belt can be inspected thoroughly. Twist the belt between the pulleys so that both sides can be viewed. Also check for fraying, and glazing which gives the belt a shiny appearance. Check the pulleys for nicks, cracks, distortion and corrosion.
8 On 4-cylinder engines with air conditioning, check the belt length – the belt must be renewed before the indicator reaches the right hand end of the slot **(see illustration 12.18)**.
9 If problems with belt squeal or slip are encountered, the belt should be renewed. If the problem continues, where a spring-loaded tensioner is fitted, it will be necessary to renew the tensioner assembly.
10 Renew any worn or damaged belt – see Chapter 5A, Section 6.

Checking/adjusting tension

4-cylinder engines without air conditioning

11 Disconnect the battery negative terminal.
12 Apply the handbrake, chock the rear roadwheels, then jack up the front of the car and support it on axle stands (see *Jacking and vehicle support*). Remove the right hand front

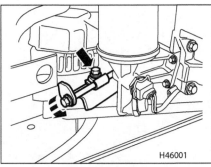

12.14b . . . and lower adjusting arm bolt, then rotate adjuster bolt (located in the end of the arm) – models without air conditioning

roadwheel and the splash shield from inside the wheel arch.
13 Check tension by applying a force of 10 kg to the belt upper run, midway between the crankshaft pulley and alternator pulley. If belt deflection is more or less than 6 mm to 8 mm, adjust the belt tension.
14 Slacken upper and lower alternator mounting bolts. Slacken adjusting link bolt. Increase tension by turning the tension adjusting bolt clockwise **(see illustrations)**. *Caution: Do not apply excessive torque to the adjusting bolt. If it is seized, apply anti-seize fluid.*
15 Tighten the mounting bolts to the specified torque. Recheck the belt tension.
16 Fit the roadwheel, and tighten the nuts to secure the wheel. Remove the stands and lower the vehicle to the ground. Use a torque wrench to tighten the roadwheel nuts to the specified torque.
17 Reconnect the battery earth lead.

4-cylinder engines with air conditioning

18 The spring-loaded roller automatically controls belt tension. Check the position of the tension indicator in the slot. The belt must be renewed before the indicator reaches the right hand end of the slot **(see illustration)**.
19 For belt renewal see Chapter 5A, Section 6.

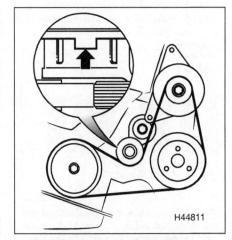

12.18 Alternator drivebelt adjustment – models with air conditioning

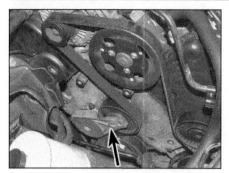

12.20 Alternator drivebelt tensioner (arrowed) – 6-cylinder engines

6-cylinder engines

20 A spring-loaded tensioner is fitted to automatically maintain the correct tension on the belt **(see illustration)**. If problems with belt squeal or slip are encountered, the belt should be renewed. If the problem continues, it will be necessary to renew the tensioner assembly.

Power steering belt – 4-cylinder engines

21 The spring-loaded roller automatically controls belt tension. Check the position of the tension indicator in the slot. The belt must be renewed before the indicator reaches the left the recess in the tensioner backplate.
22 For belt renewal see Chapter 10.

13 Exhaust system check

1 With the engine cold (at least an hour after the vehicle has been driven), check the complete exhaust system from the engine to the end of the tailpipe. The exhaust system is most easily checked with the vehicle raised on a hoist, or suitably supported on axle stands, so that the exhaust components are readily visible and accessible.
2 Check the exhaust pipes and connections for evidence of leaks, severe corrosion and damage. Make sure that all brackets and

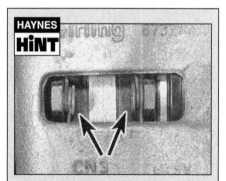

HAYNES HINT

For a quick check, the thickness of the material remaining on the brake pads can be measured through the aperture in the caliper body.

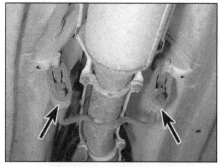

13.2 Make sure that the exhaust mountings are in good condition

mountings are in good condition, and that all relevant nuts and bolts are tight **(see illustration)**. Leakage at any of the joints or in other parts of the system will usually show up as a black sooty stain in the vicinity of the leak.
3 Rattles and other noises can often be traced to the exhaust system, especially the brackets and mountings. Try to move the pipes and silencers. If the components are able to come into contact with the body or suspension parts, secure the system with new mountings. Otherwise separate the joints (if possible) and twist the pipes as necessary to provide additional clearance.

14 Front brake check

1 Firmly apply the handbrake then jack up the front of the vehicle and support it securely on axle stands (see *Jacking and vehicle support*). Remove the front roadwheels.
2 For a quick check, the pad thickness can be carried out via the inspection hole in the front of the caliper **(see Haynes Hint)**. If any pad's friction material is worn to the specified minimum thickness or less, all four pads must be renewed as a set.
3 For a comprehensive check, the brake pads should be removed and cleaned. This will permit the operation of the caliper to be checked and the condition of the brake disc itself to be fully examined on both sides. Refer to Chapter 9 for further information.

16.1 Inspecting a driveshaft joint rubber gaiter

4 On completion refit the roadwheels, lower the vehicle to the ground and tighten the wheel nuts to the specified torque setting.

15 Rear brake check

Models with drum brakes

1 For a comprehensive check, the brake drums should be removed and cleaned. This will permit the wheel cylinders to be checked and the condition of the brake drum itself to be fully examined. Refer to Chapter 9 for further information.
2 On completion refit the roadwheels, lower the vehicle to the ground and tighten the wheel nuts to the specified torque setting.

Models with disc brakes

3 Chock the front wheels then jack up the rear of the vehicle and support it on axle stands (see *Jacking and vehicle support*).
4 For a quick check, the thickness of friction material remaining on each brake pad can be measured through the inspection aperture in the caliper body (see **Haynes Hint** for checking front brake pads in the previous Section). If any pad's friction material is worn to the specified minimum thickness or less, all four pads must be renewed as a set.
5 For a comprehensive check, the brake pads should be removed and cleaned. This will permit the operation of the caliper to be checked and the condition of the brake disc itself to be fully examined on both sides. Refer to Chapter 9 for further information.
6 On completion refit the roadwheels, lower the vehicle to the ground and tighten the wheel nuts to the specified torque setting.

16 Driveshaft and gaiter check

1 With the vehicle raised and securely supported on axle stands (see *Jacking and vehicle support*), turn the steering onto full lock then slowly rotate the roadwheel. Inspect the condition of the outer constant velocity (CV) joint rubber gaiters while squeezing the gaiters to open out the folds **(see illustration)**. Check for signs of cracking, splits or deterioration of the rubber, which may allow the grease to escape and lead to the entry of water and grit into the joint. Also check the security and condition of the gaiter retaining clips. Repeat these checks on the inner CV joints. If any damage or deterioration is found, then renew the gaiters.
2 Check the general condition of the CV joints by first holding the driveshaft and attempting to rotate the roadwheel. Repeat this check by holding the inner joint and attempting to rotate the driveshaft. Any appreciable movement

indicates wear in the joints or driveshaft splines, or a loose driveshaft nut.

17 Suspension and steering check

Front suspension and steering

1 Raise the front of the vehicle and securely support it on axle stands (see *Jacking and vehicle support*).

2 Inspect the balljoint dust covers and the steering gear rubber gaiters for splits, chafing or deterioration **(see illustration)**. Any wear of these components will cause loss of lubricant, together with dirt and water entry, resulting in rapid deterioration of the balljoints or steering gear.

3 Check the power-assisted steering (PAS) fluid hoses for chafing or deterioration, and the pipe and hose unions for fluid leakage. Also check for signs of fluid leakage under pressure from the steering gear rubber gaiters, which would indicate failed fluid seals within the steering gear.

4 Grasp the roadwheel at the 12 o'clock and 6 o'clock positions and try to rock it **(see illustration)**. Very slight free play may be felt but if the movement is appreciable then further investigation is necessary to determine the source. Continue rocking the wheel while an assistant depresses the brake pedal. If the movement is now eliminated or significantly reduced, it is likely that the hub bearings are at fault. If the free play is still evident with the brake pedal depressed, then there is wear in the suspension joints or mountings.

5 Now grasp the roadwheel at the 9 o'clock and 3 o'clock positions and try to rock it as before. Any movement felt now may again be caused by wear in the hub bearings, or in the track rod balljoints. If a balljoint is worn the visual movement will be obvious. If the inner joint is suspect it can be felt by placing a hand over the steering gear rubber gaiter and gripping the track rod. If the wheel is now rocked, movement will be felt at the inner joint if wear has taken place.

6 Using a large screwdriver or flat bar check for wear in the suspension mounting bushes by levering between the relevant suspension component and its attachment point. Some movement is to be expected as the mountings are made of rubber, but excessive wear should be obvious. Also check the condition of any visible rubber bushes, looking for splits, cracks or contamination of the rubber.

7 With the vehicle standing on its wheels, have an assistant turn the steering wheel back-and-forth about an eighth of a turn each way. There should be very little, if any, lost movement between the steering wheel and the roadwheels. If this is not the case, closely observe the joints and mountings previously described but in addition check for wear of the steering column universal joint and the steering gear itself.

17.2 Checking the condition of a steering gear rubber gaiter

Rear suspension

8 Chock the front wheels then jack up the rear of the vehicle and support it on axle stands (see *Jacking and vehicle support*).

9 Working as described for the front suspension, check the rear hub bearings and the trailing arm and lateral link bushes for wear.

Shock absorber check

10 Check for any signs of fluid leakage around the shock absorber body, or from the rubber gaiter around the piston rod. Should any fluid be noticed, the shock absorber is defective internally, and should be renewed. **Note:** *Shock absorbers should always be renewed in pairs on the same axle.*

11 To check the efficiency of the shock absorbers, bounce the vehicle at each corner. Generally speaking, the body will return to its normal position and stop after being depressed. If it rises and returns on a rebound, the shock absorber is probably suspect. Also examine the shock absorber upper and lower mountings for any signs of wear.

18 Handbrake check and adjustment

Checking

1 The handbrake should be capable of holding the parked vehicle stationary, even on steep slopes, when applied with moderate force. Equally, the handbrake must release properly, or the brakes will bind and overheat when the car is driven.

2 The mechanism should be firm and positive in feel with no trace of stiffness or sponginess from the cables and should release immediately the handbrake lever is released. If the mechanism is faulty in any of these respects then it must be checked immediately.

3 To check the handbrake setting, first apply the footbrake firmly several times. Applying normal, moderate pressure, pull the handbrake lever to the fully applied position whilst counting the number of 'clicks' produced by the handbrake ratchet mechanism. Check that the number of

17.4 Checking the condition of the steering and suspension components by rocking a roadwheel

clicks produced is as specified, if this is not the case, then adjustment is required.

Adjustment

4 To adjust the handbrake, chock the front wheels then jack up the rear of the vehicle and support it on axle stands (see *Jacking and vehicle support*). On models with rear disc brakes, remove both the rear roadwheels.

5 On models with rear disc brakes, undo the retaining bolts and remove the protective shields (where fitted) from the rear calipers. Check that the handbrake cables slide freely in their sheaths, and that the operating levers on the calipers move freely. Make sure the handbrake operating levers on the calipers are as far as they will go back against their stops (see Chapter 9 for further information).

6 Lift out the ashtray from the rear of the centre console to gain access to the handbrake adjusting nut **(see illustration)**.

7 Apply the handbrake and check that the equaliser and cables move freely and smoothly, then set the lever on the first notch of the ratchet mechanism.

8 With the lever in this position, rotate the handbrake lever adjusting nut until only a slight drag can be felt when the rear wheels are turned by hand.

9 Once this is the case, fully release the handbrake lever and check that the wheels rotate freely.

10 Check adjustment by applying the handbrake fully whilst counting the clicks emitted from the handbrake ratchet. Carry out the adjustment procedure again, if necessary.

18.6 Handbrake cable adjuster nut (arrowed) and equaliser mechanism

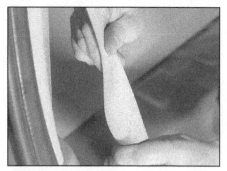

21.1 Check the webbing of each seat belt for signs of fraying, cuts or other damage

11 On models with rear disc brakes, refit the protective shields (where applicable) to the calipers and refit the roadwheels.

12 Once adjustment is correct, refit the ashtray and lower the vehicle to the ground. Tighten the roadwheels to the specified torque setting, where applicable.

19 Lock and hinge lubrication

1 Lubricate the hinges of the bonnet, doors and tailgate with some light duty oil.

2 Lightly grease the bonnet release mechanism and cable.

3 The door and tailgate latches, strikers and locks must be lubricated using only the special Rover Door Lock and Latch Lubricant supplied in small sachets. Inject 1 gram into each lock and wipe off any surplus, then apply a thin film to the latches and strikers.

4 Do not lubricate the steering lock mechanism with oil or any other lubricant, which might foul the ignition switch contacts. If the lock is stiff, try the effect of a proprietary electrical contact lubricant, rather than conventional lubricant.

5 If a sunroof is fitted, lubricate very sparingly the seal lip with Rover supplied non-staining seal grease.

20 Windscreen and number plate condition check

Refer to the *MOT test checks* described in the *Reference* Chapter, at the end of this manual.

21 Seat belt check

1 Carefully examine the seat belt webbing of each seat belt for signs of fraying, cuts or other damage, pulling the belt out to its full extent to check its entire length **(see illustration)**.

2 Check the operation of the belt buckles by fitting the belt tongue plate and pulling hard to ensure that it remains locked in position.

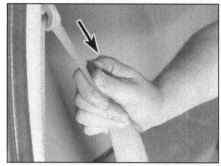

21.3 Checking the operation of the inertia reel locking mechanism

3 Check the retractor mechanism (inertia reel only) by pulling out the belt to the halfway point and jerking it downwards **(see illustration)**. The mechanism must lock immediately to prevent any further unreeling but must allow free movement during normal driving.

4 Ensure that all belt mounting bolts are securely tightened. Note that the bolts are shouldered so that the belt anchor points are free to rotate.

5 If there is any sign of damage, or any doubt about a belt's condition, then it must be renewed. If the vehicle has been involved in a collision, then any belt in use at the time must be renewed as a matter of course and all other belts checked carefully.

6 Use only warm water and non-detergent soap to clean the belts.

Caution: Never use any chemical cleaners, strong detergents, dyes or bleaches. Keep the belts fully extended until they have dried naturally and do not apply heat to dry them.

22 SRS system component check

1 Checking of the SRS/airbag system by the home mechanic is limited to a visual inspection of the outer surface of the driver and passenger airbag modules (as applicable). If the surface of the casing has sustained any damage (such as that caused by an impact, or fluid spillage for example) then the airbag system should be checked by a Rover dealer at the earliest opportunity.

2 Sit in the driver's seat and release the steering column lock. Start the engine and allow it to idle. Turn the steering wheel from lock-to-lock, whilst listening to the rotary coupler at the steering wheel hub. Any noise or roughness in operation could indicate a worn rotary coupler – refer to a Rover dealer for further advice.

3 The SRS warning lamp on the instrument panel should illuminate for about six seconds when the ignition key is turned to the 'II' position and then extinguish. If the lamp fails to extinguish, or does not illuminate at all, there may be a fault with the SRS system; the advice of a Rover dealer should be sought.

23 Road test

Instruments and electrical equipment

1 Check the operation of all instruments and electrical equipment.

2 Make sure that all instruments read correctly, and switch on all electrical equipment in turn, to check that it functions properly.

Steering and suspension

3 Check for any abnormalities in the steering, suspension, handling or road 'feel'.

4 Drive the vehicle, and check that there are no unusual vibrations or noises.

5 Check that the steering feels positive, with no excessive 'sloppiness', or roughness, and check for any suspension noises when cornering and driving over bumps.

Drivetrain

6 Check the performance of the engine, clutch, transmission and driveshafts.

7 Listen for any unusual noises from the engine, clutch and transmission.

8 Make sure that the engine runs smoothly when idling, and that there is no hesitation when accelerating.

9 On manual transmission models, check that the clutch action is smooth and progressive, that the drive is taken up smoothly, and that the pedal travel is not excessive. Also listen for any noises when the clutch pedal is depressed.

10 Check that all gears can be engaged smoothly without noise, and that the gear lever action is smooth and not abnormally vague or 'notchy'.

11 On automatic transmission models, make sure that all gearchanges occur smoothly, without snatching, and without an increase in engine speed between changes. Check that all of the gear positions can be selected with the vehicle at rest. If any problems are found, they should be referred to a Rover dealer.

12 Listen for a metallic clicking sound from the front of the vehicle, as the vehicle is driven slowly in a circle with the steering on full-lock. Carry out this check in both directions. If a clicking noise is heard, this indicates wear in a driveshaft joint (see Chapter 8).

Braking system

13 Make sure that the vehicle does not pull to one side when braking, and that the wheels do not lock when braking hard.

14 Check that there is no vibration through the steering when braking.

15 Check that the handbrake operates correctly, without excessive movement of the lever, and that it holds the vehicle stationary on a slope.

16 Test the operation of the brake servo unit as follows. Depress the footbrake four or five

times to exhaust the vacuum, and then start the engine. As the engine starts, there should be a noticeable 'give' in the brake pedal as vacuum builds-up. Allow the engine to run for at least two minutes, and then switch it off. If the brake pedal is now depressed again, it should be possible to detect a hiss from the servo as the pedal is depressed. After about four or five applications, no further hissing should be heard, and the pedal should feel considerably harder.

Every 30 000 miles or 2 years

24 Brake fluid renewal

⚠ *Warning: Brake hydraulic fluid can harm your eyes and damage painted surfaces, so use extreme caution when handling and pouring it. Do not use fluid that has been standing open for some time, as it absorbs moisture from the air. Excess moisture can cause a dangerous loss of braking effectiveness.*
Caution: On models equipped with ABS, disconnect the battery before carrying out this operation and do not reconnect the battery until after the operation is complete. Failure to do this could lead to air entering the hydraulic unit. If air enters the hydraulic unit pump it will prove very difficult (in some cases impossible) to bleed the unit. Refer to Chapter 5A when disconnecting the battery.

1 This procedure is similar to that described for the bleeding of the hydraulic system, as described in Chapter 9, except that the brake fluid reservoir should be emptied by syphoning and allowance should be made for all old fluid to be expelled when bleeding a section of the circuit.

2 Working as described in Chapter 9, open the first bleed screw in the sequence and pump the brake pedal gently until nearly all the old fluid has been emptied from the master cylinder reservoir. Top up to the MAX level on the reservoir with new fluid and continue pumping until only new fluid remains in the reservoir and new fluid can be seen emerging from the bleed screw. Old hydraulic fluid is much darker in colour than new fluid, making it easy to distinguish between them.

3 Tighten the bleed screw and top the reservoir level up to the MAX level line **(see illustration)**.

4 Work through all the remaining bleed screws in the sequence until new fluid can be seen emerging from all of them. Be careful to keep the master cylinder reservoir topped-up to above the MIN level at all times, or air may enter the system and greatly increase the length of the task.

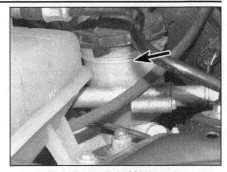

24.3 Brake fluid MAX level – arrowed

5 When the operation is complete, check that all bleed screws are securely tightened and that their dust caps are refitted. Wash off all traces of spilt fluid and recheck the master cylinder reservoir fluid level.

6 Check the operation of the brakes before taking the vehicle on the road.

7 Dispose safely of the used brake fluid with reference to *General repair procedures*.

Every 45 000 miles or 3 years

25 Air cleaner filter element renewal

4-cylinder engines

1 The air cleaner is located at the left-hand side of the engine compartment, next to the battery.

2 Release the four securing clips, then lift the upper part of the air cleaner housing to enable the element to be withdrawn **(see illustrations)**. Discard the dirty air cleaner element.

3 Wipe out the air cleaner housing and the upper cover using a clean cloth.

4 Fit the new air cleaner element, then refit the upper part of the housing and secure with the four clips.

6-cylinder engines

5 The air cleaner is located at the left-hand front of the engine compartment, next to the radiator.

6 Withdraw the air cleaner element cartridge from the top of the air cleaner housing to enable the element to be withdrawn **(see illustrations)**. Discard the dirty air cleaner element.

7 Wipe out the air cleaner cartridge and housing using a clean cloth.

8 Fit the new air cleaner element to the cartridge and slide it back into the air cleaner housing, making sure the air cleaner element is fitted correctly.

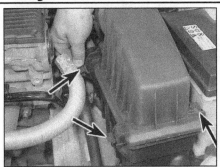

25.2a Release the retaining clips – arrowed

25.2b Withdraw the air cleaner from the housing

25.6a Slide the air filter cartridge from the housing . . .

25.6b . . . and withdraw the air cleaner

Every 60 000 miles or 4 years

26 Spark plug renewal

⚠ *Warning: Voltages produced by an electronic ignition system are considerably higher than those produced by conventional ignition systems. Extreme care must be taken when working on the system with the ignition switched on. Persons with surgically-implanted cardiac pacemaker devices should keep well clear of the ignition circuits, components and test equipment.*

1 The correct functioning of the spark plugs is vital for the correct running and efficiency of the engine. It is essential that the plugs fitted are appropriate for the engine (Rover recommendations are at the beginning of this Chapter). If this type is used and the engine is in good condition, the spark plugs should not need attention between scheduled renewal intervals. Spark plug cleaning is rarely necessary, and should not be attempted unless specialised equipment is available, as damage can easily be caused to the firing ends.

2 Spark plug removal and refitting requires a spark plug socket, with an extension which can be turned by a ratchet handle or similar. This socket is lined with a rubber sleeve, to protect the porcelain insulator of the spark plug, and to hold the plug while it is removed or inserted into the spark plug hole. A torque wrench to tighten the plugs to the specified torque will also be required.

3 Open the bonnet and, where applicable, remove the plastic engine cover from the top of the cylinder head **(see illustration)**. Note how the ignition coil wiring harnesses and HT leads are routed and secured by clips along the top of the cylinder head or inlet manifold. To prevent the possibility of mixing up the wiring/leads, it is a good idea to try to work on one spark plug at a time.

4 It is advisable to remove the dirt from the spark plug recesses using a clean brush, vacuum cleaner or compressed air before removing the plugs, to prevent dirt dropping into the cylinders.

4-cylinder engines

5 There are two coils fitted directly over the top of spark plugs 1 and 3. Spark plugs 2 and 4 are then connected to these coils by HT leads (see Chapter 5B for further information).

6 Remove the retaining bolts and remove the coil/plug cover from the camshaft cover **(see illustration)**.

7 Note the position of the HT leads and wiring cables running to the two coils and disconnect the multi-plug connectors from the both coils.

8 Disconnect the HT leads from the spark plugs in cylinders 2 and 4.

9 Undo the two retaining bolts attaching each of the two coils to the camshaft cover. Pull the coils upwards to release them from the spark plugs in cylinders 1 and 3 **(see illustration)**.

6-cylinder engines

10 Each spark plug has a separate ignition coil, either located directly over the top of the plug (rear bank) or connected by HT leads (front bank).

Rear bank

11 Note the position of the wiring cables running to the coils and disconnect the multi-plug connectors from the coils **(see illustration)**. To gain better access to the rear coils/spark plugs, remove the inlet manifold as described in Chapter 4B, Section 12.

12 Undo the two retaining bolts attaching each of the coils to the camshaft cover; pull the coils upwards to release them from the spark plugs.

Front bank

13 Note the position of the HT leads running to the spark plugs and pull them to disconnect them from the spark plugs **(see illustration)**.

All engines

14 Unscrew the plugs, ensuring that the socket is kept in alignment with each plug – if the socket is forcibly moved to either side, the porcelain top of the plug may be broken off **(see illustration)**.

15 As each plug is removed, examine it as follows – this will give a good indication of the condition of the engine. If the insulator nose of the spark plug is clean and white, with no

26.3 Remove the engine cover – 6-cylinder engines

26.6 Remove the coil/plug cover

26.9 Undo the bolts and withdraw the coil

26.11 Disconnect the multi-plug connectors from the three coils

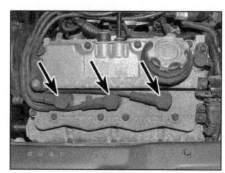

26.13 Pull the plug lead connectors from the spark plugs

26.14 Unscrewing a spark plug

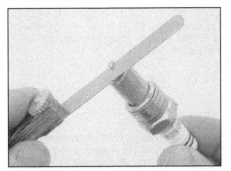

26.19a Measuring a spark plug gap using a feeler blade

26.19b Adjusting the spark plug gap using a special tool

deposits, this is indicative of a weak mixture or too hot a plug (a hot plug transfers heat away from the electrode slowly, a cold plug transfers heat away quickly).

16 If the tip and insulator nose are covered with hard black-looking deposits, then this is indicative that the mixture is too rich. Should the plug be black and oily, and then it is likely that the engine is fairly worn, as well as the mixture being too rich.

17 If the insulator nose is covered with light tan to greyish-brown deposits, then the mixture is correct and it is likely that the engine is in good condition.

18 The spark plug electrode gap is of considerable importance as, if it is too large or too small, the size of the spark and its efficiency will be seriously impaired. The gap should be set to the value given in the Specifications at the beginning of this Chapter. Where spark plugs with specially shaped multiple electrodes are used, it is not necessary or possible to adjust the electrode gap on these types.

19 Special spark plug electrode gap measuring and adjusting tools are available from most motor accessory shops **(see illustrations)**. The centre electrode should never be bent, as this may crack the insulator and cause plug failure, if nothing worse.

20 Before fitting the spark plugs, check that the threaded connector sleeves are tight (where fitted), and that the plug exterior surfaces and threads are clean.

21 Insert each spark plug into the cylinder head and screw them in by hand, taking extra care to enter the plug threads correctly **(see Haynes Hint)**.

22 When each spark plug is started correctly on its threads, screw it down until it just seats lightly, then tighten it to the specified torque wrench setting.

23 Where applicable, check the condition of the O-ring seal on the end of each ignition coil and renew them if necessary. Locate the coils over the spark plugs and secure with the retaining screws to the specified torque setting.

24 Connect the ignition coil wiring connectors or HT leads in their correct order as noted on removal. Where applicable, refit the plastic engine cover.

27 Coolant renewal

> **Warning: Wait until the engine is completely cold before starting the coolant renewal procedure. Do not allow antifreeze to come into contact with your skin or painted surfaces of the vehicle. Rinse off spills immediately with plenty of water. Never leave antifreeze lying around in an open container or in a puddle in the driveway or on the garage floor. Children and pets are attracted by its sweet smell; and antifreeze can be fatal if ingested.**

Antifreeze mixture

1 Antifreeze should always be renewed at the specified intervals. This is necessary not only to maintain the anti-freezing properties of the coolant but also to prevent corrosion that would otherwise occur, as the corrosion inhibitors in the coolant become progressively less effective.

2 Always use an ethylene glycol based antifreeze, which is suitable for use in mixed-metal cooling systems.

3 The type of antifreeze and levels of protection afforded are indicated in *Lubricants and fluids* and Specifications. To achieve the recommended 50% concentration, equal quantities of antifreeze and clean, soft water must be mixed together. It is best to make up slightly more than is actually needed to refill the cooling system, so that a supply is available for subsequent topping-up.

Caution: Always premix the antifreeze and water in a suitable container before refilling the cooling system. If the antifreeze and water are poured into the cooling system separately, they may not mix correctly and could cause localised overheating, which may lead to engine damage.

Draining

4 To drain the cooling system, remove the expansion tank filler cap then move the heater air temperature control to the maximum heat position. Where applicable, remove the plastic tray from under the engine bay. On 4-cylinder

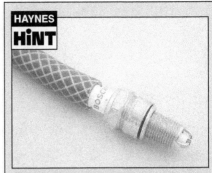

It is often difficult to insert spark plugs into their holes without cross-threading them. To avoid this possibility, fit a short length of suitable internal diameter rubber hose over the end of the spark plug. The flexible hose acts as a universal joint to help align the plug with the plug hole. Should the plug begin to cross-thread, the hose will slip on the spark plug, preventing thread damage to the cylinder head.

models, it may be necessary to remove the air cleaner assembly as described in Chapter 4A, Section 2.

5 Where applicable, remove the engine undertray, and then position a suitable container beneath the bottom hose connection on the radiator on 4-cylinder engines and below the engine oil cooler on 6-cylinder engines. Release the securing clip and carefully disconnect the bottom hose, allowing the coolant to drain into the container below. Once the system has drained completely, reconnect the bottom hose and secure with the hose clip. **Note:** *On 6-cylinder models, remove the cylinder block drain plug to allow the coolant to drain from the engine.*

Flushing

6 With time, the cooling system may gradually lose its efficiency due to the radiator core having become choked with rust, scale deposits and other sediment. To minimise this, the system should be flushed as described in the following paragraphs, whenever the coolant is renewed.

7 With the coolant drained, refill the system with fresh water. Refit the expansion tank filler cap, start the engine and warm it up to normal operating temperature, then stop it and (after allowing it to cool down completely) drain the system again. Repeat as necessary until only clean water can be seen to emerge, then refill finally with the specified coolant mixture.

8 If the specified coolant mixture has been used and has been renewed at the specified intervals, the above procedure will be sufficient to keep clean the system for a considerable length of time. If, however, the system has been neglected, a more thorough operation will be required, as follows.

9 First drain the coolant, and then disconnect the radiator top and bottom hoses from the

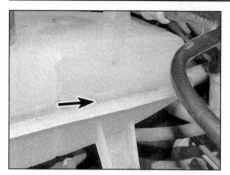

27.19 Top-up the expansion tank to the MAX level – arrowed

radiator. Insert a garden hose into the radiator top hose outlet and allow water (under LOW pressure only) to circulate through the radiator until it runs clean from the bottom outlet.

Caution: Do not flush with water under high pressure, as this may damage the radiator.

10 To flush the engine, insert the garden hose into the top hose and allow water to circulate until it runs clear from the bottom hose. If, after a reasonable period, the water still does not run clear, the cooling system should be flushed with a good proprietary cleaning agent. Bear in mind, however, that any leaks sealed in the past using a cooling system sealant additive may be weakened by this course of action, and could start to leak again.

11 In severe cases of contamination, reverse-flushing of the radiator may be necessary. To do this, remove the radiator, invert it and insert a garden hose into the bottom outlet. Continue flushing (again, using water under LOW pressure only) until clear water runs from the top hose outlet. If necessary, a similar procedure can be used to flush the heater matrix.

12 The use of chemical cleaners should be necessary only as a last resort as regular renewal of the coolant will prevent excessive contamination of the system.

Filling

13 With the cooling system drained and flushed, ensure that all radiator hoses are securely reconnected. Check all hose unions for security and all hoses for condition. Fresh antifreeze has a searching action, which will rapidly find any weaknesses in the system.

14 Prepare a sufficient quantity of the specified coolant mixture, allowing for a surplus so as to have a reserve supply for topping-up (see *Antifreeze mixture* above).

15 On 4-cylinder engines, if not already done, remove the air cleaner assembly (see Chapter 4A, Section 2) to gain access to the cooling system bleed screw in the coolant rail. Slacken the bleed screw fully, to allow trapped air to escape during refilling.

16 On 6-cylinder engines, slacken the bleed screw in the bottom hose, to allow trapped air to escape during refilling.

17 Remove the expansion tank filler cap, and then fill the system slowly through the filler neck. When coolant can be seen emerging from the bleed screw in a steady stream, tighten the bleed screw securely. Continue filling until the coolant level reaches the MAX mark on the side of the expansion tank. Refit the filler cap and tighten it securely.

18 Start the engine and run it at no more than idle speed until it has warmed-up to normal operating temperature and the radiator electric cooling fan has cut in once. Watch the temperature gauge to check for signs of overheating.

19 Stop the engine and allow it to cool down completely, then remove the expansion tank filler cap carefully and top up the tank to the MAX level **(see illustration)**. Refit the filler cap and wash off any spilt coolant from the engine compartment and bodywork with plenty of clean water.

20 After refilling, check carefully all system components for signs of coolant leaks. A label should now be attached to the radiator or expansion tank stating the type and concentration of antifreeze used and the date installed. Any subsequent topping-up should be made with the same type and concentration of antifreeze.

21 If, after draining and refilling the system, symptoms of overheating are found which did not occur previously, then the fault is almost certainly due to trapped air at some point in the system causing an airlock and restricting the flow of coolant. Usually air is trapped because the system was refilled too quickly. In some cases, airlocks can be released by tapping or squeezing the appropriate coolant hose. If the problem persists, stop the engine

and allow it to cool down completely before unscrewing the bleed screw and expansion tank filler cap, to allow the trapped air to escape.

28 Fuel filter renewal

⚠ *Warning: Petrol is extremely flammable – great care must be taken during this procedure. Before carrying out any operation on the fuel system, refer to the precautions given in 'Safety first!', and follow them implicitly. Petrol is a highly-dangerous and volatile liquid, and the precautions necessary when handling it cannot be overstressed.*

4-cylinder engines

1 The fuel filter is located on the bulkhead at the rear of the engine compartment **(see illustration)**.

2 Disconnect the battery negative terminal.

3 Position a wad of absorbent cloth beneath the inlet pipe union on the bottom of the fuel filter.

4 Using two spanners, counterhold the union on the fuel filter (to prevent damaging the fuel pipe), and **slowly** slacken the fuel pipe union nut **(see illustration)**.

⚠ *Warning: Be prepared for the escape of some fuel and take adequate fire precautions.*

5 Allow the fuel pressure to dissipate, then fully unscrew the union nut, and disconnect the fuel inlet pipe. If the new filter is not going to be fitted immediately, cover the open end of the fuel pipe union to prevent dirt entry.

6 Repeat the procedure to disconnect the fuel outlet pipe from the top of the fuel filter.

7 Release the retaining clip and withdraw the filter from the mounting bracket.

8 Collect the fuel from the filter, then dispose of the filter safely.

9 Fit the new filter using a reversal of the removal procedure, but ensure that the flow direction arrow on the side of the filter is pointing upwards **(see illustration)**, and tighten the fuel unions securely.

28.1 Fuel filter location on the bulkhead

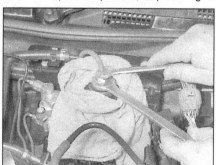

28.4 Slackening the fuel outlet pipe union

28.9 Ensure that the flow direction arrow on the side of the filter is pointing upwards

28.10 Fuel filter location on the left-hand inner wing panel

28.15 Use two spanners to counterhold the union nuts – arrowed

6-cylinder engines

10 The fuel filter is located at the left-hand side of the engine compartment, to the rear of the engine bay, below the EVAP canister **(see illustration)**.

11 Disconnect the battery negative terminal.

12 Release the EVAP canister from the inner wing panel and move it to one side.

13 Position a wad of absorbent cloth beneath the fuel hose quick-release connectors.

14 Pull back the quick-release connectors and disconnect the fuel hoses from the inlet and outlet pipes on the fuel filter. If the new filter is not going to be fitted immediately, cover the open end of the fuel pipe union to prevent dirt entry.

⚠ **Warning: Be prepared for the escape of some fuel and take adequate fire precautions.**

15 To remove the inlet and outlet pipes from the fuel filter, use two spanners to counterhold the union on the fuel filter (to prevent damaging the fuel pipe), and slacken the fuel pipe union nut **(see illustration)**.

16 Undo the fuel filter clamp bolt and withdraw the filter from the mounting bracket.

17 Collect the fuel from the filter, then dispose of the filter safely.

18 Fit the new filter using a reversal of the removal procedure, but ensure that the flow direction arrow on the side of the filter is pointing upwards towards the outlet pipe **(see**

illustration 28.9)**, and tighten the fuel unions securely.

29 Camshaft timing belt renewal

The procedure is described in Chapter 2A or 2B.

30 Transmission oil/fluid renewal

Refer to Chapter 7A or 7B.

Every 15 years, regardless of mileage

31 SRS system component renewal

1 The supplementary Restraint System (SRS), which includes the airbag(s), and seat belt pretensioners, has components which

contain pyrotechnic materials. Because these materials degrade with age, MG Rover specify that the following components must be renewed every 15 years:
  a) Driver airbag module.
  b) Passenger airbag module.
  c) Seat belt pretensioners.
  d) Rotary coupler.

2 Renewal information is given in Chapter 12. However, because of the safety critical nature of these components, and the need for special equipment to test their operation, we strongly recommend that renewal is done by an MG Rover specialist.

Notes

Chapter 1 Part B:
Routine maintenance and servicing – diesel models

Contents

Section number

Air cleaner filter element renewal 25
Air conditioning system check 11
Alarm remote keypad battery renewal 5
Auxiliary drivebelt tension and condition check. 12
Bodywork corrosion check. 4
Brake fluid renewal. 26
Camshaft timing belt renewal. 28
Coolant renewal 27
Coolant specific gravity check 7
Driveshaft check. 16
Engine oil and filter renewal 3
Exhaust system check 13
Front brake check 14
Fuel filter renewal 6
Handbrake check and adjustment 18
Heater/ventilation air intake filter renewal 24

Section number

Injection pump drivebelt renewal 29
Introduction 1
Lock and hinge lubrication. 19
Maintenance. 2
Rear brake check 15
Road test 23
Seat belt check. 21
SRS system component check 22
SRS system components renewal 31
Suspension and steering check. 17
Transmission oil/fluid level check. 8
Transmission oil/fluid renewal 30
Underbonnet and underbody hose and pipe condition check. 10
Vacuum hose condition check 9
Windscreen and number plate condition check. 20

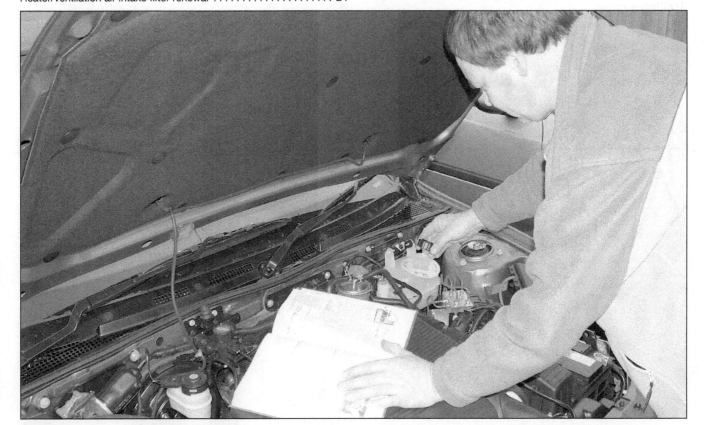

Degrees of difficulty

Easy, suitable for novice with little experience   **Fairly easy,** suitable for beginner with some experience **Fairly difficult,** suitable for competent DIY mechanic **Difficult,** suitable for experienced DIY mechanic **Very difficult,** suitable for expert DIY or professional

Lubricants and fluids

Refer to the end of *Weekly Checks* on page 0•18

Capacities

Engine oil refill and filter change	4.8 litres
Cooling system	7.0 litres (from dry)
Manual transmission	2.2 litres (from dry)/2.0 litres (drain and refill)
Automatic transmission	4.0 litres (drain and refill)
Power steering reservoir	0.35 litres
Fuel tank	55 litres
Washer system reservoir	6.0 litres

Cooling system

Antifreeze properties – 50% antifreeze (by volume):

Commences freezing	- 36°C
Frozen solid	- 48°C

Fuel system

Idle speed (for reference only)	805 ± 50 rpm

Braking system

Front and rear brake pad friction material minimum thickness	3.0 mm
Rear brake shoe friction material minimum thickness	2.0 mm
Handbrake lever travel	7 to 11 clicks

Tyre pressures

Refer to the end of *Weekly checks* on page 0•18

Torque wrench settings

	Nm	lbf ft
Automatic transmission:		
Drain plug..	45	33
Level plug..	14	10
Brake caliper bleed screws	10	7
Brake caliper guide pin bolts	27	20
Brake drum retaining screws	7	5
Engine oil drain plug......................................	25	18
Manual transmission filler/level plug:		
R65-type transmission	28	21
PG1-type transmission....................................	40	30
Roadwheel nuts	110	81
Wheel cylinder bleed screws	7	5

The maintenance intervals in this manual are provided with the assumption that you will be carrying out the work yourself. These are based on the minimum maintenance intervals recommended by the manufacturer for vehicles driven daily. If you wish to keep your vehicle in peak condition at all times, you may wish to perform some of these procedures more often. We encourage frequent maintenance because it enhances the efficiency, performance and resale value of your vehicle.

If the vehicle is driven in dusty areas, used to tow a trailer, or driven frequently at slow speeds (idling in traffic) or on short journeys, more frequent maintenance intervals are recommended.

When the vehicle is new, it should be serviced by a factory-authorised dealer service department, in order to preserve the factory warranty.

Every 250 miles or weekly
☐ Refer to *Weekly Checks*

Every 6000 miles or 6 months – whichever comes first
☐ Engine oil and filter – renew (Section 3)
Note: *Frequent oil and filter changes are good for the engine. We recommend renewing the oil and filter at these intervals, or at least twice a year.*

Every 12 000 miles or 12 months – whichever comes first
☐ Bodywork corrosion check (Section 4)
☐ Alarm remote keypad batteries – renew (Section 5)
☐ Fuel filter – renew (Section 6)
☐ Coolant specific gravity – check (Section 7)
☐ Transmission oil/fluid level – check (Section 8)
☐ Vacuum hose – check condition (Section 9)
☐ Underbonnet and underbody hoses and pipes – check condition (Section 10)
☐ Air conditioning system – check (Section 11)
☐ Auxiliary drivebelt – check condition and tension (Section 12)
☐ Exhaust system – check (Section 13)
☐ Front brake – check (Section 14)
☐ Rear brake – check (Section 15)
☐ Driveshaft and gaiter – check (Section 16)
☐ Suspension and steering – check (Section 17)
☐ Handbrake – check (Section 18)
☐ Lock and hinge lubrication (Section 19)
☐ Windscreen and number plate – check (Section 20)
☐ Seat belt – check (Section 21)
☐ SRS system component – check (Section 22)
☐ Road test (Section 23)
☐ Heater/ventilation air intake filter – renew (Section 24)

Every 24 000 miles or 2 years – whichever comes first
☐ Air cleaner – renew (Section 25)
☐ Brake fluid – renew (Section 26)

Every 48 000 miles or 4 years – whichever comes first
☐ Coolant – renew (Section 27)
☐ Camshaft timing belt – renew (models with manual tensioner for fuel injection pump drivebelt) (Section 28)
☐ Fuel injection pump drivebelt – renew (models with manual tensioner for fuel injection pump drivebelt) (Section 29)

Every 84 000 miles or 7 years – whichever comes first
☐ Camshaft timing belt – renew (models with auto tensioner for fuel injection pump drivebelt) (Section 28)
☐ Fuel injection pump drivebelt – renew (models with auto tensioner for fuel injection pump drivebelt) (Section 29)
Note: *This is the MG Rover recommendation. However, because of the serious and extensive damage which will occur to the engine if the belt breaks, we strongly recommend that belts are renewed more frequently – eg, every 48 000 miles or 4 years.*

Every 108 000 miles or 9 years – whichever comes first
☐ Transmission oil/fluid – renew (Section 30)

Every 15 years, regardless of mileage
☐ SRS components – renew (Section 31)

Underbonnet view of a turbo-diesel engine model

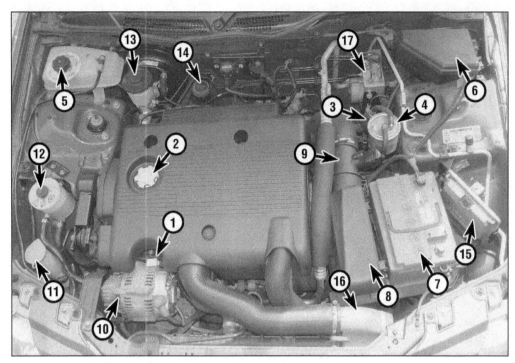

1 Engine oil level dipstick
2 Engine oil filler cap
3 Fuel system priming bulb
4 Fuel filter
5 Coolant expansion tank
6 Engine compartment fusebox
7 Battery
8 Air cleaner
9 Air mass meter
10 Alternator/vacuum pump
11 Washer fluid reservoir cap
12 Power steering fluid reservoir
13 Brake fluid reservoir/ master cylinder
14 Clutch fluid reservoir/ master cylinder
15 Engine management ECU
16 Turbo intercooler
17 ABS unit

Front underbody view of a petrol engine model – diesel similar

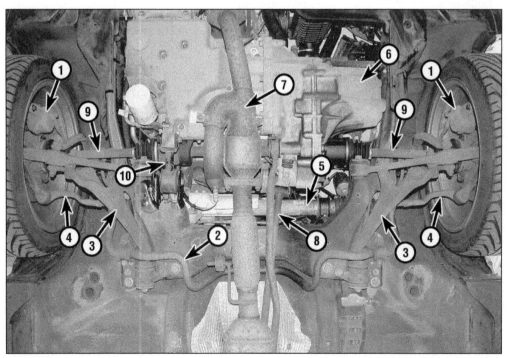

1 Brake caliper
2 Anti-roll bar
3 Suspension lower arm
4 Track rod
5 Power steering rack
6 Manual transmission
7 Exhaust system front pipe
8 Gear linkage rod
9 Driveshaft
10 Engine mounting lower steady bar

Rear underbody view of a petrol engine model – diesel similar

1 Handbrake cables
2 Rear trailing arm
3 Suspension coil/strut
4 Fuel tank
5 Suspension lower arm
6 Exhaust system tailbox
7 Trailing arm front
   compensator link
8 Anti-roll bar

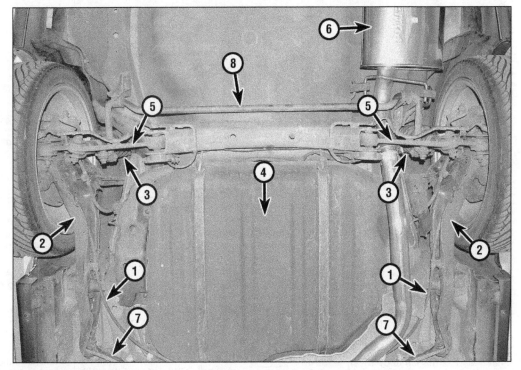

Maintenance procedures

1 Introduction

This Chapter is designed to help the home mechanic maintain his/her vehicle for safety, economy, long life and peak performance.

The Chapter contains a master maintenance schedule, referring to Sections dealing specifically with each task in the schedule, or other Chapters. Visual checks, adjustments, component renewal and other helpful items are included. Refer to the accompanying illustrations of the engine compartment and the underside of the vehicle for the locations of the various components.

Servicing your vehicle in accordance with the mileage/time maintenance schedule and the following Sections will provide a planned maintenance programme, which should result in a long and reliable service life. This is a comprehensive plan, so maintaining some items but not others at the specified service intervals will not produce the same results.

As you service your vehicle, you will discover that many of the procedures can be grouped together, because of the particular procedure being performed, or because of the close proximity of two otherwise-unrelated components to one another. For example, if the vehicle is raised for any reason, the exhaust can be inspected at the same time as the suspension and steering components.

The first step in this maintenance programme is to prepare yourself before the actual work begins. Read through all the Sections relevant to the work to be carried out, then make a list and gather together all the parts and tools required. If a problem is encountered, seek advice from a parts specialist, or a dealer service department.

2 Maintenance

1 If, from the time the vehicle is new, the routine maintenance schedule is followed closely and frequent checks are made of fluid levels and high-wear items, as suggested throughout this Manual, the engine will be kept in relatively good running condition and the need for additional work will be minimised.
2 It is possible that there will be times when the engine is running poorly due to the lack of regular maintenance. This is even more likely if a used vehicle, which has not received regular and frequent maintenance checks, is purchased. In such cases, additional work may need to be carried out, outside of the regular maintenance intervals.
3 If engine wear is suspected, a compression test will provide valuable information regarding the overall performance of the main internal components. Such a test can be used as a basis to decide on the extent of the work to

be carried out. If, for example, a compression test indicates serious internal engine wear, conventional maintenance as described in this Chapter will not greatly improve the performance of the engine, and may prove a waste of time and money unless extensive overhaul work is carried out first.
4 The following series of operations are those most often required to improve the performance of a generally poor-running engine:

Primary operations

a) Clean, inspect and test the battery (see 'Weekly checks').
b) Check all the engine-related fluids (see 'Weekly checks').
c) Check the condition and tension of the auxiliary drivebelt.
d) Check the condition of the air filter, and renew if necessary.
e) Check the fuel filter and drain off all water.
f) Check the condition of all hoses, and check for fluid leaks.

5 If the above operations do not prove fully effective, carry out the following secondary operations:

Secondary operations

a) Check the charging system (see relevant Part of Chapter 5A).
b) Check the fuel system (see relevant Part of Chapter 4C).
c) Check the preheating system (see relevant Part of Chapter 5C).

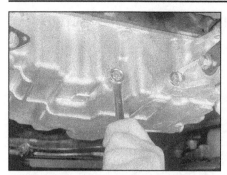

3.5 Slackening the engine oil drain plug

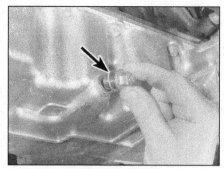

3.7 Refit the drain plug using a new sealing washer

3.10 Loosening the oil filter using an oil filter removal tool

Every 6000 miles or 6 months

3 Engine oil and filter renewal

Note: *An oil filter removal tool and a new oil drain plug sealing washer will be required for this operation.*

1 Frequent oil and filter changes are the most important preventative maintenance procedures which can be undertaken by the DIY owner. As engine oil ages, it becomes diluted and contaminated, which leads to premature engine wear.

2 Before starting this procedure, gather together all the necessary tools and materials. Also make sure that you have plenty of clean rags and newspapers handy, to mop-up any spills. Ideally, the engine oil should be warm, as it will drain more easily, and more built-up sludge will be removed with it. Take care not to touch the exhaust or any other hot parts of the engine when working under the vehicle. To avoid any possibility of scalding, and to protect yourself from possible skin irritants and other harmful contaminants in used engine oils, it is advisable to wear gloves when carrying out this work.

3 Access to the underside of the vehicle will be greatly improved if it can be raised on a lift, driven onto ramps, or jacked up and supported on axle stands (see *Jacking and vehicle support*). Whichever method is chosen, make sure that the vehicle remains level, or if it is at an angle, that the drain plug is at the lowest point. Where applicable, remove the engine/transmission undershield for access to the drain plug. The drain plug is located at the rear of the sump.

4 Remove the oil filler cap from the cylinder head cover.

5 Using a spanner, or preferably a suitable socket and bar, slacken the drain plug about half a turn **(see illustration)**. Position the draining container under the drain plug, and then remove the plug completely. If possible, try to keep the plug pressed into the sump while unscrewing it by hand the last couple of turns.

> **HAYNES HiNT** *As the plug releases from the threads, move it away sharply, so that the stream of oil from the sump runs into the container, not up your sleeve.*

6 Allow some time for the oil to drain, noting that it may be necessary to reposition the container as the oil flow slows to a trickle.

7 After all the oil has drained; wipe the drain plug and the sealing washer with a clean rag. The sealing washer should be renewed as a matter of course. Clean the area around the drain plug opening, and refit the plug complete with the new sealing washer **(see illustration)**. Tighten the plug securely, preferably to the specified torque, using a torque wrench.

8 The oil filter is located at the right-hand rear corner of the engine. Access is most easily obtained by jacking up the front of the vehicle (see *Jacking and vehicle support*).

9 Move the container into position under the oil filter.

10 Use an oil filter removal tool to slacken the filter initially, then unscrew it by hand the rest of the way **(see illustration)**. Empty the oil from the old filter into the container.

11 Use a clean rag to remove all oil, dirt and sludge from the filter sealing area on the engine. Check the old filter to make sure that the filter's rubber sealing ring has not stuck to the engine. If it has, carefully remove it.

12 Apply a light coating of clean engine oil to the sealing ring on the new filter, then screw the filter into position on the engine. Tighten the filter firmly by hand only – **do not** use any tools.

13 Remove the old oil and all tools from under the vehicle then, if applicable, lower the vehicle to the ground.

14 Fill the engine through the filler hole in the cylinder head cover, using the correct grade and type of oil (see *Lubricants and fluids*). Pour in half the specified quantity of oil first, and then wait a few minutes for the oil to drain into the sump. Continue to add oil, a small quantity at a time, until the level is up to the lower mark on the dipstick. Adding approximately 1.0 litre will bring the level up to the upper mark on the dipstick.

15 Start the engine and run it for a few minutes, while checking for leaks around the oil filter seal and the sump drain plug. Note that there may be a delay of a few seconds before the low oil pressure warning light goes out when the engine is first started, as the oil circulates through the new oil filter and engine oil galleries before the pressure builds-up.

16 Stop the engine, and wait a few minutes for the oil to settle in the sump once more. With the new oil circulated and the filter now completely full, recheck the level on the dipstick, and add more oil as necessary.

17 Dispose of the used engine oil safely.

Every 12 000 miles or 12 months

4 Bodywork corrosion check

1 Start at the front of the car and work along each body panel in turn, looking for any signs of paintwork damage. It may be possible to repair small scratches with a touch-up pen.

These should be purchased from a Rover dealer, to get an accurate colour match.

2 Larger scratches that have penetrated the primer or exposed the bare metal beneath should be repaired professionally. The Rover 45 has an extensive Anti-Corrosion Warranty, the terms of which specify how bodywork repairs must be carried out; failure to adhere to the guidelines may invalidate the warranty.

Have the damage assessed by a Rover Dealer or automotive bodywork specialist at the earliest opportunity.

3 Check each body panel for evidence of corrosion, such as raised blisters behind the paintwork and rust-coloured staining. Pay particular attention to vulnerable areas, including the wheel arches, the front edge of the bonnet, the front valence (under the front

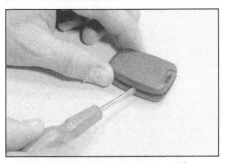

5.1a Using a flat-bladed screwdriver, carefully prise the two halves of the keypad apart . . .

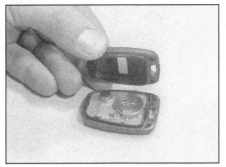

5.1b . . . to expose the battery

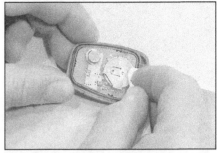

5.3 Fit the new battery, handling it with a piece of tissue paper to avoid touching the battery contact surfaces

bumper) and the lower edges of the doors. Corrosion can quickly destroy bodywork, so have any dubious-looking areas examined by a professional.

4 Jack up the front/rear car and support it securely on axle stands (see *Jacking and vehicle support*).

5 Examine the underside of the car for signs of corrosion. Look for cracking or flaking of the metal floorpan. Pay particular attention to the areas around the suspension and steering components mountings. Look for damage that may have been caused by attempting to jack up the car at incorrect jacking points.

6 Check for corrosion along the length of the side sills, which run between the front and rear wheel arches.

7 The underside of the vehicle is coated with a protective sealant, which helps to prevent corrosion. If this coating has been scraped off at any point, due to an impact or repair work, it must be re-applied as soon as possible, to protect the bodywork beneath.

5 Alarm remote keypad battery renewal

1 Place the keypad on a work surface and, using a flat-bladed screwdriver, carefully prise the two halves of the keypad apart. Take care to avoid damaging the rubber seal with the screwdriver blade **(see illustrations)**.

2 Remove the battery from the terminal clips, noting which way up it is. Press each keypad button in turn and hold them down for a few

seconds, to fully discharge the electronic components inside.

3 Obtain a new battery of the correct type and insert it between the terminal clips, ensuring that it is fitted the correct way around (the positive '+' side faces the keypad backplate). Avoid touching the contact surfaces of the battery as you do this, by handling it with a piece of tissue paper; moisture from fingertips can cause the battery surfaces to corrode **(see illustration)**.

4 Press the two halves of the keypad back together, ensuring that the rubber seal is correctly located, then check the operation of the keypad.

6 Fuel filter renewal

⚠ *Warning: Fuel is extremely flammable – great care must be taken during this procedure. Before carrying out any operation on the fuel system, refer to the precautions given in 'Safety first!', and follow them implicitly. Fuel is a highly dangerous and volatile liquid, and the precautions necessary when handling it cannot be overstressed.*

1 The fuel filter is located at the left-hand side of the engine compartment, to the rear of the battery **(see illustration)**.

2 Position a wad of absorbent cloth beneath the fuel filter.

3 Release the hose clip, and disconnect the fuel inlet hose from the top of the fuel filter

(see illustration). If the new filter is not going to be fitted immediately, clamp or cover the open end of the fuel hose to prevent dirt entry and fuel loss.

⚠ *Warning: Be prepared for the escape of some fuel and take adequate fire precautions.*

4 Repeat the procedure to disconnect the fuel outlet hose from the top of the filter **(see illustration 6.3)**.

5 Slacken the fuel filter clamp bolt, and withdraw the filter from the clamp bracket.

6 Put the fuel filter in to a container to catch any spilt fuel, then dispose of the filter safely.

7 Fit the new filter using a reversal of the removal procedure, but ensure that the hoses are correctly reconnected – fuel flow direction arrows are stamped into the filter adjacent to the fuel pipes. Ensure that the hose clips are tight and, on completion, prime the fuel system as described in Chapter 4C.

7 Coolant specific gravity check

1 Ensure that the engine has cooled completely before starting work.

2 Slowly unscrew the coolant expansion tank cap by about half a turn, allowing any residual pressure in the cooling system to reduce gradually – use a cloth to protect your hands from any escaping steam.

3 Insert a hydrometer into the expansion tank filler neck and measure the specific gravity of the coolant **(see illustration)**.

6.1 Location of diesel fuel filter

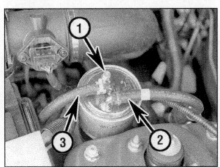

6.3 Fuel filter bleed screw (1), inlet hose (2) and outlet hose (3)

7.3 Using a hydrometer to measure the specific gravity of the coolant

8.2 Transmission filler/level plug (arrowed)

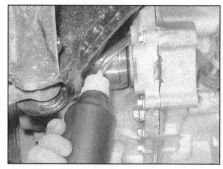

8.5 Topping-up the transmission oil level

4 The hydrometer shown in the photo incorporates an integral syringe, which allows a 'sample' of the coolant to be collected. The coloured indicator balls inside the hydrometer float or sink in the coolant sample, depending on the specific gravity.

5 If the specific gravity is too low, do not try to correct it by adding neat antifreeze, as it may not mix completely with the existing coolant and could lead to 'hot spots' in the cooling system. With reference to Section 27, partially drain the cooling system, then refill it with antifreeze and water mixed in the correct proportions.

6 If the specific gravity is too high, refer to Section 27 and partially drain the cooling system, then top-up with clean water.

8 Transmission oil/fluid level check

Manual transmission

1 Ensure that the vehicle is parked on level ground then, where applicable, remove the engine/transmission undershield to gain access to the transmission filler/level plug.

2 Remove all traces of dirt from around the filler/level plug, which is located on the left-hand side of the transmission, behind the driveshaft inboard joint **(see illustration)**. Place a suitable container beneath the plug to catch any escaping oil, then unscrew the plug and recover the sealing washer.

3 Check that the oil is level with the bottom

of the filler/level plug hole. **Note:** *Oil which has collected behind the filler/level plug will probably trickle out when the plug is removed, this can give a false impression that the level is correct.*

4 If necessary, top-up using the specified type of oil (see *Lubricants and fluids*). Refilling the transmission is an awkward operation. Allow plenty of time for the oil level to settle properly before checking it. Note that the car must be parked on flat level ground when checking the oil level.

5 Using a tube inserted through the filler/level plug hole, slowly top up the level until the oil reaches the bottom of the filler/level plug hole **(see illustration)**. Allow plenty of time for the level to stabilise.

6 When the level is correct, refit the filler/level plug, using a new sealing washer, and tighten it to the specified torque.

Automatic transmission

⚠️ *Warning: The transmission fluid may be extremely hot.*

7 Remove the engine undertray, which is secured by a number of quick-release screw fasteners.

8 The fluid level is checked with the transmission at operating temperature, and with the engine running. Starting at P, and with the footbrake firmly pressed, move the selector lever through each position. Pause in each position for a few seconds, then return to position P.

9 Clean the area around the level plug, which is located directly below the selector cable – it may even be necessary to detach the cable for better access.

10 Using a 5 mm Allen key, unscrew the filler/level plug, which will probably be very tight. Recover the sealing ring – a new one will be needed when refitting.

11 The level must be just below the bottom edge of the level plug hole (use a cranked tool such as an Allen key to check the level). With the engine running, allow any excess fluid to drain.

12 If the level is correct, refit the plug using a new sealing washer, and tighten it to the specified torque. Switch off the engine.

13 If topping-up is required, switch off the engine and remove the air cleaner as described in Chapter 4C.

14 Clean around the filler pipe on top of the transmission – it is vital that no dirt enters the transmission at any stage. Pull out the filler plug.

15 Start the engine, then slowly add clean fluid of the specified type (see *Lubricants and fluids*). Add small amounts at a time, until fluid starts to flow from the level plug hole, then refit the filler plug firmly into its pipe. Refit the air cleaner as described in Chapter 4C.

16 Move the selector lever through all positions as described in paragraph 8, and allow any excess fluid to run out.

17 When the level stabilises, stop the engine. Refit and tighten the level plug (with a new sealing washer) to the specified torque.

18 Refit the engine undertray on completion.

9 Vacuum hose condition check

1 Open the bonnet and check the condition of the vacuum hose that connects the brake servo to the vacuum pump **(see illustration)**. Look for damage in the form of chafing, melting or cracking. Check that the union nuts and T-joints (where applicable) are secure. Also examine the vacuum hoses serving the evaporative loss emission control and fuel pressure regulation systems.

2 Locate the manifold absolute pressure (MAP) sensor and the exhaust gas recirculation (EGR) solenoid valve at the rear of the engine compartment on the bulkhead. Inspect the vacuum hoses that run to the sensor and solenoid valve, ensuring that they are secure and free from damage **(see illustrations)**.

9.1 Check the condition of the brake servo vacuum hose – arrowed

9.2a Check MAP sensor vacuum pipe (arrowed) . . .

9.2b . . . and EGR solenoid valve hoses (arrowed)

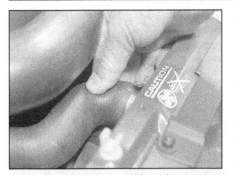

10.1 Checking the condition of a coolant hose

3 A leak in a vacuum hose means that air is being drawn into the hose (rather than escaping from it) and this makes leakage very difficult to detect. If you suspect that a vacuum hose may be leaking, the following method may help you to pinpoint it. Start the engine and allow it to idle. Hold one end of a length of narrow bore tubing close to your ear, and then run the other end along the vacuum hose. If a leak exists, you should be able to hear a hissing noise through the tubing as the air 'escapes' into the hose at the suspected leak.

10 Underbonnet and underbody hose and pipe condition check

 Warning: Refer to the safety information given in 'Safety first!' and Chapter 3, before disturbing any of the systems components.

Coolant

1 Carefully check the radiator and heater coolant hoses along their entire length. Renew any hose that is cracked, swollen or which shows signs of deterioration. Cracks will show up better if the hose is squeezed **(see illustration)**. Pay close attention to the clips that secure the hoses to the cooling system components. Hose clips that have been overtightened can pinch and puncture hoses, resulting in leakage.

2 Inspect all the cooling system components (hoses, joint faces, etc) for leaks. Where any problems of this nature are found on system components, renew the component or gasket with reference to Chapter 3.

3 A leak from the cooling system will usually show up as white or rust-coloured deposits, on the area surrounding the leak **(see Haynes Hint)**.

Fuel

4 Unlike petrol leaks, diesel leaks are fairly easy to pinpoint; diesel fuel tends to settle on the surface around the point of leakage collecting dirt, rather than evaporate. If you suspect that there is a fuel leak from the area of the engine bay, leave the vehicle overnight then start the engine from cold,

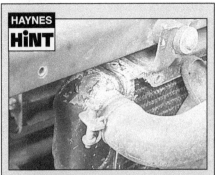

Leaks in the cooling system will usually show up as white or antifreeze-coloured deposits around the point of leakage.

and allow it to idle with the bonnet open. Metal components tend to shrink when they are cold, and rubber seals and hoses tend to harden, so any leaks may be more apparent whilst the engine is warming-up from a cold start.

5 Check all fuel lines at their connections to the fuel injection pump and fuel filter **(see illustration)**. Examine each rubber fuel hose along its length for splits or cracks. Check for leakage from the crimped joints between rubber and metal fuel lines. Examine the unions between the metal fuel lines and the fuel filter housing. Also check the area around the fuel injectors for signs of leakage.

6 To identify fuel leaks between the fuel tank and the engine bay, the vehicle should be raised and securely supported on axle stands (see *Jacking and vehicle support*). Inspect the fuel tank and filler neck for punctures, cracks and other damage. The connection between the filler neck and tank is especially critical. Sometimes a rubber filler neck or connecting hose will leak due to loose retaining clamps or deteriorated rubber.

7 Carefully check all rubber hoses and metal fuel lines leading away from the fuel tank. Check for loose connections, deteriorated hoses, kinked lines, and other damage. Pay particular attention to the vent pipes and hoses, which often loop up around the filler neck and can become blocked or kinked, making tank filling difficult. Follow the fuel supply and return lines to the front of the

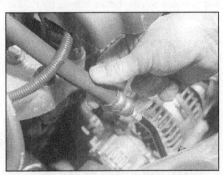

10.9 Checking a power steering fluid hose for damage

10.5 Check for fuel leaks at the fuel filter unions

vehicle, carefully inspecting them all the way for signs of damage or corrosion. Renew damaged sections as necessary.

Engine oil

8 Check the hoses leading to the engine oil cooler at the front of the engine bay for leakage. Look for deterioration caused by corrosion and damage from grounding, or debris thrown up from the road surface.

Power-assisted steering fluid

9 Examine the hose running between the fluid reservoir and the power steering pump, and the return hose running from the steering rack to the fluid reservoir. Also examine the high-pressure supply hose between the pump and the steering rack **(see illustration)**.

10 Where applicable, check the hoses leading to the PAS fluid cooler at the front of the engine bay. Look for deterioration caused by corrosion and damage from grounding, or debris thrown up from the road surface.

11 Pay particular attention to crimped unions, and the area surrounding the hoses that are secured with adjustable worm drive clips. PAS fluid is thin oil and usually red in colour.

Air conditioning refrigerant

12 The air conditioning system is filled with a liquid refrigerant, which is retained under high pressure. If the air conditioning system is opened and depressurised without the aid of specialised equipment, the refrigerant will immediately turn into gas and escape into the atmosphere. If the liquid comes into contact with your skin, it can cause severe frostbite. In addition, the refrigerant may contain substances that are environmentally damaging; for this reason, it should not be allowed to escape into the atmosphere.

13 Any suspected air conditioning system leaks should be immediately referred to a Rover dealer or air conditioning specialist. Leakage will be shown up as a steady drop in the level of refrigerant in the system – refer to Section 11 for details.

14 Note that water may drip from the condenser drain pipe, underneath the car, immediately after the air conditioning system has been in use. This is normal, and should not be cause for concern.

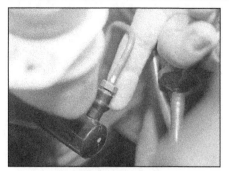

10.15 Checking a master cylinder brake pipe union for leakage

Brake fluid

15 With reference to Chapter 9, examine the area surrounding the brake pipe unions at the master cylinder for signs of leakage (see illustration). Check the area around the base of fluid reservoir, for signs of leakage caused by seal failure. Also examine the brake pipe unions at the ABS hydraulic unit. Brake fluid is an effective paint stripper, so if cracked or bubbling paintwork on or around any of the braking system components is found, suspect fluid leakage.

16 If fluid loss is evident, but the leak cannot be pinpointed in the engine bay, the brake

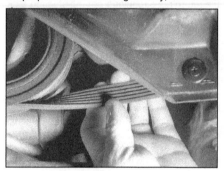

12.6 Checking the condition of the auxiliary drivebelt

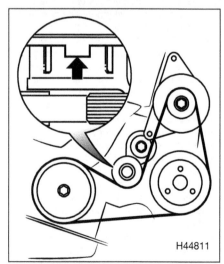

H44811

12.7 Auxiliary drivebelt and wear indicator

calipers and underbody brakelines and should be carefully checked with the vehicle raised and supported on axle stands (see *Jacking and vehicle support*). Leakage of fluid from the braking system is serious fault that must be rectified immediately.

17 Brake hydraulic fluid is a toxic substance with a watery consistency. New fluid is almost colourless, but it becomes darker with age and use.

Unidentified fluid leaks

18 If there are signs that a fluid of some description is leaking from the vehicle, but you cannot identify the type of fluid or its exact origin, park the vehicle overnight and slide a large piece of card underneath it. Providing that the card is positioned in roughly in the right location, even the smallest leak will show up on the card. Not only will this help you to pinpoint the exact location of the leak, it should be easier to identify the fluid from its colour. Bear in mind, though, that the leak may only be occurring when the engine is running!

Vacuum hoses

19 Refer to Section 9.

11 Air conditioning system check

A Rover dealer or air conditioning specialist must check the air conditioning system using dedicated test equipment.

12 Auxiliary drivebelt tension and condition check

General information

1 The auxiliary drivebelt is located at the right-hand side of the engine.

2 Due to their function and material makeup, drivebelts are prone to failure after a period of time and should therefore be inspected.

3 Since the drivebelt is located very close to the right-hand side of the engine compartment, it is possible to gain better access by raising the front of the vehicle (see *Jacking and vehicle support*) and removing the right-hand wheel, then removing the splash shield from inside the wheel arch.

4 The belt drives:
   a) *The power steering pump and the coolant pump, which are mounted in tandem in a common housing.*
   b) *The alternator, and the vacuum pump which is integral with the alternator.*
   c) *The air conditioning compressor – where fitted.* **Note:** *When air conditioning is not fitted an idler pulley, mounted on a bracket, takes the place of the compressor.*

Checking condition

5 Apply the handbrake, chock the rear roadwheels, then jack up the front of the car and support it on axle stands (see *Jacking and vehicle support*). Remove the right-hand roadwheel and the splash shield from inside the wheel arch.

6 With the engine switched off, inspect the full length of the drivebelt for cracks and separation of the belt plies (see illustration). It will be necessary to turn the crankshaft (using a socket or spanner on the crankshaft pulley bolt) in order to move the belt from the pulleys so that the full length of the belt can be inspected thoroughly. Twist the belt between the pulleys so that both sides can be viewed. Also check for fraying, and glazing which gives the belt a shiny appearance. Check the pulleys for nicks, cracks, distortion and corrosion.

7 Check the belt length – the belt must be renewed before the indicator reaches the right-hand end of the slot (see illustration).

8 A spring-loaded tensioner is fitted to automatically maintain the correct tension on the belt. If problems with belt squeal or slip are encountered, the belt should be renewed. If the problem continues, it will be necessary to renew the tensioner assembly.

9 Renew any worn or damaged belt – see Chapter 5A.

13 Exhaust system check

1 With the engine cold (at least an hour after the vehicle has been driven), check the complete exhaust system from the engine to the end of the tailpipe. The exhaust system is most easily checked with the vehicle raised on a hoist, or suitably supported on axle stands, so that the exhaust components are readily visible and accessible.

2 Check the exhaust pipes and connections for evidence of leaks, severe corrosion and damage. Make sure that all brackets and mountings are in good condition (see illustration), and that all relevant nuts and bolts are tight. Leakage at any of the joints or in other parts of the system will usually show up as a black sooty stain in the vicinity of the leak.

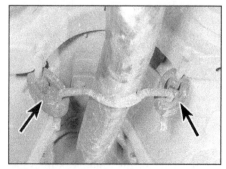

13.2 Check that the exhaust mountings are secure

3 Rattles and other noises can often be traced to the exhaust system, especially the brackets and mountings. Try to move the pipes and silencers. If the components are able to come into contact with the body or suspension parts, secure the system with new mountings. Otherwise separate the joints (if possible) and twist the pipes as necessary to provide additional clearance.

14 Front brake check

1 Firmly apply the handbrake then jack up the front of the vehicle and support it securely on axle stands (see *Jacking and vehicle support*). Remove the front roadwheels.
2 For a quick check, the pad thickness can be carried out via the inspection hole in the front of the caliper **(see Haynes Hint)**. If any pad's friction material is worn to the specified minimum thickness or less, all four pads must be renewed as a set.
3 For a comprehensive check, the brake pads should be removed and cleaned. This will permit the operation of the caliper to be checked and the condition of the brake disc itself to be fully examined on both sides. Refer to Chapter 9 for further information.
4 On completion refit the roadwheels and lower the car to the ground.

15 Rear brake check

Models with drum brakes

1 For a comprehensive check, the brake drums should be removed and cleaned. This will permit the wheel cylinders to be checked and the condition of the brake drum itself to be fully examined. Refer to Chapter 9 for further information.
2 On completion refit the roadwheels, lower the vehicle to the ground and tighten the wheel nuts to the specified torque setting.

Models with disc brakes

3 Chock the front wheels then jack up the rear of the vehicle and support it on axle stands (see *Jacking and vehicle support*).
4 For a quick check, the thickness of friction material remaining on each brake pad can be measured through the inspection aperture in the caliper body (see **Haynes Hint** for checking front brake pads in the previous Section). If any pad's friction material is worn to the specified minimum thickness or less, all four pads must be renewed as a set.
5 For a comprehensive check, the brake pads should be removed and cleaned. This will permit the operation of the caliper to be checked and the condition of the brake disc itself to be fully examined on both sides. Refer to Chapter 9 for further information.

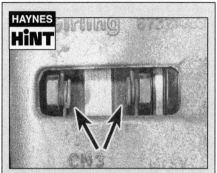

For a quick check, the thickness of the material remaining on the brake pads can be measured through the aperture in the caliper body

6 On completion refit the roadwheels, lower the vehicle to the ground and tighten the wheel nuts to the specified torque setting.

16 Driveshaft check

1 With the vehicle raised and securely supported on axle stands (see *Jacking and vehicle support*), turn the steering onto full lock then slowly rotate the roadwheel. Inspect the condition of the outer constant velocity (CV) joint rubber gaiters while squeezing the gaiters to open out the folds **(see illustration)**. Check for signs of cracking, splits or deterioration of the rubber, which may allow the grease to escape and lead to the entry of water and grit into the joint. Also check the security and condition of the gaiter retaining clips. Repeat these checks on the inner CV joints. If any damage or deterioration is found, then renew the gaiters.
2 Check the general condition of the CV joints by first holding the driveshaft and attempting to rotate the roadwheel. Repeat this check by holding the inner joint and attempting to rotate the driveshaft. Any appreciable movement indicates wear in the joints or driveshaft splines, or a loose driveshaft nut.

17 Suspension and steering check

Front suspension and steering

1 Raise the front of the vehicle and securely support it on axle stands (see *Jacking and vehicle support*).
2 Visually inspect the balljoint dust covers and the steering gear rubber gaiters for splits, chafing or deterioration **(see illustration)**. Any wear of these components will cause loss of lubricant, together with dirt and water entry, resulting in rapid deterioration of the balljoints or steering gear.

16.1 Inspecting a driveshaft joint rubber gaiter

3 Check the power-assisted steering (PAS) fluid hoses for chafing or deterioration, and the pipe and hose unions for fluid leakage. Also check for signs of fluid leakage under pressure from the steering gear rubber gaiters, which would indicate failed fluid seals within the steering gear.
4 Grasp the roadwheel at the 12 o'clock and 6 o'clock positions and try to rock it **(see illustration)**. Very slight free play may be felt but if the movement is appreciable then further investigation is necessary to determine the source. Continue rocking the wheel while an assistant depresses the brake pedal. If the movement is now eliminated or significantly reduced, it is likely that the hub bearings are at fault. If the free play is still evident with the brake pedal depressed, then there is wear in the suspension joints or mountings.
5 Now grasp the roadwheel at the 9 o'clock and 3 o'clock positions and try to rock it as

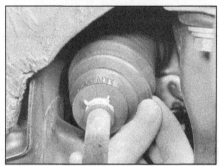

17.2 Checking the condition of a steering gear rubber gaiter

17.4 Checking the condition of the steering and suspension components by rocking a roadwheel

18.5 Handbrake cable adjuster nut (arrowed) and equaliser mechanism

before. Any movement felt now may again be caused by wear in the hub bearings, or in the track rod balljoints. If a balljoint is worn the visual movement will be obvious. If the inner joint is suspect it can be felt by placing a hand over the steering gear rubber gaiter and gripping the track rod. If the wheel is now rocked, movement will be felt at the inner joint if wear has taken place.

6 Using a large screwdriver or flat bar, check for wear in the suspension mounting bushes by levering between the relevant suspension component and its attachment point. Some movement is to be expected as the mountings are made of rubber, but excessive wear should be obvious. Also check the condition of any visible rubber bushes, looking for splits, cracks or contamination of the rubber.

7 With the vehicle standing on its wheels, have an assistant turn the steering wheel back-and-forth about an eighth of a turn each way. There should be very little, if any, lost movement between the steering wheel and the roadwheels. If this is not the case, closely observe the joints and mountings previously described but in addition, check for wear of the steering column universal joint and the steering gear itself.

Rear suspension

8 Chock the front wheels then jack up the rear of the vehicle and support it on axle stands (see *Jacking and vehicle support*).

9 Working as described for the front suspension, check the rear hub bearings and the trailing arm and lateral link bushes for wear.

Shock absorber check

10 Check for any signs of fluid leakage around the shock absorber body, or from the rubber gaiter around the piston rod. Should any fluid be noticed, the shock absorber is defective internally, and should be renewed. **Note:** *Shock absorbers should always be renewed in pairs on the same axle.*

11 To check the efficiency of the shock absorbers, bounce the vehicle at each corner. Generally speaking, the body will return to its normal position and stop after being depressed. If it rises and returns on a rebound, the shock absorber is probably suspect. Also examine the shock absorber upper and lower mountings for any signs of wear.

18 Handbrake check and adjustment

Checking

1 The handbrake should be capable of holding the parked vehicle stationary, even on steep slopes, when applied with moderate force. Equally, the handbrake must release properly, or the brakes will bind and overheat when the car is driven.

2 The mechanism should be firm and positive in feel with no trace of stiffness or sponginess from the cables and should release immediately the handbrake lever is released. If the mechanism is faulty in any of these respects then it must be checked immediately.

3 To check the handbrake setting, first apply the footbrake firmly several times. Applying normal, moderate pressure, pull the handbrake lever to the fully applied position whilst counting the number of 'clicks' produced by the handbrake ratchet mechanism. Check that the number of clicks produced is as specified, if this is not the case, then adjustment is required.

Adjustment

4 To adjust the handbrake, chock the front wheels then jack up the rear of the vehicle and support it on axle stands (see *Jacking and vehicle support*).

5 Lift out the ashtray from the rear of the centre console to gain access to the handbrake adjusting nut **(see illustration)**.

6 Apply the handbrake and check that the equaliser and cables move freely and smoothly, then set the lever on the first notch of the ratchet mechanism.

7 With the lever in this position, rotate the handbrake lever adjusting nut until only a slight drag can be felt when the rear wheels are turned by hand.

8 Once this is the case, fully release the handbrake lever and check that the wheels rotate freely.

9 Check adjustment by applying the handbrake fully whilst counting the clicks emitted from the handbrake ratchet. Carry out the adjustment procedure again, if necessary.

10 Once adjustment is correct, refit the ashtray and lower the vehicle to the ground.

19 Lock and hinge lubrication

1 Lubricate the hinges of the bonnet, doors and tailgate with some light duty oil.

2 Lightly grease the bonnet release mechanism and cable.

3 The door and tailgate latches, strikers and locks must be lubricated using only the special Rover Door Lock and Latch Lubricant supplied in small sachets. Inject 1 gram into each lock and wipe off any surplus, then apply a thin film to the latches and strikers.

4 Do not lubricate the steering lock mechanism with oil or any other lubricant, which might foul the ignition switch contacts. If the lock is stiff, try the effect of a proprietary electrical contact lubricant, rather than conventional lubricant.

5 If a sunroof is fitted, lubricate very sparingly the seal lip with Rover supplied non-staining seal grease.

20 Windscreen and number plate condition check

Refer to the *MOT test checks* described in the *Reference* Chapter, at the end of this manual.

21 Seat belt check

1 Carefully examine the seat belt webbing of each seat belt for signs of fraying, cuts or other damage, pulling the belt out to its full extent to check its entire length **(see illustration)**.

2 Check the operation of the belt buckles by fitting the belt tongue plate and pulling hard to ensure that it remains locked in position.

3 Check the retractor mechanism (inertia reel only) by pulling out the belt to the halfway point and jerking it downwards **(see illustration)**.

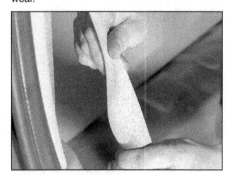

21.1 Check the webbing of each seat belt for signs of fraying, cuts or other damage

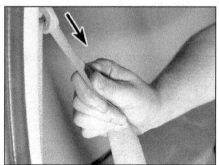

21.3 Checking the operation of the inertia reel locking mechanism

The mechanism must lock immediately to prevent any further unreeling but must allow free movement during normal driving.

4 Ensure that all belt mounting bolts are securely tightened. Note that the bolts are shouldered so that the belt anchor points are free to rotate.

5 If there is any sign of damage, or any doubt about a belt's condition, then it must be renewed. If the vehicle has been involved in a collision, then any belt in use at the time must be renewed as a matter of course and all other belts checked carefully.

6 Use only warm water and non-detergent soap to clean the belts.

Caution: Never use any chemical cleaners, strong detergents, dyes or bleaches. Keep the belts fully extended until they have dried naturally and do not apply heat to dry them.

22 SRS system component check

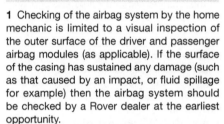

1 Checking of the airbag system by the home mechanic is limited to a visual inspection of the outer surface of the driver and passenger airbag modules (as applicable). If the surface of the casing has sustained any damage (such as that caused by an impact, or fluid spillage for example) then the airbag system should be checked by a Rover dealer at the earliest opportunity.

2 Sit in the driver's seat and release the steering column lock. On models with power steering, start the engine and allow it to idle. Turn the steering wheel from lock-to-lock, whilst listening to the rotary coupler at the steering wheel hub. Any noise or roughness in operation could indicate a worn rotary coupler – refer to a Rover dealer for further advice.

3 The SRS warning lamp on the instrument panel should illuminate for about six seconds when the ignition key is turned to the 'II' position and then extinguish. If the lamp fails to extinguish, or does not illuminate at all, there may be a fault with the SRS system; the advice of a Rover dealer should be sought.

23 Road test

Instruments and electrical equipment

1 Check the operation of all instruments and electrical equipment.

2 Make sure that all instruments read correctly, and switch on all electrical equipment in turn, to check that it functions properly.

Steering and suspension

3 Check for any abnormalities in the steering, suspension, handling or road 'feel'.

4 Drive the vehicle, and check that there are no unusual vibrations or noises.

5 Check that the steering feels positive, with no excessive 'sloppiness', or roughness, and check for any suspension noises when cornering and driving over bumps.

Drivetrain

6 Check the performance of the engine, clutch, transmission and driveshafts.

7 Listen for any unusual noises from the engine, clutch and transmission.

8 Make sure that the engine runs smoothly when idling, and that there is no hesitation when accelerating.

9 Check that the clutch action is smooth and progressive, that the drive is taken up smoothly, and that the pedal travel is not excessive. Also listen for any noises when the clutch pedal is depressed.

10 Check that all gears can be engaged smoothly without noise, and that the gear lever action is smooth and not abnormally vague or 'notchy'.

11 Listen for a metallic clicking sound from the front of the vehicle, as the vehicle is driven slowly in a circle with the steering on full-lock. Carry out this check in both directions. If a clicking noise is heard, this indicates wear in a driveshaft joint (see Chapter 8).

Braking system

12 Make sure that the vehicle does not pull to one side when braking, and that the wheels do not lock when braking hard.

13 Check that there is no vibration through the steering when braking.

14 Check that the handbrake operates correctly, without excessive movement of the lever, and that it holds the vehicle stationary on a slope.

15 Test the operation of the brake servo unit as follows. Depress the footbrake four or five times to exhaust the vacuum, and then start the engine. As the engine starts, there should be a noticeable 'give' in the brake pedal as vacuum builds-up. Allow the engine to run for at least two minutes, and then switch it off. If the brake pedal is now depressed again, it should be possible to detect a hiss from the servo as the pedal is depressed. After about four or five applications, no further hissing should be heard, and the pedal should feel considerably harder.

24 Heater/ventilation air intake filter renewal

Models with conventional heater

1 Release the fixings and remove the lower cover panel from the passenger's side of the facia.

2 Release the two securing clips and remove the cover from the heater unit housing.

3 Withdraw the filter element from the heater unit and discard it.

4 Clean the inside of the filter housing and cover, then fit a new filter using the reversal of the removal procedure.

Models with air conditioning

5 Release the fixings and remove the lower cover panel from the passenger's side of the facia.

6 Undo the two securing bolts and withdraw the glovebox from the facia panel.

7 Undo the four screws securing the glovebox lower rail and withdraw it from the facia panel.

8 Release the two securing clips and remove the cover from the evaporator/heater unit housing.

9 Withdraw the filter element from the heater unit and discard it, noting the airflow direction arrow for refitting.

10 Clean inside the filter housing and cover, then fit a new filter (noting direction arrow) using the reversal of the removal procedure.

25.2 Release the two clips – arrowed

25.3a Release the air cleaner cover securing clips . . .

25.3b . . . then lift the cover and lift out the element

Every 24 000 miles or 2 years

25 Air cleaner filter element renewal

1 The air cleaner is located at the left-hand side of the engine compartment, next to the battery.

2 Release the two clips securing the mass airflow (MAF) sensor to the air cleaner housing **(see illustration)**.

3 Release the four securing clips, then lift the upper part of the air cleaner housing to enable the element to be withdrawn **(see illustrations)**. Discard the dirty air cleaner element.

4 Wipe out the air cleaner housing and the upper cover using a clean cloth.

26.3 Brake fluid reservoir MAX level – arrowed

5 Fit the new air cleaner element, then refit the upper part of the housing and secure with the four clips.

6 Refit the MAF sensor to the air cleaner housing and secure it with the two retaining clips.

26 Brake fluid renewal

⚠️ *Warning: Brake hydraulic fluid can harm your eyes and damage painted surfaces, so use extreme caution when handling and pouring it. Do not use fluid that has been standing open for some time, as it absorbs moisture from the air. Excess moisture can cause a dangerous loss of braking effectiveness. Caution: On models equipped with ABS, disconnect the battery before carrying out this operation and do not reconnect the battery until after the operation is complete. Failure to do this could lead to air entering the hydraulic unit. If air enters the hydraulic unit pump, it will prove very difficult (in some cases impossible) to bleed the unit. Refer to Chapter 5A when disconnecting the battery.*

1 This procedure is similar to that described for the bleeding of the hydraulic system, as described in Chapter 9, except that the brake fluid reservoir should be emptied by syphoning

and allowance should be made for all old fluid to be expelled when bleeding a section of the circuit.

2 Working as described in Chapter 9, open the first bleed screw in the sequence and pump the brake pedal gently until nearly all the old fluid has been emptied from the master cylinder reservoir. Top-up to the MAX level on the reservoir with new fluid and continue pumping until only new fluid remains in the reservoir and new fluid can be seen emerging from the bleed screw. Old hydraulic fluid is much darker in colour than new fluid, making it easy to distinguish between them.

3 Tighten the bleed screw and top the reservoir level up to the MAX level line **(see illustration)**.

4 Work through all the remaining bleed screws in the sequence until new fluid can be seen emerging from all of them. Be careful to keep the master cylinder reservoir topped-up to above the MIN level at all times, or air may enter the system and greatly increase the length of the task.

5 When the operation is complete, check that all bleed screws are securely tightened and that their dust caps are refitted. Wash off all traces of spilt fluid and recheck the master cylinder reservoir fluid level.

6 Check the operation of the brakes before taking the vehicle on the road.

7 Dispose safely of the used brake fluid with reference to *General repair procedures*.

Every 48 000 miles or 4 years

27 Coolant renewal

⚠️ *Warning: Wait until the engine is completely cold before starting the coolant renewal procedure. Do not allow antifreeze to come into contact with your skin or painted surfaces of the vehicle. Rinse off spills immediately*

with plenty of water. Never leave antifreeze lying around in an open container or in a puddle in the driveway or on the garage floor. Children and pets are attracted by its sweet smell; and antifreeze can be fatal if ingested.

Antifreeze mixture

1 Antifreeze should always be renewed at the specified intervals. This is necessary not only to maintain the anti-freezing properties

of the coolant but also to prevent corrosion that would otherwise occur, as the corrosion inhibitors in the coolant become progressively less effective.

2 Always use an ethylene glycol based antifreeze, which is suitable for use in mixed-metal cooling systems.

3 The type of antifreeze and levels of protection afforded are indicated in *Lubricants and fluids* and Specifications. To achieve the recommended 50%

concentration, equal quantities of antifreeze and clean, soft water must be mixed together. It is best to make up slightly more than is actually needed to refill the cooling system, so that a supply is available for subsequent topping-up.

Caution: Always premix the antifreeze and water in a suitable container before refilling the cooling system. If the antifreeze and water are poured into the cooling system separately, they may not mix correctly and could cause localised overheating, which may lead to engine damage.

Draining

4 To drain the cooling system, remove the expansion tank filler cap then move the heater air temperature control to the maximum heat position.

5 Where applicable, remove the engine undertray, and then position a suitable container beneath the bottom hose connection, at the lower left-hand corner of the radiator. Release the hose clip and carefully pull the bottom hose off the radiator stub, allowing the coolant to drain into the container below. Once the system has drained completely, reconnect the bottom hose and secure with the hose clip.

Flushing

6 With time, the cooling system may gradually lose its efficiency due to the radiator core having become choked with rust, scale deposits and other sediment. To minimise this, the system should be flushed as described in the following paragraphs whenever the coolant is renewed.

7 With the coolant drained, refill the system with fresh water. Refit the expansion tank filler cap, start the engine and warm it up to normal operating temperature, then stop it and (after allowing it to cool down completely) drain the system again. Repeat as necessary until only clean water can be seen to emerge, then refill finally with the specified coolant mixture.

8 If the specified coolant mixture has been used and has been renewed at the specified intervals, the above procedure will be sufficient to keep clean the system for a considerable length of time. If, however, the system has

been neglected, a more thorough operation will be required, as follows.

9 First drain the coolant, and then disconnect the radiator top and bottom hoses from the radiator. Insert a garden hose into the radiator top hose outlet and allow water (under LOW pressure only) to circulate through the radiator until it runs clean from the bottom outlet.

Caution: Do not flush with water under high pressure, as this may damage the radiator.

10 To flush the engine, insert the garden hose into the top hose and allow water to circulate until it runs clear from the bottom hose. If, after a reasonable period, the water still does not run clear, the cooling system should be flushed with a good proprietary cleaning agent. Bear in mind, however, that any leaks sealed in the past using a cooling system sealant additive may be weakened by this course of action, and could start to leak again.

11 In severe cases of contamination, reverse-flushing of the radiator may be necessary. To do this, remove the radiator, invert it and insert a garden hose into the bottom outlet. Continue flushing (again, using water under LOW pressure only) until clear water runs from the top hose outlet. If necessary, a similar procedure can be used to flush the heater matrix.

12 The use of chemical cleaners should be necessary only as a last resort as regular renewal of the coolant will prevent excessive contamination of the system.

Filling

13 With the cooling system drained and flushed, ensure that all radiator hoses are securely reconnected. Check all hose unions for security and all hoses for condition. Fresh antifreeze has a searching action, which will rapidly find any weaknesses in the system.

14 Prepare a sufficient quantity of the specified coolant mixture, allowing for a surplus so as to have a reserve supply for topping-up (see *Antifreeze mixture* above).

15 Remove the expansion tank filler cap, and then fill the system slowly through the filler neck. Continue filling until the coolant level reaches the MAX mark on the side of the expansion tank. Refit the filler cap and tighten it securely.

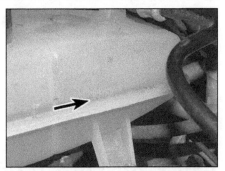

27.17 Coolant expansion tank MAX level – arrowed

16 Start the engine and run it at no more than idle speed until it has warmed-up to normal operating temperature and the radiator electric cooling fan has cut in once. Watch the temperature gauge to check for signs of overheating.

17 Stop the engine and allow it to cool down completely, then remove the expansion tank filler cap carefully and top up the tank to the MAX level **(see illustration)**. Refit the filler cap and wash off any spilt coolant from the engine compartment and bodywork with plenty of clean water.

18 After refilling, check carefully all system components for signs of coolant leaks. A label should now be attached to the radiator or expansion tank stating the type and concentration of antifreeze used and the date installed. Any subsequent topping-up should be made with the same type and concentration of antifreeze.

19 If, after draining and refilling the system, symptoms of overheating are found which did not occur previously, then the fault is almost certainly due to trapped air at some point in the system causing an airlock and restricting the flow of coolant. Usually air is trapped because the system was refilled too quickly. In some cases, airlocks can be released by tapping or squeezing the appropriate coolant hose. If the problem persists, stop the engine and allow it to cool down completely before unscrewing the expansion tank filler cap, to allow the trapped air to escape.

Every 84 000 miles or 7 years

28 Renew camshaft timing belt

29 Renew injection pump drivebelt

Renewal procedure is described in Chapter 2C.

Renewal procedure is described in Chapter 2C.

Every 108 000 miles or 9 years

30 Transmission oil/fluid renewal

Refer to Chapter 7A or 7B.

Every 15 years, regardless of mileage

31 SRS system components renewal

1 The Supplementary Restraint System (SRS), which includes the airbag(s), and seat belt pretensioners, has components which contain pyrotechnic materials. Because these materials degrade with age, MG Rover specify that the following components must be renewed every 15 years:
 a) Driver airbag module.
 b) Passenger airbag module.
 c) Seat belt pretensioners.
 d) Rotary coupler.

2 Renewal information is given in Chapter 12. However, because of the safety critical nature of these components, and the need for special equipment to test their operation, we strongly recommend that renewal is done by an MG Rover specialist.

Chapter 2 Part A:
4-cylinder petrol engine in-car repair procedures

Contents

	Section number
Camshaft cover – removal and refitting	4
Camshaft oil seals – removal and refitting	9
Camshafts and hydraulic tappets – removal and refitting	10
Compression test – description and interpretation	2
Crankshaft oil seals – removal and refitting	16
Crankshaft pulley – removal and refitting	5
Cylinder head – removal and refitting	11
Engine timing marks	3
Engine/transmission mountings – inspection, removal and refitting	18
Flywheel/driveplate – removal and refitting	17
General information and precautions	1
Oil pump – dismantling, inspection and reassembly	15
Oil pump – removal and refitting	13
Oil pump pressure relief valve – removal and refitting	14
Sump – removal and refitting	12
Timing belt and tensioner – refitting	8
Timing belt and tensioner – removal	7
Timing belt covers – removal and refitting	6

Degrees of difficulty

Easy, suitable for novice with little experience	**Fairly easy,** suitable for beginner with some experience	**Fairly difficult,** suitable for competent DIY mechanic	**Difficult,** suitable for experienced DIY mechanic	**Very difficult,** suitable for expert DIY or professional

Specifications

General

Engine type	Four-cylinder in-line, four-stroke, liquid-cooled
Designation	K16 – 16 valves, four per cylinder
Bore:	
1.4 litre engines	75.00 mm
1.6 and 1.8 litre engines	80.00 mm
Stroke:	
1.4 and 1.6 litre engines	79.00 mm
1.8 litre engine	89.30 mm
Capacity:	
1.4 litre engine	1396 cc
1.6 litre engine	1588 cc
1.8 litre engine	1796 cc
Firing order	1-3-4-2 (No 1 cylinder at timing belt end)
Direction of crankshaft rotation	Clockwise (seen from right-hand side of vehicle)
Compression ratio:	
1.4 litre engine	10.4:1
1.6 and 1.8 litre engines	10.5:1
Minimum compression pressure (typical value)	10.0 bar
Maximum compression pressure difference between cylinders (typical)	1.5 bar

Camshaft

Drive	Toothed belt from crankshaft
Belt tensioner	Automatic
Number of bearings	6 per camshaft
Bearing journal running clearance:	
Standard	0.060 to 0.094 mm
Service limit	0.15 mm
Camshaft endfloat:	
Standard	0.06 to 0.19 mm
Service limit	0.3 mm
Hydraulic tappet outside diameter	32.959 to 32.975 mm

Lubrication system

System pressure	1.7 to 3.5 bar @ idle speed
Pressure relief valve opening pressure	4.1 bar
Low oil pressure warning light comes on	0.3 to 0.5 bar
Oil pump clearances:	
Rotor end float	0.02 to 0.06 mm
Outer rotor-to-body clearance	0.28 to 0.36 mm
Rotor lobe clearance	0.05 to 0.13 mm

Torque wrench settings

	Nm	lbf ft
Alternator-to-mounting bracket nuts/bolts:		
With air conditioning	25	18
Without air conditioning	45	33
Camshaft bearing carrier bolts	10	7
Camshaft cover bolts	10	7
Camshaft oil seal cover plate bolts:		
Inlet	6	4
Exhaust	25	18
Camshaft sprocket bolt:		
M8 bolt	35	26
M10 bolt	65	48
Crankshaft pulley bolt	205	151
Cylinder head bolts:		
Stage 1	20	15
Stage 2	Angle-tighten a further 180°	
Stage 3	Angle-tighten a further 180°	
Driveplate bolts	100	74
Engine lifting bracket bolts	9	7
Engine torsion bar bolts	25	18
Engine/transmission steady bar-to-transmission/sump bolt	45	33
Flywheel bolts*	80	59
Flywheel lower cover bolts	9	7
LH hydramount-to-bracket bolt (1.8 litre manual)	100	74
LH hydramount-to-gearbox bolts (1.8 litre manual)	65	48
LH mounting bracket-to-body bolts (1.8 litre manual)	65	48
LH mounting-to-body bracket bolts (1.8 litre manual)	55	41
LH mounting-to-gearbox bolts:		
1.4 & 1.6 litre	80	59
1.8 litre automatic	55	41
LH mounting through-bolt	80	59
LH torque mounting-to-body bolts	45	33
LH torque mounting-to-mounting bracket bolts	60	44
Lower engine steady bar bolts:		
1.4 & 1.6 litre:		
Steady to engine	45	33
Through-bolt	80	59
1.8 litre	100	74
Main bearing ladder-to-cylinder block bolts:		
Stage 1	5	4
Stage 2	15	11
Oil rail-to-main bearing ladder bolts	5	4
Oil pressure warning light switch	17	13
Oil pump-to-cylinder block bolts*	10	7
Oil temperature sensor	17	13
RH hydramount-to-body bolts (1.8 litre)	45	33
RH hydramount-to-mounting bracket nut	85	63
RH mounting bracket to engine:		
1.4 & 1.6 litre (nuts*)	100	74
1.8 litre (bolts)	100	74
RH mounting through-bolt (1.4 & 1.6 litre)	75	55
RH torque mounting-to-body bolts	45	33
RH torque mounting-to-mounting bracket bolts	60	44
Roadwheel nuts	110	81
Spark plugs	25	18
Sump drain plug	28	21
Sump to bearing ladder:		
Short bolts	25	18
Long bolts	30	22
Timing belt lower cover bolts	9	7
Timing belt tensioner backplate bolt (manual tensioner)	10	7
Timing belt tensioner bolt (automatic tensioner)	25	18
Timing belt tensioner pulley bolt (manual tensioner)	45	33
Timing belt upper cover bolts	5	4
Upper engine steady bar bolts:		
Engine bolt	45	33
Gearbox bolts	10	7

Use new bolts

1 General information and precautions

How to use this Chapter

This Part of the Chapter describes those repair procedures that can reasonably be carried out on the engine whilst it remains in the vehicle. If the engine has been removed from the vehicle and is being dismantled as described in Part D of this Chapter, any preliminary dismantling procedures can be ignored.

Note that whilst it may be possible physically to overhaul items such as the piston/connecting rod assemblies with the engine in the vehicle, such tasks are not usually carried out as separate operations and usually require the execution of several additional procedures (not to mention the cleaning of components and of oilways). For this reason, all such tasks are classed as major overhaul procedures and are described in Part C of this Chapter.

Engine description

The four-cylinder in-line engine, with double overhead camshafts (DOHC) and sixteen valves, is mounted transversely at the front of the car.

The main structure of the engine consists of three major castings – the cylinder head, the cylinder block/crankcase, and the crankshaft main bearing ladder.

The three major castings are made from aluminium alloy, and are clamped together by ten long through-bolts, which perform the dual role of cylinder head bolts and crankshaft main bearing bolts. An oil rail is fitted under the main bearing ladder, and to avoid disturbing the bottom end of the engine when removing the through-bolts, the oil rail is secured independently to the main bearing ladder (by two nuts), and the main bearing ladder is secured to the cylinder block/crankcase (by ten bolts).

The crankshaft runs in five main bearings. Thrustwashers are fitted to the centre main bearing (upper half) to control crankshaft endfloat.

The connecting rods rotate on horizontally split bearing shells at their big-ends. The pistons are attached to the connecting rods by gudgeon pins, which are an interference fit in the connecting rod small-end eyes. The aluminium alloy pistons are fitted with three piston rings, comprising two compression rings and an oil control ring.

The cylinder bores are formed by renewable wet liners, which locate in the cylinder block/crankcase at their top ends. A bead of sealant around each liner prevents the escape of coolant into the sump.

The inlet and exhaust valves are each closed by coil springs and operate in guides pressed into the cylinder head. The valve seat inserts are pressed into the cylinder head and can be renewed separately if worn.

The camshafts are driven from the crankshaft by a toothed belt, with automatic tension control.

One camshaft operates two exhaust valves in each cylinder, and the other operates two inlet valves in each cylinder. The valves are opened via self-adjusting hydraulic tappets, which eliminate the need for routine checking and adjustment of valve clearances. The camshaft rotates in bearings, which are line bored directly into the cylinder head and the (bolted on) bearing carrier. This means that the cylinder head and bearing carrier are matched, and cannot be renewed separately.

The electric fuel pump is submerged in the fuel tank.

The timing belt drives the coolant pump.

Lubrication is by means of an eccentric-rotor type pump driven directly from the timing belt end of the crankshaft. The pump draws oil through a strainer located in the sump, and then forces it through an externally mounted full-flow cartridge-type oil filter into galleries in the oil rail and the cylinder block/crankcase, from where it is distributed to the crankshaft (main bearings) and camshaft. The big-end bearings are supplied with oil via internal drillings in the crankshaft, while the camshaft bearings and the hydraulic tappets receive a pressurised supply via drillings in the cylinder head. The camshaft lobes and valves are lubricated by oil splash, as are all other engine components.

Operations with engine in car

The following work can be carried out with the engine in the vehicle:

a) Compression pressure – testing.
b) Cylinder head cover – removal and refitting.
c) Crankshaft pulley – removal and refitting.
d) Timing belt covers – removal and refitting.
e) Timing belt – removal, refitting and adjustment.
f) Timing belt tensioner and sprockets – removal and refitting.
g) Camshaft oil seal(s) – renewal.
h) Camshafts and hydraulic tappets – removal, inspection and refitting.
i) Cylinder head – removal and refitting.
j) Cylinder head and pistons – decarbonising.
k) Sump – removal and refitting.
l) Oil pump – removal, overhaul and refitting.
m) Crankshaft oil seals – renewal.
n) Engine/transmission mountings – inspection and renewal.
o) Flywheel – removal, inspection and refitting.

Precautions

Note that a side effect of the through-bolt engine design is that the crankshaft cannot be rotated once the through-bolts have been slackened. During any servicing or overhaul work the crankshaft must always be rotated to the desired position before the bolts are disturbed.

2 Compression test – description and interpretation

Note: A suitable compression tester will be required for this test.

1 When engine performance is down, or if misfiring occurs which cannot be attributed to the ignition or fuel systems, a compression test can provide diagnostic clues as to the engine's condition. If the test is performed regularly it can give warning of trouble before any other symptoms become apparent.

2 The engine must be fully warmed-up to normal operating temperature, the battery must be fully-charged and the spark plugs must be removed. The aid of an assistant will be required.

3 Disable the engine management/fuel system by removing the relevant fuses from the engine compartment fusebox (see Chapter 12).

4 Fit a compression tester to the No 1 cylinder spark plug hole. The type of tester that screws into the plug thread is preferred.

5 Have the assistant hold the throttle wide open and crank the engine on the starter motor. After one or two revolutions, the compression pressure should build-up to a maximum figure and then stabilise. Record the highest reading obtained.

6 Repeat the test on the remaining cylinders, recording the pressure in each.

7 All cylinders should produce very similar pressures. Any difference greater than that specified indicates the existence of a fault. Note that the compression should build-up quickly in a healthy engine. Low compression on the first stroke, followed by gradually increasing pressure on successive strokes, indicates worn piston rings. A low compression reading on the first stroke, which does not build-up during successive strokes, indicates leaking valves or a blown head gasket (a cracked head could also be the cause). Deposits on the undersides of the valve heads can also cause low compression.

8 If the pressure in any cylinder is reduced to the specified minimum or less (Rover do not specify figures, the values given in the Specifications are typical figures for a petrol engine), carry out the following test to isolate the cause. Introduce a teaspoonful of clean oil into that cylinder through its spark plug hole and repeat the test.

9 If the addition of oil temporarily improves the compression pressure, this indicates that bore or piston wear is responsible for the pressure loss. No improvement suggests that leaking or burnt valves, or a blown head gasket, may be to blame.

10 A low reading from two adjacent cylinders is almost certainly due to the head gasket having blown between them and the presence of coolant in the engine oil will confirm this.

11 If one cylinder is about 20 percent lower than the others and the engine has a slightly rough idle; a worn camshaft lobe could be the cause.

3.4 Camshaft sprocket timing marks (A) aligned with mark (B) on camshaft belt cover

12 If the compression reading is unusually high, the combustion chambers are probably coated with carbon deposits. If this is the case, the cylinder head should be removed and decarbonised.

13 On completion of the test, refit the spark plugs and refit the fuses to the engine compartment fusebox.

3 Engine timing marks

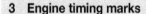

1 The crankshaft pulley, crankshaft and camshaft sprockets each have timing marks that align only at 90° BTDC. At this position, all pistons are halfway up the bores, so there is less risk of engine damage whilst working on the engine. **Note:** *These marks do not indicate TDC.* Before starting any engine

4.3 Remove coil/plug cover

4.5 Pull coils from spark plugs

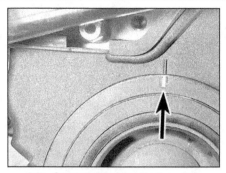

3.5a Crankshaft pulley timing mark aligned with 90° BTDC mark on camshaft belt outer cover

overhaul procedures, align the timing marks at 90° BTDC as follows.

2 Apply the handbrake, chock the rear roadwheels, then jack up the front of the car and support it on axle stands (see *Jacking and vehicle support*). Remove the right-hand front roadwheel.

3 Slacken lower bolt securing timing belt upper cover to engine. Remove the five bolts securing the upper cover to the rear cover, and remove the upper cover.

4 Using a spanner or socket on the crankshaft pulley nut, turn the crankshaft clockwise until the marks on the camshaft sprockets are aligned horizontally with the top face of the cylinder head – there is usually a mark on the rear cover which represents the top face of the head. The marks should be positioned to the right of the sprocket centres, and the EXHAUST arrows should point to the rear of the vehicle **(see illustration)**.

4.4 Pull connectors from spark plugs

4.6 Release camshaft position sensor (CMP)

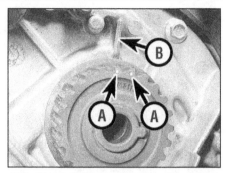

3.5b Crankshaft sprocket dots (A) aligned each side of raised rib (B) on oil pump cover

5 When these marks are aligned, the notch on the inner rim of the crankshaft pulley should be aligned with the vertical 90º BTDC mark on the on the timing belt lower cover. Similarly, if the crankshaft pulley is removed, two punched dots on the crankshaft sprocket should be aligned either side of the raised rib on the oil pump cover **(see illustrations)**.

6 Fit the roadwheel, and tighten the nuts to secure the wheel. Remove the stands and lower the vehicle to the ground. Use a torque wrench to tighten the roadwheel nuts to the specified torque.

7 Connect the battery earth lead.

4 Camshaft cover – removal and refitting

Removal

1 Disconnect the battery negative lead.

2 Release two clips and disconnect two breather hoses from the camshaft cover.

3 Remove the bolts securing coil/plug cover to camshaft cover, and remove the cover **(see illustration)**.

4 Note the position and clipping of the HT leads and cables running to the coils and camshaft position sensor. Release the HT leads, and pull the tubular connectors from the spark plugs next to the two coils **(see illustration)**.

5 Remove the two bolts attaching each coil to the camshaft cover, and pull the coils from the spark plugs **(see illustration)**.

6 Remove the bolt attaching the camshaft position sensor (CMP) to the camshaft cover. Release the sensor and position aside – note that an O-ring is fitted to the sensor **(see illustration)**.

7 Working in **reverse** order from the tightening sequence **(see illustration 4.10)**, progressively slacken and remove the bolts attaching the camshaft cover to the cylinder head.

8 Remove the cover and gasket – if the gasket is in good condition, it need not be separated from the cover.

Refitting

9 Ensure that the gasket is in good condition,

4.9 Correctly positioned gasket

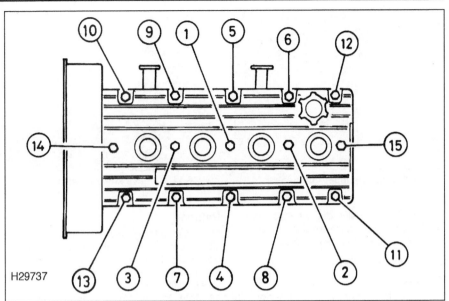

4.10 Bolt tightening sequence

and that mating faces are clean. If a new gasket is being fitted, press it onto the cover dowels, with the embossed words towards the cover. 'Exhaust man side' must be towards the exhaust manifold **(see illustration)**.

10 Ensuring that the gasket remains in place, fit the cover. Fit the retaining bolts and tighten them all finger tight. Working in the illustrated sequence, use a torque wrench to tighten the bolts to the specified torque **(see illustration)**.

11 Ensure that the CMP sensor O-ring is in good condition, and lubricate it with engine oil. Fit the CMP sensor and bolt.

12 In the positions noted before removal – fit the coils' securing bolts. Fit the HT lead tubular connectors to the plugs next to the coils – position the HT leads and cables in the grooves and clips.

13 Fit the coil cover and securing bolts. Connect the breather hoses to the cover, and reconnect the battery earth lead.

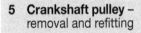

5 Crankshaft pulley – removal and refitting

Note: *When slackening or tightening the pulley securing bolt, it is necessary to prevent the crankshaft from turning. This can be done by:*
a) 1.4 and 1.6 engines: Remove the metal cover from the housing to access the flywheel.
b) 1.8 engines: Remove the starter motor to access the flywheel.

Removal

1 Disconnect the battery negative lead.

2 Apply the handbrake, chock the rear roadwheels, then jack up the front of the car and support it on axle stands (see *Jacking and vehicle support*). Remove the right-hand roadwheel.

3 Remove the alternator drivebelt (see Chapter 5A), and the power steering pump drivebelt (see Chapter 10).

1.4 and 1.6 engines

4 Remove the metal cover from the flywheel housing at the opposite side to the starter motor.

5 Have an assistant engage a suitable flat lever – such as a large screwdriver – between two teeth of the ring gear, so that when anti-clockwise effort is applied to the pulley bolt, the crankshaft will be prevented from turning.

1.8 engines

6 Remove the starter motor as described in Chapter 5A.

7 Have an assistant engage a suitable flat lever – such as a large screwdriver – between two teeth of the starter ring gear, so that when anti-clockwise effort is applied to the pulley bolt, the crankshaft will be prevented from turning.

All engines

8 Remove the pulley bolt and withdraw the pulley from the end of the crankshaft.

Refitting

9 Ensuring that mating faces are clean, fit the pulley so that the pulley notch fits over the lug on the crankshaft sprocket **(see illustration)**. Fit the washer with the largest diameter against the pulley.

5.9 Align notch in pulley and lug on sprocket

10 Lock the crankshaft, and use a torque wrench to tighten the pulley bolt to the specified torque.

1.4 and 1.6 engines

11 Remove the locking device, and fit the metal cover to the flywheel housing.

1.8 engines

12 Refit the starter motor, with reference to Chapter 5A.

All engines

13 Fit the power steering pump and alternator drivebelts – adjust the alternator belt tension, where applicable.

14 Fit the roadwheel, and tighten the nuts to secure the wheel. Remove the stands and lower the vehicle to the ground. Use a torque wrench to tighten the roadwheel nuts to the specified torque.

15 Connect the battery earth lead.

6 Timing belt covers - removal and refitting

Upper outer cover

Removal

1 Disconnect the battery negative lead.

2 Slacken lower bolt securing timing belt upper cover to engine.

3 Remove five bolts securing upper cover to rear cover, and remove the upper cover. If it is loose, remove the rubber seal **(see illustration)**.

Refitting

4 Before refitting, clean the cover.

5 Ensure that the rubber seal is correctly positioned. Fit the cover, slotting it over the lower bolt.

6.3 Remove upper outer cover

6.11 Remove lower outer cover

6.20 Removing the rear timing belt cover

6 Fit the five top bolts. Use a torque wrench to tighten the bolts to the specified torque.
7 Reconnect the battery earth lead.

Lower outer cover

Removal

8 Remove the upper cover as described in paragraphs 1 to 3.
9 Remove the crankshaft pulley as described in Section 5.
10 Remove the power steering pump belt tension roller assembly as described in Chapter 10.
11 Remove three bolts securing the lower cover to the cylinder block, and remove the cover and, if attached, the rubber seal **(see illustration)**.

Refitting

12 Before refitting, clean the cover.
13 Ensure that the rubber seal is correctly positioned. Fit the cover and the bolts. Use a torque wrench to tighten the bolts to the specified torque.
14 Refit the power steering pump belt tension roller assembly, with reference to Chapter 10.
15 Fit the crankshaft pulley. Locking crankshaft rotation as for removal, use a torque wrench to tighten the bolt to the specified torque.
16 Remove the locking device, and fit the metal cover to the flywheel housing.
17 Refit the upper outer cover as described in paragraphs 4 to 7.

Rear cover

Removal

18 Remove the outer timing belt covers as described previously in this Section.
19 Remove the timing belt and the timing belt tensioner as described in Section 7.
20 Unscrew the securing bolts, and withdraw the timing belt rear cover **(see illustration)**.

Refitting

21 Refitting is a reversal of removal, but refit the timing belt tensioner and the camshaft sprocket(s) as described in Section 8, and tighten all fixings to the specified torque wrench settings, where given.

7 Timing belt and tensioner – removal

Caution: Store and handle belt with care. Do not use a belt that has been twisted or folded – reinforcing fibres may be damaged, and the belt may fail prematurely. It is recommended that the cambelt be renewed whenever it has been removed from the vehicle.
Note: *To preserve valve timing and prevent engine damage, the camshafts must not rotate when the timing belt has been removed. An inexpensive locking tool, which fits between the teeth of the camshaft sprockets, is available from most car parts and accessory outlets.*

1 Disconnect the battery negative lead.
2 Apply the handbrake, chock the rear roadwheels, then jack up the front of the car and support it on axle stands (see *Jacking and vehicle support*). Remove the right-hand front roadwheel.
3 Where applicable, release the coolant, power steering and air conditioning hoses, which are routed past the timing belt cover, from their retaining clips and move to one side.
4 Remove the timing belt upper outer cover as described in Section 6 **(see illustrations)**.
5 Using a socket and extension bar on the crankshaft bolt, turn the crankshaft clockwise to align the camshaft sprocket timing marks at 90° BTDC – see Section 3.

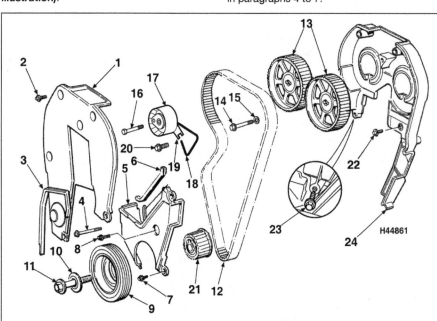

7.4a Timing belt, sprockets and covers – with automatic belt tensioner

1 *Timing belt upper outer cover*	6 *Seal*	13 *Camshaft sprockets*	18 *Index wire*
2 *Bolt*	7 *Bolt*		19 *Pointer*
3 *Seal*	8 *Bolt*	14 *Bolt*	20 *Pillar bolt*
4 *Bolt*	9 *Crankshaft pulley*	15 *Washer*	21 *Crankshaft sprocket*
5 *Timing belt lower outer cover*	10 *Washer*	16 *Timing belt tensioner bolt*	22 *Bolt*
	11 *Crankshaft pulley bolt*	17 *Timing belt tensioner*	23 *Bolt*
	12 *Timing belt*		24 *Rear cover*

6 Fit the camshaft sprocket locking tool **(see illustrations)**.

7 Remove the crankshaft pulley as described in Section 5.

8 Position a jack, with wooden block on top, under the engine sump, and adjust to support the weight of the engine and transmission.

9 On models fitted with an upper steady bar, remove the through-bolt and tilt the bar upwards clear of the mounting. Remove the bolts securing the mounting bracket to the engine. Then remove the two bolts securing rubber mounting to the body and remove the mounting assembly **(see illustrations)**.

10 On models without an upper steady bar, slacken the through-bolt securing the mounting to the body. Remove the mounting nuts which attach the mounting bracket to the engine and remove the mounting **(see illustration)**.

11 Remove and discard the timing belt tensioner retaining bolt, a new one will be required for refitting.

12 On models with an automatic tensioner, disengage the index wire from behind the pillar bolt, and remove the tensioner **(see illustration)**.

13 On models with a manual tensioner, slacken and remove the backplate clamp bolt, and remove the tensioner **(see illustration)**.

14 On models with air conditioning, hold the auxiliary drivebelt tensioner, and remove the locking pin. Allow tensioner to rotate fully anti-clockwise.

15 Remove three bolts securing lower outer cover, and remove cover and rubber seal.

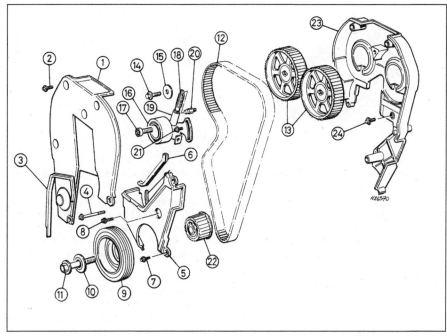

7.4b Timing belt, sprockets and covers – with manual belt tensioner

1 Timing belt upper outer cover	8 Bolt	15 Washer	20 Anchor bolt
2 Bolt	9 Crankshaft pulley	16 Timing belt tensioner pulley assembly	21 Tensioner backplate clamp bolt
3 Seal	10 Washer		
4 Bolt	11 Crankshaft pulley bolt		22 Crankshaft sprocket
5 Timing belt lower outer cover	12 Timing belt	17 Tensioner pulley Allen screw	
6 Seal	13 Camshaft sprockets	18 Tensioner pulley spring	23 Timing belt rear cover
7 Bolt	14 Bolt	19 Sleeve	24 Bolt

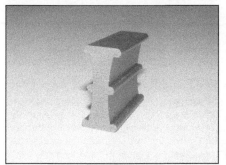

7.6a Camshaft sprocket locking tool

7.6b Sprocket locking tool in position

7.9a Tilt the steady bar upward . . .

7.9b . . . remove the mounting bracket bolts . . .

7.9c . . . and withdraw the mounting assembly

7.10 Slacken and remove the through-bolt (arrowed)

7.12 Automatic tensioner with index wire (arrowed)

16 Using fingers only, ease the timing belt off the sprockets. Discard, as a new one will be required for refitting.
Caution: Do not rotate the crankshaft with the belt removed.

8 Timing belt and tensioner – refitting

Caution: Store and handle belt with care. Do not use a belt that has been twisted or folded – reinforcing fibres may be damaged, and the belt may fail prematurely.
1 Clean the sprockets and tensioner pulley.
Caution: If the sprockets are contaminated

8.4 Manual timing belt tensioner assembly

1 Tensioner pulley
2 Backplate bolt
3 Tensioner spring and sleeve
4 Spring locating stud

8.5 Fit the timing belt, making sure all the slack is the tensioner side of the belt

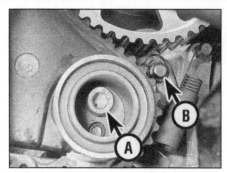

7.13 Manual tensioner pulley bolt (A) and backplate bolt (B)

with oil, they must be soaked in a bath of solvent, and washed clean. The sprockets are made of a 'sintered' material, which is porous. Any oil remaining in the material will seep out and contaminate the timing belt.
2 Ensure that the camshaft sprocket timing marks are aligned and locked.
3 On models with an automatic tensioner, fit the timing belt tensioner, locating the index wire over the new pillar bolt, and ensure that the tension lever is at 9 o'clock position. Fit a new tensioner retaining bolt, and tighten it so that it is just possible to move the tension lever **(see illustration)**.
4 On models with a manual tensioner, fit the tensioner pulley assembly into position and refit the pulley and backplate retaining bolts. Pivot the pulley fully downwards and lightly tighten the backplate bolt to hold the tensioner in position. Hook the spring onto the backplate and over its locating stud **(see illustration)**.
5 Using fingers only, fit the timing belt over the crankshaft sprocket, and then over the camshaft sprockets. **Note:** *Keep the belt taut between the crankshaft sprocket and the exhaust camshaft sprocket.* Locate the belt around the tension roller and coolant pump sprocket. Ensure that the belt is located centrally on all sprockets and roller **(see illustration)**.
6 Fit lower outer timing cover and bolts. Use a torque wrench to tighten bolts to specified torque.
7 On models with air conditioning, have an assistant rotate the auxiliary drivebelt tension

8.9a Rotate tension lever

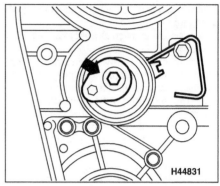

8.3 Automatic tensioner in position with index wire over pillar bolt

roller fully clockwise. Whilst the roller is held in this position, fit the locking pin into the hole in the backplate.
8 Refit crankshaft pulley as described in Section 5.
9 On models with an automatic tensioner, use a 6 mm Allen key to rotate the tension lever, and align the pointer notch with the index wire **(see illustrations)**. Whilst ensuring that the notch and index wire remain correctly aligned, use a torque wrench to tighten the tensioner bolt to the specified torque.
Caution: Ensure that the pointer notch moves towards the index wire from above. If the notch passes the index wire, release all tension and repeat the procedure.
10 On models with a manual tensioner, slacken the tensioner backplate bolt to release the tensioner and tension the timing belt. Using finger pressure to the tensioner backplate, push the pulley against the timing belt and tighten the backplate retaining bolt. Use a torque wrench to tighten the tensioner backplate bolt to the specified torque.
11 Remove the camshaft sprocket locking tool.
12 Using a suitable socket and bar on the crankshaft pulley, rotate the crankshaft two complete turns clockwise, and re-align the camshaft gear timing marks **(see illustration)**.
13 On models with an automatic tensioner, check that the pointer is correctly aligned with the index wire. If it is not correctly aligned, slacken the tensioner bolt until it is just possible to move the tensioner lever. Then, using a 6 mm

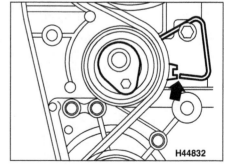

8.9b Align pointer notch with index wire

Allen key, rotate the tensioner lever clockwise until the pointer is just above the index wire and then rotate the lever anti-clockwise until the pointer is correctly aligned with the index wire. Whilst ensuring that it is correctly aligned, use a torque wrench to tighten the tensioner bolt to the specified torque.

14 On models with a manual tensioner, slacken the tensioner backplate bolt and check the timing belt is under tension from the pulley. With the belt correctly tensioned, use a torque wrench to tighten the tensioner pulley bolt and backplate retaining bolt to their specified torque.

15 Rotate the crankshaft a further two turns clockwise, align the camshaft gear timing marks, and check the tension on the timing belt is correct.

16 Refit the engine mounting assembly, use a torque wrench to tighten the bolts to the specified torque.

17 Lower and remove the jack and block from under the engine.

18 Where applicable, refit the engine mounting upper steady bar, use a torque wrench to tighten the steady bar through-bolts to the specified torque.

19 Fit the timing belt upper outer cover as described in Section 6.

20 Where applicable, secure the coolant, power steering and air conditioning hoses back into position in front of the timing belt covers.

21 Fit the roadwheel, and tighten the nuts to secure the wheel. Remove the stands and lower the vehicle to the ground. Use a torque wrench to tighten the roadwheel nuts to the specified torque.

22 Reconnect the battery earth lead.

9 Camshaft oil seals – removal and refitting

Note: *The following new parts are needed – camshaft oil seals. Right-hand (timing belt end) seals are black; left-hand (transmission end) seals are red.*

Right-hand seals

1 Remove the timing belt as described in Section 7.

9.2 With the sprocket bolts slackened, remove the locking tool (arrowed)

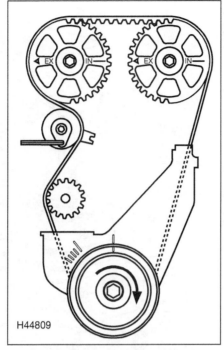

8.12 Rotate crankshaft and check camshaft alignment

2 The camshaft sprockets are identical, but they should be marked so that they can be refitted in their original positions. With the camshaft sprocket locking tool in place between the sprockets (see Section 7), slacken and remove the sprocket retaining bolts and washers. Remove the locking tool **(see illustration)**.

Caution: Do not rotate the camshafts or crankshaft.

3 Remove the sprockets from the camshafts. If the sprocket roll-pins are loose, remove them and keep them with the sprockets.

4 To collect any spilled oil or debris, pack cloths around the area under the oil seals.

5 Punch or drill two small holes opposite each other in the oil seal. Screw a self-tapping screw into each hole, and pull on the screws with pliers to remove the seal.

6 Clean and dry the seal housing and sealing surface on the camshaft. Ensure that there are no burrs or raised edges.

9.7 Using a socket to tap the camshaft oil seal into position

Caution: The new oil seals must be fitted dry. Do not lubricate the seal recess, the seal lip, or the seal running surface on the shaft.

7 With the sealing lip facing inward, carefully locate the seal over the camshaft. Using a drift or socket, which contacts only the hard outer edge of the seal, tap the seal into place until it is seated correctly in the housing **(see illustration)**.

8 Ensure that the roll-pins are correctly located in the camshafts. Fit the camshaft sprockets, washers and bolts. Use a torque wrench to tighten the bolts to the specified torque.

9 Refit and tension the timing belt as described in Section 8.

Exhaust camshaft left-hand seal

10 Disconnect the battery negative lead.

11 Remove the air cleaner assembly as described in Chapter 4A.

12 Remove the two bolts securing the cover plate, and remove the plate **(see illustration)**.

13 To collect any spilled oil or debris, pack cloths around the area under the oil seal.

14 Punch or drill two small holes opposite each other in the oil seal. Screw a self-tapping screw into each hole, and pull on the screws with pliers to remove the seal.

15 Clean and dry the seal housing and sealing surface on the camshaft. Ensure that there are no burrs or raised edges.

Caution: The new oil seal must be fitted dry. Do not lubricate the seal recess, the seal lip, or the seal running surface on the shaft.

16 With the sealing lip facing inward, carefully locate the seal over the camshaft. Using a drift or socket, which contacts only the hard outer edge of the seal, tap the seal into place until it is seated correctly in the housing.

17 Clean the cover mating faces, and fit the cover and bolts. Use a torque wrench to tighten the bolts to the specified torque.

18 Fit the air cleaner, and connect the battery earth lead.

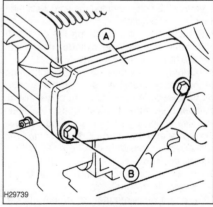

9.12 Remove exhaust camshaft left-hand cover plate

A Cover plate   *B Securing bolts*

10.7 Remove the belt inner cover retaining bolts (arrowed)

Inlet camshaft left-hand seal

Note: *The procedure for renewing the inlet camshaft oil seal is the same as that for the exhaust camshaft oil seal, except:*

19 Before removing the cover plate, disconnect the camshaft sensor multiplug. Connect the plug when the cover has been fitted.

10 Camshafts and hydraulic tappets – removal and refitting

Note: *The following new parts are needed – MG Rover sealant GUG 705963GM, camshaft oil seals. Sixteen small plastic containers, numbered one to sixteen, will be needed to store the hydraulic tappets; fill each container with clean engine oil.*

Removal

1 Disconnect the battery negative lead.

2 Disconnect the multiplug in the lead to the camshaft position sensor.

3 Remove the bolts securing the camshaft left-hand cover plates, and remove the plates.

4 Remove the timing belt as described in Section 7.

5 Remove the camshaft cover as described in Section 4.

6 Mark the camshaft sprockets so that they can be refitted in their original position. Fit the camshaft sprocket locking tool – see Section 7 – remove the bolts securing the sprockets, and remove the sprockets.

7 Remove five bolts securing the camshaft belt inner cover to the cylinder head, and remove the cover **(see illustration)**.

8 Working in the **reverse** of the tightening sequence, progressively slacken the twenty-six bolts securing the camshaft carrier to the cylinder head **(see illustration 10.19)**. When all valve spring pressure is released, remove the bolts and the carrier. **Note:** *Mark the camshafts so that they can be fitted in their original position.*

9 Lift out the camshafts, and slide off the oil seals **(see illustration)**.

10 Using a stick magnet, or rubber sucker, remove the hydraulic tappets.

Caution: Invert the tappets and place them in the numbered containers. Do not squeeze the tappet chambers together.

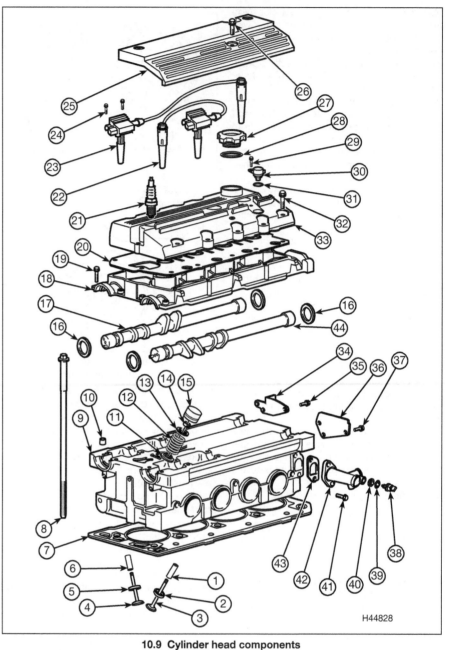

H44828

10.9 Cylinder head components

1 Exhaust valve guide	17 Inlet camshaft	31 O-ring
2 Valve seat insert – exhaust	18 Camshaft carrier	32 Bolt – camshaft cover
	19 Bolt – camshaft carrier	33 Camshaft cover
3 Exhaust valve	20 Gasket – camshaft cover	34 Bracket – multiplug
4 Inlet valve	21 Spark plug	35 Bolt – multiplug bracket
5 Valve seat insert – inlet	22 HT lead and plug tube	36 Blanking plate x 2
6 Inlet valve guide	23 Coil	37 Bolt – blanking plate
7 Gasket – cylinder head	24 Screws – coils to camshaft carrier	38 Coolant temperature sensor
8 Bolt – cylinder head	25 Coil and spark plug cover	39 Gasket
9 Cylinder head	26 Screw – coil and plug cover	40 Sealing washer
10 Locating dowel	27 Oil filler cap	41 Bolt – coolant outlet elbow
11 Valve stem oil seal	28 Seal – oil filler cap	42 Coolant outlet elbow
12 Valve spring	29 Bolt – CMP	43 Gasket – coolant outlet elbow
13 Valve spring cap	30 Camshaft position sensor (CMP)	44 Exhaust camshaft
14 Collets		
15 Hydraulic tappet		
16 Camshaft seal		

Inspection

11 Check the following components for signs of wear – eg, pitting/scoring:

Tappets, camshaft cams and bearing surfaces, camshaft carrier, tappet and bearing bores.

12 If available, a micrometer can be used to check that the outer diameter of the tappets is within specified limits.

13 Renew any worn component.

Refitting

14 Note: *Do not use a metal scraper.* Clean and dry the mating faces of the cylinder head and camshaft carrier, ensuring that all traces of old sealant are removed. Clean camshaft carrier bolt holes and dowels, and blow out oil ways.

15 Lubricate tappet bores and tappets with clean engine oil, and fit the tappets in their original bores. **Note:** *If new tappets are being fitted, they must be filled with clean engine oil before fitting.*

16 Lubricate the camshaft bearing journals and cams with clean engine oil.

17 Fit the camshafts and position the drive pin in the inlet camshaft at 4 o'clock, and the drive pin in the exhaust camshaft at 8 o'clock **(see illustration)**.

Caution: Ensure sealant is kept clear of oil feed holes and oil grooves. Assembly must be completed within 20 minutes of applying sealant.

18 Apply a continuous bead of sealant to the camshaft carrier, then spread to an even film using a roller **(see illustration)**.

19 Fit the camshaft carrier to the cylinder head, and fit the securing bolts. Use a torque wrench to tighten them progressively, and in the correct sequence, to the specified torque **(see illustration)**.

20 Clean the camshaft seal bores and running surfaces.

Caution: Oil seals must be fitted dry. Do not lubricate the seals or camshaft running surfaces.

21 With the sealing lip facing inward, carefully locate the seal over the camshaft. Using a drift or socket, which contacts only the hard outer edge of the seal, tap the seal into place until it is seated correctly in the housing **(see illustration 9.7)**.

22 Refit the camshaft cover as described in Section 4.

23 Clean the camshaft cover plates. Fit the plates and bolts. Use a torque wrench to tighten the bolts to the specified torque.

24 Connect the multiplug in the camshaft sensor lead.

25 Fit the camshaft belt inner cover and bolts. Use a torque wrench to tighten the bolts to the correct torque.

26 Refit the camshaft sprockets, and timing belt as described in Sections 9 and 8.

27 Connect the battery earth lead.

11 Cylinder head – removal and refitting

Caution: Avoid rotating the crankshaft after the cylinder head bolts have been slackened. Long through-bolts clamp together the cylinder head, cylinder block and crankshaft bearing ladder. When these are slackened, rotation of the crankshaft is difficult, or impossible.

Note: *Used with three cylinder head bolts, three large washers and tubular spacers are needed to clamp the cylinder liners after the cylinder head is removed.*

Note: *A turning/locking device for the camshaft sprockets is needed. A suitable device can be made using two pieces of flat bar – one piece approximately 36 cm long, and the other approximately 18 cm long – and three nuts and bolts. Align one end of each bar, and use one nut and bolt as a pivot for the two bars. Spread the ends of the bars to form a fork, and fit a bolt and nut through the fork end of each bar.*

10.17 Correct position of camshaft drive pins

Note: *The following new parts are needed – camshaft timing belt and, possibly, cylinder head bolts.*

Removal

1 Disconnect the battery negative lead.

2 Drain cooling system as described in Chapter 1A.

3 Remove and discard the timing belt as described in Section 7.

4 Remove the exhaust manifold heat shield.

5 Remove two nuts securing exhaust front pipe to exhaust manifold. Release pipe and discard gasket.

Models with air conditioning

6 Remove exhaust manifold as described in Chapter 4A.

All models

7 Remove the camshaft cover as described in Section 6.

8 Disconnect the following wiring harness multiplugs, with reference to Chapter 4A:

a) *Oxygen sensor (release plug from bracket).*
b) *Engine coolant temperature sensor.*
c) *Throttle position sensor.*
d) *Fuel injector harness.*
e) *Intake air temperature sensor.*
f) *Idle air control valve.*

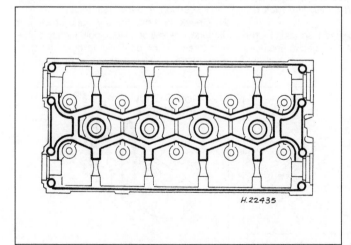

10.18 Apply a thin bead of sealant along the paths shown by the heavy black line

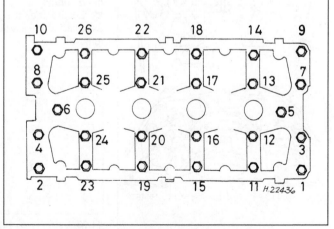

10.19 Camshaft carrier bolt tightening sequence

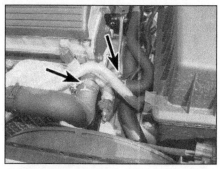

11.9 Disconnect radiator and heater hoses (arrowed) from outlet elbow

9 Slacken the securing clips, and disconnect the cooling system hoses from coolant outlet elbow **(see illustration)**.

10 Remove the securing clips, and disconnect air intake hose and purge hose from throttle housing **(see illustration)**.

11 To absorb any fuel spill, position cloths under fuel pipe connections. Depress plastic collars on hoses, and release hoses from pipes.

12 Release the throttle outer cable nut from the abutment bracket, and release the inner cable from the cam. Release the cable from the clip on the inlet manifold.

13 Depress plastic collar on the quick-release connector, and disconnect brake servo vacuum hose from inlet manifold.

14 Slacken the securing clip, and disconnect coolant expansion tank hose from inlet manifold.

15 Working in the **reverse** of the tightening sequence, progressively slacken cylinder head bolts 1 to 6 **(see illustration 11.35a)**.

16 Remove the camshaft sprocket locking device.

Caution: Do not apply tools to the sprocket teeth.

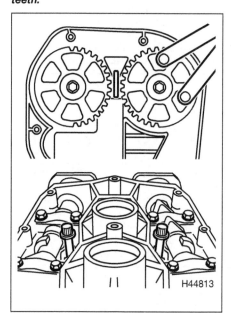

11.17 Turn the camshafts clockwise until the reluctor rings clear head bolts 7 and 8

11.10 Disconnect intake and purge hoses (arrowed) from throttle housing

17 Using the manufactured turning/locking device, engaged in two holes of the camshaft sprockets, turn the camshafts until bolts 7 and 8, under the camshaft reluctor segments, are accessible **(see illustration)**.

18 Working in the **reverse** of the tightening sequence, progressively slacken cylinder head bolts 7 to10 **(see illustration 11.35a)**. Carefully remove the bolts, and store them in their fitted order.

Caution: Bolts MUST be refitted in their original locations.

19 Avoid rotating the crankshaft after the cylinder head bolts have been removed. When these are removed, rotation of the crankshaft is difficult, or impossible. DO NOT attempt to rotate the crankshaft until the cylinder liners have been clamped in position.

20 Mark the camshaft sprockets so that they can be refitted on the correct camshaft. Using the manufactured turning/locking device to hold the sprockets, remove the sprocket securing bolts, and remove the sprockets.

21 Remove one bolt securing the dipstick support bracket. Remove five bolts securing the timing belt inner cover, and remove the cover.

Caution: Two dowels locate the cylinder head. DO NOT attempt to swivel the head, or tap it sideways. If the joint is difficult to break, use two cranked bars, fitted into two cylinder head bolt holes, and rock the head gently.

22 Ensure that the oxygen sensor, in the exhaust manifold, is not damaged during head removal.

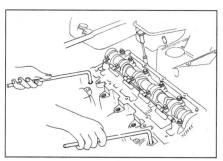

11.23 Using two cranked bars to break the cylinder head-to-cylinder block joint by rocking

23 Using assistance, remove the cylinder head, and place it on wooden blocks **(see illustration)**. Discard the gasket.

24 Remove two location dowels from the cylinder block.

Caution: When using cylinder head bolts to clamp the liners, ensure that bolts are refitted in their original locations. Fit them carefully – DO NOT drop them into the holes.

25 Using the tubular spacers, and thick washers – which will sit over the top edge of two adjacent liners – fit three cylinder bolts through the spacers and washers, and tighten them sufficiently to prevent liner movement **(see illustration)**.

Refitting

26 Clean all cylinder head related components:

Caution: Ensure that no debris is allowed to enter oil or coolant passages in the cylinder head or block. Seal them with tape or cloths.

   a) Clean mating faces of exhaust pipe and exhaust manifold.

   b) Clean the location dowels and fit them into the cylinder block.

   c) Use a hard plastic or wooden scraper to clean the mating faces of the cylinder head and cylinder block. Check mating faces for damage.

   d) Use a straight-edge and feeler gauge to check for cylinder head warp. If warp is more than 0.05 mm, the head must be skimmed or renewed.

   e) To prevent carbon, from the piston crowns, getting down the bores, smear grease around the gap. Use a hard plastic or wooden scraper to clean the piston crowns. When cleaned, wipe away the grease and carbon.

   f) Clean out the cylinder head bolt holes.

   g) Wash and dry the cylinder head bolts.

Note: If bolts have been used to clamp the liners, remove them one at time for washing and inspection, and then refit them.

27 Check the bolts for any signs of wear or damage – renew any faulty bolt. Lightly oil the bolt threads, and carefully fit them into their original holes. Screw them in finger tight.

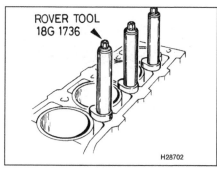

11.25 Tubular spacers and washers used to clamp liners

11.27 Measure the length of cylinder head bolts protruding above the cylinder block

11.29a Fit a new gasket over the dowels

11.29b Ensure gasket marks are correctly positioned

Measure the distance from the cylinder block surface to the underside of the bolt head. If the distance is less than 97 mm, the bolt may be re-used. If the distance is more than 97 mm, the bolt must be renewed. If several bolts are elongated, the full set should be renewed (see illustration).
Caution: If the crankshaft has been turned, check that the dots on the crankshaft sprocket are aligned either side of the raised rib on the oil pump cover.
Caution: DO NOT rotate the crankshaft after the liner clamps have been removed.
28 Remove the cylinder liner clamps.
29 Ensuring that the word TOP is uppermost, and FRONT is towards the timing belt; locate a new, dry, cylinder head gasket over the dowels (see illustrations).
30 Using assistance, locate the cylinder head on the cylinder block, ensuring that it fits over the dowels.
31 Clean and fit the timing belt inner cover. Use a torque wrench to tighten the bolts to the specified torque.
32 Align and secure the dipstick support bracket.
33 Ensure that camshaft sprocket drive pins are in position. Clean and fit the sprockets, washers and bolts. Using the locking device, hold the camshaft sprockets, and tighten the bolts to the specified torque.
34 Lightly oil the cylinder head bolt threads and underside of the heads. Being careful not to drop them, enter them into their correct holes, and tighten them finger tight.
35 Working in sequence, progressively tighten the bolts as follows (see illustrations):
Note: Rotate camshafts - as for removal - to gain access to bolts 3 and 4.
a) *Tighten all bolts to the Stage 1 torque wrench setting.*
b) *Mark each bolt to indicate a radial position reference.*
c) *Turn all bolts through 180°.*
d) *Turn all bolts through another 180°, and align radial marks.*
Caution: If any bolt is overtightened, back off 90° then realign radial marks.
36 Using the turning device, align the camshaft sprocket timing marks, and fit the sprocket locking device.

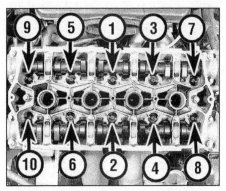
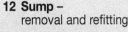

11.35a Cylinder head bolts tightening sequence

37 Completion of refitting is a reversal of the removal procedure, noting the following:
a) *Ensure all electrical multiplugs are correctly and securely connected.*
b) *Ensure all hoses and pipes are correctly and securely connected.*
c) *Fill the cooling system with the correct mix of water and antifreeze - see Chapter 1A.*
d) *Check throttle cable adjustment.*

12 Sump – removal and refitting

Note: The following new parts are needed – MG Rover sealant GUG 705963GM. Two alignment pins are needed during refit; these can be made by cutting the heads off two M8 bolts.

Removal

1 Disconnect the battery negative lead.
2 Apply the handbrake, chock the rear roadwheels, then jack up the front of the car and support it on axle stands (see *Jacking and vehicle support*). Remove the right-hand roadwheel.
3 Drain the engine oil – if necessary, see Chapter 1A. Clean and refit the drain plug, and tighten it to the specified torque. It is recommended that the oil filter is renewed.
4 Remove two nuts securing the exhaust front pipe to the exhaust manifold. Tie the pipe clear of the work area.

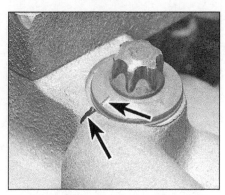

11.35b Mark bolt heads for radial position

5 On 1.8 litre engines, slacken the through-bolt securing the engine lower steady bar to the suspension crossmember. Remove the through-bolt securing the steady bar to the sump bracket, and release the bar from the bracket (see illustration).
6 Remove three bolts securing the sump rear flange to the gearbox housing.
7 Working in the **reverse** of the tightening sequence, progressively slacken and remove fourteen sump bolts (see illustration 12.16). Note that two longer bolts are fitted adjacent to the rear flange.
8 Using a mallet, tap the sump sideways to release the joint.

Refitting

9 Clean all traces of old sealant from the mating faces of the sump and bearing ladder, and clean inside the sump.

12.5 Remove steady bar through-bolt (arrowed)

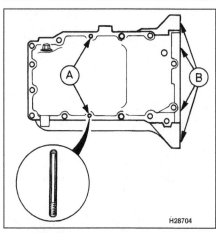

12.10 Fit two sump alignment pins

A Alignment pin locations
B Sump flange-to-cylinder block rear face alignment

10 Screw the alignment pins into the bearing ladder **(see illustration)**.
Caution: After applying sealant, sump should be refitted immediately.
11 Apply a bead of sealant to the sump mating face, then spread to an even film using a roller.
12 Locate the sump over the alignment pins. Fit two bolts at positions 5 and 6, and tighten to 4 Nm (3 lbf ft).
13 Fit ten bolts in remaining holes, ensuring that the two long bolts are fitted adjacent to the rear flange. Lightly tighten all bolts.
14 Remove the alignment pins, and fit and lightly tighten the two remaining bolts.
15 Fit three bolts securing sump rear flange to gearbox housing. Lightly tighten, and then slacken the bolts – this aligns the sump flange and gearbox housing.
16 Working in sequence, progressively tighten the bolts. Use a torque wrench to

tighten the shorter and longer bolts to their specified torque **(see illustration)**.
17 Tighten the sump flange bolts securely.
18 On 1.8 litre engines, fit the steady bar to sump bracket, and locate bolt and nut. Use a torque wrench to tighten steady bar front and rear bolts to the specified torque.
19 Clean exhaust front pipe and manifold mating faces. Using a new gasket, connect the pipe, and secure with two nuts. Use a torque wrench to tighten the nuts to the specified torque (see Chapter 4A).
20 Fit the roadwheel, and tighten the nuts to secure the wheel. Remove the stands and lower the vehicle to the ground. Use a torque wrench to tighten the roadwheel nuts to the specified torque.
21 Fill the engine with new engine oil – see Chapter 1A.
22 Reconnect the battery earth lead.

13 Oil pump – removal and refitting

Note: *The following new parts are needed – oil pump gasket, crankshaft right-hand oil seal, thread-locking compound.*

Removal

1 Remove camshaft timing belt as described in Section 7.
2 Withdraw the timing belt gear from the end of the crankshaft.
3 Slacken and remove the bolts securing the engine harness to the lower edge of the oil pump housing.
4 Remove the bolts securing oil pump to cylinder block – note the location of the M6x20 bolt **(see illustration)**.
5 To ease pump removal, remove the lower bolt from the timing belt inner cover.

6 Remove the oil pump and discard the gasket, a new one will be required for refitting.
7 Remove and discard the crankshaft oil seal from the oil pump housing.

Refitting

8 Ensuring that no debris enters the crankcase, clean the pump bolt holes in cylinder block. Clean the mating faces of the oil pump housing and cylinder block. Clean the crankshaft oil seal running surface. Clean off all traces of thread-locking compound from the pump bolts.
9 Prime the pump by injecting clean engine oil into it, and turning the rotor by hand. Turn the pump rotor to align the inner gear drive with the flats on the crankshaft.
10 Fit a new gasket (dry) to the cylinder block.
11 Fit the oil seal sleeve protection sleeve – from the seal kit – over the end of the crankshaft.
12 Locate the oil pump on the cylinder block. Fit the bolts – ensure that the M6x20 bolt is fitted in the correct location, as noted during removal. Use a torque wrench to tighten the bolts to the specified torque.
13 With the protection sleeve still in place over the crankshaft, fit a new crankshaft oil seal over the sleeve, and tap into position using a suitable tube or socket. Remove the protection sleeve.
Caution: The new oil seal must be fitted dry. Do not lubricate the seal recess, the seal lip, or the seal running surface on the shaft.
14 Refit the lower bolt to the timing belt inner cover.
15 Fit the timing belt gear to the end of the crankshaft.
16 Refit the timing belt as described in Section 8.

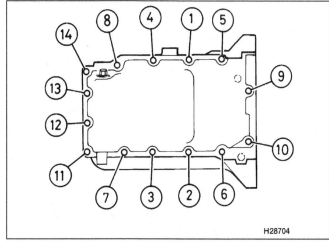

12.16 Sump bolt tightening sequence

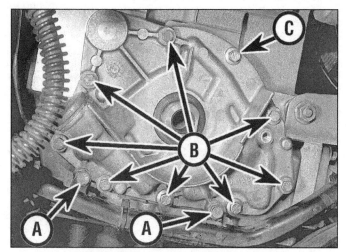

13.4 Remove pump securing bolts

A Wiring harness guide bolts
B Oil pump bolts
C M6 x 20 mm oil pump bolt

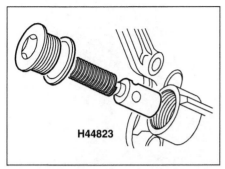

14.8 Oil pressure relief valve components

14 Oil pump pressure relief valve – removal and refitting

Note: *The following new parts are needed – relief valve Dowty sealing washer.*

Removal

1 Disconnect the battery negative lead.
2 Apply the handbrake, chock the rear roadwheels, then jack up the front of the car and support it on axle stands (see *Jacking and vehicle support*). Remove the right-hand front roadwheel.
3 Slacken the bolts securing the power steering pump pulley.
4 Remove the pump drivebelt as described in Chapter 10.
5 Undo the retaining bolts and remove the pulley from the pump.
6 Remove the nuts and bolts, and the lower bolt securing the pump to the bracket. Remove the pump from the bracket, and tie clear of the work area.
7 Remove the bolts securing the pump bracket to the cylinder block, and remove the bracket. Note the position of the M10x90 bolt, and the spacers in the bracket.
8 Remove the sealing plug and washer, spring and valve – discard the washer **(see illustration)**.
9 Check that the valve and bore are not corroded or scored. **Note:** *Light corrosion may be removed using grade 600 emery cloth soaked in oil.* Check the valve slides freely in the bore.
10 Check the spring free length equals 38.9 mm.
11 If the valve is scored, or of the spring free length is less than specified, renew the complete valve assembly.

Refitting

12 Remove all traces of locking compound from the sealing plug threads.
13 Lubricate the valve with clean engine oil and then refit the valve and spring.
14 Fit a new Dowty washer to the plug, and coat the threads with locking compound. Fit and tighten the plug.
15 Fit the power steering pump bracket and retaining bolts, ensuring that the M10x90 bolt is correctly located, as noted on removal.

16 Locate the pump in the bracket – note that the position of the spacers may need to be adjusted to allow correct location of the pump. Fit the two nuts and bolts, and the lower bolt.
17 Clean the mating faces of the pump pulley and refit the pulley to the pump, and then lightly tighten the bolts.
18 Fit the pump drivebelt as described in Chapter 10.
19 Use a torque wrench to tighten the pulley bolts to the specified torque (see Chapter 10).
20 Fit the roadwheel, remove the axle stands and then lower the vehicle to the ground. Use a torque wrench to tighten the roadwheel nuts to the specified torque.
21 Reconnect the battery earth lead.

15 Oil pump – dismantling, inspection and reassembly

Note: *If oil pump wear is suspected, check the cost and availability of new parts (only available in the form of a repair kit) against the cost of a new pump. Examine the pump as described in this Section and then decide whether renewal or repair is the best course of action. A new pump cover sealing ring, and a new pressure relief valve plug sealing ring will be required on refitting.*

Dismantling

1 Remove the oil pump as described in Section 13.
2 Unscrew the Torx screws and remove the pump cover plate. Discard the sealing ring.
3 Note the identification marks on the outer rotor then remove both the rotors from the body.

Inspection

4 Inspect the rotors for obvious signs of wear or damage and renew if necessary. If the pump body or cover plate is scored or damaged, then the complete oil pump assembly must be renewed.
5 Using feeler blades of the appropriate thickness, measure the clearance between the outer rotor and the pump body, then between the tips of the inner and outer rotor lobes (a and b respectively) **(see illustration)**.
6 Using feeler blades and a straight-edge placed across the top of the pump body and the rotors, measure the rotor endfloat (c).
7 If any measurement is outside the specified limits, the complete pump assembly must be renewed.
8 Thoroughly clean the threads of the pump cover plate securing screws.

Reassembly

9 Lubricate the pump rotors with clean engine oil and refit them to the pump body, ensuring that the identification mark on the outer rotor faces outwards (ie, towards the pump cover) **(see illustration)**.
10 Lubricate a new sealing ring with clean

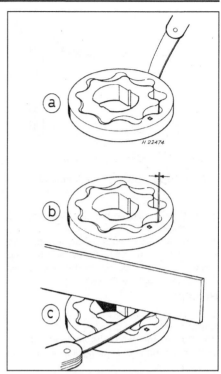

15.5 Checking oil pump rotors for wear – see text for details

engine oil, then fit the sealing ring to the pump body and refit the cover plate. Apply thread-locking compound to the threads of the cover plate screws and tighten them securely.
11 Check that the pump rotates freely, then prime it by injecting oil into its passages and rotating it. If a long time elapses before the pump is refitted to the engine, prime it again before installation.

16 Crankshaft oil seals – removal and refitting

Right-hand seal

Note: *The following new parts are needed – oil seal kit.*

Removal

1 Remove the camshaft timing belt as described in Section 7.

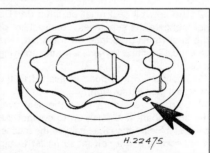

15.9 Oil pump outer rotor identification mark (arrowed)

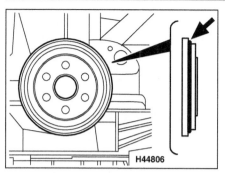

16.13 Apply a bead of sealant to oil seal

17.4 Fabricated locking tool in position

17.13 Fit new flywheel bolts

2 Withdraw the timing belt gear from the end of the crankshaft.

3 Punch, or drill, two small holes opposite each other in the seal. Screw self-tapping screws into the holes, and pull on the screws with pliers to remove the seal.

Refitting

4 Clean the seal recess.
Caution: The new oil seal must be fitted dry. Do not lubricate the seal recess, the seal lip, or the seal running surface on the shaft.

5 Fit the oil seal sleeve protection sleeve – from the seal kit – over the end of the crankshaft.

6 Fit a new crankshaft oil seal over the sleeve, and tap into position using a suitable tube or socket. Remove the protection sleeve.

7 Refit the timing belt gear to the end of the crankshaft.

8 Refit the camshaft timing belt as described in Section 8.

Left-hand seal

Note: *The following new parts are needed – oil seal, MG Rover sealant GAC 8000.*

Removal

9 Remove the flywheel as described in Section 17.

10 Using a smooth-ended flat-blade screwdriver, and taking care not to mark or damage the seal housing or crankshaft, ease the seal from the recess, and discard the seal.

Refitting

11 Clean the seal recess, and seal running surface.

12 The new oil seal must be fitted dry. Do not lubricate the seal recess, the seal lip, or the seal running surface on the shaft. The seal must be fitted immediately after applying sealant.

13 Apply a 1.5 mm bead of sealant to the new seal **(see illustration)**.

14 Using fingers only, ease the seal over the crankshaft, and push up to contact the cylinder block. Press the seal into the recess. If necessary, use a soft-faced mallet to tap the seal into place. Before topping-up oil or rotating the crankshaft, allow the sealant to cure for at least 30 minutes.

Caution: When the seal is in position, leave it to settle for at least 1 minute.

15 Refit the flywheel as described in Section 17.

16 On completion, check and top-up the engine oil.

17 Flywheel/driveplate – removal and refitting

Flywheel

Removal

Note: *The following new parts are needed – 6 flywheel retaining bolts. When slackening or tightening the flywheel securing bolts, it is necessary to prevent the flywheel from turning. This can be done by, eg:*
a) Making and fitting a locking tool.
b) Fitting a long bolt into a gearbox mounting bolt hole

1 Remove the transmission assembly as described in Chapter 7A.

2 Remove the clutch assembly as described in Chapter 6.

3 Disconnect the crankshaft position sensor multiplug. Remove the securing bolt, and remove the sensor.

4 Lock the flywheel in position **(see illustration)**. **Note:** *Use a fabricated locking tool: fit a long bolt into one of the gearbox upper mounting bolt holes and a locking plate located in the flywheel gear.*

5 Alternatively, have an assistant engage a suitable flat lever – such as a large screwdriver – between two teeth of the ring gear, and against the bolt, so that when anti-clockwise effort is applied to the flywheel bolts, the flywheel will be prevented from turning.

6 Slacken and remove the flywheel securing bolts. Discard, as new ones will be required for refitting

7 If necessary, get assistance to remove the heavy flywheel, which is located by dowels.

Refitting

8 Using a suitable thread tap, clean all old thread locking compound from the flywheel bolt holes in the crankshaft.

9 Check the condition of the clutch contact surface. If it is scored or cracked, the flywheel must be renewed.

10 Check the ring gear for broken or missing teeth. If the ring gear is damaged, either the ring gear, or the flywheel assembly, must be renewed. **Note:** *The ring gear is a shrink-fit on the flywheel, and requires controlled heating to expand it before fitting. Ring gear renewal should be carried out by an MG Rover specialist.*

11 Check the condition of the crankshaft sensor reluctor ring. If it is damaged, the flywheel must be renewed.

12 Clean the mating faces of the flywheel and crankshaft.

13 If necessary, get assistance to lift the heavy flywheel. Locate the flywheel over the dowels, and push onto the crankshaft, and fit six new bolts **(see illustration)**.

14 Lock the flywheel and, working in diagonal sequence, progressively tighten the bolts. Use a torque wrench to tighten the bolts to the specified torque.

15 Fit the crankshaft position sensor.

16 Refit the clutch assembly as described in Chapter 6.

17 Refit the gearbox assembly as described in Chapter 7A.

Driveplate

18 All procedures are essentially the same as described for the flywheel, disregarding references to the clutch. To access the driveplate, remove the automatic transmission and torque converter as described in Chapter 7B. Note that driveplate bolts are tightened to a higher torque than flywheel bolts.

18 Engine/transmission mountings – Inspection, removal and refitting

Inspection

Note: *Normally, mountings will need renewing only if the rubber has hardened or cracked, or separated from the metal backing. Dependent upon the fault, such conditions may allow excess engine movement, leading to an impression of rough running, knocking or bumping. The mountings can be visually checked for rubber deterioration, and* *separation can be checked by levering with a pry bar between the rubber and metal backing. If any fault is found, the mounting must be renewed.*

Right-hand mounting (hydramount)

Removal

1 Disconnect the battery negative lead.
2 Position a jack, with wooden block on top, under the engine sump, and adjust to support the weight of the engine and transmission.
3 Where applicable, release any pipes, hoses or wiring which are routed past the timing belt cover, from their retaining clips and move to one side.
4 On models fitted with an upper steady bar, remove the through-bolt and tilt the bar upwards clear of the mounting. Remove the bolts securing the mounting bracket to the engine. Then remove the two bolts securing rubber mounting to the body and remove the mounting assembly **(see illustrations)**.
5 On models without an upper steady bar, slacken the through-bolt securing the mounting to the body. Remove the mounting nuts, which attach the mounting bracket to the engine and remove the mounting **(see illustrations)**.

Refitting

6 Refitting is the reversal of removal, using a torque wrench to tighten the bolts to the specified torque.

Left-hand mounting

Removal

7 Disconnect the battery negative lead.
8 Position a jack, with wooden block on top, under the transmission, and adjust to support the weight of the engine and transmission.
9 Remove the battery as described in Chapter 5A.

18.4a Remove the through-bolt (arrowed) . . .

18.4b . . . and then undo the engine mounting bracket bolts (arrowed)

18.5a Remove the through-bolt (arrowed) . . .

18.5b . . . and then undo the engine mounting bracket nuts (arrowed)

10 Remove the air cleaner as described in Chapter 4A.
11 Remove two bolts securing left-hand mounting steady bar, and remove the outer part of the bar **(see illustration)**.
12 Remove two bolts securing the mounting bracket to the transmission housing **(see illustration)**.
13 Remove the through-bolt securing the mounting to the bracket on the body.
14 Lower transmission slightly and remove the mounting and rubber spacers, noting their fitted position.

Refitting

15 Refitting is the reversal of removal, making sure the rubber spacers are fitted correctly as noted on removal. Use a torque wrench to tighten the bolts to the specified torque.

Lower mounting/steady bar – 1.8 models

Removal

16 Apply the handbrake, chock the rear roadwheels, then jack up the front of the car and support it on axle stands (see *Jacking and*

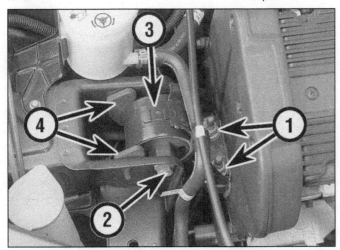

18.5c Right-hand engine mounting

1 *Mounting-to-engine bracket nuts*
2 *Through-bolt*
3 *Mounting*
4 *Rubber spacers*

18.11 Remove the steady bar bolts (arrowed)

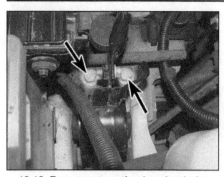

18.12 Remove mounting bracket bolts
(arrowed)

18.19 Undo the bolts (arrowed) to remove
the sump mounting bracket

vehicle support). Remove the right-hand front roadwheel and inner wing trim panel.

17 Remove the through-bolt securing the steady bar to the bracket on the front suspension crossmember/body.

18 Remove the through-bolt securing the steady bar to the bracket on the sump and withdraw the steady bar from under the vehicle.

19 To remove the mounting bracket from the sump, undo the retaining bolts **(see illustration)**.

Refitting

20 Refitting is the reversal of removal, using a torque wrench to tighten the bolts to the specified torque.

Chapter 2 Part B:
V6 engine in-car repair procedures

Contents

	Section number
Camshaft covers – removal and refitting	4
Camshaft oil seals – renewal	9
Camshafts and tappets – removal, inspection and refitting	10
Compression test – description and interpretation	2
Crankshaft oil seals – removal and refitting	18
Crankshaft pulley – removal and refitting	5
Cylinder heads – removal and refitting	11
Engine assembly/valve timing marks – general information and usage	3
Engine/transmission mountings – inspection, removal and refitting	20
Flywheel/driveplate – removal and refitting	19

	Section number
General information and precautions	1
Oil cooler – removal and refitting	17
Oil pressure switch – removal and refitting	16
Oil pump – dismantling, inspection and reassembly	15
Oil pump – removal and refitting	14
Oil pump pressure relief valve – removal and refitting	13
Sump – removal and refitting	12
Timing belt covers – removal and refitting	6
Timing belt tensioner and sprockets – removal and refitting	8
Timing belts – removal and refitting	7

Degrees of difficulty

Easy, suitable for novice with little experience	**Fairly easy,** suitable for beginner with some experience	**Fairly difficult,** suitable for competent DIY mechanic	**Difficult,** suitable for experienced DIY mechanic	**Very difficult,** suitable for expert DIY or professional

Specifications

General

Engine type	Six-cylinders in vee, twin overhead camshafts per bank, 24 valve
Designation	KV6
Bore	80.0 mm
Stroke:	
2.0 litre engine	66.2 mm
2.5 litre engine	82.8 mm
Capacity:	
2.0 litre engine	1997 cc
2.5 litre engine	2497 cc
Firing order	1-6-5-4-3-2 (No 1 cylinder at primary timing belt end, front bank)
Direction of crankshaft rotation	Clockwise (seen from right-hand side of car)
Compression ratio	10.25:1
Compression pressure (typical)	10.0 bar minimum
Compression pressure difference between cylinders (typical)	1.5 bar maximum

Camshafts

General	Direct-acting on hydraulic tappets, bearings line-bored in cylinder head
Drive	Toothed primary belt from crankshaft to inlet camshafts, automatic tensioner; two secondary toothed belts drive exhaust camshafts from rear of inlet camshafts
Bearing journal running clearance:	
Standard	0.025 to 0.059 mm
Service limit	0.100 mm
Camshaft endfloat:	
Standard	0.060 to 0.190 mm
Service limit	0.300 mm
Hydraulic tappet outside diameter	32.959 to 32.975 mm

Lubrication system

Oil pressure	1.0 bar at idle, 3.0 bar at 3000 rpm (hot)
Relief valve opening pressure	4.1 bar
Low oil pressure warning light comes on.	0.3 to 0.5 bar
Oil pump clearances:	
Outer rotor-to-body clearance	0.13 to 0.23 mm
Rotor endfloat.	0.04 to 0.09 mm

Torque wrench settings

	Nm	lbf ft
Auxiliary drivebelt top cover.	25	18
Big-end bearing cap bolts*:		
Stage 1	20	15
Stage 2	Angle-tighten a further 70°	
Camshaft bearing carrier bolts.	10	7
Camshaft cover bolts.	9	7
Camshaft sprocket bolts*:		
Stage 1	27	20
Stage 2	Angle-tighten a further 90°	
Crankshaft pulley bolt	160	118
Cylinder head bolts:		
Stage 1	25	18
Stage 2 (see text)	25	18
Stage 3	Angle-tighten a further 90°	
Stage 4	Angle-tighten a further 90°	
Dipstick tube mounting bolt.	9	7
Driveplate bolts	100	74
Engine front plate (primary timing belt end):		
Top bolts (x3)	45	33
Lower (end) bolts:		
M10 studs (x2)	45	33
M12 bolts (x5)	85	63
Engine/transmission mountings:		
Left-hand mounting through-bolt.	100	74
Left-hand mounting to body.	85	63
Left-hand mounting to transmission	85	63
Lower mounting bolts.	100	74
Right-hand hydramount to body	85	63
Right-hand lower mounting bracket to engine plate	45	33
Right-hand mounting steady (upper) bracket bolts	85	63
Right-hand mounting to body	85	63
Right-hand mounting upper cross-brace.	25	18
Right-hand upper mounting bracket bolts	100	74
Right-hand upper mounting bracket to hydramount nut	85	63
Exhaust front support bracket bolts.	25	18
Exhaust manifold-to-downpipe flange nuts	75	55
Flywheel bolts.	80	59
Flywheel end oil seal bolts*	9	7
Idler pulley bolt	45	33
Inlet manifold	25	18
Lower crankcase-to-block bolts:		
M5 bolts	9	7
M8 bolts (and nut, where fitted)	35	26
Main bearing ladder-to-cylinder block bolts*:		
Stage 1	20	15
Stage 2	Angle-tighten a further 90°	
Oil cooler:		
Cooler-to-sump bolts	45	33
Pipe unions.	26	19
Oil pick-up pipe/strainer.	25	18
Oil pressure switch.	14	10
Oil pump bolts*.	25	18
Oil pump pressure relief plug	25	18
Sump bolts.	35	26
Timing belt backplate bolts**	9	7
Timing belt tensioner mounting bolts**	25	18
Timing belt tensioner pulley bolt	45	33

* *Use new bolts*

** *Use locking compound*

1 General information and precautions

How to use this Chapter

This Part of the Chapter describes those repair procedures that can reasonably be carried out on the engine whilst it remains in the car. If the engine has been removed from the car and is being dismantled as described in Part D of this Chapter, any preliminary dismantling procedures can be ignored.

Note that whilst it may be possible physically to overhaul items such as the piston/connecting rod assemblies with the engine in the car, such tasks are not usually carried out as separate operations and usually require the execution of several additional procedures (not to mention the cleaning of components and of oilways). For this reason, all such tasks are classed as major overhaul procedures and are described in Part D of this Chapter.

Engine description

The KV6 engine is derived from the long-running K-Series engine family, and is a V6 unit mounted transversely at the front of the car with the clutch and transmission on the left-hand end. The engine has double overhead camshafts on each bank of cylinders, and is a 24 valve design.

The main structure of the engine consists of several major castings – the cylinder heads, the cylinder block/crankcase, the crankshaft main bearing ladder, lower crankcase and sump. All the castings are of aluminium alloy, with the exception of the main bearing ladder, which is made of a special aero-industry-standard alloy.

Unlike the four-cylinder K-Series engines, the KV6 does not have the extra-long cylinder head bolts which extend into the main bearing ladder. However, the more-conventional head bolts still extend into the block by 70 mm, for increased structural stiffness. The main bearing ladder is secured to the base of the block by sixteen bolts, with a cast alloy lower crankcase section below that for extra stiffness, and a cast sump 'pan' fitted below that.

The crankshaft runs in four main bearings. Thrustwashers are fitted to the rear main bearing to control crankshaft endfloat.

The connecting rods rotate on horizontally-split bearing shells at their big-ends. The pistons are attached to the connecting rods by gudgeon pins which are an interference fit in the connecting rod small-end eyes. The aluminium alloy pistons are fitted with three piston rings, comprising two compression rings and an oil control ring.

The cylinder bores are formed by renewable liners which locate in the cylinder block/crankcase at their top ends. The liners are known as 'damp' liners. To prevent the coolant escaping into the sump, the base of each liner is sealed with sealing compound.

The inlet and exhaust valves are each closed by coil springs and operate in guides pressed into the cylinder heads. The valve seat inserts are pressed into the cylinder head and can be renewed separately if worn.

Both inlet camshafts are driven by a single primary toothed timing belt, and the exhaust camshafts are each driven by a smaller secondary toothed belt from a sprocket on the rear of each inlet camshaft. The camshafts operate the valves via self-adjusting hydraulic tappets. The camshafts rotate in bearings which are line-bored directly into the cylinder head and the (bolted-on) bearing carrier. This means that the bearing carriers and cylinder heads are matched, and cannot be renewed independently. The water pump is driven by the main timing belt.

Lubrication is by means of an eccentric-rotor type pump driven directly from the right-hand (primary timing belt end) of the crankshaft. The pump draws oil through a strainer located in the sump. It then forces it through an externally-mounted full-flow cartridge-type oil filter into galleries in the oil rail and the cylinder block/crankcase, from where it is distributed to the crankshaft (main bearings) and camshafts. The big-end bearings are supplied with oil via internal drillings in the crankshaft, while the camshaft bearings and the tappets receive a pressurised supply via drillings in the cylinder heads. The camshaft lobes and valves are lubricated by oil splash, as are all other engine components. On models with air conditioning, a coolant-fed oil cooler is mounted externally on the sump, and oil circulates through two pipes to and from the oil filter housing.

Cylinder numbering

The KV6 engine is a transversely-mounted V6 unit. It will be necessary throughout this and other Chapters in the manual to refer to the cylinder head and piston positions, and this is less easy than an in-line engine. For the purposes of this manual, and hopefully for clarity, we have adopted the convention that since the 'left-hand' bank of three cylinders is the one at the front of the car, it will be called the 'front bank'. Similarly, the 'right-hand' bank, which is at the rear in the car, is the 'rear bank'.

There are timing belts at both ends of the engine, but we will maintain the convention that the 'timing belt end' refers to the KV6's primary timing belt end (opposite the transmission). When referring to the KV6's three timing belts, the 'primary' or 'main' belt is the one which drives the inlet camshafts from the crankshaft; the 'secondary' belts are the two smaller belts at the transmission end of the engine.

Using our adopted convention, No 1 cylinder is at the timing belt end on the front bank, with cylinders 3 and 5. The rear bank cylinders are numbered 2, 4 and 6 from the timing belt end.

Operations with engine in car

The following work can be carried out with the engine in the car:
a) Compression pressure – testing.
b) Camshaft covers – removal and refitting.
c) Crankshaft pulley – removal and refitting.
d) Timing belt covers – removal and refitting.
e) Timing belts – removal, refitting and adjustment.
f) Timing belt tensioner and sprockets – removal and refitting.
g) Camshaft oil seals – renewal.
h) Camshafts and tappets – removal, inspection and refitting.
i) Cylinder heads – removal and refitting.
j) Cylinder heads and pistons – decarbonising.
k) Sump – removal and refitting.
l) Oil pump – removal, overhaul and refitting.
m) Crankshaft oil seals – renewal.
n) Engine/transmission mountings – inspection and renewal.
o) Flywheel – removal, inspection and refitting.

2 Compression test – description and interpretation

Note: *A suitable compression tester will be required for this test.*

1 When engine performance is down, or if misfiring occurs which cannot be attributed to the ignition or fuel systems, a compression test can provide diagnostic clues as to the engine's condition. If the test is performed regularly it can give warning of trouble before any other symptoms become apparent.

2 The engine must be fully warmed-up to normal operating temperature, the battery must be fully-charged and the spark plugs must be removed (see Chapter 1A). The aid of an assistant will be required.

3 The fuel pump must be disabled by removing the fuel pump relay from the fusebox.

4 Fit a compression tester to the No 1 cylinder spark plug hole. The type of tester which screws into the plug thread is preferred.

5 Have the assistant hold the throttle wide open and crank the engine on the starter motor. After one or two revolutions, the compression pressure should build-up to a maximum figure and then stabilise. Record the highest reading obtained.

6 Repeat the test on the remaining cylinders, recording the pressure in each.

7 All cylinders should produce very similar pressures; a difference of more than 2 bars between any two cylinders indicates a fault. Note that the compression should build-up quickly in a healthy engine; low compression on the first stroke, followed by gradually-increasing pressure on successive strokes, indicates worn piston rings. A low compression reading on the first stroke, which does not build-up during successive

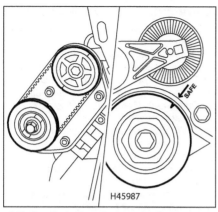

H45987

3.7 Crankshaft pulley notch aligned with SAFE arrow, and camshaft rear sprockets

strokes, indicates leaking valves or a blown head gasket (a cracked head could also be the cause). Deposits on the undersides of the valve heads can also cause low compression.

8 Although MG Rover do not specify exact compression pressures, as a guide, any cylinder pressure of below 10 bar can be considered as less than healthy. Refer to an engine specialist if in doubt as to whether a particular pressure reading is acceptable.

9 If the pressure in any cylinder is significantly low, carry out the following test to isolate the cause. Introduce a teaspoonful of clean oil into that cylinder through its spark plug hole and repeat the test.

10 If the addition of oil temporarily improves the compression pressure, this indicates that bore or piston wear is responsible for the pressure loss. No improvement suggests that leaking or burnt valves, or a blown head gasket, may be to blame.

11 A low reading from two adjacent cylinders is almost certainly due to the head gasket having blown between them and the presence of coolant in the engine oil will confirm this.

12 If one cylinder is about 20 percent lower than the others and the engine has a slightly rough idle, a worn camshaft lobe could be the cause.

13 If the compression reading is unusually high, the combustion chambers are probably coated with carbon deposits. If this is the case, the cylinder head should be removed and decarbonised.

4.1a Remove the two mounting bolts . . .

3.9a Insert the timing pin . . .

14 On completion of the test, refit the spark plugs (see Chapter 1A), reconnect the ignition coil(s) and refit the fuel pump relay.

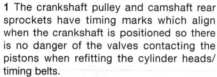

3 Engine assembly/ valve timing marks – general information and usage

1 The crankshaft pulley and camshaft rear sprockets have timing marks which align when the crankshaft is positioned so there is no danger of the valves contacting the pistons when refitting the cylinder heads/ timing belts.

2 Disconnect the battery negative terminal. If necessary, remove all the spark plugs as described in Chapter 1A to enable the engine to be easily turned over.

3 To gain access to the camshaft sprocket timing marks, remove the secondary timing belt covers, as described in Section 6.

4 Loosen the right-hand front wheel bolts. Firmly apply the handbrake, then jack up the front of the car and support it securely on axle stands (see *Jacking and vehicle support*). Remove the right-hand front wheel to improve access to the crankshaft pulley.

5 Remove the engine undertray, which is secured by a number of quick-release screw fasteners.

6 Remove the right-hand wheel arch liner as described in Chapter 11, Section 25.

7 Using a socket and extension bar on the crankshaft pulley bolt, turn the crankshaft until the notch in the pulley is aligned with the SAFE arrow. At this point, the notches in both

4.1b . . . and lift off the engine top cover

3.9b . . . and ensure it engages fully

pairs of camshaft rear sprockets should be aligned facing each other **(see illustration)**.

8 With the engine in this position, it should also be possible to lock the flywheel (driveplate on automatic transmission models) using a timing pin. The pin should be inserted through a hole in the lower crankcase flange, and it engages in a hole in the flywheel or driveplate – the MG Rover tool is 18G 1746A, but an alternative can be made from a 10 mm bolt. The critical sizes are as follows:

  1) 7.4 mm diameter for the first 12 mm length (to fit inside the flywheel or driveplate hole).

  2) 9.7 mm diameter for the next 36 mm length (to fit the hole in the crankcase lower flange).

9 Insert the tool in the relevant hole – use the inner hole to lock the driveplate, or the hole which is further out to lock the flywheel. If it will not fit immediately, turn the engine very slightly forwards or backwards from the SAFE position until it engages the flywheel/driveplate hole **(see illustrations)**.

10 If the pin is not used, a degree of safety can be achieved (on manual transmission models) by applying the handbrake firmly and engaging a gear.

11 With the crankshaft pulley and camshaft sprocket timing marks positioned as described, the engine can safely be dismantled.

4 Camshaft covers – removal and refitting

Front bank

Removal

1 Remove the engine top cover, which is secured by two bolts. Recover the washers and rubber grommets from the bolt holes, and store them for refitting **(see illustrations)**.

2 Depress the locking collars and release the two breather hoses from the cover, noting their fitted positions **(see illustration)**.

3 Check to see whether the spark plug HT leads are marked for position. Confusion when refitting is unlikely, as they are of different lengths, but if required, label the leads 1, 3 and 5 from the timing belt end. Disconnect the

4.2 Removing one of the two breather hoses

4.3a Carefully prise the HT lead end fittings upwards off the plugs. . .

4.3b . . . and unclip them from the camshaft cover

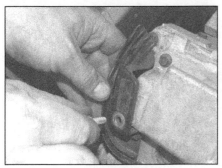

4.4 Unbolt and remove the HT lead guide clip

4.5a Disconnect the camshaft position sensor wiring plug . . .

4.5b . . . then unbolt and remove the wiring plug bracket

leads from their plugs, and unclip them from the camshaft cover **(see illustrations)**.

4 Unbolt the HT lead guide clip from the camshaft cover **(see illustration)**.

5 At the transmission end of the cover, disconnect the camshaft position sensor wiring plug, and release the plug from the mounting bracket. Unscrew the bolt securing the bracket, and remove it **(see illustrations)**.

6 To make room for the camshaft cover to be removed, remove the single bolt securing the radiator hose support bracket **(see illustration)**. Unhook the top hose. The coolant elbow at the top of the radiator hinders access to some of the cover bolts, but removing this would mean draining the coolant.

7 Progressively loosen and remove the fourteen bolts securing the camshaft cover, and lift it off with its gasket **(see illustrations)**. Discard the gasket – a new one should be used when refitting.

Refitting

8 Clean the mating surfaces of the cover and camshaft carrier. Clean inside the cover – if necessary, wash the oil separator mesh in a suitable solvent and allow to dry **(see illustration)**.

4.6 Remove the radiator top hose support bracket

9 Fit the new gasket, observing any direction-of-fitting markings. The fitted position should be evident, but any arrows should point towards the inlet manifold **(see illustration)**.

10 Refit the cover, and secure with the fourteen bolts, which should be tightened

4.7a Unbolt and lift off the camshaft cover . . .

4.7b . . . and recover the metal gasket

4.8 Ensure that the oil separator meshes are clean

4.9 Observe the direction-of-fitting marks on the new gasket

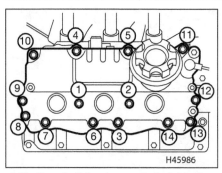

4.10 Camshaft front cover bolt tightening sequence

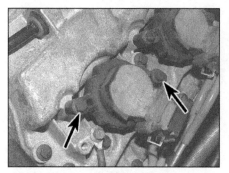

4.14a Unscrew the two bolts from each coil . . .

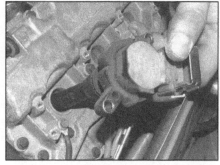

4.14b . . . then lift them off the plugs

4.15 Unscrew the bolt securing the earth lead

4.16 Disconnect the breather hose

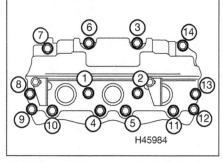

4.21 Camshaft rear cover bolt tightening sequence

progressively in sequence to the specified torque (see illustration).

11 Further refitting is a reversal of removal. Refit the breather hoses by pushing them firmly home.

Rear bank

Removal

12 Remove the upper section of the inlet manifold as described in Chapter 4B.

13 Peel up the rubber weatherseal at the rear of the engine compartment. Remove the four nuts securing the central soundproofing panel, then lift it off the wiring harness that passes through the bulkhead. Remove the two bolts and take out the access panel behind the soundproofing.

14 Release the locking clips and disconnect the wiring plugs from the three ignition coils. Though not essential, it may be wise to mark the coils for position before removing them. Remove the two bolts securing each coil, and lift them off their respective spark plugs (see illustrations).

15 Remove the bolt from the earth lead, and move the lead clear (see illustration).

16 Depress the locking collar and release the breather hose from the cover (see illustration).

17 Release the coil wiring harness from the two clips on the inlet manifold mounting bracket, and move the wiring clear.

18 Progressively loosen and remove the fourteen bolts securing the camshaft cover, and lift it off with its gasket. Discard the gasket – a new one should be used when refitting.

Refitting

19 Clean the mating surfaces of the cover and camshaft carrier. Also clean inside the cover – if necessary, wash the oil separator mesh in a suitable solvent and allow to dry.

20 Fit the new gasket, observing any direction-of-fitting markings. The fitted position should be evident, but any arrows should point towards the inlet manifold.

21 Refit the cover, and secure with the fourteen bolts, which should be tightened progressively in sequence to the specified torque (see illustration).

22 Further refitting is a reversal of removal. Refit the breather hose by pushing it firmly home.

5 Crankshaft pulley – removal and refitting

Removal

1 Loosen the right-hand front wheel bolts. Firmly apply the handbrake, and then jack up the front of the car and support it securely on axle stands (see *Jacking and vehicle support*). To improve access, remove the right-hand front wheel.

2 Remove the engine undertray, which is secured by a number of quick-release screw fasteners.

3 Remove the right-hand wheel arch liner as described in Chapter 11, Section 25.

4 If further dismantling is to be carried out, align the engine assembly/valve timing marks

as described in Section 3. However, the timing pin or bolt should be removed before loosening the crankshaft pulley bolt, as there is a risk of it shearing off otherwise. Reset the timing marks and refit the pin once the pulley has been removed, if necessary.

5 Remove the auxiliary drivebelt as described in Chapter 5A.

6 Slacken the crankshaft pulley retaining bolt. To prevent crankshaft rotation, have an assistant select top gear (manual transmission) and apply the brakes firmly. If the engine is removed from the car, it will be necessary to lock the flywheel/driveplate (see Section 19).

7 Unscrew the pulley bolt and washer, noting which way around the washer is fitted, then remove the pulley (see illustration).

Refitting

8 Fit the pulley to the crankshaft, aligning the notch in the pulley with the locating lug on

5.7 Removing the crankshaft pulley

the sprocket, then refit the retaining bolt and washer. Make sure that the tapered face of the washer is facing away from the pulley.

9 Lock the crankshaft using the method used on removal, and tighten the pulley retaining bolt to the specified torque setting.

10 Refit and tension the auxiliary drivebelt as described in Chapter 5A.

11 The remainder of refitting is a reversal of removal. Tighten the wheel bolts to the specified torque.

6 Timing belt covers – removal and refitting

1 If the timing belts are to be removed then, if not already done, set the engine to the safe position as described in Section 3.

Primary belt

Front bank upper cover

2 Remove the engine top cover, which is secured by two bolts. Recover the washers and rubber grommets from the bolt holes, and store them for refitting.

3 Loosen the right-hand front wheel bolts. Firmly apply the handbrake, and then jack up the front of the car and support it securely on axle stands (see *Jacking and vehicle support*). To improve access, remove the right-hand front wheel.

4 Remove the engine undertray, which is secured by a number of quick-release screw fasteners.

5 Remove the right-hand wheel arch liner as described in Chapter 11, Section 25.

6 If both front covers are to be removed, unbolt the engine right-hand mounting as described in Section 20.

7 Loosen the three Torx bolts securing the power steering pump pulley **(see illustration)**. Do not remove them at this stage – loosening is done now to make removing the pulley easier once the drivebelt has been removed.

8 Using the 3/8-inch square drive from a suitable socket handle in the fitting provided on the tensioner, lift the tensioner and release the drivebelt, first from the alternator and then from the remaining pulleys. If the belt is to be re-used, note any direction-of-rotation arrows.

9 Remove the three previously-loosened bolts, and take off the power steering pump pulley **(see illustration)**.

10 Unscrew the single centre Torx bolt, and take off the auxiliary drivebelt idler pulley **(see illustration)**.

11 Remove the three bolts securing the belt cover, and lift it off **(see illustration)**.

12 Refitting is a reversal of removal. Tighten all fasteners to the specified torque, where given (fit the power steering pump pulley bolts hand-tight initially, and tighten fully once the auxiliary drivebelt has been refitted).

Rear bank upper cover

13 Remove the engine right-hand mounting as described in Section 20.

6.7 Loosen the power steering pump pulley bolts with the belt fitted

6.10 Removing the auxiliary drivebelt idler pulley

14 Remove the three bolts securing the belt cover, and lift it off **(see illustrations)**.

15 Refitting is a reversal of removal. Tighten all fasteners to the specified torque, where given.

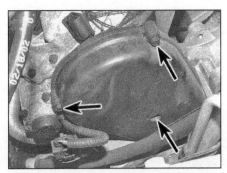

6.14a Rear bank upper cover bolts

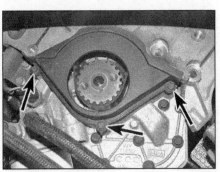

6.17a Remove the three bolts . . .

6.9 Removing the power steering pump pulley

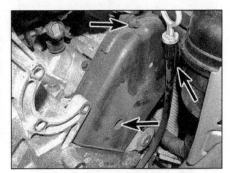

6.11 Front bank upper cover bolts

Lower cover

16 Remove the crankshaft pulley as described in Section 5.

17 Remove the three bolts securing the belt cover, and lift it off **(see illustrations)**.

6.14b Removing the rear bank upper cover

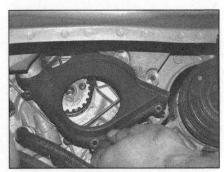

6.17b . . . and take off the lower cover

6.24 Removing the secondary belt rear bank cover

18 Refitting is a reversal of removal. Tighten all fasteners to the specified torque, where given.

Secondary belts

Front bank cover

19 Remove the air cleaner as described in Chapter 4B.
20 Remove the three bolts securing the belt cover, and lift it off.
21 Refitting is a reversal of removal.

Rear bank cover

22 Remove the battery and its tray as described in Chapter 5A.
23 Remove the inlet manifold upper section as described in Chapter 4B.
24 Remove the three bolts securing the belt cover, and lift it out **(see illustration)**.
25 Refitting is a reversal of removal.

7 Timing belts – removal and refitting

Primary belt

Note: *To fit the new belt as the manufacturers say requires the use of special camshaft locking tools that are difficult to make DIY versions of. We have provided two procedures, which should both prove satisfactory – one using the special tools and one which does not (though some home-made tools are still needed). Clearly, if the special tools can be obtained, they should be used. The primary belt's inlet sprockets are not keyed to the camshafts, so if the special tools are not available, the sprocket bolts should not be disturbed if possible. Proceed according to the relevant headings, which follow.*

1 Disconnect the battery negative lead.
2 Align the engine assembly/valve timing marks as described in Section 3.
3 Remove the belt covers as described in Section 6.
4 Remove the auxiliary drivebelt as described in Chapter 5A – this will include removal of the engine right-hand mounting, which is also necessary for other parts of this procedure.
Note: *If the engine is to be supported using the rear lifting eye, note that the eye will have to be removed when the engine front plate is removed later on.*
5 Remove the alternator as described in Chapter 5A.

6 Remove the three bolts securing the power steering pump, and move it away from its mounting bracket (which is the engine front plate), without disconnecting the hoses **(see illustrations)**.
7 Remove the auxiliary drivebelt tensioner, which is secured by two bolts **(see illustration)**.
8 Drain the engine oil as described in Chapter 1A. Remove the single bolt securing the oil dipstick tube to the block, then depress the locking collar at the base and pull the tube out of the sump (if the oil is not drained, oil spillage will result when the tube is removed) **(see illustration)**.
9 On models with air conditioning, using the information in Section 17, unbolt the oil cooler from the front of the sump – it should not be necessary to disconnect any hoses. This is necessary in order to access the air conditioning compressor mounting bolts later on.
10 On models with air conditioning, remove the three mounting bolts, then move the compressor to one side without disconnecting the hoses **(see illustrations)**. Recover the compressor heat shield, noting how it is fitted. If the oil cooler is now loosely bolted back in position, the compressor will rest on it so that the hoses are not under strain.
11 Remove the three top bolts from the engine front plate (which also serves as the alternator mounting bracket), noting that the rearmost bolt is also used to secure the engine rear lifting eye. Noting their locations, unscrew the two mounting boss/bolts and five bolts

7.6a Remove the three mounting bolts . . .

7.6b . . . and lift the pump off the engine front plate

7.7 Removing the auxiliary belt tensioner

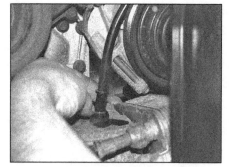

7.8 Press the collar and pull out the dipstick tube

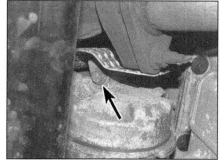

7.10a One of the three compressor mounting bolts

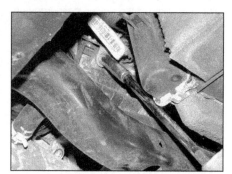

7.10b A long extension will be needed for this compressor bolt

7.11a Unscrew the three top bolts . . .

7.11b . . . the two boss/bolts . . .

7.11c . . . five lower bolts (arrowed) . . .

7.11d . . . and remove the engine front plate

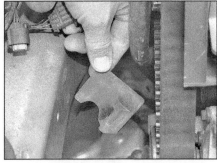

7.12a Remove the tensioner's rubber rear cover

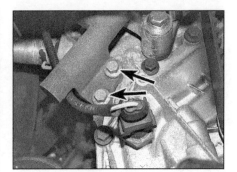

7.12b Loosen the tensioner body bolts

from the end face of the front plate. Release and remove the plate **(see illustrations)**.

12 Unclip the rubber rear cover from the timing belt tensioner (where fitted). Loosen the two tensioner mounting bolts (**do not** loosen the Allen bolt securing the tensioner pulley) **(see illustrations)**. The tensioner mounting bolts will be very stiff, due to the use of thread-lock – ensure a good-quality, close-fitting socket is used.

13 Release the belt tension by turning the tensioner pulley clockwise using a suitable Allen key in the hole provided. Holding the tensioner pulley in the released position, remove the two mounting bolts and take off the tensioner **(see illustration)**. Note: *MG Rover recommend that the tensioner should be renewed every 100 000 miles – timing belt 'kits' are usually available, which include the belts and tensioner.*

14 Make sure the timing marks are aligned

as described in Section 3, and (if removed) refit the timing pin or bolt. Before removing the belt, paint accurate camshaft sprocket alignment marks between the inlet camshaft sprockets and the timing belt backplates, to make refitting easier – this is particularly

7.13 Removing the tensioner

important if the special camshaft locking tools are not available **(see illustrations)**.

15 If the timing belt is to be refitted, mark its direction of rotation. Ease the belt off the sprockets, noting its fitted routing. **Do not** rotate the crankshaft or camshafts until the

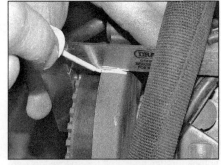

7.14a Use a straight-edge across the backplate and sprocket . . .

7.14b . . . and make alignment marks between the two

7.15a Note the routing of the belt before removal

7.15b Removing the primary timing belt

7.15c The inlet camshaft sprockets will move towards each other

7.19 Fit the camshaft sprocket and new bolt

7.20 Fit the timing belt loosely around the sprockets to begin with

7.21 Remove the exhaust camshaft end caps

7.22 Engage the special tool into the exhaust camshaft and inlet sprocket

7.23 Turn the sprockets fully clockwise

timing belt has been refitted. The sprockets will move slightly, due to the pressure of the valve springs, as the belt is removed – note how they move, as this movement will have to be reversed when the new belt is fitted (see illustrations).

16 Due to the low cost of a new belt, it is recommended that the belt be renewed as a matter of course, regardless of its apparent condition. MG Rover state that a belt which has covered more than 45 000 miles should never be refitted. If signs of oil contamination are found, trace the source of the oil leak and rectify it, then wash down the engine timing belt area and all related components to remove all traces of oil.

With special tools

17 Slacken and remove each inlet camshaft sprocket retaining bolt. If the special tools are fitted as described in paragraphs 21 and 22, they can be used to hold the sprocket while

the bolt is loosened – otherwise, use a home-made forked tool like the one depicted elsewhere in this procedure. Discard the sprocket bolts – new ones should be used when refitting.

18 Remove the sprockets and their centres/hubs, noting how the centres are fitted. Clean all removed components thoroughly.

19 Fit the centres/hubs to the sprockets, then fit the sprockets to the camshafts, using new bolts (see illustration). Tighten the bolts by hand so that the sprockets are still just able to turn on their own.

20 Fit the new belt loosely into place around the sprockets (see illustration). It does not have to be engaged with the sprockets in any way yet, but must be in place before the special tools are fitted.

21 Tap off the end cap seals from both exhaust camshafts (next to the inlet camshaft sprockets, at the primary timing belt end) (see

illustration). This is to allow the fitting of the special tools. Note that new caps should be used when refitting – however, if care is taken in their removal, this may not be necessary.

22 Fit the relevant special tools to the end of each exhaust camshaft, and engage the locating pegs in the inlet camshaft sprocket centres (see illustration).

  a) 2.0 litre engine – Tool number 12-187.
  b) 2.5 litre engine – Tool number 18G 1747-2.

23 Turn the inlet camshaft sprockets as far clockwise (viewed from the primary belt end of the engine) as they will go (see illustration).

24 Fit the timing belt to the crankshaft sprocket, then round the front idler pulley and onto the front sprocket. Turn the sprocket as little as possible anti-clockwise to make the belt fit. Feed the belt under the water pump pulley, then onto the rear sprocket, keeping the belt as taut as possible, and again not turning the sprocket more than necessary from the fully clockwise position.

25 MG Rover recommend fitting a wedge of some kind to stop the timing belt coming off the crankshaft sprocket as the tensioner is fitted. Alternatively, have an assistant on hand to hold the belt in place.

26 Using a vice with protected jaws, carefully compress the timing belt tensioner plunger until a pin (approximately 1.5 mm diameter) can be inserted through the tensioner body and plunger to lock it (see illustrations).

27 Clean the two tensioner mounting bolts, then apply a little thread-locking compound (such as Loctite 242) to their threads.

28 Turn the tensioner pulley clockwise using an Allen key (or have an assistant turn it by

7.26a Mount the tensioner in a vice with protected jaws . . .

7.26b . . . and slowly compress the plunger until the two holes are in line . . .

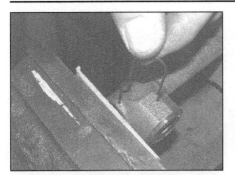

7.26c . . . then insert a pin through the body to lock the plunger

7.28a Turn the pulley clockwise, then offer the tensioner into place . . .

7.28b . . . fit and tighten the two bolts . . .

7.28c . . . then withdraw the plunger locking pin

7.29a Timing belt refitted, with special tools in place

7.29b Tighten the camshaft sprocket bolts to the specified torque . . .

hand), then offer the tensioner up behind the belt and fit the two bolts. Tighten the bolts to the specified torque, then release the pulley, remove the locking pin, and allow the tensioner to act on the belt **(see illustrations)**.

29 Tighten the two inlet camshaft sprocket bolts to the specified torque, then remove the special tools (and the wedge holding the belt on the crankshaft sprocket, if fitted) **(see illustrations)**.

Without special tools

30 Fit the timing belt around the crankshaft sprocket, then behind the front idler pulley. Using a spanner, have an assistant turn the front camshaft sprocket slightly as required to bring the timing marks into alignment (either use your own marks, or have an assistant view those on the secondary belt sprockets). Hold the sprocket in this position, and engage the belt on the sprocket teeth, keeping it as taut as possible **(see illustration)**.

31 The front sprocket will have to be held in the aligned position while the belt is fed under the water pump pulley, then the rear sprocket must be turned into alignment and held while the belt engages with the sprocket teeth. A spanner should **not** be used on the rear sprocket, as this may loosen the bolt – instead, use a home-made forked tool (or equivalent). Note that considerable pressure will be needed **(see illustration)**.

32 Once the belt is fully fitted around the tensioner pulley, the camshaft sprockets can be released slowly (to ensure the belt does not jump off, or jump a tooth). Check that the timing marks are in alignment before

proceeding, as it is possible to fit the belt exactly one tooth out.

33 Carry out the operations described in paragraphs 25 to 28. Owing to the limited access, this is a job for two people – one to

7.29c . . . then through the specified angle

7.31 . . . but the rear sprocket must be turned using a home-made forked tool

turn the pulley, and one to fit the tensioner **(see illustrations)**.

34 On completion, remove the wedge (if used) and any locking pins from the flywheel. Temporarily refit the crankshaft pulley, then

7.30 The front sprocket can be turned into alignment with a spanner . . .

7.33a Turning the tensioner pulley using an Allen key

7.33b Removing the tensioner locking pin

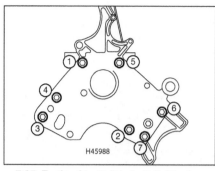

7.35 Engine front plate bolt tightening sequence

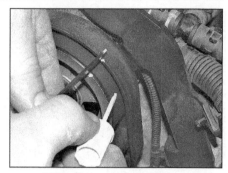

7.39a Use a straight-edge . . .

7.39b . . . to make marks on the rear inlet sprocket

7.39c Also mark the backplate and exhaust sprocket cut-out

7.40 Loosen the inlet sprocket bolt, using a forked sprocket-holding tool

turn the engine clockwise using a spanner or socket on the crankshaft pulley bolt through two complete revolutions. Check that all the sprocket marks come back into alignment (if not, the belt will have to be removed and the procedure repeated). If the secondary belts are also to be renewed, refit the flywheel locking pin.

All models

35 Offer up the engine front plate, and fit the front (end) bolts and two boss/bolts at the top. Tighten the bolts to their specified torques, working in sequence **(see illustration)**.

36 Refit the top three bolts to the engine front plate, remembering that one of the bolts is also used to secure the engine rear lifting eye. Tighten the bolts to the specified torque.

37 If a new primary timing belt has been fitted, fit new secondary belts as described later in this Section.

Secondary belts

Note: *The secondary belt sprockets are keyed to the camshafts, unlike the inlet sprockets at the primary belt end. Providing the primary timing belt is fitted, and its alignment marks are in the correct position, the secondary sprockets can safely be removed – the inlet camshaft alignment will be preserved.*

38 If not already done, align the engine assembly/valve timing marks as described in Section 3.

39 Although the secondary belt sprockets have their own marks already, they can be hard to see, so it is helpful to make extra ones on the belt backplate. Extra marks **must** be made if the special tools are not available – refer to paragraph 41 **(see illustrations)**.

Without special tools

40 Using a forked tool similar to that described in Section 8, hold the inlet camshaft

sprocket (the spoked one) and loosen the bolt **(see illustration)**. Do not attempt to loosen the sprocket bolt without such a tool, or excess load will be transferred though the inlet camshaft to the primary timing belt.

41 Before proceeding, check that accurate marks have been made between both sprockets and the belt backplate. A little paint (or typist's correction fluid) can be used to make a mark between the notch in the exhaust sprocket and the backplate. Similarly, a second line appears on the front face of the inlet sprocket, and a mark can be made on the edge of the backplate.

42 Discard the sprocket bolt (a new one is used when refitting), then remove the sprocket and slip off the belt **(see illustrations)**. **Do not** rotate the crankshaft or camshafts until the timing belt has been refitted. The exhaust camshaft will turn under pressure from the valve springs – note which way it moves, as it must be turned back when the belt is refitted.

7.42a Remove the sprocket bolt . . .

7.42b . . . then remove the inlet sprocket . . .

7.42c . . . and take the belt off the exhaust sprocket

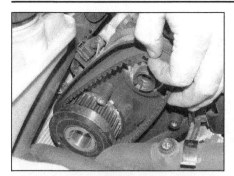

7.48 Fit the new belt round the exhaust sprocket

Slots in exhaust sprocket, for fitting home-made tool, arrowed

43 If the timing belt is to be refitted, mark its direction of rotation.

44 Due to the low cost of a new belt, it is recommended that the belt be renewed as a matter of course, regardless of its apparent condition. MG Rover state that a belt which has covered more than 45 000 miles should never be refitted. If signs of oil contamination are found, trace the source of the oil leak and rectify it, then wash down the engine timing belt area and all related components to remove all traces of oil.

45 Two home-made tools must be made up to allow refitting of the belt, as described in the following paragraphs.

46 The first tool should be made from flat bar, at least 3 mm thick, and approximately 48 mm wide – this will fit in the slots on the end of the exhaust sprocket and, with a pair of pliers, can be used (by an assistant) to turn the exhaust sprocket so the timing marks line up.

47 The second tool is a tapered pin, to fit in the end of the inlet camshaft, and used to guide the sprocket into place. The pin is approximately 10 mm diameter, 100 mm long, and should be tapered down to about 8 mm at one end.

48 Fit the new belt around the exhaust sprocket **(see illustration)**.

49 Have an assistant turn back the sprocket using the tool described in paragraph 46, until the previously-made marks come into alignment. Hold the sprocket in this position while the other sprocket is refitted. Fit the inlet sprocket inside the belt, in such a way that the alignment marks will be correctly positioned when the sprocket is fitted. Insert the tapered pin tool into the end of the inlet camshaft.

50 Slide the sprocket over the pin, and engage the key on the back of the sprocket with the corresponding notch in the end of the camshaft. This will require some effort, to overcome the tension of a new belt, but there will be a definite 'click' when the sprocket engages **(see illustrations)**.

51 Check that the timing marks made previously are in alignment, then withdraw the tapered pin and fit the new sprocket bolt, tightened by hand initially. Gently release the tool from the exhaust sprocket.

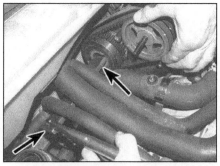

7.50a Flat bar inserted in exhaust sprocket, turned using pliers to align marks

52 When all is satisfactory, tighten the new bolt (using a forked tool to hold the sprocket) to the specified torque and angle **(see illustrations)**.

53 Repeat the procedure for the remaining secondary belt.

With special tools

54 If not already done, remove the exhaust camshaft end caps at the primary timing belt end (new caps should be used when refitting). Make an alignment mark between the exhaust camshafts and the primary belt end of each head, to use when fitting the new belt.

55 Using the special tool (12-175) placed over the sprockets to hold them, loosen the bolt from each one. Do not attempt to loosen the sprocket bolts without such a tool, or excess load will be transferred though the inlet camshaft to the primary timing belt.

7.52a Tighten the inlet sprocket bolt to the specified torque . . .

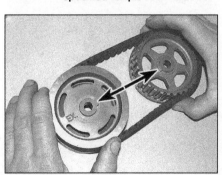

7.58 Place the sprockets face down, and fit the new belt round them

7.50b Fit the inlet sprocket over the tapered pin until the key engages

56 Remove and discard the sprocket bolts (new ones are used when refitting), and then remove the two sprockets and belt as an assembly. **Do not** rotate the crankshaft or camshafts until the timing belt has been refitted.

57 If the timing belt is to be refitted, mark its direction of rotation. Take the belt off the sprockets.

58 Place the two sprockets face down on a flat surface, so that both the keys are facing upwards, and directly opposite each other. Fit the belt around the sprockets **(see illustration)**.

59 A new belt will make the sprockets hard to fit over the camshaft ends, so the sprockets must be forced apart prior to fitting. The MG Rover tool for this is 18G 1747-1 **(see illustration)**.

60 Insert the two alignment pins (18G 1747-5)

7.52b . . . then to the specified angle

7.59 Force the sprockets apart using special tool 18G 1747-1

7.60 Fit the alignment pins into the camshafts

7.61 Fit tool 18G 1747-4 into the exhaust camshaft, at the primary belt end

7.62a Place special tool 12-175 over the sprockets . . .

7.62b . . . then fit the assembly over the alignment pins

7.63 Turn the exhaust camshaft into alignment, from the primary end

7.64a Fit the new camshaft sprocket bolt . . .

insert into the two camshaft threaded holes **(see illustration)**.

61 The exhaust camshaft will have to be turned back into alignment as the sprockets are refitted. A slot is provided in the camshaft end at the primary timing belt end, into

7.64b . . . then tighten it to the specified torque . . .

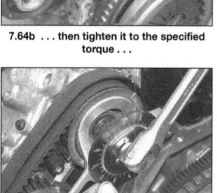

7.64c . . . and through the specified angle

which special tool 18G 1747-4 fits to turn the camshaft when required **(see illustration)**.

62 Turn the sprocket/belt assembly over, and place special tool 12-175 into position. Offer the sprockets and belt as an assembly over the alignment pins. The inlet sprocket's key should be felt to locate in the camshaft end **(see illustrations)**.

63 Have an assistant turn the exhaust cam-shaft slightly, to the previously-made alignment mark made at the primary belt end, then the exhaust sprocket should engage **(see illustration)**.

64 Withdraw the alignment pins, then fit the new camshaft sprocket bolts, and tighten by hand. Check that the sprocket marks are correctly aligned with each other before proceeding to tighten the bolts to the specified torque – hold the sprockets using the same method as removal **(see illustrations)**.

65 Repeat the procedure for the remaining secondary belt.

8.2 Use a home-made tool to hold the sprocket

Final refitting

66 Refit all removed components using a reversal of the removal procedure, noting the following points:

a) Clean the recesses in the ends of the exhaust camshafts, and fit new end cap seals (where necessary).

b) Tighten all fasteners to the specified torque.

c) Refer to Chapter 5A when refitting the alternator, and to Chapter 10 for the power steering pump.

8 Timing belt tensioner and sprockets – removal and refitting

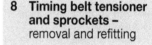

Camshaft sprockets

Primary belt

Note: It is not advisable to remove the inlet camshaft sprockets from the primary timing belt end unless a full set of special tools are available to re-align them – the sprockets at the primary timing belt end are not keyed to the camshafts. It may be possible to re-align the sprockets if enough accurate marks are made beforehand, however – the secondary belt sprockets are both keyed to their camshafts, and this could be used to provide a reference.

1 Remove the primary timing belt as described in Section 7.

2 Slacken and remove each camshaft sprocket retaining bolt, along with the centre/hub. To stop the camshaft turning, use a locking tool which fits between the sprocket spokes, which can be fabricated from two lengths of steel strip (one long, the other short) and three nuts and bolts. One nuts and bolt should form the pivot of the forked tool, with the remaining two nuts and bolts at the tips of the forks to engage with the sprocket spokes **(see illustration)**.

3 Mark the sprockets for position (front or rear bank) before removal. Remove the sprockets from the camshafts **(see illustration)**.

4 Check the sprockets for signs of wear or damage and renew if necessary.

5 Prior to refitting, check the oil seals for signs of damage or leakage. If necessary, renew as described in Section 9.

6 Refit the primary belt using the special tools as described in Section 7. Ensure that the sprockets are refitted to their original camshafts.

Secondary belt

7 The secondary belt sprockets are removed as an assembly with the belt, as described in Section 7.

8 Prior to refitting, check the oil seals for signs of damage or leakage. If necessary, renew as described in Section 9.

9 Refit the secondary belt as described in Section 7.

Crankshaft sprocket

10 Remove the primary timing belt as described in Section 7.

11 Slide the sprocket off from the end of the crankshaft, noting which way around it is fitted **(see illustration)**.

12 Refit the sprocket to the crankshaft, engaging it with the crankshaft flattened section.

13 Refit the timing belt as described in Section 7.

Tensioner body

14 The automatic tensioner is secured by two bolts, and incorporates spring plunger. This spring provides constant tension to press the pulley against the belt.

15 Gain access to the tensioner using the information in Section 7. The timing belt does not have to be removed to fit a new tensioner, though it is a good idea to fit a new belt at the same time. If the tensioner pulley is worn, or has seized, this will have damaged the belt, and a new belt should be fitted.

16 Unclip the rubber blanking plug from the rear of the timing belt tensioner. Loosen the two tensioner mounting bolts (**do not** loosen the Allen bolt securing the tensioner pulley). Release the belt tension by turning the tensioner pulley clockwise using a suitable Allen key in the hole provided. Holding the tensioner in the released position, remove the mounting bolts and take off the tensioner.

17 Using a vice with protected jaws, carefully compress the timing belt tensioner plunger until a pin (approximately 1.5 mm diameter)

8.3 Removing the primary belt camshaft sprockets

8.22a Unscrew the pulley mounting bolt . . .

can be inserted through the tensioner body and plunger to lock it.

18 Clean the two tensioner mounting bolts, then apply a little thread-locking compound (such as Loctite 242) to their threads.

19 Turn the tensioner pulley clockwise using an Allen key, then offer the tensioner up behind the belt and fit the two bolts. Tighten the bolts to the specified torque, then release the pulley, remove the locking pin, and allow the tensioner to act on the belt. Refit the tensioner's rubber plug.

20 Refit the components removed to access the tensioner, as described in Section 7.

Tensioner pulley

21 Remove the tensioner body as described previously in this Section.

22 Unscrew the pulley mounting bolt – this is below the pulley itself – and withdraw the pulley. Recover the washer fitted behind the pulley bracket **(see illustrations)**.

23 MG Rover state that the tensioner and pulley should be renewed after 100 000 miles. It's now considered good practice to renew all timing belt-related pulleys, etc, during routine belt renewal – many parts suppliers sell timing belt 'kits', which contain all the relevant items.

24 If the tensioner pulley is visibly damaged, or rough when spun by hand, a new one should be fitted.

25 Fit the tensioner, ensuring that the washer is fitted between the pulley bracket and the engine, and tighten the bolt to the specified torque.

26 Refit the tensioner body as described previously in this Section.

8.11 Removing the crankshaft sprocket

8.22b . . . and recover the washer

9 Camshaft oil seals – renewal

Primary belt end seals

1 Remove the camshaft sprockets as described in Section 8.

2 Punch or drill two small holes opposite each other in the oil seal(s). Screw a self-tapping screw into each hole, and pull on the screws with pliers to extract the seal.

3 Clean the seal housing, and polish off any burrs or raised edges, which may have caused the seal to fail.

4 The new (black) seal has a waxed outer surface, and should not be lubricated further prior to fitting. Genuine seals may be supplied with a cone-shaped tool, which slides onto the end of the camshaft. If this is not available, tape the end of the camshaft to protect the seal lips.

5 Carefully offer the seal over the camshaft and into position. Drive it into position, using a suitable tubular drift, such as a socket, which bears only on the hard outer edge of the seal **(see illustrations)**. Take care not to damage the seal lips during fitting, and note that the seal lips should face inwards.

6 Refit the camshaft sprockets as described in Section 8.

Secondary belt end seals

7 Remove the camshaft sprockets as described in Section 8.

8 Punch or drill two small holes opposite each other in the oil seal(s). Screw a self-tapping

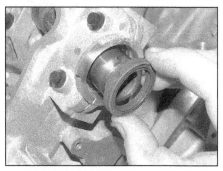

9.5a Offer the (black) seal into position . . .

9.5b . . . then tap it fully home using a suitable socket

9.11a Carefully fit the new seal over the camshaft . . .

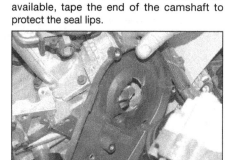

9.11b . . . and drive it home using a socket

screw into each hole, and pull on the screws with pliers to extract the seal.
9 Clean the seal housing, and polish off any burrs or raised edges, which may have caused the seal to fail.
10 The new (red) seal has a waxed outer surface, and should **not** be lubricated further prior to fitting. Genuine seals may be supplied with a cone-shaped fitting tool, which slides onto the end of the camshaft. If this is not available, tape the end of the camshaft to protect the seal lips.

10.4a Remove the bolts . . .

10.4b . . . and lift out the primary belt backplates

10.5 Removing a secondary belt backplate

10.7 Lifting out one of the exhaust camshafts

11 Carefully offer the seal over the camshaft and into position. Drive it into position, using a suitable tubular drift, such as a socket, which bears only on the hard outer edge of the seal **(see illustrations)**. Take care not to damage the seal lips during fitting, and note that the seal lips should face inwards.
12 Refit the camshaft sprockets as described in Section 8.

10 Camshafts and tappets
– removal, inspection and refitting

Removal

1 Remove the primary timing belt as described in Section 7. If both camshafts are being removed, also take off the two secondary belts (otherwise, only the belt from the relevant bank need be disturbed).
2 Remove the inlet camshaft sprockets as described in Section 8 – pay attention to the note at the start of that Section, regarding aligning the sprockets when refitting.
3 Remove the camshaft covers as described in Section 4.
4 Unscrew the bolts securing each inlet camshaft timing belt backplate, and remove them **(see illustrations)**. Each backplate may be secured by three or four bolts, depending on year of manufacture.
5 Similarly remove the backplates behind the secondary timing belt, which are secured by two bolts each **(see illustration)**.
6 Working in the **reverse** of the tightening sequence, progressively loosen the twenty-two camshaft carrier bolts on each bank, until the pressure from the valve springs is released. Remove the bolts, then lift the carriers off, noting that they are located on dowels.
7 Carefully lift the camshafts from the cylinder head **(see illustration)**. Remove the oil seals and discard them; new ones should be used on refitting. Mark the camshafts for identification – the inlet camshafts are the inner ones.
8 Obtain twenty-four small, clean plastic containers, and label them for identification. Alternatively, divide a larger container/tray into compartments. Using a sucker or magnet, withdraw each tappet in turn and place it upright in its respective container, which should then be filled with clean engine oil **(see illustration)**.
Caution: Do not interchange the tappets, and do not allow the tappets to lose oil, as they will take a long time to refill with oil on restarting the engine, which could result in incorrect valve clearances. Absolute cleanliness is essential at all times when handling the tappets.

Inspection

9 Examine the camshaft bearing surfaces and cam lobes for signs of wear ridges and scoring. Renew the camshaft if any of these conditions are apparent. Examine the condition

10.8 Using a suction tool to withdraw the hydraulic tappets

10.11 Oil the camshaft bearings in the cylinder head

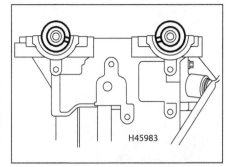

10.12 Set the camshafts so the rear sprocket notches are as shown

10.13a Clean the bearing carrier and cylinder head surfaces . . .

10.13b . . . then apply the sealant . . .

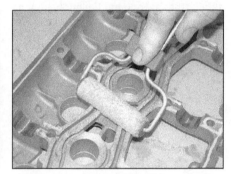

10.13c . . . and spread to a thin, even film using a roller (or a brush)

of the bearing surfaces both on the camshaft journals and in the cylinder head. If the head bearing surfaces are worn excessively, the cylinder head will need to be renewed.

10 Examine the tappet bearing surfaces which contact the camshaft lobes for wear ridges and scoring. Check the tappets and their bores in the cylinder head for signs of wear or damage. If a micrometer is available, measure the outside diameter of each tappet and compare it to the values given in the Specifications. If the engine's valve clearances have sounded noisy, particularly if the noise persists after initial start-up from cold, then there is reason to suspect a faulty tappet. If any tappet is thought to be faulty or is visibly worn it should be renewed.

Refitting

11 Liberally oil the camshaft bearings and tappets, and then refit the tappets to their

original locations in the cylinder head **(see illustration)**.

12 Lay the camshafts in position. Position the camshafts so that the camshaft sprocket locating notches at the secondary belt end are facing each other, at approximately 4 o'clock and 8 o'clock positions **(see illustration)**.

13 Ensure the mating surfaces of the camshaft bearing carrier and cylinder head are clean and dry. Apply several beads of sealant (part number GUG 705963GM) to the bearing carrier mating surface. Spread the sealant in an even film, taking care not to allow any sealant to enter the oilway grooves **(see illustrations)**.

14 Ensure that the locating dowels are in position, then refit the camshaft bearing carrier to the cylinder head **(see illustration)**. Ensure the carrier is correctly located then refit the retaining bolts, tightening them all by hand only at this stage.

15 Working in sequence, evenly and progressively tighten the retaining bolts to draw the bearing carrier squarely down into contact with the cylinder head. Once the carrier is in contact with the head, go around in sequence and tighten the retaining bolts to the specified torque **(see illustrations)**.

Caution: If the bearing carrier bolts are carelessly tightened, the carrier might break. If the carrier is broken, the complete cylinder head assembly must be renewed; the carrier is matched to the head, and is not available separately.

16 Fit new camshaft oil seals as described in Section 9.

17 Clean the timing belt backplate bolts, then apply a little thread-locking fluid (such as Loctite 242) to the threads, and tighten them to the specified torque.

18 Refit the camshaft covers as described in Section 4.

10.14 Refit the camshaft carrier onto the locating dowels

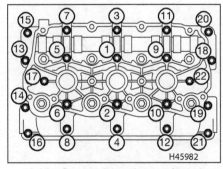

10.15a Camshaft bearing carrier bolt tightening sequence

10.15b Tightening the camshaft carrier bolts to the specified torque

11.7 Removing the timing belt backplate

19 Fit the secondary timing belt(s) as described in Section 7.
20 Refit the inlet camshaft sprockets as described in Section 8. If the secondary timing belts have been correctly fitted, the camshafts should be in the correct positions.
21 Fit the primary timing belt as described in Section 7.

11 Cylinder heads – removal and refitting

Note: *Before removing the cylinder heads, ensure that the timing belt special tools described in Section 7 are available. The inlet camshaft sprockets have to be removed, so the camshaft timing will be lost, which means the tools are essential.*
1 Depressurise the fuel system as described in Chapter 4B.

11.8a Disconnect the expansion tank hose from the radiator . . .

2 Disconnect the battery negative lead.
3 Drain the cooling system as described in Chapter 1A. Be sure to drain the cylinder block as well as removing the radiator bottom hose.
4 Remove the upper section of the inlet manifold as described in Chapter 4B.
5 Remove the primary timing belt as described in Section 7. When the primary timing belt is removed as part of a cylinder head removal procedure, a new belt **must** be fitted on reassembly.

Front bank

6 Remove the inlet camshaft sprocket as described in Section 8.
7 Remove the bolts securing the timing belt backplate, and lift it away **(see illustration)**.
8 Release the hose clips and disconnect the expansion tank bleed hoses from the tank (or

11.8b . . . and from the T-piece on top of the inlet manifold

the T-piece on top of the inlet manifold) and the radiator **(see illustrations)**.
9 Remove the expansion tank mounting bolt, then unhook the tank mounting pegs and move the tank to one side **(see illustrations)**.
10 Disconnect the radiator top hose, then release the hose from its support bracket and move to one side. Unbolt the radiator hose support bracket and remove it. Also unbolt and remove the radiator top hose connection elbow **(see illustrations)**.
11 Remove the camshaft cover from the front bank as described in Section 4.
12 Mark the ignition coils and HT leads for position. Pull back the locking collar and disconnect each coil's wiring plug. Remove the three mounting nuts and bolts from the three ignition coils serving the front bank – note that the nut for No 1 cylinder's coil also secures the earth lead. Disconnect the HT leads and remove the coils **(see illustrations)**.

11.9a Remove the expansion tank bolt . . .

11.9b . . . then disengage the tank mounting pegs

11.10a Disconnect the radiator top hose . . .

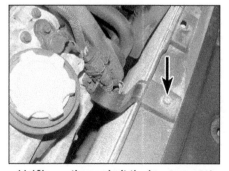

11.10b . . . then unbolt the hose support bracket . . .

11.10c . . . and the radiator coolant elbow

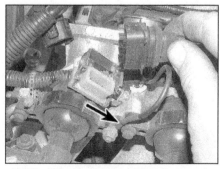

11.12a Disconnect the wiring plug – note earth lead (arrowed)

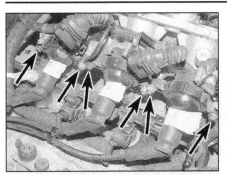

11.12b Mark the HT leads for position. Coil mounting nuts/bolts arrowed

11.12c Disconnect the HT leads and remove the coils

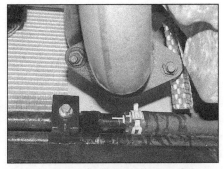

11.15 Unscrew the manifold-to-front downpipe nuts

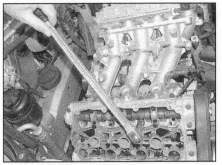

11.17a Loosen the head bolts in sequence

11.17b The rear row of bolts will come out . . .

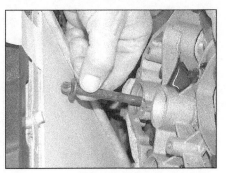

11.17c . . . but the front ones won't – note card protecting radiator

13 Disconnect the coolant bleed hose from the inlet manifold, and move the hose clear.
14 Remove the fuel rails and injectors as described in Chapter 4B, Section 11.
15 Working under the car, remove the two exhaust manifold-to-downpipe flange nuts, and separate the pipe (see illustration).
16 Before removing the front cylinder head, it's advisable to protect the radiator from possible damage – this is most easily done by taping a large piece of card over its inner face.
17 Working in the **reverse** order of the tightening sequence, progressively loosen the eight cylinder head bolts, then remove the four rear bolts. The front row of four bolts won't come out, but they can be lifted far enough to clear the head-to-block joint – by lifting them this far, then wrapping some tape around all four, the head can be lifted off (see illustrations).

11.20 Lifting off the head – note front bolts wrapped up with tape

18 The joint between the cylinder head and gasket and the cylinder block/crankcase must now be broken without disturbing the cylinder liners. Although these liners are better located and sealed than some wet-liner engines, there is still a risk of coolant and foreign matter leaking into the sump if the cylinder head is lifted carelessly. If care is not taken and the liners are moved, there is also a possibility of there seals being disturbed, causing leakage after refitting the head.
19 To break the joint, obtain two L-shaped metal bars, which fit into the cylinder head bolt holes and gently rock the cylinder head free towards the front of the car.
Caution: *Do not try to swivel the head on the cylinder block/crankcase, as it is located by dowels as well as by the tops of the liners.*
20 When the joint is broken, lift the cylinder head away, using assistance if possible as it is a heavy assembly, especially if complete with the manifolds (see illustration). Remove the gasket and discard it. Support the cylinder head on wooden blocks or stands – do not rest the lower face of the cylinder head on the work surface. Note the fitted positions of the two locating dowels, and remove them for safe-keeping if they are loose.
21 If the head bolts are to be re-used, store the bolts in order, so that they can be refitted in their original locations. The bolts can be stored by pushing them through a clearly-marked cardboard template.
22 Note that further to the warnings given at the beginning of this Section, **do not** attempt to rotate the crankshaft with the cylinder

head removed, otherwise the liners may be displaced. Operations that require the rotation of the crankshaft (eg, cleaning the piston crowns) can be carried out after fitting cylinder liner clamps (see Haynes Hint).
23 If the cylinder head is to be dismantled, remove the camshafts, as described in Section 10, then refer to the relevant Sections of Part D of this Chapter.

Rear bank

24 If only the head from the rear bank is being removed, proceed as described for the front bank, with the following differences:
a) *Remove the camshaft cover from the rear bank as described in Section 4.*
b) *Ignore paragraphs 8 to 10, as the expansion tank and radiator top hose do not have to be disturbed.*

Liner clamps can be improvised using large washers and tubular spacers, such as suitable deep sockets.

11.24a Disconnect the wiring plugs and unbolt the brackets from the rear head

11.24b Depress the collar and remove the breather pipe . . .

11.24c . . . then release the clip and disconnect the coolant hose

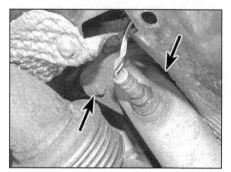

11.24d The rear manifold-to-downpipe nuts are hard to reach

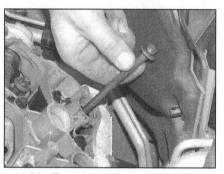

11.24e The driver's-side rear head bolt won't come out . . .

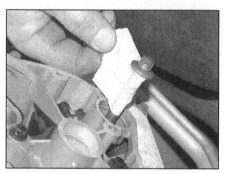

11.24f . . . so wrap some tape round it to stop it falling down

c) There is no need to protect the radiator, as described in paragraph 16.

d) There are several wiring plug brackets attached to the rear head – go round the head and disconnect the various plugs. In most cases, the wiring brackets must also be unbolted before the head is removed **(see illustration)**.

e) Disconnect the breather pipe and coolant hose from the rear inlet manifold **(see illustrations)**.

f) The rear exhaust manifold-to-downpipe nuts are tricky to reach – a long extension will be needed **(see illustration)**.

g) Only one cylinder head bolt (driver's-side rear) cannot be withdrawn before the head itself is removed. Lift the bolt up, then wrap enough tape around it to prevent it dropping back down, before removing the head **(see illustrations)**.

Preparation for refitting

25 The mating faces of the cylinder head and cylinder block/crankcase must be perfectly clean before refitting the head. Use a hard plastic or wood scraper to remove all traces of gasket and carbon. Also clean the piston crowns. Take particular care, as the soft aluminium alloy is damaged easily.

26 Make sure that the carbon is not allowed to enter the oil and water passages – this is particularly important for the lubrication system, as carbon could block the oil supply to any of the engine components. Using adhesive tape and paper, seal the water, oil and bolt holes in the cylinder block/crankcase. To prevent carbon entering the gap between

the pistons and bores, smear a little grease in the gap. After cleaning each piston, use a small brush to remove all traces of grease and carbon from the gap, then wipe away the remainder with a clean cloth. Clean all the pistons in the same way. Take great care not to move the pistons during this procedure.

27 Check the mating surfaces of the cylinder block/crankcase and the cylinder head for nicks, deep scratches and other damage. If slight, they may be removed carefully with a file, but if excessive, machining may be the only alternative to renewal.

28 If warpage of the cylinder head gasket surface is suspected, use a straight-edge to check it for distortion. Refer to Part D of this Chapter if necessary.

29 Check the condition of the cylinder head bolts, particularly their threads. Keeping all bolts in their correct fitted order, wash them and wipe dry. Check each bolt for any sign of visible wear or damage, renewing as necessary. Note that if cylinder head bolts have been used to secure the cylinder liner clamps, each bolt and clamp should be removed one at a time for checking, and refitted immediately the bolt has been inspected. Although not specified by the manufacturer, we recommend that the bolts are renewed as a complete set, regardless of their apparent condition – this is particularly recommended if the bolts have seen long service, or are known to have already been re-used once.

Refitting

30 Remove the cylinder liner clamps (where fitted) and wipe clean the mating surfaces

of the cylinder head and cylinder block/crankcase.

31 Ensure that the two locating dowels are in position at each end of the cylinder block/crankcase surface.

32 Position a new gasket on the cylinder block/crankcase surface so that its TOP mark is uppermost.

33 Keeping all the cylinder head bolts in their correct fitted order, lightly oil under the head and on the threads of each bolt.

34 Before offering the head into position, fit the bolts, which could not be withdrawn with the head in place. There's one bolt so affected on the rear head, and all four front bolts on the front head. As for removal, tape the bolts up so that they do not protrude below the gasket surface.

35 Carefully refit the cylinder head, locating it on the dowels.

36 Remove the tape from the bolts as applicable. Screw each bolt in, by hand only, until finger-tight. **Do not** drop the bolts into their holes.

37 Working progressively and in sequence, first tighten all the cylinder head bolts to the Stage 1 torque setting **(see illustration)**.

38 Once all bolts have been tightened to the Stage 1 torque, again working in sequence, tighten each bolt to the specified Stage 2 torque. **Note:** *This setting is exactly the same as the Stage 1 value, but must be carried out as described. The head gasket is of metal laminate construction, and compresses when first tightened – if Stage 2 tightening is not completed to confirm the initial torque setting, subsequent angle-tightening may*

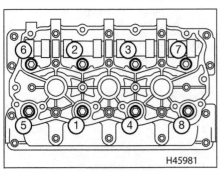

11.37 Cylinder head bolt tightening sequence

be inaccurate, giving an unevenly-tightened head.

39 Once all bolts have been tightened to the Stage 2 torque, again working in sequence, tighten each bolt through its specified Stage 3 angle, using a socket and extension bar. It is recommended that an angle-measuring gauge is used during this stage of tightening, to ensure accuracy. Alternatively, prior to tightening, use a felt-tip pen or similar to make alignment marks between each bolt head and the cylinder head.

40 Finally go around in the specified sequence again and tighten all bolts through the specified Stage 4 angle. If the bolt heads were marked prior to angle-tightening, each bolt head mark should now be directly opposite the corresponding mark on the cylinder head.

41 Refit the removed components using a

reversal of the removal procedure, noting the following points:

a) Use new gaskets/seals, as applicable.

b) Tighten all fasteners to the specified torque, where given.

c) Fit a new primary timing belt as described in Section 7. If the camshafts have not been removed, new secondary belts do not have to be fitted.

d) Refill the cooling system as described in Chapter 1A.

12 Sump – removal and refitting

Removal

1 Drain the engine oil (with reference to Chapter 1A if necessary), then clean and refit the engine oil drain plug with a new washer, tightening it to the specified torque wrench setting. If the engine is nearing the service interval when the oil and filter are due for renewal, it is recommended that the filter is also removed and a new one fitted. After reassembly, the engine can then be refilled with fresh engine oil.

2 Apply the handbrake, then jack up the front of the car and support it securely on axle stands (see *Jacking and vehicle support*).

3 Remove the right-hand front wheel arch liner, as described in Chapter 11, Section 25.

4 Remove the single bolt securing the oil dipstick tube to the block, then depress the locking collar at the base and pull the tube out of the sump **(see illustration)**.

5 Unscrew the front and rear manifold-to-downpipe nuts, and separate the joints. Remove the exhaust front pipe support bracket, which is secured by two bolts **(see illustrations)**. If care is taken, it should now be possible to move the exhaust sufficiently to access the sump mounting bolts – if not, the complete system will have to be lowered, as described in Chapter 4B.

6 Remove the engine lower mounting as described in Section 20.

7 Where applicable, unscrew the two oil cooler mounting bolts at the front of the sump, and tie the cooler forwards of the sump without disconnecting it **(see illustration)**.

8 Progressively slacken and remove the ten bolts securing the sump to the base of the lower crankcase **(see illustration)**.

9 Break the sump sealant joint by striking the sump with the palm of the hand. It is not advisable to prise between the mating faces, as this could result in a leak. If the sump is stuck, remove the drain plug, then use a sturdy screwdriver (wrapped in a rag or card to protect the drain plug threads) in the drain plug hole as a prising tool. Lower the sump away from the engine.

10 While the sump is removed, take the opportunity to check the oil pump pick-up/strainer for signs of clogging or splitting. If necessary, unbolt the pick-up/strainer and remove it from the engine along with its sealing ring. The strainer can then be cleaned easily in solvent. Inspect the strainer mesh for signs of clogging or splitting and renew if necessary.

Refitting

11 Clean all traces of sealant from the mating surfaces of the cylinder block/crankcase and sump, then use a clean rag to wipe out the sump.

12 Where necessary, fit a new sealing ring to oil pump pick-up/strainer groove then carefully refit the pipe, tightening its retaining bolt to the specified torque setting **(see illustrations)**.

13 Apply a 2 mm bead of suitable sealant (part number GUG 705963GM) to the sump mating surface, then spread this to an even film using a roller or brush **(see illustrations)**.

14 Offer up the sump to the cylinder block/crankcase, and tighten all bolts finger-tight only **(see illustration)**.

12.4 Depress the locking collar, and pull out the dipstick tube

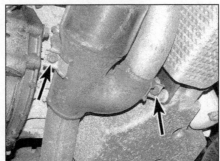

12.5a Unscrew the exhaust front pipe support bracket bolts

12.5b Exhaust front manifold-to-downpipe nuts

12.7 Unbolt and move the oil cooler clear of the sump

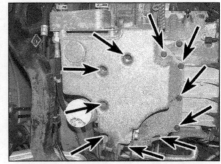

12.8 Sump bolts – seen from below

12.12a Fit a new O-ring to the groove . . .

12.12b . . . then oil and refit the oil pump pick-up

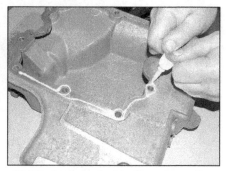

12.13a Apply sealant to the sump mating surface . . .

12.13b . . . and spread evenly with a roller or brush

12.14 Offer the sump into place, and fit the bolts finger-tight

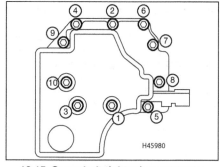

12.15 Sump bolt tightening sequence

15 Working in sequence, tighten the sump bolts to the specified torque setting **(see illustration)**.
16 Refit the oil cooler to the front of the sump, and tighten the bolts to the specified torque.
17 Refit the engine lower mounting as described in Section 20.

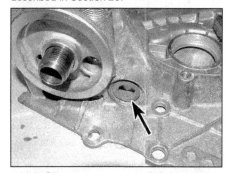

13.6 Oil pump pressure relief valve plug

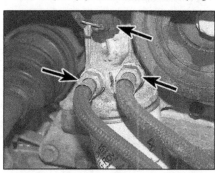

14.3 Oil pressure switch wiring plug and oil cooler unions

18 Refit the exhaust front pipe mounting bracket, tightening the bolts to the specified torque. Refit the exhaust front pipes, using a new gasket on the rear pipe, and tighten the nuts to the specified torque.
19 Clean and refit the oil dipstick tube.
20 Lower the car to the ground, and refill the engine with oil as described in Chapter 1A.

13 Oil pump pressure relief valve – removal and refitting

Removal

1 Loosen the right-hand front wheel bolts. Firmly apply the handbrake, and then jack up the front of the car and support it securely on axle stands (see *Jacking and vehicle support*). Remove the right-hand front wheel.
2 Remove the engine undertray, which is secured by a number of quick-release screw fasteners.
3 Remove the right-hand front wheel arch liner as described in Chapter 11, Section 25.
4 Place a drain container under the oil filter, then unscrew and remove the filter, referring to Chapter 1A if necessary. If the filter is not due to be changed, it can be refitted – in this case, store it upright so the oil is not lost.
5 Slacken and disconnect the two oil cooler unions. Recover and discard the O-ring seals – new ones should be fitted on reassembly.
6 Using a suitable Allen key or bit, unscrew and remove the relief valve plug – this will probably be quite tight, as thread-lock is used

when fitting **(see illustration)**. Remove the plug, and recover the spring and valve.

Refitting

7 Clean the plug, removing all traces of thread-lock. Also clean the valve, spring and the valve seating, then lubricate the valve and seating with clean oil.
8 Apply a little thread-locking fluid (such as Loctite 542) to the plug threads. Fit the valve and spring, then fit and tighten the plug to the specified torque.
9 Clean around the oil cooler unions. Reconnect the unions using new O-rings lubricated with clean engine oil, and tighten the unions to the specified torque.
10 Fit the oil filter, and tighten by hand only, referring to Chapter 1A if necessary.
11 Refit the wheel arch liner, engine undertray, and right-hand front wheel, then lower the car to the ground. Tighten the wheel bolts to the specified torque.

14 Oil pump – removal and refitting

Removal

1 Remove the crankshaft sprocket as described in Section 8.
2 Drain the engine oil, then clean and refit the engine oil drain plug with a new washer, tightening it to the specified torque.
3 Disconnect the oil pressure switch multiplug at the rear of the pump **(see illustration)**.

14.6a Remove the sixteen oil pump mounting bolts . . .

14.6b . . . then withdraw the pump . . .

14.6c . . . and recover the gasket

14.7 Prising out the crankshaft oil seal from the oil pump

14.9 Fit the new oil pump gasket

14.10 Locate the oil pump into place over the dowels

4 Place a drain container under the oil filter. Where applicable, slacken and disconnect the two oil cooler unions. Recover and discard the O-ring seals – new ones should be fitted on reassembly.

5 Unscrew and remove the oil filter – a new one should be obtained for refitting.

6 Loosen and remove the sixteen oil pump mounting bolts, then release the pump from its locating dowels and remove it with the gasket **(see illustrations)**. The gasket and bolts should both be discarded, and new ones used when refitting.

7 Remove the crankshaft oil seal from the oil pump, and obtain a new one for refitting **(see illustration)**.

Refitting

8 Ensure the mating surfaces of the oil pump and cylinder block are clean and dry. Clean all traces of locking compound from the pump mounting holes on the engine. Clean the oil seal surface on the crankshaft, and the area around the oil cooler unions.

9 Ensure the locating dowels are in position, then fit a new gasket to the cylinder block **(see illustration)**.

10 Carefully manoeuvre the oil pump into position, aligning the flats on the pump drivegear with those on the crankshaft end. Locate the pump on the dowels **(see illustration)**.

11 Fit the new oil pump bolts, and tighten progressively in sequence to the specified torque **(see illustrations)**.

12 Genuine crankshaft oil seals should come with a fitting sleeve, which sits over the

crankshaft nose **(see illustration)**. If one is not available, wrap a little tape round the sharp edge to protect the seal lips as it is fitted.

13 Fit the new oil seal (note that it should **not** be lubricated), ensuring its sealing lip is facing inwards, and ease it over the end of the

14.11a Fit the new bolts . . .

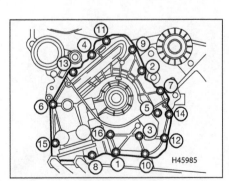

14.11c . . . using this tightening sequence

crankshaft. Press it squarely into the housing using a tubular drift (such as a socket) which bears only on the hard outer edge of the seal **(see illustrations)**. Press the seal into position so that it is flush with the housing. Remove the oil seal guide or the tape on completion.

14.11b . . . then tighten them to the specified torque . . .

14.12 Fit the oil seal fitting sleeve in place

14.13a Ease the new oil seal into place . . .

14.13b . . . and drive it home using a suitable socket

14 Reconnect the oil cooler pipe unions using new O-rings lubricated with clean engine oil, and tighten the unions to the specified torque.
15 Reconnect the oil pressure switch wiring plug.
16 Refit the crankshaft sprocket as described in Section 8.
17 On completion, refill the engine with oil and fit a new oil filter as described in Chapter 1A.

15 Oil pump – dismantling, inspection and reassembly

Note: *If oil pump wear is suspected, check the cost and availability of new parts (only available in the form of a repair kit) against the cost of a new pump. Examine the pump as described in this Section and then decide whether renewal or repair is the best course of action. The oil*
pressure relief valve can be removed with the oil pump in place, as described in Section 13.

Dismantling

1 Remove the oil pump as described in Section 14.
2 Unscrew the retaining screws and remove the pump cover plate and sealing ring **(see illustration)**.
3 Note the identification marks on the outer rotor, then remove both the rotors from the body **(see illustration)**.
4 To dismantle the pressure relief valve, slacken and remove the threaded plug and washer, then recover the valve spring and plunger.

Inspection

5 Inspect the rotors for obvious signs of wear or damage and renew if necessary. If the pump body or cover plate is scored or damaged,
then the complete oil pump assembly must be renewed.
6 Refit the rotors to the body and, using feeler blades of the appropriate thickness, measure the clearance between the outer rotor and the pump body **(see illustration)**.
7 Using feeler blades and a straight-edge placed across the top of the pump body and the rotors, measure the rotor endfloat **(see illustration)**.
8 If any measurement is outside the specified limits, the complete pump assembly must be renewed.
9 If the pressure relief valve plunger is scored, or if it does not slide freely in the pump body bore, then it must be renewed, using all the components from the repair kit.
10 Thoroughly clean the threads of the pump cover plate securing screws and renew the cover sealing ring and relief valve washer, if damaged.

Reassembly

11 Lubricate the pump rotors with clean engine oil and refit them to the pump body, ensuring that the identification mark on the outer rotor faces outwards (ie, towards the pump cover) **(see illustration)**.
12 Fit the sealing ring to the pump body and refit the cover plate. Apply thread-locking compound to the threads of the cover plate screws then refit the screws, tightening them securely **(see illustration)**.
13 Check that the pump rotates freely, then prime it by injecting oil into its passages and rotating it. If a long time elapses before the

15.2 Remove the pump cover plate screws

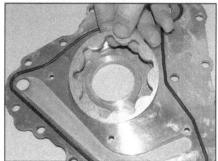

15.3 Remove the oil pump rotors

15.6 Measure the outer rotor-to-body clearance

15.7 Check the rotor endfloat with a feeler blade and straight-edge

15.11 Lubricate the pump rotors before fitting them

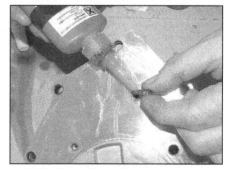

15.12 Thread-lock the oil pump cover screws

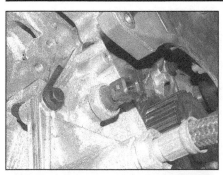

16.7 The oil pressure switch is above the oil filter

pump is refitted to the engine, prime it again before installation.

14 Refit the oil pressure relief valve plunger, ensuring that it is the correct way up, then install the spring. Fit the sealing washer to the threaded plug and tighten the plug securely.

16 Oil pressure switch –
removal and refitting

1 The oil pressure switch is a vital early warning of low oil pressure. The switch operates the oil warning light on the instrument panel – the light should come on with the ignition, and go out almost immediately when the engine starts.

2 If the light does not come on, there could be a fault on the instrument panel, the switch wiring, or the switch itself. If the light does not go out, low oil level, worn oil pump (or sump pick-up blocked), blocked oil filter, or worn main bearings could be to blame – or again, the switch may be faulty.

3 If the light comes on while driving, the best advice is to turn the engine off immediately, and not to drive the car until the problem has been investigated – ignoring the light could mean expensive engine damage.

Removal

4 Loosen the right-hand front wheel bolts. Firmly apply the handbrake, and then jack up the front of the car and support it securely on axle stands (see *Jacking and vehicle support*). Remove the right-hand front wheel.

5 Remove the engine undertray, which is secured by a number of quick-release screw fasteners.

6 Remove the right-hand front wheel arch liner as described in Chapter 11, Section 25.

7 The oil pressure switch is mounted above the oil filter (and, where applicable, above the oil cooler hoses) **(see illustration)**.

8 Disconnect the switch wiring plug.

9 Place a drain container under the switch – the amount of oil lost should be quite small.

10 Anticipating oil spillage, slowly unscrew the switch and remove it. Recover the sealing washer – a new one should be used when refitting.

11 Allow the oil to finish draining, then clean the switch threads and the switch location.

Refitting

12 Fit the switch using a new sealing washer, and tighten it to the specified torque.

13 Reconnect the wiring plug, then refit the undertray, wheel arch liner and right-hand wheel, and lower the car to the ground. Tighten the wheel bolts to the specified torque.

17 Oil cooler –
removal and refitting

Note: *The oil cooler is only fitted to models with air conditioning.*

> **HAYNES HINT** *The oil cooler is a heat exchanger, which has engine oil and coolant running through it. If the cooler fails, this will either allow oil and coolant to mix, or will cause an external leak. Check the oil and coolant levels regularly (as described in 'Weekly checks') and also look for signs of oil/ water contamination – something which normally indicates cylinder head gasket failure.*

Removal

1 Drain the engine oil and coolant, and remove the auxiliary drivebelt, as described in Chapters 1A and 5A.

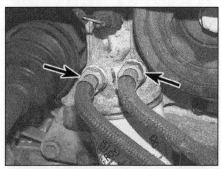

17.2a Disconnect the oil cooler unions at the oil pump . . .

17.3 Depress the collar, and pull out the dipstick tube

2 Place a drain container under the oil filter. Slacken and disconnect the two oil cooler unions on the oil pump. Recover and discard the O-ring seals – new ones should be fitted on reassembly **(see illustrations)**.

3 Remove the single bolt securing the oil dipstick tube to the block, then depress the locking collar at the base and pull the tube out of the sump **(see illustration)**.

4 Release the spring-type clips, and disconnect the two coolant hoses from the oil cooler.

5 Unscrew the two oil cooler mounting bolts, and withdraw the cooler from in front of the sump – note that it may be necessary to raise the engine on a jack to create clearance for removal **(see illustration)**.

6 Noting their fitted positions, loosen the unions and disconnect the pipes from the cooler. Remove and discard the O-ring seals.

Refitting

7 Clean around the oil cooler unions on the cooler body and oil pump.

8 Reconnect the pipe unions to their original locations on the oil cooler, using new O-rings lubricated with clean engine oil, and tighten the unions to the specified torque.

9 Offer up the cooler to the sump, then refit the mounting bolts and tighten to the specified torque.

10 Reconnect the coolant hoses to the oil cooler, and secure with the hose clips. For preference, update the spring clips with Jubilee clips.

11 Clean and refit the oil dipstick tube.

17.2b . . . and recover the O-rings

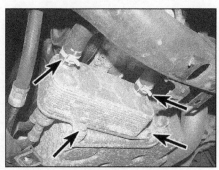

17.5 Oil cooler coolant hoses and mounting bolts

18.7a Unscrew the five mounting bolts . . .

18.7b . . . and remove the old oil seal

18.9 Fit the protector sleeve over the crankshaft

18.10 Fit the new seal over the sleeve, and press home

12 Reconnect the pipe unions to the oil pump using new O-rings lubricated with clean engine oil, and tighten the unions to the specified torque.

13 Refit the auxiliary drivebelt, refill the cooling system and engine oil, as described in Chapters 5A and 1A.

18 Crankshaft oil seals – renewal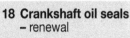

Primary timing belt end

Note: *On our project car, this oil seal was fitted after removing and refitting the oil pump – refer to Section 14.*

1 Remove the crankshaft sprocket as described in Section 8.

2 Carefully punch or drill two small holes opposite each other in the oil seal. Screw a

19.2 Home-made tool for locking the flywheel ring gear

self-tapping screw into each, and pull on the screws with pliers to extract the seal.

Caution: Great care must be taken to avoid damage to the oil pump.

3 Clean the seal housing and polish off any burrs or raised edges, which may have caused the seal to fail in the first place.

4 The new seal has a waxed outer surface, and should **not** be lubricated prior to fitting. Ease the new seal into position on the end of the shaft. Press the seal squarely into position until it is flush with the housing. If necessary, a suitable tubular drift, such as a socket, which bears only on the hard outer edge of the seal can be used to tap the seal into position. Take great care not to damage the seal lips during fitting and ensure that the seal lips face inwards; if a genuine MG Rover seal is being installed, use the seal protector supplied to protect the seal during fitting and remove the protector once the seal is correctly located.

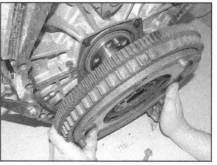

19.3 Removing the flywheel

18.11 Use five new bolts to secure the seal

5 Wash off any traces of oil, then refit the crankshaft sprocket as described in Section 8.

Flywheel end

6 Remove the flywheel or driveplate as described in Section 19.

7 Remove the five bolts securing the oil seal to the engine. Discard the seal and the bolts, as new ones must be used **(see illustrations)**.

8 Clean the seal housing, removing all traces of oil. Polish off any burrs or raised edges which may have caused the original seal to fail.

9 Genuine oil seals may be supplied with a protector sleeve for fitting – if not, wrap a little tape around the end of the crankshaft to protect the oil seal lips during fitting **(see illustration)**.

10 Offer the seal into place – note that it must **not** be lubricated. Ease the sealing lip of the seal over the crankshaft shoulder, by hand only, then press the seal evenly into it's housing until its outer flange seats evenly **(see illustration)**. If necessary, a soft-faced mallet can be used to tap the seal gently into place.

11 Fit the five new bolts, and tighten them evenly to draw the seal fully into position **(see illustration)**. Finally, tighten the bolts to the specified torque.

12 Refit the flywheel/driveplate as described in Section 19.

19 Flywheel/driveplate – removal, inspection and refitting

Flywheel

Removal

1 Remove the clutch assembly as described in Chapter 6.

2 Prevent the flywheel from turning by locking the ring gear teeth **(see illustration)**. Alternatively, bolt a strap between the flywheel and the cylinder block/crankcase. Make alignment marks between the flywheel and crankshaft using paint or a suitable marker pen.

3 Slacken and remove the six retaining bolts and remove the flywheel **(see illustration)**. **Do not** drop it, as it is very heavy.

19.7a Engage the flywheel on its locating dowel . . .

19.7b . . . then fit the bolts . . .

19.8 . . . and tighten to the specified torque

Inspection

4 If the flywheel clutch-mating surface is deeply scored, cracked or otherwise damaged, then the flywheel must be renewed, unless it is possible to have it surface-ground. Seek the advice of an engine reconditioning specialist.

5 If the ring gear is badly worn or has missing teeth, then it must be renewed. This job is best left to an engine reconditioning specialist. The temperature to which the new ring gear must be heated for installation (350°C – shown by an even light blue colour) is critical and, if not done accurately, the hardness of the teeth will be destroyed.

Refitting

6 Clean the mating surfaces of the flywheel and crankshaft, and remove all traces of locking compound from the threaded holes in the crankshaft.

7 Fit the flywheel to the crankshaft, engaging it with the crankshaft locating dowel, and fit the retaining bolts **(see illustrations)**.

8 Lock the flywheel using the method employed on dismantling then, working in a diagonal sequence, evenly and progressively tighten the retaining bolts to the specified torque wrench setting **(see illustration)**.

9 Refit the clutch assembly (see Chapter 6).

Driveplate

10 All procedures are essentially the same as described for the flywheel, disregarding references to the clutch. To access the driveplate, remove the automatic transmission as described in Chapter 7B. Note that driveplate bolts are tightened to a higher torque than flywheel bolts.

---

20 Engine/transmission mountings – inspection and renewal

Inspection

1 If improved access is required, raise the front of the car and support it securely on axle stands (see *Jacking and vehicle support*). Remove the engine undertray, which is secured by a number of quick-release screw fasteners.

2 Check the mounting rubber to see if it is cracked, hardened or separated from the metal at any point. Renew the mounting if any such damage or deterioration is evident.

3 Check that all mounting fasteners are securely tightened. Use a torque wrench to check, if possible.

4 Using a large screwdriver or a pry bar, check for wear in the mountings by carefully levering against it to check for free play. Where this is not possible, enlist the aid of an assistant to move the engine/gearbox unit back-and-forth or from side-to-side while you watch the mountings. While some free play is to be expected even from new components, excessive wear should be obvious. If excessive free play is found, check first that the fasteners are correctly secured, and then renew any worn components as described below.

Right-hand mounting

5 Firmly apply the handbrake, then jack up the front of the car and support securely on axle stands (see *Jacking and vehicle support*). Undo the fasteners and remove the engine undertray.

6 Support the weight of the engine/transmission, preferably using a hoist. Alternatively, use a trolley jack with a block of wood placed on its head, positioned underneath the engine (if this method is used, make sure the oil cooler coolant hoses are not strained or distorted as the engine is raised). Raise the engine slightly to remove all load from the mounting.

7 Remove the two bolts securing the upper cross-brace, noting that one of the bolts also secures an engine earth lead. Lift off the cross-brace **(see illustrations)**.

8 Remove the two auxiliary drivebelt upper cover bolts, and lift off the cover **(see illustrations)**.

9 The upper steady bracket is secured by

20.7a Unscrew the two cross-brace mounting bolts . . .

20.7b . . . and lift it off, noting the earth lead

20.8a Remove the two bolts . . .

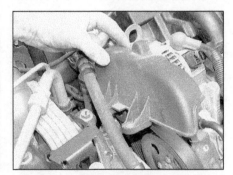

20.8b . . . and lift off the drivebelt upper cover

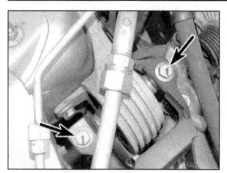

20.9a Steady bracket rear bolts . . .

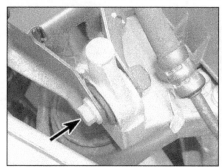

20.9b . . . and front through-bolt

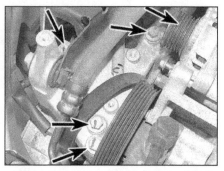

20.10a Upper mounting bracket nut and bolts

20.10b Removing the upper mounting bracket and steady bracket

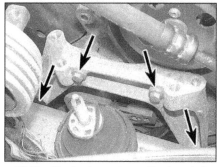

20.11a Engine lower mounting bracket bolts

20.11b Removing the engine lower mounting bracket

three bolts – two at the rear, and a through-bolt at the front **(see illustrations)**. However, the through-bolt will not come out – it hits the inner wing. Therefore, the steady bracket must be removed with the upper mounting bracket.

10 To remove the engine upper mounting bracket, unscrew the nut securing it to the hydramount, then remove the four further bolts securing it to the lower mounting bracket **(see illustrations)**.

11 The lower mounting bracket is bolted to the engine front (end) plate by four bolts, and can be removed if required **(see illustrations)**.

12 The right-hand mounting bracket on the inner wing is secured by a total of four bolts, and can be removed if required **(see illustrations)**. First, where applicable, remove the two bolts securing the air conditioning hose to the engine right-hand mounting and bonnet lock platform. Release the hose from

the mounting clips in the engine compartment as necessary, and move it clear as far as possible without disconnecting or straining it.

13 If required, the hydramount can be unscrewed from the wing, using MG Rover tool LRT-12-169 (which engages in the three slots around the mounting), or using a strap/chain wrench around the circumference of the mounting **(see illustration)**.

14 Refitting is a reversal of removal. Tighten all fasteners to the specified torque – in the case of the hydramount, torque tightening may be impossible without the special tool, so tighten securely using the same method as for removal.

Left-hand mounting

15 Remove the engine top cover, which is secured by two bolts.

16 Remove the air cleaner assembly as described in Chapter 4B.

17 Remove the battery and its tray as described in Chapter 5A.

18 Firmly apply the handbrake, then jack up the front of the car and support securely on axle stands (see *Jacking and vehicle support*). Undo the fasteners and remove the engine undertray.

19 Support the weight of the engine/transmission, preferably using a hoist. Alternatively, use a trolley jack with a block of wood placed on its head, positioned underneath the transmission (if this method is used, make sure the oil cooler coolant hoses are not strained or distorted as the engine is raised). Raise the engine slightly to remove all load from the mounting.

20 To separate the mounting, unscrew and remove the through-bolt **(see illustration)**.

21 Once the through-bolt is removed, lower the transmission until the mounting is

20.12a Two of the right-hand mounting bracket bolts . . .

20.12b . . . and a third, seen from the right-hand front wheel arch

20.13 The hydramount can be unscrewed if required

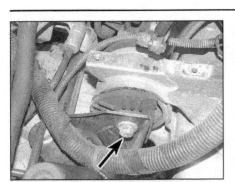

20.20 Left-hand mounting through-bolt

20.21a Left-hand mounting bracket on the inner wing – bolts arrowed

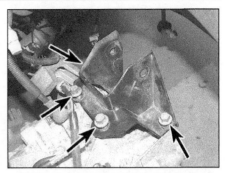

20.21b Left-hand mounting bracket on transmission

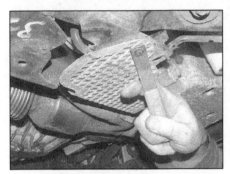

20.24a Prise out the clip . . .

20.24b . . . then remove the bolt and take off the heat shield

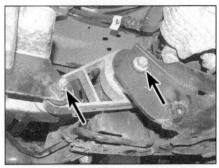

20.25 Lower mounting through-bolts

separated (again, check the oil cooler coolant hoses). If required, the two mounting brackets can now be unbolted from the body and transmission – each is secured by four bolts **(see illustrations)**.

22 Refitting is a reversal of removal. Tighten all fasteners to the specified torque.

Lower mounting

23 Firmly apply the handbrake, then jack up the front of the car and support securely on axle stands (see *Jacking and vehicle support*). Remove the engine undertray, which is secured by a number of quick-release screw fasteners.

24 Where fitted, remove the single bolt and release the clip securing the heat shield fitted at one side of the lower mounting, and withdraw it **(see illustrations)**.

25 Unscrew the two through-bolts from the lower mounting to release it, and withdraw it from the mounting brackets **(see illustration)**. Though removing the lower mounting will increase the amount of engine movement, provided they have not been disturbed, the engine will remain safely supported on its right- and left-hand mountings.

26 If required, the lower mounting bracket can be unbolted from the sump **(see illustration)**.

27 Refitting is a reversal of removal. Tighten all fasteners to the specified torque.

20.26 The lower mounting bracket is secured to the sump by two bolts

Notes

Chapter 2 Part C:
Diesel engine in-car repair procedures

Contents

	Section number
Auxiliary drivebelt tensioner – removal and refitting	22
Camshaft and hydraulic tappets – removal, inspection and refitting	13
Camshaft cover – removal and refitting	4
Camshaft oil seals – renewal	12
Compression and leakdown tests – description and interpretation	2
Crankshaft oil seals – renewal	18
Crankshaft pulley – removal and refitting	5
Cylinder head – removal and refitting	14
Engine oil cooler – removal and refitting	21
Engine timing marks – general information	3
Engine/transmission mountings – inspection, removal and refitting	20
Flywheel/driveplate – removal, inspection and refitting	19

	Section number
Fuel injection pump drivebelt – removal, inspection, refitting and adjustment	10
Fuel injection pump drivebelt cover – removal and refitting	9
Fuel injection pump drivebelt sprockets and tensioner – removal and refitting	11
General information and precautions	1
Oil pump – dismantling, inspection and reassembly	17
Oil pump – removal and refitting	16
Sump – removal and refitting	15
Timing belt – removal, inspection, refitting and adjustment	7
Timing belt covers – removal and refitting	6
Timing belt tensioner and sprockets – removal, inspection and refitting	8

Degrees of difficulty

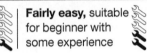

Easy, suitable for novice with little experience	Fairly easy, suitable for beginner with some experience	Fairly difficult, suitable for competent DIY mechanic	Difficult, suitable for experienced DIY mechanic	Very difficult, suitable for expert DIY or professional

Specifications

General

Engine type	Four-cylinder in-line, four-stroke, liquid-cooled
Designation:	
Turbocharged and intercooled	20T2N or 20TN2N
Bore	84.5 mm
Stroke	88.9 mm
Capacity	1994 cc
Firing order	1-3-4-2 (No 1 cylinder at timing belt end)
Direction of crankshaft rotation	Clockwise (seen from right-hand side of vehicle)
Compression ratio	19.5 : 1
Maximum power (EEC)	74 kW (101 bhp) @ 4200 rpm
Maximum torque (EEC)	240 Nm (177 lbf ft) @ 2000 rpm

Camshaft

Drive	Toothed belt from crankshaft
Number of bearings	5
Bearing journal running clearance	0.043 to 0.094 mm
Camshaft endfloat (maximum)	0.51 mm
Hydraulic tappet outside diameter	34.959 to 34.975 mm

Lubrication system

System pressure	0.7 bar @ idle speed
Pressure relief valve opening pressure	4.5 bar
Low oil pressure warning light comes on	0.4 to 0.7 bar
Oil pump clearances:	
Rotor endfloat	0.03 to 0.08 mm
Outer rotor-to-body clearance	0.05 to 0.10 mm
Rotor lobe clearance	0.025 to 0.120 mm
Pressure relief valve spring free length	38.9 mm

Torque wrench settings

	Nm	lbf ft
Auxiliary drivebelt tensioner centre bolt...............................	45	33
Camshaft bearing carrier bolts..................................	11	8
Camshaft cover bolts...	11	8
Camshaft sprocket bolt*:		
Stage 1	20	15
Stage 2	Angle-tighten through a further 90°	
Camshaft sprocket damper screws*	10	7
Crankshaft oil seal housing bolts..............................	8	6
Crankshaft pulley bolt:		
Stage 1	63	46
Stage 2	Angle-tighten through a further 90°	
Cylinder head bolts:		
Stage 1	30	22
Stage 2	65	48
Stage 3	Angle-tighten through a further 90°	
Stage 4	Angle-tighten through a further 90°	
Driveplate bolts	100	74
Flywheel bolts*:		
Stage 1	15	11
Stage 2	Angle-tighten through a further 90°	
Fuel injection pump drive (camshaft) sprocket*:		
Stage 1	20	15
Stage 2	Angle-tighten through a further 90°	
Fuel injection pump drive (camshaft) sprocket (adjuster) bolts	25	18
Fuel injection pump drivebelt backplate bolts	8	6
Fuel injection pump drivebelt tensioner pulley bolt	45	33
LH mounting-to-body bolts	45	33
LH mounting-to-bracket bolts	45	33
LH mounting-to-gearbox bracket bolts	45	33
Lower engine steady bolts	100	74
Lower engine steady bracket-to-sump bolts	85	63
Oil cooler to block:		
M8 bolts	25	18
M10 bolts	45	33
Oil cooler pipe clamp bolts	9	7
Oil cooler pipe unions..	25	18
Oil filter	17	13
Oil pressure warning light switch	15	11
Oil pressure relief valve nut	25	18
Oil pump pick-up/strainer pipe bolts	8	6
Oil pump thermostatic valve plug.............................	35	26
Oil pump-to-cylinder block bolts:		
M6 bolts	10	7
M10 bolt	45	33
RH engine mounting plate:		
Bolts	45	33
Nuts*:		
Stage 1	30	22
Stage 2	Angle-tighten through a further 120°	
RH hydramount/restraint bar-to-body bolts......................	45	33
RH mounting engine bracket-to-engine bolts	105	77
RH mounting engine bracket-to-hydramount nut	80	59
Roadwheel nuts	110	81
Sump bolts..	25	18
Sump drain plug..	25	18
Timing belt cover bolts..	5	4
Timing belt idler pulley nut	45	33
Timing belt idler pulley stud	12	9
Timing belt rear cover bolts	9	7
Timing belt tensioner pivot bolt	45	33
Timing belt tensioner pulley bolt*..............................	55	41
Upper engine steady bar bolts	100	74

* Use new bolts

1 General information and precautions

How to use this Chapter

This Part of the Chapter describes those repair procedures that can reasonably be carried out on the engine whilst it remains in the vehicle. If the engine has been removed from the vehicle and is being dismantled, as described in Part E of this Chapter, any preliminary dismantling procedures can be ignored.

Note that whilst it may be possible physically to overhaul items such as the piston/ connecting rod assemblies with the engine in the vehicle, such tasks are not usually carried out as separate operations and usually require the execution of several additional procedures (not to mention the cleaning of components and of oil ways). For this reason, all such tasks are classed as major overhaul procedures and are described in Part E of this Chapter.

Engine description

The engine is of four-cylinder, in-line type, mounted transversely at the front of the vehicle with the clutch and transmission at its left-hand end. The engine is of eight-valve single overhead camshaft type.

The crankshaft runs in five main bearings. Thrustwashers are fitted to the centre main bearing (upper half) to control crankshaft endfloat. Individual main bearing caps are used, which are bolted directly to the cylinder block.

The connecting rods rotate on horizontally-split bearing shells at their big-ends. The pistons are attached to the connecting rods by fully-floating gudgeon pins. The gudgeon pins are retained by circlips at each end. The aluminium alloy pistons are fitted with three piston rings, comprising two compression rings and an oil control ring.

The cylinders are bored directly into the cast iron cylinder block.

The inlet and exhaust valves are each closed by coil springs and operate in guides pressed into the cylinder head. The valve seat inserts are pressed into the cylinder head and can be renewed separately if worn.

The camshaft is driven by a toothed timing belt, and operates the valves via self-adjusting hydraulic tappets, thus eliminating the need for routine checking and adjustment of the valve clearances. The camshaft rotates in bearings which are line-bored directly into the cylinder head and the (bolted-on) bearing carrier. This means that the bearing carrier and cylinder head are matched, and cannot be renewed independently.

Unusually, the coolant pump is driven via a drive dog from the rear of the power steering pump, which is itself driven by the auxiliary drivebelt.

Lubrication is by means of an eccentric-rotor type pump driven directly from the timing belt end of the crankshaft. The pump draws oil through a strainer located in the sump, and then forces it through an externally mounted full-flow cartridge-type oil filter into galleries in the oil rail and the cylinder block/crankcase, from where it is distributed to the crankshaft (main bearings) and camshaft. The big-end bearings are supplied with oil via internal drillings in the crankshaft, while the camshaft bearings and the hydraulic tappets receive a pressurised supply via drillings in the cylinder head. The camshaft lobes and valves are lubricated by oil splash, as are all other engine components.

Operations with engine in car

The following work can be carried out with the engine in the vehicle:

a) Compression pressure – testing.
b) Cylinder head cover – removal and refitting.
c) Crankshaft pulley – removal and refitting.
d) Timing belt covers – removal and refitting.
e) Timing belt – removal, refitting and adjustment.
f) Timing belt tensioner and sprockets – removal and refitting.
g) Camshaft oil seals – renewal.
h) Camshaft and hydraulic tappets – removal, inspection and refitting.
i) Cylinder head – removal and refitting.
j) Cylinder head and pistons – decarbonising.
k) Sump – removal and refitting.
l) Oil pump – removal, overhaul and refitting.
m) Crankshaft oil seals – renewal.
n) Engine/transmission mountings – inspection and renewal.
o) Flywheel – removal, inspection and refitting.

2 Compression and leakdown tests – description and interpretation

Compression test

Note: A compression tester designed for diesel engines must be used for this test.

1 When engine performance is down, or if misfiring occurs which cannot be attributed to the ignition or fuel systems, a compression test can provide diagnostic clues as to the engine's condition. If the test is performed regularly, it can give warning of trouble before any other symptoms become apparent.

2 A compression tester specifically intended for diesel engines must be used, because of the higher pressures involved. The tester is connected to an adapter, which screws into the glow plug or injector hole. On these engines, an adapter suitable for use in the injector holes is preferable. It is unlikely to be worthwhile buying such a tester for occasional use, but it may be possible to borrow or hire one – if not, have the test performed by a garage.

3 Unless specific instructions to the contrary are supplied with the tester, observe the following points.

a) The battery must be in a good state of charge, the air filter must be clean, and the engine should be at normal operating temperature.
b) All the injectors or glow plugs should be removed before starting the test.
c) The stop solenoid must be disconnected, to prevent the engine from running or fuel from being discharged.

4 There is no need to hold the throttle pedal down during the test, because the diesel engine air inlet is not throttled.

5 Crank the engine on the starter motor. After one or two revolutions, the compression pressure should build-up to a maximum figure, and then stabilise. Record the highest reading obtained.

6 Repeat the test on the remaining cylinders, recording the pressure in each.

7 The cause of poor compression is less easy to establish on a diesel engine than on a petrol one. The effect of introducing oil into the cylinders ('wet' testing) is not conclusive, because there is a risk that the oil will sit in the swirl chamber or in the recess in the piston crown instead of passing to the rings. However, the following can be used as a rough guide to diagnosis.

8 All cylinders should produce very similar pressures; a difference of more than 3.0 bar between any two cylinders usually indicates a fault. Rover does not specify compression pressure figures, as a guide, any cylinder pressure of below 20 bars can be considered as less than healthy. Note that the compression should build-up quickly in a healthy engine; low compression on the first stroke, followed by gradually-increasing pressure on successive strokes, indicates worn piston rings. A low compression reading on the first stroke, which does not build-up during successive strokes, indicates leaking valves or a blown head gasket (a cracked head could also be the cause). Deposits on the undersides of the valve heads can also cause low compression.

9 A low reading from two adjacent cylinders is almost certainly due to the head gasket having blown between them; the presence of coolant in the engine oil will confirm this.

10 If the compression reading is unusually high, the combustion chambers are probably coated with carbon deposits. If this is the case, the cylinder head should be removed and decarbonised.

11 On completion of the test, refit the injectors or the glow plugs, and reconnect the stop solenoid.

Leakdown test

12 A leakdown test measures the rate at which compressed air fed into the cylinder is

3.3 The timing mark (1) on the camshaft sprocket should be aligned with the raised rib on the rear timing belt cover (2)

3.4 6.5 mm twist drill inserted through timing pin hole into flywheel

lost. It is an alternative to a compression test, and in many ways is better, since the escaping air provides easy identification of where a pressure loss is occurring (piston rings, valves or head gasket).

13 The equipment needed for leakdown testing is unlikely to be available to the home mechanic. If poor compression is suspected, have the test performed by a suitably-equipped garage.

3 Engine timing marks – general information

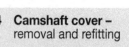

Note: *A suitable timing pin (which can be improvised using a 6.5 mm diameter twist drill) will be required for this operation.*

1 Locate the timing pinhole in the transmission mounting plate, at the rear left-hand corner of the engine. Access is difficult, and it may be necessary to move surrounding hoses and wiring to one side for access.

2 Remove the upper outer timing belt cover as described in Section 6.

3 Using a suitable socket or spanner on the crankshaft pulley bolt, turn the crankshaft until the timing mark on the camshaft sprocket is aligned with the raised rib on the rear timing belt cover **(see illustration)**.

4 It should now be possible to insert a 6.5 mm twist drill through the timing pin hole in the transmission mounting plate to engage with the timing hole in the flywheel **(see illustration)**. The crankshaft is now locked in position with No 1 piston at TDC.

4 Camshaft cover – removal and refitting

Note: *The following new parts are needed – camshaft cover gasket, intake pipe-to-intake manifold gasket.*

Removal

1 Remove the screws securing the acoustic cover to the engine, and remove the cover **(see illustration)**.

2 Remove the bolts securing the EGR cooler outlet pipe to the air intake pipe **(see illustration)**.

3 Remove the bolt securing the intake pipe to the camshaft cover bracket **(see illustration)**.

4 Remove two bolts securing the intake pipe to the inlet manifold **(see illustration)**.

5 Slacken the hose securing clip, and disconnect the intercooler top hose from the intake pipe. Release the intake pipe and discard the gasket **(see illustration)**.

6 Slacken the securing clip and disconnect the intercooler bottom hose from the turbocharger outlet pipe **(see illustration)**.

7 Remove the two bolts securing the turbocharger pipe to the engine.

8 Slacken the securing clip and remove the outlet pipe from the turbocharger outlet hose **(see illustration)**.

9 Slacken the securing clip and disconnect the engine breather hose from the camshaft cover.

10 Remove the oil filler cap, and remove the

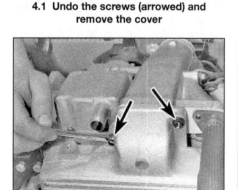

4.1 Undo the screws (arrowed) and remove the cover

4.2 Remove the EGR cooler pipe bolts (arrowed)

4.3 Remove the bolt from the camshaft cover bracket

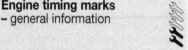

4.4 Remove the intake pipe bolts (arrowed)

4.5 Release the intake pipe from the hose

4.6 Slacken the securing clip (arrowed) and disconnect intercooler hose

bolt securing the brake servo pipe bracket to the top of the camshaft cover.

11 Remove the bolts securing the camshaft cover, and remove the cover.

12 Release the gasket from the camshaft cover and discard the gasket.

Refitting

13 Refitting is a reversal of the removal procedure, noting:
  a) *Clean the mating faces of the camshaft cover and camshaft carrier.*
  b) *Fit a new gasket to the camshaft cover, and to the intake manifold.*
  c) *Use a torque wrench to tighten all bolts to the specified torque, where given.*
  d) *Tighten the camshaft cover bolts in the correct sequence (see illustration).*

5 Crankshaft pulley – removal and refitting

Removal

1 Disconnect the battery negative terminal.

2 Apply the handbrake, chock the rear roadwheels, then jack up the front of the car and support it on axle stands (see *Jacking and vehicle support*). Remove the right hand roadwheel.

3 Remove the auxiliary drivebelt as described in Chapter 5A.

4 Insert a timing pin through the hole in the gearbox mounting plate – see Section 3. With a suitable socket or spanner on the crankshaft pulley nut, have an assistant to turn the crankshaft clockwise until the pin enters the hole in the flywheel and locks the crankshaft. Check that the timing marks on the camshaft sprocket damper, and on the timing belt rear cover, are aligned.

5 Remove the pulley securing bolt and pulley **(see illustrations)**.

Refitting

6 Ensuring that the mating faces are clean, refit the pulley and retaining bolt. Use a torque wrench to tighten the bolt to the specified torque.

7 Remove the timing pin.

6.1a Unscrew the securing bolts . . .

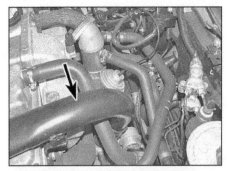

4.8 Remove outlet pipe (arrowed) from turbocharger hose

5.5a Remove pulley retaining bolt . . .

8 Refit the auxiliary drivebelt as described in Chapter 5A.

9 Fit the roadwheel, and tighten the nuts to secure the wheel. Remove the stands and lower the vehicle to the ground.

10 Use a torque wrench to tighten the roadwheel nuts to the specified torque.

11 Reconnect the battery earth lead.

6 Timing belt covers – removal and refitting

Upper outer cover

Removal

1 Unscrew the four bolts securing the upper outer timing cover to the rear cover, and withdraw the cover **(see illustrations)**.

6.1b . . . and remove the upper outer timing belt cover

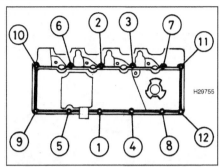

4.13 Tighten camshaft cover bolts in sequence

5.5b . . . and withdraw the pulley from the crankshaft

Refitting

2 Refitting is a reversal of removal, but make sure that the sealing strips are correctly located in the cover.

Lower outer cover

Removal

3 Disconnect the battery negative terminal.

4 Apply the handbrake, then jack up the front of the vehicle and support securely on axle stands (see *Jacking and vehicle support*). Remove the right-hand front roadwheel.

5 Remove the upper outer timing belt cover, as described previously in this Section.

6 Remove the crankshaft pulley as described in Section 5.

7 Unscrew the securing bolts, and withdraw the lower outer cover **(see illustrations)**.

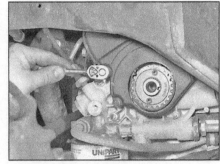

6.7a Unscrew the securing bolts . . .

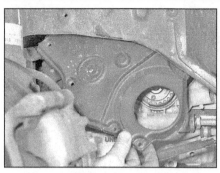

6.7b . . . and remove the lower outer timing belt cover

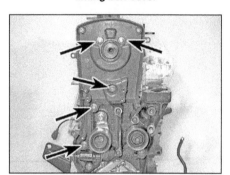

6.13a Unscrew the upper rear timing belt cover securing bolts (arrowed) – viewed with the engine removed . . .

Refitting

8 Refitting is a reversal of removal, bearing in mind the following points.

a) *Make sure that the sealing strips are correctly located in the timing belt covers.*

b) *Note that the three longer bolts fit at the bottom of the lower timing belt cover.*

c) *Refit the crankshaft pulley with reference to Section 5.*

Upper rear cover

Removal

9 Remove the outer timing belt covers as described previously in this Section.

10 Remove the timing belt as described in Section 7.

11 Remove the camshaft sprocket as described in Section 8.

12 Where applicable, release the three clips

6.23a Unscrew the two securing bolts (arrowed) . . .

6.12 Release the clips (arrowed) securing the wiring harness to the timing belt cover

6.13b . . . then remove the upper rear timing belt cover

securing the engine wiring harness to the rear timing belt cover **(see illustration)**.

13 Unscrew the five securing bolts, and remove the upper rear cover. Recover the sealing strip **(see illustrations)**.

Refitting

14 Examine the sealing strip, and renew if necessary.

15 Refit the upper rear cover, noting that the shorter securing bolts are used to secure the top of the cover to the camshaft bearing carrier. Make sure that the sealing strip is correctly located.

16 Where applicable, clip the engine wiring harness into position on the rear timing belt cover.

17 Where necessary, refit the timing belt tensioner, and the camshaft sprocket as described in Section 8.

6.23b . . . and remove the lower rear timing belt cover

18 Refit the timing belt as described in Section 7.

19 Refit the outer timing belt covers, as described previously in this Section.

Lower rear cover

Removal

20 Remove the outer timing belt covers, as described previously in this Section.

21 Remove the timing belt as described in Section 7, and the timing belt tensioner assembly as described in Section 8.

22 Unscrew the nut securing the timing belt idler pulley, and remove the pulley. Note that the mounting stud may be unscrewed with the nut.

23 Unscrew the two securing bolts, and remove the lower rear timing belt cover **(see illustrations)**. Recover the sealing strips.

Refitting

24 If the idler pulley stud was unscrewed with the nut, unscrew the nut from the stud (clamp the stud in a vice if necessary to allow the nut to be unscrewed).

25 Where applicable, clean the threads of the idler pulley stud, and the corresponding threads in the cylinder block, then apply thread-locking compound to the stud threads that screw into the cylinder block. Screw the stud into position, and tighten to the specified torque.

26 Examine the timing belt cover sealing strips, and renew if necessary.

27 Refit the lower rear timing belt cover, and tighten the securing bolts. Make sure that the sealing strips are correctly located.

28 Thoroughly clean the threads of the idler pulley nut, and then coat the threads with thread-locking compound.

29 Refit the idler pulley to the stud, then refit the nut and tighten to the specified torque.

30 Refit the timing belt as described in Section 7.

31 Refit the outer timing belt covers as described previously in this Section.

7	**Timing belt –** removal, inspection, refitting and adjustment	

Note: *Rover tool No 18G 1719 or a suitable equivalent (see text) will be required to release the timing belt tensioner during this procedure.*

Removal

1 Disconnect the battery negative terminal.

2 Lock the crankshaft at TDC (No1 cylinder) as described in Section 3. Remove the crankshaft pulley as described in Section 5.

3 Working on the right-hand side of the engine compartment, unclip any wiring or hoses, to improve access to the timing belt end of the engine.

4 Remove the right-hand engine mounting as described in Section 20.

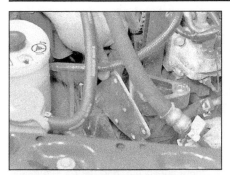

7.6 Removing the engine mounting cover plate

7.8 Slackening the bolt securing the timing belt tensioner pulley – engine removed for clarity

7.9 Prise the access plug from the rear timing belt cover – engine removed for clarity

5 Remove the outer timing belt covers, with reference to Section 6.

6 Unscrew the four securing nuts and two bolts, and remove the engine mounting cover plate **(see illustration)**.

7 If the original timing belt is to be re-used, mark the running direction on the belt, using chalk or tape. **Note:** *It is recommended that a new belt be fitted, whenever it has been removed.*

8 Slacken the bolt securing the timing belt tensioner pulley **(see illustration)**.

9 Prise the timing belt tensioner access plug from the lower rear timing belt cover **(see illustration)**.

10 A suitable tool will now be required to release the timing belt tensioner. Rover technicians use service tool 18G 1719, but a suitable alternative can be improvised using a length of M6 threaded rod or a long bolt, and a nut **(see illustration)**.

11 Insert the tool through the hole in the lower rear timing belt cover, then screw the threaded rod or bolt into the tensioner plunger, and turn the nut on the tool to draw the plunger back, relieving the tension on the timing belt tensioner pulley **(see illustration)**.

12 Once the tensioner plunger has been released, tighten the tensioner pulley bolt.

13 Slide the timing belt from the sprockets and remove the belt. **Do not** rotate the crankshaft or the camshaft until the timing belt has been refitted.

Inspection

14 Check the timing belt carefully for any signs of uneven wear, splitting or oil contamination and renew it if there is the slightest doubt about its condition. If the engine is undergoing an overhaul and has covered more than 42 000 miles since the original belt was fitted, it is advisable to renew the belt as a matter of course, regardless of its apparent condition. Note that MG Rover recommends that the belt be renewed as follows:

a) *With manual tensioner for the fuel injection pump belt, every 48 000 miles or 4 years, whichever comes first.*

b) *With automatic tensioner for the fuel injection pump belt, every 84 000 miles or 7 years, whichever comes first.*

15 If signs of oil contamination are found,

trace the source of the oil leak and rectify it, then wash down the engine timing belt area and all related components to remove all traces of oil. If the timing belt sprockets have been subjected to prolonged oil contamination, they must be soaked in a suitable solvent bath, then thoroughly washed in clean solvent before refitting (the sprockets are manufactured from a porous material which will absorb oil – the oil will eventually be released and will contaminate the new belt if the sprockets are not cleaned).

Refitting and adjustment

Note: *The manufacturer states that tensioning need only be carried out when a belt is (re)fitted. No retensioning is recommended once a belt has been fitted and therefore this operation is not included in the manufacturer's maintenance schedule. If the timing belt is thought to be incorrectly tensioned, then adjust the tension as described in the following paragraphs. If the timing belt has been disturbed, adjust its tension following the same procedure, omitting as appropriate the irrelevant preliminary dismantling/reassembly steps.*

16 Ensure that the timing marks on the camshaft sprocket and the rear timing belt cover are still aligned, and that the crankshaft is still locked in position using the timing pin inserted into the flywheel (see Section 3).

17 If a used belt is being refitted, ensure that the direction mark made on removal points in the normal direction of rotation. Fit the timing belt over the crankshaft and camshaft

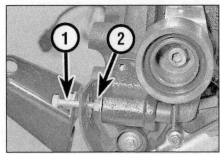

7.11 Screw the bolt (1) into the tensioner plunger, then tighten the nut (2) to draw the plunger back – engine removed for clarity

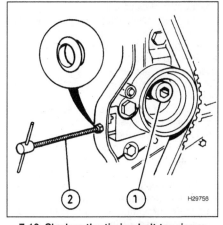

7.10 Slacken the timing belt tensioner pulley bolt (1), then use Rover tool 18G 1719 (2) or alternative to release the tensioner

sprockets and around the idler pulley, ensuring that the belt front run is taut, ie, all slack is on the tensioner pulley side of the belt, then fit the belt around the tensioner pulley. Do not twist the belt sharply during refitting and ensure that the belt teeth are correctly seated centrally in the sprockets and that the timing marks remain in alignment (see Section 3).

18 Refit the engine mounting cover plate, and tighten the securing nuts and bolts securely **(see illustration)**.

19 Refit the lower outer timing belt cover and tighten the securing bolts to the specified torque **(see illustration)**.

7.18 Refit the engine mounting cover plate – engine removed for clarity

7.19 Refitting the lower outer timing belt cover – engine removed for clarity

20 Refit the right-hand engine mounting as described in Section 20.

21 Refit the crankshaft pulley, with reference to Section 5 (do not refit the roadwheel or lower the vehicle to the ground at this stage).

22 Refit and tension the auxiliary drivebelt as described in Chapter 5A.

23 Slacken the timing belt tensioner pulley bolt.

24 Using the special tool, release the timing belt tensioner plunger, then remove the tool.

25 Lightly tighten the tensioner pulley bolt.

26 Remove the timing pin from the flywheel.

27 Using a spanner or a socket and extension bar on the crankshaft pulley bolt, rotate the crankshaft through two complete revolutions clockwise until the timing marks on the camshaft sprocket and the rear timing belt cover are aligned again.

Using an improvised tool to prevent the camshaft from rotating whilst unscrewing the sprocket bolt.

8.5a Withdraw the camshaft sprocket . . .

28 Refit the timing pin, and engage it with the flywheel.

29 Slacken the timing belt tensioner pulley bolt, and allow the tensioner to push against the belt under the force of the plunger.

30 Tighten the timing belt tensioner pulley bolt to the specified torque.

Caution: Do not exceed the specified torque setting for the tensioner pulley bolt.

31 Remove the timing pin from the flywheel.

32 Refit the upper outer timing belt cover.

33 Refit the timing belt tensioner access plug to the lower rear timing belt cover.

34 Refit the power steering fluid pipe bracket securing bolt.

35 Refit the roadwheel and lower the vehicle to the ground, then reconnect the battery negative lead.

8 Timing belt tensioner and sprockets – removal, inspection and refitting

Camshaft sprocket

Note: *The following new parts are needed – camshaft sprocket securing bolt, three sprocket damper Torx head screws.*

Removal

1 Disconnect the battery negative terminal.

2 Remove the timing belt as described in Section 7. Note that there is no need to remove the timing belt completely, provided that it is slipped from the camshaft sprocket. **Do not** rotate the crankshaft or the camshaft until the timing belt has been refitted.

3 Remove and discard three Torx head screws securing the sprocket damper, and remove the damper.

4 Slacken the camshaft sprocket retaining bolt and remove it, along with its washer. To prevent the camshaft from rotating, Rover technicians use service tool 18G 1521, but an acceptable substitute can be fabricated from two lengths of steel strip (one long, the other short) and three nuts and bolts. One nut and bolt should form the pivot of a forked tool with the remaining two nuts and bolts at the tips of the forks to engage with the sprocket spokes **(see Tool Tip)**. **Do not** allow the camshaft to rotate as the sprocket bolt is being loosened.

8.5b . . . and recover the roll-pin (arrowed) if it is loose

Discard the sprocket bolt – a new one must be used on refitting.

5 Withdraw the sprocket from the camshaft, noting the locating roll-pin **(see illustrations)**. If the roll-pin is a loose fit in the end of the camshaft, remove it and store it with the sprocket for safe-keeping.

Inspection

6 Clean the sprocket thoroughly, and renew it if it shows signs of wear, damage or cracks.

Refitting

7 Where applicable, refit the roll-pin to the end of the camshaft, ensuring that its split is facing the centre of the camshaft, then refit the sprocket (ensure that it engages with the roll-pin), ensuring that the timing marks on the sprocket and rear timing belt cover are still aligned.

8 Prevent the sprocket from rotating by using the method employed on removal, then fit a **new** sprocket securing bolt, and tighten the bolt to the specified torque setting. **Do not** allow the camshaft to turn as the bolt is tightened.

9 Fit the sprocket damper, and fit three **new** Torx head screws. Use a torque wrench to tighten the screws to the specified torque.

10 Refit and tension the timing belt as described in Section 7, and then reconnect the battery negative lead.

Crankshaft sprocket

Removal

11 Remove the timing belt as described in Section 7.

12 Remove the sprocket from the crankshaft **(see illustration)**.

Inspection

13 Clean the sprocket thoroughly, and renew it if it shows signs of wear, damage or cracks.

Refitting

14 Refit the sprocket to the crankshaft, ensuring that it locates correctly on the crankshaft flattened section. Note that the sprocket flange must be innermost. Note that the notch in the sprocket flange should be pointing vertically upwards.

15 Refit and tension the timing belt as described in Section 7, and then reconnect the battery negative lead.

8.12 Removing the crankshaft sprocket – engine removed for clarity

Tensioner assembly

Removal

16 Remove the timing belt as described in Section 7.

17 Unscrew the tensioner pulley backplate securing bolt, and the tensioner pulley bolt, and remove the tensioner – take care, as the tensioner spring and plunger will be released from their housing as the tensioner is removed **(see illustration)**.

18 Lift out the tensioner spring and plunger **(see illustration)**.

Inspection

19 Clean the tensioner assembly but do not use any strong solvent, which may enter the pulley bearing. Check that the pulley rotates freely on the backplate, with no sign of stiffness or of free play. Renew the assembly if there is any doubt about its condition or if there are any obvious signs of wear or damage. The same applies to the tensioner spring, which should be checked with great care as its condition is critical for the correct tensioning of the timing belt.

20 Check the tensioner spring for signs of distortion, and check the spring free length. If the free length is not as specified, the spring must be renewed, as its condition is critical for the correct tensioning of the timing belt.

21 Check the tensioner plunger and the housing for signs of wear and corrosion. If there is any evidence of corrosion, the housing and the plunger must be renewed – **do not** attempt to remove corrosion using emery paper or by scraping.

Refitting

22 Thoroughly clean the tensioner components, paying particular attention to the plunger and the housing.

23 Smear the plunger with a little molybdenum disulphide-based grease, then locate the spring and plunger in the housing.

24 Position the tensioner on the engine, then refit the backplate securing bolt, and the tensioner pulley bolt. Tighten the backplate securing bolt securely, but do not tighten the pulley bolt at this stage.

25 Refit and tension the timing belt as described in Section 7.

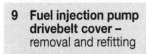

9 Fuel injection pump drivebelt cover – removal and refitting

Removal

1 Unscrew the bolts securing the engine acoustic cover to the top of the cylinder head cover, then remove the acoustic cover from the engine.

2 Remove the air cleaner assembly as described in Chapter 4C.

3 Remove the five bolts securing the drivebelt cover to the backplate, and remove the cover **(see illustrations)**.

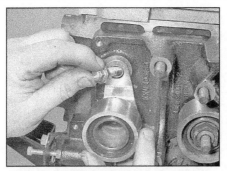

8.17 Removing the timing belt tensioner pulley assembly . . .

9.3a Undo the retaining bolts . . .

Refitting

4 Refitting is a reversal of removal.

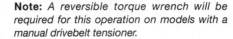

10 Fuel injection pump drivebelt – removal, inspection, refitting and adjustment

Note: *A reversible torque wrench will be required for this operation on models with a manual drivebelt tensioner.*

Removal

1 Disconnect the battery negative terminal.

2 Apply the handbrake, then jack up the front of the vehicle and support securely on axle stands (see *Jacking and vehicle support*). Remove the right-hand front roadwheel.

3 Remove the fuel injection pump drivebelt cover, as described in Section 9.

4 Rotate the crankshaft to bring No 1 piston

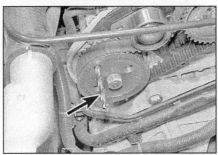

10.6 A 9.5 mm diameter twist drill (arrowed) can be used to lock the fuel injection pump sprocket in position

8.18 . . . and the spring and plunger – engine removed for clarity

9.3b . . . and withdraw the cover

to TDC, and insert the timing pin to lock the crankshaft in position, as described in Section 3.

5 A suitable locking pin must now be used to lock the fuel injection pump sprocket in position. Rover technicians use service tool 18G 1717, but an acceptable substitute can be improvised, using a 9.5 mm twist drill.

6 Push the locking tool through the hole in the fuel injection pump sprocket until it engages with the hole in the transmission mounting plate **(see illustration)**.

7 If the original fuel injection pump drivebelt is to be re-used, mark the running direction on the belt, using chalk or tape.

8 A suitable tool will now be required to hold the camshaft stationary. Rover technicians use service tool 18G 1521, but alternatively, a 3/8 inch drive breaker bar can be used – engage the square drive end of the bar with the square cut-out in the sprocket. Hold the

10.8a Engage a breaker bar with the square cut-out (arrowed) in the fuel injection pump drive sprocket . . .

10.8b ... to hold the sprocket stationary whilst slackening the sprocket adjuster bolts

10.9 Slacken the bolt securing the fuel injection pump drivebelt tensioner pulley

10.10 Slide the fuel injection pump drivebelt from the sprockets

10.14 Rotate the sprocket fully clockwise, then anti-clockwise until the belt locates in the sprocket teeth

10.16 Engage a torque wrench with the square hole in the tensioner backplate and apply the specified torque whilst tightening the tensioner pulley bolt

camshaft stationary, and slacken the four (adjuster) bolts securing the fuel injection pump drive sprocket to the camshaft **(see illustrations)**. Do not allow the camshaft to rotate as the bolts are slackened.

9 Slacken the Allen bolt securing the fuel injection pump drivebelt tensioner pulley, then move the tensioner away from the belt, and tighten the pulley bolt **(see illustration)**.

10 Slide the drivebelt from the sprockets **(see illustration)**. Do not rotate the camshaft or the fuel injection pump until the drivebelt has been refitted and tensioned.

Inspection

11 Check the fuel injection pump drivebelt carefully for any signs of uneven wear, splitting or oil contamination and renew it if there is the slightest doubt about its condition. If the engine is undergoing an overhaul and has covered more than 42 000 miles since the original belt was fitted, renew the belt as a matter of course, regardless of its apparent condition.

12 If signs of oil contamination are found, trace the source of the oil leak and rectify it, then wash down the engine timing belt area and all related components to remove all traces of oil. If the timing belt sprockets have been subjected to prolonged oil contamination, they must be soaked in a suitable solvent bath, then thoroughly washed in clean solvent before refitting (the sprockets are manufactured from a porous material which will absorb oil – the oil will eventually be

released and will contaminate the new belt if the sprockets are not cleaned).

Refitting and adjustment

Note: *The manufacturer states that tensioning need only be carried out when a belt is (re)fitted. No retensioning is recommended once a belt has been fitted and therefore this operation is not included in the manufacturer's maintenance schedule. If the belt is thought to be incorrectly tensioned, then adjust the tension as described in the following paragraphs. If the belt has been disturbed, adjust its tension following the same procedure, omitting as appropriate the irrelevant preliminary dismantling/reassembly steps.*

13 Make sure that the four (adjuster) bolts securing the fuel injection pump drive sprocket to the camshaft are just slack enough to allow the sprocket to rotate within its elongated slots – the sprocket should not be able to tip on the end of the camshaft.

14 If a used belt is being refitted, ensure that the direction mark made on removal points in the normal direction of rotation. Fit the belt over the fuel injection pump sprocket, then rotate the sprocket on the camshaft fully clockwise within the elongated slots, then anti-clockwise, until the belt locates in the sprocket teeth – this procedure must be carried out to ensure correct belt tensioning **(see illustration)**. Ensure that the lower belt run is taut, ie, all slack is on the tensioner pulley side of the belt, and then fit the belt around the tensioner pulley. Do not twist

the belt sharply during refitting and ensure that the belt teeth are correctly seated centrally in the sprockets.

15 Slacken the tensioner pulley bolt.

Manual drivebelt tensioner

16 Engage a torque wrench, with a suitable square-drive extension, with the square hole in the tensioner backplate, and apply a torque of 6 Nm (4 lbf ft), whilst tightening the tensioner pulley bolt **(see illustration)**.

17 Hold the camshaft stationary, using the tool engaged with the camshaft (timing belt) sprocket, as during removal, then tighten the four fuel injection pump drive sprocket (adjuster) bolts to the specified torque.

18 Remove the locking pins from the flywheel and the fuel injection pump sprocket.

19 Rotate the crankshaft through two complete turns clockwise, then refit the locking pin to the flywheel.

20 Check that the camshaft timing mark is aligned with the mark on the rear timing belt cover (see Section 3).

21 Slacken the four (adjuster) bolts securing the fuel injection pump drive sprocket to the camshaft, then refit the locking pin to the fuel injection pump sprocket.

22 Slacken the tensioner pulley bolt, then re-engage the torque wrench with the square hole in the tensioner backplate, and again apply a torque of 6 Nm (4 lbf ft).

23 Tighten the tensioner pulley bolt to the specified torque.

24 It is now necessary to apply an **anti-clockwise** torque to the fuel injection pump drive sprocket to ensure that the lower run of the belt is taut as the sprocket adjuster bolts are tightened. If a second torque wrench is available, apply an **anti-clockwise** torque of 25 Nm (18 lbf ft) to the sprocket centre bolt, whilst tightening the four sprocket adjuster bolts to the specified torque using a second torque wrench. If a second torque wrench is not available, apply a moderate anti-clockwise load to the sprocket centre bolt using a suitable spanner or socket, whilst tightening the sprocket adjuster bolts to the specified torque **(see illustration)**.

Automatic drivebelt tensioner

25 Rotate the tensioner **clockwise** until the index pointer passes the tension indicator.

10.24 Applying an anti-clockwise load to the pump drive sprocket centre bolt whilst tightening the adjuster bolts to the specified torque

26 Allow the tensioner to return **anti-clockwise** until the pointer is in line with the bottom edge of the tension indicator.
27 Hold the tensioner in that position and tighten it to the specified torque.

All models

28 Remove the locking pins from the flywheel and the fuel injection pump sprocket.
29 Refit the fuel injection pump drivebelt cover as described in Section 9.
30 Refit the roadwheel, then lower the vehicle to the ground and reconnect the battery negative lead.

11 Fuel injection pump drivebelt sprockets and tensioner – removal and refitting

Injection pump drive (camshaft) sprocket

Note: *A new sprocket securing bolt must be used on refitting.*

Removal

1 Remove the fuel injection pump drivebelt as described in Section 10.
2 A suitable tool will now be required to hold the camshaft stationary. Rover technicians use service tool 18G 1521, but an acceptable substitute can be fabricated from two lengths of steel strip (one long, the other short) and three nuts and bolts. One nut and bolt should form the pivot of a forked tool with the remaining two nuts and bolts at the tips of the forks to engage with the camshaft sprocket spokes **(see Tool Tip in Section 8)**. **Do not** allow the camshaft to rotate as the sprocket bolt is being loosened.
3 Hold the camshaft stationary, and slacken the centre bolt securing the fuel injection pump drive sprocket. Remove the bolt, and withdraw the sprocket from the end of the camshaft **(see illustration)**. Discard the sprocket bolt; a new bolt must be used on refitting.

Inspection

4 Clean the sprocket thoroughly, and renew it if it shows signs of wear, damage or cracks.

11.3 Removing the fuel injection pump drive (camshaft) sprocket

Refitting

5 Coat the threads of the new sprocket securing bolt with clean engine oil.
6 Locate the sprocket on the end of the camshaft, then prevent the camshaft from turning, as during removal, fit the sprocket securing bolt, and tighten the bolt to the specified torque in the two stages given (see Specifications).
7 Refit the fuel injection pump drivebelt as described in Section 10.

Injection pump sprocket

8 The procedure is described as part of the fuel injection pump removal procedure in Chapter 4C.

Tensioner

Removal

9 Remove the fuel injection pump drivebelt as described in Section 10.
10 Unscrew the tensioner pulley bolt and remove the tensioner.

Inspection

11 Clean the tensioner assembly but do not use any strong solvent, which may enter the pulley bearing. Check that the pulley rotates freely on the backplate, with no sign of stiffness or of free play. Renew the assembly if there is any doubt about its condition or if there are any obvious signs of wear or damage.

Refitting

12 Refitting is a reversal of removal, but make sure that the peg on the engine engages with the hole in the tensioner backplate **(see illustration)**. Refit the fuel injection pump drivebelt as described in Section 10.

12 Camshaft oil seals – renewal

Right-hand seal

1 Remove the camshaft sprocket as described in Section 8.
2 Punch or drill two small holes opposite each other in the oil seal. Screw a self-tapping

11.12 Make sure that the peg (arrowed) on the engine engages with the hole in the tensioner backplate

screw into each hole, and pull on the screws with pliers to extract the seal.
3 Clean the seal housing and polish off any burrs or raised edges, which may have caused the seal to fail.
4 Locate the seal against the recess, and draw the seal into position using a suitable socket and long M12 bolt, or threaded rod and bolt. Screw the bolt or threaded rod into the end of the camshaft, and turn the end of the bolt, or the nut to draw the seal into position **(see illustration 12.8)**. Alternatively, drive the seal into position using a suitable tubular drift, such as a socket, which bears only on the hard outer edge of the seal. Take care not to damage the seal lips during fitting and note that the seal lips should face inwards.
Caution: The new oil seal must be fitted dry. Do not lubricate the seal recess, the seal lip, or the seal running surface on the shaft.
5 Refit the camshaft sprocket as described in Section 8.

Left-hand seal

6 Remove the fuel injection pump drive sprocket from the end of the camshaft, and remove the fuel injection pump drivebelt tensioner, as described in Section 11.
7 Unscrew the three securing bolts, and remove the fuel injection pump drivebelt backplate.
8 Proceed as described in paragraphs 2 to 4. Ensure that the seal is fully seated in its recess **(see illustration)**.

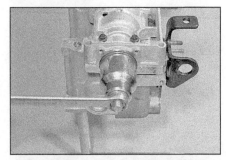

12.8 Using a socket, a length of M12 threaded rod and a nut to draw the camshaft oil seal into position – cylinder head removed

13.4a Unscrew the securing bolts . . .

13.4b . . . and remove the fuel injection pump drivebelt backplate

9 Thoroughly clean the fuel injection pump drivebelt backplate, and camshaft bearing carrier and cylinder head mating faces, then refit the backplate, and tighten the securing bolts to the specified torque.

10 Refit the fuel injection pump drivebelt tensioner, then refit the pump drive sprocket, as described in Section 11.

13 Camshaft and hydraulic tappets – removal, inspection and refitting

 HAYNES HiNT *If faulty tappets are diagnosed and the engine's service history is unknown, it is always worth trying the effect of renewing the engine oil and filter (using only good quality engine oil of the recommended viscosity and specification) before going to the expense of renewing any of the tappets.*

Note: *The following new parts are needed – MG Rover sealant kit GUG 705963GM, camshaft oil seals.*

13.8 Lifting off the camshaft bearing carrier

Removal

1 Remove the cylinder head cover, with reference to Section 4.

2 Remove the upper rear timing belt cover as described in Section 6.

3 Remove the fuel injection pump drive sprocket from the camshaft, and remove the fuel injection pump drivebelt tensioner, as described in Section 11.

4 Unscrew the three securing bolts, and remove the fuel injection pump drivebelt backplate **(see illustrations)**. Note the location of the bracket secured by one of the bolts.

5 Working in the **reverse** order of the tightening sequence **(see illustration 13.24)**, progressively slacken the camshaft bearing carrier securing bolts by 2 to 3 turns – **do not** fully slacken the bolts at this stage.

6 Using a soft-faced mallet, gently tap the bearing carrier upwards to break the sealant bond between the bearing carrier and the cylinder head. Note that the bearing carrier is located on dowels.

7 Using the same **reverse** sequence **(see illustration 13.24)**, continue to progressively slacken the bearing carrier securing bolts until all the load on the bearing carrier is relieved (the load is due to the pressure of the valve springs pushing the camshaft upwards against the bearing carrier).

Caution: If the bolts are removed completely before the load on the bearing carrier is relieved, the carrier may be suddenly released, which may cause damage to the bearing surfaces and/or the camshaft.

8 Finally remove the bolts, and lift the bearing carrier from the camshaft and cylinder head **(see illustration)**.

9 Carefully lift out the camshaft, then remove and discard the camshaft oil seals **(see illustration)**.

10 Obtain eight small, clean plastic containers and number them from 1 to 8.

11 Using a hydraulic sucker, or a small magnet, withdraw each hydraulic tappet in turn, invert it to prevent oil loss and place it in its respective container, which should then be filled with clean engine oil. **Do not** interchange the hydraulic tappets, and do not allow the hydraulic tappets to lose oil, as they will take a long time to refill with oil on restarting the engine, which could result in incorrect valve clearances.

Inspection

12 Check each hydraulic tappet for signs of obvious wear (scoring, pitting, etc) and for ovality. Renew if necessary. Using a micrometer, measure the outside diameter of the tappets – if the diameter of any tappet is outside the specified limits, it must be renewed.

13 If the engine's valve clearances have sounded noisy, particularly if the noise persists after initial start-up from cold, then there is reason to suspect a faulty hydraulic tappet. Only a good mechanic experienced in these engines can tell whether the noise level is typical, or if renewal is warranted of one or more of the tappets.

14 If the operation of any tappet is faulty, then it must be renewed.

15 Carefully remove all traces of old sealant from the mating surfaces of the camshaft bearing carrier and cylinder head, using a plastic scraper and suitable solvent if necessary. Examine the camshaft bearing journals and the cylinder head and bearing carrier bearing surfaces for signs of obvious wear or pitting. If any such signs are evident, renew the component(s) concerned.

16 To check camshaft endfloat, remove the hydraulic tappets (if not already done), carefully clean the bearing surfaces and refit the camshaft and bearing carrier. Tighten the bearing carrier bolts, in the specified order **(see illustration 13.24)**, to the specified torque wrench setting, then measure the endfloat using a Dial Test Indicator (DTI) or dial gauge mounted on the cylinder head, so that its tip bears on the front of the camshaft **(see illustration)**.

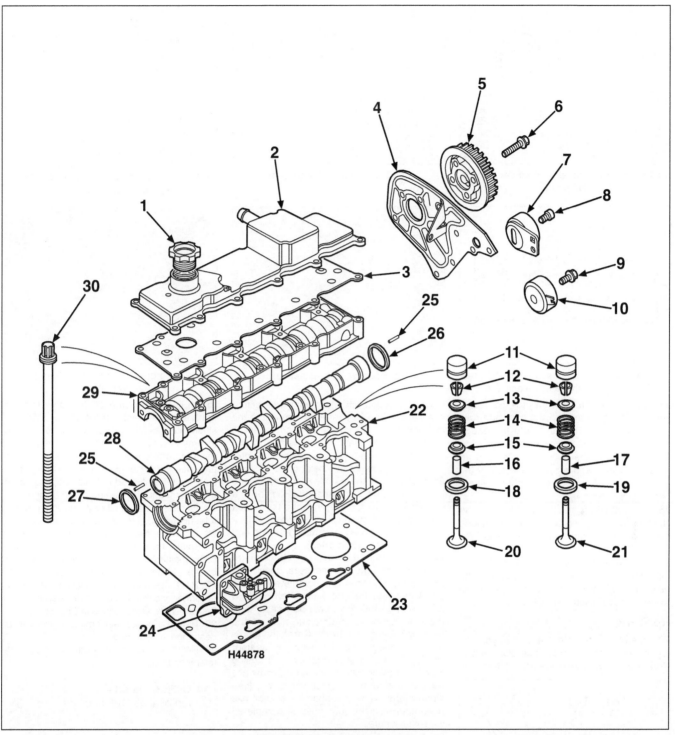

13.9 Cylinder head components

1 Oil filler cap	7 Manual fuel injection drivebelt	14 Springs	22 Cylinder head
2 Camshaft cover	tensioner	15 Lower spring seat/stem oil	23 Gasket
3 Gasket	8 Tensioner pulley bolt	seals	24 Thermostat housing
4 Fuel injection pump	9 Tensioner pulley bolt	16 Valve guide	25 Roll-pin
backplate	10 Automatic fuel injection	17 Valve guide	26 Oil seal
5 Fuel injection pump camshaft	drivebelt tensioner	18 Valve seat	27 Oil seal
sprocket	11 Tappets	19 Valve seat	28 Camshaft
6 Fuel injection pump sprocket	12 Collets	20 Valve	29 Camshaft bearing carrier
bolt	13 Spring retainers	21 Valve	30 Cylinder head bolt

13.16 Checking camshaft endfloat using a dial gauge

13.20 Liberally oil the tappets

13.21 Position the camshaft so that the roll-pin (arrowed) at the timing belt end is in the 2 o'clock position

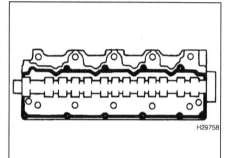

13.22a Apply a bead of sealant to the area indicated by the heavy black line

13.22b Squeeze out the sealant . . .

13.22c . . . then use a brush to spread an even film

17 Tap the camshaft fully towards the gauge, zero the gauge, then tap the camshaft fully away from the gauge and note the gauge reading. If the endfloat measured is found to be greater than the maximum specified, fit a new camshaft and repeat the check. If the clearance is still excessive, then the cylinder head must be renewed.

18 The camshaft itself should show no signs of marks, pitting or scoring on the lobe surfaces. If such marks are evident, renew the camshaft.

19 If a camshaft is renewed, extract the roll-pins from the old one and fit the pins to the new camshaft, with the split in each roll-pin towards the camshaft centreline.

Refitting

20 Liberally oil the cylinder head hydraulic tappet bores and the tappets **(see illustration)**. Note that if new tappets are being fitted, they

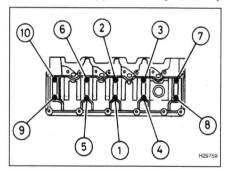

13.24 Camshaft bearing carrier securing bolt tightening sequence

must be charged with clean engine oil before installation. Carefully refit the tappets to the cylinder head, ensuring that each tappet is refitted to its original bore and is the correct way up. Some care will be required to enter the tappets squarely into their bores.

21 Liberally oil the camshaft bearings and lobes, then refit the camshaft. Position the camshaft so that the roll-pin in the timing belt sprocket end of the camshaft is in the 2 o'clock position when viewed from the right-hand end of the engine **(see illustration)**.

22 Ensure that the locating dowels are pressed firmly into their recesses, check that the mating surfaces are completely clean, unmarked and free from oil, then apply a thin bead of the recommended sealant to the cylinder head mating surfaces of the camshaft bearing carrier. Carefully follow the instructions supplied with the sealant kit. Spread the sealant to an even film using a brush or roller, taking care not to allow any sealant to enter the lubrication grooves **(see illustrations)**. Note that once the sealant has been applied, assembly must be completed within 20 minutes.

23 Refit the bearing carrier to the cylinder head, pushing it firmly into position. Fit the bearing carrier securing bolts, and tighten them finger-tight.

24 Working in sequence **(see illustration)**, progressively tighten the camshaft bearing carrier bolts by one turn at a time until the carrier touches the cylinder head evenly. Now go round again, working in the same sequence, tightening all bolts to the specified torque setting. Work only as described,

to apply the pressure of the valve springs gradually and evenly on the carrier. Wipe off all surplus sealant so that none is left to find its way into any oilways. Follow the sealant manufacturer's recommendations as to the time needed for curing – usually at least an hour must be allowed between application of the sealant and the starting of the engine.

25 Fit new camshaft oil seals, using a suitable tube or socket, with reference to Section 12.

26 Refit the fuel injection pump drivebelt backplate, then refit and tighten the securing bolts, making sure that the bracket is in place on the relevant bolt, as noted before removal.

27 Refit the fuel injection pump drivebelt tensioner and refit the pump drive sprocket to the camshaft, as described in Section 11.

28 Refit the upper rear timing belt cover as described in Section 6.

29 Refit the cylinder head cover, with reference to Section 4.

14 Cylinder head – removal and refitting

Note: *The following new parts are needed – cylinder head gasket, turbocharger oil return pipe gasket, turbocharger oil feed pipe sealing washers, camshaft sprocket bolt, fuel injection pump sprocket bolt, and possibly – cylinder head bolts.*

Note: *As they are disconnected, make a note or sketch of the position, route and clipping of all wires, harnesses, pipes and hoses.*

1 Disconnect the battery negative terminal.

14.6 Disconnect breather hose

14.7 Disconnect MAF/IAT multiplug

14.8 Remove air intake pipe

14.12 Disconnect EGR valve vacuum pipe

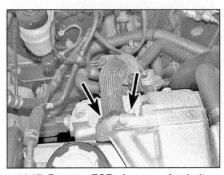

14.17 Remove EGR pipe securing bolts

14.19 Remove intake pipe

2 Undo the three retaining screws, and remove the engine acoustic cover.
3 Remove the air cleaner as described in Chapter 4C.
4 Drain the cooling system as described in Section 1B.
5 Apply the handbrake, chock the rear roadwheels, then jack up the front of the car and support it on axle stands (see *Jacking and vehicle support*).
6 Slacken the clip and disconnect the engine breather hose from the camshaft cover **(see illustration)**.
7 Disconnect the multiplug from the MAF/ IAT sensor on the air intake pipe between the air cleaner and the turbocharger **(see illustration)**.
8 Slacken the clip, and disconnect the air intake pipe from the turbocharger. Remove the air intake pipe, MAF/IAT sensor and engine breather valve assembly. Cover or plug the turbocharger intake **(see illustration)**.
9 Undo the three securing nuts, and disconnect the exhaust front pipe from the turbocharger.
10 Disconnect the boost pressure sensing pipe from the turbocharger (to the MAP sensor on the bulkhead).
11 Slacken two securing clips and disconnect two coolant pipes from the EGR cooler.
12 Disconnect the vacuum pipe from the EGR valve **(see illustration)**.
13 Slacken the securing clip, and disconnect the intercooler hose from the turbocharger outlet pipe.
14 Remove two bolts securing the turbocharger outlet pipe to the cylinder head.

15 Slacken the securing clip, and remove the outlet pipe from the turbocharger outlet hose. Cover or plug the outlet hose.
16 Slacken the securing clip, and disconnect the intercooler hose from the intake pipe.
17 Undo the two retaining bolts and disconnect the EGR pipe from the intake pipe **(see illustration)**.
18 Remove the bolt securing the intake pipe bracket to the camshaft cover.
19 Undo the two retaining bolts and remove the intake pipe from the inlet manifold **(see illustration)**.
20 Slacken and remove the banjo bolt securing the oil feed pipe to the turbocharger, remove and discard the washers.
21 Remove two bolts securing the oil drain pipe to the turbocharger, and discard the gasket **(see illustration)**.
22 Undo the two retaining bolts securing the exhaust manifold to the support bracket.

23 Slacken and remove the six bolts and six nuts securing the manifolds to the cylinder head, and remove the manifolds. Remove and discard the gasket.
24 Remove the fuel injection pump drivebelt as described in Section 10.
25 Remove the fuel injection pump drivebelt sprocket and tensioner as described in Section 11.
26 Undo the three retaining bolts from the fuel injection pump belt backplate, and remove the plate.
27 Remove the camshaft drivebelt as described in Section 7.
28 Remove the camshaft sprocket as described in Section 8.
29 Release the three clips securing the engine harness to the camshaft drivebelt rear cover.
30 Remove five bolts securing the rear cover to the cylinder head and cylinder block, and remove the cover **(see illustration)**.

14.21 Remove the turbo oil drain pipe bolts (arrowed)

14.30 Remove rear cover retaining bolts (arrowed)

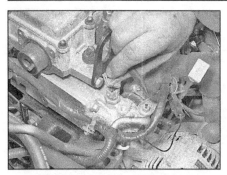

14.34 Disconnect the ECT multiplug

14.35 Disconnect temperature gauge sensor wire

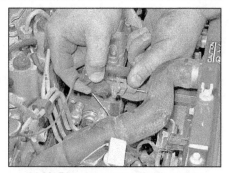

14.38 Disconnect needle lift sensor multiplug

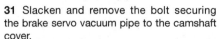

14.40 Using two spanners to slacken the injector pipes

14.42 Remove glow plug supply wire

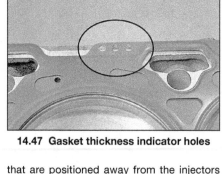

14.47 Gasket thickness indicator holes

31 Slacken and remove the bolt securing the brake servo vacuum pipe to the camshaft cover.

32 Release the securing clip, and disconnect the vacuum hose from the vacuum pump. Tie the pipe clear of the work area.

33 Remove three bolts securing the alternator upper mounting bracket, and remove the bracket.

34 Disconnect the multiplug from the Engine Coolant Temperature (ECT) sensor **(see illustration)**.

35 Disconnect the wire from the coolant temperature gauge sensor **(see illustration)**.

36 Slacken the securing clip, and disconnect the radiator top hose from the coolant outlet elbow.

37 Undo the retaining bolt attaching the dipstick tube to the outlet elbow.

38 Disconnect the multiplug from the harness for the needle lift sensor in No 1 injector **(see illustration)**.

39 Pack some absorbent cloths around the injectors to soak up any excess fuel.

Caution: To prevent damage to the injector pipes, use two spanners when slackening the connections.

40 Slacken the unions attaching the injector pipes to the injectors, and to the fuel injection pump. Carefully remove the pipes, and place them in a plastic bag. Plug the injector and fuel injection pump connections to prevent dirt ingress **(see illustration)**.

41 Disconnect the fuel spill return hose from No 3 injector. Plug the connections to prevent dirt ingress.

42 Undo the securing nut, and remove the

glow plug supply wire from No 2 glow plug **(see illustration)**.

43 Remove the twelve retaining bolts, and withdraw the camshaft cover from the cylinder head. Remove and discard the gasket.

44 Working in the **reverse** of the tightening sequence **(see illustration 14.61)**, progressively slacken and remove the ten Torx head bolts securing the cylinder head to the cylinder block.

Caution: Handle the cylinder head bolts carefully, and store them in fitted order. DO NOT remove the washers from the bolts.

45 Two dowels locate the cylinder head. The tips of the injectors and glow plugs protrude below the face of the head. DO NOT move the cylinder head sideways during removal. If necessary, carefully rock the cylinder head to release it from the cylinder block.

46 With the aid of an assistant lift off the cylinder head, and place on wooden blocks

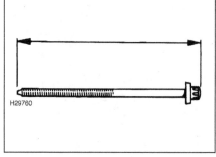

14.53 Measure the length of the bolt

that are positioned away from the injectors and glow plugs.

47 Remove the gasket, and note the number of gasket thickness indicator holes 1, 2, or 3. The new gasket must have the same number of holes **(see illustration)**.

48 Plug or tape over the oil and water passage holes in the cylinder head and cylinder block. To prevent carbon entering the gap between the piston and bore, smear a band of grease around the gap.

49 Use a hard wood or plastic scraper to remove all traces of gasket/carbon, etc, from the surfaces of the head and block. Scrape the carbon from the piston crowns. Wipe away the grease band, and wipe all surfaces.

50 Check surfaces for damage. Minor scratches are acceptable, but any more serious marking must be rectified by machining or component renewal. **Note:** *The cylinder head cannot be refaced.*

51 Check the cylinder head for distortion – see Chapter 2E.

52 Remove all tape/plugs from cylinder block and cylinder head.

53 Wash and dry the bolts. Check for signs of wear or damage. Check bolt length – if any bolt exceeds the maximum length of 243.41 mm, all bolts must be renewed **(see illustration)**.

54 Apply a light film of engine oil to the bolt threads, and the underside of the bolt heads.

Caution: DO NOT lubricate the underside of the washers.

55 Temporarily fit the crankshaft pulley bolt, and remove the crankshaft locking pin – see Section 3.

14.58 Check locating dowels (arrowed)

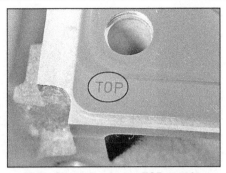

14.59 Check for gasket TOP marking

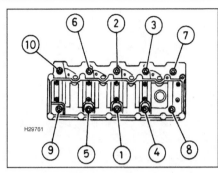

14.61 Cylinder head bolt tightening sequence

56 Using the pulley bolt, rotate the crankshaft anti-clockwise until No 1 and 4 pistons are approximately 25 mm below the face of the cylinder block.

57 Check that the camshaft drive pin is at 2 o'clock position. Remove the crankshaft pulley bolt.

58 Ensure that the two locating dowels are correctly located in the cylinder block **(see illustration)**.

Caution: ensure that the new cylinder head gasket has the same number of thickness indicator holes as the original – ie, 1, 2 or 3 holes.

59 Fit the gasket – dry – to the cylinder block, with TOP marking visible at the flywheel end **(see illustration)**.

60 With the aid of an assistant, lift the cylinder head onto the cylinder block, and locate on the dowels.

61 Carefully fit the cylinder head bolts. Use a torque wrench to tighten the bolts progressively in sequence and in the specified stages **(see illustration)**.

62 Further refitting is a reversal of the removal procedure, noting:

a) *Ensure cables, pipes, hoses and harnesses are routed and clipped as noted during removal.*

b) *Use a torque wrench to tighten all fastenings to the specified torque.*

c) *Refill the cooling system as described in Chapter 1B.*

d) *If necessary, bleed the fuel system as described in Chapter 4C.*

e) *Start the engine and check for leaks.*

Note: *If tappet noise is excessive run the engine at 2000 to 2500 rpm for 20 minutes. Do not exceed 3000 rpm until noise ceases.*

15 Sump – removal and refitting

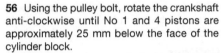

Note: *The following new parts are needed – MG Rover sealant kit GUG 705963GM, sump gasket, engine oil filter.*

Removal

1 Apply the handbrake, then jack up the front of the vehicle and support securely on axle stands (see *Jacking and vehicle support*).

2 Drain the engine oil (with reference to Chapter 1B if necessary), then clean and refit the engine oil drain plug, tightening it to the specified torque wrench setting. If the engine is nearing the service interval when the oil and filter are due for renewal, it is recommended that the filter is also removed and a new one fitted. After reassembly, the engine can then be refilled with fresh engine oil.

3 Remove the oil filter, with reference to Chapter 1B.

4 Remove the engine/transmission steady bar, as described in Section 20.

5 Unscrew the bolt securing the sump to the transmission support bracket **(see illustration)**.

6 Slacken the hose clip, and disconnect the brake vacuum pump oil drain pipe from the sump.

7 Unscrew the bolt securing the oil pipe bracket to the sump.

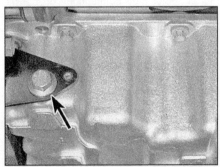

15.5 Unscrew the bolt (arrowed) securing the sump to the support bracket

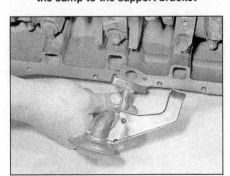

15.10b . . . and remove the oil pump pick-up/strainer pipe

8 Working in the **reverse** order to the tightening sequence **(see illustration 15.16)**, progressively slacken the sump retaining bolts then remove them.

9 Break the joint by striking the sump with the palm of the hand, then lower the sump and withdraw it. Recover the gasket and discard it.

10 With the sump removed, take the opportunity to unbolt the oil pump pick-up/strainer pipe and clean it using a suitable solvent **(see illustrations)**. Recover the O-ring, and inspect the strainer mesh for signs of clogging or splitting – renew if necessary.

Refitting

11 Clean all traces of gasket from the mating surfaces of the cylinder block/crankcase and sump, then use a clean rag to wipe out the sump and the engine interior. Clean all traces of sealant from the crankshaft oil seal housing, main bearing caps, and cylinder block.

15.10a Unscrew the securing bolts (arrowed) . . .

15.12 Refit the oil pump pick-up/strainer pipe using a new O-ring

15.13 Apply sealant (arrowed) as indicated in the text

12 Refit the oil pump pick-up/strainer pipe, using a new O-ring, and tighten the securing bolts to the specified torque **(see illustration)**.

13 Using the specified sealant (see Note at the beginning of this Section), fill the grooves on each side of the right-hand main bearing cap, and the joints between the bearing cap and the cylinder block **(see illustration)**.

14 Apply a 1 mm thick bead of sealant to the joints between the crankshaft left-hand oil seal housing, the left-hand main bearing cap and the cylinder block **(see illustration)**. **Note:** *Do not apply the sealant until immediately prior to refitting the sump, and do not spread the bead of sealant.*

15 Fit a new gasket to the sump, ensuring that the lugs on the gasket engage with the corresponding holes in the sump, then offer up the sump to the cylinder block/crankcase then refit the sump retaining bolts, and tighten the bolts finger-tight only.

16 Working in sequence **(see illustration)**, tighten the sump bolts to the specified torque setting.

17 Further refitting is a reversal of removal, bearing in mind the following points.

 a) *Tighten the bolt securing the sump to the transmission support bracket to the specified torque.*

 b) *Refit the engine/transmission steady bar, as described in Section 20.*

 c) *Fit a new oil filter and, on completion, refill the engine with oil as described in Chapter 1B.*

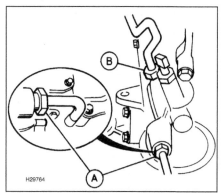

16.4 Disconnect the oil cooler pipes (A) and the turbocharger oil feed pipe (B) from the oil pump housing

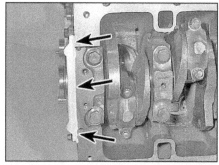

15.14 Apply sealant to the joints between the left-hand oil seal housing, the left-hand main bearing cap and the cylinder block

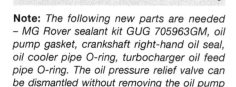

16 Oil pump –
removal and refitting

Note: *The following new parts are needed – MG Rover sealant kit GUG 705963GM, oil pump gasket, crankshaft right-hand oil seal, oil cooler pipe O-ring, turbocharger oil feed pipe O-ring. The oil pressure relief valve can be dismantled without removing the oil pump from the vehicle – see Section 17 for details.*

Removal

1 Drain the engine oil (see Chapter 1B).

2 Remove the upper and lower rear timing belt covers as described in Section 6.

3 Remove the crankshaft sprocket from the end of the crankshaft.

4 Place a suitable container beneath the oil cooler pipe connections on the oil pump housing, then unscrew the unions and disconnect the oil cooler pipes **(see illustration)**. Recover the O-rings from the pipes and discard them.

5 Similarly, slacken the union, and disconnect the turbocharger oil feed pipe from the oil pump housing. Recover the O-ring and discard it.

6 Disconnect the wiring plug from the oil pressure switch.

7 Working in the **reverse** order to the tightening sequence **(see illustration 16.20)**, unscrew the oil pump securing bolts, noting the location of the single longer securing bolt at the bottom of the pump.

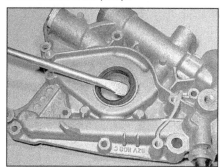

16.11 Prise the crankshaft oil seal from the oil pump

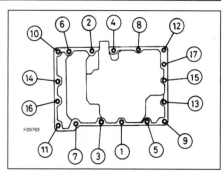

15.16 Sump bolt tightening sequence

8 Withdraw the pump from the cylinder block, and recover the Woodruff key from the crankshaft if it is loose. Recover the gasket and discard it.

Refitting

9 Make sure that the oil pump bolt holes in the cylinder block are clean and dry.

10 Clean all traces of gasket from the cylinder block and oil pump mating faces, and remove all traces of sealant from the front main bearing cap.

11 If the original oil pump is to be refitted, prise the crankshaft oil seal from the pump, and discard it **(see illustration)**.

12 The new oil seal must be fitted dry. Do not lubricate the seal recess, the seal lip, or the seal running surface on the shaft.

13 Refit the Woodruff key to the crankshaft.

14 Using the specified sealant (see Note at the beginning of this Section), apply a 1 mm thick bead of sealant to the joints between the main bearing cap and the cylinder block **(see illustrations)**.

15 Fit a new oil pump gasket to the cylinder block **(see illustration)**.

16 If a new oil pump is being fitted, it will be supplied with a new crankshaft oil seal already fitted.

17 Turn the oil pump inner rotor as necessary to align the slot in the rotor with the Woodruff key in the crankshaft.

18 Slide the oil pump over the crankshaft, ensuring that the Woodruff key engages with the slot in the oil pump inner rotor.

19 Apply thread-locking compound to the oil pump securing bolts, then refit the securing bolts, ensuring that the single longer bolt is

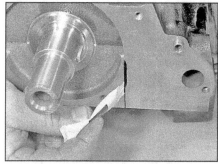

16.14a Apply a bead of sealant . . .

16.14b . . . to the joints between the main bearing cap and the cylinder block – viewed with engine removed

located at the bottom of pump in the position noted before removal.

20 Tighten the bolts to the specified torque, in sequence, noting the different torque setting for the longer bolt **(see illustration)**.

21 If the original oil pump has been refitted, fit a new crankshaft oil seal with reference to Section 18.

22 Further refitting is a reversal of removal, bearing in mind the following points.
 a) *Use new O-rings when reconnecting the turbocharger oil feed pipe and the oil cooler pipes to the pump housing.*
 b) *Refit the upper and lower rear timing belt covers as described in Section 6.*

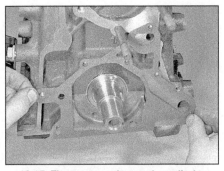

16.15 Fit a new gasket to the cylinder block – viewed with engine removed

 c) *Refill the engine with oil as described in Chapter 1B.*

17 Oil pump – dismantling, inspection and reassembly

Note: *Loctite 573 sealant, or a suitable equivalent, will be required to seal the pump cover plate to the pump body on reassembly. A new pressure relief valve threaded plug, and a new thermostatic valve plug sealing washer will be required. Thread-locking compound will be required to coat the threads of the*

pump cover plate securing screws, and the thermostatic valve plug.

1 The oil pump can be dismantled and checked as described in the following paragraphs, but no spare parts are available, and if wear or damage is found, the pump must be renewed as a complete unit.

Dismantling

2 Remove the oil pump as described in Section 16.

3 Make alignment marks between the pump cover plate and the pump body (note that some pumps have a TOP mark stamped at the top of the cover plate), then unscrew the Torx screws and remove the pump cover plate **(see illustrations)**.

4 Lift out the oil pump rotors, noting the punched identification marks on the front faces of the rotors, which face away from the cover plate **(see illustration)**.

5 The oil pressure relief valve can be dismantled, if required, without disturbing the pump. If this is to be done with the pump in position and the engine still installed in the vehicle, it will first be necessary to jack up the front of the vehicle and remove the right-hand roadwheel to gain access to the valve (see *Jacking and vehicle support*).

6 To dismantle the valve, unscrew the

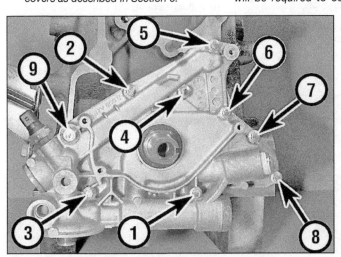

16.20 Oil pump bolt tightening sequence

17.3a Some oil pumps have a TOP marking at the top of the cover plate

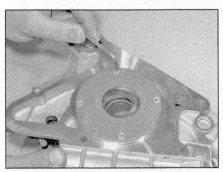

17.3b Unscrew the securing screws . . .

17.3c . . . and remove the pump cover plate

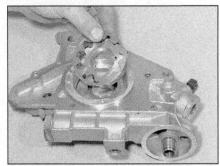

17.4 Lift out the oil pump rotors

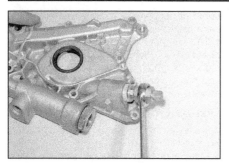

17.6a Unscrew the oil pressure relief valve threaded plug (using an oil plug drain key and a spanner) . . .

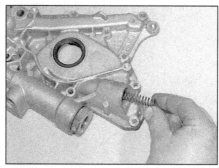

17.6b . . . then recover the valve spring . . .

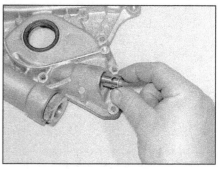

17.6c . . . and the plunger

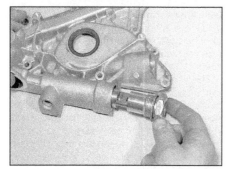

17.7a Unscrew the thermostatic valve plug . . .

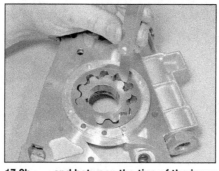

17.7b . . . then withdraw the spring and valve assembly

threaded plug and recover the valve spring and plunger **(see illustrations)**. Discard the threaded plug – a new one must be used on refitting.

7 Similarly, the thermostatic valve (which diverts

the oil to the oil cooler) can be dismantled as follows **(see illustrations)**.

a) *Unscrew the thermostatic valve plug. Recover the sealing washer and discard it.*

b) *Withdraw the spring and valve assembly from the oil pump body. Do not attempt to separate the spring from the valve.*

Inspection

8 Inspect the rotors for obvious signs of wear or damage and renew if necessary. If the pump body or cover plate is scored or damaged, then the complete oil pump assembly must be renewed.

9 Using feeler blades of the appropriate thickness, measure the clearance between the outer rotor and the pump body, then between the tips of the inner and outer rotor **(see illustrations)**.

10 Using feeler blades and a straight-edge placed across the top of the pump body and the rotors, measure the rotor endfloat **(see illustration)**.

11 If any measurement is outside the specified limits, the complete pump assembly must be renewed.

12 If the pressure relief valve plunger is scored, or if it does not slide freely in the pump body bore, then it must be renewed. Check the free length of the relief valve spring, which should be as specified.

13 Check the thermostatic valve spring for distortion and corrosion, and check that the valve slides freely in the pump body bore. If there are any signs of damage or wear to the spring or valve, the spring and valve assembly must be renewed. Thoroughly clean the threads of the valve plug, and the plug threads in the oil pump body.

Reassembly

14 Clean all traces of sealant from the mating faces of the oil pump body and the cover plate. Thoroughly clean the threads of the cover plate securing bolts, and ensure that the cover plate bolt threads in the pump body are clean and dry – **do not** use a tap to clean the threads.

15 Lubricate the pump rotors with clean engine oil and refit them to the pump body, ensuring that the punched marks on the faces of the rotors face away from the pump cover plate **(see illustration)**.

16 Apply a 1 mm bead of the specified sealant (see Note at the beginning of this Section) to the edge of the pump cover plate, then refit

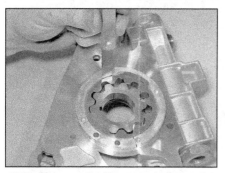

17.9a Measure the clearance between the outer rotor and the pump body . . .

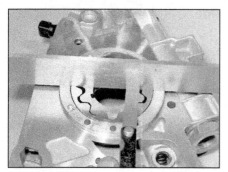

17.10 Measuring the rotor endfloat

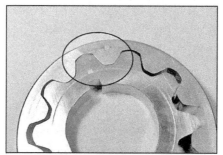

17.9b . . . and between the tips of the inner and outer rotors

17.15 The punched marks on the faces of the rotors must face away from the pump cover plate

the cover plate, ensuring that the marks made on the cover plate and pump body before removal are aligned (where applicable, the TOP marking should on the cover plate should be at the top of the pump).

17 Coat the threads of the cover plate securing screws with thread-locking compound, then refit and tighten the screws.

18 Check that the pump rotates freely, then prime it by injecting oil into its passages and rotating it. If a long time elapses before the pump is refitted to the engine, prime it again before installation.

19 Lubricate the oil pressure relief valve bore, and the spring and plunger with clean engine oil. Refit the oil pressure relief valve plunger, ensuring that it is the correct way up, and then install the spring. Fit a new threaded plug, and tighten the plug securely.

20 Lubricate the thermostatic valve, spring and the valve bore in the oil pump body with clean engine oil.

21 Clamp the oil pump body in a vice, with the thermostatic valve bore facing vertically upwards. The valve bore must be as near vertical as possible.

22 Insert the valve and spring assembly into the valve bore in the oil pump body, ensuring that the assembly is positioned centrally in the bore. The valve will not seat correctly in the valve plug if it is not positioned centrally.

23 Fit a new sealing washer to the valve plug, then coat the threads of the plug with thread-locking compound, and screw the plug into position by hand, making sure that the valve is not displaced as the plug is tightened.

24 When the plug has been fully screwed down, tighten it to the specified torque.

25 Refit the oil pump as described in Section 16.

18 Crankshaft oil seals
– renewal

Right-hand seal

1 Remove the timing belt as described in Section 7.

2 Remove the timing belt gear from the end of the crankshaft.

3 Punch or drill two small holes opposite each other in the seal. Screw a self-tapping screw into each and pull on the screws with pliers to extract the seal.

4 Clean the seal housing and polish off any burrs or raised edges, which may have caused the original seal to fail.

5 Using a suitable tubular drift, such as a socket, which bears only on the hard outer edge of the seal, drive the seal into position. To protect the seal lip, wrap a thin layer of insulating tape around the crankshaft.

Caution: Do not lubricate the seal recess, the seal lip, or the seal running surface on the shaft.

6 Remove all traces of the insulating tape,

18.11 Slide the protector sleeve, oil seal and housing assembly over the end of the crankshaft – viewed with engine removed

then slide the timing belt gear back onto the end of the crankshaft. Refit the timing belt as described in see Section 7.

Left-hand seal

Note: *The seal is integral with the oil seal housing – a complete new housing/seal assembly must be fitted.*

Note: *The following new parts are needed – oil seal/housing assembly, MG Rover sealant kit GUG 705963GM (for sump joint).*

7 Remove the flywheel as described in Section 19.

8 Remove the sump as described in Section 15.

9 Unscrew the securing bolts, and remove the crankshaft oil seal housing.

10 Thoroughly clean the oil seal running surface on the crankshaft, the oil seal housing mating faces on the cylinder block, and the bolt and dowel holes in the cylinder block.

⚠ *Warning: Do not lubricate the oil seal or the seal running surfaces on the crankshaft. The new oil seal/housing assembly will be supplied fitted with a seal protector. Do not separate the protector sleeve from the oil seal, and do not touch the oil seal lip. If the seal is inadvertently touched, it must not be fitted, as the coating applied to the seal during manufacture will be destroyed, and this may result in oil leakage.*

11 Carefully slide the seal protector sleeve, oil seal and housing assembly over the end of the crankshaft, taking care not to touch the seal lip **(see illustration)**.

12 Locate the housing against the cylinder

18.13 Crankshaft oil seal housing bolt tightening sequence

block, noting that the oil seal protector will be pushed out as the housing/seal assembly is pushed into position.

13 Refit the housing securing bolts, and tighten them to the specified torque in order **(see illustration)**.

14 Refit the sump as described in Section 15.

15 Refit the flywheel as described in Section 19.

19 Flywheel/driveplate
– removal, inspection and refitting

Flywheel

Note: *New flywheel retaining bolts must be used on refitting.*

Removal

1 Remove the clutch assembly as described in Chapter 6.

2 If not already done, turn the crankshaft until the locking pin can be inserted into the flywheel, as described in Section 3. Additionally, lock the flywheel by bolting a suitable tool to the transmission mounting plate, to engage with the flywheel ring gear teeth.

3 Slacken and remove the flywheel retaining bolts and discard them **(see illustration)**. The bolts must be renewed whenever they are disturbed.

4 Remove the flywheel **(see illustration)**, taking care not to drop it, as it is very heavy.

19.3 Unscrewing a flywheel bolt – note tool (arrowed) to prevent flywheel from turning

19.4 Lifting off the flywheel

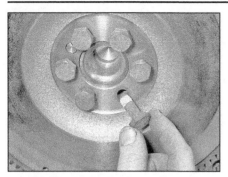

19.8 Fit new flywheel securing bolts

19.9a Tighten the flywheel bolts to the specified torque . . .

19.9b . . . then through the specified angle

Inspection

5 If the flywheel clutch mating surface is deeply scored, cracked or otherwise damaged, then the flywheel must be renewed, unless it is possible to have it surface ground. Seek the advice of a Rover dealer or engine reconditioning specialist.

6 If the ring gear is badly worn or has missing teeth, then it must be renewed. This job is best left to a Rover dealer or engine reconditioning specialist. The temperature to which the new ring gear must be heated for installation (350°C – shown by an even light blue colour) is critical and, if not done accurately, the hardness of the teeth will be destroyed.

Refitting

7 Clean the mating surfaces of the flywheel and crankshaft. Clean any remaining adhesive from the threads of the crankshaft threaded holes by carefully using a suitable tap.

8 Position the flywheel over the locating dowel in the end of the crankshaft, press it into place and fit six **new** bolts **(see illustration)**.

9 Lock the flywheel using the method employed on dismantling then, working in a diagonal sequence, progressively tighten the retaining bolts to the specified torque wrench setting in the two stages given **(see illustrations)**.

10 Refit the clutch assembly as described in Chapter 6.

Driveplate

11 All procedures are essentially the same as described for the flywheel, disregarding

references to the clutch. To access the drive-plate, remove the automatic transmission and torque converter as described in Chapter 7B. Note that driveplate bolts are not renewed and are tightened to a higher torque than flywheel bolts.

20 Engine/transmission mountings – inspection, removal and refitting

Inspection

Note: *Normally, mountings will need renewing only if the rubber has hardened or cracked, or separated from the metal backing. Dependent upon the fault, such conditions may allow excess engine movement, leading to an impression of rough running, knocking or bumping.*

Note: *The mountings can be visually checked for rubber deterioration, and separation can be checked by levering with a pry bar between the rubber and metal backing. If any fault is found, the mounting must be renewed.*

Engine lower steady bar

Removal

1 Apply the handbrake, then jack up the front of the vehicle and support securely on axle stands (see *Jacking and vehicle support*).

2 Remove the engine splash guard, with reference to Chapter 11, Section 25, if necessary.

3 Working under the vehicle, unscrew the through-bolt securing the engine steady bar to the suspension crossmember **(see illustration)**.

4 Unscrew the through-bolt securing the steady bar to the bracket on the sump, and then withdraw the steady bar **(see illustration)**.

Refitting

5 Refitting is a reversal of removal, but tighten the through-bolts to the specified torque.

Left-hand mounting

Removal

6 Disconnect the battery earth lead, and then the battery positive lead.

7 Remove the battery clamp, and lift out the battery.

8 Remove two bolts securing the engine control module (ECM) clamp to the battery tray. Tie the ECM/clamp clear of the work area

9 Remove the air cleaner as described in Chapter 4C.

10 To make access easier, remove three bolts securing the base of the battery tray, and slacken three bolts under the tray. Where applicable, release the ABS fuse holder from the battery tray, and remove the tray.

11 Apply the handbrake, chock the rear roadwheels, then jack up the front of the car and support it on axle stands (see *Jacking and vehicle support*).

12 Undo the retaining bolts and remove the engine splash guard.

13 Position a trolley jack under the transmission, with a wooden block between the jack head and transmission housing. Raise the jack to just take the weight of the engine/transmission.

14 Remove the two bolts securing the mounting to the bracket on the transmission.

15 Lower the trolley jack until it is possible to access the four mounting bolts to the vehicle body.

16 Remove the four mounting bolts in the vehicle body and withdraw the mounting.

Refitting

17 Refitting is a reversal of the removal procedure noting:

Use a torque wrench to tighten the bolts to the specified torque.

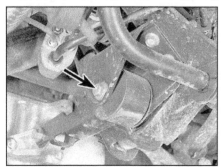

20.3 Unscrew the through-bolt (arrowed) securing the engine steady bar to the suspension crossmember

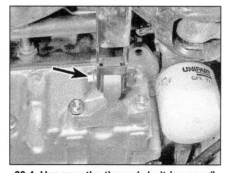

20.4 Unscrew the through-bolt (arrowed) securing the engine steady bar to the sump

Right-hand mounting

Removal

18 Disconnect the battery earth lead.
19 Apply the handbrake, chock the rear roadwheels, then jack up the front of the car and support it on axle stands (see *Jacking and vehicle support*). Remove the right-hand roadwheel.
20 Undo the retaining bolts and remove the engine splash guard.
21 Position a trolley jack under the sump, with a wooden block between the jack head and sump. Raise the jack to just take the weight of the engine/transmission.
22 Remove the through-bolt securing the upper steady bar to the mounting bracket **(see illustration)**.
23 Remove the through-bolt securing the upper steady to the body bracket, and remove the steady bar. To make access easier, undo the retaining bolts and move the power steering reservoir to one side.
24 Remove the nut securing the mounting bracket to the mounting.
25 Remove the bolts securing the mounting bracket to the engine, and remove the bracket **(see illustration)**.
26 Remove the remaining bolts securing the mounting to the body, and remove the mounting.

Refitting

27 Refit is a reversal of the removal procedure, noting:
a) *First fit the mounting to the body, and loosely tighten the nut.*
b) *Fit and align the mounting bracket, restraint bar and steady bar, and fit the bolts and nuts.*
c) *Use a torque wrench to tighten all bolts and nuts to the specified torque.*

21 Engine oil cooler – removal and refitting

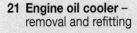

General

1 The engine coolant thermostat is located in the detachable lower housing of the cooler assembly **(see illustration)**.

20.22 Remove steady-to-mounting bracket through-bolt (arrowed)

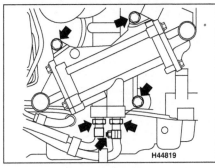

21.1 Oil cooler attachment and connections

Removal

Note: *The following new parts are needed – oil pipe O-rings.*
2 Remove the radiator as described in Chapter 3.
3 Slacken the securing clips and disconnect the following hoses:
a) *Cooler bottom hose.*
b) *Cooler top hose.*
c) *Coolant pump hose.*
d) *Hoses from coolant rails.*
4 Remove the bolt and oil pipe clamp.
5 Position a container under the cooler to collect any oil that may spill out.
6 Slacken the union nuts and disconnect the cooler oil pipes. Discard the O-rings.
7 Undo the three retaining bolts, and remove the cooler assembly **(see illustration)**.

Refitting

8 Refitting is a reversal of the removal procedure, noting:

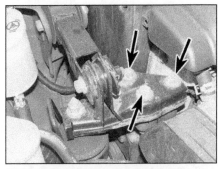

20.25 Remove the three bracket-to-engine bolts (arrowed)

21.7 Oil cooler location – viewed from underneath

a) *Fit new O-rings to the oil pipes.*
b) *Use a torque wrench to tighten the bolts and nuts to the specified torque.*
c) *Check/top-up the engine oil level.*

22 Auxiliary drivebelt tensioner – removal and refitting

Removal

1 Remove the power steering drivebelt, as described in Chapter 10.
2 Remove the centre bolt securing the tensioner to the mounting bracket, and remove the tensioner.

Refitting

3 Locate the tensioner on the dowel then fit and tighten the centre bolt to the specified torque.
4 Refit the drivebelt.

Notes

Chapter 2 Part D:
Petrol engine removal and overhaul procedures

Contents

Section number

Crankshaft – inspection 15
Crankshaft – refitting 19
Crankshaft – removal 11
Cylinder block/crankcase – cleaning and inspection. 12
Cylinder head – dismantling 7
Cylinder head – reassembly. 9
Cylinder head and valves – cleaning and inspection 8
Cylinder liners – removal and refitting 13
Engine – initial start-up after overhaul 21
Engine and transmission (4-cylinder) – removal, separation and
  refitting 4

Section number

Engine and transmission (6-cylinder) – removal, separation and
  refitting 5
Engine overhaul – dismantling sequence. 6
Engine overhaul – general information. 2
Engine overhaul – reassembly sequence. 17
Engine/transmission removal – methods and precautions 3
General information 1
Main and big-end bearings – inspection 16
Piston rings – refitting. 18
Piston/connecting rod assembly – inspection 14
Piston/connecting rod assembly – refitting 20
Piston/connecting rod assembly – removal 10

Degrees of difficulty

Easy, suitable for novice with little experience	**Fairly easy,** suitable for beginner with some experience	**Fairly difficult,** suitable for competent DIY mechanic	**Difficult,** suitable for experienced DIY mechanic	**Very difficult,** suitable for expert DIY or professional

Specifications

Cylinder block/crankcase

Material. . . . . Aluminium alloy
Cylinder liner bore diameter – 65 mm from top of bore:
  1.4 litre engines:
    Standard – grade A (Red) . . . . 74.970 to 74.985 mm
    Standard – grade B (Blue). . . . . 74.986 to 75.000 mm
  All other engines:
    Standard – grade A (Red) . . . . 80.000 to 80.015 mm
    Standard – grade B (Blue). . . . . 80.016 to 80.030 mm

Crankshaft

4-cylinder engine

Number of main bearings. 5
Main bearing journal diameter . . . . 47.986 to 48.007 mm
Main bearing journal sizes:
  Grade 1. . . . . 48.000 to 48.007 mm
  Grade 2. . . . . 47.993 to 48.000 mm
  Grade 3. . . . . 47.986 to 47.993 mm
Big-end journal diameter:
  1.4 and 1.6 litre engines . . . . 42.986 to 43.007 mm
  1.8 litre engine . . . . 47.986 to 48.007 mm
Big-end journal size grades:
  1.4 and 1.6 litre engines:
    Grade A. . . . . 43.000 to 43.007 mm
    Grade B. . . . . 42.993 to 43.000 mm
    Grade C . . . . 42.986 to 42.993 mm
  1.8 litre engine:
    Grade A. . . . . 48.000 to 48.007 mm
    Grade B. . . . . 47.993 to 48.000 mm
    Grade C . . . . 47.986 to 47.993 mm
Main bearing and big-end bearing journal maximum ovality. . . . . 0.010 mm
Main bearing and big-end bearing running clearance . . . . 0.021 to 0.049 mm
Crankshaft endfloat:
  Standard. . . . . 0.10 to 0.25 mm
  Service limit . . . . 0.34 mm
Thrustwasher thickness . . . . 2.61 to 2.65 mm

Crankshaft (continued)

6-cylinder engine

Main bearing journal diameter	67.731 to 67.749 mm
Main bearing journal size grades:	
Grade 1	67.743 to 67.749 mm
Grade 2	67.737 to 67.743 mm
Grade 3	67.731 to 67.737 mm
Main bearing ladder diameters:	
Grade A	71.600 to 71.593 mm
Grade B	71.593 to 71.586 mm
Grade C	71.586 to 71.579 mm
Big-end (crankpin) journal diameter	54.037 to 54.055 mm
Big-end (crankpin) journal size grades:	
Grade A	54.049 to 54.055 mm
Grade B	54.043 to 54.049 mm
Grade C	54.037 to 54.043 mm
Big-end housing size grades:	
Grade A	57.677 to 57.671 mm
Grade B	57.671 to 57.665 mm
Grade C	57.665 to 57.659 mm
Maximum journal ovality	0.01 mm
Main bearing running clearance	0.021 to 0.039 mm
Big-end bearing running clearance	0.022 to 0.040 mm
Crankshaft endfloat:	
Standard	0.10 to 0.30 mm
Service limit	0.40 mm
Thrustwasher thickness	2.61 to 2.65 mm

Pistons and piston rings

Piston diameter:	
1.4 litre engines:	
Grade A	74.940 to 74.955 mm
Grade B	74.956 to 74.970 mm
All other engines:	
Grade A	79.975 to 79.990 mm
Grade B	79.991 to 80.005 mm
Piston-to-bore clearance:	
1.4 litre engines	0.015 to 0.045 mm
All other engines	0.010 to 0.040 mm
Piston ring end gaps (fitted 20 mm from top of bore):	
1.4 litre engines:	
Top compression ring	0.17 to 0.37 mm
Second compression ring	0.37 to 0.57 mm
Oil control ring	0.15 to 0.40 mm
All other engines:	
Top compression ring	0.20 to 0.35 mm
Second compression ring	0.28 to 0.48 mm
Oil control ring	0.15 to 0.40 mm
Piston ring-to-groove clearance:	
1.4 litre engines:	
Top compression ring	0.040 to 0.080 mm
Second compression ring	0.030 to 0.062 mm
Oil control ring – all models	0.044 to 0.055 mm
All other engines:	
Top compression ring	0.040 to 0.072 mm
Second compression ring	0.030 to 0.062 mm
Oil control ring	0.010 to 0.180 mm

Cylinder head

Material	Aluminium alloy
Height	118.95 to 119.05 mm
Reface limit	0.20 mm
Maximum acceptable gasket face distortion	0.05 mm
Valve seat angle	45°
Valve seat width:	
Inlet	1.6 mm
Exhaust	1.2 mm

Valves

Stem diameter:
    Inlet . . . . 5.952 to 5.967 mm
    Exhaust . . . . 5.947 to 5.962 mm
Guide inside diameter . . . . 6.000 to 6.025 mm
Stem-to-guide clearance:
    Inlet:
        Standard . . . . 0.033 to 0.063 mm
        Service limit . . . . 0.110 mm
    Exhaust:
        Standard . . . . 0.038 to 0.078 mm
        Service limit . . . . 0.110 mm
Valve spring free length . . . . 50.0 mm
Valve guide fitted height . . . . 6.0 mm
Valve stem installed height:
    New . . . . 38.93 to 39.84 mm
    Service limit . . . . 40.10 mm

Torque wrench settings

Refer to Chapter 2A or 2B

1 General information

Included in this part of the Chapter are details of removing the engine/transmission unit from the vehicle and general overhaul procedures for the cylinder head, cylinder block/crankcase and all other engine internal components.

The information given ranges from advice concerning preparation for an overhaul and the purchase of new parts to detailed step-by-step procedures covering removal, inspection, renovation and refitting of engine internal components.

After Section 6, all instructions are based on the assumption that the engine has been removed from the vehicle. For information concerning in-car engine repair, as well as the removal and refitting of those external components necessary for full overhaul, refer to Part 2A or 2B of this Chapter and to Section 6. Ignore any preliminary dismantling operations described in relevant in-car-repair sections that are no longer relevant once the engine has been removed from the vehicle.

Apart from torque wrench settings, which are given at the beginning of the relevant in-car repair procedure Chapter (2A or 2B), all specifications relating to engine overhaul are at the beginning of this Part of Chapter 2.

2 Engine overhaul – general information

It is not always easy to determine when, or if, an engine should be completely overhauled, as a number of factors must be considered.

High mileage is not necessarily an indication that an overhaul is needed, while low mileage does not preclude the need for an overhaul.

Frequency of servicing is probably the most important consideration. An engine that has had regular and frequent oil and filter changes, as well as other required maintenance, should give many thousands of miles of reliable service. Conversely, a neglected engine may require an overhaul very early in its life. If a complete service does not remedy any problems, major mechanical work is the only solution.

Excessive oil consumption is an indication that piston rings, valve seals and/or valve guides are in need of attention. Make sure that oil leaks are not responsible before deciding that the rings and/or guides are worn. Perform a compression test to determine the likely cause of the problem (see Chapter 2A or 2B).

Check the oil pressure with a gauge fitted in place of the oil pressure switch and compare it with that specified (see Chapter 2A or 2B Specifications). If it is extremely low, the main and big-end bearings and/or the oil pump are probably worn out.

Loss of power, rough running, knocking or metallic engine noises, excessive valve gear noise and high fuel consumption may also point to the need for an overhaul, especially if they are all present at the same time.

An engine overhaul involves restoring all internal parts to the specification of a new engine. During an overhaul, the cylinder liners, the pistons and the piston rings are renewed. New main and big-end bearings are generally fitted and, if necessary, the crankshaft may be renewed to restore the journals. The valves are serviced as well, since they are usually in less than perfect condition at this point. While the engine is being overhauled, other components, such as the starter and alternator, can be overhauled as well. The end result should be an as-new engine that will give many trouble-free miles.

Critical cooling system components such as the hoses, thermostat and coolant pump should be renewed when an engine is overhauled. The radiator should be checked carefully to ensure that it is not clogged or leaking. Also it is a good idea to renew the oil pump whenever the engine is overhauled.

Before beginning the engine overhaul, read through the entire procedure to familiarise yourself with the scope and requirements of the job. Overhauling an engine is not difficult if you follow carefully all of the instructions, have the necessary tools and equipment and pay close attention to all specifications. However, it can be time-consuming. Plan on the vehicle being off the road for a minimum of two weeks, especially if parts must be taken to an engineering works for repair or reconditioning. Check on the availability of parts and make sure that any necessary special tools and equipment are obtained in advance. Most work can be done with typical hand tools, although a number of precision measuring tools are required for inspecting parts to determine if they must be renewed. Often the engineering works will handle the inspection of parts and offer advice concerning reconditioning and renewal.

Always wait until the engine has been completely dismantled and all components, especially the cylinder block/crankcase, the cylinder liners and the crankshaft have been inspected before deciding what service and repair operations must be performed by an engineering works. Since the condition of these components will be the major factor to consider when determining whether to overhaul the original engine or buy a reconditioned unit, do not purchase parts or have overhaul work done on other components until they have been thoroughly inspected. As a general rule, time is the primary cost of an overhaul, so it does not pay to fit worn or substandard parts.

As a final note, to ensure maximum life and minimum trouble from a reconditioned engine, everything must be assembled with care in a spotlessly clean environment.

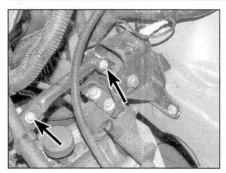

**4.11 Remove engine steady bar bolts
– arrowed**

3 Engine/transmission removal
– methods and precautions

If you have decided that the engine must be removed for overhaul or major repair work, several preliminary steps should be taken.

Locating a suitable place to work is extremely important. Adequate workspace, along with storage space for the vehicle, will be needed. If a workshop or garage is not available, at the very least a flat, level, clean work surface is required.

Cleaning the engine compartment and engine/transmission before beginning the removal procedure will help keep things clean and organised.

An engine hoist or A-frame will also be necessary. Make sure the equipment is rated in excess of the combined weight of the engine and transmission. Safety is of primary importance, considering the potential hazards involved in lifting the engine/transmission unit out of the vehicle. The engine/transmission unit is removed by lifting it out from above the engine compartment.

When removing an engine/transmission unit an assistant should always be available, as some of the procedures will need the an extra pair of hands. Advice and aid from someone more experienced would also be helpful. There are many instances when one person cannot simultaneously perform all of the operations required when lifting the unit out of the vehicle.

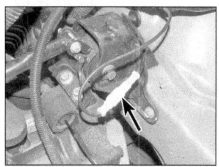

**4.12 Disconnect the wiring connector
– arrowed**

Plan the operation ahead of time. Before starting work, arrange for the hire of or obtain all of the tools and equipment you will need. Some of the equipment necessary to perform engine/transmission removal and installation safely and with relative ease are (in addition to an engine hoist) a heavy duty trolley jack, complete sets of spanners and sockets as described at the rear of this Manual, wooden blocks and plenty of rags and cleaning solvent for mopping-up spilled oil, coolant and fuel. If the hoist must be hired, make sure that you arrange for it in advance and perform all of the operations possible without it beforehand. This will save you money and time.

Plan for the vehicle to be out of use for quite a while. An engineering works will be required to perform some of the work, which the do-it-yourselfer cannot accomplish without special equipment. These places often have a busy schedule, so it would be a good idea to consult them before removing the engine in order to accurately estimate the amount of time required to rebuild or repair components that may need work.

Always be extremely careful when removing and refitting the engine/transmission unit. Serious injury can result from careless actions. Plan ahead, take your time and a job of this nature, although major, can be accomplished successfully.

4 Engine/transmission (4-cylinder) – removal, separation and refitting

Caution: Read the notes in Section 3 – 'Engine/transmission removal – methods and precautions'.
Note: *The following new parts are needed: power steering pump outlet hose O-ring and exhaust front pipe gasket. On 1.8 models only: gear selector rod roll-pin.*
Note: *Two lifting brackets, to bolt to the engine, are needed. These can be made from steel plate, and must be strong enough to carry the weight of the engine/transmission assembly. One bracket is to be bolted to the tapped hole adjacent to the dipstick tube, and the other is be bolted to the tapped holes for the exhaust camshaft rear cover plate.*
Note: *As they are disconnected, make a note or sketch of the position, route and clipping of all wires, harnesses, pipes and hoses.*

Removal

1 Disconnect both battery leads – earth lead first. Remove the battery clamp, and lift out the battery.
2 Remove the air cleaner assembly – see Chapter 4A.
3 Remove the bolts securing the engine control module (ECM) to its mounting bracket on the bulkhead. Disconnect the main engine harness multiplug from the ECM. Seal the ECM and multiplug in plastic bags, and tie clear of the work area.

4 Where applicable, release the ABS fuse holder from the battery tray. Remove three bolts from the base of the battery tray, and slacken three bolts under the tray. Lift out the tray.
5 Open the engine compartment fusebox. Remove the screw securing the positive lead to the fusebox, and disconnect the engine wiring loom multiplug in the fusebox.
6 Release two multiplugs from the bracket adjacent to the charcoal canister on the bulkhead. Disconnect the engine harness multiplugs from the main harness, and remove the engine harness from the bracket. Tie the engine harness across the top of the engine.
7 Apply the handbrake, chock the rear roadwheels, then jack up the front of the car and support it on axle stands (see *Jacking and vehicle support*). Remove the right hand front roadwheel.
8 Drain the engine oil and coolant – see Chapter 1A.
9 Drain the transmission oil/fluid – see Chapter 7A or 7B.
10 Remove the bolt securing the negative lead to the starter motor.
11 Remove two bolts attaching the engine left-hand steady bar to the engine bracket and engine mounting, and remove the steady bar **(see illustration)**.
12 Where fitted disconnect the cylindrical electrical connector adjacent to the left-hand engine mounting – the connector is in the lead going down to the roadwheel sensor at the right-hand front wheel **(see illustration)**.
13 Where applicable, disconnect the clutch fluid supply pipe from the slave cylinder, as described in Chapter 6.
14 Slacken the clips and disconnect the following hoses:
  a) *Radiator bottom hose from coolant rail.*
  b) *Radiator top hose from outlet elbow.*
  c) *Heater return hose from outlet elbow.*
  d) *Expansion tank hose from inlet manifold.*
  e) *Coolant hose from thermostat housing.*
  f) *Heater hose from coolant rail.*
15 Release the heater hose from two clips on the coolant rail and engine harness.
16 Remove two nuts securing the exhaust pipe front section to the exhaust manifold, and discard the gasket.
17 Pack some absorbent cloth around the fuel pipe connections. Depress the quick-release connectors, and disconnect the pipes with reference to Chapter 4A.
Caution: Plug the pipe connections.
18 Release the throttle outer cable nut from the abutment bracket, and then release the inner cable from the cam. Withdraw the cable releasing it from the retaining clip(s) on the inlet manifold.
19 Depress the collar on the quick-release connector, and disconnect the brake servo vacuum pipe from the inlet manifold.

Air conditioned models

20 Remove the bolt securing the air conditioning pipe to the support bracket.

21 Fit a 13 mm spanner onto the hexagon on the belt tensioner, and rotate the spanner fully clockwise. To lock in this position, fit a suitable pin – not exceeding 3 mm diameter – into the tensioner backplate.

22 Release the auxiliary drivebelt from the alternator and compressor.

23 Disconnect the air conditioning compressor multiplug.

24 Remove three bolts securing the compressor, release the compressor, and tie clear of the work area.

All models

25 Disconnect both driveshafts from the transmission – see Chapter 8.

Caution: Tie-up the driveshafts to avoid strain on the outer joints, and to keep clear the area under the engine and transmission.

26 Slacken the through-bolt securing the engine/transmission lower steady bar to the suspension crossmember. Remove the through-bolt securing the steady bar to the sump bracket, and move the bar away from the engine (see illustration).

27 Position a container under the power steering pump.

28 Slacken the clip securing the inlet hose to the pump, and disconnect the hose.

29 Remove the bolt securing the outlet hose clamp to the bracket, and disconnect the outlet hose. Discard the O-ring.

Caution: Plug the hose and pump connections.

30 On R65 transmissions, use a lever, or flat-blade screwdriver and release the balljoints from the gear selector lever, and the gearchange lever (see illustration).

31 On PG1 transmissions, remove the bolt securing the gearchange steady bar to the gearbox, and release the steady bar and washers. Remove the metal clip from the gear selector rod, and drive out the roll-pin (see illustrations).

32 Remove two bolts securing the exhaust camshaft rear cover plate to the cylinder head, and remove the plate. Use the two bolts to attach the manufactured lifting bracket. Tighten the bolt securely (see illustration).

33 Attach the other bracket to the side of the cylinder head, using the tapped hole adjacent to the dipstick tube. Tighten the bolt securely (see illustration).

34 Attach the lifting equipment to the lifting brackets, and connect to the hoist. Raise the hoist to just take the weight of the engine/transmission assembly.

35 Remove the engine right-hand and left-hand mountings – see part A of this Chapter.

36 Make a final check to ensure that all pipes, hoses, and cables, etc, have been disconnected from the engine/transmission assembly, and tied clear of the work area.

37 With the aid of an assistant, raise the hoist slightly, and tilt the engine/transmission assembly to lower the gearbox. Taking care not to damage components in the engine bay, carefully raise the engine/transmission,

4.26 Remove steady bar through-bolt – arrowed

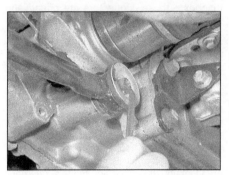

4.31a Release the gearchange steady bar . . .

and manoeuvre from the engine bay. Lower the assembly to the ground, and support on wooden blocks.

Separation

38 With the engine/transmission assembly removed, support the assembly on suitable blocks of wood, on a workbench (or failing that, on a clean area of the workshop floor).

39 To separate the transmission from the engine, first remove the starter motor with reference to Chapter 5A.

Manual transmission models

40 Progressively unscrew and remove the transmission-to-engine bolts, noting where each one goes, and the location of any brackets attached, for guidance when refitting.

41 With the help of an assistant, withdraw the transmission directly from the engine, making sure that its weight is not allowed to

4.32 Remove exhaust camshaft cover plate and attach lifting bracket

4.30 Release gear selector balljoints – R65 transmissions

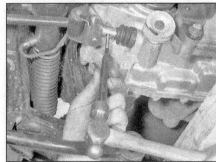

4.31b . . . and drive out the roll-pin

bear on the input shaft. Note that there are two locating dowels used.

Automatic transmission models

42 The torque converter is attached to the driveplate by four bolts, which are accessed through an aperture on the end face of the transmission. Remove the single securing bolt, and then withdraw the grommet from the access hole. Turn the engine as required to position each bolt in the aperture in turn, then unscrew and remove them.

43 Slacken and remove the bolts securing the transmission to the engine. Note the correct fitted positions of each bolt, and the necessary brackets, as they are removed to use as a reference on refitting.

44 Carefully prise the transmission off the engine, to free its locating dowels. As the transmission is removed, make sure the torque converter is kept pushed fully onto the transmission shaft.

4.33 Attach bracket to side of cylinder head

45 Once the transmission is free, secure the torque converter in position by bolting a length of metal bar to one of the housing holes.

Refitting

46 Fit the lifting equipment to the lifting brackets, and attach to the hoist.
47 With the aid of an assistant, raise the engine/transmission, and manoeuvre into the engine bay.
48 Further refitting is a reversal of the removal procedure, noting the following:
   a) Fit both engine mountings and both steady bars – see Chapter 2A.
   b) Tighten all bolts sufficiently to secure the mountings and steady bars – but not to final tightness. Release the hoist and lifting equipment.
   c) When the engine is settled on the mountings, use a torque wrench to tighten all mounting and steady bar bolts to the specified torque.
   d) Use a torque wrench to tighten all nuts and bolts to the specified torque.
   e) Fit a new O-ring the power steering outlet hose – lubricate the O-ring with PAS fluid before connecting the hose.
   f) Fit a new gasket to the exhaust pipe front section.
   g) Ensure that all cables and pipes are correctly connected, clipped and routed, as identified before removal.
   h) Fill the engine with new oil, and fill the cooling system with a 50/50 mix of water and antifreeze. If drained, fill the transmission with new oil/fluid – see Chapter 7A or 7B.
   i) Top-up and bleed the power steering system – see Chapter 10.
   j) Check/adjust the throttle cable – see Chapter 4A.

5 Engine and transmission (6-cylinder) – removal, separation and refitting

Removal

1 Park the car on firm, level ground.
2 Drain the cooling system as described in Chapter 1A.
3 Depressurise the fuel system and remove the air cleaner as described in Chapter 4B.
4 Remove the battery and its tray as described in Chapter 5A. Remove the bolts securing the engine control module (ECM) to its mounting bracket, disconnect and move it to one side.
5 Remove the bonnet as described in Chapter 11.
6 Unscrew the three bolts, and remove the air cleaner mounting bracket.
7 Release the hose clips at each end, and disconnect the bleed hose from the radiator and expansion tank. Remove the single mounting bolt, then unhook the mounting lugs and free the expansion tank from the radiator. Release the hose clip, and disconnect the

lower hose from the expansion tank, after which the tank can be removed completely.
8 Release the radiator top hose clip, and detach the hose from the radiator. Lift the hose out of its support clip, then unbolt the support clip and remove it from the radiator.
9 Referring to Chapter 5A if necessary, disconnect the starter motor wiring. Also remove the starter motor mounting bolt which secures the engine earth strap.
10 Open the engine compartment fusebox, then disconnect the main wiring multiplug and the bolts securing the battery leads.
11 Disconnect the two engine harness wiring connectors behind the engine compartment fusebox – these connectors are effectively 'screw-type', in that they unscrew from each other.
12 Release the clip and disconnect the hose from the canister-purge solenoid valve. Trace the hose from the valve, and disconnect it at the fuel rail.
13 Release the hose clips and disconnect the hoses from the coolant elbow on top of the engine.
14 Where applicable, disconnect the clutch fluid supply pipe from the slave cylinder, as described in Chapter 6.
15 On manual transmission models, referring to Chapter 7A if necessary, disconnect the gearchange cables from the selector levers and support brackets. Disconnect the reversing light switch wiring plug above the left-hand driveshaft.
16 Unbolt and remove the power steering pump – move the pump to one side, without disconnecting the fluid hoses.
17 If not already done, loosen the front wheel bolts, then jack up the front of the car and support it on axle stands. Remove the front wheels.
18 Drain the transmission oil or fluid as described in Chapter 7A or 7B.
19 On models with air conditioning, carry out the following:
   a) Remove the auxiliary drivebelt as described in Chapter 5A.
   b) Remove the Torx bolt securing the drivebelt idler pulley.
   c) Remove the oil cooler as described in Chapter 2B.
   d) Remove the three mounting bolts, and tie the air conditioning compressor to one side, without disconnecting the hoses.
20 Disconnect the oil pressure switch wiring plug (behind the crankshaft pulley).
21 Unscrew the front and rear manifold-to-downpipe nuts, and separate the joints. Remove the exhaust front pipe support bracket, which is secured by two bolts.
22 Remove the engine lower mounting as described in Chapter 2B.
23 Working in the front wheel arches, unclip the front caliper brake hose, and the ABS and pad wear sensor wiring, from the support clip. Disconnect the pad wear sensor wiring plug. Repeat this process on the other front wheel.
24 With reference to Chapter 10, disconnect

the track rod ends and lower arm balljoints from the front hubs.
25 Unscrew the two bolts securing the right-hand driveshaft bearing support bracket to the back of the engine.
26 Prise the left-hand driveshaft out of the transmission, while an assistant pulls the left-hand front wheel outwards. Recover the circlip from the end of the shaft, and obtain a new one for refitting. Tie the driveshaft to one side.
27 Similarly, pull out the right-hand driveshaft from the transmission (in this case, no prising should be required), and tie it to one side.
28 The engine is removed by lifting it out. Although this is possible without removing the radiator, clearance is tight – we recommend that the radiator's rear surface be protected with a sheet of card before proceeding further. Refitting the engine is made much easier if the radiator is removed as described in Chapter 3, but this itself is quite an involved procedure.
29 Attach the engine hoist, and raise it so that the weight of the engine is taken evenly off the mountings.
30 With the engine supported, remove the right-hand mounting completely as described in Chapter 2B.
31 Remove the left-hand mounting through-bolt, and then unbolt the left-hand mounting and bracket from the transmission and inner wing (four bolts each).
32 Raise the engine slightly on the hoist, until the heater hose on the rear of the block is accessible. Release the clip and disconnect the hose.
33 Make a final check that all necessary components have been removed, disconnected, or moved sufficiently clear. With the help of an assistant, manoeuvre the engine and transmission up and out of the engine compartment. When clear of the car, lower it to the ground. Be prepared to steady the engine when it touches down, to stop it toppling over. If the engine is lowered onto some old carpet or card, this will protect it, and make it easier to drag around as necessary.

Separation

34 With the engine/transmission assembly removed, support the assembly on suitable blocks of wood, on a workbench (or failing that, on a clean area of the workshop floor).
35 To separate the transmission from the engine, first remove the starter motor with reference to Chapter 5A.

Manual transmission models

36 Progressively unscrew and remove the transmission-to-engine bolts, noting where each one goes, and the location of any brackets attached, for guidance when refitting.
37 With the help of an assistant, withdraw the transmission directly from the engine, making sure that its weight is not allowed to bear on the input shaft. Note that there are two locating dowels used.

Automatic transmission models

38 The torque converter is attached to the driveplate by four bolts, which are accessed through an aperture on the end face of the transmission. Remove the single securing bolt, and then withdraw the grommet from the access hole. Turn the engine as required to position each bolt in the aperture in turn, then unscrew and remove them.

39 Slacken and remove the bolts securing the transmission to the engine. Note the correct fitted positions of each bolt, and the necessary brackets, as they are removed to use as a reference on refitting.

40 Carefully prise the transmission off the engine, to free its locating dowels. As the transmission is removed, make sure the torque converter is kept pushed fully onto the transmission shaft.

41 Once the transmission is free, secure the torque converter in position by bolting a length of metal bar to one of the housing holes.

Refitting

42 Refitting is a reversal of removal, noting the following additional points:
- a) Make sure that all mating faces are clean, and use new gaskets where necessary.
- b) Tighten all nuts and bolts to the specified torque setting, where given.
- c) If the transmission was removed, refit it to the engine as described in Chapter 7A or 7B, as applicable.
- d) If the radiator is not removed (see paragraph 28), take care to avoid damage to it as the engine is refitted.
- e) Delay fully tightening the engine left- and right-hand mountings until the engine has settled into place.
- f) Fit a new circlip to the groove in the inner end of the left-hand driveshaft, and ensure it fully engages as the shaft is fitted into the transmission.
- g) On manual transmission models, check the operation of the clutch on completion – the system should not require bleeding, or even topping-up, but only in theory (see Chapter 6).
- h) Refill the transmission oil or fluid, with reference to Chapter 1A.
- i) Refill the cooling system as described in Chapter 1A.
- j) Where applicable, use new washers when reconnecting the power steering pump, then fill and bleed the system as described in Chapter 10.

6 Engine overhaul – dismantling sequence

Note: *When removing external components from the engine, pay close attention to details that may be helpful or important during refitting. Note the fitted position of gaskets, seals, spacers, pins, washers, bolts and other small items.*

1 It is much easier to work on the engine if it is mounted on a portable engine stand. These stands can often be hired from a tool hire shop. Before the engine is mounted on a stand, the flywheel should be removed so that the stand bolts can be tightened into the end of the cylinder block/crankcase (**not** the main bearing ladder).

2 If a stand is not available, it is possible to dismantle the engine with it blocked up on a sturdy workbench or on the floor. Be extra careful not to tip or drop the engine when working without a stand.

3 If you are going to obtain a reconditioned engine, all external components must be removed for transfer to the new engine (just as if you are doing a complete engine overhaul yourself). These components include the following:
- a) Inlet and exhaust manifolds (relevant part of Chapter 4).
- b) Alternator/power steering pump/air conditioning compressor bracket(s) (as applicable).
- c) Coolant pump (Chapter 3).
- d) Fuel system components (relevant part of Chapter 4).
- e) Wiring harness and all electrical switches and sensors.
- f) Oil filter (Chapter 1A).
- g) Flywheel/driveplate (relevant part Chapter 2).
- h) Dipstick and tube, where applicable.
- i) Oil cooler, where applicable (relevant part of Chapter 2)
- j) Engine mounting brackets (relevant part of Chapter 2).

4 If you are obtaining a short motor (which consists of the engine cylinder block/crankcase and main bearing ladder, crankshaft, pistons and connecting rods all assembled), then the cylinder head, sump, oil pump, and timing belt will have to be removed also.

5 If you are planning a complete overhaul, the engine can be dismantled and the internal components removed in the following order given below, referring to the relevant Part of this Chapter unless otherwise stated.
- a) Inlet and exhaust manifolds (relevant part of Chapter 4).
- b) Timing belt(s), sprockets and tensioner.
- d) Cylinder head(s).

- e) Flywheel/driveplate.
- f) Sump.
- g) Oil pump.
- h) Piston/connecting rod assemblies.
- i) Crankshaft.

6 Before beginning the dismantling and overhaul procedures, make sure that you have all of the correct tools necessary. Refer to the *Tools and working facilities* Section of this manual for further information.

7 Cylinder head – dismantling

Note: *New and reconditioned cylinder heads are available from the manufacturer and from engine overhaul specialists. Due to the fact that some specialist tools are required for dismantling and inspection, and new components may not be readily available, it may be more practical and economical for the home mechanic to purchase a reconditioned head rather than dismantle, inspect and recondition the original. A valve spring compressor tool will be required for this operation.*

1 With the cylinder head(s) removed, if not already done, remove the inlet manifold as described in Chapter 4A or 4B.

2 Remove the camshafts and hydraulic tappets, as described in Chapter 2A or 2B.

3 Using a valve spring compressor tool, compress each valve spring in turn until the split collets can be removed. Release the compressor and lift off the spring retainer and spring, then use a pair of pliers to extract the spring lower seat/stem seal from the valve guide (**see illustrations**). **Note:** *If, when the valve spring compressor is screwed down, the spring retainer refuses to free and expose the split collets, gently tap the top of the tool, directly over the retainer, with a light hammer. This will free the retainer.*

4 Withdraw the valve through the combustion chamber.

5 It is essential that each valve is stored together with its collets, retainer and spring, and that all valves are kept in their correct sequence, unless they are so badly worn that they are to be renewed. If they are going to

7.3a Using a valve spring compressor to release the split collets – arrowed

7.3b Extracting the spring lower seat/stem seal

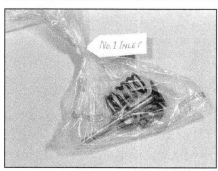

7.5 Use a labelled plastic bag to keep together and identify the valve components

be kept and used again, place each valve assembly in a labelled polythene bag or similar small container **(see illustration)**.

8 Cylinder head and valves – cleaning and inspection

1 Thorough cleaning of the cylinder head and valve components, followed by a detailed inspection, will enable you to decide how much valve service work must be carried out during the engine overhaul.

Cleaning

2 Scrape away all traces of old gasket material and sealing compound from the cylinder head.
3 Scrape away all carbon from the combustion chambers and ports, then wash the cylinder head thoroughly with paraffin or a suitable solvent.
4 Scrape off any heavy carbon deposits that may have formed on the valves, then use a power-operated wire brush to remove deposits from the valve heads and stems.

Inspection

Note: *Be sure to perform all the following inspection procedures before concluding that the services of a machine shop or engine overhaul specialist are required. Make a list of all items that require attention.*

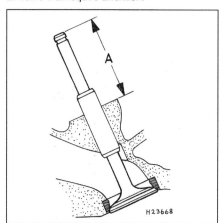

8.7 Check valve seat wear by measuring valve stem installed height (A)

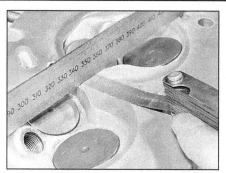

8.6a Checking a cylinder head gasket surface for distortion

Cylinder head

Note: *If the engine has been severely overheated, it is best to assume that the cylinder head is warped and to check carefully for signs of this.*

5 Inspect the head very carefully for cracks, evidence of coolant leakage and other damage. If cracks are found, a new cylinder head should be obtained.
6 Use a straight-edge and feeler blade to check that the cylinder head surface is not distorted **(see illustrations)**. If it is, it may be possible to resurface it, provided that the specified reface limit is not exceeded in so doing, or that the cylinder head is not reduced to less than the specified height.
7 Examine the valve seats in each of the combustion chambers. If they are severely pitted, cracked or burned, then they will need to be renewed or recut by an engine overhaul specialist. If they are only slightly pitted, this can be removed by grinding-in the valve heads and seats with fine valve-grinding compound as described below. To check for excessive wear, refit each valve and measure the installed height of the stem tip above the cylinder head upper surface **(see illustration)**. If the measurement is above the specified limit, repeat the test using a new valve. If the measurement is still excessive, renew the seat.
8 If the valve guides are worn, indicated by a side-to-side motion of the valve, new guides must be fitted. Measure the diameter of the existing valve stems (see below) and the bore of the guides, then calculate the clearance and compare the result with the specified value. If

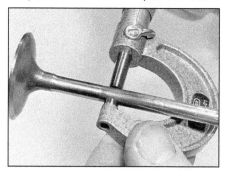

8.12 Measuring valve stem diameter

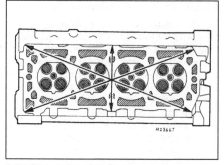

8.6b Check the cylinder head gasket surface for distortion along the paths shown

the clearance is excessive, renew the valves or guides as necessary.
9 Valve guides should be renewed by an engine overhaul specialist.
10 If the valve seats are to be recut, this must be done only after the guides have been renewed.

Valves

11 Examine the head of each valve for pitting, burning, cracks and general wear, then check the valve stem for scoring and wear ridges. Rotate the valve and check for any obvious indication that it is bent. Look for pits and excessive wear on the tip of each valve stem. Renew any valve that shows any such signs of wear or damage.
12 If the valve appears satisfactory at this stage, measure the valve stem diameter at several points by using a micrometer **(see illustration)**. Any significant difference in the readings obtained indicates wear of the valve stem. Should any of these conditions be apparent, the valve(s) must be renewed.
13 If the valves are in satisfactory condition they should be ground (lapped) into their respective seats to ensure a smooth gas-tight seal. If the seat is only lightly pitted, or if it has been recut, fine grinding compound only should be used to produce the required finish. Coarse valve-grinding compound should not be used unless a seat is badly burned or deeply pitted. If this is the case, the cylinder head and valves should be inspected by an expert to decide whether seat recutting or even the renewal of the valve or seat insert is required.
14 Valve grinding is carried out as follows. Place the cylinder head upside down on a bench.
15 Smear a trace of (the appropriate grade of) valve-grinding compound on the seat face and press a suction grinding tool onto the valve head. With a semi-rotary action, grind the valve head to its seat, lifting the valve occasionally to redistribute the grinding compound. A light spring placed under the valve head will greatly ease this operation.
16 If coarse grinding compound is being used, work only until a dull, matt even surface is produced on both the valve seat and the valve, then wipe off the used compound and repeat the process with fine compound. When

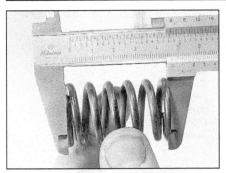

8.19 Measuring valve spring free-length

9.2 Using a socket to fit a valve stem seal

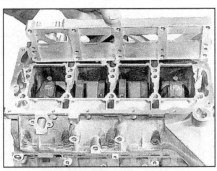

10.7a Removing the oil rail

a smooth unbroken ring of light grey matt finish is produced on both the valve and seat, the grinding operation is complete. Do not grind in the valves any further than absolutely necessary, or the seat will be prematurely sunk into the cylinder head.

17 To check that the seat has not been over-ground, measure the valve stem installed height, as described in paragraph 7.

18 When all the valves have been ground-in, carefully wash off all traces of grinding compound using paraffin or a suitable solvent.

Valve components

19 Examine the valve springs for signs of damage and discoloration and also measure their free length using vernier calipers or by comparing each existing spring with a new component **(see illustration)**.

20 Stand each spring on a flat surface and check it for squareness. If any of the springs are damaged, distorted or have lost their tension, then obtain a complete new set of springs.

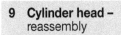

9 Cylinder head – reassembly

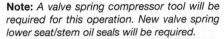

Note: *A valve spring compressor tool will be required for this operation. New valve spring lower seat/stem oil seals will be required.*

1 Lubricate the valve stems with clean engine oil and insert each valve into its original location. If new valves are being fitted, insert them into the locations to which they have been ground.

2 Working on the first valve, dip the **new** spring lower seat/stem seal in clean engine oil then carefully locate it over the valve and onto the guide. Take care not to damage the seal as it is passed over the valve stem. Use a suitable socket or metal tube to press the seal firmly onto the guide **(see illustration)**.

3 Locate the spring on the seat, followed by the spring retainer.

4 Compress the valve spring and locate the split collets in the recess in the valve stem. Use a little grease to hold the collets in place. Release the compressor, then repeat the procedure on the remaining valves.

5 With all the valves installed, rest the cylinder head on wooden blocks or stands (**do not** rest the head flat on a bench) and, using a hammer and interposed block of wood, tap the end of each valve stem to settle the components.

6 Refit the hydraulic tappets and camshafts as described in Chapter 2A or 2B.

10 Piston/connecting rod assembly – removal

Removal

4-cylinder engine

Note: *Due to the design of the engine, it will become very difficult, almost impossible; to turn the crankshaft once the cylinder head bolts have been slackened. The manufacturer accordingly states that the crankshaft will be 'tight' and should not be rotated more than absolutely necessary once the head has been removed. If the crankshaft cannot be rotated, then it must be removed for overhaul work to proceed. With this in mind, during any servicing or overhaul work the crankshaft must always be rotated to the desired position before the bolts are disturbed. Whenever the piston/ connecting rod assemblies are removed, the cylinder liners should be removed and resealed as a precaution against leakage after reassembly (see Section 13).*

1 Remove the timing belt, the camshaft sprockets and timing belt tensioner, and the timing belt rear cover, as described in Part A of this Chapter.

2 Remove the camshafts and hydraulic tappets, as described in Part A of this Chapter.

3 If not already done, rotate the crankshaft (if necessary temporarily refit the crankshaft pulley bolt and use a spanner or socket to turn the crankshaft) through a quarter-turn clockwise, until Nos 1 and 4 cylinder pistons are at TDC (No 1 piston should have been positioned 90° BTDC to remove the timing belt).

4 Remove the cylinder head, as described in Part A of this Chapter. The crankshaft cannot now be rotated. Note that there is no need to fit cylinder liner clamps, as the cylinder liners

should be removed and resealed whenever the piston/connecting rod assemblies are removed.

5 Slacken and remove the two dipstick tube retaining bolts and remove the tube from the cylinder block/crankcase.

6 Remove the sump and unbolt the oil pump pick-up/strainer pipe from the oil rail, as described in Part A of this Chapter.

7 Unscrew the two retaining nuts and remove the oil rail **(see illustrations)**.

8 Using a hammer and centre punch, paint or similar, mark each connecting rod big-end bearing cap with its respective cylinder number on the flat, machined surface provided. If the engine has been dismantled before, note carefully any identifying marks made previously **(see illustration)**. Note that No 1 cylinder is at the timing belt end of the engine.

9 Unscrew and remove the No 2 cylinder big-end bearing cap bolts and withdraw the cap, complete with bearing shell, from the connecting rod. If only the bearing shells are being attended to, push the connecting rod up and off the crankpin, ensuring that the connecting rod big-ends do not mark the cylinder bore walls, then remove the upper bearing shell. Keep the cap, bolts and (if they are to be refitted) the bearing shells together in their correct sequence. Repeat the procedure to disconnect No 3 cylinder big-end.

10 With Nos 2 and 3 cylinder big-ends disconnected, repeat the procedure (exercising great care to prevent damage to any of the components) to disconnect Nos 1 and 4 cylinder big-ends.

11 Remove the ridge of carbon from the top of each cylinder bore. Push each piston/ connecting rod assembly up and remove it from the top of the bore, ensuring that the connecting rod big-ends do not mark the cylinder bore walls.

12 Note that the number previously stamped on each bearing cap should match the cylinder number stamped (by the manufacturers) on each connecting rod, which can be read once the connecting rod has been removed. If the mark stamped on any connecting rod does not match its correct cylinder, mark or label the connecting rod immediately to avoid confusion, so that each piston/connecting rod assembly can be refitted to its original bore.

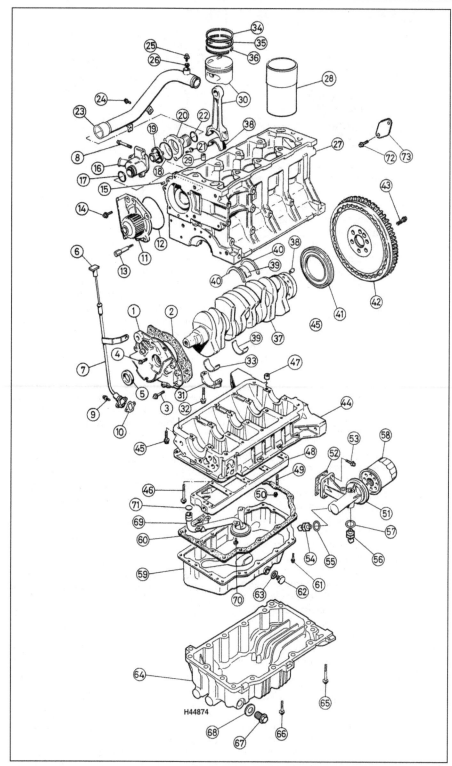

10.7b Engine bottom end components

1	Oil pump	37	Crankshaft
2	Gasket	38	Dowel
3	Screw	39	Main bearing
4	Screw		shells
5	Oil seal	40	Thrustwashers
6	Engine oil level	41	Crankshaft oil seal
	dipstick	42	Flywheel (with
7	Dipstick tube		reluctor ring)
8	Screw	43	Flywheel bolt
9	Screw	44	Main bearing
10	Gasket		ladder
11	Coolant pump	45	Bolt
12	O-ring	46	Bolt
13	Pillar bolt	47	Dowel
14	Bolt	48	Oil rail
15	Dowel pin	49	Stud
16	Thermostat	50	Nut
	housing	51	Oil filter adapter
17	O-ring	52	Gasket
18	Gasket	53	Bolt
19	Thermostat	54	Oil pressure
20	Thermostat		switch
	housing	55	Sealing washer
21	Screw	56	Oil temperature
22	O-ring		switch (if fitted)
23	Coolant rail	57	Washer
24	Screw	58	Oil filter
25	Cooling system	59	Sump
	bleed screw	60	Gasket
26	Sealing washer	61	Bolt
27	Cylinder block	62	Engine oil drain
28	Liner		plug
29	Dowel	63	Washer
30	Piston and	64	Sump
	connecting rod	65	Bolt
31	Big-end bearing	66	Bolt
	cap	67	Engine oil drain
32	Connecting rod		plug
	bolt	68	Washer
33	Big-end bearing	69	Oil pump pick-up/
	shell		strainer pipe
34	Top compression	70	Screw
	ring	71	O-ring
35	Second	72	Blanking plate
	compression ring	73	Screw
36	Oil control ring		

 HAYNES HiNT *Fit the bearing cap, shells and bolts to each removed piston/connecting rod assembly, so that they are all kept together as a matched set.*

13 Alternatively, if the engine is being completely dismantled and the cylinder head has been removed, either unbolt the main bearing ladder so that the crankshaft can be rotated with care, or remove the crankshaft completely and then remove the connecting rods and pistons.

10.8 Mark the big-end bearing caps before removal – No 4 cylinder cap shown

6-cylinder engine

14 Remove the cylinder heads, crankshaft oil seal, sump and oil pump as described in Chapter 2B.

15 Remove the single bolt securing the oil pump pick-up strainer. Withdraw it from the base of the engine, and recover the O-ring – a new one should be used when refitting.

16 Unscrew a total of eleven bolts securing the lower crankcase, noting the positions of the two smaller bolts. Some early models may have a stud and nut at the flywheel end. Remove the lower crankcase, noting that sealant is used during assembly – if possible, do not prise between the mating surfaces to free it.

17 The cylinder liners have to be removed with each piston/rod assembly – the big-ends will not pass up through the liners. Therefore, unless new liners are being fitted, mark the fitted position of each liner in the block, using paint.

18 Position the crankshaft so that the first connecting rod is accessible (it may be possible to remove the rods in pairs, if wished).

19 Using a hammer and centre-punch, paint or similar, mark each connecting rod big-end bearing cap with its respective cylinder number. On our car, the caps were numbered already, with the numbers were facing inwards. If the engine has been dismantled before, note carefully any identifying marks made previously. Refer to Chapter 2B, Section 1, for details on cylinder numbering.

20 Unscrew and remove the big-end bearing cap bolts and withdraw the cap, complete with bearing shell, from the connecting rod.

21 If only the bearing shells are being attended to, push the connecting rod up and off the crankpin, ensuring that the connecting rod big-ends do not mark the cylinder bore walls, then remove the upper bearing shell. Keep the cap, bolts and (if they are to be refitted) the bearing shells together in their correct sequence.

22 Repeat the procedure (exercising great care to prevent damage to any of the components) to remove the remaining bearing caps.

23 Using a suitable wooden drift, carefully tap the cylinder liners upwards and out of the block. Fit the bearing cap, shells and bolts to each removed piston/connecting rod assembly, so that they are all kept together as a matched set.

24 As required, the piston and connecting rod assemblies can be withdrawn from the bottom of the liner. Before doing so, however, mark the liner with its cylinder number.

Cylinder head bolts condition check

25 Check the condition of the cylinder head bolts, particularly their threads (note that if only the cylinder head has been removed, the bolts can be checked as described in Chapter 2A or 2B). Keeping all bolts in their correct fitted order, wash them and wipe dry. Check each bolt for any sign of visible wear or damage, renewing as necessary. Note that if cylinder head bolts have been used to secure the cylinder liner clamps, each bolt and clamp should be removed one at a time for checking, and refitted immediately the bolt has been tested. Lightly oil the threads of each bolt, carefully enter it into its original hole in the oil rail (**do not** drop the bolt into the hole), and screw it in, by hand only, until finger-tight.

26 If the full length of the bolt thread is engaged with the hole in the oil rail, the bolt may be re-used. If the full length of the thread is not engaged, measure the distance from the upper surface of the oil rail to the lower surface of the bolt head (**see illustration**). If the distance measured is under 378 mm, the bolt may be re-used. If the distance measured is more than 378 mm, the bolt must be renewed. Considering the task these bolts perform and the forces they must withstand, owners should consider renewing all the bolts as a matched set if more than one of the original bolts fail inspection or are close to the limit.

27 Note that if any of the cylinder head bolt threads in the oil rail are found to be damaged, then the oil rail must be renewed. Thread inserts are not an acceptable repair in this instance.

11 Crankshaft – removal

4-cylinder engine

1 Remove the following components, as described in Chapter 2A:
a) *Timing belt, sprockets, tensioner, and rear cover.*
b) *Cylinder head.*
c) *Oil pump.*
d) *Flywheel.*
e) *Sump and oil pump pick-up/strainer pipe.*

2 Slacken and remove the two dipstick tube retaining bolts and remove the tube from the cylinder block/crankcase.

11.4a Crankshaft main bearing ladder bolt slackening sequence

A *Bolts hidden in ladder flanges*
B *Location of single longer bolt*

10.26 Measure the distance from the upper surface of the oil rail to the lower surface of the bolt head

3 If cylinder liner clamps have been fitted, temporarily remove them (this is necessary because the cylinder head bolts used to secure the liner clamps screw into the oil rail), then unscrew the two retaining nuts and remove the oil rail.

4 Working in sequence, progressively unscrew the main bearing ladder retaining bolts by a turn at a time, and then withdraw the ladder. Note the locations of the two locating dowels, and the main bearing shells, which should be removed from the ladder and stored in their correct fitted order (**see illustrations**).

5 If the cylinder liners are to be left in place in the cylinder block, refit the liner clamps, noting that suitable nuts and spacers will have to be screwed onto the lower ends of the cylinder head bolts to retain the clamps (the oil rail has now been removed).

6 Using a hammer and centre punch, paint or similar, mark each connecting rod big-end bearing cap with its respective cylinder number on the flat, machined surface provided. If the engine has been dismantled before, note carefully any identifying marks made previously. Note that No 1 cylinder is at the timing belt end of the engine.

7 Working on each cylinder in turn, unscrew and remove the big-end bearing cap bolts and withdraw the cap, complete with the lower bearing shell (**see illustration**). Push the connecting rods up and off their crankpins, and then remove the upper bearing shells.

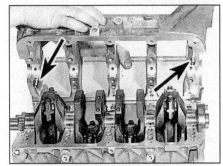

11.4b Removing the main bearing ladder – locating dowels arrowed

Keep the cap, bolts and (if they are to be refitted) the bearing shells together in their correct sequence.

8 Lift the crankshaft from the cylinder block, taking care, as this component is heavy.

9 Withdraw the two thrustwashers from the No 3 main bearing location in the cylinder block.

10 Remove the upper main bearing shells from the cylinder block, noting their locations. The bearing shells must be kept in order, along with the lower bearing shells, so that they can be refitted (if applicable) in their original locations.

11 Check the condition of the cylinder head bolts as described in Section 10.

V6 engine

12 Remove the cylinder heads, sump, oil pump and flywheel as described in Chapter 2B.

13 Remove the liners, piston and connecting rod assemblies as described in Sections 13 and 14. If no work is to be done on the pistons and connecting rods, unbolt the caps and push the pistons far enough up the liners so that the connecting rods are positioned clear of the crankshaft journals.

14 Progressively unscrew the main bearing ladder retaining bolts by a turn at a time, noting that the eight shorter bolts are fitted to the outside edges. Withdraw the ladder, noting that it is located on dowels.

15 Check the crankshaft endfloat as described in Section 15, then remove the crankshaft.

16 Withdraw the thrustwashers from the No 4 main bearing location. Noting the position of the grooved shells, remove the upper main bearing shells, which must be kept with their correct respective partners from the main bearing ladder so that all shells can be identified and (if necessary) refitted in their original locations.

12 Cylinder block/crankcase – cleaning and inspection

Note: *During any cleaning operations, take care not to score the mating surfaces of the cylinder block/crankcase, bearing ladder and oil rail. It may be necessary to use a foam action gasket remover.*

Cleaning

1 For complete cleaning, remove the cylinder liners, all external components and all electrical switches/sensors.

2 Scrape all traces of gasket from the cylinder block/crankcase, bearing ladder and oil rail, taking care not to damage the gasket/sealing surfaces.

3 Remove all oil gallery plugs (where fitted). The plugs are usually very tight and may have to be drilled out and the holes retapped. Use new plugs when the engine is reassembled.

4 If any of the castings are extremely dirty, all should be steam-cleaned.

11.7 Removing No 1 cylinder big-end bearing cap and lower bearing shell

5 After the castings have been steam-cleaned, clean all oil holes and oil galleries one more time. Flush all internal passages with warm water until the water runs clear, then dry thoroughly and apply a light film of oil to all mating faces and to the liner surfaces to prevent rusting. If you have access to compressed air, use it to speed up the drying process and to blow out all the oil holes and galleries.

 Warning: Wear eye protection when using compressed air.

6 If the castings are not very dirty, you can do an adequate cleaning job with hot soapy water and a stiff brush. Take plenty of time and do a thorough job. Regardless of the cleaning method used, be sure to clean all oil holes and galleries very thoroughly and to dry all components well. Protect the liners as described previously to prevent rusting.

7 All threaded holes must be clean to ensure accurate torque readings during reassembly. To clean all threads, run the proper size tap into each of the holes to remove rust, corrosion, thread sealant or sludge, and to restore damaged threads. If possible, use compressed air to clear the holes of debris produced by this operation. A good alternative is to inject aerosol-applied water-dispersant lubricant into each hole, using the long spout usually supplied. Always wear eye protection when cleaning out holes in this way. After cleaning, ensure that all threaded holes in the cylinder block are dry. If not already done, now is a good time to check the condition of the cylinder head bolts, as described in Section 10.

8 Apply suitable sealant to the new oil gallery plugs, and insert them into the holes in the block. Tighten them securely.

9 If the engine is not going to be reassembled right away, cover it with a large plastic bag to keep it clean. Protect the cylinder liners as described previously to prevent rusting.

Inspection

10 Inspect all castings for cracks and corrosion. Look for stripped threads. If there has been any history of internal coolant leakage, it may be worthwhile having an engine overhaul specialist check the cylinder block/crankcase with special equipment. If defects are found, have them repaired, if possible, or renew the assembly.

11 Check the bore of each cylinder liner for scuffing and scoring. If the cylinder liner walls are badly scuffed or scored, obtain new cylinder liners.

12 Measure the diameter of each cylinder liner bore 65 mm from the top of the bore, both parallel to the crankshaft axis and at right angles to it. Compare the diameter with that specified. If any measurement exceeds the service limit, then the liner must be renewed.

13 To measure the piston-to-bore clearance, either measure the relevant cylinder liner bore (as described above) and piston skirt (as described in Section 14) and subtract the skirt diameter from the bore measurement, or insert each piston into the original cylinder liner bore, select a feeler blade and slip it into the bore along with the piston. The piston must be aligned exactly in its normal attitude and the feeler blade must be between the piston and bore on one of the thrust faces, 20 mm from the bottom of the bore.

14 If the piston-to-bore clearance is excessive, new cylinder liners and corresponding pistons will be required. If the piston binds at the lower end of the bore and is loose towards the top, then the bore is tapered. If tight spots are encountered as the piston/feeler blade is rotated in the bore, then the bore is out-of-round. In either case, new liners and pistons will be required.

15 Repeat the checking procedure for the remaining pistons and cylinder liners.

16 If the bores are in reasonably good condition and not worn to the specified limits, and if the piston-to-bore clearances can be maintained properly, then it may only be necessary to renew the piston rings. In this case, **do not** attempt to hone the cylinder liner bores to allow the new rings to bed-in.

13 Cylinder liners – removal and refitting

Note: *If desired, the cylinder liners can be removed with the main bearing ladder and crankshaft fitted. MG Rover sealant kit GGC 102 is needed to seal the liners.*

Removal

1 With the pistons removed, if not already done, remove the cylinder liner clamps. **Note:** *On 6-cylinder engines the connecting rods will not pass through the liners.*

2 If the original liners are to be refitted, make alignment marks between each liner and the cylinder block to ensure that each liner can be refitted in its exact original position. Use a felt-tipped pen or paint to make the marks – **do not** etch or stamp the liners.

3 Lay the cylinder block on its side, then use hand pressure to push the cylinder liners out from the top of the cylinder block. If the liners are to be re-used, mark each one using a piece of masking tape and writing the cylinder number on the tape.

Refitting

Note: *To enable cylinder liner retaining clamps to be fitted when the liners are fitted to the cylinder block, the crankshaft and main bearing ladder must be fitted to the cylinder block.*

4 If not already done, fit the crankshaft and main bearing ladder, as described in Section 19.

5 Support the cylinder block upright on blocks of wood.

6 If not already done, thoroughly clean the cylinder liner mating faces of the cylinder block, and clean away all traces of the cylinder liner sealant. If the original liners are to be refitted, also clean all sealant from the liners, and clean the liner mating faces, taking care not to remove the alignment and identification marks made during removal.

7 Ensure that the cylinder block and liners are dry.

8 Working on the first liner to be refitted, apply a continuous 2 mm bead of sealant, from kit GGC 102, around the shoulder of the liner **(see illustration)**.

9 If the original liners are being refitted, use the marks made on removal to ensure that each liner is refitted in its original bore, in its original location.

10 Insert each liner into its bore in the cylinder block/crankcase, ensuring that the liner is square to the bore. If the original liner is being refitted, make sure that the marks made on the liner and the cylinder block are aligned. Push the liner fully down until the shoulder on the liner seats against the cylinder block. **Do not** drop the liner into position.

11 Repeat the procedure to refit the three remaining cylinder liners.

12 Cylinder liner clamps should now be fitted to prevent the liners from being disturbed before the cylinder head is refitted. The manufacturer's liner clamps are secured in place by the cylinder head bolts **(see illustrations)**. Equivalents can be improvised using large washers, tubular spacers and nuts.

---

14 Piston/connecting rod assembly – inspection

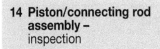

Cleaning

1 Before the inspection process can begin, the piston/connecting rod assemblies must be cleaned, and the original piston rings removed from the pistons.

2 Carefully expand the old rings over the top of the pistons. The use of two or three old feeler blades will be helpful in preventing the rings dropping into empty grooves **(see illustration)**. Be careful not to scratch the piston with the ends of the ring. The rings are brittle, and will snap if they are spread too far. They are also very sharp – protect your hands and fingers. Note that the third ring incorporates an expander. Always remove the

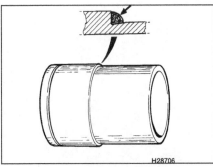

13.8 Apply a 2 mm bead of sealant around the shoulder of the liner

rings from the top of the piston. Keep each set of rings with its piston if the old rings are to be re-used. Note which way up each ring is fitted to ensure correct refitting.

3 Scrape away all traces of carbon from the top of the piston. A hand-held wire brush (or a piece of fine emery cloth) can be used, once the majority of the deposits have been scraped away.

4 Remove the carbon from the ring grooves in the piston, using an old ring. Break the ring in half to do this (be careful not to cut your fingers – piston rings are sharp). Be careful to remove only the carbon deposits – do not remove any metal, and do not nick or scratch the sides of the ring grooves. Make sure that the oil return holes in the ring grooves are clear.

5 Once the deposits have been removed, clean the piston/connecting rod assembly with paraffin or a suitable solvent, and dry thoroughly.

Inspection

6 If the pistons and cylinder liner bores are not damaged or worn excessively, the original pistons can be refitted. Measure the piston diameters, and check that they are within limits for the corresponding bore diameters. Measure the diameter of each piston at right angles to the gudgeon pin axis, 8 mm up from the bottom of the skirt.

7 If the piston-to-bore clearance is excessive (see Section 12), new cylinder liners and pistons will have to be fitted. Normal piston wear shows up as even vertical wear on the piston thrust surfaces, and slight looseness of the top ring in its groove. New piston rings should always be used when the engine is reassembled. Note that the piston and bore size grades are stamped on the piston crowns, and on the outer diameters of the cylinder liners.

8 Carefully inspect each piston for cracks around the skirt, around the gudgeon pin holes, and at the piston ring 'lands' (between the ring grooves).

9 Look for scoring and scuffing on the piston skirt, holes in the piston crown, and burned areas at the edge of the crown. If the skirt is scored or scuffed, the engine may have been suffering from overheating, and/or abnormal combustion that caused excessively high

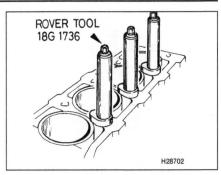

13.12a Rover cylinder liner clamps fitted to top face of cylinder block . . .

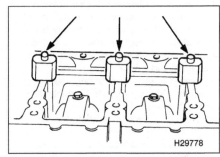

13.12b . . . retained by screwing the cylinder head bolts into nylon blocks underneath the cylinder block

operating temperatures. The cooling and lubrication systems should be checked thoroughly. Scorch marks on the sides of the pistons show that blow-by has occurred. A hole in the piston crown, or burned areas at the edge of the piston crown, indicates that abnormal combustion (pre-ignition, knocking, or detonation) has been occurring. If any of the above problems exist, the causes must be investigated and corrected, or the damage will occur again. The causes may include incorrect ignition timing, inlet air leaks or incorrect air/fuel mixture.

10 Corrosion of the piston, in the form of pitting, indicates that coolant has been leaking into the combustion chamber and/or the cylinder liner. Again, the cause must be corrected, or the problem may persist in the rebuilt engine.

11 Check the piston-to-bore clearance by measuring the cylinder bore (see Section 12)

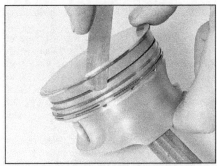

14.2 Using a feeler blade to aid removal of the piston rings

14.11 Measuring piston diameter

and the piston diameter. Measure the piston 8 mm from the bottom of the skirt, at a 90° angle to the gudgeon pin **(see illustration)**. If the piston-to-bore clearance is excessive, new cylinder liners and corresponding pistons will be required.

12 Examine each connecting rod carefully for signs of damage, such as cracks around the big-end and small-end bearings. Check that the rod is not bent or distorted. Damage is highly unlikely, unless the engine has been seized or badly overheated. Detailed checking of the connecting rod assembly can only be carried out by a Rover dealer or engine repair specialist with the necessary equipment.

13 Note that the pistons and connecting rods are only available as an assembly. If a piston or connecting rod is to be renewed, it is therefore necessary to renew all four/six complete piston/connecting rod assemblies – it is not possible to fit a new piston to an existing connecting rod.

14 Inspect the connecting rod big-end cap bolts closely for signs of wear or damage, and check that they screw easily into the connecting rods. Renew any bolt, which shows visible signs of damage or does not screw easily into position.

15 Crankshaft –
inspection

Checking endfloat

1 If crankshaft endfloat is to be checked, this must be done when the crankshaft is still installed in the cylinder block/crankcase but is free to move.

2 Check endfloat by using a dial gauge in contact with the end of the crankshaft. Push the crankshaft fully one way and then zero the gauge. Push the crankshaft fully the other way and check the endfloat. The result can be compared with the specified amount and will give an indication as to whether new thrustwashers are required.

3 If a dial gauge is not available, feeler blades can be used. First push the crankshaft fully towards the flywheel end of the engine, then use feeler blades to measure the gap between the web of No 3 crankpin and the thrustwasher. On

15.10 Measuring a crankshaft main bearing journal diameter

4-cylinder engines, the thrustwashers are only fitted to the sides of the upper centre (No 3) main bearing shell. On 6-cylinder engines the thrustwashers are fitted on the No 4 main bearing.

Inspection

4 Clean the crankshaft using paraffin or a suitable solvent, and dry it, preferably with compressed air if available. Be sure to clean the oil holes with a pipe cleaner or similar probe, to ensure that they are not obstructed.

 Warning: Wear eye protection when using compressed air.

5 Check the main and big-end bearing journals for uneven wear, scoring, pitting and cracking.

6 Big-end bearing wear is accompanied by distinct metallic knocking when the engine is running (particularly noticeable when the engine is pulling from low speed) and some loss of oil pressure.

7 Main bearing wear is accompanied by severe engine vibration and rumble – getting

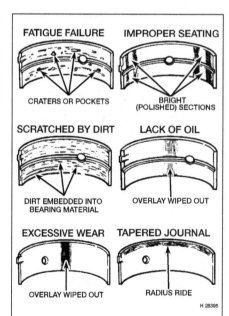

16.2 Typical bearing shell failures

progressively worse as engine speed increases – and again by loss of oil pressure.

8 Check the bearing journal for roughness by running a finger lightly over the bearing surface. Any roughness (which will be accompanied by obvious bearing wear) indicates that the crankshaft requires regrinding (where possible) or renewal.

9 If the crankshaft has been reground, check for burrs around the crankshaft oil holes (the holes are usually chamfered, so burrs should not be a problem unless regrinding has been carried out carelessly). Remove any burrs with a fine file or scraper, and thoroughly clean the oil holes as described previously.

10 Using a micrometer, measure the diameter of the main and big-end (crankpin) bearing journals, and compare the results with the Specifications **(see illustration)**. By measuring the diameter at a number of points around each journal's circumference, you will be able to determine whether or not the journal is out-of-round. Take the measurement at each end of the journal, near the webs, to determine if the journal is tapered. Compare the results obtained with those given in the Specifications.

11 Check the oil seal contact surfaces at each end of the crankshaft for wear and damage. If the seal has worn a deep groove in the surface of the crankshaft, consult an engine overhaul specialist; repair may be possible, but otherwise a new crankshaft will be required.

12 If the crankshaft journals are damaged, tapered, out-of-round or worn beyond the limits specified, the crankshaft must be renewed unless an engine overhaul specialist can be found who will regrind it and supply the necessary undersize bearing shells.

16 Main and big-end bearings
– inspection

1 Even though the main and big-end bearings should be renewed during the engine overhaul, the old bearings should be retained for close examination, as they may reveal valuable information about the condition of the engine. The bearing shells are graded by thickness, the grade of each shell being indicated by the colour code marked on it.

2 Bearing failure can occur due to lack of lubrication, the presence of dirt or other foreign particles, overloading the engine, or corrosion **(see illustration)**. Regardless of the cause of bearing failure, the cause must be corrected (where applicable) before the engine is reassembled, to prevent it from happening again.

3 When examining the bearing shells, remove them from the cylinder block/crankcase, the main bearing ladder, the connecting rods and the connecting rod big-end bearing caps. Lay them out on a clean surface in the same general position as their location in the engine.

This will enable you to match any bearing problems with the corresponding crankshaft journal.

4 Dirt and other foreign matter get into the engine in a variety of ways. It may be left in the engine during assembly, or it may pass through filters or the crankcase ventilation system. It may get into the oil, and from there into the bearings. Metal chips from machining operations and normal engine wear are often present. Abrasives are sometimes left in engine components after reconditioning, especially when parts are not thoroughly cleaned using the proper cleaning methods. Whatever the source, these foreign objects often end up embedded in the soft bearing material, and are easily recognised. Large particles will not embed in the bearing, and will score or gouge the bearing and journal. The best prevention for this cause of bearing failure is to clean all parts thoroughly, and keep everything spotlessly clean during engine assembly. Frequent and regular engine oil and filter changes are also recommended.

5 Lack of lubrication (or lubrication breakdown) has a number of interrelated causes. Excessive heat (which thins the oil), overloading (which squeezes the oil from the bearing face) and oil leakage (from excessive bearing clearances, worn oil pump or high engine speeds) all contribute to lubrication breakdown. Blocked oil passages, which usually are the result of misaligned oil holes in a bearing shell, will also oil-starve a bearing, and destroy it. When lack of lubrication is the cause of bearing failure, the bearing material is wiped or extruded from the steel backing of the bearing. Temperatures may increase to the point where the steel backing turns blue from overheating.

6 Driving habits can have a definite effect on bearing life. Full-throttle, low-speed operation (labouring the engine) puts very high loads on bearings, tending to squeeze out the oil film. These loads cause the bearings to flex, which produces fine cracks in the bearing face (fatigue failure). Eventually, the bearing material will loosen in pieces, and tear away from the steel backing.

7 Short-distance driving leads to corrosion of bearings, because insufficient engine heat is produced to drive off the condensed water and corrosive gases. These products collect in the engine oil, forming acid and sludge. As the oil is carried to the engine bearings, the acid attacks and corrodes the bearing material.

8 Incorrect bearing installation during engine assembly will lead to bearing failure as well. Tight-fitting bearings leave insufficient bearing running clearance, and will result in oil starvation. Dirt or foreign particles trapped behind a bearing shell result in high spots on the bearing, which lead to failure.

Caution: Do not touch any shell's bearing surface with your fingers during reassembly; there is a risk of scratching the delicate surface, or of depositing particles of dirt on it.

9 As mentioned at the beginning of this Section, the bearing shells should be renewed as a matter of course during engine overhaul; to do otherwise is false economy.

17 Engine overhaul – reassembly sequence

1 Before reassembly begins, ensure that all new parts have been obtained and that all necessary tools are available. Read through the entire procedure to familiarise yourself with the work involved and to ensure that all items necessary for reassembly of the engine are at hand. In addition to all normal tools and materials, it will be necessary to obtain suitable thread-locking compound, and various Rover sealants – refer to the relevant Sections in Chapter 2A or 2B for details. Carefully read the instructions supplied with the appropriate sealant kit.

2 In order to save time and avoid problems, engine reassembly can be carried out in the following order, referring to Chapter 2A or 2B when necessary. Where applicable, use new gaskets and seals when refitting the various components.

a) Crankshaft.
b) Piston/connecting rod assemblies.
c) Oil pump.
d) Sump.
e) Flywheel.
f) Cylinder head.
g) Timing belt rear cover, tensioner and sprockets, and timing belt.
h) Engine external components.

3 At this stage, all engine components should be absolutely clean and dry, with all faults repaired, and should be laid out (or in individual containers) on a completely clean work surface.

18 Piston rings – refitting

1 Before fitting new piston rings, the ring end gaps must be checked as follows.

2 Lay out the piston/connecting rod assemblies and the new piston ring sets, so that the ring sets will be matched with the same piston and cylinder during the end gap measurement and subsequent engine reassembly.

3 Insert the top ring into the first cylinder liner bore, and push it down the bore using the top of the piston. This will ensure that the ring remains square with the cylinder walls. Position the ring 20 mm from the top of the bore. Note that the top and second compression rings are different. The second ring is easily identified by the step on its lower surface.

4 Measure the end gap using feeler blades. Compare the measurements with the figures given in the Specifications **(see illustration)**.

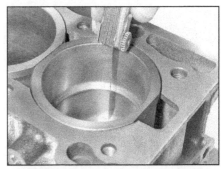

18.4 Measuring a piston ring end gap

5 If the gap is too small (unlikely if genuine Rover parts are used), it must be enlarged, or the ring ends may contact each other during engine operation, causing serious damage. Ideally, new piston rings providing the correct end gap should be fitted. As a last resort, filing the ring ends very carefully with a fine file can increase the end gap. Mount the file in a vice equipped with soft jaws, slip the ring over the file with the ends contacting the file face, and slowly move the ring to remove material from the ends. Take care, as piston rings are sharp, and are easily broken.

6 With new piston rings, it is unlikely that the end gap will be too large. If the gaps are too large, check that you have the correct rings for your engine and for the particular cylinder bore size.

7 Repeat the checking procedure for each ring in the first cylinder, and then for the rings in the remaining cylinders. Remember to keep rings, pistons and cylinders matched up.

8 Once the ring end gaps have been checked and if necessary corrected, the rings can be fitted to the pistons.

9 Check the ring-to-groove clearance by inserting the outside of each ring into the relevant groove, together with a feeler blade between the top surface of the ring and the piston land **(see illustration)**. If the grooves in the piston are excessively worn, new pistons may be required.

10 Fit the piston rings using the same technique as for removal. Fit the bottom (oil control) ring first, and work up. When fitting the oil control ring, first insert the wire expander, then fit the ring with its gap positioned 180° from the protruding wire ends of the expander.

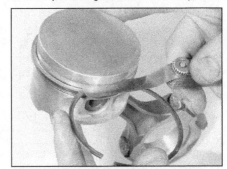

18.9 Measuring piston ring-to-groove clearance

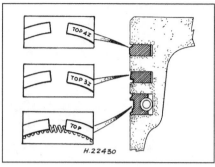

18.10a Piston ring fitting details and top surface markings

The oil control expander and ring gaps should be offset 30° either side of the gudgeon pin axis. Ensure that the rings are fitted the correct way up – the top surface of the rings is normally marked TOP **(see illustrations)**. Arrange the gaps of the top and second compression rings 120° from each other, away from the thrust side of the piston. **Note:** *Always follow any instructions supplied with the new piston ring sets – different manufacturers may specify different procedures. Do not mix up the top and second compression rings, as they have different cross-sections.*

19 Crankshaft – refitting

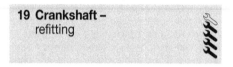

Note: *It is recommended that new main bearing shells are fitted, regardless of the*

19.9a If piston/connecting rod assemblies are refitted before main bearing ladder . . .

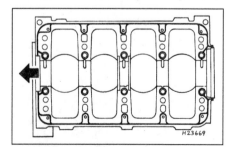

19.10 Apply sealant to the cylinder block/crankcase mating surface along the paths shown by the heavy black lines – arrow indicates timing belt end of engine

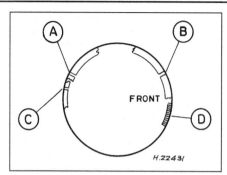

18.10b Piston ring end gap locations

    A *Top compression ring*
    B *Second compression ring*
    C *Oil control ring*
    D *Oil control ring expander*

condition of the original ones. Refer to an engine-reconditioning specialist for assistance in selecting the appropriate shells.

1 Crankshaft refitting is the first major step in engine reassembly. It is assumed at this point that the cylinder block/crankcase and crankshaft have been cleaned, inspected and repaired or reconditioned as necessary. Position the engine upside-down.

2 If temporarily refitted, remove the main bearing cap bolts, and lift out the caps. Lay the caps out in the proper order, to ensure correct installation.

3 If they are still in place, remove the old bearing shells from the block and the main bearing caps. Wipe the bearing recesses with a clean, lint-free cloth. They must be kept spotlessly clean.

19.9b . . . care is required to hold crankshaft steady while connecting rod big-end cap bolts are tightened

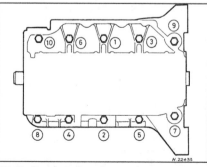

19.13 Crankshaft main bearing ladder bolt tightening sequence

4-cylinder engine

4 Clean the backs of the bearing shells, and the bearing locations in both the cylinder block/crankcase and the main bearing ladder. If new shells are being fitted, ensure that all traces of the protective grease are cleaned off using paraffin. Wipe dry the shells and connecting rods with a lint-free cloth.

5 Press the bearing shells into their locations, ensuring that the tab on each shell engages in the notch in the cylinder block/crankcase or main bearing ladder location. Take care not to touch any shell-bearing surface with your fingers.

6 Press the bearing shells into their locations, ensuring that the tab on each shell engages in the notch in the cylinder block or main bearing cap, noting the following:

  a) *Make sure that the grooved bearing shells are fitted in the upper (cylinder block) locations of Nos 2, 3 and 4 main bearings.*

  b) *If bearing shells of different grades are being fitted to the same bearing, ensure that the thicker shell is fitted in the lower (main bearing ladder) location.*

  c) *If the original bearing shells are being re-used, ensure they are refitted in their original locations.*

7 Using a little grease, stick the thrustwashers to each side of the centre (No 3) main bearing upper location. Ensure that the oilway grooves on each thrustwasher face outwards.

8 Liberally lubricate each bearing shell in the cylinder block/crankcase, and then lower the crankshaft into position. Check the crankshaft endfloat as described in Section 16.

9 Refit the piston/connecting rod assemblies to the crankshaft as described in Section 20 and position the crankshaft so the pistons are halfway up the bores **(see illustrations)**.

10 Thoroughly degrease the mating surfaces of the cylinder block and the main bearing ladder. Apply a continuous bead of sealant (part no GUG 705963GM) to the mating surface of the cylinder block/crankcase as shown, and then spread the sealant to an even film **(see illustration)**. Carefully follow the instructions supplied with the sealant.

11 Ensure the lower bearing shells are correctly fitted to the bearing ladder, and lubricate them with clean engine oil.

12 Ensure the locating dowels are in position then refit the main bearing ladder to the cylinder block, taking care to ensure that the shells are not displaced. Once the ladder is correctly located on the dowels, refit the retaining bolts, tightening them all by hand only.

13 Working in the specified sequence, go around and tighten all bolts to the specified Stage 1 torque setting, then go around again in the specified sequence and tighten them to the specified Stage 2 torque setting **(see illustration)**. **Note:** *The crankshaft cannot now be rotated until the cylinder head has been refitted.*

14 Thoroughly degrease the mating surfaces of the oil rail and the main bearing ladder.

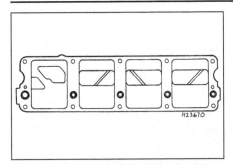

19.14 Apply sealant to the oil rail mating surfaces along the paths shown by the heavy black lines

Apply the same sealant (paragraph 10) to the oil rail mating surface as shown **(see illustration)**.

15 Refit the oil rail to the main bearing ladder and tighten its retaining nuts to the specified torque.

Caution: Do not rotate the crankshaft more than absolutely necessary, until the cylinder head bolts are tightened to the correct torque setting.

16 Refit the dipstick tube, using a new gasket, and securely tighten its retaining bolts.

17 Working as described in Chapter 2A, carry out the following procedures in order.

a) *Refit the oil pump, pick-up/strainer and sump.*
b) *Fit a new left-hand oil seal to the crankshaft and refit the flywheel.*
c) *Refit the cylinder head and camshafts.*
d) *Refit the timing belt sprockets and belt.*

18 On completion, remove the spark plugs then fit a torque wrench to the crankshaft pulley bolt and rotate the crankshaft in the normal direction of rotation. The crankshaft must rotate smoothly, without any sign of binding, and the amount of force required to rotate the crankshaft should not exceed 31 Nm (23 lbf ft). If the effort required is greater than this, the engine should be dismantled again to trace and rectify the cause. This value takes into account the increased friction of a new engine and is much higher than the actual force required to rotate a run-in engine, so do not make allowances for tight components.

6-cylinder engine

19 Clean the backs of the bearing shells,

19.23 Lubricate the bearing shells in the cylinder block with clean engine oil

19.21 Locating tab on the bearing shell – arrowed

and the bearing locations in both the cylinder block/crankcase and the main bearing ladder. If new shells are being fitted, ensure that all traces of the protective grease are cleaned off using paraffin. Wipe dry the shells and connecting rods with a lint-free cloth.

20 Press the bearing shells into their locations, taking care not to touch any shell-bearing surface with your fingers.

21 Press the bearing shells into their locations, ensuring that the tab on each shell engages in the notch in the cylinder block or main bearing cap, noting the following **(see illustration)**:

a) *Make sure that the grooved bearing shells are fitted in the upper (cylinder block) locations.*
b) *If bearing shells of different grades are being fitted to the same bearing, ensure that the thicker shell is fitted in the lower (main bearing ladder) location.*
c) *If the original bearing shells are being re-used, ensure they are refitted in their original locations.*

22 Using a little grease, stick the thrustwashers to the No 4 main bearing upper location. Ensure that the oilway grooves on each thrustwasher face outwards.

23 Liberally lubricate each bearing shell in the cylinder block/crankcase **(see illustration)**, and then lower the crankshaft into position. Check the crankshaft endfloat as described in Section 16.

24 Refit the liner/piston/connecting rod assemblies to the crankshaft as described in Section 20, and position the crankshaft so that none of the pistons is at the top of its bore.

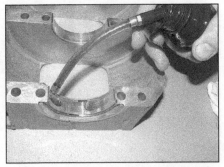

19.26 Lubricate the bearing shells in the bearing ladder with clean engine oil

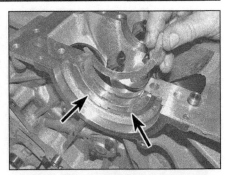

19.22 Oilways (arrowed) must face outwards

25 Thoroughly degrease the mating surfaces of the cylinder block and the main bearing ladder. Apply a bead of sealant (part no GUG 705963GM) to the mating surface of the cylinder block/crankcase, and then spread the sealant to an even film. Carefully follow the instructions supplied with the sealant.

26 Ensure the lower bearing shells are correctly fitted to the bearing ladder, and lubricate them with clean engine oil **(see illustration)**.

27 Using a little grease, stick the thrustwashers to the No 4 main bearing ladder location. Ensure that the oilway grooves on each thrustwasher face outwards **(see illustration)**.

28 Ensure the locating dowels are in position, and then refit the main bearing ladder to the cylinder block, taking care to ensure that the shells are not displaced. Once the ladder is correctly located on the dowels, refit the retaining bolts, tightening them all by hand only. Note that the eight shorter bolts are fitted to the outer positions **(see illustrations)**.

29 Working in the specified sequence, go around and tighten all bolts to the specified Stage 1 torque setting, then go around again in the specified sequence and tighten them to the specified Stage 2 angle **(see illustrations)**.

30 Thoroughly degrease the mating surfaces of the cylinder block and the lower crankcase. Apply the same sealant (paragraph 25) to the lower crankcase mating surface as shown **(see illustration)**.

31 Refit the lower crankcase, inserting the

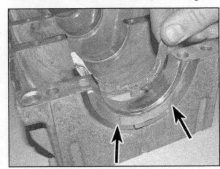

19.27 Oilways (arrowed) must face outwards

19.28a Refit the main bearing ladder . . .

19.28b . . . and the retaining bolts

19.29a Tighten the bearing ladder retaining bolts . . .

19.29b . . . using an angle gauge . . .

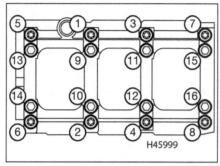

19.29c . . . in the tightening sequence shown

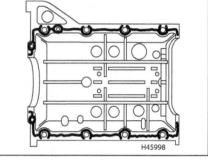

19.30 Apply sealant to the mating surfaces along the paths shown by the heavy black lines

19.31a Refit the lower crankcase . . .

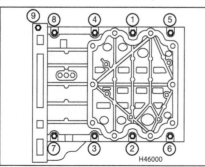

19.31b . . . and tighten the bolts in the sequence shown

two smaller bolts in their previously noted positions. Working in sequence, tighten the retaining bolts (and nut, on early models) to the specified torque **(see illustrations)**.

32 On completion of tightening, wait one minute, then go around again and retighten the M8 bolts (and nut, where fitted) to the specified torque.

33 Working as described in Part B of this Chapter, carry out the following procedures in order:

a) *Refit the oil pump, pick-up/strainer and sump.*
b) *Fit a new flywheel end oil seal to the crankshaft, and refit the flywheel/driveplate.*
c) *Refit the cylinder heads and camshafts.*
d) *Refit the timing belt sprockets and belts.*

34 On completion, remove the spark plugs and rotate the crankshaft in the normal direction of rotation. The crankshaft must rotate smoothly, without any sign of binding.

20 Piston/connecting rod assembly – refitting

Note: *It is recommended that new piston rings and big-end bearing shells are fitted regardless of the condition of the original ones. Refer to an engine reconditioning specialist for assistance in selecting the appropriate shells.*

4-cylinder engine

1 Note that the following procedure assumes that the cylinder liners have been refitted to the cylinder block/crankcase and that the crankshaft and main bearing ladder are in place. It is of course possible to refit the piston/connecting rod assemblies to the cylinder bores, to refit the crankshaft and to reassemble the piston/connecting rods on the

crankshaft before refitting the main bearing ladder (see Section 19).

2 Clean the backs of the bearing shells and the bearing recesses in both the connecting rod and the big-end bearing cap. Ensure that all traces of the protective grease are cleaned off using paraffin. Wipe dry the shells and connecting rods with a lint-free cloth.

3 Press the bearing shells into their locations, ensuring that the tab on each shell engages in the notch in the connecting rod or big-end bearing cap and taking care not to touch any shell's bearing surface with your fingers. If bearing shells of differing grades are to be fitted to the same connecting rod, the thicker shell must always be fitted in the lower (bearing cap) location.

4 Lubricate the cylinder bores, the pistons and piston rings, then lay out each piston/connecting rod assembly in its respective position.

5 Starting with assembly No 1, make sure that the piston rings are still correctly spaced (see Section 18) then clamp them in position with a piston ring compressor.

6 Insert the piston/connecting rod assembly into the top of liner No 1, ensuring that the arrow (or FRONT marking) on the piston crown faces the timing belt end of the engine. Note that the stamped marks on the connecting rod and big-end bearing cap should face the timing belt end of the engine **(see illustrations)**. Using a block of wood or hammer handle against the piston crown, tap the assembly into the liner until the piston crown is flush with the top of the liner.

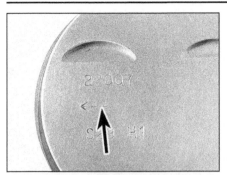

20.6a Arrow of FRONT marking on piston crown must point to timing belt end of engine

20.6b Using a piston ring compressor tool to clamp the piston rings

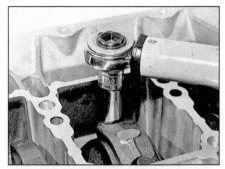

20.8a Tighten the big-end cap bolts to the specified torque setting . . .

20.8b . . . and then through the specified angle

20.10a Lubricate the piston rings with clean engine oil . . .

20.10b . . . then slide the piston ring compressor into position

7 Ensure that the bearing shell is still correctly installed. Taking care not to mark the liner bores, liberally lubricate the crankpin and both bearing shells, and then pull the piston/ connecting rod assembly down the bore and onto the crankpin. Noting that the faces with the stamped marks must match (which means that the bearing shell locating tabs abut each other), refit the big-end bearing cap, tightening the bolts finger-tight at first.

8 Evenly and progressively tighten the big-end bearing cap bolts to the specified Stage 1 torque setting, then angle-tighten each bolt through the specified Stage 2 angle. It is recommended that an angle-measuring gauge is used during this stage of the tightening, to ensure accuracy **(see illustrations)**.
Caution: Do not rotate the crankshaft more than absolutely necessary, until the cylinder head bolts are tightened to the correct torque setting.

9 Repeat the procedure for the remaining piston/connecting rod assemblies.

6-cylinder engine

10 Lubricate the piston rings, then fit the piston into a suitable ring compressor **(see illustrations)**.

11 Fit the compressor to the base of the relevant liner, and then carefully tap the piston until it is fully fitted inside the bore **(see illustration)**.

12 The cylinder number positions are clearly marked on the cylinder block, to avoid confusion **(see illustration)**.

13 Carefully clean the liner shoulders, and their seating positions in the block – it is

essential that a good seal is made when the liners are refitted – if the seal fails, the engine oil and coolant will mix **(see illustrations)**.

14 Apply a continuous bead of suitable sealant to the liner shoulder **(see illustration)**.

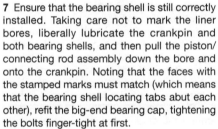

20.11 Carefully tap the piston into the cylinder

20.13a Clean around the shoulder on the liner . . .

The MG Rover specialists we spoke to recommended Blue Hylomar for this – check with your specialist or parts supplier for confirmation, however.

15 Remembering that the big-end numbers

20.12 Cylinder numbers (arrowed) marked on the cylinder block

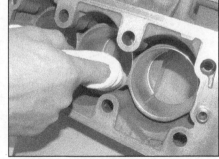

20.13b . . . and around the seat in the cylinder block

20.14 Apply a bead of sealant around the liner shoulder

20.15 Insert each piston/liner into its original position

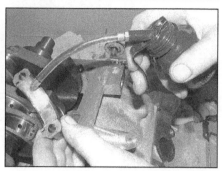

20.18 Lubricate the big-end shells with clean engine oil

20.19a Tighten the big-end cap bolts to the specified torque setting . . .

20.19b . . . and then through the specified angle

are fitted facing inwards, insert each liner/piston assembly into its original location, and ensure that the painted alignment marks line up. Seat the liner fully up to its shoulder, then ensure that it does not move, to allow the sealant to cure (see illustration).

16 Refit the liner clamps used prior to dismantling – otherwise the liners will be displaced when the big-ends are refitted to the crankshaft.

17 Lubricate the bearing and journal, then fit the first connecting rod onto the crankshaft – ensure that the liner is clamped, and move the piston as little as possible.

18 Ensure that the big-end bearing shells are in place, then lubricate and refit the big-end bearing caps to their original locations (see illustration). The manufacturer's markings should face inwards (or use those made prior to removal).

19 Lubricate the threads of the new big-end bolts with clean engine oil, then screw them into position in the connecting rod, tightening

them by hand. Evenly and progressively tighten the bolts to the specified Stage 1 torque setting, followed by angle-tightening each bolt through the specified Stage 2 angle. It is recommended that an angle-measuring gauge is used during this stage of the tightening, to ensure accuracy (see illustrations).

20 Refit the remaining big-end caps in the same way.

21 Before turning the crankshaft, make absolutely certain that all the liners are clamped. Rotate the crankshaft, and check that it turns freely, with no signs of binding or tight spots.

22 Refit the main bearing ladder and lower crankcase, as described in Section 19.

21 Engine –
initial start-up after overhaul

1 With the engine refitted to the vehicle, double-check the engine oil and coolant levels.

Make a final check to ensure that everything has been reconnected and that there are no tools or rags left in the engine compartment.

2 To prevent the engine from starting during initial cranking, remove the fuel pump fuse from the engine bay fusebox – see Wiring diagrams. Operate the starter motor and check that cranking is satisfactory, with no unusual noises. Ensure that the oil pressure warning light goes out during cranking.

3 Fit the fuel pump fuse. Note: Because fuel system components will be empty, the engine may take longer than normal to start.

4 Start the engine, and ensure that the oil pressure warning light goes off during cranking, or immediately the engine starts. Allow the engine to idle.

5 While the engine is idling, check for fuel, coolant and oil leaks. Do not be alarmed if there are some odd smells and smoke from parts getting hot and burning off oil deposits. If the hydraulic tappets have been disturbed, some valve gear noise may be heard at first; this should disappear as the oil circulates fully around the engine and normal pressure is restored in the tappets.

6 Keep the engine idling until hot coolant is felt circulating through the radiator top hose, check the ignition timing and idle speed and mixture (as appropriate), then stop the engine.

7 After a few minutes, recheck the oil and coolant levels and top-up as necessary.

8 If new pistons, rings or crankshaft bearings have been fitted, the engine must be run-in for the first 500 miles. Do not operate the engine at full throttle or allow it to labour in any gear during this period. It is recommended that the oil and filter be changed at the end of this period.

Chapter 2 Part E:
Diesel engine removal and general overhaul procedures

Contents

Crankshaft – inspection 13
Crankshaft – refitting 17
Crankshaft – removal 10
Cylinder block/crankcase – cleaning and inspection 11
Cylinder head – dismantling 6
Cylinder head – reassembly 8
Cylinder head and valves – cleaning and inspection 7
Engine – initial start-up after overhaul 19
Engine overhaul – dismantling sequence 5
Engine overhaul – general information 2

Engine overhaul – reassembly sequence 15
Engine/transmission – removal, separation and refitting 4
Engine/transmission removal – methods and precautions 3
General information 1
Main and big-end bearings – inspection 14
Piston rings – refitting 16
Piston/connecting rod assembly – inspection 12
Piston/connecting rod assembly – refitting 18
Piston/connecting rod assembly – removal 9

Degrees of difficulty

Easy, suitable for novice with little experience | **Fairly easy,** suitable for beginner with some experience | **Fairly difficult,** suitable for competent DIY mechanic | **Difficult,** suitable for experienced DIY mechanic | **Very difficult,** suitable for expert DIY or professional

Specifications

Cylinder block/crankcase
Material. . . . . Cast iron
Cylinder bore diameter . . . . 84.442 to 84.460 mm

Crankshaft
Number of main bearings 5
Main bearing journal diameter . . . . 60.703 to 60.719 mm
Big-end journal diameter . . . . 57.683 to 57.696 mm
Main bearing and big-end bearing running clearance . . . . 0.005 mm
Crankshaft endfloat . . . . 0.03 to 0.26 mm
Thrustwasher thickness . . . . 2.31 to 2.36 mm

Pistons and piston rings
Piston diameter . . . . 84.262 mm
Piston-to-bore clearance . . . . 0.18 to 0.20 mm
Piston ring end gaps (rings fitted 30 mm from top of bore):
   Top compression ring . . . . 0.25 to 0.27 mm
   Second compression ring . . . . 0.40 to 0.42 mm
   Oil control ring . . . . 0.30 to 0.32 mm
Piston ring end gaps (rings fitted to pistons):
   Top compression ring . . . . 0.30 to 0.50 mm
   Second compression ring . . . . 0.40 to 0.60 mm
   Oil control ring . . . . 0.25 to 0.50 mm
Piston ring-to-groove clearance:
   Top compression ring . . . . 0.115 to 0.135 mm
   Second compression ring . . . . 0.050 to 0.082 mm
   Oil control ring . . . . 0.050 to 0.082 mm

Gudgeon pins
Diameter . . . . 29.995 to 30.000 mm

Cylinder head and camshaft carrier

Material	Aluminium alloy
Maximum acceptable gasket face distortion	0.010 mm
Valve seat insert angle:	
Inlet	60°
Exhaust	58° to 62°
Valve seat width	1.5 mm
Valve seat insert diameter:	
Inlet	35.697 mm
Exhaust	31.05 to 31.55 mm
Cylinder head bolt length	243.41 mm

Valves

Stem diameter:	
Inlet	6.907 to 6.923 mm
Exhaust	6.897 to 6.913 mm
Guide inside diameter	6.950 to 6.963 mm
Stem-to-guide clearance (measured at valve head, with valve head extended 10 mm from seat):	
Inlet	0.056 mm
Exhaust	0.066 mm
Valve spring free length	37.0 mm
Valve guide fitted height	61.1 to 61.7 mm
Valve head recess below cylinder head face:	
Inlet	1.45 mm
Exhaust	1.35 mm

Torque wrench settings

Refer to Chapter 2C

1 General information

Included in this part of the Chapter are details of removing the engine/transmission unit from the vehicle and general overhaul procedures for the cylinder head, cylinder block/crankcase and all other engine internal components.

The information given ranges from advice concerning preparation for an overhaul and the purchase of new parts to detailed step-by-step procedures covering removal, inspection, renovation and refitting of engine internal components.

After Section 5, all instructions are based on the assumption that the engine has been removed from the vehicle. For information concerning in-car engine repair, as well as the removal and refitting of those external components necessary for full overhaul, refer to Chapter 2C and to Section 5 of this Chapter. Ignore any preliminary dismantling operations described in Chapter 2C that are no longer relevant once the engine has been removed from the vehicle.

2 Engine overhaul – general information

It is not always easy to determine when, or if, an engine should be completely overhauled, as a number of factors must be considered.

High mileage is not necessarily an indication that an overhaul is needed, while low mileage does not preclude the need for an overhaul. Frequency of servicing is probably the most important consideration. An engine that has had regular and frequent oil and filter changes, as well as other required maintenance, should give many thousands of miles of reliable service. Conversely, a neglected engine may require an overhaul very early in its life. If a complete service does not remedy any problems, major mechanical work is the only solution.

Excessive oil consumption is an indication that piston rings, valve seals and/or valve guides are in need of attention. Make sure that oil leaks are not responsible before deciding that the rings and/or guides are worn. Perform a compression or leakdown test to determine the likely cause of the problem (see Chapter 2C).

Check the oil pressure with a gauge fitted in place of the oil pressure switch and compare it with that specified. If it is extremely low, the main and big-end bearings and/or the oil pump are probably worn out.

Loss of power, rough running, knocking or metallic engine noises, excessive valve gear noise and high fuel consumption may also point to the need for an overhaul, especially if they are all present at the same time.

An engine overhaul involves restoring all internal parts to the specification of a new engine. During an overhaul, the pistons and the piston rings are renewed. New main and big-end bearings are generally fitted and, if necessary, the crankshaft may be renewed to restore the journals (see illustration). The valves are serviced as well, since they are usually in less than perfect condition at this point. While the engine is being overhauled, other components, such as the distributor, starter and alternator, can be overhauled as well. The end result should be an as-new engine that will give many trouble-free miles.

Critical cooling system components such as the hoses, thermostat and coolant pump should be renewed when an engine is overhauled. The radiator should be checked carefully to ensure that it is not clogged or leaking. Also it is a good idea to renew the oil pump whenever the engine is overhauled.

Before beginning the engine overhaul, read through the entire procedure to familiarise yourself with the scope and requirements of the job. Overhauling an engine is not difficult if you follow carefully all of the instructions, have the necessary tools and equipment and pay close attention to all specifications. However, it can be time-consuming. Plan on the vehicle being off the road for a minimum of two weeks, especially if parts must be taken to an engineering works for repair or reconditioning. Check on the availability of parts and make sure that any necessary special tools and equipment are obtained in advance. Most work can be done with typical hand tools, although a number of precision measuring tools are required for inspecting parts to determine if they must be renewed. Often the engineering works will handle the inspection of parts and offer advice concerning reconditioning and renewal.

Always wait until the engine has been completely dismantled and all components, especially the cylinder block/crankcase and the crankshaft, have been inspected before deciding what service and repair operations must be performed by an engineering works. Since the condition of these components will be the major factor to consider when determining whether to overhaul the original engine or buy a reconditioned unit, do not purchase parts or have overhaul work done on other components until they have been

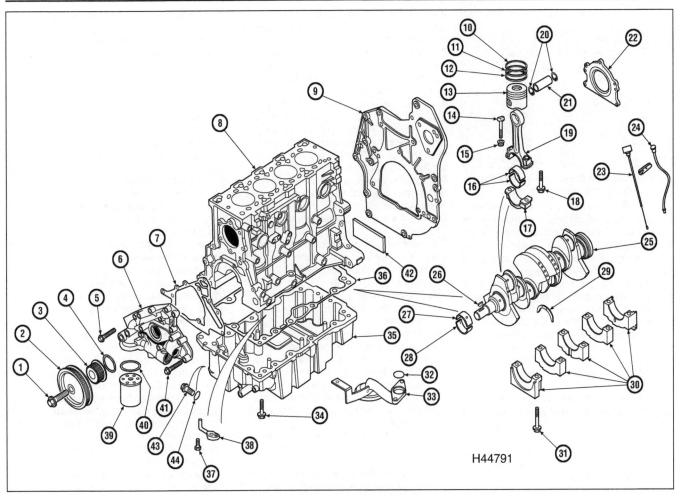

2.6 Cylinder block components

1   Crankshaft pulley bolt
2   Crankshaft pulley
3   Camshaft belt drive gear
4   Crankshaft right-hand
    seal
5   Bolt – M10
6   Oil pump
7   Gasket – oil pump
8   Cylinder block
9   Gearbox adapter plate
10 Top compression ring
11 2nd compression ring

12 Oil control ring
13 Piston
14 Bolt – connecting rod –
    Type A engines
15 Nut – connecting rod –
    Type A engines
16 Big-end bearing shells
17 Big-end cap
18 Bolt – connecting rod –
    Type B and C engines
19 Connecting rod
20 Gudgeon pin circlips

21 Gudgeon pin
22 Crankshaft left-hand oil seal
    and housing
23 Dipstick
24 Dipstick tube
25 Crankshaft
26 Woodruff key
27 Main bearing upper shell
28 Main bearing lower shell
29 Thrustwasher
30 Main bearing caps
31 Main bearing cap bolt

32 O-ring
33 Oil strainer and pick-up
    tube
34 Bolt – sump
35 Sump
36 Gasket – sump
37 Banjo bolt
38 Oil squirt jet
39 Oil filter
40 Oil filter O-ring
41 Bolt – M10

thoroughly inspected. As a general rule, time is the primary cost of an overhaul, so it does not pay to fit worn or substandard parts.

As a final note, to ensure maximum life and minimum trouble from a reconditioned engine, everything must be assembled with care in a spotlessly clean environment.

3 Engine/transmission removal – methods and precautions

If you have decided that the engine must be removed for overhaul or major repair work, several preliminary steps should be taken.

Locating a suitable place to work is extremely important. Adequate workspace, along with storage space for the vehicle, will be needed. If a workshop or garage is not available, at the very least a flat, level, clean work surface is required.

Cleaning the engine compartment and engine/transmission before beginning the removal procedure will help keep things clean and organised.

An engine hoist or A-frame will also be necessary. Make sure the equipment is rated in excess of the combined weight of the engine and transmission. Safety is of primary importance, considering the potential hazards involved in lifting the engine/transmission unit

out of the vehicle. The engine/transmission unit is removed by lowering it out from under the front of the vehicle.

If a novice is removing the engine/transmission unit, a helper should be available. Advice and aid from someone more experienced would also be helpful. There are many instances when one person cannot simultaneously perform all of the operations required when lowering the unit out of the vehicle.

Plan the operation ahead of time. Before starting work, arrange for the hire of or obtain all of the tools and equipment you will need. Some of the equipment necessary to perform engine/transmission removal and installation safely and with relative ease are (in addition

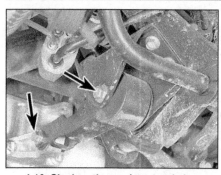

4.10 Slacken the engine steady bar mounting bolts – arrowed

to an engine hoist) a heavy duty trolley jack, complete sets of spanners and sockets as described at the back of this Manual, wooden blocks and plenty of rags and cleaning solvent for mopping-up spilled oil, coolant and fuel. If the hoist must be hired, make sure that you arrange for it in advance and perform all of the operations possible without it beforehand. This will save you money and time.

Plan for the vehicle to be out of use for quite a while. An engineering works will be required to perform some of the work, which you cannot accomplish without special equipment. These places often have a busy schedule, so it would be a good idea to consult them before removing the engine in order to accurately estimate the amount of time required to rebuild or repair components that may need work.

Always be extremely careful when removing and refitting the engine/transmission unit. Serious injury can result from careless actions. Plan ahead, take your time and a job of this nature, although major, can be accomplished successfully.

4 Engine/transmission – removal, separation and refitting

Caution: Read the notes in Section 3 – 'Engine/transmission removal – methods and precautions'.

Note: *On models with air conditioning, it will be necessary to disconnect the refrigerant lines in order to remove the engine/transmission unit from the vehicle. Have the refrigerant discharged by an air conditioning specialist before starting work and have ready some caps and plugs to plug the hose/pipe end fittings whilst the engine is removed. On completion it will be necessary to have the system recharged by an air conditioning specialist.* **Do not** *operate the air conditioning system whilst it is discharged.*

Note: *The engine can be removed from the car only as a complete unit with the transmission.*

Removal

1 On models with air conditioning, have the refrigerant discharged by an air conditioning specialist.

2 On all models, park the vehicle on firm, level ground then remove the bonnet as described in Chapter 11.

3 Release the retaining clips and remove the plastic cover from the top of the engine, taking care not to lose the grommets which are fitted to the cover mountings.

4 Chock the rear wheels and firmly apply the handbrake, then jack up the front of the vehicle (see *Jacking and vehicle support*). Securely support it on axle stands, bearing in mind the note at the start of this Section, and remove both front roadwheels.

5 Undo the retaining screws and fasteners and remove the undercover from beneath the engine/transmission unit.

6 Drain the cooling system as described in Chapter 1B.

7 If the engine or transmission is to be dismantled, working as described in Chapter 1B, first drain the engine/transmission oil.

8 Referring to Chapter 4C, carry out the following procedures.

  a) *Remove the air cleaner housing and intake duct.*

  b) *Remove the exhaust front pipe.*

  c) *Release the retaining clips and disconnect the fuel feed and return hoses from the pipes on the left-hand end of the rear of the engine. Plug the hose and pipe ends to minimise fuel loss and prevent the entry of dirt into the system. Mop-up all spilt fuel.*

  d) *Remove the injection system airflow meter and electronic control module (ECM).*

  e) *Disconnect the wiring connectors from the injection pump, the fuel injector needle lift sensor (fitted to No 1 injector) and the crankshaft sensor.*

  f) *On models not fitted with an intercooler, disconnect the accelerator cable from the injection pump and position it clear of the engine.*

  g) *On models with an intercooler, remove the ducts linking the intercooler to the turbocharger and manifold.*

9 Referring to Chapter 5A, carry out the following operations.

  a) *Remove the battery, mounting tray and bracket.*

  b) *Disconnect the wiring from the starter motor.*

  c) *Disconnect the wiring from the alternator.*

10 Slacken and remove the engine mounting rear steady bar bolts and remove the bar from the rear of the sump **(see illustration)**.

11 Disconnect the wiring connector from the exhaust gas recirculation (EGR) solenoid valve (see Chapter 4C) and the oil pressure switch then unclip the wiring harness from the right-hand end of the engine unit.

12 Disconnect the wiring connectors from the coolant temperature sensors, which are screwed into the thermostat housing on the front of the cylinder head. Unclip the wiring harness and position it clear of the engine unit.

13 Unscrew the terminal nut and disconnect the glow plug feed wiring from No 2 glow plug. Refit the nut to the glow plug for safekeeping.

14 Disconnect the wiring connector from the radiator cooling fan.

15 Referring to Chapter 7A, carry out the following procedures.

  a) *Drain the transmission oil (if not already done) or be prepared for oil spillage as the engine/transmission unit is removed.*

  b) *Disconnect the gearchange selector and steady rods from the transmission unit.*

  c) *Disconnect the wiring connector from the vehicle speed sensor and reversing light switch.*

  d) *Unbolt the earth lead from the front of the transmission housing.*

16 Unclip the engine wiring harness from the left-hand end of the cylinder head and position it clear of the engine.

17 Release the retaining clip and disconnect the servo unit vacuum hose, which is situated at the right-hand end of the camshaft cover. Also disconnect the vacuum hose from the EGR valve.

18 Release the retaining clip and disconnect the radiator top and bottom hoses from the cylinder head and oil cooler. Also disconnect the heater coolant hose from the pipe on the left-hand end of the rear of the cylinder head.

19 Referring to Chapter 6, trace the clutch hydraulic pipe back from the master cylinder to its quick-release fitting on the bulkhead. Wipe clean and disconnect the two halves of the fitting. Mop-up any spilt fluid and take precautions not to allow any dirt to enter the hydraulic system; the hose fittings are fitted with valves to prevent fluid loss when they are disconnected.

20 Referring to Chapter 10, disconnect the feed pipe and return hose from the power steering pump and free the pipe from the engine. Locate the feed pipe union at the rear of the engine then slacken the union nut and separate the pipe and hose so the pipe is free to be removed with the engine. Plug the pipe/hose ends and pump unions to minimise fluid loss and prevent the entry of dirt into the hydraulic system.

21 Referring to Chapter 8, disconnect the driveshaft inner ends from the transmission unit. Note that it is not necessary to remove the driveshafts completely, they can be left attached to the hub assemblies and released as the hub is pulled outwards.

Caution: Do not allow the shafts to hang down under their own weight as this could damage the constant velocity joints/gaiters.

22 Release the fuel filter from its mounting bracket and position it clear of the engine/transmission unit.

23 On models with air conditioning, trace the refrigerant pipes/hoses back from the compressor to the unions at the front of the engine and bulkhead. Slacken the union nuts and disconnect both pipes/hoses, noting the sealing rings. Free both pipes from any relevant clips/ties so they are free to be removed with the engine unit. Recover the sealing ring from each union and plug the hose/pipe ends to prevent the entry of dirt and moisture into the air conditioning system. Discard all sealing rings, new ones must be used on refitting. Also disconnect the wiring connector from the air conditioning compressor.

24 On all models, manoeuvre the engine hoist into position, and attach it to the lifting brackets bolted onto the cylinder head. Raise the hoist until it is supporting the weight of the engine.

25 Remove the engine/transmission right-hand and left-hand mounting assemblies as described in Chapter 2C, Section 20.

26 Make a final check that any components which would prevent the removal of the engine/transmission from the car have been removed or disconnected. Ensure that components such as the driveshafts are secured so that they cannot be damaged on removal.

27 Raise the engine/transmission assembly out of position, making sure that nothing is trapped, taking great care not to damage the radiator. Enlist the help of an assistant during this procedure, as it may be necessary to tilt the assembly slightly to clear the body panels. Great care must be taken to ensure that no components are trapped and damaged during the removal procedure.

28 Once the engine is high enough, lift it out over the front of the body, and lower the unit to the ground.

Separation

29 With the engine/transmission assembly removed, support the assembly on suitable blocks of wood, on a workbench (or failing that, on a clean area of the workshop floor).

30 Undo the retaining bolts and remove the starter motor from the transmission (see Chapter 5A).

31 Ensure that both engine and transmission are adequately supported, then slacken and remove the remaining bolts securing the transmission housing to the engine mounting plate. Note the correct fitted positions of each bolt (and the relevant brackets) as they are removed, to use as a reference on refitting.

32 Carefully withdraw the transmission from the engine, ensuring that the weight of the transmission is not allowed to hang on the input shaft while it is engaged with the clutch friction disc.

33 If they are loose, remove the locating dowels from the engine or transmission, and keep them in a safe place.

Refitting

34 If the engine and transmission have been separated, perform the operations described below in paragraphs 35 to 38. If not, proceed as described from paragraph 39 onwards.

35 Referring to Chapter 6, apply a smear of molybdenum disulphide grease (Rover recommend the use of Molykote BR2 plus, G-n plus or G-Rapid plus) to the clutch release bearing, fork and guide sleeve contact surfaces and check the operation of the clutch release mechanism. Also apply a smear of grease to the transmission input shaft splines; **do not** apply too much grease otherwise the clutch friction plate may be contaminated.

36 Ensure the locating dowels are correctly positioned then carefully offer the transmission to the engine, until the locating dowels are engaged. Ensure that the weight of the transmission is not allowed to hang on the input shaft as it is engaged with the clutch friction disc.

37 Refit the transmission housing-to-engine bolts, ensuring that all the necessary brackets are correctly positioned, and tighten them to the specified torque setting.

38 Refit the starter motor and tighten its mounting bolts to the specified torque (see Chapter 5A).

39 Reconnect the hoist and lifting tackle to the engine lifting brackets. With the aid of an assistant, lift the assembly over the engine compartment.

40 The assembly should be tilted as necessary to clear the surrounding components, as during removal; lower the assembly into position in the engine compartment, manipulating the hoist and lifting tackle as necessary.

41 Refit the right-hand and left-hand mounting assemblies as described in Chapter 2C, Section 20. Tighten the right-hand mounting steady rod bolts by hand only at this stage; tighten them to the specified torque once the vehicle is resting on its wheels and all other items are correctly reconnected.

42 The remainder of the refitting procedure is a direct reversal of the removal sequence, noting the following points:

a) Ensure that all wiring is correctly routed and retained by all the relevant retaining clips and that all connectors are correctly and securely reconnected.

b) Ensure that all disturbed hoses are correctly reconnected, and securely retained by their retaining clips.

c) Renew the transmission differential oil seals (see Chapter 7A) before refitting the driveshafts.

d) Renew all power steering/air conditioning pipe/hose union sealing rings and tighten the union nuts/bolts to the specified torque.

e) Refill the transmission with the correct quantity and type of oil, as described in Chapter 7A and 'Lubricants and fluids'. If the oil was not drained, top-up the level as described in Chapter 1B.

f) Refill the engine with oil (Chapter 1B) and also refill the cooling system.

g) Prime and bleed the fuel system and adjust the accelerator cable (models not fitted with an intercooler only) as described in Chapter 4C.

h) On models with air conditioning, have the system recharged with refrigerant by an air conditioning specialist.

5 Engine overhaul – dismantling sequence

Note: *When removing external components from the engine, pay close attention to details that may be helpful or important during refitting. Note the fitted position of gaskets, seals, spacers, pins, washers, bolts and other small items.*

1 It is much easier to work on the engine if it is mounted on a portable engine stand. These stands can often be hired from a tool hire shop. Before the engine is mounted on a stand, the flywheel should be removed so that the stand bolts can be tightened into the end of the cylinder block/crankcase.

2 If a stand is not available, it is possible to dismantle the engine with it blocked up on a sturdy workbench or on the floor. Be extra careful not to tip or drop the engine when working without a stand.

3 If you are going to obtain a reconditioned engine, all external components must be removed for transfer to the new engine (just as if you are doing a complete engine overhaul yourself). These components include the following **(see illustrations)**:

a) Alternator/brake vacuum pump assembly.

b) Air conditioning compressor (where applicable).

c) Power steering pump/coolant pump assembly.

d) Coolant outlet elbow.

e) Dipstick tube.

f) Fuel injection pump, drivebelt, fuel

5.3a Unscrew the securing bolts . . .

5.3b . . . and remove the transmission mounting plate

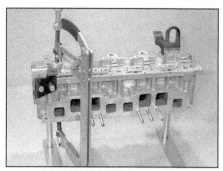

6.3a Using a valve spring compressor tool . . .

6.3b . . . compress the valve spring until the split collets can be removed

6.5 Place each valve assembly in a labelled polythene bag

injectors, glow plugs, and associated fuel system components.
g) All electrical switches and sensors.
h) Inlet and exhaust manifolds.
i) Oil pipes, coolant pipes and brackets.
j) Oil cooler.
k) Oil filter.
l) Engine mounting brackets.
m) Flywheel.
n) Transmission mounting plate.
o) Ancillary mounting brackets.

4 If you are obtaining a short motor (which consists of the engine cylinder block/crankcase, crankshaft, pistons and connecting rods all assembled), then the fuel injection pump drivebelt, timing belt, cylinder head, sump, oil pump and oil cooler will have to be removed also.

5 If you are planning a complete overhaul, the engine can be dismantled and the internal components removed in the following order:
a) Inlet and exhaust manifolds.
b) Timing and injection pump belts, sprockets, tensioner, and timing belt rear covers.
c) Cylinder head.
d) Flywheel.
e) Sump.
f) Oil pump.
g) Piston/connecting rod assemblies.
h) Crankshaft.

6 Before beginning the dismantling and overhaul procedures, make sure that you have all of the correct tools necessary.

6 Cylinder head – dismantling

Note: New and reconditioned cylinder heads are available from the manufacturer and from engine overhaul specialists. Due to the fact that some specialist tools are required for dismantling and inspection, and new components may not be readily available, it may be more practical and economical for the home mechanic to purchase a reconditioned head rather than dismantle, inspect and recondition the original. A valve spring compressor tool will be required for this operation.

1 With the cylinder head removed, if not already done, remove the fuel injectors (see Chapter 4C) and the glow plugs (see Chapter 5C), then proceed as follows.

2 Remove the camshaft and hydraulic tappets, as described in Chapter 2C.

3 Using a valve spring compressor tool, compress each valve spring in turn until the split collets can be removed. Release the compressor and lift off the spring retainer and spring, then use a pair of pliers to extract the spring lower seat/stem seal (see illustrations).

> **HAYNES HINT**
> If, when the valve spring compressor is screwed down, the spring retainer refuses to free and expose the split collets, gently tap the top of the tool directly over the retainer with a light hammer. This will free the retainer.

4 Withdraw the valve through the combustion chamber.

5 It is essential that each valve is stored together with its collets, retainer and spring, and that all valves are kept in their correct sequence, unless they are so badly worn that they are to be renewed. If they are going to be kept and used again, place each valve assembly in a labelled polythene bag or similar small container (see illustration). Note that No 1 valve is nearest to the timing belt end of the engine.

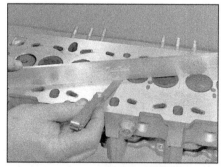

7.6 Use a straight-edge and feeler blade to check the cylinder head for distortion

7 Cylinder head and valves – cleaning and inspection

Note: If the engine has been severely overheated, it is best to assume that the cylinder head is warped and to check carefully for signs of this.

Note: Be sure to perform all the following inspection procedures before concluding that the services of a machine shop or engine overhaul specialist are required. Make a list of all items that require attention.

1 Thorough cleaning of the cylinder head and valve components, followed by a detailed inspection, will enable you to decide how much valve service work must be carried out during the engine overhaul.

Cleaning

2 Scrape away all traces of old gasket material and sealing compound from the cylinder head.

3 Scrape away all carbon from the combustion chambers and ports, then wash the cylinder head thoroughly with paraffin or a suitable solvent.

4 Scrape off any heavy carbon deposits that may have formed on the valves, then use a power-operated wire brush to remove deposits from the valve heads and stems.

Inspection

Cylinder head

5 Inspect the head very carefully for cracks, evidence of coolant leakage and other damage. If cracks are found, a new cylinder head should be obtained.

6 Use a straight-edge and feeler blade to check that the cylinder head surface is not distorted (see illustration). Note that the cylinder head cannot be refaced, and must be renewed if the surface is distorted beyond the specified limit.

7 Examine the valve seats in each of the combustion chambers. If they are severely pitted, cracked or burned, then they will need to be renewed or recut by an engine overhaul specialist. If they are only slightly pitted, this can be removed by grinding-in the valve heads

and seats with fine valve-grinding compound as described below. To check for excessive wear, refit each valve and measure the recess of the valve head below the surface of the cylinder head. This can be carried out with a dial gauge, or with a straight-edge and feeler blades **(see illustration)**. If the measurement is above the specified limit, the valve and the valve seat insert must be renewed.

8 If the valve guides are worn, indicated by a side-to-side motion of the valve, new guides and valves must be fitted. Measure the diameter of the existing valve stems (see below) and the bore of the guides, then calculate the clearance and compare the result with the specified value. If the clearance is excessive, renew the valves and guides as necessary. Note that the valve guides can only be renewed twice – if the guides need to be renewed for the third time, the cylinder head must be renewed. A mark on the camshaft side of the cylinder head, adjacent to the valve guide will be present if the valve guide has been renewed before: '+' indicates that the guide has been renewed once before, and '-' indicates that the guide has been renewed twice before.

9 Valve guide renewal is best carried out by an engine overhaul specialist, as the cylinder head must be evenly heated to remove and fit the guides, and the guides must be accurately reamed once fitted.

Valves

10 Examine the head of each valve for pitting, burning, cracks and general wear, then check the valve stem for scoring and wear ridges. Rotate the valve and check for any obvious indication that it is bent. Look for pits and excessive wear on the tip of each valve stem. Renew any valve that shows any such signs of wear or damage.

11 If the valve appears satisfactory at this stage, measure the valve stem diameter at several points by using a micrometer **(see illustration)**. Any significant difference in the readings obtained indicates wear of the valve stem. Should any of these conditions be apparent, the valve(s) must be renewed.

12 If the valves are in satisfactory condition they should be ground (lapped) into their respective seats to ensure a smooth gas-tight seal. If the seat is only lightly pitted, or if it has been recut, fine grinding compound only should be used to produce the required finish. Coarse valve-grinding compound should not be used unless a seat is badly burned or deeply pitted. If this is the case, the cylinder head and valves should be inspected by an expert to decide whether seat recutting or even the renewal of the valve or seat insert is required.

13 Valve grinding is carried out as follows. Place the cylinder head upside down on a bench.

14 Smear a trace of (the appropriate grade of) valve-grinding compound on the seat face and press a suction grinding tool onto

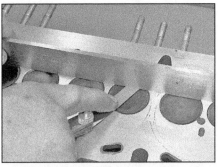
7.7 Checking the recess of a valve head below the surface of the cylinder head

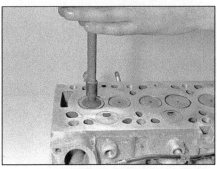
7.14 Grinding-in a valve using a suction grinding tool

the valve head. With a semi-rotary action, grind the valve head to its seat, lifting the valve occasionally to redistribute the grinding compound **(see illustration)**. A light spring placed under the valve head will greatly ease this operation.

15 If coarse grinding compound is being used, work only until a dull, matt even surface is produced on both the valve seat and the valve, then wipe off the used compound and repeat the process with fine compound. When a smooth unbroken ring of light grey matt finish is produced on both the valve and seat, the grinding operation is complete. Do not grind in the valves any further than absolutely necessary, or the seat will be prematurely sunk into the cylinder head.

16 To check that the seat has not been over-ground, measure the valve head recess, as described in paragraph 7.

17 When all the valves have been ground-

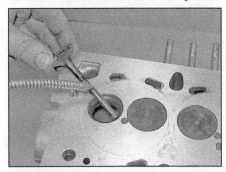
8.1 Lubricate the valve stems with clean engine oil

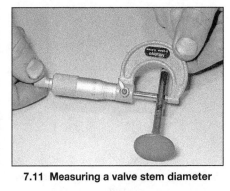
7.11 Measuring a valve stem diameter

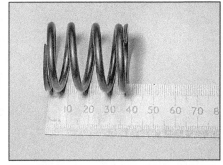
7.18 Measuring a valve spring free length

in, carefully wash off all traces of grinding compound using paraffin or a suitable solvent.

Valve components

18 Examine the valve springs for signs of damage and discoloration and also measure their free length using vernier calipers or a rule, or by comparing each existing spring with a new component **(see illustration)**.

19 Stand each spring on a flat surface and check it for squareness. If any of the springs are damaged, distorted or have lost their tension, then obtain a complete new set of springs.

20 Check the hydraulic tappets as described in Part C of this Chapter.

8 Cylinder head – reassembly

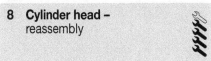

Note: *A valve spring compressor tool will be required for this operation. New valve spring lower seat/stem oil seals will be required.*

1 Lubricate the valve stems with clean engine oil and insert each valve into its original location **(see illustration)**. If new valves are being fitted, insert them into the locations to which they have been ground.

2 Working on the first valve, dip the **new** spring lower seat/stem seal in clean engine oil then carefully locate it over the valve and onto the guide. Take care not to damage the seal as it is passed over the valve stem. Press the seal firmly onto the guide **(see illustration)**.

8.2 Fitting a valve spring lower seat/stem seal

8.3a Refit the spring . . .

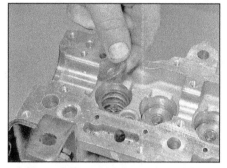

8.3b . . . followed by the spring retainer

8.4 Compress the spring and fit the split collets into place

3 Locate the spring on the seat, followed by the spring retainer **(see illustrations)**.

4 Compress the valve spring and locate the split collets in the recess in the valve stem **(see illustration)**. Use a little grease to hold the collets in place. Release the compressor, then repeat the procedure on the remaining valves.

5 With all the valves installed, rest the cylinder head on wooden blocks or stands (**do not** rest the head flat on a bench) and, using a hammer and interposed block of wood, tap the end of each valve stem to settle the components.

6 Refit the hydraulic tappets and camshaft as described in Chapter 2C.

9 Piston/connecting rod assembly – removal

Note: *The big-end bearing caps may be*

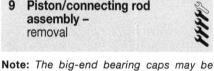

9.3 Connecting rod and big-end cap identification markings

secured to the connecting rods by nuts, or bolts, depending on engine type. On engines where the big-end bearing caps are secured by bolts, 'fracture-split' connecting rod/bearing cap assemblies are fitted (big-end bearing caps secured by bolts) – each connecting rod/bearing cap is manufactured as a one-piece component, and then 'fractured' to give the connecting rod and bearing cap. On engines with fracture-split assemblies, each bearing cap is therefore perfectly matched to its respective connecting rod, and the big-end bolts are offset to prevent incorrect fitting of the bearing cap.

1 Remove the cylinder head as described in Chapter 2C.

2 Remove the sump and oil pick-up pipe, as described in Chapter 2C.

3 If the connecting rods and big-end caps are not marked to indicate their positions in the cylinder block (ie, marked with cylinder

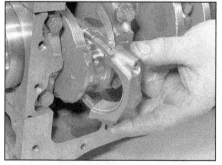

9.4 Removing a big-end bearing cap

numbers), centre-punch them at adjacent points either side of the cap/rod joint. Note to which side of the engine the marks face **(see illustration)**.

4 Unscrew the big-end cap nuts or bolts (as applicable) from the first connecting rod, and remove the cap **(see illustration)**. Tape the cap and the shell together to enable subsequent examination. Similarly, the big-end cap nuts or bolts (as applicable) must be kept in their original locations, with their original connecting rod/bearing cap assemblies (refit the nuts/bolts once the relevant piston/connecting rod assembly has been removed).

5 Check the top of the cylinder bore for a wear ridge. If evident, carefully scrape it away with a ridge reamer tool; otherwise the piston rings may jam against the ridge as the piston is pushed out of the block.

6 Place the wooden handle of a hammer against the bottom of the connecting rod, and push the piston/rod assembly up and out of the cylinder bore. Take care to keep the connecting rods clear of the cylinder bore walls, and be careful not to damage the piston oil spray jets fitted to the cylinder block. Recover the bearing shell, and tape it to the connecting rod if it is to be re-used.

7 Remove the remaining three assemblies in a similar way. Rotate the crankshaft as necessary to bring the big-end nuts or bolts (as applicable) to the most accessible position.

10 Crankshaft – removal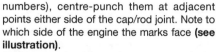

Note: *A dial gauge will be required to check crankshaft endfloat.*

1 Remove the flywheel, and the crankshaft left-hand oil seal, as described in Chapter 2C.

2 Remove the pistons and connecting rods, as described in Section 9.

3 Remove the oil pump as described in Chapter 2C.

4 Invert the cylinder block so that the crankshaft is uppermost.

5 Before removing the crankshaft, check the endfloat using a dial gauge in contact with the end of the crankshaft. Push the crankshaft fully one way, and then zero the gauge. Push the crankshaft fully the other way, and check the endfloat **(see illustration)**. The result should be compared with the specified limit, and will give an indication as to whether new thrust bearing shells are required.

6 The main bearing caps are normally numbered 1 to 5 from the timing belt end of the engine **(see illustration)**. If the bearing caps are not marked, centre-punch them to indicate their locations, and note to which side of the engine the marks face.

7 Starting with the centre bearing cap, and working progressively outwards, unscrew and remove the main bearing cap bolts. Keep all the bolts in their fitted order.

8 Using the fingers only, rock each main bearing cap until it is released from its locating dowels (see illustration). Do not tap the bearing caps sideways to release them. Recover the bearing shells if they are loose, and tape them to their respective caps.

9 Lift the crankshaft from the crankcase. Take care, the crankshaft if heavy! Take care not to damage the piston oil spay jets fitted to the cylinder block.

10 Extract the upper bearing shells, and identify them for position. Similarly, extract the two thrustwashers from the centre bearing location (see illustration).

11 Cylinder block/crankcase – cleaning and inspection

Cleaning

1 Before proceeding, unscrew the securing bolts, and remove the piston oil spray jets from the cylinder block (see illustration). Note that each spray jet is located by a roll-pin.

2 For complete cleaning, ideally the core plugs should be removed, where fitted. Drill a small hole in the plugs, then insert a self-tapping screw, and pull out the plugs using a pair of grips or a slide hammer (see illustration). Also remove all external components (senders, sensors, brackets, etc).

3 Scrape all traces of gasket from the cylinder block, taking particular care not to damage the cylinder head and sump mating faces.

4 Remove all oil gallery plugs, where fitted. The plugs are usually very tight – they may have to be drilled out and the holes retapped. Use new plugs when the engine is reassembled.

5 If the block is extremely dirty, it should be steam-cleaned.

6 If the block has been steam-cleaned, clean all oil holes and oil galleries one more time on completion. Flush all internal passages with warm water until the water runs clear. Dry the block thoroughly, and wipe all machined surfaces with light oil. If you have access to compressed air, use it to speed the drying process, and to blow out all the oil holes and galleries.

 Warning: Wear eye protection when using compressed air.

7 If the block is relatively clean, an adequate cleaning job can be achieved with hot soapy water and a stiff brush. Take plenty of time, and do a thorough job. Regardless of the cleaning method used, be sure to clean all oil holes and galleries very thoroughly, dry the block completely, and coat all machined surfaces with light oil.

8 The threaded holes in the cylinder block must be clean, to ensure accurate torque readings when tightening fixings during reassembly. Run the correct-size tap (which can be determined from the size of

10.5 Checking crankshaft endfloat using a dial gauge

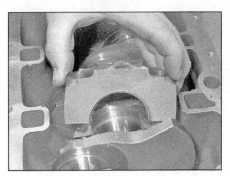

10.8 Removing a main bearing cap

the relevant bolt) into each of the holes to remove rust, corrosion, thread sealant or other contamination, and to restore damaged threads (see illustration). If possible, use compressed air to clear the holes of debris produced by this operation. Do not forget to clean the threads of all bolts and nuts as well.

9 After coating the mating surfaces of the new core plugs with suitable sealant, fit them to the cylinder block. Make sure that they are driven in straight and seated correctly, or leakage could result. Special tools are available to fit the core plugs, but a large socket, with an outside diameter that will just fit into the core plug, will work just as well.

10 Where applicable, apply suitable sealant to the new oil gallery plugs, and insert them into the relevant holes in the cylinder block. Tighten the plugs securely.

11 Thoroughly clean the piston oil spray jets and their securing bolts. Examine the spray

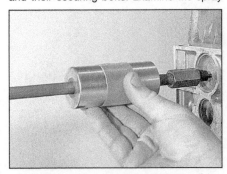

11.2 Removing a core plug using a slide hammer

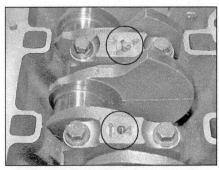

10.6 Main bearing cap identification markings

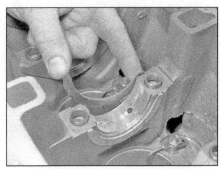

10.10 Extract the thrustwashers from the centre main bearing location

jets for damage or distortion, and renew if necessary. Ensure that the oil spray jets are clear, and that the locating roll-pins are in position in the cylinder block, then refit the spray jets, ensuring that they locate with the roll-pins. Apply a little thread-locking fluid to

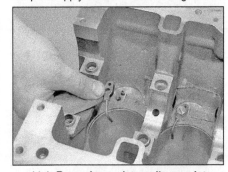

11.1 Removing a piston oil spray jet

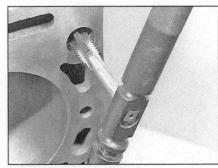

11.8 Clean out the threaded holes in the cylinder block using the correct-size tap

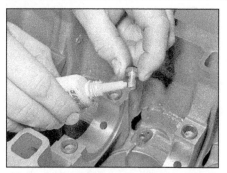

11.11 Apply thread-locking fluid to the oil spray jet securing bolts

the threads of each oil spray jet securing bolt, then refit the bolt and tighten to the specified torque **(see illustration)**.

Caution: Ensure that the thread-locking fluid does not enter the oil hole in the oil spray jet securing bolt.

12 If the engine is to be left dismantled for some time, refit the main bearing caps, tighten the bolts finger-tight, and cover the cylinder block with a large plastic bag to keep it clean and prevent corrosion.

Inspection

13 Visually check the block for cracks, rust and corrosion. Look for stripped threads in the threaded holes (it may be possible to recut stripped threads using a suitable tap). If there has been any history of internal coolant leakage, it may be worthwhile asking an engine overhaul specialist to check the block using special equipment. If defects are found, have the block repaired if possible; otherwise a new block may be the only option.

14 Examine the cylinder bores for taper, ovality, scoring and scratches. Start by carefully examining the top of the cylinder bores. If they are at all worn, a very slight ridge will be found on the thrust side. This marks the top of the piston ring travel.

15 Measure the bore diameter of each cylinder approximately 70 mm from the top of the bore, parallel to the crankshaft axis **(see illustration)**.

16 Next, measure the bore diameter at right angles to the crankshaft axis. Compare the results with the figures given in the Specifications.

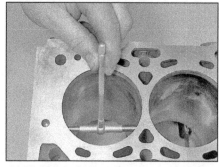

11.15 Measuring a cylinder bore diameter using an internal micrometer

17 Repeat the procedure for the remaining cylinders.

18 If the cylinders wear exceeds the permitted tolerances, or if the cylinder walls are badly scored or scuffed, then the cylinder block and pistons **must** be renewed. Note that it is not possible to rebore the cylinder block, as only one size of piston is available for this engine. Similarly, **do not** attempt to hone or 'glaze-bust' the cylinder bores.

12 Piston/connecting rod assembly – inspection

1 Before the inspection process can begin, the piston/connecting rod assemblies must be cleaned, and the original piston rings removed from the pistons.

2 Carefully expand the old rings over the top of the pistons. The use of two or three old feeler blades will be helpful in preventing the rings dropping into empty grooves **(see illustration)**. Take care, however, as piston rings are sharp.

3 Scrape away all traces of carbon from the top of the piston. A hand-held wire brush, or a piece of fine emery cloth, can be used once the majority of the deposits have been scraped away.

4 Remove the carbon from the ring grooves in the piston, using an old ring. Break the ring in half to do this (be careful not to cut your fingers – piston rings are sharp). Be very careful to remove only the carbon deposits – do not remove any metal, and do not nick or scratch the sides of the ring grooves.

5 Once the deposits have been removed, clean the piston/connecting rod assembly with paraffin or a suitable solvent, and dry thoroughly. Make sure that the oil return holes in the ring grooves are clear.

6 If the pistons and cylinder bores are not damaged or worn excessively, the original pistons can be refitted. Normal piston wear shows up as even vertical wear on the piston thrust surfaces, and slight looseness of the top ring in its groove. New piston rings should always be used when the engine is reassembled.

7 Carefully inspect each piston for cracks around the skirt, at the gudgeon pin bosses, and at the piston ring lands (between the ring grooves).

8 Look for scoring and scuffing on the thrust faces of the piston skirt, holes in the piston crown, and burned areas at the edge of the crown. If the skirt is scored or scuffed, the engine may have been suffering from overheating, and/or abnormal combustion ('pinking') which caused excessively-high operating temperatures. The cooling and lubrication systems should be checked thoroughly. A hole in the piston crown, or burned areas at the edge of the piston crown indicates that abnormal combustion (pre-ignition, pinking, knocking, or detonation) has been occurring. If any of the above problems exist, the causes must be investigated and corrected, or the damage will occur again. The causes may include incorrect fuel injection pump timing, inlet air leaks, or a faulty fuel injector.

9 Corrosion of the piston, in the form of pitting, indicates that coolant has been leaking into the combustion chamber and/or the crankcase. Again, the cause must be corrected, or the problem may persist in the rebuilt engine.

10 Check the piston-to-bore clearance by measuring the cylinder bore (see Section 11) and the piston diameter. Measure the piston 44 mm from the bottom of the skirt, at a 90° angle to the gudgeon pin. Note that the measurement should be made on the bare metal surfaces of the piston skirt, **not** on the graphite-coated areas **(see illustrations)**. Subtract the piston diameter from the bore diameter to obtain the clearance. If

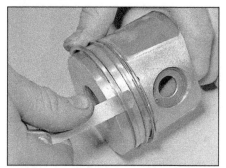

12.2 Removing a piston ring with the aid of a feeler blade

12.10a Measure the diameter of the pistons . . .

12.10b . . . across the bare metal surfaces (arrowed) of the piston skirt

12.14a Prise out the circlips . . .

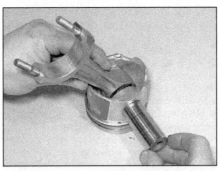

12.14b . . . and push the gudgeon pin from the piston

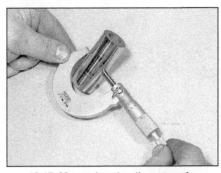

12.17 Measuring the diameter of a gudgeon pin

this is greater than the figures given in the Specifications, and the cylinder bore diameter is within limits, new pistons must be fitted. If the cylinder bore is worn beyond the specified limits, the block and pistons **must** be renewed. Note that it is not possible to rebore the cylinder block, as only one size of piston is available for this engine. Similarly, **do not** attempt to hone or glaze-bust the cylinder bores.

11 Alternatively, the piston-to-bore clearance can be measured as follows. Invert the piston, and slide it into the relevant cylinder bore, with the arrow on the piston crown pointing towards the flywheel end of the cylinder block. Position the piston with the bottom of the skirt 25 mm below the top of the cylinder bore. Using a feeler blade, measure the clearance between the piston skirt and the left-hand side of the cylinder bore (when viewed with the cylinder block inverted, from the timing belt end of the cylinder block).

12 Examine each connecting rod carefully for signs of damage, such as cracks around the big-end and small-end bearings. Check that the rod is not bent or distorted. Damage is highly unlikely, unless the engine has been

seized or badly overheated. Detailed checking of the connecting rod assembly can only be carried out by a Rover dealer or engine repair specialist with the necessary equipment.

13 The gudgeon pins are of the floating type, secured in position by two circlips. The pistons and connecting rods can be separated as follows.

14 Using a small flat-bladed screwdriver, prise out the circlips, and push out the gudgeon pin **(see illustrations)**. Hand pressure should be sufficient to remove the pin. Identify the piston and rod to ensure correct reassembly. Discard the circlips – new ones **must** be used on refitting.

15 Examine the gudgeon pin and connecting rod small-end bearing for signs of wear or damage. It should be possible to push the gudgeon pin through the connecting rod bush by hand, without noticeable play. If the connecting rod bush is worn, the connecting rod must be renewed – it is not possible to renew the bushes.

16 Similarly, check the fit of the gudgeon pin in its relevant piston. The pin must be a tight sliding fit, with no perceptible side play.

17 Measure the diameter of the gudgeon pin **(see illustration)**. If the diameter is less than the specified limit, or if excessive side play in the piston is evident, the gudgeon pin and piston must be renewed as an assembly.

18 Repeat the checking procedure for the remaining pistons, connecting rods and gudgeon pins.

19 The connecting rods themselves should not be in need of renewal, unless seizure

or some other major mechanical failure has occurred. Check the alignment of the connecting rods visually, and if the rods are not straight, take them to an engine overhaul specialist for a more detailed check.

20 Examine all components, and obtain any new parts from your Rover dealer. If new pistons are purchased, they will be supplied complete with gudgeon pins and circlips. Circlips can also be purchased individually. Note that on models with fracture split connecting rod/bearing cap assemblies (big-end bearing caps secured by bolts), if a connecting rod requires renewal, it can only be renewed as an assembly with the relevant bearing cap.

21 Position the piston in relation to the connecting rod, as follows **(see illustrations)**.

a) *On models where the big-end bearing caps are secured by nuts, the bearing shell tag recess in the connecting rod should be positioned to the left of the arrow on the piston crown, when the piston is viewed from the flywheel end.*

b) *On models where the big-end bearing caps are secured by bolts, the cast boss on the connecting rod should be positioned on the same side of the assembly as the arrow on the piston crown.*

22 Apply a smear of clean engine oil to the gudgeon pin. Slide it into the piston and through the connecting rod small-end. Check that the piston pivots freely on the rod, then secure the gudgeon pin in position with two new circlips. Ensure that each circlip is correctly located in its groove in the piston.

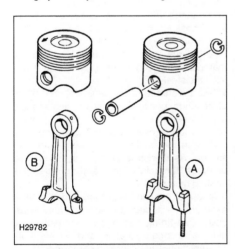

12.21a Piston and connecting rod identification

A *Assembly with big-end bearing cap secured by nuts*
B *Assembly with big-end bearing cap secured by bolts*

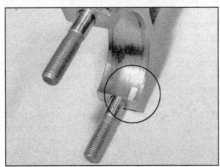

12.21b Where the bearing caps are secured by nuts, the bearing shell tag recess in the connecting rod . . .

12.21c . . . should be positioned to the left of the arrow on the piston crown when the piston is viewed from the flywheel end

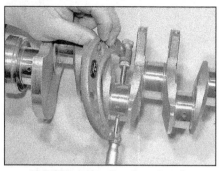

13.6 Measuring the diameter of a crankshaft big-end bearing journal

23 On engines where the big-end bearing caps are secured by nuts, using the fingers only, check that each big-end bearing cap nut rotates freely on the threads of its respective bolt. If any nut is tight, then both bolts and nuts from the relevant connecting rod must be renewed.

24 On engines where the big-end bearing caps are secured by bolts, using the fingers only, check that each bolt turns freely in its connecting rod. If there is any sign of binding in the threads, the bolts must be renewed.

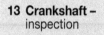

13 Crankshaft – inspection

1 Clean the crankshaft using paraffin or a suitable solvent, and dry it, preferably with compressed air if available. Be sure to clean the oil holes with a pipe cleaner or similar probe, to ensure that they are not obstructed.

 Warning: Wear eye protection when using compressed air.

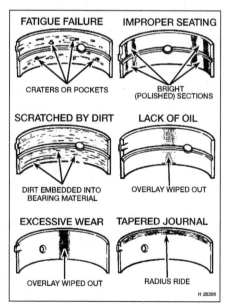

14.2 Typical bearing failures

2 Check the main and big-end bearing journals for uneven wear, scoring, pitting and cracking.

3 Big-end bearing wear is accompanied by distinct metallic knocking when the engine is running (particularly noticeable when the engine is pulling from low revs), and some loss of oil pressure.

4 Main bearing wear is accompanied by severe engine vibration and rumble – getting progressively worse as engine revs increase – and again by loss of oil pressure.

5 Check the bearing journal for roughness by running a finger lightly over the bearing surface. Any roughness (which will be accompanied by obvious bearing wear) indicates that the crankshaft requires renewing.

6 Using a micrometer, measure the diameter of the main and big-end bearing journals, and compare the results with the Specifications at the beginning of this Chapter **(see illustration)**. By measuring the diameter at a number of points around each journal's circumference, you will be able to determine whether or not the journal is out-of-round. Take the measurement at each end of the journal, near the webs, to determine if the journal is tapered. If the crankshaft journals are damaged, tapered, out-of-round or excessively worn, the crankshaft must be renewed. It is not possible to regrind the crankshaft.

7 Check the oil seal contact surfaces at each end of the crankshaft for wear and damage. If the seal has worn an excessive groove in the surface of the crankshaft, consult an engine overhaul specialist, who will be able to advise whether a repair is possible, or whether a new crankshaft is necessary.

14 Main and big-end bearings – inspection

1 Even though the main and big-end bearings **must** be renewed during the engine overhaul, the old bearings should be retained for close examination, as they may reveal valuable information about the condition of the engine.

2 Bearing failure can occur due to lack of lubrication, the presence of dirt or other foreign particles, overloading the engine, or corrosion **(see illustration)**. Regardless of the cause of bearing failure, the cause must be corrected (where applicable) before the engine is reassembled, to prevent it from happening again.

3 When examining the bearing shells, remove them from the cylinder block/crankcase, the main bearing caps, the connecting rods and the connecting rod big-end bearing caps. Lay them out on a clean surface in the same general position as their location in the engine. This will enable you to match any bearing problems with the corresponding crankshaft journal.

4 Dirt and other foreign matter gets into the engine in a variety of ways. It may be left in the engine during assembly, or it may pass through filters or the crankcase ventilation system. It may get into the oil, and from there into the bearings. Metal chips from machining operations and normal engine wear are often present. Abrasives are sometimes left in engine components after reconditioning, especially when parts are not thoroughly cleaned using the proper cleaning methods. Whatever the source, these foreign objects often end up embedded in the soft bearing material, and are easily recognised. Large particles will not embed in the bearing, and will score or gouge the bearing and journal. The best prevention for this cause of bearing failure is to clean all parts thoroughly, and keep everything spotlessly clean during engine assembly. Frequent and regular engine oil and filter changes are also recommended.

5 Lack of lubrication (or lubrication breakdown) has a number of interrelated causes. Excessive heat (which thins the oil), overloading (which squeezes the oil from the bearing face) and oil leakage (from excessive bearing clearances, worn oil pump or high engine speeds) all contribute to lubrication breakdown. Blocked oil passages, which usually are the result of misaligned oil holes in a bearing shell, will also oil-starve a bearing, and destroy it. When lack of lubrication is the cause of bearing failure, the bearing material is wiped or extruded from the steel backing of the bearing. Temperatures may increase to the point where the steel backing turns blue from overheating.

6 Driving habits can have a definite effect on bearing life. Full-throttle, low-speed operation (labouring the engine) puts very high loads on bearings, tending to squeeze out the oil film. These loads cause the bearings to flex, which produces fine cracks in the bearing face (fatigue failure). Eventually, the bearing material will loosen in pieces, and tear away from the steel backing.

7 Short-distance driving leads to corrosion of bearings, because insufficient engine heat is produced to evaporate off the condensed water and corrosive gases. These products collect in the engine oil, forming acid and sludge. As the oil is carried to the engine bearings, the acid attacks and corrodes the bearing material.

8 Incorrect bearing installation during engine assembly will lead to bearing failure as well. Tight-fitting bearings leave insufficient bearing running clearance, and will result in oil starvation. Dirt or foreign particles trapped behind a bearing shell result in high spots on the bearing, which lead to failure.

9 As mentioned at the beginning of this Section, the bearing shells must be renewed during engine overhaul, regardless of their condition.

15 Engine overhaul – reassembly sequence

1 Before reassembly begins, ensure that all new parts have been obtained and that all necessary tools are available. Read through the entire procedure to familiarise yourself with the work involved and to ensure that all items necessary for reassembly of the engine are at hand. In addition to all normal tools and materials, it will be necessary to obtain suitable thread-locking compound, and various Rover sealants – refer to the relevant Sections in this Part of the Chapter and Part C for details. Carefully read the instructions supplied with the appropriate sealant kit.

2 In order to save time and avoid problems, engine reassembly can be carried out in the following order, referring to Part C of this Chapter when necessary. Where applicable, use new gaskets and seals when refitting the various components.

a) Crankshaft.
b) Piston/connecting rod assemblies.
c) Oil pump.
d) Sump.
e) Crankshaft left-hand oil seal and flywheel.
f) Cylinder head.
g) Timing belt rear cover, tensioner and sprockets, and timing belt.
h) Engine external components.

3 At this stage, all engine components should be absolutely clean and dry, with all faults repaired, and should be laid out (or in individual containers) on a completely clean work surface.

16 Piston rings – refitting

1 Before fitting new piston rings, the ring end gaps must be checked as follows.

2 Lay out the piston/connecting rod assemblies and the new piston ring sets, so that the ring sets will be matched with the same piston and cylinder during the end gap measurement and subsequent engine reassembly.

3 Insert the top ring into the first cylinder bore, and push it down the bore using the top of the piston. This will ensure that the ring remains square with the cylinder walls. Position the ring 30 mm from the top of the bore. Note that the top and second compression rings are different. The second ring is easily identified by the step on its lower surface.

4 Measure the end gap using feeler blades (see illustration). Compare the measurements with the figures given in the Specifications.

5 If the gap is too small (unlikely if genuine Rover parts are used), it must be enlarged, or the ring ends may contact each other during engine operation, causing serious damage. Ideally, new piston rings providing

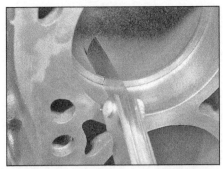

16.4 Measuring a piston ring end gap

the correct end gap should be fitted. As a last resort, the end gap can be increased by filing the ring ends very carefully with a fine file. Mount the file in a vice equipped with soft jaws, slip the ring over the file with the ends contacting the file face, and slowly move the ring to remove material from the ends.

Caution: Take care, as the piston rings are sharp, and are easily broken.

6 With new piston rings, it is unlikely that the end gap will be too large. If the gaps are too large, check that you have the correct rings for your engine and for the particular cylinder bore size.

7 Repeat the checking procedure for each ring in the first cylinder, and then for the rings in the remaining cylinders. Remember to keep rings, pistons and cylinders matched up.

8 Once the ring end gaps have been checked and if necessary corrected, the rings can be fitted to the pistons.

9 Fit the piston rings using the same technique as for removal. Fit the bottom (oil control) ring first, and work up. Ensure that the rings are fitted the correct way up – the top surface of the rings is normally marked TOP (see illustration). Arrange the gaps of the top and second compression rings 120° from each other, away from the thrust side of the piston. **Note:** *Always follow any instructions supplied with the new piston ring sets – different manufacturers may specify different procedures. Do not mix up the top and second compression rings, as they have different cross-sections.*

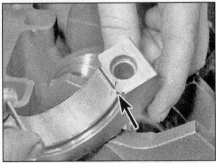

17.4a Ensure that the tab (arrowed) engages with the notch in the main bearing cap

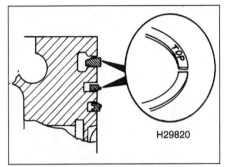

16.9 Piston ring fitting details

17 Crankshaft – refitting

Note: *New main bearing shells must be fitted on reassembly.*

1 After inspecting the crankshaft, and renewing it if necessary, as described in Section 13, proceed as follows.

2 Check that the main bearing cap locating dowels are in position in the cylinder block, and that the main bearing cap bolt holes are clean and dry.

3 Clean the backs of the new bearing shells, and the bearing locations in both the cylinder block/crankcase and the main bearing caps. Ensure that all traces of the protective grease are cleaned off the new bearing shells using paraffin. Wipe the shells dry with a lint-free cloth.

4 Press the bearing shells into their locations in the cylinder block and bearing caps, noting that the bearing shells with the oil grooves fit into the upper locations (in the cylinder block/ crankcase). Take care not to touch any shell-bearing surface with your fingers. Ensure that the tab on each lower shell engages in the notch in the main bearing cap. The shells in the cylinder block/crankcase have no locating tabs, so make sure that they are located centrally and squarely in their respective positions (see illustrations).

5 Using a little grease, stick the thrustwashers to each side of the centre main bearing upper location in the cylinder block/crankcase.

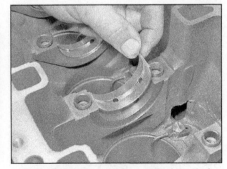

17.4b Press the bearing shells into their locations in the cylinder block . . .

17.4c . . . making sure that they are located centrally

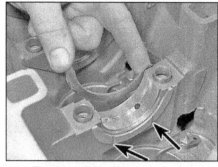

17.5 Ensure that the oil grooves (arrowed) on the thrustwashers face outwards

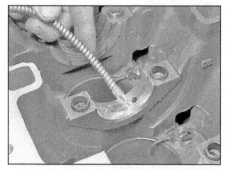

17.6 Lubricate the bearing shells in the cylinder block/crankcase

17.8 Oil the threads of the main bearing cap bolts

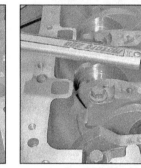

17.9 Tighten the main bearing cap bolts to the specified torque

Ensure that the oilway grooves on each thrustwasher face outwards (see illustration).

6 Liberally lubricate each bearing shell in the cylinder block/crankcase, and then lower the crankshaft into position (see illustration).

7 Lubricate the bearing shells in the bearing caps, and the crankshaft journals, then fit the bearing caps, ensuring that they engage with the locating dowels.

8 Ensure that the threads of the main bearing cap bolts are clean, then oil the threads of the bolts, and screw them into their original locations, finger-tight only at this stage (see illustration).

9 Working from the centre main bearing cap outwards, progressively tighten the bearing cap bolts to the specified torque (see illustration).

10 Now rotate the crankshaft, and check that it turns freely, with no signs of binding or tight spots.

11 Check the crankshaft endfloat with reference to Section 10. If the endfloat exceeds the specified limit, remove the crankshaft and fit new thrustwashers. If, with the new thrustwashers fitted, the endfloat is still excessive, the crankshaft must be renewed.

12 Refit the oil pump as described in Chapter 2C.

13 Refit the pistons and connecting rods as described in Section 18.

14 Refit the crankshaft left-hand oil seal and the flywheel as described in Chapter 2C.

18 Piston/connecting rod assembly – refitting

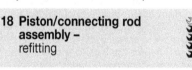

Caution: Two different types of big-end bearing shells are available, one type for

models with fracture-split connecting rod/ big-end cap assemblies (big-end bearing caps secured by bolts), and one for models with conventional connecting rod/big-end cap assemblies (big-end bearing caps secured by nuts). The two bearing shell types are not interchangeable, and it is vital that the correct bearing shells are fitted, depending on engine type – if in doubt, refer to a Rover dealer for advice.

Note: *New big-end bearing shells must be fitted on reassembly.*

1 After inspecting the crankshaft, and renewing it if necessary, as described in Section 13, proceed as follows.

2 Clean the backs of the new bearing shells, and the bearing locations in both the connecting rods and the big-end bearing caps. Ensure that all traces of the protective grease are cleaned off the new bearing shells using paraffin. Wipe the shells dry with a lint-free cloth.

3 Press the bearing shells into their locations. On models where the big-end caps are secured by nuts, ensure that the locating tab on each shell engages with the notch in the connecting rod or big-end cap. On models where the big-end caps are secured by bolts, the shells have no locating tabs, so make sure that they are located centrally and squarely in their respective positions in the connecting rods and bearing caps (see illustrations). Take care not to touch any shell-bearing surface with your fingers.

4 Liberally lubricate the big-end bearing journals on the crankshaft.

5 Lubricate No 1 piston and piston rings, and check that the ring gaps are correctly positioned. The gaps of the top and second compression rings should be arranged 120° from each other, away from the thrust side of the piston.

6 Liberally lubricate the cylinder bore with clean engine oil.

7 Fit a ring compressor to No 1 piston, then insert the piston and connecting rod into the cylinder bore so that the base of the compressor stands on the block. With the crankshaft big-end bearing journal positioned at its lowest point, tap the piston carefully into the cylinder bore with the wooden handle of a hammer (see illustration). Note that the

18.3a Where the big-end caps are secured by nuts, the locating tab (arrowed) on each shell must engage with the notch in the connecting rod

18.3b Where the big-end caps are secured by bolts, the bearing shells must be located centrally in the bearing caps

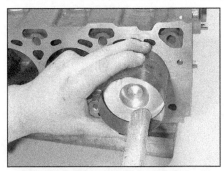

18.7 Refitting a piston/connecting rod assembly using a piston ring compressor and a hammer handle

arrow on the piston crown must point towards the timing belt end of the engine. Check that the cutout in the piston skirt is positioned above the oil spray jet location. Take care not to allow the connecting rod (and the big-end bolts) to contact the cylinder bore.

8 Guide the connecting rod onto the big-end bearing journal, taking care not to displace the bearing shell, and then refit the big-end bearing cap. On engines where the big-end bearing caps are secured by nuts, make sure that the tapered portion of the machined flat on the cap is facing towards the timing belt end of the engine. On engines where the big-end bearing caps are secured by bolts, make sure that the identification marks on the connecting rod and big-end cap are on the same side of the engine.

9 Lubricate the threads of the big-end studs or bolts (as applicable) with clean engine oil, then fit the nuts or bolts (as applicable), and tighten to the specified torque wrench setting

(see illustration). Note: *The torque wrench setting for engines where the big-end bearing caps are secured by nuts is different to that for engines where the bearing caps are secured by bolts.*

10 Repeat the procedure to refit the remaining three piston/connecting rod assemblies.

11 Refit the oil pick-up pipe and the sump, as described in Chapter 2C.

12 Refit the cylinder head as described in Chapter 2C.

19 Engine –
initial start-up after overhaul

1 With the engine refitted to the vehicle, double-check the engine oil and coolant levels. Make a final check to ensure that everything has been reconnected and that there are no tools or rags left in the engine compartment.

2 To prevent the engine from starting during initial cranking, remove the fuel pump fuse from the engine bay fusebox – see *Wiring diagrams*. Operate the starter motor and check that cranking is satisfactory, with no unusual noises. Ensure that the oil pressure warning light goes out during cranking.

3 Prime the fuel system – see Chapter 4C.

4 Fit the fuel pump fuse. **Note:** *Because fuel system components will be empty, the engine may take longer than normal to start.*

5 When the preheating indicator lamp has gone out, start the engine, and ensure that the oil pressure warning light goes off during cranking, or immediately the engine starts. Allow the engine to idle.

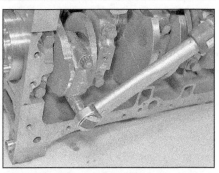

18.9 Tightening a big-end bearing cap nut to the specified torque

6 While the engine is idling, check for fuel, coolant and oil leaks. Do not be alarmed if there are some odd smells and smoke from parts getting hot and burning off oil deposits. If the hydraulic tappets have been disturbed, some valve gear noise may be heard at first; this should disappear as the oil circulates fully around the engine and normal pressure is restored in the tappets.

7 Keep the engine idling until hot coolant is felt circulating through the radiator top hose, then stop the engine.

8 After a few minutes, recheck the oil and coolant levels and top-up as necessary.

9 If new pistons, rings or crankshaft bearings have been fitted, the engine must be run-in for the first 500 miles. Do not operate the engine at full throttle or allow it to labour in any gear during this period. It is recommended that the oil and filter be changed at the end of this period.

Notes

Chapter 3
Cooling, heating and ventilation systems

Contents

Air conditioning compressor drivebelt – inspection, adjustment
  and renewal 12
Air conditioning system – general information and precautions 13
Air conditioning system components – removal and refitting 14
Coolant pump – removal and refitting 5
Coolant pump housing (diesel engines) – removal and refitting 6
Cooling system hoses – renewal 2
Cooling system electrical switches – general information, testing,
  removal and refitting. 8
Electric cooling fan – removal and refitting 7
General information and precautions. 1
Heater components – removal and refitting. 9
Heater controls – removal, refitting and adjustment 11
Heater/ventilation intake filter – renewal 10
Radiator and expansion tank – removal, inspection and refitting . . . 3
Thermostat – removal, testing and refitting 4

Degrees of difficulty

Easy, suitable for novice with little experience	Fairly easy, suitable for beginner with some experience	Fairly difficult, suitable for competent DIY mechanic	Difficult, suitable for experienced DIY mechanic	Very difficult, suitable for expert DIY or professional

Specifications

General

System type . . . . Pressurised, pump-assisted thermo-syphon with front mounted radiator and electric cooling fan(s)

Cap opening pressure:
  Petrol models:
    4-cylinder models . . . . 0.9 to 1.2 bar
    6-cylinder models . . . . 1.4 bar
  Diesel models. . . . . 0.9 to 1.2 bar

Thermostat

Type . . . . Wax element
Start of opening temperature:
  Petrol models . . . . 88 ± 2°C
  Diesel models. . . . . n/a
Full-open temperature:
  Petrol models:
    4-cylinder models . . . . 100 ± 2°C
    6-cylinder models . . . . 96 ± 2°C
  Diesel models. . . . . 82 ± 5°C

Cooling fan(s)

	On	Off
Operating temperature:		
All models without air conditioning	104°C	98°C
Petrol models with air conditioning:		
4-cylinder models:		
Low-speed	104°C	98°C
High-speed	112°C	106°C
6-cylinder models:		
Low-speed	95°C	93.5°C
High-speed	114°C	112°C
Diesel models with air conditioning:		
Low-speed	104°C	94°C
High-speed	112°C	106°C

Fan type:
  Petrol models:
    4-cylinder models . . . . 2 speed, thermostatically-controlled with 7 blades
    6-cylinder models . . . . Variable speed, ECM-controlled with 11 blades x 2
  Diesel models. . . . . 2 speed, thermostatically-controlled with 6 blades

Air conditioning

Compressor type	Delphi Harrison V5e
Oil type	Sanden SP-10 or Unipart SP-10
Oil quantity	220 cm³ ± 15
Refrigerant type	R 134a
Refrigerant quantity	650g ± 35

Torque wrench settings

	Nm	lbf ft
Cooling system		
Coolant pump bolts (petrol models):		
4-cylinder models	10	7
6-cylinder models	9	7
Coolant pump bolts (diesel models):		
Coolant pump housing bolts	45	33
Coolant pump cover-to-housing bolts	10	7
Coolant rail-to-cylinder block bolts	25	18
Cooling fan housing-to-radiator bolts	9	7
Cylinder block drain plug (6-cylinder petrol models)	20	15
Engine coolant temperature (ECT) sensor:		
Petrol models:		
4-cylinder engines	15	11
6-cylinder engines	17	13
Diesel models	14	10
Expansion tank-to-body bolts	9	7
Intercooler-to-radiator bolts	25	18
Radiator upper mounting bracket bolts	9	7
Radiator upper mounting bracket mounting bolts (diesel models)	25	18
Thermostat housing bolt(s):		
Petrol models:		
4-cylinder models	9	7
6-cylinder models	18	13
Diesel models	10	7
Heating system		
Heater unit-to-bulkhead mounting nuts:		
6 mm	10	7
10 mm	22	16
Air conditioning system		
Compressor refrigerant pipe union bolt	35	26
Compressor-to-mounting bracket bolts	25	18
Condenser mounting bolts	9	7
Condenser refrigerant pipe union screws	9	7
Receiver/drier clamp bracket screws	10	7
Receiver/drier refrigerant pipe union	9	7
Refrigerant pressure sensor	12	9

1 General information and precautions

General information

The cooling system is of the pressurised type, consisting of a front-mounted radiator with cooling fan(s) at the rear of the radiator, a translucent expansion tank mounted on the right-hand inner wing, a thermostat and a centrifugal coolant pump, as well as the connecting hoses (see illustrations). The coolant pump is driven by the engine timing belt on petrol models. On diesel models, the coolant pump arrangement is unusual: the pump itself is mounted in a housing that is shared with the power steering pump. Drive is taken indirectly from the auxiliary drivebelt via a shaft that extends into the coolant pump housing from the rear of the power steering pump.

The electric cooling fan on 4-cylinder engines is thermostatically controlled, on 6-cylinder engines there are two fans, which are controlled by the Engine Control Module (ECM).

The cooling system is of the by-pass type, allowing coolant to circulate around the engine while the thermostat is closed. With the engine cold, the thermostat closes off the coolant feed from the bottom radiator hose. Coolant is then drawn into the engine via the heater matrix, inlet manifold and from the top of the cylinder block. This allows some heat transfer, by conduction, to the radiator through the top hose whilst retaining the majority of heat within the cylinder block.

The siting of the thermostat in the intake rather than the outlet side of the system ensures that the engine warms-up quickly by circulating a small amount of coolant around a shorter tract. This also prevents temperature build-up in the cylinder head prior to the thermostat opening.

When the coolant reaches a predetermined temperature, the thermostat opens and the coolant is allowed to flow freely through the top hose to the radiator. As the coolant circulates through the radiator, it is cooled by the in-rush of air when the vehicle is in forward motion. Airflow is supplemented by the action of the electric cooling fan when necessary. Upon reaching the bottom of the radiator, the coolant is now cooled and the cycle is repeated.

With the engine at normal operating temperature, the coolant expands and some of it is displaced into the expansion tank. This coolant collects in the tank and is returned to the radiator when the system cools.

The electric cooling fan mounted behind the radiator is controlled by the Engine

**1.1a Cooling system component layout
– 4-cylinder petrol engine**

1 Hose
2 Heater control valve
3 Expansion tank
4 Hose
5 Hose
6 Bleed screw
7 Bottom hose
8 Electric cooling fan and cowling
9 Hose
10 Radiator
11 Coolant outlet elbow
12 Hose
13 Coolant pump
14 Hose
15 Thermostat housing
16 Hose

Control Module (ECM). At a predetermined temperature the coolant sensor gives a signal to the ECM, which then actuates the fan.

Precautions

Cooling system

When the engine is hot, the coolant in the cooling system is under high pressure. The increased pressure raises the boiling point of the coolant and this allows the coolant to circulate at temperatures close to 100°C without actually boiling. If the pressure is reduced suddenly, eg, by removing the expansion tank filler cap, the coolant will boil very rapidly, resulting in boiling water and steam being ejected through the expansion tank filler neck. This can happen very quickly and the risk of scalding is high.

For this reason, do not attempt to remove the expansion tank filler cap or to disturb any part of the cooling system whilst the engine is hot. Allow the engine to cool for several hours after switching off. When removing the expansion tank filler cap, as a precaution cover the cap with a thick layer of cloth to avoid

**1.1b Cooling system component layout –
6-cylinder petrol engine models**

1 Top hose
2 Bottom hose
3 Radiator
4 Engine and condenser cooling fans
5 Oil cooler
6 Bottom hose
7 Pipe – engine to expansion tank
8 Pipe – radiator to expansion tank
9 Heater return hose connector
10 Hose – heater return to thermostat
11 Expansion tank
12 Hose – engine to heater control valve
13 Heater control valve
14 Hose – heater supply
15 Hose – heater return
16 Pipe – RH inlet manifold to expansion tank
17 Expansion pipe connector
18 Pipe – LH inlet manifold to expansion tank

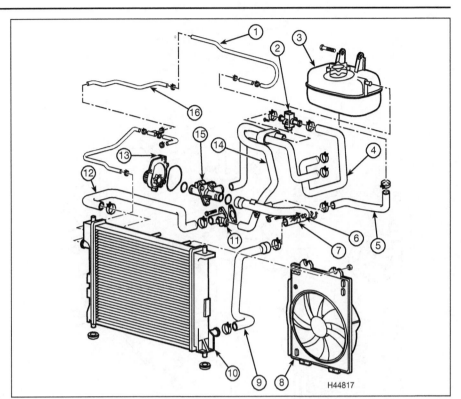
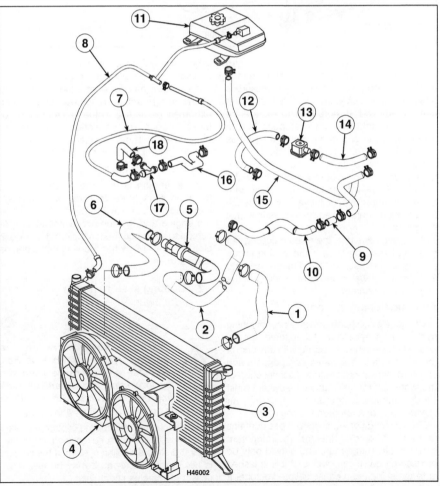

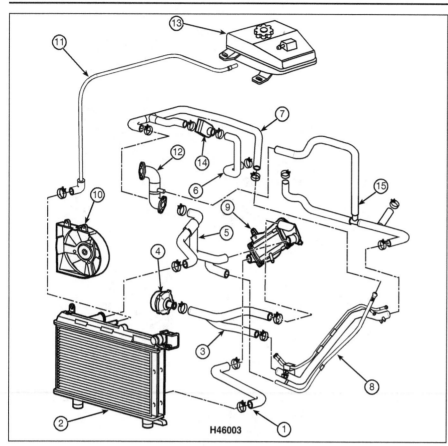

H46003

1 Bottom hose
2 Radiator
3 Hose – coolant pump inlet
4 Coolant pump
5 Top hose
6 Hose – control valve to heater
7 Hose – coolant rail to EGR cooler
8 Coolant rail
9 Engine oil cooler
10 Cooling fan and cowl (without air conditioning)
11 Pipe – radiator to expansion tank
12 EGR cooler
13 Expansion tank
14 Heater control valve
15 Hose – expansion tank to coolant rail

scalding, and slowly unscrew the filler cap until a hissing sound can be heard. When the hissing has stopped, showing that pressure is released, slowly unscrew the filler cap until it can be removed. If more hissing sounds are heard, wait until they have stopped before unscrewing the cap completely. At all times keep well away from the filler opening.

Do not allow antifreeze to come in contact with your skin or painted surfaces of the vehicle. Rinse off spills immediately with plenty of water. Never leave any antifreeze lying around in unmarked bottles, as it is fatal if ingested.

If the engine is hot, the electric cooling fan may start rotating even if the engine is not running, so be careful to keep hands, hair and loose clothing well clear when working in the engine compartment.

Air conditioning system

On models equipped with an air conditioning system, it is necessary to observe special precautions whenever dealing with any part of the system, it's associated components and any items which necessitate disconnection of the system. If for any reason the system must be disconnected, entrust this task to your Rover dealer or a refrigeration engineer.

The air conditioning system pipes contains pressurised liquid refrigerant. The refrigerant is potentially dangerous, and should only be handled by qualified persons. If it is splashed onto the skin, it can cause severe frostbite. It is not itself poisonous, but in the presence of a naked flame (including a cigarette), it forms a poisonous gas. Uncontrolled discharging of the refrigerant is dangerous and is also extremely damaging to the environment. For these reasons, disconnection of any part of the system without specialised knowledge and equipment is not recommended.

Electric cooling fan

If the engine is hot, the electric cooling fan (two fans fitted to 6-cylinder models) may start rotating without warning even if the engine and ignition are switched off. Be careful to keep your hands, hair and any loose clothing well clear when working in the engine compartment.

2 Cooling system hoses
– renewal

> ⚠ **Warning: Never work on the cooling system when it is hot. Release any pressure from the system by loosening the expansion tank cap, having first covered it with a cloth to avoid any possibility of scalding.**

1 If inspection of the cooling system reveals a faulty hose, then it must be renewed as follows.
2 First drain the cooling system. If the coolant is not due for renewal, it may be re-used if collected in a clean container.

3 To disconnect any hose, use a screwdriver to slacken the clips then move them along the hose clear of the outlet. Carefully work the hose off its outlets. Do not attempt to disconnect any part of the system when still hot.
4 Note that the radiator hose outlets are fragile. Do not use excessive force when attempting to remove the hoses. If a hose proves stubborn, try to release it by rotating it on its outlets before attempting to work it off. If all else fails, cut the hose with a sharp knife then slit it so that it can be peeled off in two pieces. Although expensive, this is preferable to buying a new radiator.
5 When fitting a hose, first slide the clips onto the hose then work the hose onto its outlets.

> **HAYNES HINT** *If the hose is stiff, use soap as a lubricant or soften it by first soaking it in boiling water whilst taking care to prevent scalding.*

6 Work each hose end fully onto its outlet, check that the hose is settled correctly and is properly routed, then slide each clip along the hose until it is behind the outlet flared end before tightening it securely.
7 Refill the system with coolant.
8 Check carefully for leaks as soon as possible after disturbing any part of the cooling system.

3 Radiator and expansion tank
– removal, inspection and refitting

Radiator removal

4-cylinder petrol engines

1 Disconnect the battery negative terminal (refer to *Disconnecting the battery* in the Reference Section of this manual).
2 Drain the cooling system as described in Chapter 1A. **Note:** *After draining the cooling*

system, leave the bottom hose disconnected at this point.

3 Remove the radiator cooling fan as described in Section 7. **Note:** On models without air conditioning, the radiator can be removed with the cooling fan attached.

4 Slacken the securing clips, and disconnect the top hose and the expansion tank hose from the top of the radiator.

5 Support the radiator, then remove the two bolts securing the radiator top mounting brackets to the upper crossmember, and then remove the brackets.

6 Disengage the radiator from the lower rubber mountings and carefully withdraw it from the engine bay.

6-cylinder petrol engines

7 Disconnect the battery negative terminal (refer to *Disconnecting the battery* in the Reference Section of this manual).

8 Apply the handbrake, then jack up the front of the vehicle and support securely on axle stands (see *Jacking and vehicle support*). **Note:** *The radiator will need to be withdrawn from underneath the vehicle, make sure the vehicle is raised to a sufficient height.*

9 Drain the cooling system as described in Chapter 1A. **Note:** *After draining the cooling system, leave the bottom hose disconnected at this point.*

10 Remove the air cleaner assembly as described in Chapter 4A.

11 Remove the front bumper as described in Chapter 11.

12 Disconnect the bottom hose from the radiator and remove it from the vehicle. **Note:** *The other end of the bottom hose was attached to the engine oil cooler, this should have been disconnected for draining the cooling system.*

13 Undo the mounting bolts and disconnect the transmission cooler pipe from the bottom of the radiator. Plug the open ends to prevent dirt ingress. Remove and discard the O-ring seal, a new one will be required for refitting.

14 Undo the mounting bolts and disconnect the fluid cooler pipe from the top of the radiator. Plug the open ends to prevent dirt ingress. Remove and discard the O-ring seal, a new one will be required for refitting.

15 Slacken the securing clips, and disconnect the top hose and the expansion tank hose from the top of the radiator.

16 Remove the two bolts securing the radiator top mounting brackets to the upper crossmember, and then remove the brackets.

17 Release the fluid cooler hose quick-release couplings from across the bottom of the radiator and move them clear of the radiator.

18 Support the radiator, then remove the two bolts securing each of the lower radiator mountings to the crossmember, and then remove the mountings.

19 Carefully release, and manoeuvre the radiator out from the engine bay from underneath the vehicle.

3.28 Undo the two expansion tank mounting bolts – arrowed

Diesel engines

20 Disconnect the battery negative terminal (refer to *Disconnecting the battery* in the Reference Section of this manual).

21 Drain the cooling system as described in Chapter 1B. **Note:** *After draining the cooling system, leave the bottom hose disconnected at this point.*

22 Remove the intercooler as described in Chapter 4C.

23 Remove the radiator cooling fan as described in Section 7.

24 Slacken the securing clips, and disconnect the top hose and the expansion tank hose from the top of the radiator.

25 Remove the retaining bolt and upper mounting bracket from the top of the radiator.

26 Carefully lift the radiator from the lower mountings and remove it from the engine bay.

Expansion tank removal

27 Slacken the securing clip and disconnect the hose from the top of the expansion tank.

28 Remove the two bolts securing the expansion tank to the inner wing panel **(see illustration)**, and then pull it forward to release it from the bulkhead.

29 Lift the expansion tank up, slacken the securing clip and disconnect the coolant feed hose from the bottom of the expansion tank. Position a container under the expansion tank to collect the coolant as the hose is removed.

30 The expansion tank can now be removed from the vehicle.

Inspection

Radiator

31 If the radiator has been removed due to suspected blockage, reverse-flush it as described in the relevant part of Chapter 1. Clean dirt and debris from the radiator fins, using a low-pressure air line (in which case, wear eye protection) or a soft brush. Be careful, as the fins are sharp, and can be easily damaged.

32 If necessary, a radiator specialist can perform a 'flow test' on the radiator, to establish whether an internal blockage exists.

33 A leaking radiator must be referred to a specialist for permanent repair. Do not attempt to weld or solder a leaking radiator, as damage to the plastic components may result.

> **HAYNES HiNT** *Minor leaks from the radiator can be cured using a suitable sealant with the radiator in situ.*

34 If the radiator is to be sent for repair or renewed, remove all hoses, and the cooling fan switch (where fitted).

35 Inspect the condition of the radiator mounting rubbers, and renew them if necessary.

Expansion tank

36 Empty any remaining coolant from the tank and flush it with fresh water to clean it. If the tank is leaking it must be renewed but it is worth first attempting a repair using a proprietary sealant or suitable adhesive.

37 The expansion tank cap should be cleaned and checked whenever it is removed. Check that its sealing surfaces and threads are clean and undamaged and that they mate correctly with those of the expansion tank.

38 The cap's performance can only be checked by using a cap pressure-tester (cooling system tester) with a suitable adaptor. On applying pressure, the cap's pressure relief valve should hold until the specified pressure is reached, at which point the valve should open.

39 If there is any doubt about the cap's performance, then it must be renewed. Ensure that the new one is of the correct type and rating for your engine.

Refitting

40 Refitting is a reversal of removal, bearing in mind the following points:

a) Take care not to damage the radiator fins (nor the condenser/intercooler, where applicable) during refitting.

b) Where applicable, refit the front bumper with reference to Chapter 11.

c) On completion, refill the cooling system as described in Chapter 1A or 1B.

4 Thermostat – removal, testing and refitting

Removal

1 Disconnect the battery negative terminal (refer to *Disconnecting the battery* in the Reference Section of this manual).

2 Drain the cooling system as described in Chapter 1A or 1B. Where applicable, undo the retaining bolts/nuts and remove the engine undertray.

4-cylinder petrol engines

3 Note that access to the thermostat is very limited. It may be easier to raise the front of the vehicle and to work from underneath, ensuring that the vehicle is securely supported on axle stands (see *Jacking and vehicle support*).

4 Unbolt the coolant rail from the rear of the cylinder block/crankcase, then slacken the

4.4 Disconnect the coolant rail and heater return hoses (arrowed) from the rear of the thermostat housing

4.5 Slacken and withdraw the bolt that secures the thermostat housing to the engine block

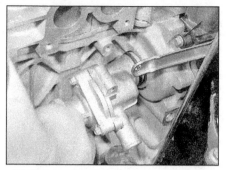

4.6 Release the thermostat housing from the pump and remove it from the vehicle (inlet manifold removed)

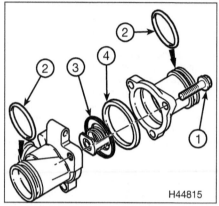

4.8 Thermostat components – petrol engines

1 Bolt	3 Thermostat
2 O-ring seals	4 Rubber seal

4.11 Remove the hoses from the thermostat housing

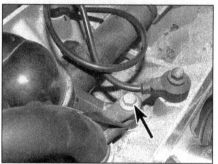

4.13 Undo the bolt (arrowed) from the coolant elbow

4.14 Remove the coolant elbow from the cylinder block

clips and disconnect the heater return hose and coolant rail hose from the thermostat housing **(see illustration)**.

5 Slacken and withdraw the bolt that secures the thermostat housing to the engine block. Note that on some models, the bolt also secures the dipstick tube support bracket in place **(see illustration)**.

6 Release the thermostat housing from the rear of the coolant pump and remove it from the vehicle **(see illustration)**.

7 Remove the O-ring seals from the housing stubs and discard them – new seals must be used on refitting.

8 Slacken and remove the three thermostat housing cover bolts, and then lift off the housing cover. Remove the thermostat together with its rubber seal **(see illustration)**.

6-cylinder petrol engines

Note: *The thermostat is part of the thermostat*

4.15 Disconnect the thermostat housing from the connecting pipe

housing and can only be renewed as a complete assembly.

9 Remove the inlet manifold as described in Chapter 4B.

10 Release the engine wiring harness from the two securing clips.

11 Slacken the securing clips, and disconnect the bottom hose and heater hose from the thermostat housing **(see illustration)**.

12 Slacken the securing clip and disconnect the top hose from the coolant elbow at the side of the thermostat housing.

13 Undo the retaining bolt which secures the thermostat housing and the coolant elbow to the cylinder block **(see illustration)**.

14 Withdraw the coolant elbow from the cylinder block **(see illustration)**.

15 Withdraw the thermostat housing from the cylinder block and release it from the connecting pipe to the coolant pump **(see illustration)**.

16 Remove the O-ring seals from the coolant elbow, thermostat housing and connecting pipe and discard them – new seals must be used on refitting.

Diesel engines

Note: *The thermostat is housed in the lower part of the engine oil cooler.*

17 Apply the handbrake, chock the rear roadwheels, then jack up the front of the car and support it on axle stands (see *Jacking and vehicle support*).

18 Slacken the securing clip and release the coolant hose from the thermostat housing.

19 Release the securing clip and remove the vacuum pump oil return hose from the sump.

20 Undo the three bolts securing the thermostat housing to the oil cooler housing, and remove it from the engine.

21 Remove the thermostat and the O-ring seal from the oil cooler housing. Discard the seal – a new one must be used on refitting **(see illustration)**.

Testing

22 If the thermostat remains in the open position at room temperature, then it is faulty and must be renewed.

23 To test it fully, suspend the (closed) thermostat on a length of string in a container of cold water, with a thermometer beside it.

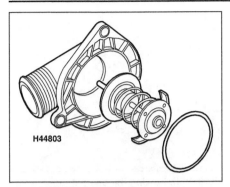

**4.21 Thermostat components –
diesel engines**

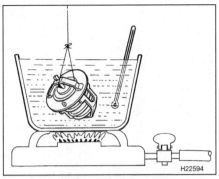

4.23 Testing the thermostat

**4.24 The stamped marking (arrowed)
indicates the temperature at which the
thermostat starts to open**

Ensure that neither touches the side of the container **(see illustration)**.
24 Heat the water and check the temperature at which the thermostat begins to open. Compare this value with that specified. Continue to heat the water until the thermostat is fully open. The temperature at which this should happen is stamped in the unit's end **(see illustration)**. Remove the thermostat and measure the height of the fully-opened valve, then allow the thermostat to cool down and check that it closes fully.
25 If the thermostat does not open and close as described, if it sticks in either position, or if it does not open at the specified temperature, then it must be renewed.

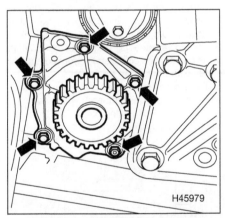

**5.7 Remove the coolant pump bolts
– arrowed**

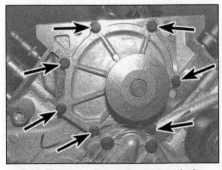

**5.10 Remove the coolant pump bolts
– arrowed**

Refitting

26 Refitting is a reversal of the removal procedure, noting:
a) Make sure all the mating faces and thermostat components are clean before refitting.
b) Ensure that the thermostat is fitted the correct way round, with the spring facing into the housing and it is correctly seated in the housing.
c) Where applicable, fit a new rubber seal to the thermostat
d) Fit new O-ring seals to the housing and connecting pipe stubs. Lubricate seals with rubber grease.
e) Use a torque wrench to tighten the screws to the specified torque.
f) On completion, refill the cooling system as described in Chapter 1A or 1B.

5 Coolant pump – removal and refitting

Removal

1 Coolant pump failure is usually indicated by coolant leaking from the gland behind the pump bearing, or by rough and noisy operation, usually accompanied by excessive pump spindle play. If the pump shows any of these symptoms then it must be renewed as follows.
2 Disconnect the battery negative terminal (refer to *Disconnecting the battery* in the Reference Section of this manual).

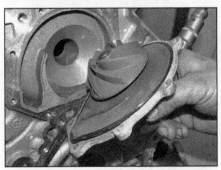

5.11a Withdraw the coolant pump . . .

3 Drain the cooling system as described in Chapter 1A or 1B. Where applicable, undo the retaining bolts/nuts and remove the engine undertray.
4 Apply the handbrake, chock the rear roadwheels, then jack up the front of the car and support it on axle stands (see *Jacking and vehicle support*).

4-cylinder petrol models

5 Remove the timing belt, with reference to Chapter 2A.
6 Unscrew the single bolt securing the rear of the coolant pump to the upper timing belt inner cover. It may also be necessary to undo the dipstick bracket retaining bolt from the top of the thermostat housing.
7 Unscrew the five bolts securing the coolant pump to the cylinder block/crankcase **(see illustration)**. There are different length bolts fitted; note their positions to ensure correct refitting.
8 Withdraw the coolant pump from the locating dowels and discard its sealing ring (this should be renewed whenever it is disturbed).

6-cylinder petrol engines

9 Remove the timing belt, with reference to Chapter 2B.
10 Unscrew the seven bolts securing the coolant pump to the cylinder block/crankcase **(see illustration)**. Note their positions to ensure correct refitting.
11 Withdraw the coolant pump from the cylinder block and discard its sealing ring (this should be renewed whenever it is disturbed) **(see illustrations)**.

5.11b . . . and remove the sealing ring

5.14 Disconnect the hose (arrowed) from the rear of the coolant pump – diesel models

5.15 Removing coolant pump housing cover – diesel models

5.16 Withdrawing the coolant pump from its housing – diesel models

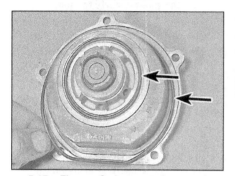

5.17a Fit new O-ring seals (arrowed) – diesel models . . .

5.17b . . . and the pump housing cover – diesel models

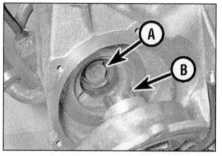

5.17c Power steering pump drive lugs (A) must engage with those on the front of the coolant pump (B) – diesel model

Diesel models

12 Remove the alternator as described in Chapter 5A.

13 Slacken the hose securing clips and remove the top hose from the vehicle.

14 Loosen the securing clip and disconnect the hose from the coolant pump housing cover **(see illustration)**.

15 Progressively slacken and withdraw the five securing bolts (noting their fitted position) then remove the coolant pump housing cover. Collect the O-ring seal from the housing and discard it – a new seal must be used on refitting **(see illustration)**.

16 Withdraw the coolant pump from its housing. Collect the two O-ring seals and discard them – new seals must be used on refitting **(see illustration)**.

Refitting

17 Refitting is a reversal of removal, noting the following points **(see illustrations)**:

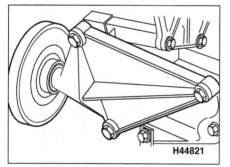

6.7 Remove idler pulley bracket

a) Make sure all the mating faces and coolant pump components are clean before refitting.
b) Use new O-ring seals and coat them with rubber grease.
c) Tighten all bolts to the specified torque setting.
d) Where applicable, refit the timing belt with reference to Chapter 2A or 2B.
e) On diesel models, refit the alternator as described in Chapter 5A.
f) On completion, refill the cooling system as described in Chapter 1A or 1B.

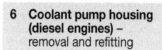

6 Coolant pump housing (diesel engines) – removal and refitting

Removal

1 Disconnect the battery negative terminal (refer to *Disconnecting the battery* in the Reference Section of this manual).

2 Drain the cooling system as described in Chapter 1B. Where applicable, undo the retaining bolts/nuts and remove the engine undertray.

3 Apply the handbrake, chock the rear roadwheels, then jack up the front of the car and support it on axle stands (see *Jacking and vehicle support*).

4 Slacken the three power steering pump pulley retaining bolts. Do not remove them completely at this point.

5 Remove the brake servo vacuum pump as described in Chapter 9.

6 Slacken the securing clip and disconnect the hose from the coolant pump.

7 Remove the three mounting bolts from the auxiliary drivebelt idler pulley bracket, and remove it from the engine **(see illustration)**.

8 The power steering pump pulley retaining bolts can now be completely removed and the pulley withdrawn from the pump.

9 To gain better access, undo the mounting bolt from the power steering pipe securing bracket on the inner wing panel, and move the pipe to one side.

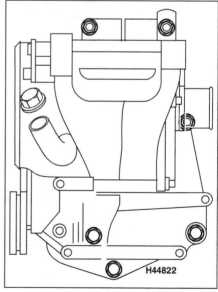

6.11 Remove pump housing bolts

10 Undo the Allen bolt from the auxiliary belt tensioner and withdraw the tensioner from the coolant pump housing.

11 Remove the five bolts securing the power steering pump to the coolant pump housing, remove the support bracket and fasten the power steering pump to one side **(see illustration)**.

12 Remove the six bolts securing the coolant pump housing to the cylinder block, release the housing from the locating dowels and turn it through 90° to withdraw it from the vehicle **(see illustration)**.

13 Remove the O-ring seal from the coolant pump housing and discard it – a new seal must be used on refitting.

Refitting

14 Refitting is a reversal of removal, bearing in mind the following points:
   a) Lubricate the housing new O-ring with rubber grease.
   b) Use a torque wrench to tighten all fastenings to the correct torque.
   c) Refit the brake servo vacuum pump as described in Chapter 9.
   d) On completion, refill the cooling system as described in Chapter 1B.

7 Electric cooling fan – removal and refitting

Removal

1 Disconnect the battery negative terminal (refer to *Disconnecting the battery* in the Reference Section of this manual). Where fitted, remove the plastic engine acoustic cover.

4-cylinder petrol engines – without air conditioning

2 Trace the wiring back from the cooling fan and disconnect the fan harness multiplug.

3 Unclip the top hose from the support bracket on the top of the cooling fan cowl and move it to one side.

4 Remove two lower nuts and the two upper nuts securing the fan housing to the radiator.

5 Release the fan assembly from the studs on the radiator and carefully withdraw it from the engine bay.

6.12 Pump housing location – arrowed

4-cylinder petrol engines – with air conditioning

6 Drain the cooling system as described in Chapter 1A. Where applicable, undo the retaining bolts/nuts and remove the engine undertray.

7 Remove the air cleaner assembly as described in Chapter 4A.

8 Disconnect the multiplug from the radiator cooling fan motor.

9 Slacken the hose securing clips and remove the top hose from the vehicle, releasing it from any retaining clips.

10 Disconnect the multiplug from the coolant temperature sensor located in the coolant outlet elbow on the engine.

11 Undo the mounting bolt from the air conditioning pipe securing bracket on the cooling fan housing, and move the pipe to one side.

12 Remove two lower nuts and the two upper nuts securing the fan housing to the radiator.

13 Release the fan assembly from the studs on the radiator and carefully withdraw it from the engine bay.

6-cylinder petrol engines

14 Apply the handbrake, chock the rear roadwheels, then jack up the front of the car and support it on axle stands (see *Jacking and vehicle support*).

15 Remove the front bumper as described in Chapter 11.

16 Undo the four retaining bolts and remove the crossmember from across the front of the vehicle **(see illustration)**.

17 Undo the two bonnet safety catch securing bolts **(see illustration)**, and remove it from the upper crossmember.

18 Disconnect the multiplugs from the two radiator cooling fan motors.

19 Undo the mounting bolts (one at each side) from the cooling fan and condenser assembly.

20 Undo the mounting bolts from the two lower mounting brackets **(see illustration)**.

21 Remove the two upper mounting bolts securing the fan housing to the condenser.

22 The fan housing can now be unclipped from the condenser and removed from the vehicle.

23 To remove the fan from the housing release the wiring harness from the fan housing, undo the motor retaining screws and remove the fan assembly.

Diesel engines

24 Remove the air cleaner assembly as described in Chapter 4C.

25 Remove the turbo intercooler as described in Chapter 4C.

26 Slacken the securing clips and completely remove the upper and lower intercooler hoses from the inlet manifold and the turbocharger outlet pipe.

27 Disconnect the fan harness multiplug.

28 Remove two bolts securing the top of the fan assembly housing.

29 Release the assembly from the lower mounting point, and carefully remove the fan assembly.

Refitting

30 Refitting is a reversal of removal, bearing in mind the following points:
   a) Refit the air cleaner assemblies, front bumper and diesel turbo intercooler as described in the relevant Chapter.
   b) Where applicable, refill the cooling system as described in Chapter 1A.

8 Cooling system electrical switches – information, testing, removal and refitting

Information

Radiator cooling fan relay

1 The operation of the radiator cooling fan(s) is controlled by the Engine Control

7.16 Undo the two bolts (arrowed) – left-hand side shown

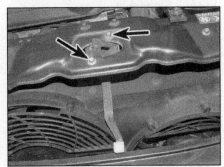

7.17 Undo the bonnet safety catch bolts (arrowed)

7.20 Lower mounting bracket (arrowed) – left-hand side shown

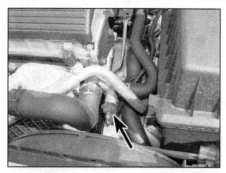

8.3a Engine coolant temperature (ECT) sensor location – 4-cylinder petrol engines

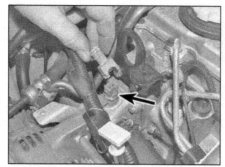

8.3b Engine coolant temperature (ECT) sensor location – diesel engines

8.12 Engine compartment fusebox

module (ECM) via a relay. On models with air conditioning, the fan has a slow- and high-speed setting, controlled when the air conditioning is switched on. **Note:** *If there is a fault on the slow-speed circuit, the fan will run at the high-speed setting, see specifications.*

2 Depending on model, the relay is either located in the engine compartment fuse/relay box or the shroud around the cooling fan; see Chapter 12 for cooling system wiring diagram.

Engine coolant temperature sensor

3 On 4-cylinder petrol engines, the engine coolant temperature sensor is located in the cooling system outlet elbow at the transmission side of the cylinder head. On diesel engines, it is in the coolant elbow on the front of the engine at the timing belt side of the cylinder head **(see illustrations)**.

4 On 6-cylinder engines, the coolant temperature sensor is located between the two banks of cylinders between cylinders 3 and 6.

5 The temperature gauge is fed with a regulated 5 volts feed (via the ignition switch and a fuse) and the sensor controls the gauge earth. The sensor contains a thermistor – an electronic component whose electrical resistance decreases at a predetermined rate as its temperature rises. When the coolant is cold, the sensor resistance is high, current flow through the gauge is reduced, and the gauge needle points towards the blue (cold) end of the scale. As the coolant temperature rises and the sensor resistance falls, current flow increases, and the gauge needle moves towards the upper end of the scale. If the sensor is faulty, it must be renewed. This type of sensor is a Negative Temperature Coefficient (NTC) thermistor, which is in contact with the engine coolant.

6 On models with a temperature warning light, the light is fed with a voltage from the instrument panel. The sender controls the light earth. The sender is effectively a switch, which operates at a predetermined temperature to earth the light and complete the circuit. If the light is fitted in addition to a gauge, the senders for the gauge and light are incorporated in a single unit, with two wires, one each for the light and gauge earths.

Testing

7 If the gauge develops a fault, first check the other instruments; if they do not work at all; check the instrument panel electrical feed. If the readings are erratic, there may be a fault in the voltage stabiliser, which will necessitate renewal of the stabiliser (the stabiliser is integral with the instrument panel printed circuit board – see Chapter 12). If the fault lies in the temperature gauge alone, check it as follows.

8 If the gauge needle remains at the cold end of the scale when the engine is hot, disconnect the sender wiring plug, and earth the relevant wire to the engine. If the needle then deflects when the ignition is switched on, the sender unit is proved faulty, and should be renewed. If the needle still does not move, remove the instrument panel (Chapter 12) and check the continuity of the wire between the sender unit and the gauge, and the feed to the gauge unit. If continuity is shown, and the fault still exists, then the gauge is faulty, and the gauge unit should be renewed.

9 If the gauge needle remains at the hot end of the scale when the engine is cold, disconnect the sender wire. If the needle then returns to the cold end of the scale when the ignition is switched on, the sender unit is proved faulty, and should be renewed. If the needle still does not move, check the remainder of the circuit as described previously.

10 The same basic principles apply to testing the warning light. The light should illuminate when the relevant sender wire is earthed.

Removal and refitting

Radiator cooling fan relay

11 For relays located in the shroud around the cooling fan; disconnect the wiring connector, release the retaining clip and remove the relay from the shroud.

12 For relays located in the engine compartment fuse/relay box; remove the fusebox cover and withdraw the relay to release it from the fuse/relay box **(see illustration)**.

Engine coolant temperature sensor

Note: *Loctite 577 is needed to seal the sensor threads on types of sensor without sealing washers.*

13 Partially drain the cooling system to below the level of the coolant temperature sensor.

See Chapter 1A or 1B for information on draining the cooling system.

14 On 6-cylinder engines it will be necessary to remove the thermostat as described in Section 4 of this Chapter, to access the engine coolant temperature sensor.

15 Disconnect the wiring connector, and then unscrew the sensor from the cylinder head outlet elbow (4-cylinder engines) or between the cylinder banks (6-cylinder engines) and remove.

16 Refit the temperature sensor into the coolant housing using a reversal of the removal procedure. Tighten to the specified torque setting. **Note:** Clean and degrease the sensor threads, and apply a smear of Loctite 577 or new sealing washer, before refitting.

17 On completion, top-up or refill the cooling system, with reference to *Weekly checks,* Chapter 1A or 1B.

9 Heater components – removal and refitting

Heater unit

Removal

1 Drain the cooling system as described in Chapter 1A or 1B. Where applicable, undo the retaining bolts/nuts and remove the engine undertray.

2 Working in the engine compartment, slacken the hose clips and disconnect the heater supply and return hoses from the matrix outlets on the bulkhead **(see illustration)**.

9.2 Disconnecting the supply and return hoses on engine compartment bulkhead

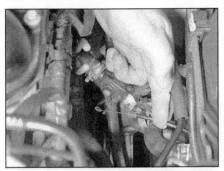

9.3 Disconnecting the heater valve control cable

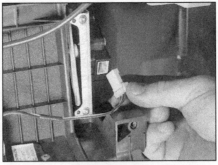

9.6 Disconnect the wiring connector from the air duct

9.7 Undo the mounting bolts . . .

9.8 . . . and withdraw the air duct

9.13 Undo the nuts securing the heater unit to the mounting studs on the bulkhead

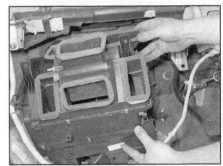

9.14 Carefully lift the heater unit off its mounting studs and remove it from the vehicle

3 Where fitted, disconnect the heater cable inner from the heater valve and free the cable outer from its retaining clip **(see illustration)**.
4 Slacken and remove the heater mounting nut, which is situated just above the matrix outlet pipes.
5 Working inside the vehicle, remove the facia panel as described in Chapter 11.
6 Release the vehicle wiring harness from the clip at the front of the heater unit and disconnect the wiring multiplug connector **(see illustration)**.
7 Remove the securing screws and detach the heater duct from the heater outlet and blower motor **(see illustration)**.
8 Remove the air duct from the lower part of the heater unit **(see illustration)**.
9 Undo the two retaining bolts and move the inertia switch/relay bracket clear of the steering column support beam.
10 Undo the seven mounting bolts and withdraw the steering column support beam from the vehicle.
11 Release the wiring loom from the securing clips on the left-hand side of the heater housing and the aerial lead from the securing clips along the top of the heater housing.
12 Remove the retaining clip at the lower part of the heater unit where it secures to the floor tunnel ducting.
13 Unscrew the two nuts that secure the upper part of the heater unit to the mounting studs on the bulkhead **(see illustration)**.
14 Carefully withdraw the heater unit off its mounting studs and release it from the lower tunnel air ducts and remove it from the vehicle

(see illustration). Keep the unit in the upright position to prevent any coolant still inside the heater matrix from leaking out.

Refitting

15 Refitting is a reversal of removal, bearing in mind the following points:
a) *Ensure that the heater ducts are securely connected to the unit so that there are no air leaks or gaps.*
b) *Check the operation of all heater cables before refitting the facia, ensuring that the relevant component moves smoothly from the fully-open to the fully-closed position. If necessary, adjustments can be made by releasing the relevant retaining clip and repositioning the cable outer.*
c) *Ensure that the heater hoses are correctly reconnected and are securely held by the retaining clips.*

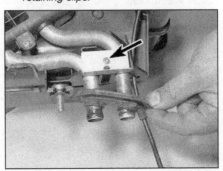

9.17 Remove the rubber grommet and the pipe retaining screw – arrowed

d) *Tighten the heater mounting nuts/bolts securely.*
e) *On completion, refill the cooling system as described in Chapter 1A or 1B.*

Heater matrix

Removal

16 Remove the heater unit as described in paragraphs 1 to 14.
17 Remove the rubber grommet from the inlet and outlet pipes on the heater matrix **(see illustration)**
18 Undo the screw securing the pipe bracket to the heater unit and remove the bracket **(see illustration 9.17)**.
19 Slacken and remove the two matrix cover retaining screws, then remove the cover and withdraw the matrix from the heater unit **(see illustrations)**.
20 If the matrix is leaking, it is best to obtain

9.19a Remove the cover . . .

9.19b ... and withdraw the matrix from the heater unit

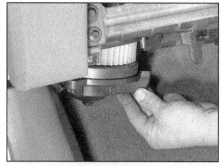

9.23 Remove the blower motor from the air duct ...

9.24 ... and disconnect the wiring connector

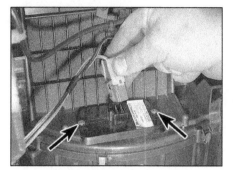

9.28a Disconnect the wiring connector, undo the two screws (arrowed) ...

9.28b ... and withdraw the resistor

a new or reconditioned unit, as home repairs are seldom successful. If it is blocked, it can sometimes be cleared by reverse flushing using a garden hose. Use a proprietary radiator cleaning product if absolutely necessary.

Refitting

21 Refitting is a reverse of the removal procedure.

Heater blower motor

Removal

22 Disconnect the battery negative terminal (refer to *Disconnecting the battery* in the Reference Section of this manual).
23 Slacken the three securing screws and withdraw the motor from the blower unit **(see illustration)**.
24 As the heater blower motor is lowered, unplug the motor wiring connector **(see illustration)**.

Refitting

25 Refitting is a reverse of the removal procedure.

Heater blower motor resistor

Removal

26 Release the fixings and remove the lower cover panel from the passenger's side of the facia.
27 Open the glovebox, then undo the two securing bolts and withdraw the glovebox from the facia panel.
28 Disconnect the wiring connector, then undo the two retaining screws and remove the resistor from the front of the heater assembly **(see illustrations)**.

Refitting

29 Refitting is a reverse of the removal procedure.

Heater valve

Removal

30 Working in the engine compartment, disconnect the cable inner from the heater valve and free the cable outer from the retaining clip **(see illustration 9.3)**.
31 Either drain the cooling system (see Chapter 1A or 1B) or clamp the coolant hoses on each side of the coolant valve to minimise the loss of coolant.
32 Slacken the hose securing clips, then disconnect the two hoses from the heater valve. **Note:** *Use a container to catch any coolant which may still be in the hoses as they are disconnected.*
33 Undo the retaining nut/bolt from the heater valve mounting bracket and remove it from the engine compartment.

Refitting

34 Refitting is a reversal of the removal procedure. On completion, check the heater cable operates smoothly and replenish the cooling system (see Chapter 1A or 1B).

---

10 Heater/ventilation intake filter – renewal

Models with conventional heating

1 Release the fixings and remove the lower cover panel from the passenger's side of the facia.
2 Release the two securing clips and remove the cover from the heater unit housing.
3 Withdraw the filter element from the heater unit and discard it.
4 Clean the inside of the filter housing and cover, then fit a new filter using the reversal of the removal procedure.

Models with air conditioning

5 Release the fixings and remove the lower cover panel from the passenger's side of the facia.
6 Open the glovebox, then undo the two securing bolts and withdraw the glovebox from the facia panel.
7 Undo the four screws securing the glovebox lower rail and withdraw it from the facia panel.
8 Release the two securing clips and remove the cover from the evaporator/heater unit housing.
9 Withdraw the filter element from the heater unit and discard it, noting the airflow direction arrow for refitting.
10 Clean inside the filter housing and cover, then fit a new filter (noting direction arrow) using the reversal of the removal procedure.

---

11 Heater controls – removal, refitting and adjustment

Removal

1 Refer to Chapter 11 and remove the front centre console assembly from the facia panel.
2 With the heater control knobs set in the fully anti-clockwise position, disconnect the air distribution control cable and the temperature control cables from the levers on the right-hand side of the heater unit. Make a note of each cable's fitted position to aid refitting **(see illustration)**.
3 Slacken and remove the four securing screws and withdraw the heater control panel from the facia slightly **(see illustrations)**.
4 Disconnect the multiplug connectors from the rear of the heater control panel as they become accessible (3 connectors on models with a conventional heating system, 4 on models with air conditioning) **(see illustration)**.

5 Fully withdraw the control panel from the facia, feeding the control cables through the facia aperture.

6 If the control panel or switches are to be renewed, proceed as described in the following paragraphs.

7 Carefully prise the heater control knobs from the front of the control panel.

8 Remove the securing screws and withdraw the heater fan switch and cable control units from the rear of the control panel.

9 Where applicable, transfer the new switch, knobs and cable control unit to the new heater control panel.

Refitting and adjustment

10 Refitting is a reversal of removal, noting the following points:
- a) *Set the heater control knobs in the fully anti-clockwise position, before reconnecting the control cables.*
- b) *Check the operation of all heater controls before refitting the centre console*
- c) *Refit the front centre console with reference to Chapter 11.*

12 Air conditioning compressor drivebelt – inspection, adjustment and renewal

Inspection and adjustment

1 Refer to Chapter 1A or 1B, as applicable.

Renewal

2 On petrol models, the air conditioning compressor is driven by the same drivebelt as the alternator; refer to the information given in Chapter 5A.

3 On diesel models, all ancillaries are driven by a single auxiliary drivebelt; its renewal is described in Chapter 5A.

13 Air conditioning system – general information and precautions

General information

An air conditioning system is available on most models. It enables the temperature of incoming air to be lowered; it also dehumidifies the air, which makes for rapid demisting and increased comfort.

The cooling side of the system works in the same way as a domestic refrigerator. Refrigerant gas is drawn into a belt-driven compressor, and passes into a condenser in front of the radiator, where it loses heat and becomes liquid. The liquid passes through an expansion valve to an evaporator, where it changes from liquid under high pressure to gas under low pressure. This change is accompanied by a drop in temperature, which cools the evaporator. The refrigerant returns to the compressor and the cycle begins again **(see illustrations)**.

11.2 Disconnect the control cables (arrowed) from the heater unit

11.3a Remove the securing screws from heater control panel . . .

11.3b . . . and withdraw it from the facia

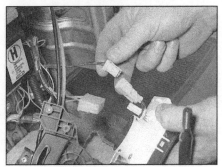

11.4 Unplug the wiring connectors from the rear of the heater control panel

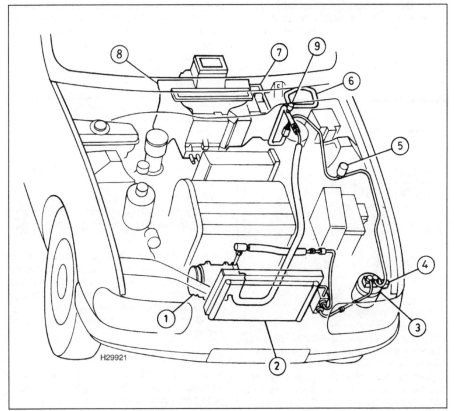

13.2a Air conditioning system layout

1 Compressor	4 Trinary pressure switch	7 Evaporator
2 Condenser	5 High pressure connection	8 Heater housing
3 Receiver/drier	6 Blower unit	9 Low pressure connection

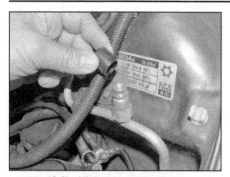

13.2b High-pressure valve – all models

13.2d Low-pressure valve – 6-cylinder petrol models

Air blown through the evaporator passes to the air distribution unit, where it is mixed with hot air blown through the heater matrix, to achieve the desired temperature in the passenger compartment. The heating side of the system works in the same way as on models without air conditioning.

Precautions

⚠ *Warning: The refrigerant is potentially dangerous, and should only be handled by qualified*

TOOL TiP

Many car accessory shops sell one-shot air conditioning recharge aerosols. These generally contain refrigerant, compressor oil, leak sealer and system conditioner. Some also have a dye to help pinpoint leaks.

⚠ *Warning: These products must only be used as directed by the manufacturer, and do not remove the need for regular maintenance.*

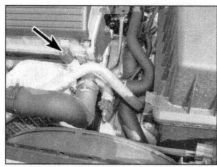

13.2c Low-pressure valve – 4-cylinder petrol models

13.2e Low-pressure valve – diesel models

persons. If it is splashed onto the skin, it can cause frostbite. It is not itself poisonous, but in the presence of a naked flame (including a cigarette) it forms a poisonous gas.

Uncontrolled discharging of the refrigerant is dangerous, and damaging to the environment. It follows that a Rover dealer or an air conditioning specialist must only carry out any work on the air conditioning system that involves opening the refrigerant circuit.

Do not operate the air conditioning system if it is known to be short of refrigerant; the compressor may be damaged (see **Tool tip**).

14 Air conditioning system components – removal and refitting

⚠ *Warning: The air conditioning system must be professionally discharged before carrying out any of these procedures (see Section 13). Cap or plug the pipe/lines as soon as they are disconnected to prevent the entry of moisture.*

Compressor removal

Note: *The following new parts are needed – O-rings for air conditioning pipes, refrigerant oil to lubricate the O-rings.*

1 To remove the compressor completely, the air conditioning system must be discharged before unscrewing the unions, see Section 13.
Note: *If necessary, the compressor can be unbolted and moved to one side (without*

disconnecting its flexible pipes), after removing the drivebelt and disconnecting the wiring plug connector.
2 Disconnect the battery negative terminal (refer to *Disconnecting the battery* in the Reference Section of this manual).
3 Remove the auxiliary drivebelt as described in Chapter 1A or 1B. **Note:** *On diesel models, slacken the three power steering pump pulley retaining bolts (do not remove at this point), before removing the auxiliary belt.*

4-cylinder petrol engines

4 Disconnect the multiplug connector from the compressor clutch.
5 With the system discharged, slacken and remove the bolt securing the air conditioning pipe union to the compressor, and release the pipe union. Discard the O-ring seals on removal, as new seals will be required for refitting.
Caution: Plug or cap all pipes and connections to prevent ingress of dirt or moisture into the system.
6 Slacken and remove the upper compressor mounting bolt and the two lower mounting bolts attaching the compressor to the support bracket.
7 Remove the compressor from the support bracket and withdraw it from under the vehicle.

6-cylinder petrol engines

8 Remove the engine oil cooler as described in Chapter 2B.
9 Remove the right-hand engine mounting (hydramount) as described in Chapter 2B.
10 If not already done, undo the retaining bolt securing the low-pressure pipe to the lower part of the engine-mounting bracket on the cylinder block **(see illustration)**.
11 Release the two cable ties securing the air conditioning pipe to the power steering hose.
12 With the system discharged, slacken and remove the bolt securing the air conditioning low pressure pipe union to the compressor, and release the pipe union. Discard the O-ring seals on removal, as new seals will be required for refitting.
13 With the system discharged, slacken and remove the bolt securing the air conditioning high-pressure pipe union to the compressor, and release the pipe union. Discard the O-ring

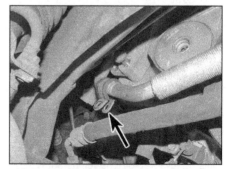

14.10 Air conditioning low-pressure pipe bracket – arrowed

seals on removal, as new seals will be required for refitting.

Caution: Plug or cap all pipes and connections to prevent ingress of dirt or moisture into the system.

14 Disconnect the multiplug connector from the compressor clutch.

15 Slacken and remove the two mounting bolts, securing the compressor and heat shield. Remove the heat shield from the compressor.

16 Undo the remaining compressor mounting bolt and remove the compressor from the support bracket and withdraw it from under the vehicle.

Diesel engines

17 Remove the right-hand engine mounting (hydramount) as described in Chapter 2C.

18 Raise the engine slightly, remove the power steering pump pulley retaining bolts and remove the pulley

19 Release the power steering fluid reservoir from its mounting bracket and empty the fluid into a container.

20 Slacken and remove the bolt securing the high pressure pipe to the power steering pump, release the pipe union and catch any spilt fluid. **Note:** *Use two spanners (one to counter-hold the union) when removing or refitting the power steering pipe.*

21 Slacken the securing clip and disconnect the intercooler hose from the turbocharger outlet pipe.

22 Undo the bolt securing the air conditioning pipe to the bracket on the coolant rail.

23 Disconnect the multiplug connector from the compressor clutch.

24 With the system discharged, slacken and remove the bolt securing the air conditioning pipe union to the compressor, and release the pipe union. Discard the O-ring seals on removal, as new seals will be required for refitting.

Caution: Plug or cap all pipes and connections to prevent ingress of dirt or moisture into the system.

25 Remove the upper mounting bolt from the compressor, which also secures the power steering pipe retaining bracket. Make sure the power steering pipe is located safely out of the way of the compressor.

26 Undo the two remaining compressor mounting bolts, remove the compressor from the support bracket and withdraw it from under the vehicle.

Compressor refitting

Caution: If a new compressor is being fitted, it will be filled with a quantity of special oil (which is more than the recommended quantity of oil). Before fitting, an exact amount of oil must be drained. This should only be done by an MG Rover dealer, or air conditioning specialist who know the recommended quantity of oil.

27 Refitting is a reversal of removal, noting the following points:

14.45 Location of receiver/drier – behind left-hand headlight, with battery tray removed

a) *Have the quantity of oil in the compressor checked at an MG Rover dealer or air conditioning specialist.*

b) *Make sure all pipes and components are clean before refitting.*

c) *Fit new O-ring seals to the pipe connections.*

d) *Refit the auxiliary drivebelt with reference to Chapter 1A or 1B.*

e) *Have the system recharged at an MG Rover dealer or air conditioning specialist.*

f) *Tighten all mounting nuts/bolts to their specified torque setting.*

Condenser

Note: *The following new parts are needed – O-rings for air conditioning pipes, refrigerant oil to lubricate the O-rings.*

Removal

28 Disconnect the battery negative terminal (refer to *Disconnecting the battery* in the Reference Section of this manual).

29 Apply the handbrake, chock the rear roadwheels, then jack up the front of the car and support it on axle stands (see *Jacking and vehicle support*). Where applicable, undo the retaining bolts/nuts and remove the engine undertray.

30 Remove the front bumper as described in Chapter 11.

31 On 6-cylinder petrol engines, to gain better access, undo the four retaining bolts and remove the crossmember from across the front of the vehicle.

32 Undo the bonnet safety catch securing bolts, and remove it from the upper crossmember. If required unclip the bonnet release cable from its retaining clip.

33 Disconnect the multiplugs from the two cooling fan motors.

34 With the system discharged, slacken and remove the bolts securing the air conditioning pipe union to the condenser, and release the pipe union. Discard the O-ring seals on removal, as new seals will be required for refitting.

Caution: Plug or cap all pipes and connections to prevent ingress of dirt or moisture into the system.

35 Undo the mounting bolts (one at each side) from the cooling fan and condenser assembly.

36 The cooling fan and condenser and can now be withdrawn from the lower mountings and removed from the vehicle.

Refitting

37 Refitting is a reversal of removal, noting the following points:

a) *Make sure all pipes and components are clean before refitting.*

b) *Fit new O-ring seals to the pipe connections.*

c) *Have the system recharged at an MG Rover dealer or air conditioning specialist.*

Condenser fan and motor

Removal

38 Remove the condenser as described in paragraphs 28 to 36.

39 Undo two bolts securing the cooling fan assembly to the condenser, release the fan assembly and carefully remove it from the condenser.

40 To remove the fan from the housing release the wiring harness from the fan housing, undo the motor retaining screws and remove the fan assembly.

Refitting

41 Refitting is a reversal of the removal procedure, noting:

a) *Make sure all pipes and components are clean before refitting.*

b) *Fit new O-ring seals to the pipe connections.*

c) *Have the system recharged at an MG Rover dealer or air conditioning specialist.*

Receiver/drier unit

Note: *Rover recommends that the receiver/drier unit must be renewed whenever the air conditioning system is discharged.*

Removal

42 Disconnect the battery negative terminal (refer to *Disconnecting the battery* in the Reference Section of this manual).

43 Remove the air cleaner assembly.

44 For easier access, remove the battery and battery tray as described in Chapter 5A.

45 Disconnect the multiplug from the refrigerant pressure sensor **(see illustration)**.

46 With the system discharged, slacken and remove the bolts securing the air conditioning pipe union to the receiver/drier, and release the pipe union.

47 Discard the O-ring seals on removal, as new seals will be required for refitting.

Caution: Plug or cap all pipes and connections to prevent ingress of dirt or moisture into the system.

48 Undo two bolts securing the receiver/drier unit mounting bracket to the body panel.

49 Remove the refrigerant pressure sensor, and discard the O-ring from the sensor, a new one will be required for refitting.

50 If required, slacken the two securing screws on the mounting bracket and remove it from the receiver/drier unit.

14.53 Air conditioning pipes – arrowed

14.68 Trinary pressure switch location (arrowed) in top of receiver/drier

Refitting

51 Refitting is a reversal of the removal procedure, noting:

a) *Make sure all pipes and components are clean before refitting.*

b) *Fit new O-ring seals to the pipe connections.*

c) *Have the system recharged at an MG Rover dealer or air conditioning specialist.*

Evaporator

Removal

52 Disconnect the battery negative terminal (refer to *Disconnecting the battery* in the Reference Section of this manual).

53 Working under the bonnet, slacken and remove the bolt securing the air conditioning pipe connection at the side of the brake ABS unit **(see illustration)**. An extension with a universal joint will be required to get to this connector.

54 Working inside the vehicle, release the fixings and remove the lower cover panel from the passenger's side of the facia.

55 Undo the two securing bolts and withdraw the glovebox from the facia panel.

56 Undo the four screws securing the glovebox lower rail and withdraw it from the facia panel.

57 Disconnect the two wiring connectors from the evaporator thermostat.

58 Working your way around the evaporator assembly remove the five securing screws from around the housing and the one retaining nut at the upper edge of the housing

59 With the aid of an assistant (working under the bonnet), disconnect the air conditioning pipe connector from the evaporator. Discard the O-rings from the connector pipe, as new ones will be required for refitting.

60 Withdraw the evaporator assembly from between the heater unit casing, removing the drain tube as the evaporator housing is removed.

61 To remove the evaporator from the housing first remove the heater/ventilation intake filter as described in Section 10.

62 Undo the five retaining screws and release the three securing clips to remove the upper part of the evaporator housing from the lower. Note the position of the retaining screws for refitting, as some are longer than others.

63 Withdraw the temperature sensor probe

from inside the lower part of the evaporator housing, then slide the evaporator out from the lower part of the housing.

64 To remove the expansion valve from the evaporator, first undo the Allen bolt and remove the adaptor from the expansion valve. Then remove two further Allen bolts and remove the expansion valve from the evaporator. Discard the O-rings from the between the adaptor and expansion valve and between the expansion valve and the evaporator, as new ones will be required for refitting.

Refitting

65 Refitting is a reversal of the removal procedure, noting:

a) *Make sure all pipes and components are clean before refitting.*

b) *Fit new O-ring seals to the pipe connections and expansion valve.*

c) *Have the system recharged at an MG Rover dealer or air conditioning specialist.*

Temperature sensor probe

66 The temperature sensor probe is located inside the evaporator housing next to the evaporator. To remove the temperature sensor probe, follow the procedures as described in paragraphs 52 to 63.

Expansion valve

67 The expansion valve is located inside the evaporator housing on the evaporator inlet and outlet pipe connector. To remove the expansion valve, follow the procedures as described in paragraphs 52 to 64.

Trinary pressure switch

68 Since the receiver/drier must be renewed whenever the air conditioning system is opened, the removal and refitting procedure for the trinary pressure switch is the same as that given for the receiver/drier **(see illustration)**. Refer to paragraphs 42 to 51.

Chapter 4 Part A:
Fuel and exhaust systems – 4-cylinder petrol engines

Contents

Section number

Accelerator cable – removal, refitting and adjustment 4
Accelerator pedal – removal and refitting. 5
Air cleaner assembly – removal and refitting 2
Exhaust system – general information and component renewal 13
Fuel injection system – depressurising and priming 7
Fuel injection system – general information. 6
Fuel injection system – testing and adjustment. 9

Section number

Fuel injection system components – removal and refitting 11
Fuel pump/fuel gauge sender unit – removal and refitting. 8
Fuel tank and filler neck – removal, inspection and refitting 3
General information and precautions. 1
Manifolds – removal and refitting 12
Throttle body – removal and refitting 10

Degrees of difficulty

Easy, suitable for novice with little experience	**Fairly easy,** suitable for beginner with some experience	**Fairly difficult,** suitable for competent DIY mechanic	**Difficult,** suitable for experienced DIY mechanic	**Very difficult,** suitable for expert DIY or professional

Specifications

General
System type . . . . Rover modular engine management system (MEMS 3) multi-point fuel injection system integrated with ignition system

Fuel pump
Type . . . . Electric roller vane pump in fuel tank
Maximum delivery pressure . . . . 4.1 bar
Regulated injection pressure . . . . 3.0 ± 0.2 bar

Idle settings (not adjustable – for reference only)
Idle speed. . . . . 825 ± 50 rpm
Idle mixture (CO content) . . . . Less than 0.5 %

Torque wrench settings

	Nm	lbf ft
Camshaft position (CMP) sensor bolt	9	7
Crankshaft position sensor-to-flywheel housing bolt.	6	4
Engine control module (ECM)-to-bracket nuts.	4	3
Engine coolant temperature (ECT) sensor to housing	15	11
Exhaust joint nuts and bolts	50	37
Exhaust manifold securing nuts.	45	33
Fuel feed pipe-to-fuel rail bolts	10	7
Fuel pump/gauge sender-to-fuel tank nuts	9	7
Fuel rail-to-manifold bolts	5	4
Heated oxygen sensor (HO_2S) to manifold/exhaust system	55	41
Idle air control valve (IACV)-to-manifold screws	6	4
Inlet manifold securing nuts and bolts.	17	13
Intake air temperature (IAT) sensor to manifold	7	5
Throttle body-to-inlet manifold bolts	9	7
Throttle position sensor securing screws.	2	1

1 General information and precautions

General information

The operation of the fuel injection system is described in more detail in Section 6.

Fuel is supplied from a tank mounted under the rear of the vehicle by an electric fuel pump mounted in the tank. The fuel pump also incorporates the fuel level gauge sender unit. The fuel passes through a filter to the fuel injection system, which incorporates various sensors, actuators and an engine control module (ECM) **(see illustration)**.

The inducted air passes through an air cleaner, which incorporates a paper filter element to filter out potentially harmful particles (serious internal engine damage can be caused if foreign particles enter through the air intake system).

The engine control module (ECM) controls both the fuel injection system and the ignition system, integrating the two into a complete engine management system. Refer to Chapter 5B for details of the ignition side of the system.

The exhaust system incorporates a catalytic converter to reduce exhaust gas emissions.

Further details can be found in Chapter 4D, along with details of the other emission control systems and components.

Precautions

Before disconnecting any fuel lines, or working on any part of the fuel system, the system must be depressurised as described in Section 7.

Care must be taken when disconnecting the fuel lines. When disconnecting a fuel union or hose, loosen the union or clamp screw slowly to avoid sudden uncontrolled fuel spillage. Take adequate fire precautions.

When working on fuel system components, scrupulous cleanliness must be observed, and care must be taken not to introduce any foreign matter into fuel lines or components.

After carrying out any work involving disconnection of fuel lines, it is advisable to check the connections for leaks; pressurise the system by switching the ignition on and off several times.

Electronic control units are very sensitive components, and certain precautions must be taken to avoid damage to these units as follows.
• When carrying out welding operations on the vehicle using electric welding equipment, the battery and alternator should be disconnected.

• Although the underbonnet-mounted modules will tolerate normal underbonnet conditions, they can be adversely affected by excess heat or moisture. If using welding equipment or pressure-washing equipment in the vicinity of an electronic module, take care not to direct heat, or jets of water or steam, at the module. If this cannot be avoided, remove the module from the vehicle, and protect its wiring plug with a plastic bag.
• Before disconnecting any wiring, or removing components, always ensure that the ignition is switched off.
• Do not attempt to improvise fault diagnosis procedures using a test lamp or multimeter, as irreparable damage could be caused to the module.
• After working on fuel injection/engine management system components, ensure that all wiring is correctly reconnected before reconnecting the battery or switching on the ignition.

Leaded fuel will damage the catalytic converter, so unleaded fuel must be used at all times. In addition, if unburnt fuel enters the catalytic converter, this may result in overheating and irreparable damage to the catalytic converter.

Damage to the catalytic converter may result if the following precautions are not observed:

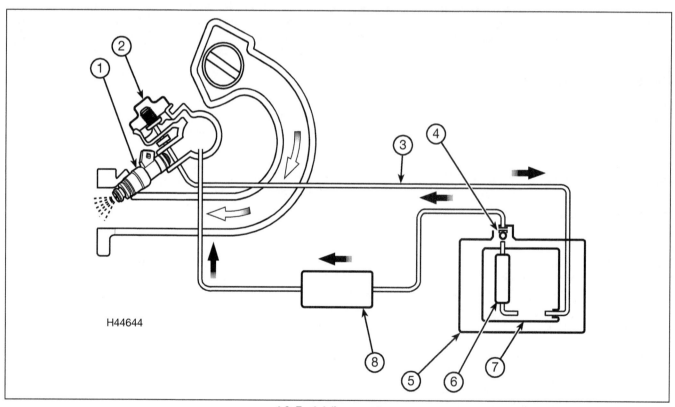

H44644

1.2 Fuel delivery system

1 Injectors	3 Fuel return line	6 Fuel pump
2 Fuel pressure regulator	4 Non-return valve	7 Swirl pot
	5 Fuel tank	8 Fuel filter

• Consult an approved dealer as soon as possible in the event of misfiring, irregular engine running after a cold start, a significant loss of engine power, or any other malfunction which may indicate a fault in the ignition system. If it is necessary to continue driving, do so for a short time at low engine speed, without labouring the engine.

• Avoid frequent cold starts one after another.

• Avoid actuation of the starter for an unnecessarily long time during starting.

• Do not allow the fuel tank to become empty.

• Do not attempt to start the engine by push- or tow-starting – use jump leads (see *Jump starting*).

⚠ *Warning: Many of the procedures in this Chapter require the disconnection of fuel line connections, and the removal of components, which may result in some fuel spillage. Before carrying out any operation on the fuel system, refer to the precautions given in 'Safety first!' at the beginning of this manual, and follow them implicitly. Petrol is a highly-dangerous and volatile liquid, and the precautions necessary when handling it cannot be overstressed.*

2 Air cleaner assembly – removal and refitting

Removal

1 Remove the battery as described in Chapter 5A.

2 Release the hose clip, and disconnect the air intake trunking from the throttle body **(see illustration)**.

3 Unscrew the two bolts securing the air cleaner to the battery tray **(see illustration)**.

4 Release the air intake tube from the bottom of the air cleaner, then remove the air cleaner assembly from the engine compartment.

Refitting

5 Refitting is a reversal of removal.

3 Fuel tank and filler neck – removal, inspection and refitting

Fuel tank

Note: *During removal, note the locations and routing of all hoses to aid refitting.*

Removal

1 Disconnect the battery negative lead. **Note:** *Before disconnecting the battery, refer to 'Disconnecting the battery' at the rear of this manual.*

2 Chock the front wheels, then jack up the rear of the vehicle and support securely on axle stands (see *Jacking and vehicle support*).

2.2 Release the retaining clip – arrowed

3 Syphon the fuel from the tank into a clean metal container which can be sealed. Alternatively, working under the car, disconnect an accessible fuel line connection at the tank, and drain the fuel into a suitable container.

⚠ *Warning: This procedure should be carried out in a well-ventilated area, and it is vital to take adequate fire precautions – refer to 'Safety first!' for further details.*

4 Free the fuel pump wiring connector from its retaining clip at the rear of the fuel tank and disconnect the wiring connector.

5 Slacken and remove the retaining screws and fasteners and remove the protective cover from the left-hand side of the fuel tank to gain access to the fuel pipes and breather hose **(see illustration)**.

6 Slacken the hose clips and disconnect the breather hose and fuel filler neck from the fuel

2.3 Remove the two bolts – arrowed

tank **(see illustration)**. Plug or cap the hoses to prevent dirt ingress.

7 Release the quick-fit connectors and disconnect the fuel feed and return hoses from the pipes under the rear of the vehicle **(see illustration)**. Plug or cap the open ends of the hoses and pipes to prevent dirt entry.

8 Release the securing clip and disconnect the breather hose from the pipe **(see illustration)**.

9 Place a trolley jack under the fuel tank, with a block of wood between the jack and the fuel tank.

10 Working at the rear of the fuel tank, unscrew the locknuts, and then unscrew the two fuel tank strap securing nuts **(see illustration)**.

11 Ensure that the jack is supporting the fuel tank, and then release the fuel tank straps from the brackets on the body.

12 With the aid of an assistant, lower the fuel tank and withdraw the fuel tank from under the vehicle.

3.5 Remove the protective cover from the left-hand side of the fuel tank

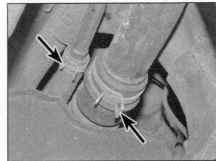

3.6 Release the clips (arrowed) and disconnect the hoses from the fuel tank

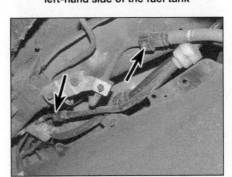

3.7 Disconnect the fuel feed and return hoses (arrowed) from the pipes

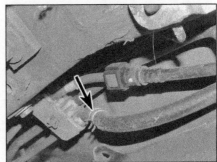

3.8 Release the clip (arrowed) and disconnect the breather hose

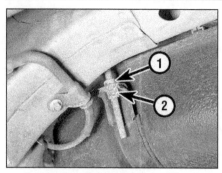

3.10 Fuel tank strap locknut (1) and securing nut (2)

Inspection

13 If the tank contains sediment or water, it may be cleaned out using two or three rinses with paraffin. Shake vigorously using several changes of paraffin, but before doing so remove the fuel pump/gauge sender unit (see Section 8).

⚠️ *Warning: This procedure should be carried out in a well-ventilated area, and it is vital to take adequate fire precautions – refer to 'Safety first!' for further details.*

14 Any repairs to the fuel tank should be carried out by a professional. Do not under any circumstances attempt to weld or solder a fuel tank. Removal of residual fuel vapour requires several hours of specialist cleaning.

Refitting

15 Refitting is a reversal of removal, but

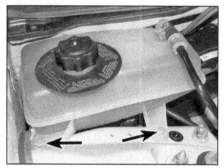

4.1 Undo the two expansion tank mounting bolts – arrowed

4.3 . . . then slide the cable end fitting from the throttle lever

3.17 Remove the inner wheel arch liner

ensure that all hoses are reconnected to their correct locations as noted before removal, and use new hose clips if necessary.

Fuel filler neck

Removal

16 Chock the front wheels, then jack up the rear of the vehicle and support securely on axle stands (see *Jacking and vehicle support*). Remove the left-hand rear roadwheel.
17 Remove the securing screws, and withdraw the rear left-hand wheel arch liner **(see illustration)**.
18 Remove the fuel filler cap and undo the three retaining nuts securing the filler neck surround to the body **(see illustration)**.
19 Working under the vehicle, slacken the hose clips, and disconnect the breather hose and the filler hose from the fuel filler neck **(see illustration 3.6)**.

4.2 Slide the cable adjuster from the bracket . . .

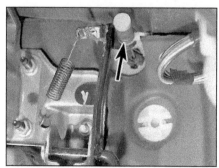

4.7 Unclip the inner cable (arrowed) from the upper end of the pedal

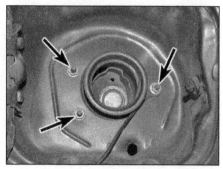

3.18 Undo the three retaining nuts – arrowed

⚠️ *Warning: Be prepared for fuel spillage, and have a suitable container ready to catch any fuel which may be released as the filler hose is disconnected.*

20 Halfway up the filler neck tube, undo the bolt securing the filler neck to the inner body panel, and then withdraw the filler neck assembly from under the wheel arch.

Refitting

21 Refitting is a reversal of removal.

| 4 | Accelerator cable – removal, refitting and adjustment | |

Removal

1 Undo the two retaining bolts **(see illustration)** and release the coolant expansion tank from the bulkhead and move it to one side.
2 Slide the cable adjuster from the bracket on the throttle body/inlet manifold **(see illustration)**.
3 Slide the cable end fitting from the groove in the throttle lever, and disconnect the cable from the lever **(see illustration)**.
4 Working your way along the accelerator cable, release it from any retaining clips.
5 Working at the engine compartment bulkhead, turn the collar on the accelerator cable through 90°, and release the cable from the bulkhead.
6 Working inside the vehicle, remove the pocket from the driver's side of the facia panel. Undo the three retaining screws and remove the lower facia trim panel from the below the steering column.
7 Reach up under the facia, and pull the end of the cable forwards from the pedal, then squeeze the securing lugs and remove the plastic cable securing clip from the end of the pedal. Release the end of the cable from the pedal **(see illustration)**.
8 Pull the cable through the bulkhead into the engine compartment, and withdraw the cable from the vehicle.

Refitting

9 Refitting is a reversal of removal, but

smear the bulkhead grommet with rubber grease and, on completion, check the cable adjustment as described in the following paragraphs.

Adjustment

Note: *Do not attempt to adjust the throttle stop screw during this procedure and make sure the cable is routed correctly.*

10 Slide the cable adjuster from the bracket on the inlet manifold/throttle body, then position the cable adjuster against the rear of the bracket.

11 Hold the throttle lever on the throttle body in the fully closed position, ensuring that the cam on the throttle lever rests against the throttle stop screw.

12 Turn the cable adjuster as necessary until all freeplay is removed from the cable, without moving the throttle lever.

13 Slide the adjuster back into position in the bracket.

14 Have an assistant fully depress the accelerator pedal, and check that the throttle lever moves to the fully open position, and returns to the fully closed position when the pedal is released.

5 Accelerator pedal – removal and refitting

Removal

1 Working inside the vehicle, remove the pocket from the driver's side of the facia panel. Undo the three retaining screws and remove the lower facia trim panel from the below the steering column.

2 Reach up under the facia, and pull the end of the cable forwards from the pedal, then squeeze the securing lugs and remove the plastic cable securing clip from the end of the pedal. Release the end of the cable from the pedal **(see illustration 4.7).**

3 Using a suitable pair of pliers, unhook the return spring from the top of the pedal.

4 Undo the retaining bolt/nut and then remove the pedal assembly from the mounting bracket.

Refitting

5 Refitting is a reversal of removal, but make sure that the accelerator cable is fitted correctly – see Section 4.

6 Fuel injection system – general information

The amount of fuel delivered and the injection timing is controlled by the Modular Engine Management System (MEMS 3), which also controls the ignition system (see Chapter 5B).

Fuel is supplied from the rear-mounted fuel tank by an electric pump mounted in the tank, via a fuel filter, to the fuel rail. A fuel pressure regulator mounted on the fuel rail maintains a constant fuel pressure to the fuel injectors. Excess fuel is returned from the regulator to the tank.

The fuel rail acts as a reservoir for the four fuel injectors, which inject fuel into the cylinder inlet tracts, upstream of the inlet valves. The injectors operate in pairs – the injectors for Nos 1 and 4 cylinders operate simultaneously, as do the injectors for Nos 2 and 3 cylinders.

The injectors are electronically controlled by the Engine Control Module (ECM). Each injector has a solenoid which, when energised by a pulse from the ECM, lifts the injector needle and fuel is sprayed into the cylinder.

6.6 Engine management system components

1 Fuel pressure regulator
2 Inertia switch
3 Malfunction indicator lamp
4 Engine Control Module – ECM
5 Idle Air Control valve – IAC
6 Fuel filter
7 Fuel rail
8 Throttle housing
9 Engine compartment fusebox
10 Main relay
11 Air conditioning relay
12 Fuel pump relay
13 Purge valve and canister
14 Crankshaft position sensor – CKP
15 Air filter
16 Throttle position sensor – TP
18 Catalytic converter
19 Cooling fan relay
20 Engine Coolant Temperature sensor – ECT
21 Intake Air Temperature sensor – IAT
22 Camshaft Position sensor – CMP
23 Oxygen sensor – HO$_2$S*
24 Pre-catalyst
25 Engine oil temperature sensor
26 Engine oil pressure switch
27 Ignition coils
28 Injectors x 4
29 Manifold Absolute Pressure sensor – MAP
29 Oxygen sensor – HO$_2$S
* Certain models only

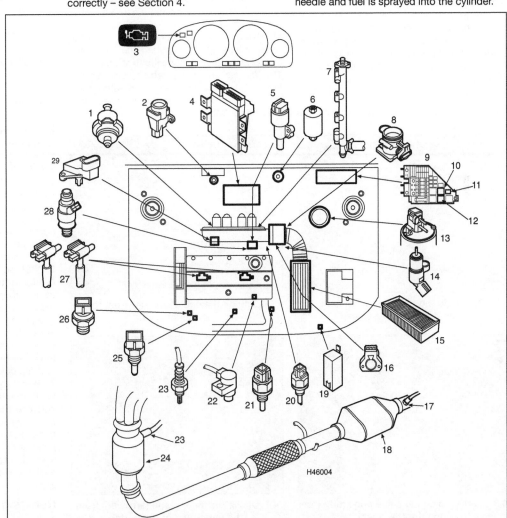

H46004

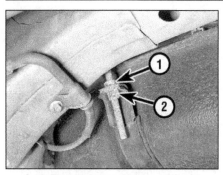

3.10 Fuel tank strap locknut (1) and securing nut (2)

3.17 Remove the inner wheel arch liner

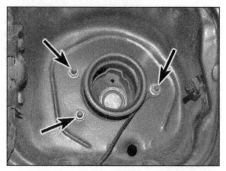

3.18 Undo the three retaining nuts – arrowed

Inspection

13 If the tank contains sediment or water, it may be cleaned out using two or three rinses with paraffin. Shake vigorously using several changes of paraffin, but before doing so remove the fuel pump/gauge sender unit (see Section 8).

⚠️ *Warning: This procedure should be carried out in a well-ventilated area, and it is vital to take adequate fire precautions – refer to 'Safety first!' for further details.*

14 Any repairs to the fuel tank should be carried out by a professional. Do not under any circumstances attempt to weld or solder a fuel tank. Removal of residual fuel vapour requires several hours of specialist cleaning.

Refitting

15 Refitting is a reversal of removal, but

ensure that all hoses are reconnected to their correct locations as noted before removal, and use new hose clips if necessary.

Fuel filler neck

Removal

16 Chock the front wheels, then jack up the rear of the vehicle and support securely on axle stands (see *Jacking and vehicle support*). Remove the left-hand rear roadwheel.

17 Remove the securing screws, and withdraw the rear left-hand wheel arch liner **(see illustration)**.

18 Remove the fuel filler cap and undo the three retaining nuts securing the filler neck surround to the body **(see illustration)**.

19 Working under the vehicle, slacken the hose clips, and disconnect the breather hose and the filler hose from the fuel filler neck **(see illustration 3.6)**.

⚠️ *Warning: Be prepared for fuel spillage, and have a suitable container ready to catch any fuel which may be released as the filler hose is disconnected.*

20 Halfway up the filler neck tube, undo the bolt securing the filler neck to the inner body panel, and then withdraw the filler neck assembly from under the wheel arch.

Refitting

21 Refitting is a reversal of removal.

---

4 Accelerator cable – removal, refitting and adjustment

Removal

1 Undo the two retaining bolts **(see illustration)** and release the coolant expansion tank from the bulkhead and move it to one side.

2 Slide the cable adjuster from the bracket on the throttle body/inlet manifold **(see illustration)**.

3 Slide the cable end fitting from the groove in the throttle lever, and disconnect the cable from the lever **(see illustration)**.

4 Working your way along the accelerator cable, release it from any retaining clips.

5 Working at the engine compartment bulkhead, turn the collar on the accelerator cable through 90°, and release the cable from the bulkhead.

6 Working inside the vehicle, remove the pocket from the driver's side of the facia panel. Undo the three retaining screws and remove the lower facia trim panel from the below the steering column.

7 Reach up under the facia, and pull the end of the cable forwards from the pedal, then squeeze the securing lugs and remove the plastic cable securing clip from the end of the pedal. Release the end of the cable from the pedal **(see illustration)**.

8 Pull the cable through the bulkhead into the engine compartment, and withdraw the cable from the vehicle.

Refitting

9 Refitting is a reversal of removal, but

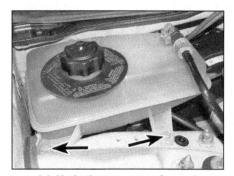

4.1 Undo the two expansion tank mounting bolts – arrowed

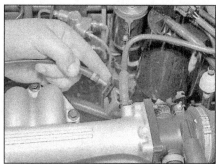

4.2 Slide the cable adjuster from the bracket . . .

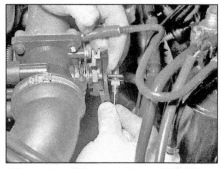

4.3 . . . then slide the cable end fitting from the throttle lever

4.7 Unclip the inner cable (arrowed) from the upper end of the pedal

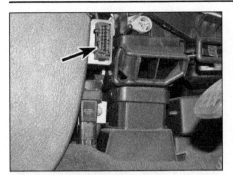

9.3 Diagnostic wiring connector – viewed from driver's side footwell

Adjustment

4 Experienced home mechanics with access to a tachometer and an accurately calibrated exhaust gas analyser may be able to check the exhaust CO level and the idle speed. However, if either of these settings is found to be in need of adjustment, the vehicle must be taken to a Rover dealer for further testing.
5 No manual adjustment of the exhaust CO level or idle speed is possible.

10 Throttle body – removal and refitting

Note: *The following new parts are needed: throttle body O-ring, silicone grease.*
Note: *On completion, the engine may need to be retuned by an MG Rover dealer, using special electronic equipment.*

Removal

1 Disconnect the battery negative lead. **Note:** *Before disconnecting the battery, refer to 'Disconnecting the battery' at the rear of this manual.*
2 Slacken the hose clip securing the air intake hose to the throttle body, and then disconnect it from the throttle body **(see illustration)**.
3 Disconnect the hose from the idle air control valve (IACV).
4 Disconnect the wiring plug from the throttle position sensor (TPS) **(see illustration)**.
5 Release the hose clip(s), and disconnect the breather hose(s) from the throttle body.
6 Slide the cable adjuster from the bracket on the inlet manifold/throttle body.
7 Slide the cable end fitting from the groove in the throttle lever, and disconnect the cable from the lever.
8 Unscrew the four securing bolts, and withdraw the throttle body from the inlet manifold. Recover the O-ring and discard it.

Refitting

9 Clean the mating faces of the throttle body and inlet manifold.
10 Lubricate a new O-ring with silicone grease, and fit it to the throttle body.
11 Locate the throttle body on the inlet manifold, and fit the four bolts into position.

10.2 Release the air intake hose retaining clip – arrowed

12 Working in following sequence, use a torque wrench to tighten the bolts as follows **(see illustration):**
  1) First tighten to 4 Nm.
  2) Then back off one flat.
  3) Finally tighten to 9 Nm.
13 The remaining refitting is a reversal of the removal procedure.
14 If necessary, arrange engine tuning by an MG Rover dealer.

11 Fuel injection system components – removal and refitting

Fuel rail and injectors

Note: *The following new parts are needed – injector O-rings, silicone grease.*

Removal

1 Disconnect the battery negative lead. **Note:** *Before disconnecting the battery, refer to 'Disconnecting the battery' at the rear of this manual.* Remove the engine oil dipstick.
2 Depressurise the fuel system as described in Section 7.
3 Release the securing clip and disconnect the vacuum pipe from the fuel pressure regulator,
4 Pack absorbent cloth under the fuel rail. Disconnect the fuel supply hose from the fuel rail. Plug the pipe connections.
5 Remove two bolts securing the fuel rail to the inlet manifold.
6 Release the fuel rail and injectors from the inlet manifold, and remove the injector spacer.
7 Disconnect the multiplugs from the injectors and remove the fuel rail complete with injectors.
8 Release the spring clips securing the injectors to the fuel rail, and remove the injectors.
9 Remove and discard two O-rings from each injector. Cover both ends of each injector with a protective cap to prevent dirt ingress.

Refitting

10 Refitting is a reversal of the removal procedure, noting:
  a) *Lubricate new O-rings with silicone grease and fit them to the injectors.*

10.4 Disconnect the throttle position sensor wiring connector – arrowed

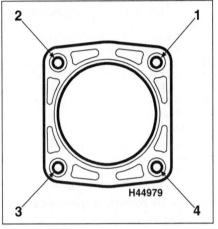

10.12 Bolt tightening sequence

  b) *Use a torque wrench to tighten the fuel rail bolts to the specified torque.*

Fuel pressure regulator

11 The fuel pressure regulator is integral with the fuel rail, and cannot be removed separately. If the fuel regulator is faulty, the complete fuel rail/regulator assembly must be renewed.

Idle air control valve

Note: *A new O-ring and suitable silicone grease will be required on refitting.*

Removal

12 The idle air control valve (IAC) is located at the rear of the engine on the intake manifold **(see illustration)**.

11.12 Idle air control (IAC) valve

11.14 Disconnect the air hose (arrowed) from the throttle body

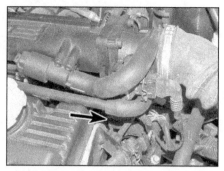

11.17 Intake air temperature (IAT) sensor location

11.23 Engine coolant temperature (ECT) sensor location

13 Disconnect the battery negative lead, and then disconnect the wiring plug from the valve.

14 Disconnect the air hose from the throttle body **(see illustration)**.

15 Remove the four screws securing the valve to the inlet manifold, and then withdraw the valve from the manifold. Recover the O-ring and discard it, a new one will be required for refitting.

Refitting

16 Refitting is a reversal of removal, tightening the valve securing screws to the specified torque setting. Use a new O-ring and lubricate the O-ring with a little silicone grease.

Intake air temperature sensor

Removal

17 The intake air temperature (IAT) sensor is located at the left-hand rear of the inlet manifold under the throttle body assembly **(see illustration)**.

18 Release the wiring connector from the bracket at the end of the cylinder head, to give access to the sensor. Disconnect the multiplug from the sensor.

19 Unscrew the sensor from the inlet manifold.

Refitting

20 Before refitting the sensor, clean the threads and the mating face in the inlet manifold.

21 Fit the sensor to the inlet manifold and tighten the specified torque.

22 Reconnect the multiplug to the sensor and refit the wiring connector to the bracket

on the cylinder head. Reconnect the battery earth lead.

Coolant temperature sensor

Note: *Loctite 577 is needed to seal the sensor.*

Removal

23 The engine coolant temperature (ECT) sensor is screwed into the side of the coolant outlet elbow **(see illustration)**. **Note:** *The temperature gauge sensor is screwed into the underside of the coolant outlet elbow.*

24 Disconnect the battery negative lead. **Note:** *Before disconnecting the battery, refer to 'Disconnecting the battery' at the rear of this manual.*

25 Disconnect the multiplug from the sensor.

26 Locate a container under the sensor to collect coolant, and then unscrew the sensor from the housing.

Refitting

27 Refitting is a reversal of the removal procedure, noting:
  a) *Clean and degrease the sensor threads, and apply a smear of Loctite 577.*
  b) *Use a torque wrench to tighten the sender to the specified torque.*
  c) *Top-up the coolant level.*

Throttle position sensor

Note: *Whenever the sensor is removed or renewed, a 'throttle initialisation' procedure must be carried out. This can only be done by an MG Rover dealer, using special electronic equipment. Therefore, it is recommended that remove/refit or renewal of the sensor should be done by an MG Rover dealer.*

Note: *The following new parts are needed – two Torx head screws and wave washers.*

Removal

28 Disconnect the battery negative lead. **Note:** *Before disconnecting the battery, refer to 'Disconnecting the battery' at the rear of this manual.*

Caution: The sensor can easily be damaged. Handle it with care. Do not twist, or apply leverage to the sensor.

29 Disconnect the air hose from the throttle body to access the throttle position sensor **(see illustration)**.

30 Disconnect the multiplug from the throttle position (TP) sensor **(see illustration)**.

31 Remove and discard the two screws and wave washers securing the sensor to the throttle housing.

32 Remove the plate from across the sensor, and pull the sensor from the throttle spindle.

Refitting

33 Clean the mating faces of the throttle housing and sensor.

Caution: When pushing the sensor onto the throttle spindle, use fingers only, and apply pressure to the shaded area only.

34 Align the flat on the sensor with the flat on the throttle spindle, and push the sensor onto the spindle **(see illustration)**.

35 Rotate the sensor in an anti-clockwise direction to align the screw holes.

Caution: Do not rotate the sensor in clockwise direction. Rotate only anti-clockwise, and do not rotate beyond the sensor internal stops.

11.29 Disconnect the air hose – arrowed

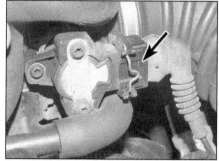

11.30 Disconnect the throttle sensor wiring connector – arrowed

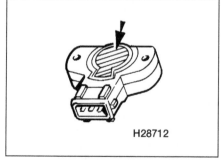

H28712

11.34 Apply pressure to the shaded area only

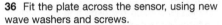

11.41 Manifold absolute pressure (MAP) sensor – arrowed

11.48 Disconnect the wiring connector – arrowed

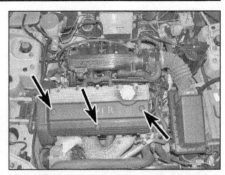

11.55 Undo the camshaft cover bolts – arrowed

36 Fit the plate across the sensor, using new wave washers and screws.

37 Tighten the screws to the specified torque – DO NOT exceed the specified torque.

38 Reconnect the wiring multiplug to the sensor.

39 Connect the battery earth lead.

40 Check that throttle operation is correct, and then arrange to have throttle initialisation carried out by an MG Rover dealer

Manifold absolute pressure sensor

Removal

41 The manifold absolute pressure (MAP) sensor is located on the forward face of the inlet manifold **(see illustration)**.

42 Release the cover from over the sensor wiring and disconnect the wiring multiplug from the sensor.

43 Undo the two retaining screws and remove the sensor from the inlet manifold.

Refitting

44 Clean the sensor and manifold mating faces.

45 Refit the MAP sensor to the manifold, and secure with the two retaining screws.

46 Connect the wiring multiplug to the sensor, and refit the cover over the wiring.

Heated oxygen sensor

Note: *The following new parts are needed – sensor sealing washer, exhaust manifold gasket.*

Removal

47 Remove the exhaust manifold heat shield – see Section 12.

48 Disconnect the wiring connector for the oxygen sensor **(see illustration)**.

49 Unscrew the sensor from the exhaust manifold, and discard the sealing washer.

Refitting

50 Clean the sensor and manifold threads, and fit a new sealing washer to the sensor.

51 Fit the sensor to the manifold and tighten to the specified torque.

52 Reconnect the wiring multiplug connector for the oxygen sensor.

53 Fit the exhaust manifold heat shield with reference to Section 12.

Camshaft position sensor

Removal

54 Disconnect the battery negative lead.
Note: *Before disconnecting the battery, refer to 'Disconnecting the battery' at the rear of this manual.*

55 Remove three bolts securing the coil cover the camshaft cover, and remove the coil cover **(see illustration)**.

56 Release the camshaft position (CMP) sensor cable from the retaining bracket, and disconnect the multiplug.

57 Remove the bolt securing the sensor to the camshaft cover. Release the cable from the clip, and remove the sensor **(see illustration)**.

Refitting

58 Before refitting, clean the mating faces of sensor and camshaft cover.

59 Refit the sensor and tighten to the specified torque.

60 Reconnect the multiplug and secure the cable back in its bracket.

61 Fit the coil cover and tighten the bolts securely.

62 Connect the battery earth lead.

Engine Control Module

Note: *If a new ECM is to be fitted it will need to be programmed with the code from the anti-theft security unit before the engine can be started. This can be done only by an MG Rover dealer using special equipment.*

Removal

63 Disconnect the battery negative lead.
Note: *Before disconnecting the battery, refer to 'Disconnecting the battery' at the rear of this manual.*

64 Remove the four nuts securing the engine control module (ECM) to the mounting bracket on the bulkhead. On later models, there is a cover plate on the lower part of the ECM; this has the two lower retaining nuts on the inside of the mounting bracket **(see illustrations)**.

65 Release the clip securing the wiring loom to the mounting bracket and lift the ECM out of its bracket. Disconnect the wiring multiplugs as the ECM is removed.

11.57 Remove the camshaft position (CMP) sensor

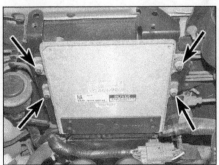

11.64a Engine control module (ECM) mounting nuts

11.64b Engine control module (ECM) mounting nuts – later models

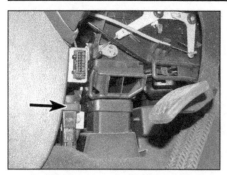

11.67 Fuel inertia cut-off switch location – arrowed

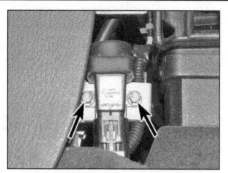

11.69 Undo the two bolts – arrowed

Refitting

66 Refitting is a reversal of the removal procedure.

Fuel inertia cut-off switch

Removal

67 The switch is located inside the driver's side footwell behind the centre console to the left of the clutch pedal (see illustration).

68 Disconnect the battery negative lead, and then disconnect the wiring plug from the switch.

69 Remove the two securing bolts (see illustration) and withdraw the switch from its mounting bracket.

Refitting

70 Refitting is a reversal of removal, but ensure that the switch is reset by pressing the button on the top of the switch.

Crankshaft position sensor

Removal

71 Disconnect the battery negative lead. Note: Before disconnecting the battery, refer to 'Disconnecting the battery' at the rear of this manual.

72 The crankshaft position (CKP) sensor is mounted at the rear of the flywheel housing (to the left-hand end of the engine) (see illustration). To improve access to the sensor, apply the handbrake, then jack up the front of the vehicle and support securely on axle stands (see Jacking and vehicle support).

73 Disconnect the wiring plug from the sensor.

74 Unscrew the bolt securing the sensor to the flywheel housing, then remove the sensor.

Refitting

75 Thoroughly clean the mating faces on the sensor and housing, then refit the sensor using a reversal of the removal procedure and tightening its bolt to the specified torque setting.

12 Manifolds – removal and refitting

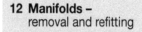

Note: Make a note of the routing and connections of all hoses, pipes and cables.

Inlet manifold

Note: The following new parts are needed – manifold gasket.

Removal

1 Disconnect the battery negative lead. Note: Before disconnecting the battery, refer to 'Disconnecting the battery' at the rear of this manual.

2 Drain the cooling system – see Chapter 1A.

3 Position absorbent cloth around the fuel feed and return hose connections. Release the connectors, and disconnect fuel feed and return hoses.

Caution: Plug the connections to prevent dirt ingress.

4 Release/slacken the clips and disconnect the following hoses:
a) Air intake hose, and breather hose from throttle body.
b) Purge hose from inlet manifold.
c) Idle air control (IAC) hose to throttle body.
d) Coolant hose from inlet manifold.

5 Release cables and disconnect the following multiplugs:
a) Throttle position (TP) sensor.
b) Idle air control (IAC) valve.
c) Manifold absolute pressure (MAP) sensor.

6 Release the accelerator cable and fuel return pipe from the securing clips on the inlet manifold.

7 Release the accelerator cable adjustment nut from the mounting bracket, and then release the inner cable from the throttle linkage.

8 Release the retaining clips and disconnect the breather hose and brake servo hose from the inlet manifold.

9 Remove the three retaining screws, and remove the coil/plug cover.

10 Undo the two bolts securing the right-hand ignition coil to the cylinder head, and release the coil from the spark plug. Disconnect the coil multiplugs, and release the coil wiring harness from the retaining clips.

11 Release the injector multiplug wiring connector from the bracket on the left-hand side of the cylinder head, and disconnect the connector.

12 Working in the reverse of the tightening sequence, progressively slacken and remove the four bolts and three nuts securing the manifold to the cylinder head (see illustration 12.15).

13 Remove the manifold, and discard the gasket (see illustration).

Refitting

14 Clean the mating faces of the manifold and cylinder head, and ensure that metal inserts are fitted in the inlet manifold stud and bolt holes.

15 Using a new gasket, locate the manifold against the cylinder head, and fit the nuts and bolts. Use a torque wrench to tighten the nuts and bolts, in sequence, to the specified torque (see illustration).

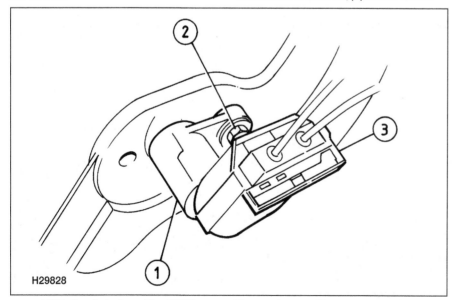

H29828

11.72 Crankshaft position (CKP) sensor (1), securing bolt (2) and wiring plug (3)

16 The remaining refitting is a reversal of the removal procedure, noting:
  a) *Refill the cooling system with a 50/50 mixture of water and antifreeze.*
  b) *Check/adjust accelerator cable operation.*

Exhaust manifold

Note: *The following new parts are needed – manifold gasket.*

Removal

17 Disconnect the battery negative lead.
Note: *Before disconnecting the battery, refer to 'Disconnecting the battery' at the rear of this manual.*

18 On models with air conditioning, remove the exhaust manifold heat shield as described in paragraphs 25 to 34. On models without air conditioning, undo the two bolts and one nut from the heat shield and withdraw the heat shield from the manifold.
19 Undo the two retaining nuts, and disconnect the exhaust front pipe from the exhaust manifold.
20 Release the oxygen sensor multiplug from the bracket on the left-hand side of the cylinder head, and disconnect the wiring plug connector.
21 Working in the **reverse** of the tightening sequence, progressively slacken the five nuts securing the manifold to the cylinder head, and remove the manifold, and discard the gasket **(see illustration 12.23)**.

Refitting

22 Clean the mating faces of the manifold and cylinder head, and fit a new gasket the studs in the cylinder head.
23 Locate the manifold against the cylinder head, and fit the nuts. Use a torque wrench to tighten the nuts and bolts, in sequence, to the specified torque **(see illustration)**.
24 The remaining refitting is a reversal of the removal procedure.

Exhaust manifold heat shield

Removal

25 Disconnect the battery negative lead.
Note: *Before disconnecting the battery, refer to 'Disconnecting the battery' at the rear of this manual.*
26 Remove the splash shield from under the vehicle.
27 Slacken and remove the bolt securing the heat shield to the exhaust flange bracket.
28 Remove the nut and bolt securing the heat shield to the alternator and manifold brackets.
29 Fit a 13 mm spanner on the alternator belt tension pulley, and rotate the pulley fully clockwise to release belt tension. Lock in this position with a 3 mm pin pushed into the tensioner backplate.
30 Release the drivebelt from the alternator.
31 Remove the top bolt securing the alternator, and slacken the lower bolt.

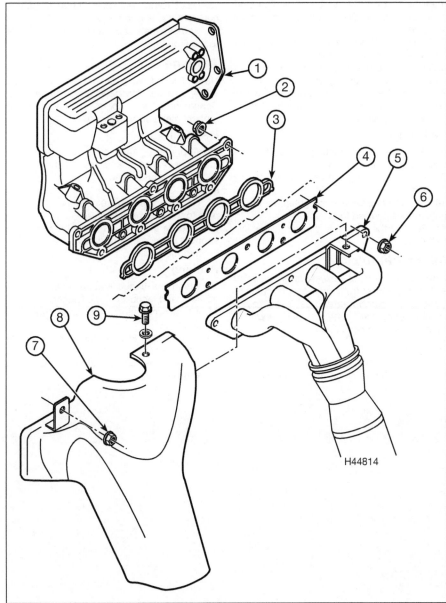

12.13 Manifold component layout

1 Inlet manifold	4 Gasket – exhaust manifold	7 Nut
2 Nuts x 3 and bolts x 4	5 Exhaust manifold	8 Heat shield – exhaust manifold
3 Gasket – inlet manifold	6 Nut x 5	9 Bolt and washer x 2

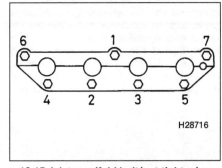

H28716

12.15 Inlet manifold bolt/nut tightening sequence

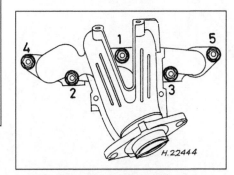

H.22444

12.23 Exhaust manifold nut tightening sequence

32 Tilt the alternator forward to gain access the alternator bracket.

33 Remove the bolt securing the bracket. Turn the bracket clear of the alternator, and remove the bracket.

34 Remove the alternator bracket stud, and manoeuvre the heat shield from the engine.

Refitting

35 Refitting is a reversal of the removal procedure, noting:

a) *Ensure that the drivebelt locates correctly in the grooves of all pulleys.*

b) *Relieve tension on the locking pin, and remove the pin from the tension pulley. Ensure that the pulley rotates to tension the belt correctly.*

c) *Use a torque wrench to tighten nuts and bolts to the specified torque.*

13 Exhaust system –
general information and component renewal

1 The exhaust system comprises three pipe sections – front, intermediate and tail. The pipe assemblies are connected to each other by flanges, secured by two nuts, and sealed with gaskets. The whole assembly is suspended on rubber mountings attached to the body.

2 The front pipe, which connects to the exhaust manifold, includes a catalytic converter. To reduce engine vibration in the exhaust system, a corrugated pipe section, covered by metal braiding, is located between the manifold connecting flange and converter.

3 The intermediate and tail pipes each incorporate a silencer, which contain baffle plates and expansion chambers designed to reduce engine exhaust noise.

Note: *Renewing the complete system: Apply the handbrake, chock the rear road wheels, then jack up the front of the car as high as possible, and support it on axle stands (see*

'Jacking and vehicle support'). Because of rust and corrosion, it may be quicker to separate pipe sections by cutting through them, instead of trying to slacken and remove the flange securing nuts.

Front pipe

Note: *The following new parts are needed – manifold flange gasket, front pipe-to-intermediate pipe gasket. Depending on their condition, new mounting rubbers may also be needed.*

Removal

4 Apply the handbrake, chock the rear roadwheels, then jack up the car and support it on axle stands (see *Jacking and vehicle support*).

5 Remove the two nuts securing the front pipe to the exhaust manifold.

6 Remove the two nuts attaching the front pipe to the intermediate pipe.

7 Release the mounting rubber from the support bracket, and remove the front pipe. Discard the gaskets.

Refitting

8 Clean the flange mating faces, fit new gaskets, and reconnect pipe flanges.

9 Fit the mounting rubbers to the body brackets.

10 Use a torque wrench to tighten the flange nuts to the specified torque.

11 Remove the stands, and lower the vehicle to the ground.

Intermediate pipe

Note: *The following new parts are needed – flange gaskets: front pipe-to-intermediate pipe, and intermediate pipe-to-tail pipe. Depending on their condition, new mounting rubbers may also be needed.*

Removal

12 Apply the handbrake, chock the rear roadwheels, then jack up the car and support

it on axle stands (see *Jacking and vehicle support*).

13 Remove the two nuts securing the tail pipe to the intermediate pipe.

14 Remove the two nuts attaching the intermediate pipe to the front pipe.

15 Release two mounting rubbers from the support brackets, and remove the intermediate pipe. Discard the gaskets.

Refitting

16 Clean the flange mating faces, fit new gaskets, and reconnect pipe flanges.

17 Fit the mounting rubbers to the body brackets.

18 Use a torque wrench to tighten the flange nuts to the specified torque.

19 Remove the stands, and lower the vehicle to the ground.

Tail pipe

Note: *The following new parts are needed – flange gasket intermediate pipe-to-tail pipe. Depending on their condition, new mounting rubbers may also be needed.*

Removal

20 Apply the handbrake, chock the rear roadwheels, then jack up the car and support it on axle stands (see *Jacking and vehicle support*).

21 Remove the two nuts securing the tail pipe to the intermediate pipe.

22 Release three mounting rubbers from the support brackets, and remove the tail pipe. Discard the gasket.

Refitting

23 Clean the flange mating faces, fit new gaskets, and reconnect pipe flanges.

24 Fit the mounting rubbers to the body brackets.

25 Use a torque wrench to tighten the flange nuts to the specified torque.

26 Remove the stands, and lower the vehicle to the ground.

Chapter 4 Part B:
Fuel and exhaust systems – V6 engines

Contents

Section number

Accelerator cable – removal, refitting and adjustment............ 5
Accelerator pedal – removal and refitting...................... 6
Air cleaner assembly – removal and refitting 2
Cruise control – general information and component renewal 14
Exhaust system – general information and component renewal 16
Fuel filler flap release cables – removal and refitting 4
Fuel injection system – depressurising 7
Fuel injection system – testing and adjustment................. 9
Fuel injection system components – removal and refitting 11

Section number

Fuel pump/fuel gauge sender unit – removal and refitting......... 8
Fuel tank and filler neck – removal, inspection and refitting 3
General information and precautions.......................... 1
Manifolds – removal and refitting............................ 12
Throttle body – removal and refitting 10
Traction control system – general information and component
  renewal 15
Variable induction system – general information and component
  renewal 13

Degrees of difficulty

Easy, suitable for novice with little experience	Fairly easy, suitable for beginner with some experience	Fairly difficult, suitable for competent DIY mechanic	Difficult, suitable for experienced DIY mechanic	Very difficult, suitable for expert DIY or professional

Specifications

General
System type .... Siemens engine management system, sequential multi-point fuel injection system, variable inlet manifold geometry, integrated with ignition system

Fuel pump
Type .... Electric roller vane pump in fuel tank
Operating pressure.................................... 3.5 bar

Idle settings (for reference only)
Idle speed... 750 ± 50 rpm
Idle mixture (CO content) .... Less than 0.5 %

Torque wrench settings

	Nm	lbf ft
Air cleaner mounting bracket...........................	45	33
Air conditioning compressor mounting bolts.....................	25	18
Camshaft position sensor bolt...........................	10	7
Engine coolant temperature sensor...........................	17	13
Engine lower mounting through-bolts...........................	100	74
Engine right-hand mounting upper crossbrace	25	18
Exhaust clamp nuts...........................	48	35
Exhaust crossbrace bolts...........................	25	18
Exhaust flange-to-manifold nuts	75	55
Exhaust manifold-to-head nuts	45	33
Exhaust pipe-to-manifold nuts...........................	40	30
Exhaust support strap nuts/bolts...........................	22	16
Fuel rail-to-manifold bolts	9	7
Fuel tank mounting bolts	24	18
Fuel tank unit locking ring	38	28
Inlet manifold-to-head bolts...........................	25	18
Inlet manifold upper section bolts	18	13
Knock sensor mounting bolts	25	18
Oxygen sensors	55	41

1 General information and precautions

General information

The fuel and ignition systems are controlled by the Siemens engine management system. For more information on the ignition side of the system, refer to Chapter 5B, but note that most of the system sensors are deemed to have a dual role, and will be covered in this Chapter **(see illustration)**.

Fuel is supplied from the rear-mounted fuel tank by an electric pump mounted in the tank, via an in-line fuel filter on the left-hand inner wing, to the two plastic fuel rails. The rail serving the rear bank has a pressure damper, and a steel crossover tube joins the two rails. Unlike many earlier injection systems, no fuel return system is fitted. The fuel rails act as a reservoir for the six fuel injectors, which inject fuel onto the back of the inlet valves.

The injectors operate sequentially in firing order, with fuel being injected during each cylinder's induction stroke. The injectors are electronically controlled by the Engine Control Module (ECM). Each injector has a solenoid which, when energised by a pulse from the ECM, lifts the injector needle and fuel is sprayed into the cylinder. The duration of the pulse determines the length of time the needle is lifted and, therefore, the amount of fuel injected. Pulse duration is calculated by the ECM, and is constantly varying to match engine operating and ambient conditions.

The fuelling and ignition timing calculation is based on information supplied to the ECM by the following sensors:

a) *Throttle position sensor (TP) – mounted on the throttle body, the sensor provides a signal representing the amount and rate of throttle opening – ie, driver demand.*

b) *Crankshaft position sensor (CKP) – supplies a signal representing the speed and angular position of the crankshaft.*

c) *Camshaft position sensor (CMP) – attached to the camshaft cover on the front bank, the sensor provides a signal representing the angular position of the camshaft, in relation to the angular position of the crankshaft.*

d) *Manifold absolute pressure (MAP) – located on the throttle body, supplies a signal representing the air pressure in the inlet manifold, which is used to determine the amount of air entering the cylinders. Built-in air temperature sensor monitors inlet air temperature.*

e) *Engine coolant temperature (ECT) – located in the top of the engine block. The sensor provides a coolant temperature signal.*

f) *Oxygen sensors – one is located in each front pipe, upstream of the 'starter' catalytic converter, with later models having a third sensor located in the exhaust pipe, downstream of the main converter. The sensors provide signals representing the amount of oxygen in the exhaust gas, and allow the ECM to precisely control the air/fuel ratio around the ideal combustion ratio of 14.7:1.*

g) *Knock sensors – one per bank, located between the two banks. Detects combustion 'knock' or 'pinking', typically caused by over-advanced ignition timing.*

Idle speed is controlled by the ECM via an idle air control valve (IACV), which varies the amount of air bypassing the throttle valve. Fine control of idle speed is further achieved by small variations in ignition timing.

Information on engine loads, such as the power steering and air conditioning systems, is provided by the power steering pressure sensor and by the ambient air temperature sensor. Vehicle speed information is provided to the ECM from the four ABS wheel sensors

Failure of certain sensors – either complete loss of signal, or sending an abnormal signal, will cause the ECM to default to preprogrammed values. In most cases this will be noticeable as poor or erratic engine performance, and the engine management warning light on the instrument panel will come on. If the crankshaft position (CKP) sensor signal is lost, the engine will not run.

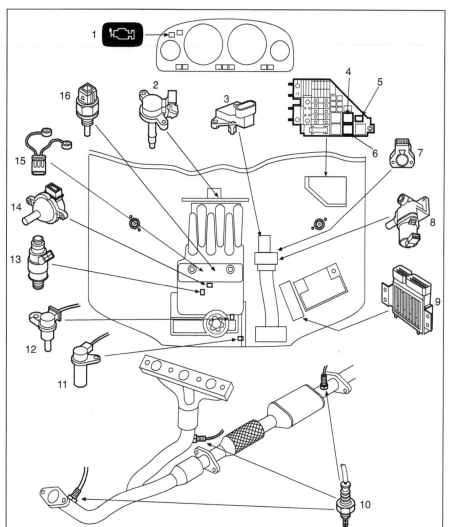

1.1 Engine management system components

1 Malfunction indicator lamp (MIL)
2 Ignition coils – rear bank
3 Intake air temperature sensor/manifold absolute pressure sensor – IAT/MAP
4 Main relay
5 Air conditioning relay
6 Fuel pump relay
7 Throttle position sensor – TP
8 Idle air control valve – IAC
9 Engine control module – ECM
10 Heated oxygen sensors (x3) – HO_2S
11 Crankshaft position sensor – CKP
12 Camshaft position sensor – CMP
13 Injectors x 6
14 Ignition coils – front bank
15 Knock sensors
16 Engine coolant temperature sensor – ECT

2.1 Remove the two bolts – arrowed

2.2 Remove the inlet hose from the air filter housing

2.3a Disconnect air intake duct from lower part of housing – arrowed

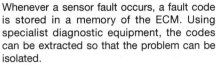

2.3b Housing lower locating grommet – arrowed

2.4a Air intake duct between the air cleaner housing and the air resonator box

2.4b Undo the two retaining bolts to remove the resonator

Whenever a sensor fault occurs, a fault code is stored in a memory of the ECM. Using specialist diagnostic equipment, the codes can be extracted so that the problem can be isolated.

All models are fitted with a fuel inertia cut-off switch (see Section 11), which cuts off the fuel supply in the event of the car being involved in an impact – the interior lights will be on all the time until the switch is reset. The engine cannot be started if the switch is activated – the switch must be reset manually.

The inlet manifold features variable-length inlet tracts, for optimum torque at all engine speeds and loads. The system is controlled by the ECM – for more details, see Section 13.

Precautions

• Before disconnecting any fuel lines, or working on any part of the fuel system, the system must be depressurised as described in Section 7.
• Care must be taken when disconnecting the fuel lines. When disconnecting a fuel union or hose, loosen the union or clamp screw slowly, to avoid sudden uncontrolled fuel spillage. Take adequate fire precautions.
• When working on fuel system components, scrupulous cleanliness must be observed, and care must be taken not to introduce any foreign matter into fuel lines or components.
• After carrying out any work involving disconnection of fuel lines, it is advisable to check the connections for leaks; pressurise the system by switching the ignition on and off several times.
• Before disconnecting any wiring, or

removing components, always ensure at least that the ignition is switched off – better still, disconnect the battery. If this is not done, and a component is disconnected when 'live', it could be damaged – or a fault code may be stored, which would then have to be cleared to regain normal operation.
• Do not attempt to improvise fault diagnosis procedures using a test light or multimeter, as irreparable damage could be caused to the module.

> ⚠ **Warning:** *Many of the procedures in this Chapter require the disconnection of fuel line connections, and the removal of components, which may result in some fuel spillage. Before carrying out any operation on the fuel system, refer to the precautions given in 'Safety first!' at the beginning of this manual, and follow them implicitly. Petrol is a highly-dangerous and volatile liquid, and the precautions necessary when handling it cannot be overstressed.*

2 Air cleaner assembly – removal and refitting

1 Undo the two retaining bolts from the front cross panel at the front of the air cleaner housing **(see illustration)**.
2 Slacken the large hose clips and disconnect the throttle body inlet hose from the air cleaner cover **(see illustration)**.
3 The air cleaner housing can now be lifted out. It is located in a grommet at the lower

part of radiator, and must be released from the air intake duct at the base **(see illustrations)**.
4 There is an air resonator box positioned behind the front bumper on the left-hand side of the vehicle. If required, remove the front bumper as described in Chapter 11, then release the air duct and undo the two retaining bolts to remove the air resonator box **(see illustrations)**.
5 Refitting is a reversal of removal. Ensure that the hose clips are tightened securely; otherwise this will produce an air leak.

3 Fuel tank and filler neck – removal, inspection and refitting

Refer to Chapter 4A.

4 Fuel filler flap release cables – removal and refitting

Refer to Chapter 11, Section 17.

5 Accelerator cable – removal, refitting and adjustment

Note: *On models with traction control, this procedure applies only to the primary cable. Refer to Section 15 for information on the secondary cable.*

Removal

1 Slide the cable end fitting from the groove

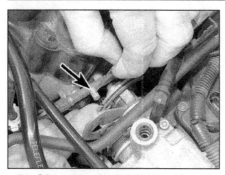

5.1 Slide out and unhook the cable end fitting – arrowed

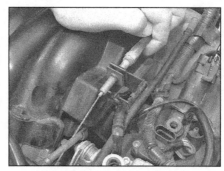

5.2 Lift out the cable adjuster

in the throttle lever, and disconnect the cable from the lever **(see illustration)**.
2 Slide the cable adjuster from the bracket on the throttle body/inlet manifold **(see illustration)**.
3 Release the cable from the clip on the inlet manifold **(see illustration)**.
4 Working at the engine compartment bulkhead, turn the collar on the accelerator cable through 90°, and release the cable from the bulkhead.
5 Remove the trim panel fitted above the pedals, which is secured by two screws at the top, and two push-fasteners at the bottom.
6 Reach up under the facia, and pull the end of the cable forwards from the pedal, then squeeze the securing lugs and remove the plastic cable securing clip from the end of the pedal. Release the end of the cable from the pedal **(see illustration)**.
7 Pull the cable through the bulkhead into the engine compartment, and withdraw the cable from the car.

Refitting

8 Refitting is a reversal of removal, but smear the bulkhead grommet with rubber grease and, on completion, check the cable adjustment as described in the following paragraphs.

Adjustment

9 Slide the cable adjuster from the bracket on the inlet manifold/throttle body, then position the cable's square adjuster against the rear of the bracket.
10 Hold the throttle lever on the throttle body

in the fully closed position, ensuring that the cam on the throttle lever rests against the throttle stop screw.
11 Turn the cable adjuster as necessary until all freeplay is removed from the cable, without moving the throttle lever.
12 Slide the adjuster back into position in the bracket.
13 Have an assistant fully depress the accelerator pedal, and check that the throttle lever moves to the fully open position, and returns to the fully closed position when the pedal is released.

6 Accelerator pedal – removal and refitting

Removal

1 Working inside the vehicle, remove the pocket from the driver's side of the facia panel. Undo the three retaining screws and remove the lower facia trim panel from the below the steering column.
2 Reach up under the facia, and pull the end of the cable forwards from the pedal, then squeeze the securing lugs and remove the plastic cable securing clip from the end of the pedal. Release the end of the cable from the pedal.
3 Using a suitable pair of pliers, unhook the return spring from the top of the pedal.
4 Undo the retaining bolt/nut and then

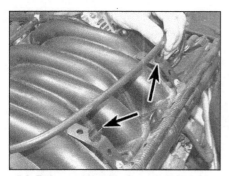

5.3 Release the cable from the retaining clips – arrowed

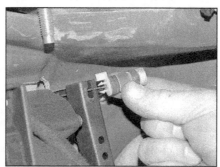

5.6 Pull out the cable end fitting, and unhook from the pedal

remove the pedal assembly from the mounting bracket.

Refitting

5 Refitting is a reversal of removal, but make sure that the accelerator cable is fitted correctly – see Section 5.

7 Fuel injection system – depressurising

⚠ *Warning: The following procedure will merely relieve the pressure in the fuel system – remember that fuel will still be present in the system components, and take precautions accordingly before disconnecting any of them.*

1 The fuel system referred to in this Chapter is defined as the fuel tank and tank-mounted fuel pump/fuel gauge sender unit, the fuel injectors, fuel pressure damper, and the metal pipes and flexible hoses of the fuel lines between these components. All these contain fuel, which will be under pressure while the engine is running and/or while the ignition is switched on.
2 The pressure will remain for some time after the ignition has been switched off, and must be relieved before any of these components is disturbed for servicing work.
3 The simplest depressurisation method is to disconnect the fuel pump electrical supply by removing the fuel pump fuse (make sure the ignition is off – it's a 20 amp fuse in position number 10, in the engine compartment fusebox. Check with wiring diagrams in Chapter 12) and starting the engine. Allow the engine to idle until it stops through lack of fuel. If it won't start, turn the engine over once or twice on the starter to ensure that all pressure is released. Switch off the ignition on completion. Remember to refit the fuse when work is complete – the ignition must be off when this is done.
4 Before opening the fuel system, **always** disconnect the battery negative lead, and move the lead away from the battery (see *Disconnecting the battery*).
5 When opening any high-pressure fuel union, wrap absorbent cloth around the union, then **slowly** slacken the union nut. Allow the fuel pressure to dissipate, and then retighten the union nut.
6 Note that, once the fuel system has been depressurised and drained (even partially), it will take significantly longer to restart the engine – perhaps several seconds of cranking – before the system is refilled and pressure restored. To avoid this, the system can be 'primed' before starting by switching the ignition on a few times – each time this is done, the fuel pump should be heard running for a short time. If the pump does not stop running, this may indicate a leak in the system – investigate before starting the engine.

8 Fuel pump/fuel gauge sender unit – removal and refitting

Refer to Chapter 4A.

9 Fuel injection system – testing and adjustment

Testing

1 If a fault appears in the fuel injection system, first ensure that all the system wiring connectors are securely connected and free from corrosion. Ensure that the fault is not due to poor maintenance; ie, check that the air cleaner filter element is clean, that the spark plugs are in good condition and correctly gapped (see Chapter 1A), that the cylinder compression pressures are correct (see Chapter 2B), and that the engine breather hoses are clear and undamaged (see Chapter 4D).

2 If the engine will not start, check that the fuel inertia cut-off switch has not operated (see Section 11). Push the switch button behind the centre console from the driver's side footwell, to reset if necessary.

3 If these checks fail to reveal the cause of the problem, the car should be taken to a garage with diagnostic equipment for testing. A wiring connector is provided behind the centre console, into which a special electronic diagnostic tester can be plugged (see illustration). The tester should locate the fault quickly and simply, avoiding the need to test all the system components individually, which is time-consuming, and also carries a risk of damaging the ECM.

Adjustment

4 Experienced home mechanics with access to a tachometer and an accurately calibrated exhaust gas analyser may be able to check the exhaust CO level and the idle speed. However, if either of these settings is found to be in need of adjustment, the car must be taken to a garage with diagnostic equipment for further testing.

5 No manual adjustment of the exhaust CO level or idle speed is possible.

10 Throttle body – removal and refitting

Note: *On completion, the throttle body may need to be set up using diagnostic equipment, in order to function correctly. This is particularly the case if a new or secondhand unit is being fitted.*

Removal

1 Ensure that the ignition is switched off (take out the key).

2 Remove the air cleaner as described in Section 2.

3 Loosen the hose clip on the throttle body, and remove the inlet air duct, pulling off the smaller hose from the idle air control valve at the same time (see illustration).

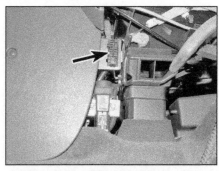

9.3 Diagnostic wiring connector – viewed from driver's side footwell

4 Depress the locking collars, and pull out the breather and vacuum pipes from the throttle body and idle air control valve, noting their fitted positions (see illustrations).

5 Slide out the accelerator cable's square adjuster from the bracket on the inlet manifold/throttle body, then slide the cable end fitting from the groove in the throttle lever, and disconnect the cable from the lever – refer to Section 5 if necessary (see illustration).

6 On models with traction control, release the secondary accelerator cable from its bracket and the throttle cam (refer to Section 15 if necessary). Disconnect the multiplug from the secondary throttle position sensor.

7 On models with cruise control, disconnect the vacuum hose from the cruise control actuator.

8 Disconnect the wiring plugs from the primary throttle position sensor and idle air control valve (see illustration).

10.3 Removing the inlet air duct

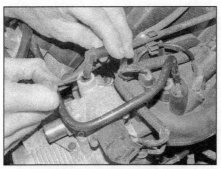

10.4a Release the locking collar to disconnect the vacuum pipe . . .

10.4b . . . and pull the vacuum pipe from the throttle body . . .

10.4c . . . and release locking collar for breather hose

10.5 Disconnect the accelerator cable from the throttle linkage

10.8 Disconnect the throttle sensor and air valve wiring plugs

10.9a Throttle body upper . . .

10.9b . . . and lower Torx screws

9 Unscrew the four Torx bolts, and withdraw the throttle body from the inlet manifold **(see illustrations)**. Recover the seal from the inlet manifold and discard it.

10 If a new throttle body is being fitted, the following components should be removed from it and transferred to the new unit:

a) *Cruise control actuator (Section 14).*

b) *Secondary throttle position sensor and secondary accelerator cable bracket – models with traction control (Section 15).*

c) *Primary throttle position sensor (Section 11).*

d) *Idle air control valve (Section 11).*

Refitting

11 Clean the mating faces of the throttle body and inlet manifold.

12 Fit a new seal to the throttle body.

13 Locate the throttle body on the inlet

manifold, then fit and securely tighten the four bolts.

14 The remaining refitting is a reversal of the removal procedure.

15 If the engine does not run properly on completion (after a reasonable period has been given for the engine to 'relearn' its settings), it may be necessary to have the engine set up using diagnostic equipment at a suitably-equipped garage.

11 Fuel injection system components – removal and refitting

1 Before disconnecting any fuel injection wiring plugs, ensure that the ignition is switched off (take out the key). If any component is disconnected 'live', it could introduce a fault code in the ECM memory.

Better still, disconnect the battery negative lead, and move the lead away from the battery (see *Disconnecting the battery*).

Fuel rails and injectors

2 Depressurise the fuel system as described in Section 7.

3 Remove the inlet manifold upper section as described in Section 12.

4 Disconnect the fuel pipe from the front fuel rail – this will require careful use of a small screwdriver to release its retaining clip **(see illustration)**.

5 Mark the ignition coils for position. Remove the three mounting nuts and bolts from the three ignition coils serving the front bank – note that one of the bolts also secures the earth lead. Lift out the coils and place to one side **(see illustrations)**.

6 Where applicable, release the two clips and two bolts securing the fuel injector protection plate, and lift the plate out – the two bolts are also used to secure the rear fuel rail.

7 Disconnect the injector multiplugs, noting that one of the rear injectors is fitted the 'wrong' way round. Unscrew the two bolts from the front fuel rail, and two more from the rear rail, if not already done **(see illustrations)**.

8 Disconnect the vacuum pipe from the fuel pressure damper, and cut the clips securing the injector wiring harness to the rear fuel rail. Ease out the two fuel rails, noting that there will be resistance from the injector O-rings. Note the crossover pipe fitted between the rails, which means the two rails must be lifted out evenly, to avoid damage. Place the two

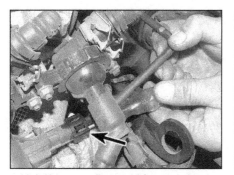

11.4 Use a small screwdriver to release the fuel rail rigid pipe

11.5a Coils position marked with masking tape – note earth lead (arrowed)

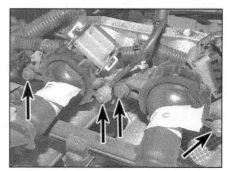

11.5b Each coil is secured by a nut and a bolt

11.7a Disconnect the injector wiring plugs

11.7b One of the rear injectors (arrowed) is reversed

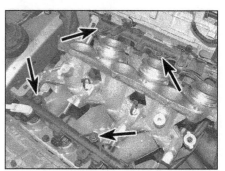

11.7c Front and rear fuel rail bolts

11.8a Carefully cut the clips securing the fuel rail wiring harness . . .

11.8b . . . then ease out the rails evenly, and remove them as a pair

11.9a Slide out the spring clip . . .

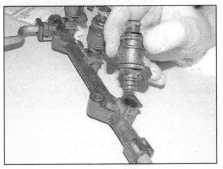

11.9b . . . then ease each injector out of the fuel rail

11.9c Recover the O-ring seals – new ones must be used

11.10 Each injector should have three new O-rings

fuel rail and injector assemblies carefully to one side **(see illustrations)**.

9 Release the spring clips securing the injectors to the fuel rail, and remove the injectors. Remove and discard the three O-rings from each injector **(see illustrations)**. Cover both ends of each injector with a protective cap.

10 Refitting is a reversal of the removal procedure, noting the following points:

a) *Use new injector O-rings, lubricated with a little light oil before fitting them to the injectors* **(see illustration)**.

b) *Tighten the fuel rail bolts to the specified torque, noting that those for the rear bank also secure the injector protection plate.*

Fuel pressure damper

Note: *On later models, the damper is an integral part of the rear fuel rail, and cannot be removed.*

11 The fuel pressure damper is mounted on the fuel rail serving the rear bank, and is intended to reduce the effects of pressure variations in the fuel supplied from the tank-mounted pump.

12 Depressurise the fuel system as described in Section 7.

13 Remove the inlet manifold upper section as described in Section 12.

14 Mark the ignition coils for position. Remove the three mounting nuts and bolts from the three ignition coils serving the front bank – note that one of the bolts also secures the earth lead. Lift out the coils and place to one side.

15 Where applicable, release the two clips and two bolts securing the fuel injector protection plate, and lift the plate out – the two bolts are also used to secure the rear fuel rail.

16 Disconnect the pressure damper vacuum pipe. The damper is retained by a large spring

clip – squeeze together the legs at one side of the clip, and withdraw it **(see illustration)**.

17 Anticipating some fuel spillage, pull the damper out of the fuel rail, and recover the O-rings.

18 Refitting is a reversal of removal. Use new O-rings, and ensure the damper is securely clipped into the fuel rail.

Idle air control valve

19 The idle air control valve is located on top of the throttle body.

20 Disconnect the wiring plug from the valve.

21 Depress the locking collar, and pull out the control valve's vacuum hose **(see illustration)**. The air bypass hose, which is part of the main air inlet duct, just pulls off.

22 Remove the two Allen screws securing the valve to the throttle body, and then withdraw the valve from the manifold **(see illustration)**. Recover the gasket and discard it.

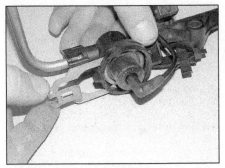

11.16 Removing the pressure damper retaining clip

11.21 Release locking collar (arrowed) to disconnect the vacuum hose

11.22 Idle air control valve Allen screws

11.26a Disconnect the wiring plug next to the thermostat housing . . .

11.26b . . . then unscrew and remove the coolant temperature sensor

11.30 Disconnect the wiring plug . . .

11.31 . . . then withdraw the sensor from the transmission

23 Refitting is a reversal of removal, using a new gasket and tightening the valve securing screws securely.

Coolant temperature sensor

24 The engine coolant temperature sensor (ECT) sensor is screwed into the top of the engine.

25 Remove the air cleaner and inlet manifold upper section.

26 Disconnect the sensor multiplug, then unscrew and remove the switch **(see illustrations)**. Recover the sealing washer – a new one should be obtained for refitting.

27 Refitting is a reversal of the removal procedure, noting the following points:

a) Clean the sensor and the mating face on the block, and use a new sealing washer.

b) Tighten the sensor to the specified torque.

c) Refit the thermostat as described in Chapter 3.

Crankshaft position sensor

28 The sensor is mounted at the front edge of the transmission bellhousing (at the left-hand end of the engine).

29 Release the front edge of the engine undertray, which is secured by a number of quick-release screw fasteners.

30 Disconnect the wiring plug above the sensor **(see illustration)**.

31 Unscrew the single bolt securing the sensor to the bellhousing, then remove the sensor **(see illustration)**.

32 Thoroughly clean the mating faces on the sensor and housing, and then refit the sensor using a reversal of the removal procedure.

Throttle position sensor

Note: Whenever the sensor is removed or renewed, a 'throttle initialisation' procedure must be carried out, to ensure correct operation afterwards – also see paragraph 38.

As this requires the use of diagnostic equipment, it may be advisable to have work involving this sensor carried out by a suitably-equipped garage or specialist.

33 The sensor is mounted on the side of the throttle body.

34 Remove the battery and its tray as described in Chapter 5A.

35 Disconnect the multiplug from the sensor.

36 Remove and discard two Torx screws and wave washers securing the sensor to the throttle housing – discard the washers and screws, as new ones should be used when refitting **(see illustration)**.

37 Remove the sensor specification plate, and pull the sensor from the throttle spindle without twisting it.

38 The sensor's inner section should not be turned while it is removed – if the same unit is being refitted, this minimises the need for the sensor to be 'initialised' on completion.

Caution: The sensor can easily be damaged, especially during fitting – handle it with care. Ensure, for example, that the machined flat on the throttle spindle is accurately aligned with the corresponding one inside the sensor. If nothing has been moved, and the original sensor is being refitted, it should only be necessary to align the mounting screw holes.

39 Clean the mating faces of the throttle housing and sensor.

40 Align the flat on the sensor with the flat on the throttle spindle, and push the sensor gently onto the spindle. If a new sensor is being fitted, rotate the sensor in an anti-clockwise direction to align the screw holes – **do not** turn it clockwise, nor beyond its internal stop. If possible, set the new sensor to the same position as the one just removed.

41 Fit the specification plate, with new wave washers and Torx screws. Tighten the screws securely.

42 Connect the multiplug to the sensor.

43 Operate the throttle linkage by hand a few times, and check that both idle and full-throttle positions appear to be available.

44 Run the engine and test the operation of the sensor. If the idle quality has suffered, and does not improve even after giving the system time to 're-learn' its values, throttle initialisation may be required – this requires diagnostic equipment.

Camshaft position sensor

45 Remove the two bolts and unclip the engine top cover. Recover the washers and rubber grommets from the bolt holes, and store them for refitting.

46 The sensor is screwed into the front bank of the engine, and is located next to the oil filler cap **(see illustration)**. Trace the sensor wiring to the end of the cylinder head, to the wiring plug.

47 Disconnect the wiring plug, then unscrew the single bolt securing the sensor in position, and withdraw it from the cylinder head **(see illustrations)**. Recover the sensor's O-

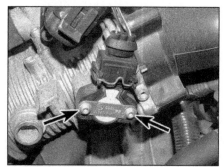

11.36 Throttle position sensor wiring plug and Torx screws (arrowed)

11.46 Camshaft position sensor location

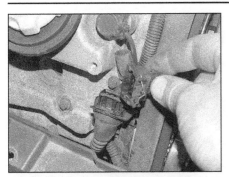

11.47a Disconnect the wiring plug connector . . .

11.47b . . . then unbolt and remove the camshaft position sensor

11.48a Slide out the wiring plug . . .

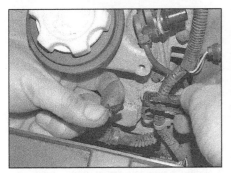

11.48b . . . then unbolt and remove the bracket

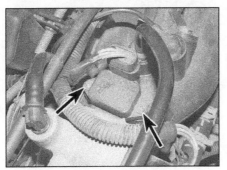

11.50 The MAP sensor is behind the idle air control valve – screws arrowed

11.51 Disconnecting the MAP sensor wiring plug

ring seal – a new one should be used when refitting.

48 To remove the sensor completely, slide the other half of the wiring plug out of the bracket, then unscrew the bolt securing the bracket to the head, and remove it to free the sensor wiring behind **(see illustrations)**.

49 Refitting is a reversal of removal, noting the following points:

a) *Clean the mating faces of the sensor and cylinder head.*

b) *Lubricate a new seal with engine oil, and tighten the bolt securely.*

c) *Ensure that the sensor wiring is routed as before, behind the wiring plug bracket.*

Manifold absolute pressure sensor

Note: *This sensor has a built-in inlet air temperature sensor.*

50 The MAP sensor is located behind the idle air control valve **(see illustration)**.

51 Disconnect the sensor wiring plug **(see illustration)**.

52 Remove the two screws and lift the sensor off.

53 Refitting is a reversal of removal. Clean the sensor and manifold mating faces prior to fitting.

Oxygen sensors

54 Refer to Chapter 4A, Section 11. The procedure for removing the oxygen sensor is the same as for 4-cylinder engines. **Note:** *There are two oxygen sensors fitted to 4-cylinder engines and three oxygen sensors fitted to 6-cylinder engines.*

Fuel inertia cut-off switch

55 The switch is located inside the driver's side footwell behind the centre console to the left of the clutch pedal **(see illustration)**.

56 Disconnect the battery negative lead, and then disconnect the wiring plug from the switch.

57 Remove the two securing bolts **(see illustration)** and withdraw the switch from its mounting bracket.

58 Refitting is a reversal of removal, but ensure that the switch is reset by pressing the button on the top of the switch.

Power steering pressure switch

59 The switch is located at the rear of the power steering pump.

60 Remove the two bolts, and lift off the engine right-hand mounting's upper crossbrace.

61 Disconnect the multiplug from the switch.

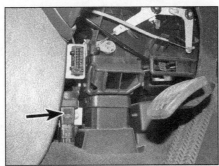

11.55 Location of fuel inertia cut-off switch

62 Position a container under the switch to catch any lost fluid. Unscrew the switch, and remove it. Recover the O-ring – a new one should be used when refitting.

63 Refitting is a reversal of removal, noting the following points:

a) *Use a new O-ring, lubricated with power steering fluid.*

b) *Tighten the switch to the specified torque – counterhold the union with another spanner as this is done.*

c) *Tighten the engine mounting crossbrace bolts to the specified torque.*

Canister purge valve

64 Refer to Chapter 4D.

Engine control module

Note: *If a new module is to be fitted, it will need to be programmed with the code from the anti-theft security unit before the engine*

11.57 Undo the two bolts – arrowed

11.66 Undo the three mounting nuts – arrowed

can be started. This can only be done using diagnostic equipment, and it may therefore be advisable to have this work carried out by a suitably-equipped garage or specialist.

65 Disconnect the battery negative lead,

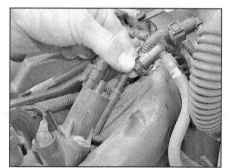

12.4a Disconnect the two hoses, noting their fitted positions . . .

12.4b . . . and the wiring plug from the purge valve

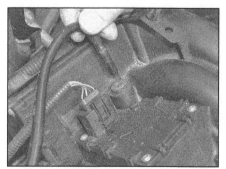

12.5c . . . and disconnect the brake servo vacuum hose

undo the battery clamp bolt and remove the battery (see *Disconnecting the battery*). This is **essential** – if the ECM wiring plug is disconnected (or reconnected) 'live', the module could be damaged.

66 Remove the three retaining nuts and remove the engine control module from the mounting bracket **(see illustration)**.

67 Slide the ECM wiring plug locking clip to the side, then disconnect it and remove the module **(see illustration)**.

68 Refitting is a reversal of removal. Ensure that the module wiring plugs are securely reconnected.

12 Manifolds – removal and refitting

Inlet manifold upper chamber

1 Remove the two bolts and unclip the engine top cover. Recover the washers and rubber grommets from the bolt holes, and store them for refitting.

2 Remove the air cleaner as described in Section 2.

3 Remove the battery and its tray as described in Chapter 5A.

4 Disconnect the two hoses and the wiring plug from the canister purge valve **(see illustrations)**.

5 Depress the locking collars, and pull out the breather and vacuum pipes from the throttle body and idle air control valve, noting their fitted positions. Similarly disconnect the brake

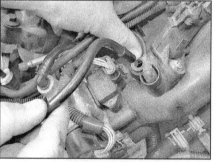

12.5a Depress the locking collars, and remove the breathers . . .

12.6a Disconnect the wiring plugs from the throttle body . . .

11.67 Slide the locking clips sideways, and disconnect the wiring plug

servo vacuum hose from the inlet manifold **(see illustrations)**.

6 Referring to Section 11 as necessary, disconnect the wiring plugs from the throttle position sensor(s), idle air control valve and MAP sensor **(see illustrations)**. Unclip the wiring harness and move it clear.

7 Where applicable, disconnect the vacuum hose from the cruise control actuator, and unclip it from the manifold.

8 Referring to Section 5, disconnect the accelerator cable(s) from the throttle body.

9 Noting how they are routed, unclip the vacuum and breather hoses from the top of the engine, removing them as a complete assembly with the T-piece. Also disconnect the hoses from the front cylinder head **(see illustrations)**.

10 Disconnect the wiring plugs from the variable induction system motors on the right-hand side of the manifold **(see illustration)**.

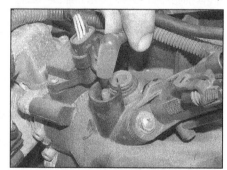

12.5b . . . and pull off the vacuum pipe from the throttle body . . .

12.6b . . . and from the MAP sensor

12.9a Disconnect the breather hoses from the front . . .

12.9b . . . and rear cylinder heads . . .

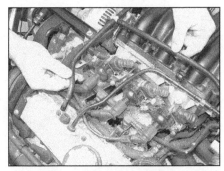

12.9c . . . and remove them as an assembly where possible

12.10 Disconnect the VIS motor wiring plugs

Remove the screws securing the wiring harness brackets.
11 Remove the two screws securing the wiring harness to the back of the manifold, and move the harness clear **(see illustration)**.
12 Unscrew the bolt securing each manifold

12.13 Unclip the rear ignition coil wiring harness from the manifold

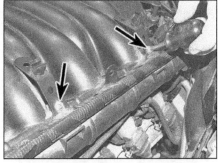

12.11 Remove the screws (arrowed) securing the wiring harness

support bracket to the rear bank's camshaft cover – there are two, but they are quite hard to reach **(see illustration)**.
13 Release the two clips securing the rear bank's ignition coil wiring harness to the upper manifold mounting brackets **(see illustration)**.

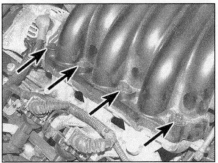

12.14 Unscrew the four manifold mounting bolts

12.12 Unscrew the bolts from the two manifold rear support brackets

14 Progressively loosen and remove the four bolts securing the upper manifold to the front inlet manifold **(see illustration)**.
15 Lift the upper section off the front and rear manifolds, This is made very difficult, due to resistance from the three large O-rings – prise the upper section carefully, and pack progressively larger (non-metal) wedges in the resulting gap until the O-rings release **(see illustrations)**.
16 Remove the upper manifold seals and the O-rings from the rear inlet manifold – new seals and O-rings will be needed for refitting **(see illustrations)**.
17 Refitting is a reversal of removal, noting the following points:
a) Clean the mating surfaces, and fit new seals and O-rings **(see illustration)**.
b) Align the upper chamber with the manifolds, then fit and tighten the four bolts to the specified torque.

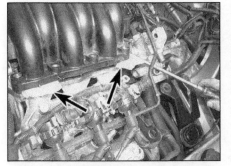

12.15a Carefully prise the manifold at each end, and insert wedges . . .

12.15b . . . until the manifold is freed from the large O-rings . . .

12.15c . . . and can be lifted off

12.16a Remove the upper manifold seals . . .

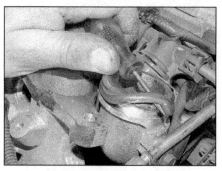

12.16b . . . and the O-rings

12.17 Fit new seals and O-rings when refitting

c) Ensure that all hoses are correctly routed and reconnected as noted before removal.

d) Adjust the accelerator cable(s) if necessary, as described in Section 5.

Inlet manifold

Front

18 Drain the cooling system as described in Chapter 1A.

19 Remove the fuel rail as described in Section 11.

20 Depress the locking collar and pull out the breather hose from the front inlet manifold.

21 Release the hose clip and disconnect the coolant hose from the manifold.

22 Progressively loosen and remove the seven bolts securing the front inlet manifold to the head **(see illustration)**.

23 Lift off the inlet manifold, and recover the gasket – a new one will be needed for refitting.

24 Refitting is a reversal of removal, noting the following points:
a) Clean the mating surfaces, and fit a new gasket.
b) Starting from the centre and working outwards, progressively tighten the manifold bolts to the specified torque.
c) Refill the cooling system as described in Chapter 1A.

Rear

25 Drain the cooling system as described in Chapter 1A.

26 Remove the fuel rail as described in Section 11.

27 Depress the locking collar and pull out the vacuum hose from the rear inlet manifold.

28 Release the hose clip and disconnect the coolant hose from the manifold.

29 Progressively loosen and remove the seven bolts securing the front inlet manifold to the head.

30 Lift off the inlet manifold, and recover the gasket – a new one will be needed for refitting. Remove the bolt securing the hose bracket to the manifold.

31 Refitting is a reversal of removal, noting the following points:
a) Clean the mating surfaces, and fit a new gasket **(see illustrations)**.
b) Starting from the centre and working outwards, progressively tighten the manifold bolts to the specified torque.
c) Refill the cooling system as described in Chapter 1A.

Exhaust manifolds

32 Jack up the front of the car, and support it on axle stands (see *Jacking and vehicle support*).

33 Remove the engine undertray, which is secured by a number of quick-release screw fasteners.

34 Unhook the front section of the exhaust from its rubber mountings **(see illustration)**.

35 Remove the two bolts securing the front downpipe to the support bracket under the engine **(see illustration)**.

36 Remove the two nuts from each of the manifold-to-downpipe flanges, and separate the joints **(see illustration)**. Discard the flange gaskets – new ones must be used when refitting. Lower the downpipe clear, but support it so the pipe is not under strain.

37 If removing the front manifold on models with air conditioning, remove the oil cooler as described in Chapter 2B. Unscrew the three air conditioning compressor mounting bolts,

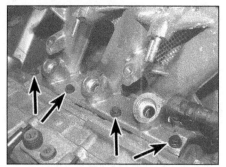

12.22 Four of the seven front inlet manifold bolts

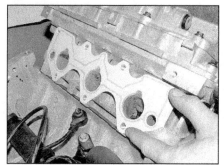

12.31a Fit a new gasket . . .

12.31b . . . then refit the rear manifold, and tighten the bolts

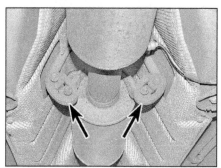

12.34 Unhook the exhaust from the front rubber mountings

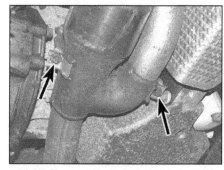

12.35 Remove the two exhaust support bracket bolts

and tie the compressor to one side without disconnecting the hoses.

38 Progressively loosen and remove the four nuts securing the front or rear manifold to the cylinder head **(see illustration)**. Remove the manifold from the studs, and recover the gasket – a new one must be used when refitting. If the manifold nuts are in poor condition, new ones should be obtained for reassembly – in this case, also consider fitting new studs.

39 If any studs were removed with the nuts, these can be refitted to the head using two nuts tightened against each other. If any studs have to be refitted (or renewed, if their threads are in poor condition), apply a little thread-locking fluid to their threads before screwing them into the head.

40 Refitting is a reversal of removal, noting the following points:

a) *Clean the mating surfaces, and fit a new manifold gasket* **(see illustration)**.

b) *Progressively tighten the manifold nuts to the specified torque* **(see illustration)**.

c) *Fit new downpipe flange gaskets, and tighten their nuts to the specified torque.*

d) *Tighten the two downpipe-to-support bracket bolts to the specified torque.*

e) *On completion, run the engine and check for exhaust leaks from the disturbed joints.*

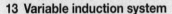

13 Variable induction system – general information and component renewal

General information

1 The inlet manifold features variable-length inlet tracts, for optimum torque at all engine speeds and loads.

2 Variable Induction System (VIS) valves, known as the balance valve and the power valves, are operated via the ECM by two motors on the right-hand side of the inlet manifold.

3 From the throttle body, a Y-shaped section feeds air into the two plenum chambers which serve each bank of three cylinders. At the end of the two plenum chambers is the balance valve, which allows the chambers to be connected together, giving an inlet tract length

12.36 Remove the manifold-to-downpipe nuts

12.40a Fit a new manifold gasket . . .

of up to 500 mm. The tract in each plenum chamber also has a power valve fitted 350 mm along its length, which, when opened, diverts the air to a third plenum, thus shortening the inlet tract. One motor can operate all six power valves simultaneously, by means of a rod.

4 In the event of a failure in part of the system, the engine will typically lack bottom-end torque. Apparently, the most likely reason for failure will be one of the VIS motors, which can be renewed quite easily as described in the following paragraphs.

VIS motors

Removal

5 Disconnect the multiplug from the motor to be removed **(see illustration)**.

6 Remove the four mounting screws, and lift the motor from the inlet manifold upper chamber **(see illustrations)**. Recover the

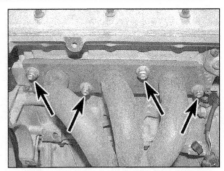

12.38 Exhaust manifold mounting nuts

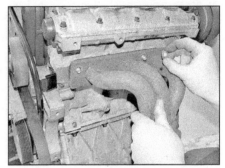

12.40b . . . then refit the manifold and tighten the nuts

seal fitted to each motor – if they are in good condition, they can be re-used.

Refitting

7 Clean the motor and inlet manifold mating faces, and check that the seal is fitted to the motor.

8 Locate the motor drive pin into the groove, and make sure the seal is correctly located on the manifold.

9 Fit and securely tighten the motor mounting screws, then reconnect the multiplug.

14 Cruise control – general information and component renewal

1 The cruise control system fitted to some models offers the means of automatically maintaining any speed selected by the driver (from 22 to 125 mph), without using

13.5 Disconnect the VIS motor wiring plug

13.6a Remove the mounting screws (arrowed) . . .

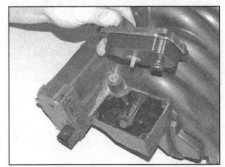

13.6b . . . and lift out the motor

14.20a Disconnect the clutch switch wiring plug . . .

14.20b . . . then pull the switch from its bracket

the accelerator pedal. This is useful for long periods of motorway cruising, and/or as a means of avoiding speeding convictions.

2 The system works via a vacuum actuator attached to the throttle cam, operated by a vacuum pump via its own ECU. When the facia master switch is pressed, the system becomes active. Once the desired speed has been reached, using the SET+ control on the steering wheel, the speed can be selected, and then increased. Once this has been done, the speed is controlled by the vacuum actuator, which opens and closes the throttle automatically in response to changing road conditions – information on the current vehicle speed is provided by the ABS wheel sensors. The system can be deactivated by pressing the brake or clutch (or on automatic transmission models, by selecting N), or by using the RES steering wheel control – afterwards, the RES control can be used to have the system resume the previously-set speed.

Vacuum actuator

3 Remove the two bolts and unclip the engine top cover. Recover the washers and rubber grommets from the bolt holes, and store them for refitting.
4 Remove the air cleaner as described in Section 2.
5 Disconnect the vacuum hose from the actuator on the side of the throttle body.
6 Unscrew the mounting nut, then detach the operating rod from the throttle cam and remove the actuator.
7 Refitting is a reversal of removal. Check the condition of the vacuum hose before refitting it – any cracks or splits will result in partial or non-operation of the system.

Vacuum pump

8 The vacuum pump is located on the left-hand inner wing (left as seen from the driver's seat).
9 Jack up the front of the car, and support it on axle stands (see *Jacking and vehicle support*).
10 Remove the engine undertray, which is secured by a number of turn-buckle fasteners.
11 Disconnect the pump motor wiring plug, and the vacuum supply hose.
12 Unscrew the two mounting bolts and

remove the pump from the car, together with its mounting bracket.
13 The pump is attached to its bracket by three rubber mountings – release these to remove the pump completely.
14 Refitting is a reversal of removal. Check the condition of the vacuum hose before refitting it – any cracks or splits will result in partial or non-operation of the system.

Master switch

15 Taking care not to mark the facia, prise out the trim panel which sits over the central row of switches – this is secured by four clips.
16 Unclip the switch from the facia, then disconnect the wiring plug behind and remove it.
17 Refitting is a reversal of removal.

Steering wheel switches

18 The steering wheel switches for the cruise control are removed with the horn switches, as described in Chapter 12, Section 4.

Clutch switch

19 Remove the trim panel fitted above the pedals, which is secured by two screws at the top, and two push-fasteners at the bottom.
20 Disconnect the wiring plug, then pull out the clutch switch from the pedal bracket, and remove it **(see illustrations)**.
21 Refitting is a reversal of removal. Fully depress the clutch pedal and hold it down, then manoeuvre the switch into position. Slide the switch as far as it will go into the bracket, then **slowly** release the clutch pedal and allow it to return to its starting position. **Note:** *If the pedal is released too quickly, the switch will be incorrectly adjusted.*

ECU and interface

22 Ensure that the ignition is switched off (take out the key).
23 Remove the glovebox as described in Chapter 11.
24 The ECU is a small unit to the left of the fuse panel, secured by two bolts; the interface unit is smaller still, and mounted above it.
25 Swing the required unit's wiring plug locking lever to the left, and disconnect the wiring multiplug.
26 If removing the ECU, unscrew the two mounting bolts, and withdraw the unit.

27 To remove the interface unit, release the clip securing it to the mounting bracket, and remove it.
28 Refitting is a reversal of removal.

15 Traction control system – general information and component renewal

1 The traction control system fitted to some V6 models is intended to reduce the tendency for the front wheels to spin under hard acceleration, or when driving on slippery surfaces. The system is largely a feature of the anti-lock braking system (ABS) – see Chapter 9. From the wheel sensors, the ABS ECU checks for wheelspin by comparing the speed of each front (driven) wheel with the rear (non-driven) wheel on the same side. If required, the front brakes are applied lightly and evenly, until the front wheel speeds normalise.
2 In addition, when the wheelspin condition is detected, engine power is reduced by the engine control module (ECM), or by the traction control ECU, in one of three ways:
1) *First, the ignition is retarded by the ECM.*
2) *A secondary throttle system is used, to progressively restrict the airflow into the engine. A second throttle plate is fitted inside the throttle body, operated via cable by an actuator controlled by the traction control ECU. The plate is fully-open by default, but can be closed as required.*
3) *If further reduction in power is required, the ECM alters the fuelling.*

3 The system is active every time the engine is started, but can be switched off using a facia-mounted switch if the driver prefers.

Secondary throttle position sensor

4 The procedure is identical to the (primary) throttle position sensor, described in Section 11.

Secondary accelerator cable

Removal

5 Remove the air cleaner assembly as described in Section 2.
6 Slide the cable adjuster from the bracket on the throttle body/inlet manifold.
7 Slide the cable end fitting from the groove in the throttle lever, and disconnect the cable from the lever.
8 Noting its routing, unclip the cable from the top of the inlet manifold, and trace it back to the actuator.
9 Unclip and open the access flap on the top of the actuator, then unhook the cable end fitting from the drivegear.
10 Release the clip and detach the outer cable from the actuator, and remove it.

Refitting

11 Refitting is a reversal of removal.

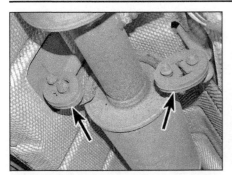

16.11 Unhook the exhaust front mountings

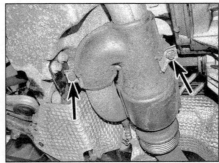

16.12 Unbolt the exhaust support from the bottom of the engine

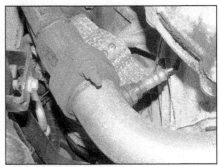

16.14 Exhaust front downpipe flange

Adjustment

12 If not already done, remove the air cleaner as described in Section 2.

13 Slide the cable adjuster from the bracket on the throttle body, then position the cable's square adjuster against the rear of the bracket.

14 Ensure the secondary throttle plate is in the fully-open position, and that the cam on the throttle lever rests against the stop.

15 Turn the cable adjuster as necessary until all freeplay is removed from the cable, without moving the throttle lever.

16 Slide the adjuster back into position in the bracket.

17 Refit the air cleaner as described in Section 2.

Secondary throttle actuator

Removal

18 Remove the secondary accelerator cable as described previously in this Section.

19 Disconnect the multiplug from the base of the actuator.

20 Unscrew the three nuts securing the actuator mounting bracket to the bulkhead, and withdraw it.

21 If required, the actuator can be separated from the mounting bracket after unscrewing the two bolts.

Refitting

22 Refitting is a reversal of removal. Refit and adjust the cable as described previously in this Section.

16 Exhaust system –
general information and component renewal

1 The exhaust system fitted at the factory is a one-piece item, with two catalytic converters and three silencer boxes. A three-branch manifold is fitted to each bank of cylinders, and the two manifolds merge into a single pipe ahead of the 'starter' catalytic converter, which is fitted upstream of the main catalytic converter.

2 Repair sections are available for the centre and tail silencer boxes, but to fit them on the factory original system requires that the pipe

is cut at precisely the right point – for this reason, owners may prefer to have exhaust work carried out by an exhaust specialist. Where these repair sections have been fitted previously, references to cutting can be ignored, as the pipes can be separated by loosening the clamps.

3 The front pipe, which connects to the exhaust manifolds, includes the two catalytic converters, and three oxygen sensors.

4 The intermediate/tail section incorporates three silencers, which contain baffle plates and expansion chambers designed to reduce engine exhaust noise.

5 In the first instance, establish which section needs to be renewed, and what service sections are available.

6 Renewal of each section involves essentially the same process – owners may prefer to remove the complete system initially, as this should make working on it easier.

Front pipe

7 Jack up the front of the car, and support it on axle stands (see *Jacking and vehicle support*).

8 Remove the engine undertray, which is secured by a number of quick-release screw fasteners.

9 Offer up the new pipe as a guide for cutting, then clean and mark the pipe for cutting.

10 Cut the pipe through squarely, using a proper pipe-cutting tool if available.

11 Unhook the front section of the exhaust from its rubber mountings **(see illustration)**.

12 Remove the two bolts securing the front downpipe to the support bracket under the engine **(see illustration)**.

13 Trace the wiring from the three oxygen sensors (one below each manifold flange, and another behind the main catalytic converter) back to the wiring connectors, and disconnect it so that the sensors can be removed with the front pipe. Typically, the wiring plugs are mounted high up on the engine.

14 Remove the two nuts from each of the manifold-to-downpipe flanges, and separate the joints **(see illustration)**. Discard the flange gaskets – new ones must be used when refitting. Lower the downpipe clear.

15 De-burr the cut pipe, then fit the pipe clamp loosely in position.

16 As necessary, unscrew and transfer the oxygen sensors to the new pipe section – note that, where applicable, new sealing washers should be used. If possible, tighten the sensors to the specified torque.

17 Offer up the new section into the pipe clamp, and set it in place.

18 Fit new flange gaskets, and tighten the flange nuts by hand.

19 Refit the two bolts underneath securing the downpipe to its support bracket, and tighten them to the specified torque.

20 Tighten the downpipe flange nuts and the pipe clamp nuts to the specified torque.

21 Reconnect the oxygen sensor wiring.

22 Refit the engine undertray, then lower the car to the ground.

Intermediate pipe

23 Apply the handbrake, then jack up the car and support it on axle stands (see *Jacking and vehicle support*). For the best access, if enough axle stands are available, the car should be raised front and rear.

24 Remove the engine undertray, which is secured by a number of quick-release screw fasteners.

25 Offer up the new pipe as a guide for cutting, then clean and mark the pipe for cutting.

26 Cut the pipe through squarely front and rear, using a proper pipe-cutting tool if available.

27 In the centre of the car, unscrew a total of ten bolts and remove the three crossbraces fitted below the exhaust.

28 Unhook the exhaust from its rubber mountings, and lower it to the floor.

29 De-burr the cut pipes, then fit the pipe clamps loosely in position.

30 Offer the new section into place, and hook it onto the rubber mountings. With the system 'settled' in place (and not touching the floor or suspension components), tighten the clamp nuts to the specified torque.

31 Refit the three crossbraces, and tighten the bolts to the specified torque.

32 Refit the engine undertray, then lower the car to the ground.

Tail pipe

33 Jack up the rear of the car, and support it on axle stands (see *Jacking and vehicle support*).

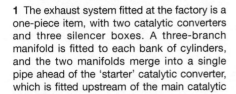

34 Offer up the new section, and mark the pipe for cutting (if the tail section has been replaced previously, loosen the clamp nuts).

35 Where applicable, cut the pipe through squarely, using a proper pipe-cutting tool if available.

36 Unscrew the nut and bolt each side securing the silencer support strap, then lower the strap and silencer.

37 Where applicable, de-burr the cut end of pipe, and fit the clamp loosely in to place.

38 Offer in the new section, and hand-tighten the clamp nuts.

39 Refit the support strap, and tighten the nuts/bolts to the specified torque.

40 With the new section 'settled' in place, tighten the clamp nuts to the specified torque.

41 Lower the car to the ground to complete.

Chapter 4 Part C:
Fuel and exhaust systems – diesel engines

Contents

Section number

Accelerator cable – removal, refitting and adjust. 4
Accelerator pedal – removal and refitting. 5
Air cleaner assembly – removal and refitting 2
Electronic Diesel Control (EDC) system components – removal and
   refitting 12
Exhaust system – general information and component renewal 18
Fuel gauge sender unit – removal and refitting 8
Fuel injection control system – general information. 6
Fuel injection pump – removal and refitting 10
Fuel injection system – testing and adjustment 9

Section number

Fuel injectors – testing, removal and refitting. 11
Fuel system – priming and bleeding. 7
Fuel tank and fuel filler neck – removal and refitting 3
General information and precautions. 1
Intercooler – removal and refitting 16
Manifolds – removal and refitting. 17
Turbocharger – description and precautions 13
Turbocharger – examination and overhaul 15
Turbocharger – removal and refitting 14

Degrees of difficulty

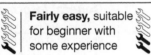

Easy, suitable for novice with little experience	**Fairly easy,** suitable for beginner with some experience	**Fairly difficult,** suitable for competent DIY mechanic	**Difficult,** suitable for experienced DIY mechanic	**Very difficult,** suitable for expert DIY or professional

Specifications

General

System type	Electronic diesel control (EDC) system direct diesel injection system Rear-mounted fuel tank, high-pressure pump with common-rail, direct injection, turbocharger
Type	Bosch EDC15M
Firing order	1-3-4-2 (No 1 cylinder at timing belt end of engine)

Fuel system data

Fuel injection pump	Bosch electronic VP30
Idle speed (not adjustable):	
Without intercooler.	850 ± 50 rpm
With intercooler	805 ± 50 rpm
Glow plug:	
Make.	Beru
Type	0100226 184
Injectors:	
Make.	Bosch
Type	2-stage needle lift injectors (sensing on number one injector)
Opening pressure	
1st stage.	210 bar
2nd stage	380 bar
Maximum pressure rating.	1400 bar
Maximum no load engine speed	5300 rpm

Torque wrench settings

	Nm	lbf ft
Catalytic converter-to-front pipe nuts	50	37
Crankshaft position (CKP) sensor bolt	9	7
Engine control module (ECM) bolts	4	3
Engine coolant temperature (ECT) sensor	15	11
Exhaust front pipe-to turbocharger nuts	50	37
Exhaust/inlet manifold to cylinder head:		
Bolts	33	24
Nuts	25	18
Fuel injection pump fuel feed and return pipe unions	25	18
Fuel injection pump mounting bracket nuts and bolts	25	18
Fuel injection pump securing nuts	25	18
Fuel injection pump sprocket nut	60	44
Fuel injection pump vacuum pipe union	25	18
Fuel injector clamp bolt	25	18
Fuel injector feed pipe unions	27	20
Fuel injector return pipe unions	10	7
Fuel shut-off solenoid	20	15
Intercooler-to-radiator bolts	25	18
Manifold absolute pressure (MAP) sensor nut	9	7
Turbocharger oil feed pipe-to-turbo bolt	20	15
Turbocharger oil drain pipe-to-turbo nuts	10	7
Turbocharger oil drain union to cylinder block	20	15
Throttle position (TP) mounting bracket-to-body nuts	10	7
Throttle position (TP) sensor-to-mounting bracket nuts	4	3
Turbocharger outlet pipe-to-cylinder head bolts:		
M6	10	7
M8	25	18
Turbocharger-to-exhaust manifold nuts	25	18

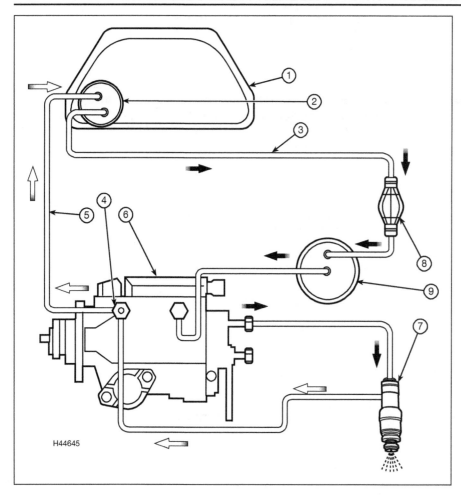

H44645

1 General information and precautions

General information

The operation of the fuel injection system is described in more detail in Section 6.

Fuel is supplied from a tank mounted under the rear of the vehicle, and then passes through a filter to the fuel injection pump, which delivers the fuel to the injectors **(see illustration)**. The injection pump is controlled by an engine control module (ECM) on the basis of information provided by various sensors.

The inducted air passes through an air cleaner, which incorporates a paper filter element to filter out potentially harmful particles (serious internal engine damage can be caused if foreign particles enter through the air intake system).

The engine control module (ECM) controls both the fuel injection pump and the preheating system, integrating the two into a complete engine management system. Refer to Chapter 5C for details of the preheating side of the system.

1.2 Fuel delivery system

1 Fuel tank
2 Swirl pot
3 Fuel supply line
4 Bleed screw
5 Fuel return line
6 Fuel injection pump (FIP)
7 Fuel injector
8 Priming bulb
9 Fuel filter

The exhaust system incorporates a catalytic converter to reduce exhaust gas emissions. Further details can be found in Chapter 4D, along with details of the other emission control systems and components.

Precautions

⚠️ **Warning: It is necessary to take certain precautions when working on the fuel system components,** particularly the fuel injectors and high-pressure pump. Before carrying out any operations on the fuel system, refer to the precautions given in 'Safety first!' at the beginning of this manual. Allow the engine to cool for 5 to 10 minutes to ensure that both the fuel pressure and temperature are at a minimum.

⚠️ **Warning: Exercise extreme caution when working on the high-pressure fuel system. Do** not attempt to test the fuel injectors or disconnect the high-pressure lines with the engine running. Never expose the hands or any part of the body to injector spray, as the high working pressure can cause the fuel to penetrate the skin, with possibly fatal results. You are strongly advised to have any work, which involves testing the injectors under pressure carried out by a dealer or fuel injection specialist.

• When working on fuel system components, scrupulous cleanliness must be observed, and care must be taken not to introduce any foreign matter into fuel lines or components.
• After carrying out any work involving disconnection of fuel lines, it is advisable to check the connections for leaks; pressurise the system by cranking the engine several times.
• Electronic control units are very sensitive components, and certain precautions must be taken to avoid damage to these units as follows.
• When carrying out welding operations on the vehicle using electric welding equipment, the battery and alternator should be disconnected.
• Although the underbonnet-mounted modules will tolerate normal underbonnet conditions, they can be adversely affected by excess heat or moisture. If using welding equipment or pressure-washing equipment in the vicinity of an electronic module, take care not to direct heat, or jets of water or steam, at the module. If this cannot be avoided, remove the module from the vehicle, and protect its wiring plug with a plastic bag.
• Before disconnecting any wiring, or removing components, always ensure that the ignition is switched off.
• Do not attempt to improvise fault diagnosis procedures using a test lamp or multimeter, as irreparable damage could be caused to the module.
• After working on fuel injection/engine management system components, ensure that all wiring is correctly reconnected before

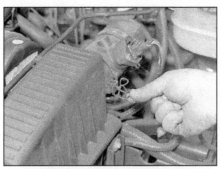

2.3 Release the air cleaner clips

reconnecting the battery or switching on the ignition.
• Damage to the catalytic converter may result if the following precautions are not observed:
a) Consult an approved dealer as soon as possible in the event of misfiring, irregular engine running after a cold start, or a significant loss of engine power. If it is necessary to continue driving, do so for a short time at low engine speed, without labouring the engine.
b) Avoid frequent cold starts one after another.
c) Avoid actuation of the starter for an unnecessarily long time during starting.
d) Do not allow the fuel tank to become empty.
e) Do not attempt to start the engine by push- or tow starting – use jump leads (see 'Jump starting').

2 Air cleaner assembly – removal and refitting
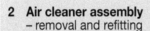

Note: *The following new parts are needed – air cleaner-to-IAT/MAF sensor housing O-ring.*

Removal

1 Disconnect the battery negative lead (refer to *Disconnecting the battery* in the Reference Chapter), and then the positive lead.
2 Remove the battery clamp and lift out the battery.
3 Release the two clips securing the air cleaner upper housing to the mass airflow (MAF) sensor housing on the air intake pipe **(see illustration)**.
4 Remove the two bolts securing the air cleaner to the battery carrier **(see illustration)**.
5 As the air cleaner assembly is lifted, release the air intake pipe from under the air cleaner lower housing.
6 Remove the air cleaner assembly from the engine compartment.

Refitting

7 Refitting is a reversal of the removal procedure, noting:
a) Make sure the air cleaner housing is located correctly

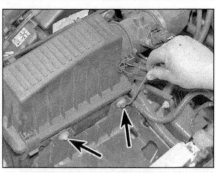

2.4 Remove two securing bolts

b) Fit a new O-ring to the MAF sensor housing.

3 Fuel tank and fuel filler neck – removal and refitting

Refer to Chapter 4A.

4 Accelerator cable – removal, refitting and adjust

Removal

1 Disconnect the battery negative lead (refer to *Disconnecting the battery* in the Reference Chapter).
2 Release the outer cable adjustment nut from the throttle position sensor, mounting bracket **(see illustration)**.
3 Release the inner cable from the cam on the throttle position sensor.
4 Undo the two mounting bolts from the cooling system expansion tank, release it from the bulkhead and move it to one side.
5 At the bulkhead, turn the accelerator cable outer collar through 90°, and release it from the bulkhead.
6 Working inside the vehicle, release the securing clips, and remove the trim panel from under the facia on the driver's side.
7 Depress the nylon clips, and disconnect the inner cable from the accelerator pedal.
8 Working inside the engine compartment, withdraw the accelerator cable from the vehicle.

4.2 Remove adjustment nut (arrowed) from bracket

Refitting

9 Refitting is a reversal of the removal procedure, noting:
a) *Feed the cable assembly through the bulkhead and connect the inner cable to the accelerator pedal.*
b) *Smear rubber grease on both sides of the rubber seal, and secure the cable to the bulkhead.*
c) *Carry out the cable adjustment, as described in this Section.*

Adjust

Note: *Make sure the accelerator cable is correctly routed before adjusting the cable.*
10 Release the outer cable adjustment nut from the mounting bracket and hold it against the outer face of the bracket.
11 Hold the sensor cam in the fully closed position, and turn the adjustment nut until all slack is removed from the inner cable.
12 The adjustment nut can then be fitted back into the mounting bracket.

13 Check that the cam moves to the full throttle position when the pedal is pressed down.
14 Connect the battery earth lead.

---

5 Accelerator pedal –
removal and refitting

Removal

1 Working inside the vehicle, remove the pocket from the driver's side of the facia panel. Undo the three retaining screws and remove the lower facia trim panel from the below the steering column.
2 Reach up under the facia, and pull the end of the cable forwards from the pedal, then squeeze the securing lugs and remove the plastic cable securing clip from the end of the pedal. Release the end of the cable from the pedal.
3 Using a suitable pair of pliers, unhook the return spring from the top of the pedal.

4 Undo the retaining bolt/nut and then remove the pedal assembly from the mounting bracket.

Refitting

5 Refitting is a reversal of removal, but make sure that the accelerator cable is fitted correctly – see Section 4.

---

6 Fuel injection control system
– general information

The amount of fuel delivered, and the injection timing is controlled by the Electronic Diesel Control system (EDC) which also controls the preheat system, Exhaust Gas Recirculation system (EGR) and fuel cut-off solenoid for engine stop.

The fuelling, and injection timing, calculation is based on information supplied to the ECM by the following sensors **(see illustration):**
a) *Crankshaft position sensor (CKP) sends signal representing the crankshaft speed and position.*
b) *Fuel injector needle lift sensor. Incorporated in number one injector, sends signal representing the start of No 1 cylinder injection sequence.*
c) *Engine coolant temperature (ECT).*
d) *Manifold absolute pressure (boost pressure) sensor (MAP), sends signal representing the pressure of the air entering the engine. The signal is used in conjunction with the intake air temperature sensor to calculate the volume of oxygen in the air.*
e) *Roadspeed sensor sends a signal representing the vehicle roadspeed, which operates the speedometer, and provides a signal to the ECM for idle stabilisation.*
f) *Throttle pedal position sensor (TP). The sensor is a potentiometer, which provides an electrical signal to the ECM representing the amount and rate of throttle opening – ie, driver demand.*
g) *Throttle control is 'drive by wire'. The sensor is connected to the pedal by a Bowden cable, and to the ECM by electrical cable.*
h) *Brake pedal switch, when closed by brake application, sends brake-applied signal.*
i) *Intake air temperature/Mass airflow sensor (IAT/MAF), supplies separate signals representing the mass airflow and intake air temperature.*

Signals from these sensors are constantly updated and processed by the ECM. The resultant calculations are compared with preprogrammed 'maps' that provide datum points for the amount of fuel required and injection timing, for many combinations of engine operating conditions.

Failure of certain sensors – either complete loss of signal, or sending an abnormal signal, will cause the ECM to default to

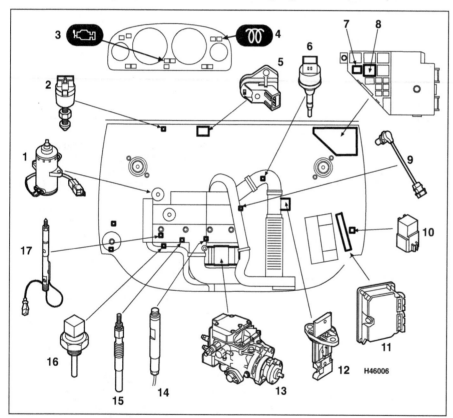

6.2 Electronic Diesel Control (EDC) components

1 *Throttle position sensor – TP*
2 *Brake pedal switch*
3 *Glow plug warning lamp*
4 *Engine malfunction lamp – MIL*
5 *Manifold absolute pressure sensor – MAP (Turbo boost pressure)*
6 *Roadspeed sensor*
7 *Air conditioning compressor clutch relay*
8 *Main relay*
9 *Crankshaft position sensor – CKP*
10 *Glow plug relay*
11 *Engine Control Module – ECM*
12 *Intake air temperature/mass airflow sensor – IAT/MAF*
13 *Fuel injection pump – FIP*
14 *Standard fuel injector x 3*
15 *Glow plug x 4*
16 *Engine coolant temperature sensor – ECT*
17 *Fuel injector with needle lift sensor*

preprogrammed values. In most cases this will be noticeable as poor or erratic engine performance.

Whenever a sensor fault occurs, the engine malfunction warning lamp, on the instrument panel is lit and a fault code is stored in a memory of the ECM. Using specialist diagnostic equipment, the codes can be extracted by MG Rover dealers.

7 Fuel system – priming and bleeding

⚠️ **Warning: Refer to the warning in Section 1 before proceeding.**

1 After any operation which requires the disconnection of any fuel hose, it is necessary to prime and bleed the fuel system; the priming pump is located in the left-hand rear corner of the engine compartment, where it is fitted to the fuel filter inlet pipe.

2 Position wads of absorbent rag around the fuel filter then slacken the bleed screw which is fitted to the top of the fuel filter **(see illustration)**. Gently squeeze and release the pump until fuel which is free of air bubbles is flowing out of the filter. Once all traces of air have been removed, squeeze and hold the pump then securely tighten the bleed screw before releasing the pump. Remove the rag from around the filter and mop-up any spilt fuel.

3 Turn on the ignition switch and gently squeeze and release the pump until resistance is felt. Once the lines are full of fuel (indicated by the resistance felt when the pump is squeezed), stop pumping and turn off the ignition.

4 Depress the accelerator pedal to the floor then start the engine as normal (this may take longer than usual, especially if the fuel system has been allowed to run dry – operate the starter in ten second bursts with 5 seconds rest in between each operation). Run the engine at a fast idle speed for a minute or so to purge any remaining trapped air from the fuel lines. After this time the engine should idle smoothly at a constant speed.

5 If the engine idles roughly, then there is still some air trapped in the fuel system. Increase the engine speed again for another minute or so then recheck the idle speed. Repeat this procedure as necessary until the engine is idling smoothly.

8 Fuel gauge sender unit – removal and refitting

⚠️ **Warning: Refer to the warning in Section 1 before proceeding.**

Removal

1 The fuel gauge sender unit is mounted in the top of the fuel tank, and cannot be accessed with the tank in place.

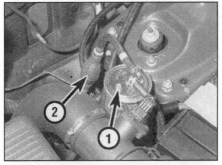

7.2 Slacken the bleed screw (1) and pump the rubber priming bulb (2)

2 Remove the fuel tank as described in Chapter 4A, Section 3.

3 Unclip the fuel pump wiring harness from the securing clips along the top of fuel tank.

4 Release the securing clips, and disconnect the fuel feed and return hoses from the fuel sender unit. Plug or cover the open ends of the hoses and pipes to prevent dirt entry.

5 Unscrew the six nuts securing the sender unit to the fuel tank.

6 Carefully withdraw the sender unit from the fuel tank, taking care not to damage the sender unit float. Recover the sealing ring.

Refitting

7 Examine the condition of the sealing ring, and renew if necessary, then thoroughly clean the mating faces of the tank and the sender unit.

8 Refitting is a reversal of removal, but if necessary renew the fuel hose clips and, on completion, refit the fuel tank with reference to Section 3.

9 Fuel injection system – testing and adjustment

Testing

1 If a fault appears in the fuel injection system, first ensure that all the system wiring connectors are securely connected and free from corrosion. Ensure that the fault is not due to poor maintenance; ie, check that the air cleaner filter element is clean, that the cylinder compression pressures are correct (see Chapter 2C), and that the engine breather hoses are clear and undamaged (see Chapter 4D).

2 If the engine will not start, check the condition of the glow plugs (see Chapter 5C).

3 If these checks fail to reveal the cause of the problem, the vehicle should be taken to a Rover dealer for testing. A diagnostic wiring connector is provided on a bracket under the facia, into which a special electronic diagnostic tester can be plugged **(see illustration)**. The tester should locate the fault quickly and simply, avoiding the need to test all the system components individually, which is time-consuming, and also carries a risk of damaging the ECM.

9.3 Diagnostic wiring connector – viewed from driver's side footwell

Adjustment

4 Idle speed, maximum speed and fuel injection pump timing are all controlled by the ECM, and no manual adjustment is possible.

10 Fuel injection pump – removal and refitting

Caution: Be careful not to allow dirt into the injection pump or injector pipes during this procedure. New sealing rings should be used on the fuel pipe banjo unions when refitting.

Note: *Refer to the warning in Section 1 before proceeding.*

Removal

1 Disconnect the battery negative lead (refer to *Disconnecting the battery* in the Reference Chapter).

2 Remove the screws securing the engine acoustic cover, and remove it from the top of the engine.

3 Slacken the clip and disconnect the intercooler bottom hose from the air intake pipe **(see illustration)**.

4 Remove two bolts and release the EGR cooler pipe from the air intake pipe **(see illustration)**.

5 Slacken and remove the mounting bolt securing the intake pipe to the cylinder head.

6 Remove two bolts securing the intake pipe to the inlet manifold and remove the intake pipe **(see illustration)**. Discard the gasket a new one will be required for refitting.

10.3 Disconnect intercooler hose

10.4 Undo the two EGR cooler pipe bolts – arrowed

10.6 Remove the intake pipe

10.12 Sprocket locking pin (drill bit) in position

10.14 Disconnect the sensor multi-plug

10.18 Slacken injector pipe unions, using two spanners

7 Drain the cooling system as described in Chapter 1B.

8 Slacken the securing clips and remove the intercooler inlet and outlet hoses from the engine bay.

9 Slacken the securing clips and remove the cooling system radiator top hose.

10 Slacken the clip and remove the radiator top hose from the oil cooler housing.

11 Remove the fuel injection pump (FIP) drivebelt as described in Chapter 2C.

12 Ensure that the sprocket is locked in position using the Rover special locking pin tool 12-185 (a 9.5 mm twist drill or similar can be used). Remove the three Torx head retaining bolts and withdraw the flywheel/sprocket from the pump shaft **(see illustration)**.

13 Slacken the retaining nut and disconnect the wiring connector from No 2 glow plug.

14 Release the injector needle lift sensor multiplug from the fuel injection pump

10.19 Removing the injector pipes

10.21 Remove support bracket bolts (1) and nuts (2)

mounting bracket, and disconnect the plug from the engine harness **(see illustration)**.

15 Disconnect the wiring connector multiplug from the fuel injection pump. Working your way along the wiring harness, release it from any securing brackets.

Caution: Cap or plug the open connections, to reduce fuel loss, and to prevent the entry of dirt. Pack absorbent cloth around the fuel pipe connections to soak up excess fuel spillage.

16 Slacken and remove the fuel feed, and return pipes from the fuel injection pump. Discard the sealing washers, as new ones will be required for refitting.

17 Disconnect the fuel return pipe from No 3 injector.

Caution: To prevent injector pipe damage, use two spanners when slackening the unions.

18 Using two spanners to counterhold the

injector, slacken the injector pipe unions at the injectors and fuel injection pump **(see illustration)**.

19 Starting with injector pipes 1 and 2, disconnect the unions and remove the pipes from the engine, then remove injector pipes 3 and 4 **(see illustration)**.

20 Undo the mounting bolt attaching the dipstick bracket the coolant elbow, and move the dipstick to one side.

21 Remove four bolts securing the fuel injection pump support bracket to the cylinder block, and the two nuts securing the bracket to the fuel injection pump. Then move the bracket to one side **(see illustration)**.

22 Remove two Torx head bolts and one nut securing the fuel injection pump to the adapter plate. Remove the fuel injection pump and withdraw the mounting bracket.

Refitting

23 Refitting is a reversal of the removal procedure, noting:

  a) *Use a torque wrench to tighten all fastenings to the specified torque.*

  b) *Clean the mating faces of the fuel injection pump and adaptor plate.*

  c) *Position fuel injection pump mounting bracket, before refitting the fuel pump.*

  d) *Fit No 3 and 4 injector pipes first, followed by No 1 and 2 pipes.*

  e) *Fit a new fuel injection pump belt as described in Chapter 2C.*

  f) *Prime and bleed the fuel system as described in Section 7. Run the engine, and check for fuel leaks.*

  g) *On completion, top-up the cooling system as described in 1B.*

11 Fuel injectors –
testing, removal and refitting

Caution: Be careful not to allow dirt into the injectors or injector pipes during this procedure. New sealing washers should be used on the injectors when refitting.

Note: *Refer to the warning in Section 1 before proceeding.*

Removal

1 Disconnect the battery negative lead (refer

to *Disconnecting the battery* in the Reference Chapter).

2 Remove the screws securing the engine acoustic cover, and remove it from the top of the engine.

3 Slacken the clip and disconnect the intercooler bottom hose from the air intake pipe.

4 Remove two bolts and release the EGR cooler pipe from the air intake pipe **(see illustration 10.4)**.

5 Slacken and remove the mounting bolt securing the intake pipe to the cylinder head.

6 Remove two bolts securing the intake pipe to the inlet manifold and remove the intake pipe **(see illustration 10.6)**. Discard the gasket a new one will be required for refitting.

7 Disconnect the needle lift sensor multiplug from No 1 injector **(see illustration 10.14)**. **Note:** *A fuel injector needle lift sensor is incorporated in number one injector; this sends a signal to the ECM, representing the start of No 1 cylinder injection sequence.*
Caution: Cap or plug the open connections, to reduce fuel loss, and to prevent the entry of dirt. Pack absorbent cloth around the fuel pipe connections to soak up excess fuel spillage.

8 Slacken and remove the fuel return hose banjo bolts from the injectors **(see illustration)**. Discard the sealing washers, as new ones will be required for refitting.
Caution: To prevent injector pipe damage, use two spanners when slackening the unions.

9 Using two spanners to counterhold the injector, slacken the injector pipe unions at the injectors and fuel injection pump **(see illustration 10.18)**.

10 Disconnect the injector pipes from the injectors and move them to one side, taking care not to damage them. Cap the ends of the pipes to prevent dirt ingress.

11 Undo the injector clamp plate securing bolts and withdraw the injectors from the cylinder head **(see illustrations)**. Discard the sealing washers, as new ones will be required for refitting.

Refitting

12 Refitting is a reversal of the removal procedure, noting:

12.1 Crankshaft position (CKP) sensor location (arrowed) – engine removed for clarity

11.8 Remove the fuel return hose

11.11b . . . and withdraw the injectors

a) *Clean the injectors and injector seats in the cylinder head.*
b) *Fit new injector sealing washers with the domed surface of the washer against the injector* **(see illustration)**.
c) *Tighten injector securing bolts and fuel pipes to the specified torque.*

12 Electronic Diesel Control (EDC) system components – removal and refitting

Crankshaft position sensor

Removal

1 The CKP sensor is mounted at the rear of the flywheel housing (at the left-hand end of the engine) **(see illustration)**.

2 Disconnect the battery negative lead (refer to *Disconnecting the battery* in the Reference Chapter).

3 Release the wiring connector from its mounting bracket and disconnect the multiplug to the sensor.

4 Unscrew the sensor securing bolt, then withdraw the sensor from its housing.

Refitting

5 Refitting is a reversal of removal, tightening the sensor securing bolt to the specified torque setting.

Coolant temperature sensor

6 The engine coolant temperature sensor removal and refitting details can be found in Chapter 3, Section 8.

11.11a Remove the clamp plates . . .

11.12 Fit new injector sealing washers in the cylinder head

Fuel pump temperature sensor

7 There is a fuel pump temperature sensor, which is integral with the fuel injection pump ECU. This cannot be renewed separately.

Intake air temperature/ mass airflow sensor

Note: *The following new parts are needed – sensor O-ring seal.*

Removal

8 The IAT/MAF sensor is located in the air intake hose between the air cleaner and turbocharger **(see illustration)**.

9 Disconnect the battery negative lead (refer to *Disconnecting the battery* in the Reference Chapter).

10 Release the securing clip and disconnect the multiplug from the sensor.

11 Slacken the clip securing the air intake hose to the sensor assembly

12.8 IAT/MAF sensor location in air duct

12.17 Throttle position sensor (TPS) location

12.25 Manifold absolute pressure (MAP) sensor location

12.31 Engine control module (ECM) location

12 Release the two clips securing the sensor assembly to the air cleaner housing.
13 Withdraw the sensor assembly from the air intake hose and discard the O-ring seal.

Refitting

14 Refitting is a reversal of the removal procedure, noting a new O-ring seal will need to be fitted to the sensor assembly.

Fuel injector needle lift sensor

15 The needle lift sensor is an integral part of the No 1 cylinder fuel injector, and cannot be renewed separately. Fuel injector removal and refitting is covered in Section 11.

Vehicle speed sensor

16 The engine control module receives a vehicle speed signal from the same vehicle speed sensor used to provide a signal to the speedometer. Sensor removal and refitting details can be found in Chapter 7A.

Throttle position sensor

Removal

17 The TP sensor is located on the inside of the suspension turret at the right-hand side of the engine compartment (see illustration).
18 Disconnect the battery negative lead (refer to *Disconnecting the battery* in the Reference Chapter).

19 Unscrew the two bolts securing the heat shield to the sensor mounting bracket.
20 Slide the accelerator outer cable adjuster nut from the mounting bracket, and release the inner cable from the cam on the sensor.
21 Release the wiring connector from the mounting bracket and disconnect the multiplug to the sensor.
22 Unscrew the two mounting bracket securing bolts and withdraw the sensor and mounting bracket from the vehicle.
23 To remove the sensor from the mounting bracket undo the two securing nuts, and remove the sensor.

Refitting

24 Refitting is a reversal of removal, noting the accelerator cable will need to be reconnected and adjusted as described in Section 4.

Manifold absolute pressure sensor

Removal

25 The MAP sensor is located at the rear of the engine compartment on the bulkhead next to the EGR solenoid valve (see illustration).
26 Disconnect the battery negative lead (refer to *Disconnecting the battery* in the Reference Chapter).
27 Disconnect the wiring multiplug and the vacuum hose from the MAP sensor.

28 Undo the retaining nut and remove the sensor from the mounting bracket on the bulkhead.

Refitting

29 Refitting is a reversal of removal, tightening the sensor securing nut to the specified torque.

Brake pedal switch

30 The engine control module receives a signal from the brake light switch, which indicates when the brakes are being applied. Brake light switch removal and refitting details can be found in Chapter 9.

Engine Control Module (ECM)

Note: *If a new ECM is to be fitted, it will need to be programmed with the code from the anti-theft security unit before the engine can be started. Only an MG Rover dealer using special equipment can do this.*

Removal

31 The ECM is located at the left-hand front of the engine compartment, next to the battery (see illustration).
32 Disconnect the battery negative lead (refer to *Disconnecting the battery* in the Reference Chapter).
33 Undo the securing nut and remove the mounting bracket from the rear of the ECM.
34 Withdraw the ECM and push the two wiring connector, locking clips inwards to release and disconnect two multiplugs.

Refitting

35 Refitting is a reversal of the removal procedure, noting it may be necessary to arrange programming of the module at an MG Rover dealer.

13 Turbocharger – description and precautions

Turbocharger assembly

By increasing the volume of air fed into the engine, the turbocharger allows a greater amount of fuel to be injected and burnt efficiently. The result is an increase in engine efficiency and power output, and a reduction in exhaust emissions.

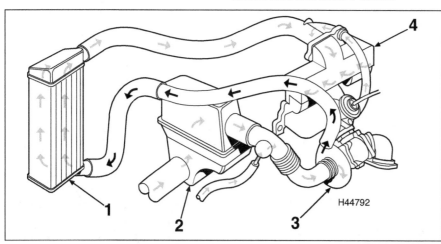

H44792

13.4 Air intake system

1 *Intercooler* 2 *Air cleaner* 3 *Turbocharger* 4 *Intake manifold*

14.6a Unscrew the bolts (arrowed) securing the turbocharger pipe to the cylinder head . . .

14.6b . . . and the rear of the cylinder head

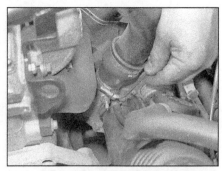

14.7 slacken the clip securing the hose to the turbocharger and remove

The turbocharger has a single shaft in a specially-shaped housing. The housing is divided into two non-connecting chambers – one chamber housing a turbine wheel, and the other housing a compressor wheel. Both wheels are fixed to the single shaft.

Before passing into the exhaust outlet system, the engine exhaust gas passes through the turbine chamber, and spins the turbine wheel at high speed. Fixed to the other end of the common shaft, the compressor wheel also spins at high speed.

Before entering the intake manifold, the intake air enters the compressor housing and is compressed by the spinning compressor wheel. This increases the density of the air, and allows more to be forced into the engine. Consequently, more fuel can be burnt efficiently **(see illustration opposite)**.

Boost pressure (the pressure in the inlet manifold) is limited by a wastegate, which diverts the exhaust gas away from the turbine wheel in response to a pressure-sensitive actuator.

The turbo shaft is pressure-lubricated by an oil feed pipe from the main oil gallery. The shaft 'floats' on a cushion of oil. A drain pipe returns the oil to the sump.

Intercooling

The air compression process raises the temperature of the air, so it expands and becomes less dense.

To counteract this drawback, after leaving the turbocharger, and before entering the engine, the air is passed through an intercooler.

The intercooler, mounted by the side of the cooling system radiator, is an air-to-air heat exchanger. Construction and operation of the intercooler is similar to that of the cooling system radiator. Engine intake air from the turbocharger, passing through the core tubes of the intercooler, is cooled by outside air passing across fins attached the core tubes.

As the volume of air entering the engine is the same, it is effectively taking in a greater mass of air than before, meaning that more fuel can be burnt.

Precautions

• The turbocharger operates at extremely high speeds and temperatures. Certain precautions

must be observed to avoid premature failure of the turbo or injury to the operator.

• Do not operate the turbo with any parts exposed. Foreign objects falling onto the rotating vanes could cause excessive damage and (if ejected) personal injury.

• Do not race the engine immediately after start-up, especially if it is cold. Give the oil a few seconds to circulate.

• Always allow the engine to return to idle speed before switching it off – do not blip the accelerator and switch off, as this will leave the turbo spinning without lubrication.

• Allow the engine to idle for several minutes before switching off after a high-speed run.

• Observe the recommended intervals for oil and filter changing, and use a reputable oil of the specified quality. Neglect of oil changing, or use of inferior oil, can cause carbon formation on the turbo shaft and subsequent failure.

14 Turbocharger – removal and refitting

Note: *A new oil drain pipe gasket, a new exhaust front section-to-turbocharger elbow gasket, and new oil feed pipe sealing washers will be required on refitting.*

Removal

1 Disconnect the battery negative lead (refer to *Disconnecting the battery* in the Reference Chapter).

2 Apply the handbrake, then jack up the front

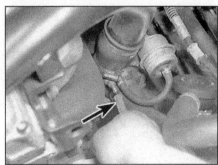

14.8 Disconnecting the MAP sensor pipe (arrowed) from the turbocharger

of the vehicle and support securely on axle stands (see *Jacking and vehicle support*).

3 Remove the screws securing the engine acoustic cover, and remove it from the top of the engine.

4 Working under the vehicle, remove the exhaust front pipe section with reference to Section 18.

5 Slacken the securing clips, and remove the intake hose from the turbocharger to the IAT/MAF sensor.

6 Unscrew the two bolts securing the turbocharger outlet pipe to the front and rear of the cylinder head **(see illustrations)**.

7 Slacken the securing clips and remove the turbocharger outlet pipe from across the top of the engine **(see illustration)**.

8 Disconnect the manifold absolute pressure (MAP) sensor pipe from the turbocharger **(see illustration)**.

9 Unscrew the union banjo bolt, and disconnect the oil feed pipe from the top of the turbocharger **(see illustration)**. Be prepared for some oil spillage, then recover and discard the sealing washers.

10 Slacken and remove the two bolts securing the oil drain pipe to the bottom of the turbocharger **(see illustration)**. Be prepared for some oil spillage, then recover and discard the gasket. If required, the oil drain pipe can now be disconnected from the cylinder block and removed from the engine.

11 Remove the two mounting bolts securing the turbocharger to the support bracket **(see illustration)**.

12 Support the turbocharger, and then unscrew the three nuts securing the

14.9 Turbocharger oil feed pipe union bolt (arrowed)

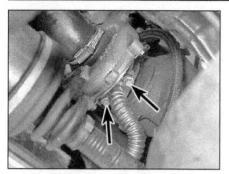

14.10 Unscrew the two bolts (arrowed) securing the oil drain pipe

14.11 Unscrew the two bolts (arrowed) from the mounting bracket

14.12 Turbocharger securing nuts (arrowed)

turbocharger to the exhaust manifold. Withdraw the turbocharger assembly out from the rear of the engine **(see illustration)**.

Refitting

13 Refitting is a reversal of removal, bearing in mind the following points:
   a) *Thoroughly clean the mating faces of the turbocharger and the manifold.*
   b) *Tighten all fixings to the specified torque, where applicable.*
   c) *Thoroughly clean the mating faces of the oil drain pipe and the turbocharger, and use a new gasket when reconnecting the pipe.*
   d) *Reconnect the exhaust front section to the turbocharger, using a new gasket, with reference to Section 18.*
   e) *Introduce a small amount of clean engine oil into the top of the turbocharger, then reconnect the turbocharger oil feed pipe, using new sealing washers.*
   f) *Run the engine at idle speed, and check the turbocharger oil unions for leakage. Rectify any problems without delay.*
   g) *After the engine has been run, check the engine oil level, and top-up if necessary.*

15 Turbocharger –
examination and overhaul

1 With the turbocharger removed, inspect the housing for cracks or other visible damage.
2 Spin the turbine or the compressor wheel to verify that the shaft is intact and to feel for excessive shake or roughness. Some play is normal since in use the shaft is 'floating' on a film of oil. Check that the wheel vanes are undamaged.
3 The wastegate and actuator are integral with the turbocharger, and cannot be checked or renewed separately. Consult a Rover dealer or other specialist if it is thought that the wastegate may be faulty.
4 If the exhaust or induction passages are oil-contaminated, the turbo shaft oil seals have probably failed. (On the induction side, this will also have contaminated the intercooler, which if necessary should be flushed with a suitable solvent.)

5 No DIY repair of the turbo is possible. A new unit may be available on an exchange basis.

16 Intercooler –
removal and refitting

Removal

1 Disconnect the battery negative lead (refer to *Disconnecting the battery* in the Reference Chapter).
2 Remove the screws securing the engine acoustic cover, and remove it from the top of the engine.
3 Remove the air cleaner assembly as described in Section 2.
4 Where fitted, remove the two retaining bolts from the trim panel across the top of the radiator and remove it from the vehicle.
5 Slacken the securing clips and disconnect the top and bottom hoses from the intercooler.
6 Remove the upper and lower mounting bolts securing the intercooler in place **(see illustration)**.
7 Release the intercooler from the lower mounting, and remove it from the engine compartment.

Refitting

8 Refitting is a reversal of the removal procedure.

16.6 Intercooler upper mounting bolt – arrowed

17 Manifolds –
removal and refitting

Removal

1 The intake and exhaust manifolds share a common gasket **(see illustration)**. To enable a new gasket to be fitted, both manifolds must be removed.
2 Disconnect the battery negative lead (refer to *Disconnecting the battery* in the Reference Chapter).
3 Remove the screws securing the engine acoustic cover, and remove it from the top of the engine.
4 Apply the handbrake, then jack up the front of the vehicle and support securely on axle stands (see *Jacking and vehicle support*).
5 Drain the cooling system as described in Chapter 1B.
6 Remove the turbocharger as described in Section 14 of this Chapter.
7 Slacken the clip and disconnect the intercooler bottom hose from the air intake pipe.
8 Remove two bolts and release the EGR cooler pipe from the air intake pipe **(see illustration)**.
9 Slacken and remove the mounting bolt securing the intake pipe to the cylinder head.
10 Remove two bolts securing the intake pipe to the inlet manifold and remove the intake pipe **(see illustration)**. Discard the gasket, a new one will be required for refitting.
11 Slacken the securing clip, and disconnect the breather hose from the cylinder head cover.
12 Disconnect the vacuum pipe from the exhaust gas recirculation (EGR) valve.
13 Slacken the securing clips and disconnect the coolant hoses from the EGR cooler.
14 Slacken the six nuts and six bolts securing the exhaust manifold to the cylinder head. Support the manifolds and remove the nuts and bolts, noting the locations of the washers **(see illustration)**.
15 Carefully withdraw the manifolds from the cylinder head, exhaust manifold first. Recover and discard the gasket, a new one will be required for refitting.

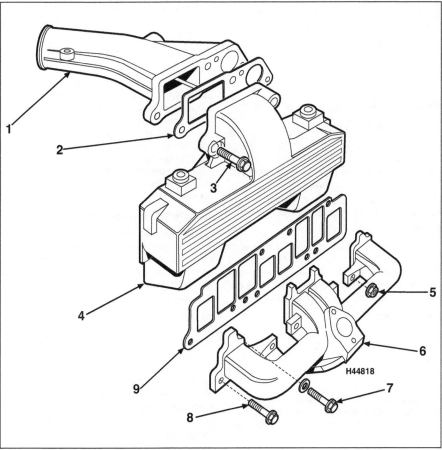

17.1 Manifold component layout

1 Air intake pipe	4 Inlet manifold	8 Bolt x 2
2 Gasket – intake pipe to	5 Nut x 6	9 Gasket – inlet and
inlet manifold	6 Exhaust manifold	exhaust manifold
3 Bolt x 2	7 Bolt and washer x 4	

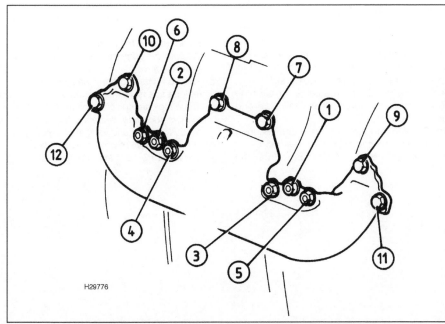

17.18 Manifold securing nut and bolt tightening sequence

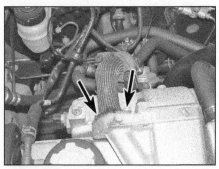

17.8 Unscrew the two EGR pipe bolts – arrowed

17.10 Remove the air intake pipe

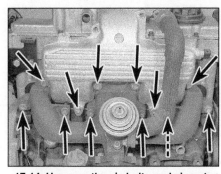

17.14 Unscrew the six bolts and six nuts (arrowed) – engine removed for clarity

Refitting

16 Thoroughly clean the mating faces of the manifolds and the cylinder head, and then position a new gasket on the cylinder head studs.

17 Manoeuvre the manifolds into position, then refit the securing nuts and bolts, ensuring that the washers are in place as noted before removal.

18 Tighten the inlet and exhaust manifold securing nuts and bolts to the specified torque (note that the torques for the nuts and bolts are different), in sequence **(see illustration)**.

19 Further refitting is a reversal of removal, bearing in mind the following points.

a) Ensure that the cylinder head and manifold mating surfaces are clean and use a new gasket.

b) Tighten all fixings to the specified torque, where applicable.

c) Refit the turbocharger with reference to Section 14.

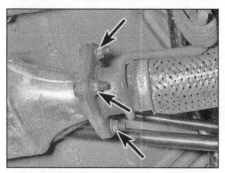

18.6 Unscrew the exhaust front section-to-catalytic converter nuts – arrowed

d) *Ensure that any vacuum/breather hoses are correctly reconnected as noted before removal.*

e) *Ensure that any wiring or hose brackets/clips are positioned as noted before removal.*

f) *On completion, top-up the cooling system as described in 1B.*

18 Exhaust system – general information and component renewal

1 The exhaust system comprises three pipe sections – front, intermediate and tail, and a catalytic converter. The pipe assemblies, and converter, are connected to each other by flanges, secured by studs and nuts, and sealed with gaskets. The whole assembly is suspended on rubber mountings attached to the body.

2 To reduce engine vibration in the exhaust system, a corrugated pipe section, covered by metal braiding, is located in the front pipe.

3 The tail pipe incorporates a silencer, which contains baffle plates and expansion chambers designed to reduce engine exhaust noise.

Note: *If renewing the complete system:*

a) *Raise the vehicle as high as possible, and support securely on axle stands (see 'Jacking and vehicle support').*

b) *Because of rust and corrosion, it may be quicker to separate pipe sections by cutting through them, instead of trying to slacken and remove the flange securing nuts.*

18.7 Undo the front pipe-to-turbocharger nuts – arrowed

Caution: Ensure that the exhaust has cooled sufficiently to avoid burns.

Removal

4 To remove the system or part of the system, first jack up the front or rear of the car, and support it on axle stands (see *Jacking and vehicle support*). Alternatively, position the car over an inspection pit, or on car ramps.

Front pipe

Note: *The following new parts are needed – manifold flange gasket, front pipe-to-catalytic converter pipe gasket. Depending on their condition, new mounting nuts and rubbers may also be needed*

5 Remove the engine undertray.

6 Slacken and remove the three nuts securing the front pipe to the catalytic converter **(see illustration)**.

7 Remove the three nuts securing the front pipe to the turbocharger/manifold **(see illustration)**.

8 Release the mounting rubber from the pipe bracket and remove the front pipe from under the vehicle. Discard the gaskets.

Intermediate pipe

Note: *The following new parts are needed – flange gaskets: catalytic converter-to-intermediate pipe and intermediate pipe-to-tail pipe. Depending on their condition, new mounting rubbers may also be needed*

9 Remove the three nuts securing tail pipe to intermediate pipe. Release tail pipe and discard gasket.

10 Slacken and remove three nuts securing intermediate pipe to catalytic converter.

11 Release the intermediate pipe from the rubber mountings and remove intermediate pipe from under the vehicle. Discard the gaskets.

Tail pipe/silencer

Note: *The following new parts are needed – flange gasket intermediate pipe-to-tail pipe. Depending on their condition, new mounting rubbers may also be needed.*

12 Slacken and remove the three nuts securing the tail pipe/silencer to the intermediate pipe.

13 Release three mounting rubbers from the support brackets, and remove the tail pipe/silencer from under the vehicle. Discard the gasket.

Catalytic converter

Note: *The following new parts are needed – flange gasket: front pipe-to-converter and converter-to-intermediate pipe. Depending on their condition, new mounting rubbers may also be needed.*

Removal

14 Remove the three nuts securing the converter to the intermediate pipe, and three nuts securing the converter to the front pipe.

Caution: The converter can be easily damaged. Ensure that it is adequately supported during removal.

15 Release and lower the catalytic converter from both flanges, and then withdraw it from under the vehicle. Discard the gaskets.

Refitting

16 Each section is refitted, by reversing the removal sequence, noting the following points:

a) *Ensure that all traces of corrosion have been removed from the flanges, and renew all necessary gaskets.*

b) *Inspect the rubber mountings for signs of damage or deterioration, and renew as necessary.*

c) *When refitting the front flexible pipe to the catalytic converter, ensure that a new gasket is fitted.*

d) *Prior to tightening the exhaust system fasteners, ensure that all rubber mountings are correctly located, and that there is adequate clearance between the exhaust system and vehicle underbody.*

e) *On completion, remove the axle stands and lower the vehicle to the ground.*

Chapter 4 Part D:
Emission control systems

Contents

Section number

Catalytic converter – general information and precautions 4
Diesel engine emission control systems – testing and component
renewal 3

Section number

General information 1
Petrol engine emission control systems – testing and component
renewal 2

Degrees of difficulty

Easy, suitable for novice with little experience	**Fairly easy,** suitable for beginner with some experience	**Fairly difficult,** suitable for competent DIY mechanic	**Difficult,** suitable for experienced DIY mechanic	**Very difficult,** suitable for expert DIY or professional

Specifications

Torque wrench setting	Nm	lbf ft
Exhaust gas recirculation (EGR) valve and cooler bolts (diesel engines) .	25	18

1 General information

Provided that the engine is correctly maintained, and is in good mechanical condition, the control systems will keep emissions within legal limits.

All models are fitted with the following control systems to reduce engine emissions released into the atmosphere **(see illustrations):**

Petrol engines

Crankcase emission control

When the engine is running, a certain amount of combustion gas passes the pistons – 'blow-by' gases – and enters the crankcase. The amount of blow-by is dependent on the overall condition/wear of the engine.

When crankcase emission control is fitted, the blow-by gases from the crankcase are mixed with inlet air, and burned in the combustion chambers.

Ventilation is via the oil drain passages in the cylinder block and cylinder head, and two ports in the camshaft cover (two ports in each camshaft cover on 6-cylinder models):

a) The larger port is connected by a plastic tube (and rubber hose on 4-cylinder models) to the throttle body, upstream of the throttle disc.

b) The smaller port is connected by a rubber hose (4-cylinder models) or plastic pipes (6-cylinder models) to the inlet manifold. These have a restrictor and gauze oil separator to prevent oil being drawn from the camshaft cover.

When the engine is running at idle, the throttle disc is closed; this causes a depression and draws crankcase gases into

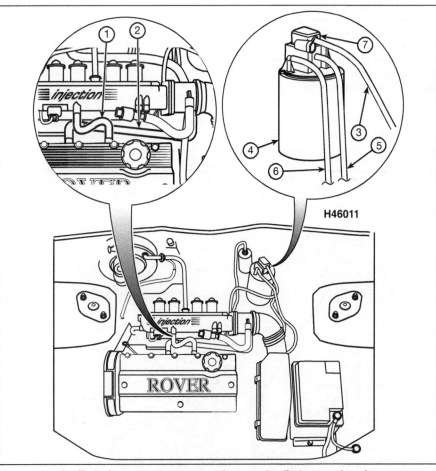

1.2a Emission control component layout – 4-cylinder petrol engines

1   Crankcase breather hose to inlet manifold
2   Crankcase breather hose to throttle body
3   Vent line to inlet manifold
4   EVAP canister
5   Vent line to atmosphere
6   Vent line from fuel tank
7   Purge valve

H46011

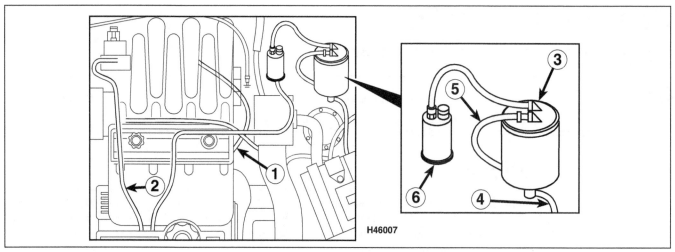

1.2b Emission control component layout – 6-cylinder petrol engines

1 *Crankcase breather hose to inlet manifold*
2 *Crankcase breather hose to throttle body*
3 *EVAP canister*
4 *Vent line to atmosphere*
5 *Vent line from fuel tank*
6 *Purge valve*

the inlet manifold. From the upstream side of the disc, clean air is drawn into the crankcase to limit crankcase depression.

With the engine running and the throttle disc wide open, both the upstream and downstream sides of the disc and ports are subjected to similar weak depression. Crankcases gases are drawn out of both ports, with most being drawn via the larger port into the throttle body.

Exhaust emission control

To minimise the amount of pollutants which escape into the atmosphere, all models are fitted with a catalytic converter in the exhaust system. The system has oxygen sensors in the exhaust system to provide the engine control module ECM with constant feedback, enabling the ECM to adjust the mixture to provide the best possible conditions for the converter to operate. The main components used in catalytic converters on petrol models are platinum, rhodium and palladium.

The efficient operation of the catalytic converter is dependent upon careful control of the oxygen content of the exhaust gas. This is achieved by using heated oxygen sensors (HO_2S), upstream and downstream of the catalytic converter.

a) *An upstream sensor measures oxygen content in the exhaust system before it goes through the catalytic converter.*
b) *A downstream sensor sends a signal to the ECM to monitor the condition of the catalytic converter.*

Evaporative emissions (EVAP) control

The EVAP system reduces the level of hydrocarbons released into the atmosphere from fuel vapour.

The main components are – EVAP charcoal canister, a two-way valve, a purge valve and connecting vent pipes.

Fuel vapour, created in the fuel tank as the fuel heats up, is held in the tank until pressure is sufficient to open the outward venting side of the two-way valve. When the valve opens excess vapour is released through a fuel cut-off valve into the vent pipes and into the EVAP canister. Charcoal in the canister absorbs and stores fuel from the vapour, and air with very little fuel vapour being vented to the atmosphere.

The canister and charcoal have a limited capacity, so fuel is purged via the purge valve into the inlet manifold, where it is burned during combustion. The purge valve is located in the top of the EVAP canister on 4-cylinder engines and on the inlet manifold on 6-cylinder engines.

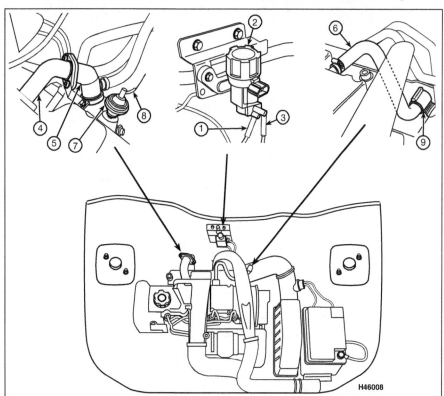

1.2c Emission control component layout – diesel engines

1 *Vacuum line from brake vacuum servo*
2 *EGR solenoid*
3 *Vacuum line from EGR valve*
4 *EGR cooler to inlet manifold pipe*
5 *EGR cooler*
6 *Crankcase breather hose*
7 *EGR valve*
8 *Vacuum line to EGR solenoid*
9 *Crankcase pressure limiting valve*

On 6-cylinder engines, vent pipes are used to attach the purge valve to the EVAP canister. The ECM operates the purge valve, when the engine is above a certain temperature and speed, the valve is opened. The outside air is then drawn through the charcoal and into the inlet manifold

When the fuel tank cools and pressure is reduced, the inward venting side of the two-way valve opens, and outside air is drawn through the EVAP canister, and into the tank.

Diesel engines

Crankcase emission control

When the engine is running, a certain amount of combustion gas passes the pistons – 'blow-by' gases – and enters the crankcase. The amount of blow-by is dependent on the overall condition/wear of the engine.

When crankcase emission control is fitted, the blow-by gases from the crankcase are mixed with inlet air, and burned in the combustion chambers.

Ventilation is via the oil drain passages in the cylinder block and cylinder head, and a port in the camshaft cover. The port on the camshaft cover is then connected to the crankcase pressure limiter valve on the turbocharger intake pipe by a rubber vent hose. The crankcase pressure limiter valve limits the depression produced in the crankcase. To prevent oil being drawn into the vent hose, there's a gauze oil separator inside the camshaft cover.

When the engine is running, the depression in the turbocharger intake pipe draws gases through the camshaft cover port and limiter valve. As engine speed increases, the depression in the intake pipe increases and progressively closes the limiter valve, to maintain a fairly constant and safe pressure in the crankcase.

Exhaust emission control

To minimise the amount of pollutants, which escape into the atmosphere, all models are fitted with a catalytic converter in the exhaust system. The main component used in catalytic converters on diesel models is platinum.

Exhaust Gas Recirculation (EGR)

Under certain running conditions, the vacuum-operated EGR valve on the exhaust manifold, diverts exhaust gases into the inlet manifold, where they are used in the combustion process.

The main result of this is to reduce combustion temperatures and, therefore, oxides of nitrogen (NOx) emissions.

From the EGR valve, gases pass to the inlet manifold via a cooler, and a corrugated and insulated metal pipe. Engine coolant, passing through the EGR cooler, reduces the temperature of the exhaust gases to further reduce emissions.

The valve is operated by a solenoid located on the engine bay bulkhead; this gets its vacuum supply from the brake servo pump. The solenoid is controlled by the ECM, which gets a signal from the mass airflow (MAF) sensor.

2.3a Charcoal canister/purge valve – 4-cylinder engines

2 Petrol engine emission control systems – testing and component renewal

Crankcase emission control

1 The components of this system require no attention other than to check that the hose(s) are clear and undamaged at regular intervals.
Note: *When removing hoses to check for condition or blockage, make sure their fitted positions are noted for reassembly.*

Evaporative emission control

Testing

2 If the system is thought to be faulty, disconnect the hoses from the charcoal canister and purge control valve and check that they are clear by blowing through them. Full testing of the system can only be carried out using specialist diagnostic equipment, which is connected to the engine management system diagnostic wiring connector. If the purge control valve or charcoal canister are thought to be faulty, they must be renewed.

Charcoal canister renewal

Note: *Note the locations of the hoses on the canister before removal to ensure correct refitting.*
3 The charcoal canister is located on the left-hand side of the engine compartment, on the suspension turret **(see illustrations)**.
4 Disconnect the battery negative terminal (refer to *Disconnecting the battery* in the Reference Section of this manual).

2.13 Disconnect the wiring connector and the vent hose from the purge valve

2.3b Charcoal canister – 6-cylinder engines

5 Trace the outlet hose back from the canister to the inlet manifold. Release the retaining clip and disconnect the hose from the manifold/throttle housing.
6 Trace the inlet hose back from the canister, then release the retaining clip and disconnect the hose from the fuel tank vent pipe.
7 Release the canister breather/vent hose from the securing clips.
8 On 4-cylinder models, disconnect the wiring connector multiplug from the purge valve (mounted on the top of the canister).
9 Slacken the mounting bracket bolt and withdraw the canister along with the vent hoses.
10 Refitting is a reverse of the removal procedure, ensuring the hoses are correctly and securely reconnected, as noted before removal.

Purge valve renewal

Note: *On 4-cylinder models, the valve is integral with the charcoal canister, and cannot be renewed separately. If the valve is faulty, the complete charcoal canister assembly must be renewed.*
11 Disconnect the battery negative terminal (refer to *Disconnecting the battery* in the Reference Section of this manual).
12 Disconnect the wiring connector multiplug from the purge valve.
13 Squeeze together the quick-release connection on the top of the purge valve to remove the vent hose **(see illustration)**.
14 Slacken and remove the retaining screw and washer from the purge valve and withdraw the valve from the inlet manifold **(see illustration)**.

2.14 Undo the purge valve securing screw – arrowed

3.4 Crankcase pressure limiting valve – arrowed

15 Refitting is a reverse of the removal procedure, ensuring the valve and the mating surfaces are clean.

Exhaust emission control

Testing

16 The performance of the catalytic converter can be checked by measuring the exhaust gases using an exhaust gas analyser.

17 If the exhaust gas CO level is too high, the vehicle should be taken to a Rover dealer so that the engine management system, particularly the heated oxygen sensor (HO_2S), can be thoroughly checked using the special diagnostic equipment. If no fault is found in the engine management system, the fault must be in the catalytic converter, which must be renewed.

Catalytic converter renewal

18 The catalytic converter is part of the exhaust system, refer to Chapter 4A or 4B.

Oxygen sensor renewal

19 Refer to Chapter 4A or 4B, Section 11.

---

3 Diesel engine emission control systems – testing and component renewal

---

Crankcase emission control

Testing

1 The components of this system require no attention other than to check that the hose(s) are clear and undamaged at regular intervals.

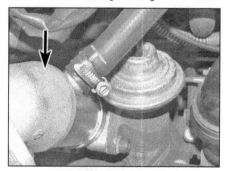

3.20 EGR cooler location

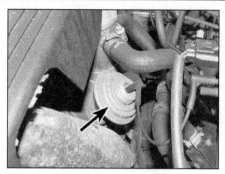

3.13 EGR valve location

2 If the system is thought to be faulty, firstly, check that the hoses are unobstructed and not damaged. On high-mileage cars, particularly when regularly used for short journeys, a sludge-like deposit may be evident inside the system hoses and oil separators. If excessive deposits are present, the relevant component(s) should be removed and cleaned.

3 Periodically inspect the system components for security and damage, and renew them as necessary.

Crankcase pressure limiting valve renewal

4 Slacken the retaining clip and disconnect the breather hose from the valve (see illustration).

5 Slacken the retaining clip, then ease the valve out from the intake pipe, and remove it from the engine compartment. Note the orientation of the valve to ensure correct refitting.

6 Refitting is the reverse of removal, ensuring that the valve is orientated correctly, as noted before removal.

Exhaust emission control

Testing

7 The performance of the catalytic converter can be checked by measuring the exhaust gases using an exhaust gas analyser which is suitable for diesel engines.

8 Before assuming that the catalytic converter is faulty, the vehicle should be taken to a Rover dealer so that the engine management system and the fuel injectors can be thoroughly

3.24 EGR solenoid valve location

checked using the special diagnostic equipment. If no fault is found in the engine management system or the fuel injectors, the fault must be in the catalytic converter, which must be renewed.

Catalytic converter renewal

9 The catalytic converter is part of the exhaust system, refer to Section 18 in Part C of this Chapter.

Exhaust Gas Recirculation

Testing

10 System testing can only be carried out by MG Rover dealers, using special diagnostic equipment connected to the EDC system.

EGR valve renewal

Note: *The following new parts are needed – two EGR valve gaskets.*

11 Disconnect the battery negative terminal (refer to *Disconnecting the battery* in the Reference Section of this manual).

12 Remove the screws securing the engine acoustic cover, and remove it from the top of the engine.

13 The EGR valve is mounted on top of the exhaust manifold, at the rear of the engine (see illustration). Disconnect the vacuum pipe from the valve.

14 Remove two retaining bolts securing the valve to the EGR cooler, and the two securing the valve to the exhaust manifold.

15 Remove the EGR valve from the exhaust manifold/cooler and discard the gaskets.

16 Refitting is the reverse of removal, using new gaskets and ensuring that the bolts are tightened to their specified torque setting.

EGR cooler renewal

Note: *The following new parts are needed – two EGR cooler gaskets.*

17 Disconnect the battery negative terminal (refer to *Disconnecting the battery* in the Reference Section of this manual).

18 Remove the screws securing the engine acoustic cover, and remove it from the top of the engine.

19 Drain the cooling system as described in Chapter 1B.

20 Slacken the securing clips and disconnect two coolant hoses from the EGR cooler (see illustration).

21 Remove two retaining bolts securing the cooler to the EGR valve, and the two securing the cooler to the EGR pipe.

22 Remove the cooler from the EGR valve/ manifold and discard the gaskets.

23 Refitting is the reverse of removal, using new gaskets and ensuring that the bolts are tightened to their specified torque setting.

EGR solenoid valve renewal

24 The valve is located at the rear of the engine compartment on the bulkhead, next to the MAP sensor (see illustration).

25 Disconnect the battery negative terminal (refer to *Disconnecting the battery* in the Reference Section of this manual).

26 Remove the screws securing the engine acoustic cover, and remove it from the top of the engine.

27 Disconnect the wiring connector multiplug from the solenoid valve.

28 Release the two vacuum hoses and disconnect them from the solenoid valve, noting their locations to ensure correct refitting.

29 Unscrew the two securing bolts, and withdraw the valve from its mounting bracket.

30 Refitting is a reversal of removal, but make sure that the hoses are correctly reconnected as noted before removal.

4 Catalytic converter – general information and precautions

General information

1 The catalytic converter reduces harmful exhaust emissions by chemically converting the more poisonous gases to ones that (in theory at least) are less harmful. The chemical reaction is known as an 'oxidising' reaction, or one where oxygen is 'added'.

2 Inside the converter is a honeycomb structure, made of ceramic material and coated with the precious metals palladium, platinum and rhodium (the 'catalyst' which promotes the chemical reaction). The chemical reaction generates heat, which itself promotes the reaction – therefore, once the car has been driven several miles, the body of the converter will be very hot.

3 The ceramic structure contained within the converter is understandably fragile, and will not withstand rough treatment. Since the converter runs at a high temperature, driving through deep standing water (in flood conditions, for example) is to be avoided, since the thermal stresses imposed when plunging the hot converter into cold water may well cause the ceramic internals to fracture, resulting in a 'blocked' converter – a common cause of failure. A converter that has been damaged in this way can be checked by shaking it (do not strike it) – if a rattling noise is heard, this indicates probable failure.

Precautions

4 The catalytic converter is a reliable and simple device which needs no maintenance in itself, but there are some facts of which an owner should be aware if the converter is to function properly for its full service life.

Petrol engine

a) DO NOT use leaded petrol or LRP in a car equipped with a catalytic converter – the lead will coat the precious metals, reducing their converting efficiency and will eventually destroy the converter.

b) Always keep the ignition and fuel systems well-maintained in accordance with the manufacturer's schedule.

c) Consult an approved dealer as soon as possible in the event of misfiring, irregular engine running after a cold start, a significant loss of engine power, or any other malfunction which may indicate a fault in the ignition system. If it is necessary to continue driving, do so for a short time at low engine speed, without labouring the engine.

d) DO NOT switch off the ignition at high engine speeds.

e) DO NOT push- or tow-start the car – this will soak the catalytic converter in unburned fuel, causing it to overheat when the engine does start. Use jump leads (see 'Jump starting').

f) Avoid frequent cold starts one after another.

g) DO NOT allow the fuel tank to become empty.

h) DO NOT use fuel or engine oil additives – these may contain substances harmful to the catalytic converter.

i) DO NOT continue to use the car if the engine burns oil to the extent of leaving a visible trail of blue smoke.

j) Remember that the catalytic converter operates at very high temperatures. DO NOT, therefore, park the car in dry undergrowth, over long grass or piles of dead leaves after a long run.

k) Remember that the catalytic converter is FRAGILE – do not strike it with tools during servicing work.

l) In some cases a sulphurous smell (like that of rotten eggs) may be noticed from the exhaust. This is common to many catalytic converter-equipped cars and once the car has covered a few thousand miles the problem should disappear. This may also depend on the fuel used.

m) The catalytic converter, used on a well-maintained and well-driven car, should last for between 50 000 and 100 000 miles – if the converter is no longer effective it must be renewed.

Diesel engine

5 The catalytic converter fitted to diesel models is simpler than that fitted to petrol models, but it still needs to be treated with respect to avoid problems:

a) DO NOT use fuel or engine oil additives – these may contain substances harmful to the catalytic converter.

b) DO NOT continue to use the car if the engine burns (engine) oil to the extent of leaving a visible trail of blue smoke.

c) Remember that the catalytic converter operates at very high temperatures. DO NOT, therefore, park the car in dry undergrowth, over long grass or piles of dead leaves after a long run.

d) Driving through deep water should be avoided if possible. The sudden cooling effect will fracture the ceramic honeycomb, damaging it beyond repair.

e) Remember that the catalytic converter is FRAGILE – do not strike it with tools during servicing work, and take care handling it when removing it from the car for any reason.

f) If a substantial loss of power is experienced, remember that this could be due to the converter being blocked. This can occur simply as a result of high mileage, but may be due to the ceramic element having fractured and collapsed internally (see general information, paragraph 3). A new converter is the only cure in this instance.

g) The catalytic converter, used on a well-maintained and well-driven car, should last at least 100 000 miles – if the converter is no longer effective, it must be renewed.

Notes

Chapter 5 Part A:
Starting and charging systems

Contents

	Section number
Alternator – testing, removal and refitting	5
Auxiliary drivebelt – removal and refitting	6
Battery – removal and refitting	3
Battery – testing and charging	2
Charging system – testing	4
General information and precautions	1

	Section number
Ignition switch – removal and refitting	10
Oil pressure warning light switch – removal and refitting	11
Starter motor – removal and refitting	8
Starter motor – testing and overhaul	9
Starting system – testing	7

Degrees of difficulty

Easy, suitable for novice with little experience	Fairly easy, suitable for beginner with some experience	Fairly difficult, suitable for competent DIY mechanic	Difficult, suitable for experienced DIY mechanic	Very difficult, suitable for expert DIY or professional

Specifications

System type .... 12 volt, negative earth

Battery
Type:
1.4 and 1.6 litre petrol engines	Yuasa H4 (Sealed for life)
1.8, 2.0 and 2.5 litre petrol engines	Yuasa H5 (Sealed for life)
Diesel engines	Yuasa H6 (Sealed for life)

Capacity/rating (nominal) .... 63 Ah
Charge condition:
Poor	11.5 volts
Normal	12.0 volts
Good	12.7 volts

Alternator
Type:
1.4, 1.6 and 1.8 litre petrol engines	Bosch
2.0 and 2.5 litre petrol engines	Nippon Denso
Diesel engines	Nippon Denso

Output rating (nominal):
1.4 and 1.6 litre petrol engines	75 amps
1.8 litre petrol engines	85 amps
2.0 and 2.5 litre petrol engines	75 amps
Diesel engines	85 amps

Starter motor
Type:
1.4, 1.6 and 1.8 litre petrol engines (manual transmission)	Bosch
1.8 litre petrol engines (automatic transmission)	Nippon Denso
2.0 and 2.5 litre petrol engines	Nippon Denso
Diesel engines	Nippon Denso

Power rating (nominal):
1.4 litre petrol engines	0.8 kW
1.6 litre petrol engines	0.9 kW
1.8 litre petrol engines:	
Manual transmission	1.0 kW
Automatic transmission	1.2 kW
2.0 and 2.5 litre petrol engines	1.8 kW
Diesel engines	1.8 kW

Torque wrench settings

	Nm	lbf ft
4-cylinder petrol engines		
Alternator mounting bracket-to-engine bolt/nut	25	18
Alternator pulley nut	25	18
Alternator-to-mounting bracket nuts/bolts:		
With air conditioning	25	18
Without air conditioning	45	33
Battery cable-to-alternator nut	8	6
Battery cable-to-starter solenoid nut	13	10
Drivebelt tensioner bolt		
M8	25	18
M10	45	33
Right-hand engine torque mounting (1.4 and 1.6 litre engines):		
Torque mounting-to-mounting bracket bolts	60	44
Torque mounting-to-body bolts	45	33
Starter motor bolts/nuts:		
1.4 & 1.6 litre	45	33
1.8 litre (manual transmission)	85	63
1.8 litre (automatic transmission)	25	18
Starter motor support bracket nuts	25	18
6-cylinder petrol engines		
Battery cable-to-starter solenoid nut:		
Manual transmission	13	10
Automatic transmission	9	7
Cambelt cover bolts	25	18
Engine mountings:		
Mounting bracket to engine bolts	45	33
Upper mounting bracket-to-engine bracket bolts	100	74
Upper mounting bracket-to-engine mounting nut	85	63
Engine steady bar mounting bolts	100	74
Starter motor bolts/nuts:		
Manual transmission	85	63
Automatic transmission	45	33
Diesel engines		
Alternator lower fixing bolt/nut	45	33
Alternator mounting bracket-to-coolant elbow bolts	25	18
Alternator upper fixing bolt	25	18
Auxiliary drivebelt idler pulley bolts (without air conditioning)	25	18
Auxiliary drivebelt tensioner bolt	45	33
Battery cable to-alternator stud	4	3
Drivebelt tensioner bolt	25	18
Starter motor bolts	80	59

1 General information and precautions

General information

The engine electrical system consists mainly of the charging and starting systems. Because of their engine-related functions, these components are covered separately from the body electrical devices such as the lights, instruments, etc (which are covered in Chapter 12). On petrol engine models refer to Part B for information on the ignition system, and on diesel models refer to Part C for information on the preheating system.

The electrical system is of the 12 volt negative earth type.

The battery is of the low maintenance or 'maintenance-free' (sealed for life) type and is charged by the alternator, which is belt-driven from the crankshaft pulley.

The starter motor is of the pre-engaged type incorporating an integral solenoid. On starting, the solenoid moves the drive pinion into engagement with the flywheel ring gear before the starter motor is energised. Once the engine has started, a one-way clutch prevents the motor armature being driven by the engine until the pinion disengages from the flywheel.

Further details of the various systems are given in the relevant Sections of this Chapter. While some repair procedures are given, the usual course of action is to renew the component concerned. The owner whose interest extends beyond mere component renewal should obtain a copy of the *Automotive Electrical & Electronic Systems Manual*, available from the publishers of this manual.

Precautions

It is necessary to take extra care when working on the electrical system to avoid damage to semi-conductor devices (diodes and transistors), and to avoid the risk of personal injury. In addition to the precautions given in *Safety first!* at the beginning of this manual, observe the following when working on the system:

• *Always remove rings, watches, etc, before working on the electrical system.* Even with the battery disconnected, capacitive discharge could occur if a component's live terminal is earthed through a metal object. This could cause a shock or nasty burn.

• *Do not reverse the battery connections.* Components such as the alternator, electronic control units, or any other components having semi-conductor circuitry could be irreparably damaged.

• If the engine is being started using jump leads and a slave battery, connect the batteries *positive-to-positive* and *negative-to-negative* (see *Jump starting*). This also applies when connecting a battery charger.

• Never disconnect the battery terminals, the alternator, any electrical wiring or any test instruments when the engine is running.

• Do not allow the engine to turn the alternator when the alternator is not connected.

• Never 'test' for alternator output by 'flashing' the output lead to earth.

• Never use an ohmmeter of the type incorporating a hand-cranked generator for circuit or continuity testing.

• Always ensure that the battery negative lead is disconnected when working on the electrical system.

• Before using electric-arc welding equipment on the car, disconnect the battery, alternator and components such as the fuel injection/ignition electronic control unit to protect them from the risk of damage.

The audio unit fitted as standard equipment by Rover is equipped with a built-in security code to deter thieves. If the power source to the unit is cut, the anti-theft system will activate. Even if the power source is immediately reconnected, the unit will not function until the correct security code has been entered. Therefore, if you do not know the correct security code for the audio unit **do not** disconnect the battery negative terminal of the battery or remove the unit from the vehicle.

2 Battery –
testing and charging

Testing

Standard and low maintenance battery

1 If the vehicle covers a small annual mileage, it is worthwhile checking the specific gravity of the electrolyte every three months to determine the state of charge of the battery. Use a hydrometer to make the check and compare the results with the following table. Note that the specific gravity readings assume an electrolyte temperature of 15°C; for every 10°C below 15°C subtract 0.007. For every 10°C above 15°C add 0.007.

	Ambient temperature:	
	above 25°C	below 25°C
Fully-charged	1.210 to 1.230	1.270 to 1.290
70% charged	1.170 to 1.190	1.230 to 1.250
Discharged	1.050 to 1.070	1.110 to 1.130

2 If the battery condition is suspect, first check the specific gravity of electrolyte in each cell. A variation of 0.040 or more between any cells indicates loss of electrolyte or deterioration of the internal plates.

3 If the specific gravity variation is 0.040 or more, the battery should be renewed. If the cell variation is satisfactory but the battery is discharged, it should be charged as described later in this Section.

Maintenance-free battery

4 In cases where a 'sealed for life' maintenance-free battery is fitted, topping-up and testing of the electrolyte in each cell is not possible. The condition of the battery can therefore only be tested using a battery condition indicator or a voltmeter.

5 If testing the battery using a voltmeter, connect the voltmeter across the battery and compare the result with those given in the Specifications under 'charge condition'. The test is only accurate if the battery has not been subjected to any kind of charge for the previous six hours. If this is not the case, switch on the headlights for 30 seconds, then wait four to five minutes before testing the battery after switching off the headlights. All other electrical circuits must be switched off, so check that the doors and tailgate are fully shut when making the test.

6 If the voltage reading is less than 12.0 volts, then the battery is discharged, whilst a reading of 12.2 to 12.4 volts indicates a partially discharged condition.

7 If the battery is to be charged, remove it from the vehicle (Section 3) and charge it as described later in this Section.

Charging

Note: *The following is intended as a guide only. Always refer to the manufacturer's recommendations (often printed on a label attached to the battery) before charging a battery.*

Standard and low maintenance battery

8 Charge the battery at a rate of 3.5 to 4 amps and continue to charge the battery at this rate until no further rise in specific gravity is noted over a four hour period.

9 Alternatively, a 'trickle charger' charging at the rate of 1.5 amps can safely be used overnight.

10 Specially rapid 'boost' charges that are claimed to restore the power of the battery in 1 to 2 hours are not recommended, as they can cause serious damage to the battery plates through overheating.

11 While charging the battery, note that the temperature of the electrolyte should never exceed 37.8°C.

Maintenance-free battery

12 This battery type takes considerably longer to fully recharge than the standard type, the time taken being dependent on the extent of discharge, but it can take anything up to three days.

13 A constant voltage type charger is required to be set, when connected, to 13.9 to 14.9 volts with a charger current below 25 amps. Using this method, the battery should be useable within three hours, giving a voltage reading of 12.5 volts, but this is for a partially-discharged battery and, as mentioned, full charging can take considerably longer.

14 If the battery is to be charged from a fully-discharged state (condition reading less than 12.2 volts), have it recharged by your Rover dealer or local automotive electrician, as the charge rate is higher and constant supervision during charging is necessary.

3 Battery –
removal and refitting

Note: *Refer to 'Disconnecting the battery' in the Reference Section of this manual before proceeding.*

Removal

1 The battery is located on the left-hand side front of the engine compartment.

2 Slacken the clamp nut and disconnect the negative (earth) lead clamp from the battery terminal **(see illustration)**.

3 Lift the insulation cover and disconnect the positive terminal lead **(see illustration)** in the same way as the negative.

4 Unscrew the bolt and remove the battery retaining clamp, the battery can then be lifted out from the engine compartment **(see illustrations)**.

3.2 Disconnect the earth lead

3.3 Disconnect the positive lead

3.4a Unscrew the bolt (arrowed) to remove the retaining clamp . . .

3.4b . . . and lift the battery from the engine compartment

3.5a Move the ECM to one side . . .

3.5b . . . undo the three retaining bolts . . .

3.5c . . . and withdraw the battery tray

5 To remove the battery tray, first unbolt the engine control module (ECM) and move it to one side, then remove the three bolts from the base of the tray **(see illustrations)**.

6 On models fitted with cruise control, it will be necessary to unbolt the cruise control vacuum pump from the side of the battery tray.

Refitting

7 Refitting is a reversal of removal, but smear petroleum jelly on the terminals after reconnecting the leads to reduce corrosion. Always reconnect the positive lead first, and the negative lead last.

4 Charging system – testing

Note: *Refer to the warnings given in 'Safety*

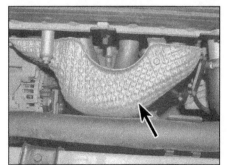

5.4 Remove exhaust manifold heat shield

first!' and in Section 1 of this Chapter before starting work.

1 If the ignition warning light fails to illuminate when the ignition is switched on, first check the alternator wiring connections for security. If satisfactory, check that the warning light bulb has not blown, and that the bulbholder is secure in its location in the instrument panel (see Chapter 12). If the light still fails to illuminate, check the continuity of the warning light feed wire from the alternator to the bulbholder. If all is satisfactory, the alternator is at fault and should be renewed or taken to an auto-electrician for testing and repair.

2 If the ignition warning light illuminates when the engine is running, stop the engine and check that the drivebelt is correctly tensioned (see Chapter 1A or 1B) and that the alternator connections are secure. If all is so far satisfactory, have the alternator checked by an auto-electrician.

5.7a Slacken the upper through-bolt – arrowed

3 If the alternator output is suspect even though the warning light functions correctly, the regulated voltage may be checked as follows.

4 Connect a voltmeter across the battery terminals and start the engine.

5 Increase the engine speed until the voltmeter reading remains steady; the reading should be approximately 13.2 to 14.8 volts, and no more than 14.8 volts.

6 Switch on as many electrical accessories (eg, the headlights, heated rear window and heater blower) as possible, and check that the alternator maintains the regulated voltage at around 13.2 to 14.8 volts.

7 If the regulated voltage is not as stated, the fault may be due to worn brushes, weak brush springs, a faulty voltage regulator, a faulty diode, a severed phase winding or worn or damaged slip-rings. The alternator should be renewed or taken to an auto-electrician for testing and repair.

5 Alternator – testing, removal and refitting

Testing

1 If the alternator is thought to be suspect, it should be removed from the vehicle and taken to an auto-electrician for testing on specialist equipment. However, check on the cost of repairs before proceeding, as it may prove more economical to obtain a new or exchange alternator. **Note:** *At the time of writing, no spare brushes are available from Rover dealers.*

Removal

2 Disconnect the battery negative terminal (refer to *Disconnecting the battery* in the Reference Section of this manual).

3 Where fitted remove the screws securing the engine acoustic cover, and remove it from the top of the engine.

4-cylinder petrol engine models without air conditioning

4 To give better access, undo the retaining nut and bolts and remove the heat shield from the top of the exhaust manifold **(see illustration)**.

5 Undo the nut securing the battery cable to the rear of the alternator, and release the cable.

6 Disconnect the electrical wiring multiplug connector from the rear of the alternator.

7 Slacken the nut on the through-bolt attaching the alternator to the upper mounting bracket **(see illustrations)**, do not remove at this point.

8 Slacken the nut and bolt securing the alternator to the adjusting bracket **(see illustration)**.

9 Release drivebelt tension by turning the adjusting bolt anti-clockwise – the adjusting bolt screws into the end of the adjusting bracket **(see illustration)**.

Caution: Do not apply excessive torque

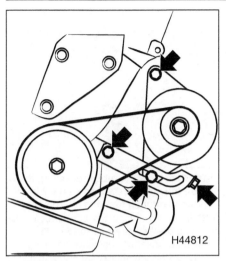

5.7b Alternator drive arrangement –
fixing points arrowed

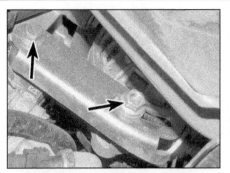

5.8 Slacken the alternator adjusting
bracket nut and bolt – arrowed

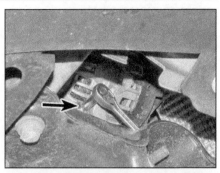

5.9 Turn adjusting bolt in the end of the
adjusting bracket – arrowed

*to the bolt. If it is seized, apply anti-seize
compound.*

10 Release the drivebelt from the alternator
pulley.

11 Remove the alternator upper mounting
through-bolt and nut, release the alternator
from the mounting bracket and withdraw it
from the vehicle.

12 To remove the alternator pulley, use an 8 mm
Allen key to hold the alternator shaft still, while
using a special pulley securing nut tool (Rover
tool -18G 1653) to remove the securing nut.

4-cylinder petrol engine models with air conditioning

13 Apply the handbrake, chock the rear
roadwheels, then jack up the front of the car
and support it on axle stands (see *Jacking and
vehicle support*).

14 Where fitted, undo the retaining screws
and remove the splash shield from under the
engine.

15 Working in the engine compartment,
undo the upper retaining nut and bolts from
the exhaust manifold heat shield and move it
away from the engine.

16 Remove the auxiliary drivebelt as
described in Section 6 of this Chapter.

17 Slacken and remove the alternator upper
mounting bolt.

18 Slacken the alternator lower mounting
nut.

19 Pivot the alternator forwards and remove
the alternator upper mounting bracket bolt
(see illustration).

20 If not already done, release the heat shield
from the mounting bracket stud and remove
the alternator upper mounting bracket from
the engine.

21 Using a stud extractor (or two nuts locked
together) remove the mounting bracket stud
from the cylinder head **(see illustration)**, and
then withdraw the heat shield upwards away
from the exhaust manifold.

22 Remove the plastic cap and undo the nut

5.19 Undo the upper alternator bracket
bolt – arrowed

securing the battery cable to the rear of the
alternator, and release the cable.

23 Disconnect the electrical wiring multiplug
connector from the rear of the alternator.

24 Remove the alternator lower through-bolt,
and then release the alternator from the lower
mounting bracket. There is a metal sleeve/
spacer fitted in the lower bracket, which
makes the alternator a tight fit. This sleeve/
spacer may need to be tapped out slightly
to allow the alternator to be refitted **(see
illustration)**.

25 To remove the alternator pulley, use an 8 mm
Allen key to hold the alternator shaft still, while
using a special pulley securing nut tool (Rover
tool -18G 1653) to remove the securing nut.

6-cylinder petrol engine models

26 Apply the handbrake, chock the rear
roadwheels, then jack up the front of the car
and support it on axle stands (see *Jacking and
vehicle support*).

5.24 Sleeve/spacer in alternator lower
mounting bracket

5.21 Using two nuts locked together to
remove the bracket stud

27 Where fitted, undo the retaining screws
and remove the splash shield from under the
engine.

28 Working under the vehicle, slacken the
engine lower steady bar retaining bolts.
Remove the bolt securing the steady bar to
the sump bracket and swivel the steady bar
from the engine.

29 Remove the auxiliary drivebelt as
described in Section 6 of this Chapter.

30 Remove the rubber cap and undo the
nut securing the battery cable to the rear of
the alternator, and release the cable **(see
illustration)**.

31 Disconnect the electrical wiring multiplug
connector from the rear of the alternator.

32 Slacken and remove the alternator upper
mounting bolt.

33 Slacken the alternator lower mounting
bolt, and then carefully move the engine
forward (making sure it is safely supported

5.30 Disconnect the wiring from the
alternator

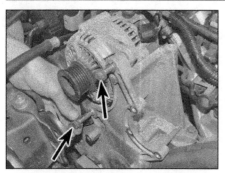

5.33 Remove the two mounting bolts (arrowed) from the alternator

5.34 Remove the alternator from the mounting bracket

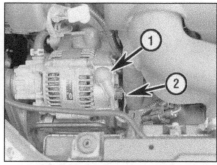

5.36 Peel back the rubber cover (1), then undo the nut and disconnect the wiring connector (2) from the alternator

on the jack). When the lower mounting bolt is clear of the body panel, withdraw it from the alternator **(see illustration)**.

34 The alternator can now be released from its mounting bracket and withdrawn from the vehicle **(see illustration)**.

Diesel engine models

35 Remove the auxiliary drivebelt as described in Section 6 of this Chapter.

36 Remove the plastic cap and undo the nut securing the battery cable to the rear of the alternator, and release the cable **(see illustration)**.

37 Disconnect the electrical wiring multiplug connector from the rear of the alternator.

38 Slacken and remove the retaining bolt securing the brake servo vacuum pipe to the top of the camshaft cover.

39 Undo the four retaining bolts securing the brake vacuum pump to the alternator **(see illustration)**.

40 Slacken and remove the alternator upper mounting bolt **(see illustration)**.

41 Remove the alternator lower mounting bolt **(see illustration)**. Carefully release the alternator from the brake vacuum pump as it is being removed from the engine compartment.

Refitting

42 Refitting is a reversal of the removal procedure, noting:
  a) Use a torque wrench to tighten any fastenings to their specified torque.
  b) On diesel models, clean the mating face between the alternator and brake vacuum pump.

c) Refit the auxiliary drivebelt with reference to Section 6.

6 Auxiliary drivebelt – removal and refitting
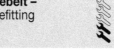

1 Disconnect the battery negative terminal (refer to *Disconnecting the battery* in the Reference Section of this manual).

2 Where fitted, remove the screws securing the engine acoustic cover, and remove it from the top of the engine.

3 Chock the rear wheels and apply the handbrake. Jack up the front of the vehicle, and support securely on axle stands (see *Jacking and vehicle support*). Remove the right-hand front roadwheel and where applicable, remove the wheel arch liner.

4 Where fitted, undo the retaining screws and remove the splash shield from under the engine.

4-cylinder petrol engine models without air conditioning

Removal

5 Remove the power steering pump drivebelt as described in Chapter 10.

6 On 1.4 and 1.6 litre engines, undo the four retaining bolts and remove the torque mounting from under the right-hand front wing.

7 Slacken the alternator upper mounting nut and bolt and also the lower bolt securing the alternator adjustment bracket to the engine.

8 Slacken the nut on the alternator to the adjusting bracket **(see illustration 5.8)**.

9 Release drivebelt tension by turning the adjusting bolt anti-clockwise – the adjusting bolt screws into the end of the adjusting bracket **(see illustration 5.9)**.

Caution: Do not apply excessive torque to the bolt. If it seized, apply anti-seize compound.

10 Release the belt from the pulleys and remove it from the vehicle.

Refitting

11 Refitting is a reversal of the removal procedure, noting:
  a) Make sure that all pulleys are clean and check for any damage.
  b) Check and adjust the tension of the drivebelt as described in Chapter 1A, Section 12.
  c) Use a torque wrench to tighten any fastenings to their specified torque.

4-cylinder petrol engine models with air conditioning

Removal

12 Remove the power steering pump drivebelt as described in Chapter 10.

13 On 1.4 and 1.6 litre engines, undo the four retaining bolts and remove the torque mounting from under the right-hand front wing.

14 Fit a 13 mm spanner to the hexagon on the belt tensioner, and rotate fully clockwise to release belt tension.

15 Lock the tensioner in this position by

5.39 Undo the four bolts (arrowed) – alternator removed for clarity

5.40 Removing the upper mounting bolt

5.41 Lower mounting bolt and nut – arrowed

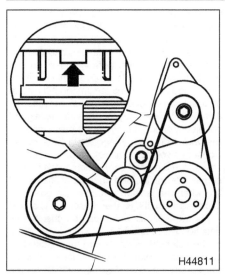

6.19 Renew belt before indicator reaches the right-hand end of the slot – arrowed

fitting a 3 mm diameter locking-pin through a hole in the tensioner backplate.

16 Release the belt from the pulleys and tensioner, and remove the belt.

Refitting

17 Make sure that all pulleys are clean and check for any damage, then fit the new belt around the pulleys.

18 Use the 13 mm spanner to relieve tension on the locking pin, and remove the pin. Release the spanner, and allow the tension pulley to rest on the belt.

19 Ensure that the indicator marking on the tensioner falls within the 'gauge' recessed into the tensioner backplate **(see illustration)**. Check and adjust the tension of the drivebelt as described in Chapter 1A, Section 12.

20 Fit the roadwheel, engine undertray, engine cover and wheel arch liner as required. Remove the stands, and lower the vehicle to the ground.

21 Use a torque wrench to tighten the roadwheel nuts to the specified torque.

22 Reconnect the battery earth lead.

6-cylinder petrol engine models

Removal

23 Undo the two retaining bolts and remove the power steering reservoir from the right-hand inner wing panel. Move the reservoir to one side, without disconnecting the pipes **(see illustration)**.

24 Slacken and remove the retaining bolts from the upper engine steady bar and remove it from across the top of the right-hand engine mounting **(see illustration)**.

25 Place a jack beneath the engine, with a block of wood on the jack head. Raise the jack until it is supporting the weight of the engine. Alternately, attach an engine support bar to the lifting brackets and support the weight of the engine with the bar across the engine bay.

26 Undo the two retaining bolts and remove

6.23 Remove the power steering fluid reservoir and move it to one side

the timing belt upper cover from the engine mounting bracket **(see illustration)**.

27 With the engine supported from underneath, slacken and remove the three mounting bolts and nut from the top of the upper engine mounting bracket and withdraw the bracket from the engine **(see illustration)**.

28 Remove the securing bolts from the engine mounting bracket and position the power steering pipe and air conditioning pipe to one side.

29 Slacken and remove the four engine mounting bracket retaining bolts and withdraw the mounting bracket from the engine **(see illustration)**.

30 Using a 3/8" square drive socket bar/ratchet, turn the auxiliary drivebelt tensioner anti-clockwise and release the auxiliary belt from around the pulleys **(see illustration)**. Note the routing of the belt, before it is removed.

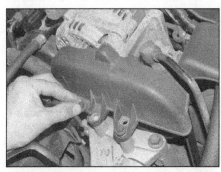

6.26 Undo the two cover retaining bolts

6.29 Removing the engine mounting bracket

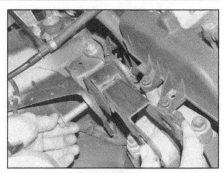

6.24 Removing the upper steady bar

31 With the belt removed, carefully release the pressure on the tensioner and let it come back to its stop.

Refitting

32 Make sure that all pulleys are clean and check for any damage.

33 Fit the 3/8" square drive socket bar to the tensioner pulley **(see illustration)**, as described in the removal procedure and use it rotate the tensioner assembly anti-clockwise to the limit of its travel.

34 Whilst holding the tensioner in the fully-rotated position, pass the new drivebelt around the pulleys as noted on removal, ensuring that the 'vee' pattern on the drive surface of the belt engages correctly with the grooves on each of the pulleys.

35 Manoeuvre the flat surface of the belt under the tensioner pulley, then slowly release the pressure on the 3/8" square drive socket bar, until the tensioner roller contacts the drivebelt.

6.27 Removing the upper engine mounting bracket

6.30 Release the tension and remove the auxiliary belt

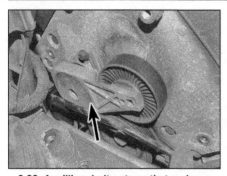

6.33 Auxilliary belt automatic tensioner – arrowed

36 Using a spanner on the crankshaft pulley bolt, turn the crankshaft through one revolution to allow the belt tension to be evenly distributed and check that the belt is correctly engaged with the pulleys.

37 The remainder of the refitting procedure is a reversal of the removal, noting:
a) *Check and adjust the tension of the drive-belt as described in Chapter 1A, Section 12.*
b) *Use a torque wrench to tighten any fastenings to their specified torque.*

Diesel engine models

Removal

38 Working through the right-hand wheel arch, fit a 15 mm spanner to the tensioner pulley bolt and use it to rotate the whole tensioner assembly clockwise, so that the tension on the drivebelt is released.

39 Hold the tension pulley in this position and release the auxiliary drivebelt from around the pulleys. Note the routing of the belt before it is removed. Where fitted, undo the retaining bolt(s) and remove the shield from above the alternator/pump pulley **(see illustration)**.

40 With the belt removed, carefully release the pressure on the tensioner and let it come back to its stop.

Refitting

41 Make sure that all pulleys are clean and check for any damage.

42 Fit a spanner to the tensioner pulley bolt (as described in *Removal*) and use it rotate the whole tensioner assembly clockwise to the limit of its travel.

43 Whilst holding the tensioner in the fully-rotated position, pass the new drivebelt around the pulleys as noted on removal, ensuring that the 'vee' pattern on the drive surface of the belt engages correctly with the grooves on each of the pulleys.

44 Manoeuvre the flat surface of the belt under the tensioner pulley. Using the ring spanner, slowly release the tensioner assembly, until it contacts the drivebelt.

45 Using a spanner on the crankshaft pulley bolt, turn the crankshaft through one revolution to allow the belt tension to be evenly distributed and check that the belt is correctly engaged with both pulleys. If necessary, check and adjust the tension of the drivebelt as described in Chapter 1B, Section 12.

6.39 Pulley shield – arrowed

46 Fit the roadwheel, engine undertray, engine cover and wheel arch liner as required. Remove the stands, and lower the vehicle to the ground.

47 Use a torque wrench to tighten the roadwheel nuts to the specified torque.

48 Reconnect the battery earth lead.

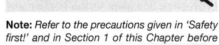

7 Starting system – testing

Note: *Refer to the precautions given in 'Safety first!' and in Section 1 of this Chapter before starting work.*

1 If the starter motor fails to operate when the ignition key is turned to the appropriate position, the following possible causes may be to blame.
a) *The battery is faulty.*
b) *The electrical connections between the switch, solenoid, battery and starter motor are somewhere failing to pass the necessary current from the battery through the starter to earth.*
c) *The solenoid is faulty.*
d) *The starter motor is mechanically or electrically defective.*

2 To check the battery, switch on the headlights. If they dim after a few seconds, this indicates that the battery is discharged – recharge (see Section 2) or renew the battery. If the headlights glow brightly, turn the ignition switch to the start position, and observe the lights. If they dim, then this indicates that current is reaching the starter motor; therefore the fault must lie in the starter motor. If the lights continue to glow brightly (and no clicking sound can be heard from the starter motor solenoid), this indicates that there is a fault in the circuit or solenoid – see following paragraphs. If the starter motor turns slowly when operated, but the battery is in good condition, then this indicates that either the starter motor is faulty, or there is considerable resistance somewhere in the circuit.

3 If a fault in the circuit is suspected, disconnect the battery leads (including the earth connection to the body), the starter/solenoid wiring and the engine/transmission earth strap. Thoroughly clean the connections,

and reconnect the leads and wiring, then use a voltmeter or test lamp to check that full battery voltage is available at the battery positive lead connection to the solenoid, and that the earth is sound. Smear petroleum jelly around the battery terminals to prevent corrosion – corroded connections are amongst the most frequent causes of electrical system faults.

4 If the battery and all connections are in good condition, check the circuit by disconnecting the wire from the solenoid blade terminal. Connect a voltmeter or test lamp between the wire end and a good earth (such as the battery negative terminal), and check that the wire is live when the ignition switch is turned to the 'start' position. If it is, then the circuit is sound – if not, the circuit wiring can be checked as described in Chapter 12.

5 The solenoid contacts can be checked by connecting a voltmeter or test lamp between the battery positive feed connection on the starter side of the solenoid, and earth. When the ignition switch is turned to the 'start' position, there should be a reading or lighted bulb, as applicable. If there is no reading or lighted bulb, the solenoid is faulty and should be renewed.

6 If the circuit and solenoid are proved sound, the fault must lie in the starter motor. In this event, it may be possible to have the starter motor overhauled by a specialist, but check on the cost of spares before proceeding, as it may prove more economical to obtain a new or exchange motor.

8 Starter motor – removal and refitting

Removal

All engines

1 Disconnect the battery negative terminal (refer to *Disconnecting the battery* in the Reference Section of this manual).

2 Where fitted remove the screws securing the engine acoustic cover, and remove it from the top of the engine.

3 Remove the air cleaner assembly.

4 Chock the rear wheels and then apply the handbrake. Jack up the front of the vehicle, and support securely on axle stands (see *Jacking and vehicle support*). Remove the right-hand front roadwheel and, where applicable, remove the wheel arch liner.

5 Where fitted, undo the retaining screws and remove the splash shield from under the engine.

6 Remove the plastic cap and undo the nut securing the battery cable to the rear of the starter solenoid, and release the cable **(see illustration)**.

7 Disconnect the push-on connector from the starter solenoid.

1.4 and 1.6 litre engines

8 Remove the starter motor upper securing

bolt, and disconnect the earth lead **(see illustration)**.
9 Remove the two lower securing bolts, and remove the starter motor **(see illustration)**.

1.8 litre engines with manual transmission

10 Remove the securing nut from the lower starter motor bolt, and withdraw the bolt from the transmission housing.
11 Remove the securing nut from the upper starter motor bolt, and withdraw the bolt from the transmission housing.
12 The starter motor can then be withdrawn from the transmission housing.

1.8 litre engines with automatic transmission

13 Remove the three bolts securing the flywheel front cover plate and withdraw the plate from the transmission housing.
14 Remove the two starter motor securing bolts, and withdraw it from the transmission housing.

6-cylinder engines with manual transmission

15 Release the charcoal canister from its mounting bracket on the left-hand inner wing panel to gain better access to the starter motor.
16 Remove the lower starter motor bolt from the transmission housing.
17 Slacken and remove the upper starter motor securing bolt **(see illustration)**, and then withdraw the starter motor from the transmission housing. Note the position of any wiring brackets, secured by the starter motor mounting bolts for refitting.

6-cylinder engines with automatic transmission

18 Remove the battery and battery tray with reference to Section 3 of this Chapter.
19 Remove the three securing bolts, and withdraw the starter motor from the transmission housing.

Diesel engine models

20 Disconnect the wiring multiplug from the mass airflow (MAF) sensor in the air intake pipe **(see illustration)**.
21 Slacken the securing clip and disconnect the breather hose from the camshaft cover.
22 Slacken the securing clip and disconnect the air intake hose from the turbocharger and move the air intake hose to one side.
23 Remove two bolts securing the starter motor and remove it **(see illustration)**.

Refitting

24 Refitting is a reversal of the removal procedure, noting:
a) Clean the mating faces of the starter motor and flywheel housing.
b) Use a torque wrench to tighten all nuts and bolts to the specified torque.

9 Starter motor – testing and overhaul

If the starter motor is thought to be suspect, it should be removed from the vehicle and taken to an auto-electrician for testing. Most auto-electricians will be able to supply and fit

brushes at a reasonable cost. However, check on the cost of repairs before proceeding, as it may prove more economical to obtain a new or exchange motor.

10 Ignition switch – removal and refitting

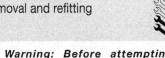

⚠️ *Warning: Before attempting removal of the ignition switch, carefully read the precautions about the SRS system in Chapter 12.*

Removal

1 Disconnect the battery negative terminal (refer to *Disconnecting the battery* in the Reference Section of this manual).
2 Undo the three retaining screws and remove the lower facia trim panel from the driver's side of the vehicle.
3 Undo the three retaining screws and remove the steering column lower and upper shrouds.
4 Trace the wiring back from the ignition switch and, depending on type of switch fitted, either disconnect the two wiring multiplugs from the fusebox, or the single wiring multiplug from the facia main wiring harness.
5 Working along the underside of the steering column, unclip the ignition switch wiring harness from the securing clips.
6 Undo the two ignition switch securing screws and withdraw it from the back of the steering lock assembly.

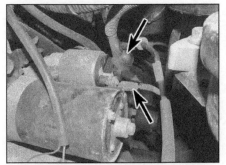

8.6 Disconnect the wiring connectors (arrowed) – 6-cylinder model shown

8.8 Starter motor upper mounting bolt – arrowed

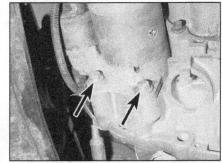

8.9 Starter motor lower mounting bolts – arrowed

8.17 Starter motor upper mounting bolt – arrowed

8.20 Disconnect the wiring connector from the MAF sensor – arrowed

8.23 Removing the starter motor – engine removed for clarity

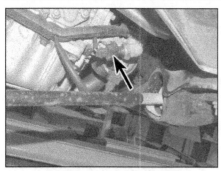

11.1 Oil pressure switch (and oil temperature sensor) location – 4-cylinder petrol engines

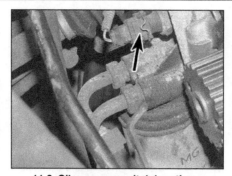

11.2 Oil pressure switch location – 6-cylinder petrol engines

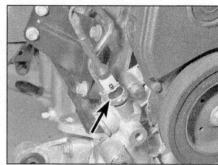

11.3 Oil pressure switch location – diesel engines

Refitting

7 Refitting is a reversal of the removal procedure.

11 Oil pressure warning light switch – removal and refitting

Location

4-cylinder petrol engines

1 The oil pressure switch is screwed – at an angle – into the oil filter housing. Also screwed into the filter housing, adjacent to the pressure switch, is an oil temperature sensor, which is used by the engine management system **(see illustration)**.

6-cylinder petrol engines

2 The oil pressure switch is screwed into the top of the oil filter housing **(see illustration)**.

Diesel engines

3 The oil pressure switch is screwed into the top of the oil filter housing **(see illustration)**.

Removal

4 Disconnect the battery negative terminal (refer to *Disconnecting the battery* in the Reference Section of this manual).

5 Jack up the front of the vehicle, and support securely on axle stands (see *Jacking and vehicle support*). Remove the right-hand front road wheel and inner wing panel.

6 On diesel engine models, remove the engine undertray.

7 Disconnect the multiplug from the switch.

8 Position a container under the switch to catch any oil that will leak out.

9 Unscrew the switch from the housing.

Refitting

10 Refitting is a reversal of the removal procedure, noting:

  a) *Clean and dry the switch threads.*
  b) *Tighten the switch securely.*
  c) *Check/top-up the engine oil level – see 'Weekly Checks'.*

Chapter 5 Part B:
Ignition system – petrol engines

Contents

	Section number		Section number
General information and precautions	1	Ignition system – testing	2
Ignition HT coils (4-cylinder engines) – removal and refitting	3	Ignition timing – checking and adjustment	5
Ignition HT coils (6-cylinder engines) – removal and refitting	4	Spark plug renewal	See Chapter 1A

Degrees of difficulty

Easy, suitable for novice with little experience	**Fairly easy,** suitable for beginner with some experience	**Fairly difficult,** suitable for competent DIY mechanic	**Difficult,** suitable for experienced DIY mechanic	**Very difficult,** suitable for expert DIY or professional

Specifications

General

System type:

4-cylinder engines .... Rover modular engine management system version 3 (MEMS 3) ignition system integrated with indirect multi-point fuel injection system

6-cylinder engines .... Siemens engine management system, sequential multi-point fuel injection system, variable inlet manifold geometry, integrated with ignition system

Firing order

4-cylinder engines .... 1-3-4-2 (No 1 cylinder at timing belt end)

6-cylinder engines .... 1-6-5-4-3-2 (front bank 1, 3 and 5; rear bank 2, 4 and 6)

Torque wrench settings

	Nm	lbf ft
Ignition coil securing bolts/nuts	9	7
Spark plugs to cylinder head	25	18

1 General information and precautions

The ignition system produces the sparks to ignite the fuel/air mixture in each cylinder at precisely the right moment. The system is controlled by the Engine Control Module (ECM), which is the main component of the Engine Management System (EMS).

The 4-cylinder engines have two coils – one serving two cylinders. The two coils are attached to the camshaft cover above the spark plugs for cylinders 1 and 3. In this system, each cylinder is paired with the cylinder opposite in the firing order – 1 and 4, and 2 and 3. The ends of each coil secondary windings are attached to spark plugs for the paired opposites. These two plugs are in cylinders which are at Top Dead Centre (TDC) at the same time – one cylinder at TDC on the compression stroke, and the other at TDC on the exhaust stroke. When the ECM switches off the primary winding supply, high voltage is supplied to both plugs simultaneously to complete the series circuit. The spark created by the plug in the cylinder on exhaust stroke is, of course, not needed, so this method of firing is known as a 'wasted spark' system. Because the polarity of the primary and secondary windings is fixed, one plug fires in a 'conventional' direction – ie, from centre electrode to side electrode, and the other plug fires in reverse – from side electrode to centre electrode.

The 6-cylinder engines have six coils – one per cylinder. The coils on the rear bank of cylinders are attached to the camshaft cover above the spark plugs for cylinders 2, 4 and 6. The coils on the front bank of cylinders are remote mounted coils attached to the inlet manifold and have HT leads to the spark plugs for cylinders 1, 3 and 5.

Ignition timing

The precise point at which the spark is needed is constantly monitored and adjusted by the ECM. The ignition timing profile for a wide range of engine operating conditions is developed during engine testing, and programmed into the ECM. The ignition timing is not adjustable.

Precautions

Refer to the precautions to be observed given in Chapter 4A, Section 1.

⚠ *Warning: The HT voltage generated by an electronic ignition system is extremely high and, in certain circumstances, could prove fatal. Take care to avoid receiving electric shocks from the HT side of the ignition system. Do not handle HT leads, or touch the distributor or coil, when the engine is running. If tracing faults in the HT circuit, use well-insulated tools to manipulate live leads. Persons with surgically implanted cardiac pacemaker devices should keep well clear of the ignition circuits, components and test equipment.*

2 Ignition system – testing

⚠ *Warning: DO NOT attempt to check for a spark by holding a HT cable a short distance from an earth point. The voltages are extremely high, and can easily cause serious injury or death. In addition, electronic components will be damaged.*
Caution: Electronic components are easily damaged by wrong connections, or attempted connection of unsuitable test equipment.
Note: *If simple visual checks do not reveal the cause of any fault, the engine management system should have a full diagnostic check performed by and MG Rover dealer.*

1 If an engine management system fault is suspected, carry out the following checks:
  a) *Loose or dirty electrical connections/ plugs.*
  b) *Chafing/frayed wiring.*
  c) *HT voltage tracking due to dampness.*
  d) *Air cleaner filter clean.*
  e) *Engine breather hoses correctly fitted, and clear.*
  f) *Coils and connections secure.*
  g) *Spark plugs in good condition.*
  h) *If the engine will not start, check that the fuel cut-off switch has not been triggered.*

3 Ignition HT coils (4-cylinder engines) – removal and refitting

Removal

1 Disconnect the battery negative lead. **Note:** *Before disconnecting the battery, refer to 'Disconnecting the battery' at the rear of this manual.*
2 Remove three bolts securing coil/plug cover to camshaft cover, and remove the cover **(see illustration)**.
3 Note the position and clipping of the HT leads and cables running to the coils. Release the HT leads, and pull the tubular connectors from the spark plugs next to the two coils **(see illustration)**.
4 Remove the two bolts attaching each coil to the camshaft cover, and pull the coils from the spark plugs **(see illustration)**.
5 Withdraw the coil from the top of the spark plug, disconnect the wiring connector and remove the HT lead from each coil **(see illustration)**.

Refitting

6 Refitting is a reversal of the removal procedure, noting:
  a) *Ensure that all cables are correctly connected, routed and clipped.*
  b) *Use a torque wrench to tighten the coil securing bolts to the specified torque.*

3.2 Remove coil/plug cover

3.3 Pull the HT lead connector from the spark plug

3.4 Remove the two coil bolts . . .

3.5 . . . and withdraw the coil

4.1 Removing the engine acoustic cover

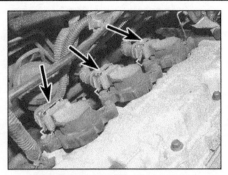

4.4 Wiring connectors – arrowed

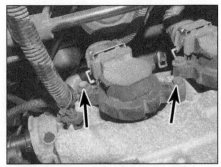

4.5a Undo the two bolts (arrowed) . . .

4.5b . . . and withdraw the coil

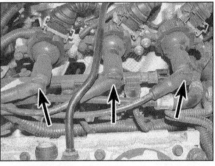

4.6 Disconnect the HT leads – arrowed

4.8 Earth lead securing nut – arrowed

4 Ignition HT coils (6-cylinder engines) – removal and refitting

Removal

1 Disconnect the battery negative lead. **Note:** *Before disconnecting the battery, refer to 'Disconnecting the battery' at the rear of this manual.* Undo the retaining screws and remove the engine acoustic cover **(see illustration).**

2 Each spark plug has a separate ignition coil, either located directly over the top of the plug (rear bank) or connected by HT leads (front bank).

Rear bank

3 To gain better access, remove the inlet manifold as described in Chapter 4B, Section 12.

4 Note the position of the wiring cables running to the coils and disconnect the multiplug connectors from the coils **(see illustration).**

5 Undo the two retaining bolts attaching each of the coils to the camshaft cover; pull the coils upwards to release them from the spark plugs **(see illustrations).**

Front bank

6 Note the position of the HT leads running to each spark plug and pull them to disconnect them from the coils **(see illustration).**

7 Note the position of the wiring cables running to the coils and disconnect the multiplug connectors from the coils.

8 Undo the retaining nut and disconnect the earth lead, noting its position for refitting **(see illustration).**

9 Undo the retaining bolt and nut attaching each of the coils to the inlet manifold and remove the coil.

Refitting

10 Refitting is a reversal of the removal procedure, noting:
  a) *Ensure that all cables are correctly connected, routed and clipped.*
  b) *Use a torque wrench to tighten the coil securing bolts to the specified torque.*

5 Ignition timing – checking and adjustment

The ignition timing profile is programmed into the ECM and cannot be adjusted.

Chapter 5 Part C:
Preheating system – diesel engines

Contents

	Section number		Section number
General description	1	Glow plugs – removal, inspection and refitting	3
Glow plug relay – removal and refitting	4	Preheating system – testing	2

Degrees of difficulty

Easy, suitable for novice with little experience	**Fairly easy,** suitable for beginner with some experience	**Fairly difficult,** suitable for competent DIY mechanic	**Difficult,** suitable for experienced DIY mechanic	**Very difficult,** suitable for expert DIY or professional

Specifications

Glow plugs

Type .... Beru 0100226 184

Torque wrench settings	Nm	lbf ft
Glow plugs	20	15

---

1 General description

To assist cold starting, diesel engines have a preheating system controlled by the Engine Control Module (ECM), which is the main component of the Electronic Diesel Control system (EDC).

A glow plug for each cylinder is installed in the cylinder head. Glow plugs are miniature electric heating elements with a heated probe at one end and an electrical connection at the other. The probe is positioned to preheat air and fuel spray entering the cylinder. Preheating improves fuel ignition and combustion, and so improves engine starting in cold weather.

The glow plugs are connected in parallel to a supply from a relay switched by the ECM, and the circuit is completed to earth via the plug bodies.

When the ignition switch is turned to position II, the relay is energised. Voltage is fed to the glow plugs, which heat up rapidly, and an indicator lamp on the instrument panel is lit, this is known as preheating. The length of time the relay is energised is determined by the coolant temperature signal fed to the ECM. At the end of the calculated time, the relay is de-energised, and the indicator lamp goes out. If the starter motor is operated before preheating is complete, the relay is de-energised and the lamp goes out.

After the engine has been started, the glow plugs remain supplied with a current. This is known as post-heating phase, which occurs immediately after the engine has been started, and the period of post-heating depends on the temperature of the coolant.

3.3 Remove the nuts and disconnect the cables

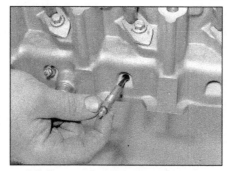

3.5 Remove the glow plugs from the cylinder head

4.1 Glow plug relay location – arrowed

2 Preheating system – testing

Caution: Electronic components are easily damaged by wrong connections, or attempted connection of unsuitable test equipment.
Note: *If the following checks do not reveal the cause of any fault, the engine management system should have a full diagnostic check performed by an MG Rover dealer.*

1 If the preheating system is thought to be faulty, carry out the following checks on the glow plugs.

2 Connect a voltmeter or 12 volt test lamp between the glow plug supply cable, and a good earth point on the engine.

Caution: Make sure that the live connection is kept well clear of the engine and bodywork.

3 Have an assistant activate the system by turning the ignition key to the second position, and check that battery voltage is applied to the glow plug electrical connection. Note the time for which the warning light is lit, and the total time for which voltage is applied before the system cuts out.

4 If there is no supply at all at the glow plugs, the relay, ECU or associated wiring is at fault, see Chapter 12.

5 To locate a faulty glow plug, first operate the preheating system to allow the glow plugs to reach working temperature, then disconnect the battery negative cable and position it away from the battery terminal.

6 Disconnect the main supply cable and the interconnecting wire or strap from the top of the heater plugs. Be careful not to drop the nuts and washers.

7 Measure the electrical resistance between the glow plug terminal and the engine earth. A reading of anything more than a few ohms indicates that the glow plug is defective.

8 As a final check, remove the glow plugs and inspect them visually, as described in the following Section.

9 If this does not locate the fault, take the vehicle to a Rover dealer or diesel specialist who will have the diagnostic equipment necessary to pin-point the fault.

3 Glow plugs – removal, inspection and refitting

Note: *If glow plug No 4 is to be removed, the fuel injection pump must be removed first to access it.*

Removal

1 Disconnect the battery negative terminal (refer to *Disconnecting the battery* in the Reference Section of this manual).

2 To access number four glow plug, remove the fuel injection pump as described in Chapter 4C, Section 10.

3 Remove the terminal nuts and washers attaching the cables to the glow plugs, and disconnect the cables **(see illustration)**. Note the fitted position of the main feed cable to the glow plug.

4 Clean the area around the base of the glow plugs to prevent dirt getting into the cylinders.

5 Unscrew and remove the glow plugs from the cylinder head **(see illustration)**.

Inspection

6 Inspect the plugs for any sign of damage. Burnt or eroded tips may be caused by incorrect injector spray pattern. Have the injectors tested if this sort of damage is found.

7 If the heater plugs are in good physical condition, check them electrically using a 12 volt test lamp or continuity tester as described in the previous Section.

Caution: If the plugs are working, the tip will get red hot after a few seconds. Ensure that all connections are tight. Secure the plug so that it cannot touch any other component whilst voltage is applied, or whilst it is still hot. Allow the plug to cool before handling.

8 The heater plugs can be energised by applying 12 volts to them to verify that they heat up evenly and in the required time. Observe the following precautions.

a) Support the heater plug by clamping it carefully in a vice or self-locking pliers. Remember it will become red hot.

b) Make sure that the power supply or test lead incorporates a fuse or overload trip to protect against damage from a short-circuit.

c) After testing, allow the heater plug to cool for several minutes before attempting to handle it.

9 A heater plug in good condition will start to glow red at the tip after drawing current for 5 seconds or so. Any plug that takes much longer to start glowing, or which starts glowing in the middle instead of at the tip indicates the glow plug is defective.

Refitting

10 Refitting is a reversal of the removal procedure, noting:

a) Clean the plugs and seating area in the cylinder head.

b) Apply anti-seize compound to the plug threads.

c) Use a torque wrench to tighten the plugs to the specified torque.

d) Ensure that the main feed cable is connected to the glow plug noted on removal.

4 Glow plug relay – removal and refitting

Removal

1 The relay is attached to a bracket on the left-hand inner wing panel next to the engine control module (ECM) **(see illustration)**.

2 Disconnect the battery negative terminal (refer to *Disconnecting the battery* in the Reference Section of this manual).

3 Undo the retaining nut and release the relay from the mounting bracket, and disconnect the wiring connector.

Refitting

4 Refitting is a reversal of the removal procedure.

Chapter 6
Clutch

Contents

Section number

Clutch assembly – removal, inspection and refitting 5
Clutch hydraulic system – bleeding 7
Clutch master cylinder – removal and refitting 3
Clutch pedal – removal and refitting 2

Section number

Clutch release components – removal, inspection and refitting 6
Clutch slave cylinder – removal and refitting 4
General information 1

Degrees of difficulty

Easy, suitable for novice with little experience	**Fairly easy,** suitable for beginner with some experience	**Fairly difficult,** suitable for competent DIY mechanic	**Difficult,** suitable for experienced DIY mechanic	**Very difficult,** suitable for expert DIY or professional

Specifications

General

Type . . . . Single dry friction disc with diaphragm spring pressure plate, hydraulically-operated release bearing

Friction disc

Diameter:
  1.4, and 1.6 litre petrol engine models . . . . 200 mm
  1.8 litre petrol engine models . . . . 215 mm
  2.0 and 2.5 litre petrol engine models . . . . 228 mm
  Diesel engine models . . . . 228 mm
Minimum friction material thickness . . . . 1.5 mm
Minimum rivet head depth below surface of friction material . . . . 0.1 mm

Pressure plate

Maximum surface distortion . . . . 0.2 mm

Torque wrench settings

	Nm	lbf ft
Clutch pressure plate-to-flywheel bolts:		
1.4 and 1.6 litre petrol engine models	18	13
All other petrol and diesel engine models	25	18
Clutch release fork-to-shaft bolt (PG1-type transmission)	29	21

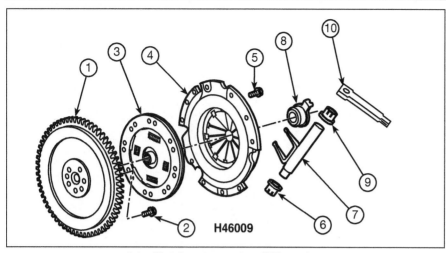

1.1a Clutch components – R65 gearbox

1 Flywheel	5 Pressure plate bolts	8 Release bearing
2 Flywheel bolts	6 Release fork lower bush	9 Release fork upper bush
3 Clutch friction disc	7 Release fork and shaft	10 Release lever
4 Clutch pressure plate		

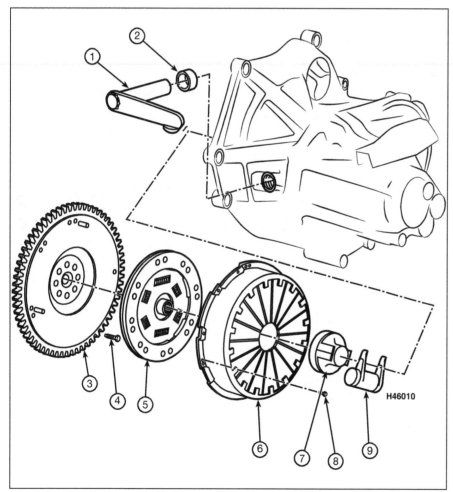

1.1b Clutch components – PG1 gearbox

1 Release lever	4 Flywheel bolts	7 Release bearing
2 Oil seal – release shaft	5 Clutch friction disc	8 Pressure plate bolts
3 Flywheel	6 Clutch pressure plate	9 Release fork

1 General information

The clutch is of single dry plate type, and consists of a friction disc, a pressure plate and a release bearing; all of these components are contained in the large cast-aluminium alloy bellhousing, sandwiched between the engine and the transmission **(see illustrations)**.

The friction disc is free to slide along the splines of the transmission input shaft and is held in position between the flywheel and the pressure plate by the pressure exerted on the pressure plate by the diaphragm spring. Friction lining material is riveted to both sides of the friction disc. Spring cushioning between the friction linings and the hub absorbs transmission shocks, and helps to ensure a smooth take-up of power as the clutch is engaged.

The release bearing is located on a guide sleeve at the front of the transmission. The bearing is free to slide on the sleeve, under the action of the release arm that pivots inside the clutch bellhousing.

The release mechanism is hydraulic, operated by a master cylinder and a slave cylinder. The hydraulic master cylinder is located at the top of the clutch pedal bracket on the bulkhead, and the slave cylinder is mounted on the transmission housing by the clutch release lever.

When the clutch pedal is depressed, the hydraulic fluid actuates the release lever. The release lever pushes the release bearing forwards, to bear against the centre of the diaphragm spring, thus pushing the centre of the diaphragm spring inwards. The diaphragm spring acts against the fulcrum rings in the cover. When the centre of the spring is pushed in, the outside of the spring is pushed out, so allowing the pressure plate to move backwards away from the friction disc.

When the clutch pedal is released, the diaphragm spring forces the pressure plate into contact with the friction linings on the friction disc. This simultaneously pushes the friction disc forwards on its splines, forcing it against the flywheel. The friction disc is now firmly sandwiched between the pressure plate and the flywheel, and drive is taken up. Also when the clutch pedal is released, excess fluid is expelled through the master cylinder into the fluid reservoir.

Note: *The clutch hydraulic system is sealed for life and should require no regular maintenance or topping-up.*

⚠ *Warning: Hydraulic fluid is poisonous; wash off immediately and thoroughly in the case of skin contact, and seek immediate medical advice if any fluid is swallowed or gets into the eyes. Certain types of hydraulic fluid are flammable, and may ignite when allowed into contact with hot components; when servicing any hydraulic system, it is safest to assume that the fluid is flammable, and to take precautions against the risk of fire as though it is petrol that is being handled. Hydraulic fluid is also an effective paint stripper, and will attack plastics; if any is spilt, it should be washed off immediately, using copious quantities of fresh water. Finally, it is hygroscopic (it absorbs moisture from the air) – old fluid may be contaminated and unfit for further use. When topping-up or renewing the fluid, always use the recommended type, and ensure that it comes from a freshly-opened sealed container.*

2.2 Remove the retaining clip (arrowed) and withdraw the clevis pin

2.3 Remove the pivot bolt and nut – arrowed

2 Clutch pedal – removal and refitting

Removal

1 Release the retaining clips and then remove the cover from under the driver's side of the facia.
2 Remove the retaining clip and withdraw the clevis pin securing the clutch pedal to the master cylinder pushrod. Discard the retaining clip; a new one should be used on refitting **(see illustration)**.
3 Slacken and remove the pivot bolt and nut securing the pedal to the mounting bracket **(see illustration)**, then manoeuvre the pedal out from the mounting bracket. Release the return spring from the pedal as it is removed, if any parts are worn or damaged then check for the availability of new parts.

Refitting

4 Manoeuvre the pedal assembly into position, ensuring it is correctly engaged with the pushrod clevis. As the pedal is moved into position attach the return spring.
5 Refit the pivot bolt and nut and tighten securely.
6 Insert the clevis pin and secure it in position in the master cylinder pushrod with the new retaining clip.
7 Check the operation of the clutch pedal then refit the cover under the facia panel.

3 Clutch master cylinder – removal and refitting

Note: *Refer to the warning in Section 1 before proceeding.*

Removal

1 Disconnect the battery negative terminal (refer to *Disconnecting the battery* in the Reference Section of this manual).
2 On 4-cylinder petrol models, it may be necessary to undo the retaining nuts and remove the engine control module (ECM) from the bulkhead, at the rear of the engine compartment. Carefully move it to one side to access the master cylinder **(see illustrations)**.
3 Using special tool (Rover 18G 1593), disconnect the quick-release coupling at the end of the hydraulic pipe. **Note:** *The quick-release couplings have a valve inside, to help prevent the loss of fluid*
4 Place some absorbent cloth below the pipe connections on the master cylinder, to soak up any fluid still in the system.
5 Working inside the vehicle on the driver's side, undo the retaining screws and unclip the lower trim panel from the facia panel.
6 Release the spring clip and withdraw the clevis pin from the master cylinder pushrod to the clutch pedal **(see illustration 2.2)**.
7 Slacken and remove the two clutch master cylinder mounting nuts **(see illustration)**.
8 Working inside the engine compartment, withdraw the master cylinder and rotate it 45° clockwise to remove it from the bulkhead.

Refitting

9 Refitting is a reversal of removal, noting the following points:
 a) Check the condition of the quick-release connectors, and renew if necessary.
 b) Ensure that all fluid hose connections are clean, and are securely made.
 c) If required, fill and bleed the clutch system on completion, as described in Section 7.
 d) Check the clutch system is operating correctly with no leaks.

4 Clutch slave cylinder – removal and refitting

Note: *Refer to the warning in Section 1 before proceeding.*

Removal

1 Remove the air cleaner as described in Chapter 4A, 4B or 4C, depending on model.
2 Disconnect the quick-release coupling at the slave cylinder end of the hydraulic pipe using special tool (Rover 18G 1593). **Note:** *The quick-release couplings have a valve inside, to help prevent the loss of fluid*
3 Place some absorbent cloth below the pipe connections, to soak up any fluid still in the system.
4 Release the locking collar, which secures the slave cylinder to the mounting bracket on the transmission **(see illustration)**.
5 Unclip the slave cylinder from the mounting

3.2a Engine control module – 4-cylinder petrol models

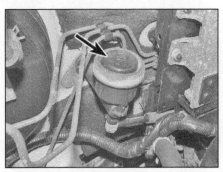
3.2b Clutch master cylinder – location

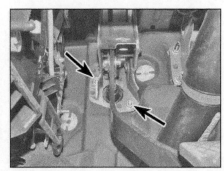
3.7 Undo the two mounting nuts – arrowed

bracket and release the pushrod from the lever, then remove it from the transmission.

Refitting

6 Refitting is a reversal of removal, noting the following points:
 a) Check the condition of the quick-release connectors, and renew if necessary.
 b) Ensure that all fluid hose connections are clean, and are securely made.
 c) If required, fill and bleed the clutch system on completion, as described in Section 7.
 d) Check the clutch system is operating correctly with no leaks.
 e) Refit the air cleaner.

5 Clutch assembly – removal, inspection and refitting

⚠ Warning: Dust created by clutch wear and deposited on the clutch components may contain asbestos, which is a health hazard. DO NOT blow it out with compressed air, or inhale any of it. DO NOT use petrol (or petroleum-based solvents) to clean off the dust. Brake system cleaner or methylated spirit should be used to flush the dust into a suitable receptacle. After the clutch components are wiped clean with rags, dispose of the contaminated rags and cleaner in a sealed, marked container.

Note: *Although some friction materials may no longer contain asbestos, it is safest to*

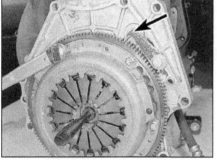

5.3 Flywheel locking tool – arrowed

5.5 Withdraw the pressure plate and friction disc – 6-cylinder engine shown

4.4 Locking collar (arrowed) for slave cylinder

assume that they do, and to take precautions accordingly.

Removal

1 Remove the transmission, as described in Chapter 7A.

2 If the original clutch is to be refitted, make alignment marks between the clutch pressure plate and the flywheel, so that the clutch can be refitted in its original position.

3 To prevent the flywheel from turning, use a flywheel-locking tool, or alternatively position a screwdriver over the dowel on the cylinder block and engage it with one of the teeth on the starter ring gear **(see illustration)**.

4 Progressively unscrew the bolts securing the pressure plate to the flywheel **(see illustration)**.

5 Withdraw the pressure plate from the flywheel, complete with friction disc, noting which way round the friction disc is fitted – the

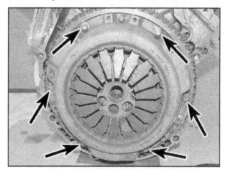

5.4 Remove the bolts – arrowed

5.7 Using a vernier gauge to check the depth of the lining

side of the disc facing the flywheel is normally marked 'Flywheel side' **(see illustration)**. **Caution: Be prepared to catch the clutch friction disc, which will drop out as the pressure plate assembly is withdrawn from the flywheel.**

Inspection

Note: *Due to the amount of work necessary to remove and refit clutch components, it is usually considered good practice to renew the clutch friction disc, pressure plate assembly and release bearing as a matched set, even if only one of these is actually worn enough to require renewal. It is also worth considering the renewal of the clutch components on a preventative basis if the engine and/or transmission have been removed for some other reason.*

6 With the clutch assembly removed, clean off all traces of dust using a dry cloth, working in a well-ventilated atmosphere. When cleaning clutch components, read first the warning at the beginning of this Section.

⚠ Warning: Asbestos dust is harmful, and must not be inhaled.

7 Examine the linings of the friction disc for wear and loose rivets, and for distortion, cracks, broken damping springs (where applicable) and worn splines. The surface of the friction linings may be highly glazed, but, as long as the friction material pattern can be clearly seen, this is satisfactory. If there is any sign of oil contamination, indicated by a continuous, or patchy, shiny black discolouration, the plate must be renewed. The source of the contamination must be traced and rectified before fitting new clutch components; typically, a leaking crankshaft oil seal or transmission input shaft oil seal – or both – would be to blame (renewal procedures are given in the relevant Part of Chapter 2 and Chapter 7A respectively). The plate must also be renewed if the lining thickness has worn down to, or just above, the level of the rivet heads **(see illustration)**.

8 Check the machined faces of the flywheel and pressure plate. If either is grooved, or heavily scored, renewal is necessary. The

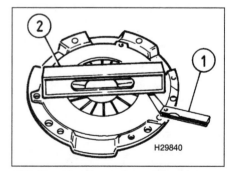

5.8 Checking the surface of the pressure plate for flatness using a straight-edge and feeler blades

1 Feeler blades   2 Straight-edge

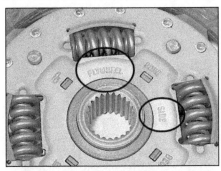

5.12a Check for markings (circled) on the friction disc which should face the flywheel . . .

5.12b . . . or GEARBOX, which should face the transmission

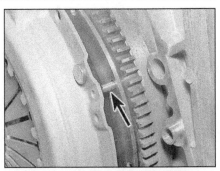

5.13 Ensure that the pressure plate locates over the dowels (arrowed) on the flywheel

pressure plate must also be renewed if any cracks are apparent, or if the diaphragm spring is damaged or its pressure suspect. Check the surface of the pressure plate for flatness using a straight-edge and feeler blades – renew the pressure plate if the distortion is excessive (see illustration).

9 With the clutch removed, it is advisable to check the condition of the release bearing, as described in Section 6.

Refitting

10 If new clutch components are to be fitted, where applicable, ensure that all anti-corrosion preservative is cleaned from the friction material on the disc, and the contact surfaces of the pressure plate.

11 It is important to ensure that no oil or grease gets onto the friction disc linings, or the pressure plate and flywheel faces. It is advisable to refit the clutch assembly with clean hands, and to wipe down the pressure plate and flywheel faces with a clean rag before assembly begins.

12 Apply a smear of molybdenum disulphide grease to the splines of the friction disc hub, then offer the plate to the flywheel, with the 'Flywheel side' marking facing the flywheel. On some clutches it may have 'Gearbox' marked on the transmission side of the clutch disc (see illustrations). Hold the friction disc against the flywheel while the pressure plate assembly is offered into position.

13 Fit the pressure plate assembly, where applicable aligning the marks on the flywheel (if the original pressure plate is re-used). Ensure that the pressure plate locates over the dowels on the flywheel (see illustration). Insert the securing bolts and washers, and tighten them finger-tight, so that the friction disc is gripped, but can still be moved.

14 The friction disc must now be centralised, so that when the engine and transmission are mated, the transmission input shaft splines will pass through the splines in the friction disc hub.

15 Centralisation can be carried out by inserting a round bar or a long screwdriver through the hole in the centre of the friction disc, so that the end of the bar rests in the spigot bearing in the centre of the crankshaft. Where possible, use a blunt instrument, but

if a screwdriver is used, wrap tape around the blade to prevent damage to the bearing surface. Moving the bar sideways or up-and-down as necessary, move the friction disc in whichever direction is necessary to achieve centralisation. With the bar removed, view the friction disc hub in relation to the hole in the centre of the crankshaft and the circle created by the ends of the diaphragm spring fingers. When the hub appears exactly in the centre, all is correct.

16 Alternatively, a clutch-aligning tool can be used to eliminate the guesswork; these can be obtained from most accessory shops. The normal type consists of a spigot bar with several different adapters, but a home-made aligning tool can be fabricated from a length of metal rod or wooden dowel which fits closely inside the spigot bearing in the crankshaft, and has insulating tape wound around it to match the diameter of the friction disc splined hole (see illustration).

17 A more recent type of aligning tool works by clamping the friction disc to the pressure plate before locating the two items on the flywheel. Rover recommends this type of alignment tool for the 6-cylinder petrol engines.

18 When the friction disc is centralised, tighten the pressure plate retaining bolts gradually in a diagonal sequence, to the specified torque. Remove the flywheel locking tool and the friction disc alignment tool.

19 Refit the transmission as described in Chapter 7A.

6 Clutch release components – removal, inspection and refitting

Release bearing

1 Remove the transmission, as described in Chapter 7A.

2 Disengage the bearing from the release fork, then pull the bearing forwards, and slide it from the guide sleeve in the transmission bellhousing (see illustration).

3 Spin the release bearing, and check it for excessive roughness. Hold the outer race, and attempt to move it laterally against the inner race. If any excessive movement or roughness

5.16 Using a clutch alignment tool to centralise the friction disc

is evident, renew the bearing. If a new clutch has been fitted, it is wise to renew the release bearing as a matter of course.

4 Clean and then lightly grease the release bearing contact surfaces on the release fork. Similarly, lightly grease the guide sleeve.

5 Slide the bearing into position on the guide sleeve, and then engage the bearing with the release lever.

6 Refit the transmission as described in Chapter 7A.

Release fork and lever

R65-type transmission

Note: A new release lever securing roll-pin will be required on refitting.

7 Remove the release bearing, as described previously in this Section.

8 Using a suitable pin-punch, drive out the roll-pin securing the release lever to the

6.2 Removing the clutch release bearing – R65-type transmission

6.8 Driving out the roll-pin securing the release lever – R65-type transmission

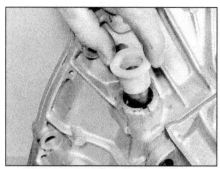

6.9 Removing a release fork shaft pivot bush – R65-type transmission

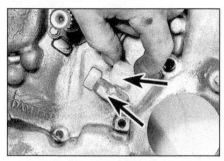

6.13 Align the pivot bush locating tags with the slots in the transmission casing (arrowed)

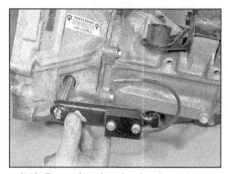

6.18 Removing the clutch release lever shaft – PG1-type transmission

6.24 Refitting the clutch release fork – PG1-type transmission

6.26 Refitting the clutch release bearing – PG1-type transmission

release fork shaft, then slide the release lever from the shaft, noting its fitted position (see illustration).

9 Slide the release fork shaft upwards, and remove the shaft bushes from the transmission casing, noting their fitted position (see illustration).

10 Withdraw the release fork shaft from the transmission, then Inspect the release bearing contact faces, and the pivot faces on the release fork and shaft for wear. Renew if excessive wear is evident.

11 Examine the pivot bushes, and renew if necessary.

12 Clean the components thoroughly, then smear the release fork shaft with a little molybdenum disulphide grease.

13 Slide the release fork shaft into position in the transmission, then fit the bushes, ensuring that the locating tags on the bushes engage with the slots in the transmission casing, as noted on removal (see illustration).

14 Slide the release fork shaft into position, then fit the release lever to the shaft (in the position noted on removal), and secure with a new roll-pin.

15 Refit the release bearing as described previously in this Section.

PG1-type transmission

16 Remove the release bearing, as described previously in this Section.

17 Unscrew the bolt (and recover the washer) securing the release fork to the release lever shaft

18 Slide the release lever shaft from the transmission, and withdraw the release fork, noting their fitted position (see illustration). Inspect the release bearing contact faces, and the pivot faces on the release fork and shaft for wear. Renew if excessive wear is evident.

19 Examine the pivot bushes in the transmission casing for wear. If necessary the bushes can be renewed, as follows.

20 Carefully prise the lower bush from the transmission casing.

21 To remove the upper bush, carefully cut a longitudinal slot in the inner face of the bush, opposite the split in the bush, then prise the bush from the transmission casing.

22 Carefully drive the new bushes into position in the casing, using a suitable metal tube or socket (take care not to distort the bushes during fitting).

23 Clean the components thoroughly, then smear the release fork shaft with a little molybdenum disulphide grease.

24 Position the release fork in the transmission casing (in the position noted on removal), then slide the release lever shaft into position, passing it through the fork (see illustration). Note that the release lever faces away from the clutch housing.

25 Align the holes in the release fork and shaft, then refit the fork securing bolt, ensuring that the washer is in place, and tighten to the specified torque.

26 Refit the release bearing as described previously in this Section (see illustration).

7 Clutch hydraulic system – bleeding

The clutch hydraulic system is a sealed system and never requires topping-up or bleeding, even after the hydraulic pipes have been disconnected. The hydraulic pipes have quick-release couplings at each end, which have a valve inside, to help prevent the loss of fluid. If a problem develops then either the master cylinder or slave cylinder is faulty and renewal is the only option.

Chapter 7 Part A:
Manual transmission

Contents

Section number

Gearchange linkage – removal, refitting and adjustment 3
General information 1
Manual transmission – removal and refitting 7
Manual transmission oil – draining and refilling 2

Section number

Manual transmission overhaul – general information 8
Oil seals – renewal 4
Reversing light switch – testing, removal and refitting 5
Vehicle speed sensor – removal and refitting 6

Degrees of difficulty

Easy, suitable for novice with little experience	Fairly easy, suitable for beginner with some experience	Fairly difficult, suitable for competent DIY mechanic	Difficult, suitable for experienced DIY mechanic	Very difficult, suitable for expert DIY or professional

Specifications

General

Type	Manual, five forward speeds and reverse. Synchromesh on all forward speeds

Designation:
1.4 and 1.6 litre petrol engine models	Rover R65
1.8, 2.0 and 2.5 litre petrol engine models	Rover PG1
Diesel engine models	Rover PG1

Transmission code:
1.4 litre	5C 39 WUR
1.6 litre	5C 37 WUC
1.8 litre	C6 BP
2.0 and 2.5 litre	C6 BKUH
Diesel	S6 BNU

Gear ratios:

R65-type transmission:
1st	3.417:1
2nd	1.947:1
3rd	1.333:1
4th	1.054:1
5th	0.854:1
Reverse	3.583:1

PG1-type transmission:

Petrol engine models:
1st	3.167:1
2nd	1.842:1
3rd	1.308:1
4th	1.033:1
5th	0.765:1
Reverse	3.000:1

Diesel engine models:
1st	3.250:1
2nd	1.895:1
3rd	1.222:1
4th	0.848:1
5th	0.649:1
Reverse	3.000:1

Final drive ratio:
1.4 litre petrol engines	3.937:1
1.6 litre petrol engines	3.765:1
1.8, 2.0 and 2.5 litre petrol engines	3.938:1
Diesel engines	3.937:1

Lubrication

Recommended oil and capacity	See end of *Weekly checks*

Torque wrench settings

	Nm	lbf ft
R65-type transmission		
Drain plug	25	18
Engine steady bar-to-transmission bolts	25	18
Filler/level plug	28	21
Flywheel front cover plate bolts	9	7
Flywheel rear cover plate bolt	9	7
Gear selector mounting-to-body bolts	22	16
Gearchange linkage-to-crossmember bolts	24	18
LH engine mounting-to-body bolts	55	41
Release bearing guide sleeve/seal bolts	5	4
Reversing light switch	25	18
Transmission mounting bracket-to-engine mounting bolts	60	44
Transmission mounting through-bolt	85	63
Transmission-to-engine bolts	85	63
Transmission-to-engine sump bolts	45	33
PG1-type transmission		
Drain plug	45	33
Earth lead-to-transmission bolt	25	18
Engine-to-differential bolt	85	63
Filler/level plug	40	30
Front closing plate nuts and bolts	85	63
Gear selector mounting-to-body bolts	22	16
Gearchange steady bar to transmission	10	7
LH engine mounting-to-transmission bolts	100	74
LH mounting-to-body bracket through-bolt	85	63
Reversing light switch	25	18
Transmission lifting eye bolt	45	33
Transmission mounting bracket-to-transmission bolts	60	44
Transmission-to-engine sump bolts	45	33
Transmission-to-engine/mounting plate nuts and bolts	85	63

1 General information

The 5-speed transmission is contained in a casing bolted to the left-hand end of the engine and consists of the transmission and final drive differential – often called a transaxle.

Drive is transmitted from the crankshaft via the clutch to the input shaft, which has a splined extension to accept the clutch friction disc, and rotates in sealed ball-bearings. From the input shaft, drive is transmitted to the output shaft, which rotates in a roller bearing at its right-hand end, and a sealed ball-bearing at its left-hand end. From the output shaft, the drive is transmitted to the differential crownwheel, which rotates with the differential case and planetary gears, thus driving the sun gears and driveshafts. The rotation of the planetary gears on their shaft allows the inner roadwheel to rotate at a slower speed than the outer roadwheel when the car is cornering.

The input shaft runs in parallel with the output shaft. The input shaft and output shaft gears are in constant mesh, and selection of gears is by sliding synchromesh hubs which lock the appropriate gears to the shafts. In the neutral position, the output shaft gear pinions rotate freely, so that drive cannot be transmitted to the crownwheel.

Gear selection is via a floor-mounted lever and selector mechanism. The selector mechanism causes the appropriate selector fork to move its respective synchrosleeve along the shaft to lock the gear pinion to the synchro-hub. Since the synchro-hubs are splined to the gearshaft, this locks the pinion to the shaft, so that drive can be transmitted. To ensure that gearchanging can be made quickly and quietly, a synchromesh system is fitted to all forward gears, consisting of baulk rings and spring-loaded fingers, as well as the gear pinions and synchro-hubs. The synchromesh cones are formed on the mating faces of the baulk rings and gear pinions.

2 Manual transmission oil – draining and refilling

Note: *New filler/level plug and drain plug sealing washers must be used when refitting the plugs.*

1 This operation is much quicker and more efficient if the car is first taken on a journey of sufficient length to warm the engine/transmission up to normal operating temperature.

2 Park the car on level ground, and switch off the ignition. To improve access during draining, apply the handbrake, and then jack up the front of the car and support it securely on axle stands (see *Jacking and vehicle support*). Note that the car must be lowered to the ground and level, to ensure accuracy, when refilling and checking the oil level.

3 Where applicable, remove the engine/transmission undershield to gain access to the filler/level and drain plugs.

4 Remove all traces of dirt from around the filler/level plug, which is located on the left-hand side of the transmission behind the driveshaft inboard joint. Unscrew the plug and recover the sealing washer **(see illustrations)**.

5 Position a suitable container under the drain plug, which is also situated on the left-hand side of the transmission below the driveshaft joint.

6 Unscrew the drain plug and allow the oil to drain into the container. If the oil is hot, take precautions against scalding. Clean both the

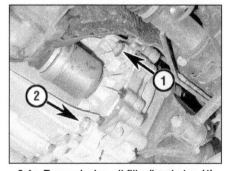

2.4a Transmission oil filler/level plug (1) and drain plug (2) locations – R65-type transmission

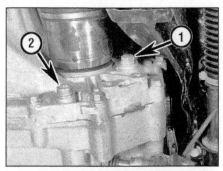

2.4b Transmission oil filler/level plug (1) and drain plug (2) locations – PG1-type transmission

filler/level plug and the drain plug, taking care to wipe any metallic particles off the magnetic inserts. Recover the sealing washers from the plugs, and discard them.

7 When the oil has finished draining, clean the drain plug threads in the transmission casing, fit a new sealing washer to the plug, and refit the drain plug. Tighten the plug to the specified torque. It the car was raised for the draining operation, now lower it to the ground.

8 Refilling the transmission is an awkward operation. Allow plenty of time for the oil level to settle properly before checking it. **Note:** *The car must be parked on flat level ground when checking the oil level.*

9 Using a tube inserted through the filler/level plug hole, slowly refill the transmission with the specified type of oil, until the level reaches the bottom of the filler/level plug hole. Allow plenty of time for the level to stabilise, see Chapter 1A or 1B, Section 8, for further information.

10 When the level is correct, refit the filler/level plug, using a new sealing washer, and tighten it to the specified torque.

3 Gearchange linkage
– removal, refitting and adjustment

R65-type transmission

Removal

1 Apply the handbrake, then jack up the front of the vehicle and support securely on axle stands (see *Jacking and vehicle support*). Where applicable, remove the engine/transmission undershield.

2 Although not strictly necessary, access to the gearchange linkage can be improved if the exhaust front pipe is first removed, as described in Chapter 4A.

3 Using a large flat-bladed screwdriver, carefully prise the gear linkage rod balljoints from the gear selector levers on the transmission, taking care not to damage the balljoints or their gaiters **(see illustration)**. Make a note of the location of each linkage rod (to ensure correct refitting), note which way round they are fitted, then detach both

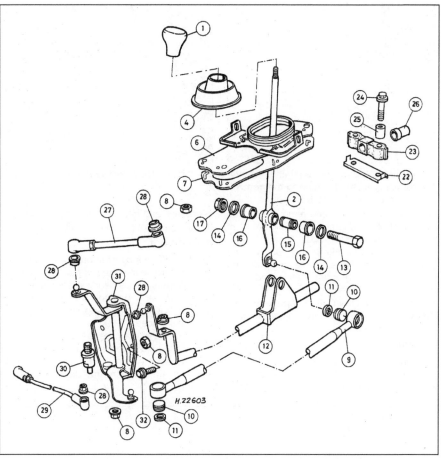

3.3 Gearchange linkage assembly – R65-type transmission

Note: *On some models, rods 27 and 29 are not adjustable*

1 Gearchange lever knob	11 Rubber seal	24 Bolt
2 Gearchange lever	12 Control rod	25 Spacer
4 Rubber cover	13 Pivot bolt	26 Bush
6 Mounting plate	14 Thrustwasher	27 Upper link rod
7 Seal	15 Spacer	28 Dust cover
8 Nut	16 Bush	29 Lower link rod
9 Selector rod	17 Nut	30 Bucket joint
10 Ball housing	22 Mounting plate	31 Bellcrank assembly
	23 Mounting rubber	32 Bolt

rod balljoints from the bellcrank assembly and remove the rods from the vehicle.

4 Prise the gear selector rod from the balljoints on the gearchange lever and bellcrank assembly, and manoeuvre the selector rod out from underneath the vehicle **(see illustration)**.

5 Working inside the vehicle, remove the centre console as described in Chapter 11.

6 With the console removed, carefully peel the rubber gaiter from the base of the gearchange lever, and slide the gaiter up the lever to gain access to the control rod pivot bolt and nut. Unscrew the nut, and remove the pivot bolt and thrustwashers.

7 Working underneath the vehicle, unscrew the nut securing the front of the control rod to the bellcrank pivot, then unscrew the two bolts and remove the retaining plate securing the rear of the control rod mounting to the

body **(see illustration)**. Remove the mounting assembly, taking care not to lose its spacers, then manoeuvre the control rod out from underneath the vehicle.

3.4 Prising the gear selector rod from the balljoint on the gearchange lever

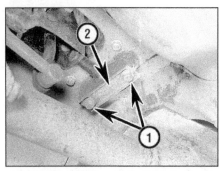

3.7 Unscrew the two bolts (1) and remove the retaining plate (2) securing the control rod mounting to the body

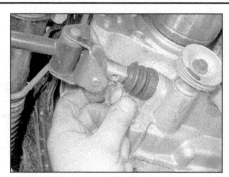

3.14a Remove the metal clip . . .

3.14b . . . then drive out the roll-pin securing the selector rod to the selector shaft

8 If necessary, slacken and remove the three mounting bolts and remove the bellcrank from the suspension crossmember.

9 If necessary, slacken and remove the gearchange lever housing retaining nuts and remove the seal, mounting plate and lever assembly from the vehicle.

10 Thoroughly clean all components and check them for wear or damage, renewing all worn or faulty items.

Refitting

11 Refitting is the reverse of the removal procedure, but check the linkage balljoints for wear and damage, and fit new components as necessary, and apply a smear of grease to all the linkage pivot points and balljoints.

Adjustment

12 If a stiff, sloppy or imprecise gearchange leads you to suspect that a fault exists within the linkage, first dismantle it completely and check for wear or damage, then reassemble it, applying a smear of the approved grease to all bearing surfaces.

13 If this does not cure the fault, the vehicle should be examined by an expert, as the fault must lie within the transmission itself. There is no adjustment, as such, in the linkage.

PG1-type transmission

Note: *A new gear selector rod-to-selector shaft roll-pin will be required on refitting.*

Removal

14 Remove the metal clip from the gear selector rod-to-selector shaft joint to expose the roll-pin, then drive out the roll-pin using a suitable pin punch, and release the selector rod from the selector shaft **(see illustrations)**.

15 Unscrew and remove the nut and pivot bolt securing the selector rod to the base of the gearchange lever, and remove the selector rod from the vehicle **(see illustration)**.

16 Working inside the vehicle, remove the centre console as described in Chapter 11, then release the gearchange lever rubber gaiter from the housing and slide it up the lever.

17 Working underneath the vehicle, unscrew and remove the bolts and retaining plate securing the gearchange steady rod rear mounting to the body. Remove the mounting rubber from the steady rod, taking care not to lose its spacers.

18 Unscrew and remove the bolt securing the gearchange steady rod to the transmission, and recover the washers **(see illustrations)**. Manoeuvre the steady rod and gearchange lever assembly out from underneath the vehicle – if necessary, the two can then be separated.

19 If necessary, slacken and remove the retaining nuts and remove the gearchange lever plate assembly and seal.

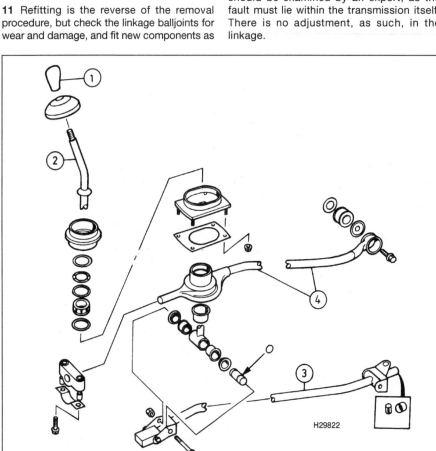

3.15 Gearchange linkage assembly – PG1-type transmission

1 Gearchange lever knob
2 Gearchange lever
3 Gear selector rod
4 Gearchange steady rod

3.18a Unscrew the bolt securing the gearchange steady rod to the transmission . . .

20 Thoroughly clean all components and check them for wear and damage, renewing components if necessary.

Refitting

21 Refitting is a reversal of the removal, but use a new roll-pin to secure the gear selector rod to the selector shaft, and apply a smear of grease to all the linkage pivot points.

Adjustment

22 No adjustment of the gearchange linkage is possible.

4 Oil seals – renewal

Driveshaft oil seals

1 Apply the handbrake, then jack up the front of the car and support it securely on axle stands (see *Jacking and vehicle support*). Remove the appropriate front roadwheel, where applicable remove the engine/transmission undershield.

2 Drain the transmission oil as described in Section 2, or be prepared for some oil loss as the driveshaft is removed.

3 Referring to Chapter 8, disconnect the driveshaft from the transmission. Note that it is not necessary to remove the driveshaft completely; the shaft can be left attached to the hub assembly and slid off from the differential gear splines as the hub assembly is pulled outwards. **Note:** *Do not allow it to hang down under its own weight as this could damage the constant velocity joints/gaiters.*

4 Clean the area around the differential oil seal, then carefully prise the oil seal from the transmission using a large flat-bladed screwdriver (**see illustration**).

5 Remove all traces of dirt from the area around the oil seal aperture, then apply a smear of grease to the outer lip of the new oil seal.

6 Ensure that the seal is correctly positioned, with its sealing lip facing inwards, and drive it squarely into position, using a suitable tubular drift (such as a socket), which bears only on the hard outer edge of the seal (**see illustration**). Ensure that the seal is seated correctly in the transmission recess.

7 Reconnect the inboard end of the driveshaft as described in Chapter 8.

8 Refill/top-up the transmission with the specified type of oil, and check the oil level as described in Section 2.

9 Refit the roadwheel and lower the car to the ground and tighten the roadwheel bolts to the specified torque.

Input shaft oil seal

R65-type transmission

Note: *The following new parts are needed – release bearing guide sleeve (the seal is integral with the sleeve), three securing bolts for the release bearing guide sleeve.*

3.18b . . . and recover the washers

10 Remove the transmission as described in Section 7.

11 Disengage the release bearing from the release fork, then pull the bearing forwards, and slide it from the guide sleeve in the transmission bellhousing (**see illustration**).

12 Remove the three bolts securing the guide sleeve to the transmission casing (**see illustration**). Discard the bolts, as new ones will be required for refitting.

13 Remove the guide sleeve/seal from the transmission casing and discard.

14 Fit new guide sleeve/seal over the input shaft, and align the bolt holes, fit the three new securing bolts and tighten to the specified torque setting.

15 Fit the release bearing over the guide sleeve and secure to release fork.

16 Refit the transmission as described in Section 7.

4.4 Levering out a driveshaft oil seal – R65-type transmission

4.11 Remove the release bearing

PG1-type transmission

17 To renew the input shaft oil seal, the transmission must be dismantled. This task should therefore be entrusted to a Rover dealer or transmission specialist.

Gear selector shaft oil seal

R65-type transmission

Note: *A new selector lever-to-shaft roll-pin will be required on refitting.*

18 Access to the selector shaft seal is greatly improved with the transmission removed. If the transmission is fitted to the vehicle, proceed as follows. If the transmission has been removed, proceed to paragraph 23.

19 Apply the handbrake, then jack up the front of the vehicle and support securely on axle stands (see *Jacking and vehicle support*). Remove the left-hand front roadwheel, where applicable remove the engine/transmission undershield.

20 Release the charcoal canister from its mounting bracket on the inner wing panel and move it to one side.

21 Using a large flat-bladed screwdriver, carefully prise the gear linkage rod balljoint from the gear selector lever on the transmission, taking care not to damage the balljoint.

22 If required, to make access easier, undo the retaining bolts and remove the damper fork from the lower suspension arm and the base of the damper unit, with reference to Chapter 10.

23 Working under the left-hand front wheel

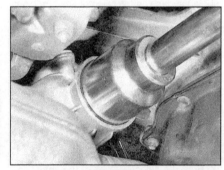

4.6 Fitting a driveshaft oil seal using a socket – R65-type transmission

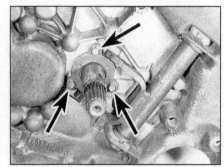

4.12 Remove guide sleeve bolts – arrowed

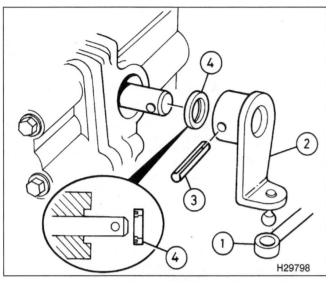
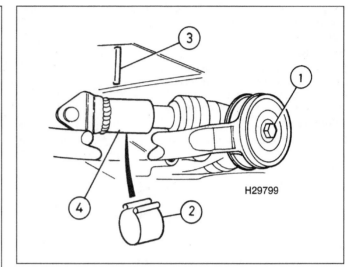

4.23 Gearchange selector shaft oil seal fitting details –
R65-type transmission

1 Link rod   3 Roll-pin
2 Selector lever   4 Oil seal

4.31 Gearchange selector shaft oil seal renewal –
PG1-type transmission

1 Gearchange steady bar   3 Roll-pin
  securing bolt   4 Selector rod
2 Metal clip

arch, use a suitable punch, and if necessary an extension piece, to drive out the roll-pin securing the selector lever to the shaft **(see illustration)**. Discard the roll-pin, a new one will be required for refitting.

24 Withdraw the selector lever from the shaft, then carefully prise the seal from the recess in the transmission casing, taking great care not to damage the shaft or casing.

25 Before fitting a new seal, check the seal rubbing surface on the selector shaft for signs of burrs, scratches or other damage which may have caused the seal to fail in the first place. It may be possible to polish away minor faults of this sort using fine abrasive paper, however, more serious defects will require the renewal of the shaft.

26 Lubricate the new seal with a smear of clean transmission oil, then ease the seal into position. Press the seal squarely into position, using a socket, which bears only on the hard outer edge of the seal, ensuring that the seal lip faces inwards.

27 Refit the selector lever to the shaft, and secure it in position with a new roll-pin.

28 If the transmission is fitted to the vehicle

proceed as follows, otherwise refit the transmission.

a) Press the gear linkage rod balljoint into position on the selector lever.
b) Refit the charcoal canister back to the mounting bracket on the inner wing panel.
c) Refit the left-hand lower damper fork with reference to Chapter 10.
d) Refit the roadwheel and lower the vehicle to the ground.

PG1-type transmission

Note: *A new selector lever-to-shaft roll-pin will be required on refitting.*

29 Apply the handbrake, then jack up the front of the vehicle and support it securely on axle stands (see *Jacking and vehicle support*). Where applicable, remove the engine/ transmission undershield.

30 Unscrew the bolt securing the gearchange steady bar to the transmission. Recover the two washers.

31 Remove the metal clip from the gear selector rod-to-selector shaft joint to expose the roll-pin **(see illustration)**.

32 Drive out the roll-pin using a suitable pin

punch, then release the selector rod from the selector shaft, and move the rod and the gearchange steady bar to one side. Discard the roll-pin a new one will be required for refitting.

33 If the transmission oil has not been drained, have a container ready to catch any escaping oil.

34 Slide the gaiter from the selector shaft, and carefully prise the seal from the recess in the transmission casing, taking great care not to damage the shaft or casing **(see illustrations)**.

35 Before fitting a new seal, check the seal rubbing surface on the selector shaft for signs of burrs, scratches or other damage which may have caused the seal to fail in the first place. It may be possible to polish away minor faults of this sort using fine abrasive paper, however, more serious defects will require the renewal of the selector shaft.

36 Lubricate the new seal with clean transmission oil, and ease it over the end of the selector shaft. Press the seal squarely into the transmission housing using a tube (such as a socket), which bears only on the hard outer edge of the seal.

37 Slide the gaiter onto the shaft, ensuring that the lip on the gaiter engages with the oil seal.

38 Connect the selector rod onto the shaft, and secure using a new roll-pin. Refit the metal clip over the selector shaft and roll-pin.

39 Refit the bolt securing the gearchange steady bar to the transmission, ensuring that the washers are in place, and then tighten the bolt to the specified torque.

40 Lower the vehicle to the ground, then refill/ top-up the transmission with the specified type of oil and check the oil level as described in Section 2.

4.34a Slide the gaiter from the selector shaft . . .

4.34b . . . and carefully prise out the oil seal

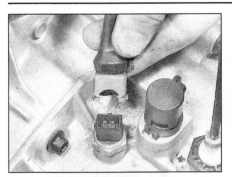

5.1a Reversing light switch –
R65-type transmission

5.1b Reversing light switch (arrowed)
– PG1-type transmission

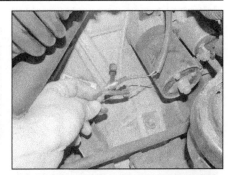

5.9 Disconnect the reversing light switch
wiring connectors – PG1-type transmission

5 Reversing light switch
– testing, removal and refitting

Testing

1 The reversing light circuit is controlled by a plunger-type switch, located in the top of the transmission casing on R65-type transmissions, or in the front of the transmission casing on PG1-type transmissions **(see illustrations)**. If a fault develops in the circuit, first ensure that the circuit fuse has not blown.

2 To test the switch, first disconnect the wiring connector. Use a multimeter (set to the resistance function), or a battery-and-bulb test circuit, to check that there is continuity between the switch terminals only when reverse gear is selected. If this is not the case, and there are no obvious breaks or other damage to the wires, the switch is faulty, and must be renewed.

R65-type transmission

Note: *A new sealing washer will be required on refitting.*

Removal

3 Disconnect the battery negative terminal (refer to *Disconnecting the battery* in the Reference Section of this manual).

4 To improve access to the switch, remove the air cleaner assembly as described in Chapter 4A.

5 Disconnect the switch wiring connector, then unscrew the switch and remove it from the top of the transmission. Recover the

sealing washer and discard it as a new one will be required for refitting.

Refitting

6 Refitting is a reversal of removal, using a new sealing washer, and tighten the switch to the specified torque setting.

PG1-type transmission

Note: *A new sealing washer will be required on refitting.*

Removal

7 Disconnect the battery negative terminal (refer to *Disconnecting the battery* in the Reference Section of this manual).

8 Apply the handbrake, then jack up the front of the vehicle and support it securely on axle stands (see *Jacking and vehicle support*). Where necessary, remove the engine/transmission undershield to gain access to the switch.

9 Trace the wiring back from the switch, freeing it from any relevant retaining clips, and separate the two halves of the wiring connectors **(see illustration)**.
Caution: Be prepared for possible transmission fluid loss when the switch is removed, and have ready a suitable plug to plug the aperture in the transmission whilst the switch is removed.

10 Clean the area around the switch, and then unscrew the switch and recover and discard the sealing washer. If necessary, plug the switch aperture to minimise fluid loss.

Refitting

11 Refitting is a reversal of removal, using a new sealing washer and tighten the switch to

the specified torque setting. If transmission fluid was lost during the removal procedure, check the transmission oil level and top-up if necessary as described in Section 2.

6 Vehicle speed sensor
– removal and refitting

Note: *This type of speed sensor is not required on all models, as other sensors determine the vehicle speed, depending on the type of engine management used.*

Removal

1 Where fitted, the vehicle speed sensor is mounted on the top of the transmission housing, next to the inboard end of the right-hand driveshaft **(see illustration)**.

2 Disconnect the battery negative terminal (refer to *Disconnecting the battery* in the Reference Section of this manual).

3 To gain access to the speedometer sensor, apply the handbrake then jack up the front of the vehicle and support it securely on axle stands (see *Jacking and vehicle support*).

4 Disconnect the wiring connector from the vehicle speed sensor then unscrew the sensor securing nut, and remove the sensor from the top of the speedometer drive assembly **(see illustration)**.

5 Slacken and remove the retaining bolt, and withdraw the speedometer drive assembly from the transmission housing, along with its O-ring **(see illustration)**. Discard the o-ring, as a new one will be required for refitting.

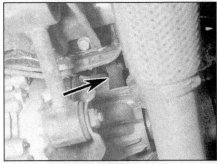

6.1 Vehicle speed sensor location
– arrowed

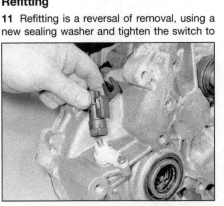

6.4 Removing the vehicle speed sensor

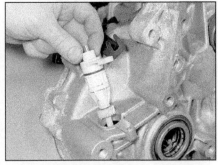

6.5 Removing the speedometer drive
assembly

7.11 Disconnecting the gear linkage balljoints

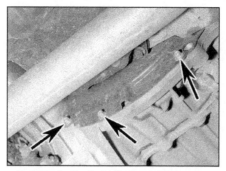

7.12 Undo the bolts (arrowed) from the front cover plate

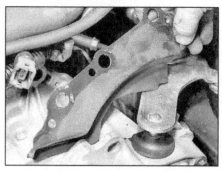

7.14 Remove the rear cover plate

Refitting

6 Lubricate a new O-ring with a smear of clean transmission oil then fit the O-ring to the speedometer drive housing.

7 Ease the speedometer drive assembly into position in the transmission, ensuring that the drive and driven pinions are correctly engaged. Refit and tighten the retaining bolt.

8 Fit the speed sensor to the top of the drive assembly, ensuring that the sensor drive pin is correctly engaged with the pinion, and securely tighten the sensor securing nut.

9 Reconnect the wiring connector to the speed sensor then lower the vehicle to the ground, and reconnect the battery negative lead.

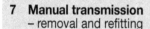

7 Manual transmission – removal and refitting

Note: *An assistant will be required to carry out this procedure.*

Removal

1 Disconnect the battery negative terminal (refer to *Disconnecting the battery* in the Reference Section of this manual).

2 Remove the battery and battery tray as described in Chapter 5A, Section 3.

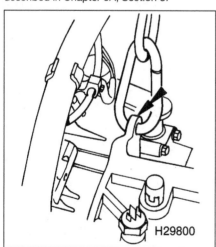

7.16 Attach the lifting eye to transmission

3 Remove the air cleaner assembly and hoses as described in the relevant part of Chapter 4. On diesel models, remove the mass airflow (MAF) sensor, with reference to Chapter 4C.

4 Remove the starter motor as described in Chapter 5A, Section 8.

5 Apply the handbrake, chock the rear roadwheels, then jack up the front of the car and support it on axle stands (see *Jacking and vehicle support*). Remove the both front roadwheels. **Note:** *When jacking the vehicle and supporting it on axle stands, make sure there is enough room to get the transmission out from under the vehicle.*

6 Drain the transmission oil with reference to Section 2. Refit drain plug with new washer when the oil has drained, and tighten to the specified torque setting.

7 Disconnect the inboard ends of both drive-shafts from the transmission as described in Chapter 8. **Note:** *Do not allow the shafts to hang down under their own weight as this could damage the constant velocity joints/gaiters.*

8 Disconnect the quick-release coupling at the slave cylinder end of the hydraulic pipe using a special tool (See Chapter 6, Section 4, for further information).

1.4 and 1.6 litre petrol engine models

9 Undo the retaining bolts and remove the air cleaner mounting bracket from the top of the transmission housing. Unclip any wiring from the bracket as it is removed.

10 Disconnect the multiplug connector from the reversing light switch.

11 Carefully disconnect the gear linkage rod balljoints from the gearchange levers (see

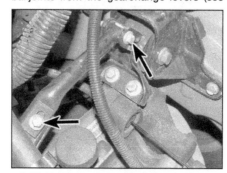

7.17 Undo the two bolts (arrowed) from the engine steady bar

Section 3), and tie them clear of the work area **(see illustration)**.

12 Remove the three bolts securing the flywheel front cover plate to the transmission housing, and remove the cover plate **(see illustration)**. Unclip the starter wiring from the securing clip as the cover is removed.

13 Disconnect the multiplug connector from the vehicle speed sensor.

14 Remove the three bolts securing the rear engine mounting bracket to the transmission and remove the flywheel rear cover plate **(see illustration)**.

15 Release the charcoal canister from its mounting bracket on the inner wing panel and move it to one side.

16 Place a jack with a block of wood beneath the engine, to take the weight of the engine. Alternatively, attach a hoist or support bar to the engine lifting eyes to take the engine weight **(see illustration)**. Also place a trolley jack and block of wood beneath the transmission, and raise the jack to take the weight of the transmission.

17 Remove the two bolts attaching the engine left-hand steady bar to the engine bracket and engine mounting, and remove the steady bar **(see illustration)**.

18 Undo the retaining bolts and remove the left-hand engine/transmission mounting, with reference to Chapter 2A.

19 Undo the retaining bolts and disconnect the left-hand lower suspension arm from the body panel. See Chapter 10 for further information.

20 Where applicable, remove the retaining bolts from the air conditioning pipe mounting bracket on the front of the transmission housing and move it to one side.

21 With the jack positioned beneath the transmission taking the weight, slacken and remove the remaining nuts and bolts securing the transmission housing to the engine. Work your way around the circumference of the transmission housing, noting the correct fitted positions of each nut/bolt, and the necessary brackets, as they are removed (this will be useful as a reference on refitting). Make a final check that all components have been disconnected, and are positioned clear of the transmission so that they will not hinder the removal procedure. *Caution: Do not allow the transmission to hang on the clutch shaft.*

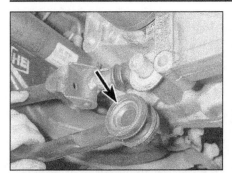

7.27 Disconnect the engine steady bar

7.29 Tie the gear selector rod to one side

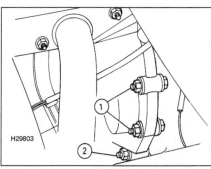

7.33 Unscrew the nuts and bolts (1) securing the flywheel front cover plate and the remaining transmission-to-engine nut and bolt (2)

22 With the aid of an assistant, move the trolley jack and transmission to the left, to free it from its locating dowels. Once the transmission is free, lower the jack and manoeuvre the unit out from under the car. Remove the locating dowels from the transmission or engine if they are loose, and keep them in a safe place.

1.8 litre petrol engine models

Note: *A new gear selector rod-to-selector shaft roll-pin will be required on refitting.*
23 Remove the left-hand centre engine/transmission mounting as described in Chapter 2A.
24 Undo the retaining bolt and disconnect the earth cable from the transmission.
25 Trace the wiring back from the reversing light switch and disconnect the two wiring connectors.
26 Disconnect the multiplug connector from the vehicle speed sensor.
27 Unscrew the bolt securing the gearchange steady bar to the transmission **(see illustration)**. Recover the two washers.
28 Remove the metal clip from the gear selector rod-to-selector shaft joint to expose the roll-pin.
29 Drive out the roll-pin using a suitable pin punch, then release the selector rod from the selector shaft, and move the rod and the gearchange steady bar to one side **(see illustration)**. Discard the roll-pin, a new one will be required for refitting.
30 Where applicable, remove the retaining bolts from the air conditioning pipe mounting bracket on the front of the transmission housing and move it to one side.
31 Place a jack with a block of wood beneath the engine, to take the weight of the engine. Alternatively, attach a hoist or support bar to the engine lifting eyes to take the engine weight. Also place a trolley jack and block of wood beneath the transmission, and raise the jack to take the weight of the transmission.
32 Unscrew the two upper engine-to-transmission retaining bolts.
33 Remove the three bolts securing the flywheel front cover plate to the transmission housing, and remove the cover plate **(see illustration)**.
34 With the jack positioned beneath the transmission taking the weight, slacken and

remove the remaining nuts and bolts securing the transmission housing to the engine. Work your way around the circumference of the transmission housing, noting the correct fitted positions of each nut/bolt, and the necessary brackets, as they are removed (this will be useful as a reference on refitting). Make a final check that all components have been disconnected, and are positioned clear of the transmission so that they will not hinder the removal procedure.
Caution: Do not allow the transmission to hang on the clutch shaft.
35 With the aid of an assistant, move the trolley jack and transmission to the left, to free it from its locating dowels. Once the transmission is free, lower the jack and manoeuvre the unit out from under the car. Remove the locating dowels from the transmission or engine if they are loose, and keep them in a safe place.

2.0 and 2.5 litre petrol engine models

Note: *A new gear selector rod-to-selector shaft roll-pin will be required on refitting.*
36 Undo the retaining bolt and disconnect the earth cable from the transmission **(see illustration)**.
37 Trace the wiring back from the reversing light switch and disconnect the two wiring connectors.
38 Unscrew the bolt securing the gearchange steady bar to the transmission. Recover the two washers.
39 Remove the metal clip from the gear selector rod-to-selector shaft joint to expose the roll-pin.

7.36 Disconnect the earth lead – arrowed

40 Drive out the roll-pin using a suitable pin punch, then release the selector rod from the selector shaft, and move the rod and the gearchange steady bar to one side (see Section 3). Discard the roll-pin, a new one will be required for refitting.
41 Remove the exhaust front pipe as described in Chapter 4B.
42 Place a jack with a block of wood beneath the engine, to take the weight of the engine. Alternatively, attach a hoist or support bar to the engine lifting eyes to take the engine weight. Also place a trolley jack and block of wood beneath the transmission, and raise the jack to take the weight of the transmission.
43 Undo the retaining bolts and remove the left-hand engine/transmission mounting **(see illustration)**, with reference to Chapter 2B. The transmission will need to be lowered slightly on the trolley jack to access the two lower mounting bolts.
44 With the jack positioned beneath the transmission taking the weight, slacken and remove the remaining nuts and bolts securing the transmission housing to the engine. Work your way around the circumference of the transmission housing, noting the correct fitted positions of each nut/bolt, and the necessary brackets, as they are removed (this will be useful as a reference on refitting). Make a final check that all components have been disconnected, and are positioned clear of the transmission so that they will not hinder the removal procedure. **Note:** *The lower transmission bolts which are adjacent to the*

7.43 Left-hand engine/transmission mounting – arrowed

exhaust mounting bracket cannot be removed fully.

Caution: Do not allow the transmission to hang on the clutch shaft.

45 With the aid of an assistant, move the trolley jack and transmission to the left, to free it from its locating dowels. Once the transmission is free, lower the jack and manoeuvre the unit out from under the car. Remove the locating dowels from the transmission or engine if they are loose, and keep them in a safe place.

Diesel engine models

Note: *A new gear selector rod-to-selector shaft roll-pin will be required on refitting.*

46 Slacken the securing clip and disconnect the breather pipe from the camshaft cover.

47 If not already done, undo the retaining bolts and remove the air cleaner mounting bracket from the engine compartment.

48 Release the locking collar, which secures the slave cylinder to the mounting bracket on the transmission. Press down on the pushrod and unclip the slave cylinder from the mounting bracket and remove it from transmission and move it to one side.

49 Undo the retaining bolt and disconnect the earth cables from the transmission.

50 Trace the wiring back from the reversing light switch, locate the wiring connector(s), and separate the two halves of the wiring connector(s).

51 Unscrew the nut/bolt securing the air conditioning pipe to the coolant rail bracket on the transmission mounting plate. Lift and secure the coolant rail, to clear the transmission housing for removal.

52 Unscrew the bolt securing the gearchange steady bar to the transmission. Recover the two washers.

53 Remove the metal clip from the gear selector rod-to-selector shaft joint to expose the roll-pin.

54 Drive out the roll-pin using a suitable pin punch, then release the selector rod from the selector shaft, and move the rod and the gearchange steady bar to one side (see Section 3). Discard the roll-pin, a new one will be required for refitting.

55 Disconnect the multiplug connector from the vehicle speed sensor.

56 Release the fuel filter from its mounting bracket on the inner wing panel and move it to one side.

57 Place a jack with a block of wood beneath the engine, to take the weight of the engine. Alternatively, attach a hoist or support bar to the engine lifting eyes to take the engine weight. Also place a trolley jack and block of wood beneath the transmission, and raise the jack to take the weight of the transmission.

58 Undo the retaining bolts and remove the left-hand engine/transmission mounting, with reference to Chapter 2C. The transmission will need to be lowered slightly on the trolley jack to access the two lower mounting bolts.

59 Unscrew the four bolts securing the transmission to the mounting plate and the engine/transmission reinforcing bracket **(see illustration)**.

60 Unscrew the two bolts securing the clutch slave cylinder bracket to the transmission housing and remove.

61 With the jack positioned beneath the transmission taking the weight, slacken and remove the remaining upper bolt securing the transmission housing to the engine. Work your way around the circumference of the transmission housing, noting the correct fitted positions of each nut/bolt, and the necessary brackets, as they are removed (this will be useful as a reference on refitting). Make a final check that all components have been disconnected, and are positioned clear of the transmission so that they will not hinder the removal procedure.

Caution: Do not allow the transmission to hang on the clutch shaft.

62 With the aid of an assistant, move the trolley jack and transmission to the left, to free it from its locating dowels on the mounting plate. Once the transmission is free, lower the jack and manoeuvre the unit out from under the car. Remove the locating dowels from the transmission housing or mounting plate if they are loose, and keep them in a safe place.

Refitting

63 Clean the mating faces of the engine and flywheel housing.

64 Check that the clutch friction disc is centralised as described in Chapter 6.

65 Apply a little high melting-point grease to the splines of the transmission input shaft. Do

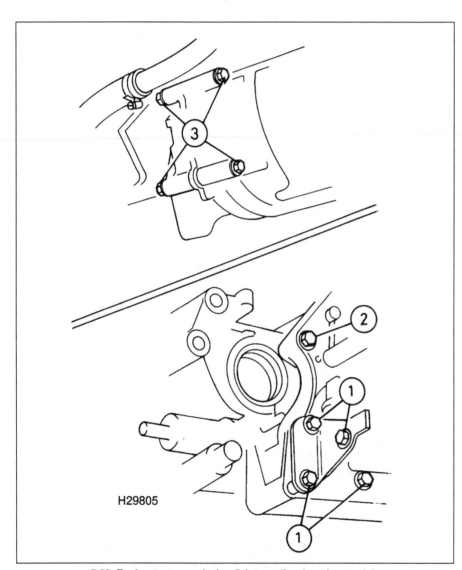

H29805

7.59 Engine-to-transmission fixings – diesel engine models

1 *Lower transmission-to-mounting plate bolts*
2 *Rear transmission-to-mounting plate bolt*
3 *Transmission-to-mounting plate nuts and bolts*

not apply too much, as this may contaminate the clutch.

66 With the aid of an assistant, position the transmission under the vehicle, and secure it to the lifting equipment.

67 Ensure that the locating dowels are in place in the engine/mounting plate, then carefully offer the transmission to the engine until the locating dowels are engaged, ensuring that the weight of the transmission is not allowed to hang on the input shaft as it is engaged with the clutch friction disc.

68 Refit the transmission-to-engine/mounting plate nuts and bolts, and tighten them to their specified torque setting.

69 Further refitting is a reversal of removal, bearing in mind the following points:

a) Tighten all fixings to the specified torque, where applicable.

b) Refit the left-hand engine/transmission mounting as described in Chapter 2A, 2B or 2C, as applicable.

c) Where applicable, refit the left-hand front suspension tie-rod as described in Chapter 10.

d) Reconnect the driveshafts to the transmission as described in Chapter 8.

e) Where applicable, use a new roll-pin when reconnecting the gear selector rod to the selector shaft.

f) On 2.0 and 2.5 litre petrol engine models, reconnect the exhaust front section to the manifold with reference to Chapter 4B.

g) Refit the starter motor as described in Chapter 5A.

h) On completion, refill the transmission with oil as described in Section 2.

8 Manual transmission overhaul – general information

Overhauling a manual transmission unit is a difficult and involved job for the DIY home mechanic. In addition to dismantling and reassembling many small parts, clearances must be precisely measured and, if necessary, changed by selecting shims and spacers. Internal transmission components are also often difficult to obtain, and in many instances, extremely expensive. Because of this, if the transmission develops a fault or becomes noisy, the best course of action is to have the unit overhauled by a specialist repairer, or to obtain an exchange reconditioned unit.

Nevertheless, it is not impossible for the more experienced mechanic to overhaul the transmission, provided that the necessary special tools are available, and the job is done in a deliberate step-by-step manner, so that nothing is overlooked.

The tools necessary for an overhaul include internal and external circlip pliers, bearing pullers, a slide hammer, a set of pin punches, a dial test indicator, and possibly a hydraulic press. In addition, a large, sturdy workbench and a vice will be required.

During dismantling of the transmission, make careful notes of how each component is fitted, to make reassembly easier and more accurate.

Before dismantling the transmission, it will help if you have some idea of what area is malfunctioning. Certain problems can be closely related to specific areas in the transmission, which can make component examination and renewal easier. Refer to the Fault finding Section of this manual for more information.

Notes

Chapter 7 Part B:
Automatic transmission

Contents

Section number

Automatic transmission – removal and refitting 6
Automatic transmission fluid level check . . . . . . .See Chapter 1A or 1B
Automatic transmission fluid – renewal 11
Automatic transmission overhaul – general information 7
Fluid cooler – removal and refitting 8
Fluid seals – renewal 9

Section number

General information 1
Inhibitor switch – description, removal, refitting and adjustment 5
Selector cable – removal, refitting and adjustment 3
Selector indicator – removal and refitting 4
Selector mechanism – removal and refitting 2
Transmission ECU – removal and refitting 10

Degrees of difficulty

Easy, suitable for novice with little experience 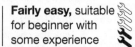	Fairly easy, suitable for beginner with some experience	Fairly difficult, suitable for competent DIY mechanic	Difficult, suitable for experienced DIY mechanic	Very difficult, suitable for expert DIY or professional

Specifications

General

Type	Jatco, five forward speeds and reverse

Ratios:

First.	3.474 : 1
Second	1.948 : 1
Third	1.247 : 1
Fourth	0.854 : 1
Fifth.	0.685 : 1
Reverse	2.714 : 1
Final drive ratio	4.150 : 1

Torque wrench settings

	Nm	lbf ft
Engine/transmission mountings:		
Left-hand mounting through-bolt	100	74
Left-hand mounting to body	85	63
Left-hand mounting to transmission	85	63
Lower mounting through-bolts	100	74
Fluid cooler mounting bracket bolts	9	7
Fluid drain plug.	45	33
Fluid filler/level plug	14	10
Fluid hose unions to transmission	18	13
Fluid pan bolts	7	5
Selector cable bracket to transmission	25	18
Selector housing-to-floor Torx bolts	9	7
Selector lever-to-transmission selector shaft nut.	25	18
Torque converter access plate bolts	9	7
Torque converter-to-driveplate bolts	45	33

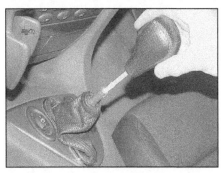

2.1 Pull up sharply to remove the selector lever knob

1 General information

A 5-speed fully automatic transmission is available as an option on many models. The transmission consists of a torque converter, an epicyclic geartrain, and hydraulically-operated clutches and brakes.

The torque converter provides a fluid coupling between the engine and transmission, acts as an automatic 'clutch', and also provides a degree of torque multiplication when accelerating. To improve economy, the torque converter has a 'lock-up' facility under low-load conditions (such as when cruising), which eliminates the small degree of slip which would otherwise be present.

Three modes of operation are available: Normal (economy), Sport or Snow, displayed by symbols in the instrument panel, and selected using the mode switch on the facia panel. In Sport mode, the software programme makes the transmission more responsive, and allows upshifts to happen at higher engine speeds for better acceleration. The Snow mode, designed for winter driving, makes starting off easier in slippery conditions (2nd gear is used), and the transmission upshifts at lower engine speeds to reduce wheelspin.

Sophisticated adaptive software programming of the transmission control unit enables it to recognise driving situations such as towing, downhill overrun, steep mountain roads, etc, and select the optimum shift strategies for each.

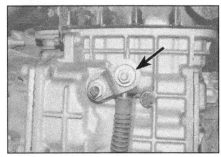

3.4a Slacken the selector inner cable clamp nut (arrowed) at the transmission end of the cable . . .

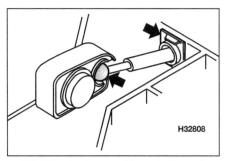

2.6 Selector inner cable end fitting at the selector lever, and outer cable clip (arrowed)

Due to the complexity of the automatic transmission, any repair or overhaul work must be entrusted to a suitably-qualified transmission specialist, with the necessary specialist equipment and knowledge for fault diagnosis and repair. Refer to the *Fault finding* Section at the end of this manual for further information.

2 Selector mechanism – removal and refitting

Removal

1 With the lever in neutral (N), pull up sharply to disengage the selector knob's securing tab, and remove the selector knob **(see illustration)**.
2 Unclip the selector lever gaiter trim panel from the centre console, then disconnect two wiring plugs and lift the panel and gaiter off the selector lever.
3 Referring to the relevant part of Chapter 4, either lower the front half of the exhaust system, or (for the best access) remove the whole system. The exhaust's central heat shield must be removed for access to the selector mechanism.
4 Remove the nine bolts securing the centre heat shield and remove the heat shield from under the car.
5 Unscrew the four Torx bolts securing the selector mechanism to the underside of the car. Lower the mechanism through the floor.

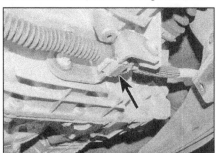

3.4b . . . and remove the outer cable-to-transmission bracket retaining clip (arrowed)

6 Pull off the rubber boot from the selector mechanism. Slide the barrelled end of the inner cable from the selector lever, pull out the retaining clip and release the outer cable from the selector housing **(see illustration)**.

Refitting

7 Refitting is a reversal of removal. Adjust the selector cable as described in Section 3 on completion.

3 Selector cable – removal, refitting and adjustment

Removal

1 Remove the selector mechanism as described in Section 2.
2 Release the selector cable from the retaining clips on the car body.
3 Where applicable, unscrew the two bolts and remove the cable support bracket from the transmission.
4 Slacken the selector inner cable clamp nut at the transmission end of the cable, and remove the outer cable-to-transmission bracket retaining clip **(see illustrations)**. Remove the cable.

Refitting

5 Refitting is a reversal of removal. Adjust the cable as described below.

Adjustment

6 Park the car on level ground, switch off the ignition, and apply the handbrake firmly. Jack up the front of the car and support it securely on axle stands (see *Jacking and vehicle support*).
7 Remove the engine undertray, which is secured by a number of quick-release screw fasteners.
8 Slacken the selector inner cable clamp nut at the transmission end of the cable **(see illustration 3.4a)**.
9 Move the selector lever in the passenger compartment into position P.
10 Move the selector lever on the transmission fully clockwise to engage the P position.
11 At the transmission end, gently pull the inner cable to eliminate any slack, and then tighten the inner cable clamp nut securely.
12 Check that all selector lever operation is correct, and that the engine can only be started in positions P and N.
13 Refit the engine undertray, and lower the car to the ground.

4 Selector indicator – removal and refitting

Removal

1 Remove the selector lever trim panel as described in Section 2, paragraphs 1 and 2.

It is possible to prise the indicator out from above **(see illustration)**, but to save any damage to the panel it would be safer to press it out from below.

2 Squeeze the tabs on the underside of the selector indicator, and lift it out of the panel **(see illustration)**.

Refitting

3 Refitting is a reversal of removal.

---

5 Inhibitor switch –
description, removal, refitting and adjustment

Description

1 The starter inhibitor switch is screwed into the top of transmission casing. The function of the switch ensures that the engine can only be started with the selector lever in either the N or the P positions, therefore preventing the engine from being started with the transmission in gear. If at any time it is noted that the engine can be started with the selector lever in any position other than N or P, then it is likely that the inhibitor function of the switch is faulty, or the selector cable adjustment is incorrect (see Section 3).

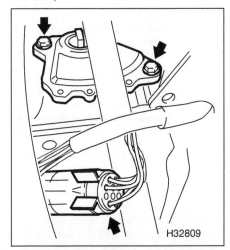

5.6 Release the inhibitor switch wiring plug from the clip, and undo the two bolts (arrowed)

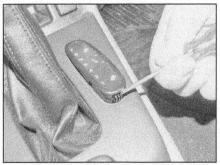

4.1 Releasing locking tab using a small screwdriver

Removal

2 On petrol engine models, remove the air cleaner as described in Chapter 4A or 4B.

3 Park the car on level ground, switch off the ignition, and apply the handbrake firmly. Jack up the front of the car and support it securely on axle stands (see *Jacking and vehicle support*).

4 Remove the engine undertray, which is secured by a number of quick-release screw fasteners.

5 Move the selector lever to position N.

6 Release the inhibitor switch wiring plug from the retaining clip on the transmission fluid pan, and disconnect it **(see illustration)**.

7 Unscrew the two retaining bolts and remove the switch from the transmission casing.

Refitting

8 Commence refitting by cleaning the switch, and the switch mating face in the transmission casing.

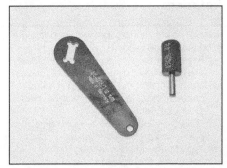

5.16a MG Rover inhibitor switch aligning tools

4.2 Squeeze the tabs under the panel and remove the selector indicator

9 Align the internal lugs with the mark on the inhibitor switch.

10 Align the two lugs of the switch with the machined grooves in the selector lever shaft, and fit the switch. Do not tighten the switch bolts at this stage.

11 Reconnect the switch wiring plug, and refit the connector to the retaining clip.

12 Carry out the adjustment procedure.

Adjustment

13 On petrol engine models, if not already done, remove the air cleaner as described in Chapter 4A or 4B.

14 Ensure the selector lever is in position N.

15 Slacken the inhibitor switch bolts.

16 Fit special tool 44-018 over the selector lever shaft, and rotate the switch so that the tool alignment pin can be inserted through the tool lever, and into the inhibitor switch. If the special tool is not available, a suitable homemade equivalent can be fabricated **(see illustrations)**.

17 Tighten the inhibitor switch bolts securely, and remove the alignment tool.

18 Check the inhibitor switch operation by attempting to start the engine with the selector lever in positions other than P or N.

---

6 Automatic transmission
– removal and refitting

Caution: The transmission is a heavy and awkward assembly, and care should be taken to avoid personal injury during its

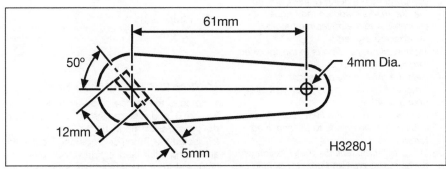

5.16b If the MG Rover tool is not available, make an equivalent using the dimensions shown

61mm

50°

12mm

5mm

4mm Dia.

H32801

5.16c Aligning tool and pin fitted to inhibitor switch

removal. It is recommended that this task is only undertaken with the help of an assistant. Read through the entire procedure before starting work.

1 Park the car on firm, level ground.

2 Remove the air cleaner and throttle body as described in Chapter 4B.

3 Remove the battery and its tray, and the starter motor, as described in Chapter 5A.

4 Remove the bonnet as described in Chapter 11.

5 Unclip the two transmission wiring multiplugs from the brackets on the front of the transmission, then disconnect them by twisting them apart.

6 Disconnect the crankshaft position sensor wiring plug, then unscrew the sensor mounting bolt from the front of the transmission and withdraw the sensor.

7 Remove the two bolts, and withdraw the stepped closing plate above the right-hand driveshaft.

8 Bolt two suitable lifting eyes to the transmission casing. Alternatively, the transmission can be removed just by supporting it from below.

9 Raise the front of the car sufficiently to allow the transmission to be lowered out and withdrawn from underneath.

10 Remove the driveshafts as described in Chapter 8.

11 Slacken the selector inner cable clamp nut at the transmission end of the cable, and remove the outer cable-to-transmission bracket retaining clip. Where applicable, remove the two bolts from the cable support bracket on the transmission. Move the selector cable clear.

12 Turn the engine so that the first of the four torque converter bolts is accessible, in the aperture above the right-hand driveshaft.

13 Mark the relationship of the driveplate to the torque converter, to aid refitment. Rotate the crankshaft using a spanner or socket on the crankshaft pulley to access, and unscrew the four torque converter bolts one at a time.

14 Loosen all of the transmission-to-engine bolts by half a turn only. There are seven in total – one or more of these bolts will have been removed earlier in the procedure. A nut and bolt is at the front.

15 Loosen the union nuts, then disconnect the two fluid cooler unions from the transmission – note their positions for refitting. Recover the O-rings (new ones will be needed for refitting) and plug or tape over the open connections.

16 Support the transmission from below using a substantial jack with a flat piece of wood on top of it. Another jack will be required to support the engine – alternatively, use an engine support bar for this, located in the bonnet side channels on the inner wings.

17 Make a final check from below and above that there is nothing left attached to the transmission, nor anything in the way which would prevent the unit from being lowered out.

18 Loosen and remove the engine/transmission left-hand mounting through-bolt, then remove the four bolts securing the mounting bracket to the top of the transmission.

19 Lower the engine on the jack, and remove the transmission mounting bracket.

20 If lifting eyes were fitted to the transmission, unbolt and remove the transmission mounting bracket from the inner wing, then attach the lifting equipment to them, and take the weight.

 Before removing the transmission from the engine, it is helpful for refitting to paint or scratch an alignment mark or two across the engine/transmission, so that the transmission can be offered up in approximately the right alignment to engage the dowels.

21 With the help of an assistant to steady the transmission, remove the bolts securing it to the engine. Note that the unit is also mounted on two dowels – if necessary; carefully prise the transmission away from the engine to free it.

22 Withdraw the transmission off the engine, taking care that its weight is not allowed to hang on the input shaft. Once it is free, while an assistant keeps it steady on the jack, lower it to the ground (or, if a hoist is used, the jack can be removed before lowering). With the help of your assistant, remove it from under the car.

Refitting

23 The transmission is refitted using a reversal of the removal procedure, bearing in mind the following points:

a) If required, the torque converter fluid seal can be renewed as described in Section 9.

b) Make sure that the torque converter is correctly fitted to the transmission input shaft (see Section 9).

c) Ensure the locating dowels are correctly positioned prior to installation.

d) Align the torque converter with the driveplate, and tighten the securing bolts to the specified torque. If the original torque converter and driveplate components are being refitted, ensure that the marks made on the torque converter and the driveplate before removal are aligned.

e) Tighten all nuts and bolts to the specified torque (where given).

f) Refit the driveshafts as described in Chapter 8, renewing the inner joint circlips prior to refitting.

g) Fit new O-rings to the fluid cooler hoses, and tighten the unions to the specified torque.

h) On completion, refill the transmission with the specified type and quantity of fluid (see 'Lubricants and fluids') as described in Section 11.

7 Automatic transmission overhaul – general information

In the event of a fault occurring on the transmission, it is first necessary to determine whether it is of an electrical, mechanical or hydraulic nature, and to achieve this, special test equipment is required. It is therefore essential to have the work carried out by a suitably-equipped specialist if a transmission fault is suspected.

Do not remove the transmission from the car for possible repair before professional fault diagnosis has been carried out, since most tests require the transmission to be in the car.

8 Fluid cooler – removal and refitting

1 Remove the front bumper as described in Chapter 11.

2 Slacken and remove the two upper mounting bolts for the cooling fan(s) and condenser. Using cable ties, secure the cooling fan, condenser and radiator to the upper body cross panel.

3 Undo the four retaining bolts and remove the two lower radiator mounting brackets.

4 Position a suitable container under the fluid cooler connections and release the cooler from the body panel and cooling fan housing.

5 Release the quick-fit couplings from the fluid cooler and remove the cooler from the car. Cap or plug the pipe connections to prevent dirt ingress and move the pipes to one side.

6 If a new cooler is being fitted, remove the mounting bushes and washers from the mounting brackets at each end of the cooler.

7 Refitting is a reversal of removal, noting the following points:

a) If the fluid temperature sensor was removed, use a new sealing washer.

b) Clean the fluid cooler unions, and fit new O-rings, lubricated with transmission fluid.

c) On completion, check and top-up the transmission fluid level.

9 Fluid seals – renewal

Torque converter fluid seal

1 Remove the transmission as described in Section 6, and slide the torque converter from the transmission input shaft.

2 Discard the O-ring seal from the input shaft and, using a flat-bladed screwdriver, prise the fluid seal from the input shaft housing. Note the fitted depth of the seal.

3 Ensure that the fluid seal recess in the

transmission, and the torque converter spigot are clean and dry. Lubricate the new fluid seal with clean transmission fluid, and fit it to the transmission. Use a tubular drift that bears only on the hard outer edge of the seal. Fit the seal squarely into the housing, with the inner lip facing the transmission.

4 Fit a new O-ring to the transmission input shaft.

5 Position the torque converter over the input shaft, and check that it is fully located **(see illustration).**

Driveshaft fluid seals

6 Working as described in Chapter 8, remove the driveshaft on the side concerned.

7 Carefully prise the seal out of the transmission using a large flat-bladed screwdriver.

8 Remove all traces of dirt from the area around the seal aperture. The new seal has a waxed outer surface, and should **not** be lubricated prior to fitting. Ensure the seal is correctly positioned, with its sealing lip facing inwards, and drive it squarely into position, using a suitable tubular drift (such as a socket), which bears only on the hard outer edge of the seal.

9 Ensure the seal is correctly located in the transmission housing, then refit the driveshaft as described in Chapter 8.

10 Top-up the transmission with the specified type of fluid (see *Lubricants and fluids*) as described in Chapter 1A or 1B.

---

10 Transmission ECU – removed and refitting

Removal

1 Disconnect the battery negative lead, and move the lead away from the battery (see *Disconnecting the battery*).

2 Working in the passenger's front footwell, release the fixings and remove the trim panel from the bottom of the A-pillar.

3 Disconnect the wiring connector from the ECU.

4 Unscrew the two mounting bolts and remove the ECU from its location.

Refitting

5 Refitting is a reversal of removal.

---

11 Automatic transmission fluid – renewal

⚠ **Warning: The transmission fluid may be extremely hot.**

1 The fluid should ideally be drained with the transmission at operating temperature. For this reason, it is advisable to wear gloves for this procedure, to protect your hands from hot fluid and surrounding components.

2 Remove the air cleaner assembly. Pull out the plug from the fluid filler pipe on top of the transmission.

3 Park the car on level ground, and remove the engine undertray, which is secured by a number of quick-release screw fasteners. If possible, leave the car on the ground – if the car is raised for better access underneath, it must be level to ensure accurate refilling.

4 Position a container (of at least 4.0 litre capacity) under the transmission drain plug, which is a hex-headed bolt at the rear of the housing. Clean the area around the drain plug.

5 Remove the drain plug, and recover the sealing washer – a new one should be obtained for refitting.

6 When the fluid has finished draining, refit the drain plug with a new washer, and tighten it to the specified torque.

7 Clean around the filler pipe on top of the transmission – it is vital that no dirt enters the transmission at any stage.

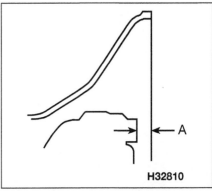

9.5 Showing the torque converter fitted depth (A) of 4mm

8 Slowly add 3.5 to 4.0 litres of clean fluid of the specified type (see *Lubricants and fluids*) through the filler pipe, then clean and refit the filler plug.

9 Start the engine. With the footbrake firmly pressed, move the selector lever through each position. Pause in each position for a few seconds, then return to position P.

10 Clean the area around the level plug, which is located directly below the selector cable – it may even be necessary to detach the cable for better access. Position a container under the level plug.

11 Using a 5 mm Allen key, unscrew the filler/level plug, which will probably be very tight. Recover the sealing ring – a new one will be needed when refitting.

12 Allow any excess fluid to run out. If none emerges, add a little fluid through the filler pipe on top of the transmission, until it just runs from the level hole. Move the selector through all its positions, finishing at P, then wait for the excess fluid to run out.

13 When the level stabilises, stop the engine. Refit and tighten the level plug (with a new sealing washer) to the specified torque.

14 Refit the engine undertray on completion.

Notes

Chapter 8
Driveshafts

Contents

Section number

Driveshaft overhaul – general information and inspection 2
Driveshaft rubber gaiters – renewal 5
General information and precautions 1

Section number

Left-hand driveshaft – removal and refitting 3
Right-hand driveshaft – removal and refitting 4

Degrees of difficulty

Easy, suitable for novice with little experience	Fairly easy, suitable for beginner with some experience	Fairly difficult, suitable for competent DIY mechanic	Difficult, suitable for experienced DIY mechanic	Very difficult, suitable for expert DIY or professional

Specifications

Driveshafts

Type . . . . Unequal-length solid steel shafts, splined to inner and outer constant velocity joints, dynamic damper on both shafts

Torque wrench settings	Nm	lbf ft
Driveshaft retaining nut	180	133
Roadwheel nuts	110	81

1 General information and precautions

General information

Drive is transmitted from the differential to the front wheels by means of two driveshafts of unequal length. Both driveshafts are splined at their outer ends to accept the wheel hubs, and are threaded so that each hub can be fastened by a large retaining nut. The inner end of each driveshaft is splined to accept the differential sun gear and has a groove to accept the circlip, which secures the driveshaft to the sun gear **(see illustration)**.

Constant velocity (CV) joints are fitted to both ends of each driveshaft to ensure the smooth and efficient transmission of drive at all possible angles as the roadwheels move up-and-down with the suspension and as they turn from side-to-side under steering.

The inner CV joints are a tripod type of joint with spherical bushing to reduce sliding resistance. The outer CV joint is of the ball-and-cage type, both joints are sealed with rubber gaiters, which are pre-packed with grease.

On diesel models, a dynamic damper is fitted to each driveshaft to reduce vibrations and resonance **(see illustration)**.

On V6 petrol models, the right-hand driveshaft is a two-piece shaft, which is supported by an intermediate bearing, located at the rear of the cylinder block.

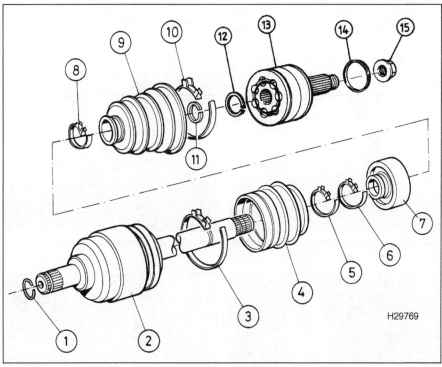

1.1 Driveshaft assembly

1	Circlip	5	Small gaiter retaining clip	10	Large gaiter retaining clip
2	Inner joint and shaft assembly	6	Damper clip	11	Stopper ring
3	Large gaiter retaining clip	7	Dynamic damper	12	Circlip
4	Gaiter	8	Small gaiter retaining clip	13	Outer joint assembly
		9	Gaiter	14	Seal
				15	Driveshaft nut

H29769

1.4 Dynamic damper (arrowed) on the driveshaft

Precautions

• The driveshaft retaining nuts are extremely tight; ensure the car is securely supported when slackening and tightening them.

• The only new parts listed are the inner CV joint/driveshaft assemblies, the outer CV joint assemblies and the rubber gaiters. The gaiters are supplied in a kit with the necessary sachets of grease and clips.

• If any CV joint is worn or damaged, it cannot be reconditioned and must be renewed. In the case of the inner joints, this means that the complete joint/shaft assembly must be renewed.

2 Driveshaft overhaul – general information and inspection

1 Refer to the relevant Part of Chapter 1 and if

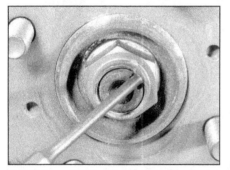

3.3 Using a hammer and punch to release driveshaft nut staking

3.7 Pull swivel hub outwards and disengage driveshaft outer CV joint

the checks carried out indicate wear, proceed as follows.

2 Remove the roadwheel trim. If the staking is still effective, the driveshaft nut should be correctly tightened. If in doubt, use a torque wrench to check that the nut is securely fastened and restake it. Refit the wheel trim. Repeat this check on the remaining driveshaft nut.

3 Road test the vehicle and listen for a metallic clicking from the front as the vehicle is driven slowly in a circle on full lock. If a clicking noise is heard, this indicates wear in the outer CV joint.

4 Outer CV joints can be dismantled and inspected for wear as described in Section 5. Check on the availability of components before dismantling a joint.

5 If vibration, consistent with roadspeed, is felt through the vehicle when accelerating, there is a possibility of wear in the inner CV joints.

3 Left-hand driveshaft – removal and refitting

Note: *A balljoint separator tool will be required for this operation.*

Removal

1 Chock the rear wheels, firmly apply the handbrake then jack up the front of the vehicle and support it on axle stands (see *Jacking and vehicle support*). Remove the appropriate front roadwheel.

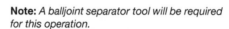

3.5 Removing the damper fork

3.9 Carefully lever driveshaft inner CV joint out of housing

2 Drain the transmission oil as described in Chapter 7A or 7B.

3 Using a hammer and suitable punch, tap back the staking securing the driveshaft retaining nut to the groove in the CV joint **(see illustration)**. **Note:** *A new driveshaft retaining nut will be required for refitting.*

4 Have an assistant firmly depress the brake pedal to prevent the front hub from rotating then, using a socket and extension bar, slacken and remove the driveshaft retaining nut. Discard the nut.

5 With reference to Chapter 10, undo the retaining bolts and remove the damper fork **(see illustration)** from the lower suspension arm and the base of the damper unit.

6 Extract the split pin and undo the nut securing the lower suspension arm balljoint to the swivel hub. Remove the nut and release the balljoint tapered shank using a universal balljoint separator.

7 Carefully pull the swivel hub assembly outwards and withdraw the driveshaft outer CV joint from the hub assembly **(see illustration)**. If necessary, the shaft can be tapped out of the hub using a soft-faced mallet.

Caution: Take care to avoid damaging the driveshaft threads.

8 On automatic models, disconnect the multiplug wiring connector from the inhibitor switch on the top of the transmission and move it to one side.

9 To release the inner CV joint, insert a suitable flat bar between the joint and transmission housing, then carefully lever the joint out of position, whilst taking great care not to damage the driveshaft oil seal **(see illustration)**.

10 Support the inner CV joint, keeping it horizontal, whilst withdrawing it from the transmission, to ensure the oil seal is not damaged.

11 Remove the driveshaft from the vehicle and discard the circlip from the inner splines. **Note:** *A new circlip will be required for refitting.*

Refitting

12 Before fitting the driveshaft, examine the transmission housing driveshaft oil seal for signs of damage or deterioration and, if necessary, renew it (see Chapter 7A or 7B).

3.13a Inspect outer CV joint seal (arrowed) . . .

3.13b . . . and renew the Inner CV joint circlip – arrowed

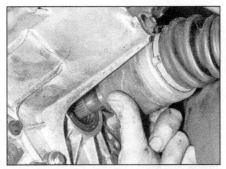

3.15 Refit driveshaft inner CV joint, taking care not to damage driveshaft oil seal

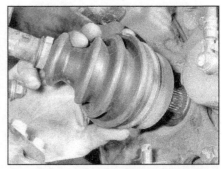

3.16 Engage the outer CV joint with swivel hub

3.20a Fit the new driveshaft nut . . .

3.20b . . . and tighten it to the specified torque

3.20c Stake driveshaft nut firmly into the groove in the CV joint

13 Renew the circlip, which is fitted to the groove in the inner CV joint splines, as a matter of course (see illustrations).

14 Thoroughly clean the driveshaft splines and the apertures in the transmission and hub assembly. Check that all gaiter clips are securely fastened.

15 Ensure that the circlip fitted to the inner CV joint is located securely in its groove, then locate the joint splines with those of the differential sun gear, taking great care not to damage the oil seal. Keeping it horizontal, push the joint fully into the transmission (see illustration). Check that the joint is securely retained by the circlip by trying to pull the shaft outwards.

16 Locate the outer CV joint splines with those of the swivel hub and slide the joint back into position in the hub (see illustration).

17 Insert the lower suspension arm balljoint into the swivel hub and tighten the retaining nut to the specified torque (see Chapter 10). Secure the nut in position using a new split pin.

18 On automatic models, reconnect the multiplug wiring connector to the inhibitor switch.

19 With reference to Chapter 10, refit the damper fork to the lower suspension arm and the base of the damper unit, and tighten the retaining bolts.

20 Fit the new driveshaft retaining nut and tighten it to the specified torque setting whilst an assistant firmly depresses the brake pedal. Release the brake, check that the hub rotates freely, and then stake the nut firmly into the groove on the CV joint using a suitable punch (see illustrations).

21 Refit the roadwheel then lower the vehicle to the ground and tighten the wheel nuts to the specified torque.

22 Refill the transmission with the correct type and quantity of oil, then check that the level is correct as described in Chapter 7A or 7B.

4 Right-hand driveshaft – removal and refitting

Note: A balljoint separator tool will be required for this operation.

Removal

1 Chock the rear wheels, firmly apply the handbrake then jack up the front of the vehicle and support it on axle stands (see Jacking and vehicle support). Remove the appropriate front roadwheel.

2 Drain the transmission oil as described in Chapter 7A or 7B.

3 Using a hammer and suitable punch, tap back the staking securing the driveshaft retaining nut to the groove in the CV joint (see illustration 3.3). **Note:** A new driveshaft retaining nut will be required for refitting.

4 Have an assistant firmly depress the brake pedal to prevent the front hub from rotating, then using a socket and extension bar, slacken and remove the driveshaft retaining nut. Discard the nut.

5 With reference to Chapter 10, undo the retaining bolts and remove the damper fork from the lower suspension arm and the base of the damper unit.

6 On V6 petrol models, undo the retaining bolts from the driveshaft intermediate bearing, located at the rear of the cylinder block.

7 Extract the split pin and undo the nut securing the lower suspension arm balljoint to the swivel hub. Remove the nut and release the balljoint tapered shank using a universal balljoint separator.

8 Carefully pull the swivel hub assembly outwards and withdraw the driveshaft outer CV joint from the hub assembly. If necessary, the shaft can be tapped out of the hub using a soft-faced mallet.

Caution: Take care to avoid damaging the driveshaft threads.

9 On all models except V6 petrol models, unscrew the two bolts securing the lower engine steady bar to the engine and the suspension crossmember and remove it from under the vehicle.

10 On all models except V6 petrol models, unscrew the bolt securing the gearchange steady bar to the transmission. Recover the two washers.

11 To release the inner CV joint, insert a suitable flat bar between the joint and transmission housing, then carefully lever the joint out of position, whilst taking great care not to damage the driveshaft oil seal.

12 Support the inner CV joint, keeping it horizontal, whilst withdrawing it from the transmission, to ensure the oil seal is not damaged.

13 Remove the driveshaft from the vehicle and discard the circlip (except V6 petrol models) from the inner splines. **Note:** A new circlip will be required for refitting.

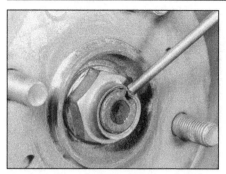

4.24 Use a punch to stake the driveshaft retaining nut

Refitting

14 Before fitting the driveshaft, examine the transmission housing driveshaft oil seal for signs of damage or deterioration and, if necessary, renew it (see Chapter 7A or 7B).

15 On all models except V6 petrol models, renew the circlip, which is fitted to the groove in the inner CV joint splines as a matter of course **(see illustration 3.13b)**. Ensure that the circlip is located securely in its groove.

16 Thoroughly clean the driveshaft splines and the apertures in the transmission and hub assembly. Check that all gaiter clips are securely fastened.

17 Locate the inner joint splines with those of the differential sun gear, taking great care not to damage the oil seal. Keeping it horizontal, push the joint fully into the transmission. Where applicable, check that the joint is securely retained by the circlip by trying to pull the shaft outwards.

18 Locate the outer CV joint splines with those of the swivel hub and slide the joint back into position in the hub.

19 Insert the lower suspension arm balljoint into the swivel hub and tighten the retaining nut to the specified torque (see Chapter 10). Secure the nut in position using a new split pin.

20 On V6 petrol models, refit the driveshaft intermediate bearing, to the rear of the cylinder block and tighten the retaining bolts.

21 With reference to Chapter 10, refit the damper fork to the lower suspension arm and the base of the damper unit, and tighten the retaining bolts.

22 On all models except V6 petrol models, secure the gearchange steady bar to the transmission, not forgetting to fit the two washers, and tighten the retaining bolt.

23 On all models except V6 petrol models, refit the lower engine steady bar to the engine and suspension crossmember, and then tighten the retaining bolts.

24 Fit the new driveshaft retaining nut and tighten it to the specified torque setting whilst an assistant firmly depresses the brake pedal. Release the brake, check that the hub rotates freely, and then stake the nut firmly into the groove on the CV joint using a suitable punch **(see illustration)**.

25 Refit the roadwheel then lower the vehicle to the ground and tighten the wheel nuts to the specified torque.

26 Refill the transmission with the correct type and quantity of oil, then check that the level is correct as described in Chapter 7A or 7B.

5 Driveshaft rubber gaiters – renewal

Outer joint

Removal

1 Remove the driveshaft as described in Section 3 or 4, as applicable.

2 Secure the driveshaft in a vice equipped with soft jaws and release the two rubber gaiter retaining clips by raising the locking tangs with a screwdriver and releasing the end of the clip with a pair of pliers. If necessary, the gaiter retaining clips can be cut to release them **(see illustration)**. Discard the retaining clips, as new ones will be required for refitting.

3 Slide the rubber gaiter down the shaft to expose the outer CV joint and clean out as much of the old grease as possible.

4 Using a soft-faced mallet, sharply strike the inner member of the joint to drive it off the end of the shaft **(see illustration)**. The outer joint is retained on the driveshaft by a circular section circlip and striking the joint in this manner forces the circlip into its groove, so allowing the joint to slide off.

5 Once the joint assembly has been removed, remove the circlip from the groove in the driveshaft splines and discard it. A new circlip must be fitted on reassembly.

6 The rubber gaiter can now be withdrawn from the driveshaft.

7 With the CV joint removed from the driveshaft, thoroughly clean the joint using paraffin or a suitable solvent and dry it thoroughly. Inspect the joint as follows.

8 Move the inner splined driving member from side-to-side to expose each ball in turn at the top of its track. Examine the balls for cracks, flat spots or signs of surface pitting.

9 Inspect the ball tracks on the inner and outer members. If the tracks have widened, the balls will no longer be a tight fit. At the same time check the ball cage windows for wear or cracking between the windows.

10 If, on inspection, any of the CV joint components are found to be worn, or damaged, it will be necessary to renew the complete joint assembly, since no components are available separately. If the joint is in satisfactory condition, obtain a repair kit consisting of a new gaiter, retaining clips and the correct type and quantity of grease.

Refitting

11 Tape over the splines on the end of the drive-shaft, then fit the small retaining clip onto the gaiter and carefully slide the gaiter onto the shaft.

12 Remove the tape, then ensuring that the stopper ring is securely located in its groove, fit a new circlip to the groove in the driveshaft splines **(see illustration)**. Engage the help of an assistant for the following operations.

13 Position the CV joint over the splines on the driveshaft until it abuts the circlip.

14 Using two small screwdrivers placed one either side of the circlip, compress the clip and at the same time have your assistant firmly strike the end of the joint with a soft-faced mallet. This should not require an undue amount of force. If the joint does not spring into place, remove it, reposition the circlip and try again. Do not force the joint; otherwise the circlip will be damaged.

15 Check that the circlip holds the joint securely on the driveshaft end then pack the joint with the grease supplied. Work the grease well into the ball tracks whilst twisting the joint and fill the rubber gaiter with any excess.

16 Ease the gaiter over the joint and place the large retaining clip in position. Ensure that the gaiter is correctly located in the grooves on both the driveshaft and CV joint.

5.2 Cutting gaiter clips to release them

5.4 Driving outer CV joint off driveshaft end

5.12 Ensure stopper ring and new circlip are correctly located before fitting outer CV joint

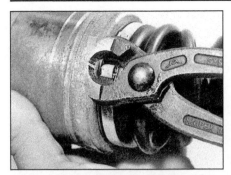

5.17 Using correct tool to tighten gaiter clip – side-cutters can be used if care is exercised

5.22 Cutting inner CV joint clip to release it

5.26 Pack inner CV joint with grease supplied in gaiter kit

17 Using a pair of pliers, pull the large retaining clip and fold it over until the end locates between the two raised tangs. Hold the clip in this position and bend the tangs over to lock the clip in position. Remove any slack in the gaiter retaining clip by carefully compressing the raised section of the clip. In the absence of the special tool, a pair of side-cutters may be used **(see illustration)**. Secure the small retaining clip using the same procedure.

18 Check that the CV joint moves freely in all directions, and then refit the driveshaft as described in Section 3 or 4, as applicable.

Inner joint

Removal

19 Remove the outer CV joint and gaiter as described in paragraphs 1 to 6.

20 Mark the position of the dynamic damper on the driveshaft, as reference for refitting. Clean and lubricate the length of the shaft to aid removal.

21 On diesel models, release the retaining clip and slide the dynamic damper along the driveshaft to remove it. Make a note of the position of the damper for refitting.

 HAYNES HiNT *Use liquid soap as a lubricant if necessary to aid damper removal and clean off any rust deposits or similar using emery cloth.*

22 Release the inner joint gaiter retaining clips and slide the gaiter off the shaft **(see illustration)**.

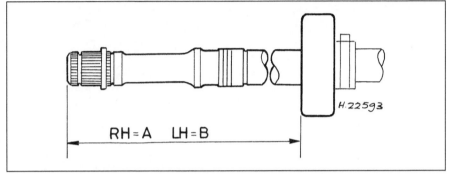

5.28 Position dynamic damper specified distance from outer end of driveshaft

A Right-hand driveshaft – 221 to 227 mm   B Left-hand driveshaft – 201 to 207 mm

23 Thoroughly clean the joint using paraffin, or a suitable solvent, and dry it thoroughly. Inspect the joint as described in paragraphs 8 and 9.

24 If, on inspection, the CV joint components are found to be worn, or damaged, it will be necessary to renew the complete joint and shaft assembly, since the inner joint is not available separately. If the joint is in satisfactory condition, obtain a repair kit consisting of a new gaiter, retaining clips and the correct type and quantity of grease. Although not strictly necessary, it is also recommended that the outer CV joint gaiter is renewed, regardless of its apparent condition.

Refitting

25 Make sure the shaft is clean and free from any rust or sharp edges which may damage the gaiter.

26 Pack the joint with the grease supplied

in the gaiter kit. Work the grease well into the ball tracks whilst twisting the joint **(see illustration)**.

27 Slide the inner joint gaiter along the driveshaft and locating it in the grooves on the joint and shaft. Fit both the large and small retaining clips, securing the clips in position as described in paragraph 17. Check that the joint moves freely in all directions.

28 On diesel models, lubricate the shaft and position a new retaining clip on the dynamic damper flange. Slide the dynamic damper onto the shaft so that its clip flange is innermost (faces the inner CV joint). Position the damper as noted on removal **(see illustration)**, and then secure it in position with the retaining clip. See illustration for fitted dimensions.

29 Remove any surplus lubricant from the shaft and refit the outer CV joint as described in paragraphs 11 to 18.

Notes

Chapter 9
Braking system

Contents

Section number

Anti-lock Braking System (ABS) – component removal and refitting 25
Brake pedal – removal and refitting 2
Brake proportioning valve – testing, removal and refitting. 13
Brake servo vacuum pump (diesel models) – removal and refitting. . 26
Front brake caliper – removal and refitting. 11
Front brake disc – inspection, removal and refitting 12
Front brake pads – inspection 9
Front brake pads – renewal 10
General information and precautions. 1
Handbrake cables – removal and refitting 23
Handbrake lever – removal and refitting. 22
Hydraulic fluid – level check and renewal 5
Hydraulic pipes and hoses – inspection and renewal 7

Section number

Hydraulic system – bleeding 6
Master cylinder – removal and refitting 8
Rear brake caliper – removal and refitting 20
Rear brake disc – inspection, removal and refitting 21
Rear brake drum – removal, inspection and refitting 16
Rear brake pads – inspection. 18
Rear brake pads – renewal. 19
Rear brake shoes – inspection. 14
Rear brake shoes – renewal 15
Rear wheel cylinder – removal and refitting 17
Stop-lamp switch – removal, refitting and adjustment. 24
Vacuum servo unit – testing, removal and refitting 3
Vacuum servo unit check valve – removal, testing and refitting 4

Degrees of difficulty

Easy, suitable for novice with little experience	Fairly easy, suitable for beginner with some experience	Fairly difficult, suitable for competent DIY mechanic	Difficult, suitable for experienced DIY mechanic	Very difficult, suitable for expert DIY or professional

Specifications

Braking system

Type . . . . Servo-assisted hydraulic circuit, split diagonally with anti-lock braking system (ABS). Disc front brakes. Disc or drum rear brakes, depending on model. On diesel models, vacuum provided by alternator-driven pump. Cable-operated handbrake, acting on rear brakes

Front brakes

Type	Disc, with sliding caliper
Disc type:	
1.4 and 1.6 litre petrol models	Solid
1.8, 2.0 and 2.5 litre petrol models	Ventilated
Diesel models.	Solid
Disc diameter:	
Rover 45 models	262 mm
MG ZS models	280 mm
Disc wear limit:	
Solid.	11.00 mm
Ventilated	19.00 mm
Maximum disc run-out.	0.04 mm
Brake pad friction material minimum thickness.	3.0 mm

Rear drum brakes

Type	Drum with leading and trailing shoes
Drum diameter:	
New	203 mm
Maximum diameter after machining.	204 mm
Maximum drum ovality.	0.012 mm
Brake shoe friction material minimum thickness	2.0 mm
ABS rear wheel sensor-to-reluctor ring	0.5 mm
Handbrake lever travel	7 to 11 clicks

Rear disc brakes

Type . . . .   Disc, with sliding caliper
Disc diameter:
   Rover 45 models . . . .   239 mm
   MG ZS models . . . .   260 mm
Disc wear limit . . . .   8.0 mm
Maximum disc run-out . . . .   0.10 mm
Brake pad friction material minimum thickness . . . .   3.0 mm
Handbrake lever travel . . . .   7 to 11 clicks

Torque wrench settings

	Nm	lbf ft
ABS front wheel sensor retaining bolt	6	4
ABS modulator mounting nuts.	21	15
ABS modulator union nuts	14	10
ABS rear wheel sensor retaining bolts (drum)	45	33
ABS rear wheel sensor retaining screws (disc)	6	4
ABS wheel sensor wiring bracket/cover bolts	10	7
Caliper bleed screw	10	7
Caliper bracket-to-hub mounting bolts	108	80
Caliper guide pin bolt	27	20
Caliper hydraulic hose union bolt.	34	25
Disc retaining screws	10	7
Drum retaining screws	7	5
Handbrake cable retaining plate bolts	22	16
Handbrake lever-to-floorpan bolts	22	16
Handbrake warning light switch screw	5	4
Master cylinder brake pipe union nuts.	19	14
Master cylinder-to-servo unit nuts	15	11
Proportioning valve mounting bolts	10	7
Proportioning valve hydraulic pipe union nuts	19	14
Roadwheel nuts	110	81
Servo hydraulic hose union nut (diesel models).	12	9
Servo-to-bulkhead nuts	13	10
Servo vacuum hose-to-inlet manifold union bolt	50	37
Vacuum pump-to-alternator bolts (diesel models).	8	6
Wheel cylinder bleed screw	7	5
Wheel cylinder brake pipe union	19	14
Wheel cylinder-to-backplate bolts	8	6

1 General information and precautions

General information

The brakes are operated by hydraulic pressure. For safety, the hydraulic system is split diagonally into two circuits – LH front with RH rear, and RH front with LH rear. Failure in any one circuit does not affect the other.

Pressure on the footbrake operates the two independent sections of a tandem master cylinder. Fluid pressure from the master cylinder is supplemented by vacuum assistance. On petrol engine vehicles, vacuum is provided by inlet manifold depression. On diesel engine vehicles, vacuum is provided by a vacuum pump attached to the alternator.

To reduce the possibility of rear wheel lock-up during severe braking, a brake pressure proportioning valve limits the pressure applied to the rear brakes. Pressure to the front brakes also passes through the proportioning valve, but this is for distribution only.

All models are fitted with front disc brakes, actuated by single piston, sliding-type calipers which ensure that equal pressure is applied to each disc pad. The brake discs may be solid or ventilated, depending on variant (see Specifications).

Rear drum or disc brakes may be fitted, depending on model. The drum brakes incorporate leading and trailing shoes, which are actuated by twin piston wheel cylinders. A self-adjusting mechanism is incorporated, to automatically compensate for brake shoe wear. As the brake shoe linings wear, the footbrake operation automatically operates the adjuster mechanism quadrant, which effectively lengthens the shoe strut and repositions the brake shoes to remove the lining-to-drum clearance.

The rear disc brakes are actuated by a single piston sliding caliper, which incorporates a mechanical handbrake mechanism.

On all models, the handbrake is operated by a floor-mounted lever and employs twin cables to provide an independent mechanical means of rear brake application.

Anti-lock Braking System

ABS reduces the possibility of skidding, by preventing wheel lock-up on loose/slippery surfaces. The system comprises a modulator block, which contains an ABS Electronic Control Unit (ECU), hydraulic solenoid valves and accumulators, and an electrically-driven return pump. One sensor is fitted to each roadwheel (see illustration). The purpose of the system is to prevent wheel locking during heavy braking. This is achieved by automatic release of the brake on the relevant (locking) wheel, followed by reapplication of the brake.

The solenoid valves are controlled by the ECU, which receives signals from the four roadwheel sensors, which in turn monitor the speed of rotation of each wheel. By comparing these speed signals from the four wheels, the ECU can determine the speed at which the vehicle is travelling. It can then use this speed to determine when a wheel is decelerating at an abnormal rate compared to the speed of the vehicle and therefore predict when a wheel is about to lock. During normal operation, the system functions in the same way as a non-ABS braking system.

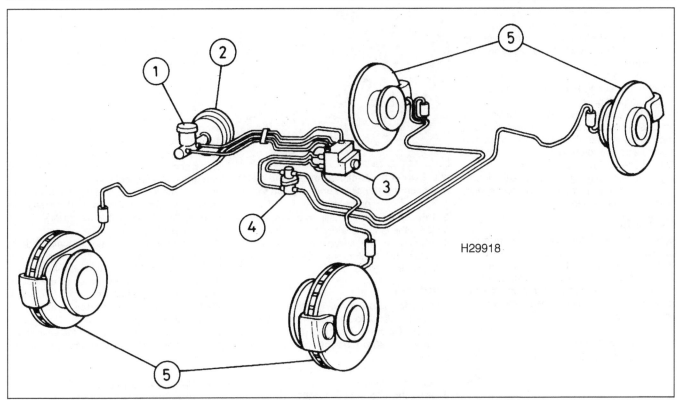

1.8 Anti-lock braking system (ABS) – component layout

1 *Master cylinder*
2 *Vacuum servo unit*

3 *Modulator block and ECU*
4 *Brake pressure proportioning valve*

5 *Reluctor ring and wheel sensor*

If the ECU senses that a wheel is about to lock, the ABS system enters the 'pressure maintain' phase. The ECU operates the relevant solenoid valve in the modulator block which then isolates the brake caliper on the wheel which is about to lock from the master cylinder, effectively sealing in the hydraulic pressure.

If the speed of rotation of the wheel continues to decrease at an abnormal rate, the ABS system then enters the 'pressure decrease' phase, where the electrically-driven return pump operates and pumps the hydraulic fluid back into the master cylinder, releasing pressure on the brake caliper/wheel cylinder so that the brake is released. Once the speed of rotation of the wheel returns to an acceptable rate, the pump stops and the solenoid valve opens thereby allowing the hydraulic master cylinder pressure to return to the caliper/wheel cylinder, which then reapplies the brake. This cycle can be carried out at up to 10 times a second.

The action of the solenoid valves and return pump creates pulses in the hydraulic circuit. When the ABS system is functioning, these pulses can be felt through the brake pedal.

The solenoid valves connected to the front calipers operate independently, but the valve connected to the rear calipers, together with the proportioning valve, operates both calipers (or wheel cylinders in the case of models with rear drum brakes) simultaneously.

Operation of the ABS system is entirely dependent on electrical signals. To prevent the system responding to any inaccurate signals, a built-in safety circuit monitors all signals received by the ECU. If a spurious signal or low battery voltage is detected, the ABS system is automatically shut down and the warning lamp on the instrument panel is illuminated to inform the driver that the ABS system is not operational. Under these circumstances, the braking system operates as a conventional, non-ABS braking system.

If a fault does develop in the ABS system the vehicle must be taken to a Rover dealer for fault diagnosis and repair. Check first, however, that the problem is not due to loose or damaged wiring connections, or badly routed wiring picking up false signals from the ignition system.

Precautions

• Hydraulic fluid is poisonous. Wash off immediately and thoroughly in the case of skin contact and seek immediate medical advice if any fluid is swallowed or gets into the eyes. Certain types of hydraulic fluid are inflammable and may ignite if brought into contact with hot components.

• When servicing any hydraulic system, it is safest to assume that the fluid is flammable and to take precautions against the risk of fire, as though it were petrol being handled. Hydraulic fluid is also an effective paint stripper and will attack plastics. If any is spilt, it should be washed off immediately using copious quantities of fresh water.

• Hydraulic fluid is hygroscopic, that is, it absorbs moisture from the air. Brake fluid that has become contaminated with water may boil under heavy braking, causing brake fade and so must be considered unfit for further use. When topping-up or renewing fluid, always use the recommended type and ensure that it comes from a newly opened container.

• When working on brake components, take care not to disperse brake dust into the air, or to inhale it, since it may contain asbestos, which is a health hazard.

• When servicing any part of the system, work carefully and methodically. Also observe scrupulous cleanliness when overhauling any part of the hydraulic system. Always renew components (in axle sets, where applicable) if in doubt about their condition and use only genuine Rover parts, or at least those of known good quality.

2 Brake pedal – removal and refitting

Removal

1 Working inside the vehicle, undo the three screws and remove the right-hand lower facia panel. Release the stud clips and lower the felt panel to expose the pedal mountings.

2 Extract the R-clip and clevis pin securing the servo unit pushrod to the brake pedal **(see illustration)**.

3 Using pliers, carefully unhook the brake pedal return spring from the pedal to release all the spring tension.

4 Slacken and remove the nut and washers (as applicable) from the brake pedal pivot bolt then withdraw the pivot bolt and remove the brake pedal and return spring.

5 Examine all brake pedal components for signs of wear, paying particular attention to the pedal bushes, pivot bolt and return spring, renewing as necessary.

Refitting

6 Refitting is a reverse of the removal procedure. Lubricate the bushes, pivot bolt and clevis pin with multi-purpose grease.

7 On completion, check the operation of the pedal and ensure that it returns smoothly to its 'at rest' position under the pressure of the return spring.

3 Vacuum servo unit – testing, removal and refitting

Testing

1 To test the operation of the servo unit, depress the footbrake several times to exhaust the vacuum, then start the engine whilst keeping the pedal firmly depressed. As the engine starts, there should be a noticeable 'give' in the brake pedal as the vacuum builds-up. Allow the engine to run for at least two minutes then switch it off. If the brake pedal is now depressed it should feel normal, but further applications should result in the pedal feeling firmer, with the pedal stroke decreasing with each application.

2 If the servo does not operate as described, inspect and test the servo unit check valve as described in Section 4.

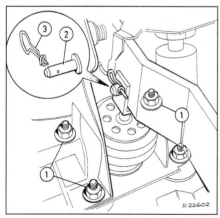

3.11 Remove the four flange nuts

1 Servo unit mounting nuts
2 Pushrod clevis pin
3 R-clip

2.2 Extract the R-clip (arrowed) and clevis pin securing the servo unit pushrod to the brake pedal

3 If the servo unit still fails to operate satisfactorily, the fault lies within the unit itself.

4 Repairs to the servo unit may not be possible and it will require renewing, check with your local Rover dealer.

Removal

Note: *The following new parts are needed – clevis pin securing clip, servo unit gasket.*

Caution: Do not adjust the domed nut on the servo pushrod, as this is preset in the factory.

5 Remove the brake master cylinder as described in Section 8.

6 Undo the two retaining bolts, release the coolant expansion bottle from the bulkhead and move it to one side.

7 Working inside the vehicle, remove the pocket from the driver's side of the facia panel. Undo the three retaining screws and remove the lower facia trim panel from the below the steering column.

8 Pull back the carpet from the lower part of the steering column and remove the two securing studs from the steering column gaiter.

9 Release the two securing clips from the steering column gaiter and remove it from the vehicle.

10 Remove and discard the spring-clip from the clevis pin, which connects the servo unit push-rod to the brake pedal. Remove the clevis pin.

11 Remove four flange nuts securing the servo unit to the engine bay bulkhead **(see illustration)**.

12 From inside the engine compartment, disconnect the vacuum hose from the servo unit **(see illustration)**.

13 Remove the servo unit from the engine compartment and the servo-to-bulkhead gasket. Discard gasket, a new one will be required for refitting.

Refitting

14 Check the vacuum hose for damage or deterioration – renew if required.

15 Fit a new gasket to the servo unit. **Note:** *The gasket must be the correct MG Rover part.*

Caution: The correct servo gasket must be fitted, as it acts as a spacer between the servo and the bulkhead.

16 Locate the servo unit into place, and fit

the retaining nuts – check that the push-rod fork locates correctly over the brake pedal. Use a torque wrench to tighten the nuts to the specified torque.

17 Working inside the vehicle, apply a small amount of grease and fit the clevis pin to the pedal and pushrod. Secure the pin with a new spring clip.

18 Refit the steering column gaiter and secure it with the two securing clips.

19 Secure the lower part of the steering column gaiter in place with the two securing studs and refit the carpet around the lower part of the steering column.

20 Refit the lower facia trim panel below the steering column and tighten the three retaining screws. Refit the pocket to the driver's side of the facia panel.

21 Working inside the engine compartment, refit the coolant expansion bottle to the bulkhead and tighten the two retaining bolts.

22 Connect the vacuum hose to the servo; ensuring that it is a tight fit.

23 Refit the brake master cylinder as described in Section 8.

24 Start the engine and check for leaks at the vacuum connection, and check operation of the brakes.

4 Vacuum servo unit check valve – removal, testing and refitting

Note: *The vacuum servo unit check valve is only available as part of the vacuum hose assembly. Do not try to remove the valve, the servo unit connection or the inlet manifold union from the hose, or air leaks may ensue, necessitating renewal of the hose assembly.*

Removal

1 Carefully release the hose connection from the vacuum servo unit **(see illustration 3.12)**.

2 On petrol models, release the locking collar and withdraw the vacuum hose from the inlet manifold **(see illustration)**.

3 On diesel models, release the hose clip and disconnect the vacuum hose from the pipe connection on the vacuum pump.

Testing

4 Examine the hose for damage, splits,

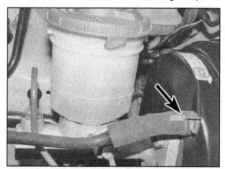

3.12 Vacuum hose on servo unit – arrowed

cracks or general deterioration. Make sure that the check valve inside the hose is working correctly by blowing through the hose from the servo unit connection end. Air should flow in this direction but not when blown through from the inlet manifold union. Renew the hose and check valve assembly if at all suspect.

5 Examine the servo unit sealing grommet for signs of damage or deterioration and renew if necessary.

Refitting

6 On petrol models, make sure the locking clip on the inlet manifold is secure and make a tight seal on the vacuum hose.

7 On diesel models, reconnect the hose to the vacuum pump pipe and secure it in position with the securing clip.

8 Carefully ease the hose onto the connection on the servo unit, taking care not to damage the hose and make a tight seal.

9 On completion, start the engine and check the vacuum hose-to-servo unit connection for signs of air leaks.

5 Hydraulic fluid –
level check and renewal

Refer to *Weekly Checks* and Chapter 1A or 1B.

6 Hydraulic system –
bleeding

⚠ **Warning: Refer to the 'Precautions' given at the end of Section 1, before handling brake fluid.**
Caution: Hydraulic fluid is an effective paint stripper and will attack plastics. If any is spilt onto painted components or bodywork, it should be washed off immediately with clean, warm water.

General

1 The correct operation of any hydraulic system is only possible after removal of all air from the components and circuit. This is achieved by bleeding the system.

2 During the bleeding procedure, add only clean, unused hydraulic fluid of the recommended type; never re-use fluid that has already been bled from the system. Ensure that sufficient fluid is available before starting work.

3 If there is any possibility of incorrect fluid being already in the system, the brake components and circuit must be flushed completely with uncontaminated, correct fluid and new seals should be fitted to the various components.

4 If hydraulic fluid has been lost from the system, or air has entered because of a leak, then ensure that the fault is cured before proceeding further.

5 Park the vehicle on level ground, chock the

roadwheels to prevent movement and then release the handbrake. Start the engine and allow it to idle.

6 Check that all pipes and hoses are secure, unions tight and bleed screws closed. Clean any dirt from around the bleed screws.

7 Unscrew the master cylinder reservoir cap and top the master cylinder reservoir up to the MAX level line. Refit the cap loosely and remember to maintain the fluid level at least above the MIN level line throughout the procedure or there is a risk of air being drawn into the system during the bleeding procedure.

8 There is a number of one-man, do-it-yourself brake bleeding kits currently available from motor accessory shops. It is recommended that one of these kits is used whenever possible as they greatly simplify the bleeding operation and also reduce the risk of expelled air and fluid being drawn back into the system. If such a kit is not available, then the basic (two-man) method must be used which is described in detail below.

9 If a kit is to be used, prepare the vehicle as described previously and follow the kit manufacturer's instructions as the procedure may vary slightly according to the type being used. Generally, they are as outlined below in the relevant sub-section.

10 Whichever method is used, the same sequence must be followed (paragraphs 11 and 12) to ensure the removal of all air from the system.

Bleeding sequence

11 If the system has been only partially disconnected and suitable precautions were taken to minimise fluid loss, it should be necessary only to bleed that part of the system (ie: the primary or secondary circuit).

12 If the complete system is to be bled, then it should be done working in the following sequence:
  1) Left-hand front brake.
  2) Right-hand rear brake.
  3) Right-hand front brake.
  4) Left-hand rear brake.

Bleeding

Basic (two-man) method

13 Collect a clean glass jar, a suitable length of plastic or rubber tubing which is a tight fit over the bleed screw and a ring spanner to fit the screw. The help of an assistant will also be required.

14 Remove the dust cap from the first screw in the sequence. Fit the spanner and tube to the screw, place the other end of the tube in the jar and pour in sufficient fluid to cover the end of the tube.

15 Ensure that the master cylinder reservoir fluid level is maintained at least above the MIN level line throughout the procedure.

16 Have the assistant fully depress the brake pedal several times to build-up pressure, and then maintain it on the final stroke.

4.2 Release the vacuum pipe locking clip – arrowed

17 While pedal pressure is maintained, unscrew the bleed screw (approximately one turn) and allow the fluid and air to flow into the jar. The assistant should maintain pedal pressure, following it down to the floor if necessary and should not release it until instructed to do so. When the flow stops, tighten the bleed screw again, release the pedal slowly and recheck the reservoir fluid level.

18 Repeat the steps given in paragraphs 16 and 17 until the fluid emerging from the bleed screw is free from air bubbles. If the master cylinder has been drained and refilled and air is being bled from the first screw in the sequence, allow approximately five seconds between cycles for the master cylinder passages to refill.

19 When a flow of clean air-free fluid is passing into the container and, whilst the pedal is held down, tighten the bleed screw securely – do not overtighten the screw. Remove the tube and fit the dust cap

20 Repeat the procedure on the remaining screws in the sequence until all air is removed from the system and the brake pedal feels firm again.

Using a one-way valve kit

21 As their name implies, these kits consist of a length of tubing with a one-way valve fitted to prevent expelled air and fluid being drawn back into the system. Some kits include a translucent container, which can be positioned so that the air bubbles can be more easily seen flowing from the end of the tube **(see illustration)**.

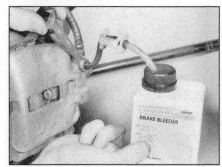
6.21 Using a one-way valve kit to bleed the braking system

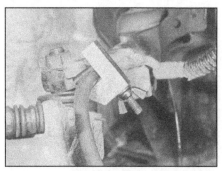

7.4 Using a brake hose clamp to minimise fluid loss

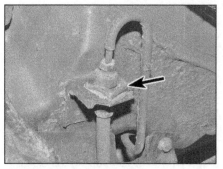

7.5 Spring clip (arrowed) securing brake pipe connection

22 The kit is connected to the bleed screw, which is then opened. The user returns to the driver's seat and depresses the brake pedal with a smooth, steady stroke and slowly releases it. This sequence is repeated until the expelled fluid is clear of air bubbles.

23 Note that these kits simplify work so much that it is easy to forget the master cylinder reservoir fluid level. Ensure that this is maintained at least above the MIN level line at all times.

Using a pressure bleeding kit

24 These kits are usually operated by the reservoir of pressurised air contained in the spare tyre, although note that it will probably be necessary to reduce the pressure to a lower limit than normal. Refer to the instructions supplied with the kit.

25 By connecting a pressurised, fluid-filled container to the master cylinder reservoir, bleeding can be carried out simply by opening each bleed screw in turn (in the specified sequence) and allowing the fluid to flow out until no more air bubbles can be seen in the expelled fluid.

26 This method has the advantage that the large reservoir of fluid provides an additional safeguard against air being drawn into the system during bleeding.

27 Pressure bleeding is particularly effective when bleeding 'difficult' systems or when bleeding the complete system at the time of routine fluid renewal.

All methods

28 When bleeding is complete and firm pedal feel is restored, wash off any spilt fluid, tighten

7.6 Using a brake pipe spanner (arrowed) to unscrew a union nut

the bleed screws securely and refit their dust caps.

29 Check the hydraulic fluid level and top-up if necessary (see *Weekly checks*).

30 Discard any hydraulic fluid that has been bled from the system, as it will not be fit for re-use.

31 Check the feel of the brake pedal. If it feels at all spongy, air must still be present in the system and further bleeding is required. Failure to bleed satisfactorily after a reasonable repetition of the bleeding procedure may be due to worn master cylinder seals.

7 Hydraulic pipes and hoses – inspection and renewal

⚠ **Warning: Refer to the 'Precautions' given at the end of Section 1, before handling brake fluid.**

Inspection

1 The hydraulic pipes, hoses, hose connections and pipe unions should be regularly examined.

2 First check for signs of leakage at the pipe unions, and then examine the flexible hoses for signs of cracking, chafing and fraying.

3 The brake pipes should be examined carefully for signs of dents, corrosion or other damage. Corrosion should be scraped off and, if the depth of pitting is significant, the pipes renewed. This is particularly likely in those areas underneath the vehicle body where the pipes are exposed and unprotected.

Removal

4 If any pipe or hose is to be renewed, minimise fluid loss by removing the master cylinder reservoir cap and then tightening it down onto a piece of polythene (taking care not to damage the sender unit) to obtain an airtight seal. Alternatively, flexible hoses can be sealed, by using a proprietary brake hose clamp, while metal brake pipe unions can be plugged (if care is taken not to allow dirt into the system) or capped immediately they are disconnected **(see illustration)**. Place a wad of rag under any union that is to be disconnected to catch any spilt fluid.
Caution: Do not use a G-clamp on the

brake hose, as the edges of the jaws may pinch the hose internally and cause it to fail. If a proprietary brake hose clamp is not available, fit two old sockets over the jaws of a pair of Mole grips then use them to clamp the brake hose. The rounded edges of the socket will prevent the jaws damaging the brake hose.

5 If a flexible hose is to be disconnected, unscrew the brake pipe union nut before removing the spring clip **(see illustration)**, which secures the hose to its mounting bracket.

6 To unscrew the union nuts it is preferable to obtain a proprietary brake pipe spanner of the correct size **(see illustration)**. These spanners are available from most large motor accessory shops. Failing this, a close-fitting open-ended spanner will be required, though if the nuts are tight or corroded, their flats may be rounded-off if the spanner slips. In such a case, a self-locking wrench is often the only way to unscrew a stubborn union but it follows that the pipe and the damaged nuts must be renewed on reassembly. Always clean a union and surrounding area before disconnecting it. If disconnecting a component with more than one union, make a careful note of the connections before disturbing any of them.

7 If a brake pipe is to be renewed, then it can be obtained from a Rover dealer, already cut to length and with the union nuts and end flares in place. All that is then necessary is to bend it to shape, following the line of the original, before fitting it to the vehicle. Alternatively, most motor accessory shops can make up brake pipes from kits but this requires very careful measurement of the original to ensure that the new one is of the correct length. The safest answer is usually to take the original to the shop as a pattern.

Refitting

8 On refitting, do not overtighten the union nuts. The specified torque wrench settings, where given, are not high and it is not necessary to exercise brute force to obtain a sound joint; brake union threads are very fine and can easily be accidentally stripped. When refitting flexible hoses, always renew any sealing washers used.

9 Ensure that the pipes and hoses are correctly routed with no kinks and that they are secured in the clips or brackets provided.

10 After fitting, remove the polythene from the reservoir (or remove the plugs or clamps, as applicable), and bleed the hydraulic system as described in Section 6. Wash off any spilt hydraulic fluid, and check the system carefully for fluid leaks.

8 Master cylinder – removal, and refitting

⚠ **Warning: Refer to the 'Precautions' given at the end of Section 1, before handling brake fluid.**

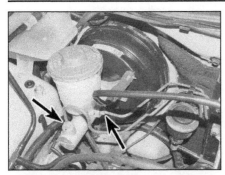

8.2 Master cylinder brake pipe unions – arrowed

Removal

1 Remove the master cylinder reservoir cap, having disconnected the sender unit wiring connectors, and syphon all hydraulic fluid from the reservoir. Do **NOT** syphon the fluid by mouth, as it is poisonous but use a syringe or an old antifreeze tester. Alternatively, open any convenient bleed screw in the system and gently pump the brake pedal to expel the fluid through a plastic tube connected to the bleed screw.

2 Wipe clean the area around the brake pipe unions on the side of the master cylinder and place absorbent rags beneath the pipe unions to catch any surplus fluid. Unscrew the two union nuts and carefully withdraw the two metal hydraulic pipes from the master cylinder **(see illustration)**. Plug or tape over the pipe ends and master cylinder orifices to minimise loss of brake fluid and to prevent the entry of dirt into the system. Wash off any spilt fluid immediately with clean water.

3 On diesel models, remove the bolt securing the support bracket to the inner wing panel.

4 Slacken and remove the two nuts and spring washers securing the master cylinder to the vacuum servo unit, then withdraw the unit from the engine compartment. On diesel models, remove the support bracket from the master cylinder retaining studs.

5 Remove the O-ring (where fitted) from the rear of the master cylinder and discard it; a new one will be required for refitting.

Refitting

6 Remove all traces of dirt from the master cylinder and servo unit mating surfaces, then fit a new O-ring to the groove on the master cylinder body.

7 Fit the master cylinder to the servo unit, ensuring that the servo unit pushrod enters the master cylinder bore centrally. Refit the master cylinder washers and mounting nuts and tighten them to the specified torque.

8 On diesel models, refit the support bracket to the brake servo mounting studs/nuts and tighten mounting bolt in inner wing panel.

9 Wipe clean the brake pipe unions then refit them to the master cylinder ports and tighten them to the specified torque setting.

10 Refill the master cylinder reservoir with new fluid and bleed the hydraulic system, as described in Section 6.

9 Front brake pads – inspection

Refer to the information given in Chapter 1A or 1B.

10 Front brake pads – renewal

⚠️ *Warning: Renew both sets of front brake pads at the same time. Never renew the pads on only one wheel as uneven braking may result. The dust created by pad wear may contain asbestos, which is a health hazard. Never blow it with compressed air or inhale it. An approved filtering mask should be worn when working on the brakes. DO NOT use petroleum-based solvents to clean brake parts the rubber sealing components may be damaged; use brake cleaner or methylated spirit only.*

Removal

1 Chock the rear wheels, firmly apply the handbrake then jack up the front of the vehicle and support it on axle stands (see *Jacking and vehicle support*). Remove both front roadwheels.

2 Remove the caliper lower guide pin bolt **(see illustration)**, pivot the caliper away from the disc to gain access to the brake pads and

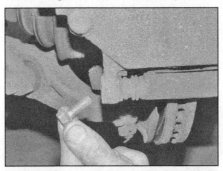

10.2 Remove caliper lower guide pin bolt

10.4 Removing pads complete with shims

secure it to the suspension strut using a piece of wire.

3 Remove the circular shim, which is fitted to the caliper piston **(see illustration)**.

4 Remove the brake pads from the caliper mounting bracket whilst noting the correct position of the pad retainer springs and pad shims **(see illustration)**.

5 Measure the thickness of friction material remaining on each brake pad **(see illustration)**. If either pad is worn at any point to the specified minimum thickness or less, all four pads must be renewed. Also, the pads should be renewed if any are fouled with oil or grease as there is no satisfactory way of degreasing friction material once contaminated. If any of the brake pads are worn unevenly or fouled with oil or grease, trace and rectify the cause before reassembly. New brake pad kits are available from Rover dealers and include new shims and pad retainer springs.

6 If the brake pads are still serviceable, carefully clean them using a clean, fine wire brush or similar, paying particular attention to the sides and back of the metal backing. Clean out the grooves in the friction material (where applicable) and pick out any large embedded particles of dirt or debris. Carefully clean the pad retainer springs and the pad locations in the caliper body and mounting bracket.

Refitting

7 Prior to fitting the pads, check that the guide pins are free to slide easily in the caliper bracket and check that the rubber guide pin gaiters are undamaged **(see illustration)**.

10.3 Removing circular shim from caliper piston

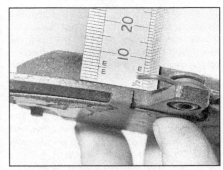

10.5 Measuring thickness of brake pad friction material

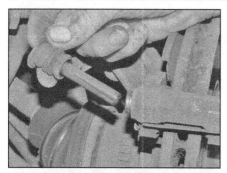

10.7 Check condition of guide pins and gaiters before refitting pads

10.8 Fit pad retainer springs to caliper bracket

10.9 Apply brake grease to shim

10.11 Using special tool to push the piston into the caliper

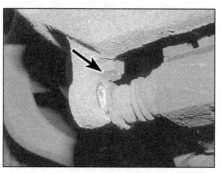

10.12 Align flat on the guide pin with flat on caliper housing – arrowed

Brush the dust and dirt from the caliper and piston but **do not** inhale it, as it is injurious to health. Inspect the dust seal around the piston for damage and the piston for evidence of fluid leaks, corrosion or damage. Renew as necessary.

8 On refitting, first fit the pad retainer springs to the caliper mounting bracket **(see illustration)**.

9 Apply a thin smear of high-temperature brake grease or anti-seize compound to the sides and back of each pad's metal backing and to those surfaces of the caliper body and mounting bracket which support the pads. Fit the shims to the back of both pads and apply a thin smear of grease (Molykote M77 or similar) to both sides of each shim. Do not allow the grease to foul the friction material **(see illustration)**.

10 Install the brake pads in the caliper mounting bracket, ensuring that the friction material is against the disc.

11 If new brake pads have been fitted, the caliper piston must be pushed back into the cylinder to make room for them. Fit the bleed bottle and tube to the bleed screw on the caliper you are working on, open the bleed screw and carefully draw the piston in, preferably using a G-clamp or, alternatively, using a flat bar or screwdriver as a lever **(see illustration)**. As the piston is retracted, the fluid will be pushed out of the bleed screw and into a bleed bottle. Tighten the bleed screw when the piston is fully retracted. Keep a careful watch on the fluid level in the reservoir to make sure the fluid level stays between the MAX and MIN level lines on the reservoir.

12 Apply a thin smear of the recommended lubricant (see above) to the circular shim and fit the shim to the caliper piston. Pivot the caliper body down over the brake pads then refit the bottom guide pin bolt and tighten it to the specified torque wrench setting. Make sure the flats on the guide pin sleeves align with the caliper housing **(see illustration)**.

13 Check that the caliper body slides smoothly in the mounting bracket, and then depress the brake pedal repeatedly until the pads are pressed into firm contact with the brake disc and normal (non-assisted) pedal pressure is restored.

14 Repeat the above procedure on the remaining front brake caliper.

15 Refit the roadwheels, then lower the vehicle to the ground and tighten the roadwheel nuts to the specified torque setting.

16 On completion, check the hydraulic fluid level (see *Weekly checks*).

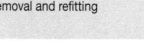

11 Front brake caliper – removal and refitting

 Warning: Refer to the 'Precautions' given at the end of Section 1, before handling brake fluid.

Removal

1 Chock the rear wheels, firmly apply the handbrake, jack up the front of the vehicle and support on axle stands (see *Jacking and vehicle support*). Remove the appropriate front roadwheel.

2 Minimise fluid loss either by removing the master cylinder reservoir cap and then tightening it down onto a piece of polythene to obtain an airtight seal (taking care not to damage the sender unit), or by using a brake hose clamp or a similar tool to clamp the flexible hose.

Caution: Do not use a G-clamp on the brake hose, as the edges of the jaws may pinch the hose internally and cause it to fail. If a proprietary brake hose clamp is not available, fit two old sockets over the jaws of a pair of Mole grips then use them to clamp the brake hose. The rounded edges of the socket will prevent the jaws damaging the brake hose.

3 Clean the area around the union, then undo the brake hose union bolt and disconnect the hose from the caliper, place absorbent rags beneath the pipe union to catch any surplus fluid. Plug the end of the hose and the caliper orifice to prevent dirt entering the hydraulic system. Discard the sealing washers as they must be renewed whenever disturbed.

4 Unscrew the two caliper guide pin bolts whilst, if necessary, using a slim open-ended spanner to prevent the guide pins themselves from rotating **(see illustration opposite)**.

5 Carefully lift the caliper assembly off the brake pads and remove the circular shim from the caliper piston. Note that the brake pads need not be disturbed and can be left in position in the caliper mounting bracket.

Refitting

6 Refit the circular shim to the piston and carefully slide the caliper into position over the brake pads. Refit the caliper guide pin bolts and tighten them to the specified torque setting.

7 Position a new sealing washer on each side of the hose union and refit the brake hose union bolt. Ensure that the brake hose union is correctly positioned between the lugs on the caliper then tighten the union bolt to the specified torque setting.

8 Remove the brake hose clamp, where fitted, and bleed the hydraulic system. Providing the precautions described were taken to minimise brake fluid loss, it should only be necessary to bleed the relevant front brake, see Section 6.

9 Refit the roadwheel then lower the vehicle to the ground and tighten the roadwheel nuts to the specified torque.

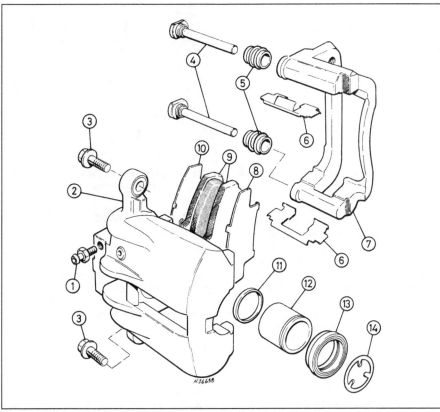

11.4 Front brake caliper components

1 Bleed screw	6 Pad retainer spring	10 Outer pad shim
2 Caliper body	7 Caliper mounting	11 Piston seal
3 Guide pin bolt	bracket	12 Piston
4 Guide pin	8 Inner pad shim	13 Dust seal
5 Gaiter	9 Brake pads	14 Circular shim

12 Front brake disc –
inspection, removal and refitting

Note: *If either brake disc requires renewal, both should be renewed at the same time to ensure even and consistent braking. In principle, new pads should be fitted also.*

Inspection

1 Chock the rear wheels, firmly apply the handbrake, jack up the front of the vehicle and support on axle stands (see *Jacking and vehicle support*). Remove the appropriate front roadwheel.

2 Slowly rotate the brake disc so that the full area of both sides can be checked. Remove the brake pads if better access is required to the inboard surface. Light scoring is normal in the area swept by the brake pads but if heavy scoring is found, then the disc must be renewed. The only alternative to this is to have the disc surface-ground until it is flat again, but this must not reduce the disc to less than the minimum thickness specified.

3 It is normal to find a lip of rust and brake dust around the disc's perimeter. This can be scraped off if required. If, however, a lip has formed due to excessive wear of the brake pad swept area, particularly on the outer edge of the disc, then the disc's thickness must be measured by using a micrometer **(see illustration)**. Take measurements at several places around the disc at the inside and outside of the pad swept area. If the disc has worn at any point to the specified minimum thickness or less, then it must be renewed. Note that a large variation in the thickness of the disc around its circumference may be caused by poor disc seating and can cause brake judder.

4 If the disc is thought to be warped, it can be checked for run-out (at a point 10.0 mm in from the disc's outer edge) by either using a dial gauge mounted on any convenient fixed point, while the disc is slowly rotated, or by using feeler blades to measure (at several points all around the disc) the clearance between the disc and a fixed point, such as the caliper mounting bracket **(see illustration)**. If the measurements obtained are at the specified maximum or beyond, the disc is excessively warped and must be renewed. However, it is worth checking first that the hub bearing is in good condition. Also, try the effect of removing the disc, cleaning the hub and disc mating surfaces and turning the disc through 180° to reposition it on the hub. If run-out is still excessive, the disc must be renewed.

5 Check the disc for cracks, especially around the stud holes, and any other wear or damage. Renew it if any of these are found.

Removal

6 If not already done, proceed as described in paragraph 1.

7 Unscrew the two bolts securing the brake caliper mounting bracket to the hub carrier, and slide the caliper assembly, complete with pads, off the disc (if necessary, pull the caliper body outwards, away from the centre of the car – this will push the piston back into its bore to allow the pads to pass over the disc). Using a piece of wire or string, tie the caliper to the front suspension coil spring, to avoid placing any strain on the hydraulic brake hose or pad wear sensor wiring **(see illustration)**.

12.3 Using a micrometer to measure brake disc thickness

12.4 Using a dial gauge to check brake disc run-out

12.7 Remove caliper assembly and secure it safely to one side

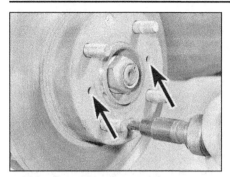

12.9a Removing disc retaining screws (jacking holes arrowed)

12.9b Drawing off a disc using two 8 mm bolts

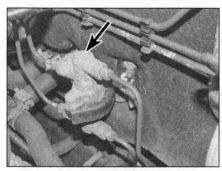

13.1 Brake proportioning valve (arrowed) – diesel model shown

8 If the same disc is to be refitted, use chalk or paint to mark the relationship of the disc to the hub.

9 Remove the screws securing the brake disc to the hub, and then remove the disc by lightly tapping its rear face with a hide or plastic mallet. If the disc is a tight fit on the hub, it can be drawn off the hub by screwing two bolts into the threaded holes provided in the brake disc **(see illustrations)**.

Refitting

10 Thoroughly clean the mating surfaces of the hub and brake disc, using a wire brush or fine grade emery paper. Remove all traces of brake dust and corrosion to ensure that the disc seats correctly.

11 The remainder of the refitting procedure is the reverse of the removal procedure, noting the following:

a) *Where applicable, observe the disc alignment markings made during removal.*

b) *If a new disc is being fitted, use a suitable solvent to wipe any preservative coating from the disc.*

c) *Fit and tighten the brake disc screws to their specified torque.*

d) *Check the disc run-out, as described in paragraph 4.*

e) *Fit the brake caliper and mounting bracket, tighten the bolts to the specified torque setting.*

f) *Refit the roadwheel, then lower the vehicle to the ground and tighten the roadwheel bolts to the specified torque.*

g) *On completion, depress the brake pedal several times to bring the brake pads into contact with the disc.*

13 Brake proportioning valve
– testing, removal and refitting

Warning: Refer to the 'Precautions' given at the end of Section 1, before handling brake fluid.

Testing

1 The valve is mounted on the engine compartment bulkhead **(see illustration)**.

2 Specialist equipment is required to check valve performance. If the valve is thought to

be faulty, the vehicle should be taken to a suitably-equipped Rover dealer for testing. However, in the event of an internal failure, brake fluid may seep from the valve, which is situated to the side of the two heater hose unions. Repairs are not possible; if the valve is thought to be faulty, it must be renewed.

Removal

3 Disconnect the sender unit wiring connector and unscrew the master cylinder reservoir filler cap. Place a piece of polythene over the filler neck and securely refit the cap (taking care not to damage the sender unit). This will minimise brake fluid loss during subsequent operations. As an added precaution, place absorbent rags beneath the proportioning valve brake pipe unions.

4 Wipe clean the area around the four brake pipe unions on the proportioning valve, then make a note of how the pipes are arranged for reference on refitting. Unscrew the union nuts and carefully withdraw the four pipes away from the valve. Plug or tape over the pipe ends and valve orifices to minimise the loss of brake fluid and to prevent the entry of dirt into the system. Wash off any spilt fluid immediately with cold water.

5 Slacken and remove the two bolts which secure the valve to the bulkhead, and then remove it from the engine compartment.

Refitting

6 Refit the proportioning valve to the bulkhead and tighten its mounting bolts to the specified torque.

7 Wipe the brake pipe unions clean and refit them to the valve, using the notes made on dismantling to ensure they are correctly positioned. Tighten the union nuts to the specified torque.

8 Remove the polythene from the master cylinder reservoir filler neck and bleed the hydraulic system as described in Section 6.

14 Rear brake shoes
– inspection

Refer to the information given in Chapter 1A or 1B as applicable.

15 Rear brake shoes –
renewal

Warning: Brake shoes must be renewed on both rear wheels at the same time. Never renew the shoes on only one wheel as uneven braking may result.

Removal

1 Remove the brake drum as described in Section 16.

2 Working carefully and noting all precautions (See Section 1), remove all traces of brake dust from the brake drum, backplate and shoes.

3 Measure the thickness of friction material remaining on each brake shoe at several points. If either shoe is worn at any point to the specified minimum thickness or less, all four shoes must be renewed as a set. Also, the shoes should be renewed if any are fouled with oil or grease as there is no satisfactory way of degreasing friction material once it is contaminated.

4 If any of the brake shoes are worn unevenly or fouled with oil or grease, trace and rectify the cause before reassembly.

5 To remove the brake shoes, first remove the shoe retainer springs and pins, using a pair of pliers to press in each retainer clip until it can be rotated through 90° and released. Ease the shoes out one at a time from the lower pivot point to release the tension of the return spring, then disconnect the lower return spring from the leading shoe. Ease the upper end of both shoes out from their wheel cylinder locations, and disconnect the handbrake cable from the trailing shoe. The brake shoes and adjuster strut assembly can now be manoeuvred out of position and away from the backplate **(see illustrations)**. Do not depress the brake pedal until the brakes are reassembled. Wrap a strong elastic band around the wheel cylinder pistons to retain them.

Caution: Take great care to avoid damaging the wheel cylinder seals when removing the brake shoes.

6 With the brake shoe assembly on the work surface, make a note of the fitted positions of

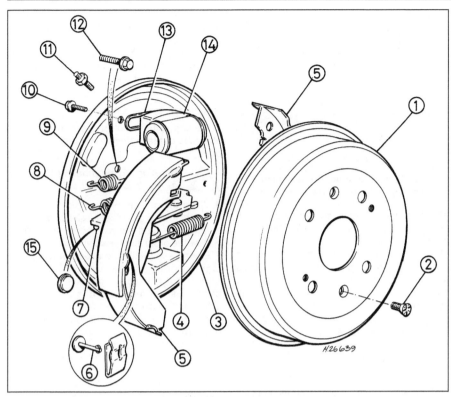

15.5b Remove brake shoe retainer springs . . .

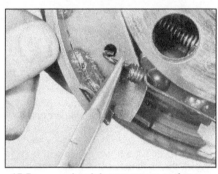

15.5c . . . unhook lower return spring . . .

15.5a Rear drum brake assembly

1 Brake drum	6 Shoe retaining pin spring clip	11 Bleed screw
2 Drum securing screw	7 Adjuster strut assembly	12 Backplate securing screw
3 Backplate	8 Strut return spring	13 Seal
4 Lower return spring	9 Upper return spring	14 Wheel cylinder
5 Brake shoes	10 Wheel cylinder securing screw	15 Grommet

the adjuster strut and springs to use as guide on reassembly **(see illustration)**. Carefully ease the adjuster strut from its slot in the trailing shoe and remove the short spring, which secures the two components together. Detach the upper return spring and separate the shoes and strut.

7 Examine the adjuster strut assembly for signs of wear or damage, paying particular attention to the adjuster quadrant and knurled wheel. If damaged, the strut assembly must be renewed. Renew all the brake shoe return springs regardless of their apparent condition.

8 Peel the rubber protective caps on the wheel cylinder back to check for fluid leaks or other damage. Check that both cylinder pistons are free to move easily.

Refitting

Caution: Do not allow lubricant to come into contact with the brake linings or dust covers.

9 Clean the backplate, and apply a thin smear of Molykote 111, or anti-seize compound, to all the surfaces which contact the shoes, including the adjuster and wheel cylinder pistons.

10 Ensure the handbrake lever stop on the

trailing shoe is correctly engaged with the lever and is pressed tight against the brake shoe **(see illustration)**.

11 Fully extend the adjuster strut quadrant and fit the leading brake shoe into the adjuster strut slot, ensuring that the strut spring and knurled wheel are situated on the underside of the strut assembly. Using a screwdriver, move the quadrant away from the knurled wheel and set it in the minimum adjustment position.

12 Fit the upper return spring to its respective location on the leading shoe. Fit the trailing shoe to the upper return spring and carefully ease the shoe into position in the adjuster strut slot. Once in position, fit the small spring which secures the trailing shoe to the strut assembly.

13 Remove the elastic band fitted to the wheel cylinder and manoeuvre the shoe and strut assembly into position on the backplate. Locate the upper end of both shoes with the

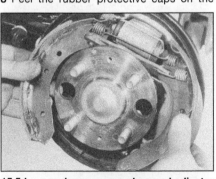

15.5d . . . and manoeuvre shoe and adjuster strut assembly away from backplate

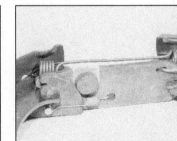

15.6 Correct fitted positions of adjuster strut and springs

15.10 Ensure handbrake stop lever is correctly located

15.14 Reset adjuster strut prior to refitting drum

wheel cylinder pistons and fit the handbrake cable to the trailing shoe operating lever. Fit the lower return spring to both shoes and ease the shoes into position on the lower pivot point.

14 Tap the shoes to centralise them with the backplate, then refit the shoe retainer pins and springs and secure them in position with the retainer clips. Check that the adjuster quadrant is still in the minimum adjuster position and if necessary, reset as follows. Place a block of wood between the trailing shoe and hub, to prevent the shoe moving forwards, then lever the leading shoe away from the hub to release the brake shoe return spring pressure on the adjuster quadrant. With the shoe held in this position, reset the quadrant to the minimum adjustment setting **(see illustration)**. Once the adjuster strut is correctly set, ease the leading shoe back into position then remove the block of wood and check that the shoes are still central.

15 Refit the brake drum (as described in section 16) and repeat the above operation on the remaining rear brake assembly.

16 On completion, apply the footbrake repeatedly to set the shoe-to-drum clearance, until normal (non-assisted) brake pedal operation returns.

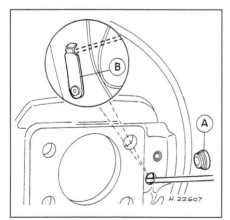

16.4a Releasing handbrake mechanism stop lever

Remove rubber grommet (A) and use small screwdriver to depress handbrake lever stop (B)

16.3 Removing brake drum retaining screws – threaded holes arrowed

17 Check handbrake cable operation and, if necessary, adjust as described in Chapter 1A or 1B.

18 Refit the roadwheels then lower the vehicle to the ground and tighten the roadwheel nuts to the specified torque.

19 Check and if necessary top-up the hydraulic fluid level (see *Weekly checks*).

16 Rear brake drum – removal, inspection and refitting

Note: *If either brake drum requires renewal, both should be renewed at the same time to ensure even and consistent braking.*

Removal

1 Chock the front wheels then jack up the rear of the vehicle and support it on axle stands (see *Jacking and vehicle support*). Remove the appropriate rear wheel.

2 If the same drum is to be refitted, use chalk or paint to mark the relationship of the drum to the hub.

3 With the handbrake firmly applied to prevent drum rotation, unscrew the drum retaining screws **(see illustration)**. Fully release the handbrake cable and withdraw the drum.

4 If the drum will not pull away, first check that the handbrake is fully released. If the drum will still not come away, remove the grommet from the rear of the backplate and, using a small screwdriver, disengage the handbrake lever stop from behind the lever

16.4b Brake drum can be drawn off hub by using two 8 mm bolts

to increase the shoe-to-drum clearance. If removal is still difficult, it can be drawn off the shoes by screwing two bolts into the threaded holes provided in the drum **(see illustrations)**. If the drum is still held firm, slacken the handbrake cable, adjusting nut (see Section 23).

Inspection

5 Using a suitable solvent, carefully remove all traces of brake dust from inside the brake drum.

⚠ *Warning: Avoid inhaling the dust, as it is injurious to health.*

6 Clean the outside of the drum and check it for obvious signs of wear or damage such as cracks around the roadwheel stud holes. Renew the drum if necessary.

7 Examine carefully the inside of the drum. Light scoring of the friction surface is normal but if heavy scoring is found, the drum must be renewed. It is usual to find a lip on the drum's inboard edge, which consists of a mixture of rust and brake dust. This should be scraped away to leave a smooth surface, which can be polished with fine (120 to 150 grade) emery paper. If, however, the lip is due to the friction surface being recessed by excessive wear, then the drum must be renewed.

8 If the drum is thought to be excessively worn or oval, its internal diameter must be measured at several points by using an internal micrometer. Take measurements in pairs, the second at right angles to the first, and compare the two to check for signs of ovality. Provided that it does not enlarge the drum to beyond the specified maximum diameter, it may be possible to have the drum refinished by skimming or grinding but if this is not possible, the drums on both sides must be renewed.

Refitting

9 Refitting is the reverse of the removal procedure, noting the following:
  a) *On fitting a new brake drum, use a suitable solvent to remove any preservative coating that may have been applied to its interior.*
  b) *If the existing drum is to be refitted, use a clean wire brush to remove all traces of dirt, brake dust and corrosion from the mating surfaces of the drum and the hub flange.*
  c) *Align the marks made on removal (where applicable).*
  d) *Tighten the drum retaining screws to their specified torque wrench settings.*
  e) *Refit the roadwheel, then lower the vehicle to the ground and tighten the roadwheel bolts to the specified torque.*
  f) *On completion, operate the handbrake and brake pedal several times to check their operation.*

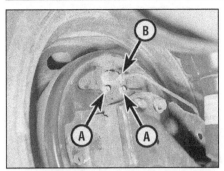

17.3 Wheel cylinder retaining bolts (A) and brake pipe union nut (B)

17 Rear wheel cylinder
– removal and refitting

Removal

1 Remove the brake shoes as described in Section 15.

2 Minimise fluid loss by removing the master cylinder reservoir cap and then tightening it down onto a piece of polythene to obtain an airtight seal (taking care not to damage the sender unit), or by using a brake hose clamp or a similar tool to clamp the flexible hose.

Caution: Do not use a G-clamp on the brake hose, as the edges of the jaws may pinch the hose internally and cause it to fail. If a proprietary brake hose clamp is not available, fit two old sockets over the jaws of a pair of Mole grips then use them to clamp the brake hose. The rounded edges of the socket will prevent the jaws damaging the brake hose.

3 Wipe away all traces of dirt around the brake pipe union at the rear of the wheel cylinder and unscrew the union nut, place an absorbent rag beneath the pipe union to catch any surplus fluid. Carefully ease the pipe out of the wheel cylinder and plug or tape over its end to prevent dirt entry **(see illustration)**.

4 Unscrew the two wheel cylinder retaining bolts from the rear of the backplate and remove the cylinder, noting the rubber sealing ring which is fitted between the cylinder and backplate.

Refitting

5 Fit a new sealing ring to the rear of the wheel cylinder and place the cylinder in position on the backplate.

6 Refit the wheel cylinder retaining bolts and tighten them to the specified torque.

7 Tighten the brake pipe union nut and, where applicable, remove the clamp from the flexible brake hose.

8 Refit the brake shoes as described in Section 15.

9 Bleed the hydraulic braking system with reference to Section 6. If precautions were taken to minimise fluid loss, it should only be necessary to bleed the relevant rear brake.

10 On completion, check that both footbrake and handbrake function correctly before taking the vehicle on the road.

18 Rear brake pads –
inspection

Refer to Chapter 1A or 1B.

19 Rear brake pads –
renewal

Warning: Renew both sets of front brake pads at the same time. Never renew the pads on only one wheel as uneven braking may result. The dust created by pad wear may contain asbestos, which is a health hazard. Never blow it with compressed air or inhale it. An approved filtering mask should be worn when working on the brakes. DO NOT use petroleum-based solvents to clean brake parts the rubber sealing components may be damaged; use brake cleaner or methylated spirit only.

Removal

1 Chock the front wheels then jack up the rear of the vehicle and support on axle stands (see *Jacking and vehicle support*). Remove the rear roadwheels.

2 Undo the two bolts securing the caliper shield in position, and then withdraw the shield from the rear of the caliper.

3 Remove both caliper guide pin bolts whilst, if necessary, using a slim open-ended spanner to prevent the guide pins from rotating. Lift the caliper away from the disc, noting the position of the pad retaining spring clip which is fitted between the caliper and the pads. Secure the caliper to the suspension strut using a piece of wire to avoid straining the hydraulic hose **(see illustration overleaf)**.

4 Remove the brake pads from the caliper mounting bracket whilst noting the correct fitted positions of the brake pads, pad retainer springs and pad shims.

5 Measure the thickness of friction material remaining on each brake pad **(see illustration 10.5)**. If either pad is worn at any point to the specified minimum thickness or less, all four pads must be renewed. Also, the pads should be renewed if any are fouled with oil or grease as there is no satisfactory way of degreasing friction material once contaminated. If any of the brake pads are worn unevenly or fouled with oil or grease, trace and rectify the cause before reassembly. New brake pad kits are available from Rover dealers and include new shims and pad retainer springs.

6 If the brake pads are still serviceable, carefully clean them using a clean, fine wire brush or similar, paying particular attention to the sides and back of the metal backing. Clean

out the grooves in the friction material (where applicable) and pick out any large embedded particles of dirt or debris. Carefully clean the pad retainer springs and the pad locations in the caliper body and mounting bracket.

Refitting

7 Prior to fitting the pads, check that the guide pins are free to slide easily in the caliper bracket and check that the rubber guide pin gaiters are undamaged. Brush the dust and dirt from the caliper and piston but **do not** inhale it, as it is injurious to health. Inspect the dust seal around the piston for damage and the piston for evidence of fluid leaks, corrosion or damage. Renew as necessary.

8 On refitting, first fit the pad retainer springs to the caliper mounting bracket.

9 Apply a thin smear of Molykote M77 compound to the sides and back of each pad's metal backing and to those surfaces of the caliper body and mounting bracket which bear on the pads. In the absence of the specified lubricant, a good quality high-temperature brake grease or anti-seize compound may be used. Fit the shims to the back of both pads, noting that the smaller shim must be fitted to the piston side pad, and apply a thin smear of lubricant to the back of each shim.

Caution: Do not allow lubricant to foul the friction material.

10 Install the brake pads in the caliper mounting bracket, ensuring that the friction material is against the disc and the pad with the smaller shim attached is fitted on the inside.

11 If new pads have been fitted, it will be necessary to retract the piston fully into the caliper bore by rotating it in a clockwise direction. This can be achieved by using a suitable pair of circlip pliers as a peg spanner or by fabricating a peg spanner for the task. Fit the bleed bottle and tube to the bleed screw on the caliper you are working on, open the bleed screw and carefully rotate the piston in a clockwise direction. As the piston is retracted, the fluid will be pushed out of the bleed screw and into a bleed bottle. Tighten the bleed screw, when the piston is fully retracted. Keep a careful watch on the fluid level in the reservoir to make sure the fluid level stays between the MAX and MIN level lines on the reservoir.

12 Ensure the pad retaining spring clip is in position (as noted on removal), and then slide the caliper into position in its mounting bracket. When fitting the caliper, ensure that the lug on the rear of the piston side pad is located in one of the slots in the piston. Refit the caliper guide pin bolts and tighten them to the specified torque setting.

13 Depress the footbrake to bring the piston into contact with the pads then check that the lug on the piston side pad is still located in one of the slots in the piston. If necessary, remove the caliper and adjust the piston position by turning it clockwise, as described above.

14 Refit the shield to the rear of the caliper and tighten the two retaining bolts.

15 Repeat the above procedure on the remaining rear brake caliper.
16 Once both calipers have been done, depress the brake pedal a few times, until normal (non-assisted) pedal operation returns, then apply the handbrake a few times, to check

handbrake adjustment. Check the operation of the handbrake and, if necessary, adjust the cable as described in Chapter 1A or 1B.
17 Refit the roadwheels, then lower the vehicle to the ground and tighten the roadwheel nuts to the specified torque setting.

18 On completion, check the hydraulic fluid level (see *Weekly checks*).

20 Rear brake caliper – removal and refitting

⚠️ *Warning: Refer to the 'Precautions' given at the end of Section 1, before handling brake fluid.*

Removal

1 Chock the front wheels, then jack up the rear of the vehicle and support on axle stands (see *Jacking and vehicle support*). Remove the rear wheel.
2 Undo the two bolts securing the caliper shield in position, and then withdraw the shield from the rear of the caliper.
3 Extract the spring clip and clevis pin securing the handbrake cable to the caliper handbrake lever, then remove the clip securing the outer cable to its mounting bracket and detach the handbrake cable from the caliper **(see illustration)**.
4 Minimise fluid loss by removing the master cylinder reservoir cap and then tightening it down onto a piece of polythene to obtain an airtight seal (taking care not to damage the sender unit), or by using a brake hose clamp or similar tool to seal off the flexible brake hose.
Caution: Do not use a G-clamp on the brake hose, as the edges of the jaws may pinch the hose internally and cause it to fail. If a proprietary brake hose clamp is not available, fit two old sockets over the jaws of a pair of Mole grips then use them to clamp the brake hose. The rounded edges of the socket will prevent the jaws damaging the brake hose.
5 Clean the area around the hose union, then undo the brake hose union bolt and disconnect the hose from the caliper **(see illustration)**, place an absorbent rag beneath the pipe union to catch any surplus fluid. Plug the end of the hose and the caliper orifice to prevent dirt entering the hydraulic system. Discard the sealing washers as they must be renewed whenever disturbed.
6 Remove both the caliper guide pin bolts whilst, if necessary, using a slim open-ended

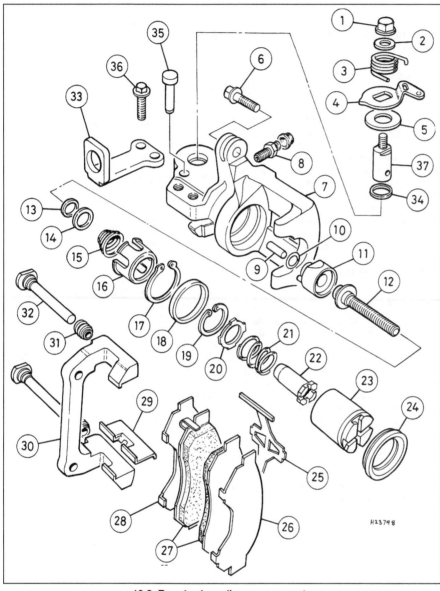

19.3 Rear brake caliper components

1 Handbrake lever retaining nut	13 Bearing	27 Brake pads
2 Washer	14 Spring seat	28 Outer pad shim
3 Return spring	15 Spring	29 Pad spring
4 Handbrake operating lever	16 Spring cover	30 Caliper mounting bracket
5 Dust seal	17 Circlip	31 Gaiter
6 Guide pin bolt	18 Piston seal	32 Guide pin
7 Caliper body	19 Circlip	33 Handbrake cable mounting bracket
8 Bleed screw	20 Thrustwasher	34 Cam washer
9 Pushrod	21 Spring	35 Pin
10 O-ring	22 Adjuster nut	36 Bolt
11 Adjusting bolt piston	23 Piston	37 Handbrake mechanism cam
12 Adjusting bolt	24 Dust seal	
	25 Pad spring	
	26 Inner pad shim	

20.3 Spring clip and clevis pin (arrowed) securing the handbrake cable to the lever

spanner to prevent the guide pins from rotating, then lift the caliper away from the disc **(see illustration)**. Note the fitted position of the pad retaining spring clip, which is fitted between the caliper and the pads. **Note:** *The brake pads need not be disturbed and can be left in position in the caliper mounting bracket.*

Refitting

7 Ensure the pad retaining spring clip is in position (as noted on removal), and then slide the caliper into position in its mounting bracket. When fitting the caliper, ensure that the lug on the rear of the piston side pad is located in one of the slots in the piston. Refit the caliper guide pin bolts and tighten them to the specified torque setting.

8 Position a new sealing washer on each side of the hydraulic hose union and refit the brake hose union bolt. Ensure that the brake hose union is correctly positioned between the lugs on the caliper then tighten the union bolt to the specified torque setting.

9 Remove the brake hose clamp, where fitted, and bleed the hydraulic system, with reference to Section 6. Providing the precautions described were taken to minimise brake fluid loss, it should only be necessary to bleed the relevant rear brake.

10 Refit the handbrake cable outer to its mounting bracket and secure it in position with the retaining clip. Ensure the return spring is located in the groove in the operating lever then refit the handbrake cable-to-lever clevis pin and secure it in position with the spring clip.

11 Depress the footbrake to bring the piston into contact with the pads then check that the lug on the piston side pad is still located in one of the slots in the piston. If necessary, remove the caliper and adjust the piston position by turning it clockwise, as described in Section 19.

12 Refit the shield to the rear of the caliper and tighten the two retaining bolts.

13 If necessary, adjust the handbrake cable as described in Chapter 1A or 1B.

14 Refit the roadwheels, then lower the vehicle to the ground and tighten the roadwheel nuts to the specified torque setting.

15 On completion, check the hydraulic fluid level (see *Weekly checks*).

21 Rear brake disc –
inspection, removal and refitting

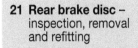

Note: *If either brake disc requires renewal, both should be renewed at the same time to ensure even and consistent braking. In principle, new pads should be fitted also.*

Inspection

1 Inspect the rear brake discs as described for the front discs, in Section 12, paragraphs 1 to 5.

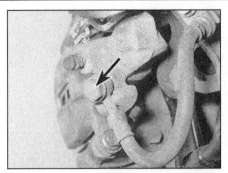

20.5 Flexible brake hose union – arrowed

Removal

2 Chock the front wheels, then jack up the rear of the vehicle and support on axle stands (see *Jacking and vehicle support*). Remove the appropriate rear roadwheel.

3 Undo the two bolts securing the caliper shield in position, and then withdraw the shield from the rear of the caliper.

4 Undo the two bolts securing the caliper mounting bracket to the trailing arm assembly and slide the caliper assembly off the disc. Using a piece of wire or string, tie the caliper to the coils of the rear suspension strut to avoid placing any strain on the hydraulic brake hose.

5 If the same disc is to be refitted, use chalk or paint to mark the relationship of the disc to the hub.

6 Remove the screws securing the brake disc to the hub, and then remove the disc by lightly tapping its rear face with a hide or plastic mallet. If the disc is a tight fit on the hub, it can be drawn off the hub by screwing two bolts into the threaded holes provided in the brake disc.

Refitting

7 Thoroughly clean the mating surfaces of the hub and brake disc, using a wire brush or fine grade emery paper. Remove all traces of brake dust and corrosion to ensure that the disc seats correctly.

8 The remainder of the refitting procedure is the reverse of the removal procedure, noting the following:

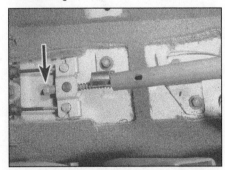

22.4 Handbrake adjustment nut – arrowed

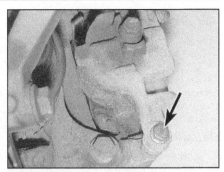

20.6 Rear brake calliper lower guide pin bolt

a) *Where applicable, observe the disc alignment markings made during removal.*

b) *If a new disc has been fitted, use a suitable solvent to wipe any preservative coating from the disc.*

c) *Tighten the disc retaining screws to their specified torque wrench settings.*

d) *Fit the brake caliper and mounting bracket, and tighten the bolts to the specified torque setting.*

e) *Refit the roadwheel, then lower the vehicle to the ground and tighten the roadwheel bolts to the specified torque.*

f) *On completion, depress the brake pedal several times to bring the brake pads into contact with the disc.*

22 Handbrake lever –
removal and refitting

Removal

1 With the vehicle parked on level ground, chock the roadwheels so that the vehicle cannot move.

3 From inside the vehicle prise out the cover from the top of the rear centre console section to gain access to the two retaining screws. Undo the two screws at the rear of the console (one at each side) and remove the rear console section.

3 Remove the handbrake lever rubber gaiter and disconnect the wiring connector from the lever warning lamp switch.

4 Slacken and remove the handbrake cable adjusting nut from the rear of the lever and undo the bolts securing the handbrake lever assembly to the floorpan **(see illustration)**.

5 Lift the handbrake assembly out of position, noting the location of the spring, which is fitted on the handbrake lever adjusting rod.

6 If required, undo the retaining screw and remove the handbrake warning light switch from the handbrake lever.

Refitting

7 Refitting is a reverse of the removal procedure. Prior to refitting the handbrake lever rubber gaiter, adjust the handbrake cable as described in Chapter 1A or 1B.

23 Handbrake cables – removal and refitting

1 The handbrake cable consists of two sections (right- and left-hand), which are linked to the lever assembly by an equaliser plate. Each section can be removed individually.

Removal

2 Firmly chock the front wheels then jack up the rear of the vehicle and support it on axle stands (see *Jacking and vehicle support*). Remove the relevant rear wheel.
3 From inside the vehicle prise out the cover from the top of the rear centre console section to gain access to the two retaining screws. Undo the two screws at the rear of the console (one at each side) and remove the rear console section.
4 Slacken and remove the handbrake cable adjusting nut from the rear of the lever and disconnect the equaliser plate **(see illustration)**, noting the spring which is fitted to the lever adjusting rod.
5 Undo the two bolts securing the cable outer retaining plate to the floor panel **(see illustration)**. Remove the retaining plate then detach the relevant cable inner from the equaliser plate.

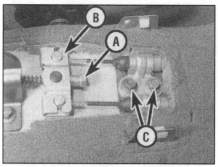

23.4 Handbrake cable adjusting nut (A), equaliser plate (B) and outer cable retaining plate bolts (C)

6 Pull the carpet back from around the rear of the handbrake lever and release the cable rubber grommet from the floor panel.
7 Working under the vehicle, release the rubber mountings from the rear of the exhaust system and carefully lower the system down onto an axle stand.
8 Undo the retaining bolts and withdraw the fuel tank heat shield, from under the vehicle.
9 Working your way along the handbrake cable, undo the retaining bolts from the cable securing clips **(see illustration)** and pull the handbrake cable out from the rubber grommets in the floor panel.

10 On models equipped with rear drum brakes; remove the relevant rear brake drum as described in Section 16. Remove the trailing shoe retainer spring and pin, using a pair of pliers to press in the retainer clip, rotate through 90° and release it from the pin. Ease the trailing shoe out of the lower pivot point to release the tension of the return spring, then disconnect the lower return spring from both shoes. Disconnect the handbrake cable from the trailing shoe, and then use a ring spanner to compress the handbrake cable retaining tangs and withdraw the cable from the rear of the backplate **(see illustration)**.
11 On models equipped with rear disc brakes, remove the brake caliper shield retaining bolts and withdraw the shield from the caliper. Extract the spring clip and clevis pin securing the handbrake cable to the caliper handbrake lever, then remove the clip securing the outer cable to its mounting bracket and release the handbrake cable from the caliper.
12 Once the cable is free, withdraw it from underneath the vehicle and, if necessary, repeat the procedure for the remaining cable section on the other side of the vehicle.

Refitting

13 Refitting is a reversal of the removal sequence noting the following:
a) Lubricate all exposed linkages and cable pivots with good quality multi-purpose grease.
b) Ensure the cable outer grommet is correctly located in the floor panel and

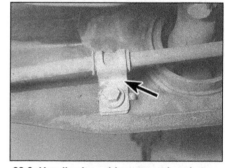

23.9 Handbrake cable support bracket on the trailing arm

23.10 Using a ring spanner to compress the outer cable retaining tangs

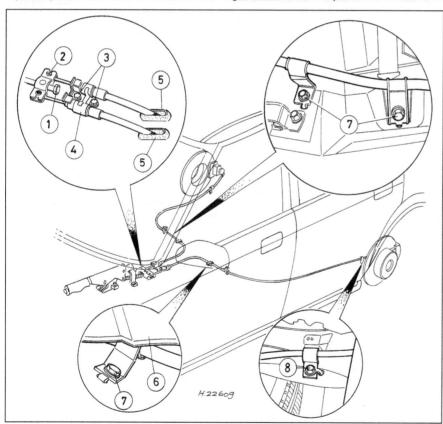

23.5 Handbrake mechanism layout

1 Handbrake cable adjuster nut
2 Equaliser plate
3 Bolts
4 Cable retaining plate
5 Grommet
6 Exhaust heat shield
7 Bolts – cable-to-body
8 Bolts – cable-to-trailing arm

that all retaining bolts are tightened to the specified torque.

c) On models with rear drum brakes, relocate the trailing shoe and refit the brake drum, with reference to Section 15.

d) On models with rear disc brakes, reconnect the handbrake cable, with reference to Section 20.

e) Prior to refitting the rear centre console section, adjust the handbrake cable as described in Chapter 1A or 1B.

24 Stop-lamp switch – removal, refitting and adjustment

Removal

1 Working inside the vehicle, remove the pocket from the driver's side of the facia panel. Undo the three retaining screws and remove the lower facia trim panel from the below the steering column.

2 Disconnect the wiring connector from the stop-lamp switch at the top of the brake pedal **(see illustration)**.

3 On manual adjusting stop-lamp switches, slacken the locknut and unscrew the switch from the pedal bracket.

4 On automatic adjusting stop-lamp switches, rotate the switch clockwise to release it from the pedal bracket.

Refitting

5 On manual adjusting stop-lamp switches, carry out the adjustment of the switch as described in paragraphs 10 to 12.

6 On automatic adjusting stop-lamp switches, rotate the switch anti-clockwise and secure it in the pedal bracket.

7 Reconnect the wiring connector to the stop-lamp switch.

8 Before refitting the facia trim panel, switch on the ignition, press the brake pedal and check the operation of the brake lights.

9 Refit the lower facia trim panel below the steering column and tighten the three retaining screws. Refit the pocket to the driver's side of the facia panel.

Adjustment (manual type)

10 Screw the switch into position in the

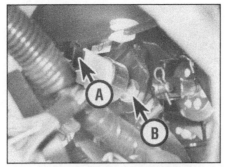

24.2 Stop-lamp switch wiring connector (A) and locknut (B)

mounting bracket at the top of the pedal, until the plunger is fully depressed.

11 Rotate the switch back approximately quarter of a turn to give a clearance of 0.3 mm, between the plunger and the pedal.

12 Once the stop-lamp switch is correctly adjusted, hold the switch stationary and tighten the locknut securely.

13 Follow the procedures as described in paragraphs 7 to 9.

25 Anti-lock Braking System (ABS) – component removal and refitting

⚠ **Warning: After any work on the ABS system or components, system operation must be checked by an MG Rover dealer using special diagnostic equipment. Refer to the 'Precautions' given at the end of Section 1, before handling brake fluid.**

ABS hydraulic modulator

1 Disconnect the battery negative terminal (refer to *Disconnecting the battery* in the Reference Section of this manual).

2 Apply the handbrake, chock the rear roadwheels, then jack up the front of the car and support it on axle stands (see *Jacking and vehicle support*)

3 Connect a bleed tube to the bleed screw on the front right-hand caliper and place the other end of the tube in a container. Open the bleed screw and pump the brake pedal to expel fluid from the master cylinder. Tighten the bleed screw.

4 Repeat the above operation (paragraph 3) to the front left-hand caliper.

5 Pull the locking clip outwards, and disconnect the multiplug from the ECU on the brake modulator.

6 Clean around the pipe connections, and position cloths under the modulator to absorb fluid spills.

7 Disconnect four brake pipes from the top of the modulator, and the two brake pipes from the front of the modulator **(see illustration)**.

Caution: Make a note of how the six pipes are connected to the modulator, as reference for refitting. Plug or cap the connections immediately after disconnection, to prevent any dirt ingress.

8 Slacken the two nuts (one at each) side securing the modulator to the mounting bracket.

9 Withdraw the modulator, and release it from the lower bush removing it from the engine compartment.

Caution: DO NOT attempt to dismantle the modulator – special equipment is needed.

10 Refitting is a reversal of the removal procedure, noting:

a) Use a torque wrench with suitable adapters to tighten mounting nuts and pipe connections to the specified torque.

b) Ensure that the six pipes are correctly connected as noted before removal.

c) Bleed the brake system as described in Section 6.

d) Have the operation of the ABS system tested by an MG Rover dealer.

Front wheel sensor

11 Chock the rear wheels, firmly apply the handbrake, jack up the front of the vehicle and support on axle stands (see *Jacking and vehicle support*). Remove the appropriate front roadwheel.

12 From inside the engine compartment, disconnect the relevant sensor wiring connector from under the ABS modulator unit. Unclip the wiring from the securing clips inside the engine compartment, noting the routing of the cable.

13 From inside the wheel arch, pull the sensor wiring lead through the grommet in the inner wing panel, then slacken and remove the two bolts securing the sensor unit to the wheel hub **(see illustrations)**. Remove the sensor and lead assembly.

25.7 Anti-lock braking System (ABS) modulator

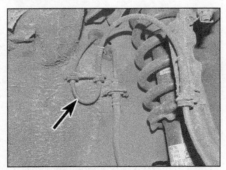

25.13a Release the wiring (arrowed) from the securing brackets . . .

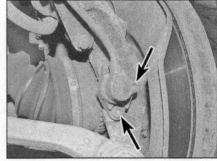

25.13b . . . and undo the retaining screws – arrowed

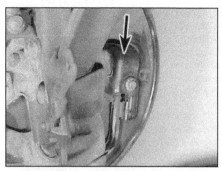

25.18 ABS sensor cover plate – arrowed

14 Refitting is the reverse of the removal procedure, noting the following:
  a) Ensure that the sensor and hub sealing faces are clean
  b) Refit the sensor and tighten its retaining bolts to the specified torque.
  c) Ensure the sensor wiring is secured and correctly routed.

Rear wheel sensor

Models with disc brakes

15 Chock the front wheels then jack up the rear of the vehicle and support it on axle stands (see *Jacking and vehicle support*). Remove the appropriate roadwheel.
16 Trace the wiring back from the sensor to the wiring connector, then free the connector from its retaining clip and disconnect it.
17 Working your way along the length of the sensor wiring, undo the bolts from the securing clips to release the sensor wiring lead, noting the routing of the cable.
18 Slacken and remove the bolt securing the wiring bracket to the sensor cover, then undo the two retaining bolts and remove the sensor cover **(see illustration)**.

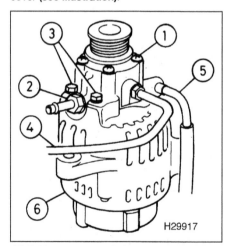

H29917

26.5 Vacuum pump is located on the front of the alternator

1	Vacuum pump	3	Vacuum pump mounting bolts
2	Vacuum stub to servo unit	4	Oil feed pipe
		5	Oil return hose
		6	Alternator

19 Undo the screws securing the sensor to the rear hub assembly and remove it from the vehicle.
20 Refitting is the reverse of the removal procedure, noting the following:
  a) Ensure the sensor and hub sealing faces are clean before installing the sensor.
  b) Tighten the sensor retaining screws to the specified torque.
  c) Ensure the sensor wiring is secured and correctly routed.

Models with drum brakes

21 With reference to Sections 15 and 16, remove the relevant brake drum and brake shoes from the backplate.
22 Trace the wiring back along the suspension components to the wiring connector, then free the connector from its retaining clip and disconnect it.
23 Working your way along the length of the sensor wiring, undo the bolts from the securing clips to release the sensor wiring lead, noting the routing of the cable.
24 Slacken and remove the two sensor adaptor mounting bolts, then slacken the two remaining bolts securing the backplate to the hub assembly. With the backplate plate loose, the sensor harness at the rear of the backplate can now be released from its retaining clip.
25 Withdraw the sensor and adaptor from the backplate, release the sensor wiring from the grommet in the backplate and withdraw the sensor wiring lead.
26 If required, slacken the lockscrew in the adapter plate to release the sensor.
27 Fit the new sensor to the adapter plate, then pass the wiring lead through the backplate aperture and press the grommet into place. Fit sensor/adaptor plate in position on the backplate and tighten the two retaining bolts to the specified torque.
28 Slacken the adapter lockscrew then, using a feeler blade, adjust the position of the sensor in the adapter so that the clearance between the tip of the sensor and the reluctor ring is 0.5 mm. On completion, tighten the adapter lockscrew.
29 The remainder of the refitting procedure is a reversal of removal, noting the following points:
  a) Ensure that the sensor wiring connector is securely refitted.
  b) Refit the sensor wiring securely into their

26.8 Remove the four securing bolts (arrowed) and detach the vacuum pump from the front of the alternator

retaining clips, making sure it is routed correctly.
  c) Refit the brake shoes and drum with reference to Sections 15 and 16 respectively.

Reluctor rings

30 The reluctor rings are not available as separate items. The front rings are available only as an integral part of the outer constant velocity joint assembly and the rear rings are available only as an integral part of the rear hub.

26 Brake servo vacuum pump (diesel models) – removal and refitting

Removal

1 Disconnect the battery negative terminal (refer to *Disconnecting the battery* in the Reference Section of this manual).
2 Raise the front of the car, support it securely on axle stands (see *Jacking and vehicle support*) and remove the right-hand front roadwheel.
3 Remove the fixings and withdraw the undertray from the underside of the engine compartment.
4 Remove the auxiliary drivebelt with reference to Chapter 5A, Section 6. **Note:** *On some models it may be necessary to remove the alternator completely as described in Chapter 5A, Section 5.*
5 Slacken the oil feed union pipe and disconnect it from the vacuum pump **(see illustration)**.
Caution: Be prepared for some oil spillage; position a drain container under the union and pad the surrounding area with absorbent rags.
6 Release the securing clip and disconnect the vacuum hose from the vacuum pump.
7 Slacken the securing clip and disconnect the vacuum pump oil return hose from the pipe to the sump.
8 Undo the four bolts securing the vacuum pump to the front of the alternator **(see illustration)**, and then remove the vacuum pump from the engine compartment.
Caution: Plug or cap the connections immediately after disconnection, to prevent any dirt ingress.

Refitting

9 Refitting is a reversal of removal, noting the following points:
  a) Ensure that the vacuum pump-to-alternator bolts are tightened to the specified torque.
  b) Where applicable, refit the alternator and auxiliary belt as described in chapter 5A.
  c) Ensure that all oil supply and return unions are clean before reconnection, and tighten the union nuts securely.
  d) On completion, reconnect the battery and check the operation of the brake system.

Chapter 10
Suspension and steering

Contents

Section number

Front hub bearings – checking and renewal 3
Front shock absorber/coil spring assembly – removal, overhaul
    and refitting 4
Front suspension anti-roll bar – removal and refitting 6
Front suspension upper and lower control arms – removal,
    overhaul and refitting 5
Front swivel hub assembly – removal and refitting 2
General information and precautions 1
Power steering drivebelt – removal and refitting 23
Power steering oil cooler – removal and refitting 19
Power steering pump – removal and refitting 18
Power steering system – bleeding 20
Rear hub and bearings – checking, removal and refitting 7

Section number

Rear stub axle – removal and refitting 8
Rear suspension anti-roll bar – removal and refitting 12
Rear suspension lateral links – removal, inspection and refitting . . . 10
Rear suspension shock absorber – removal, overhaul and refitting . 9
Rear suspension trailing arm – removal and refitting 11
Steering column – removal and refitting 14
Steering gear – removal, overhaul and refitting 17
Steering gear rubber gaiters – renewal 16
Steering lock – removal and refitting 15
Steering wheel – removal and refitting 13
Track rod end – removal and refitting 21
Wheel alignment and steering angles 22

Degrees of difficulty

Easy, suitable for novice with little experience	Fairly easy, suitable for beginner with some experience	Fairly difficult, suitable for competent DIY mechanic	Difficult, suitable for experienced DIY mechanic	Very difficult, suitable for expert DIY or professional

Specifications

Front suspension

Type	Fully independent, double wishbone with dampers and coil springs. Anti-roll bar fitted
Anti-roll bar diameter	24 mm
Front coil springs:	
Total coils:	
R45	10.5
MG ZS	9.07
Wire diameter:	
R45	12.45 mm ± 0.05 mm
MG ZS	13.43 mm ± 0.05 mm
Nominal height to wheel arch from hub centre – at unladen weight:	
R45	365 mm ± 15 mm
MG ZS	345 mm ± 15 mm

Rear suspension

Type	Independent, wishbone with damper and coil springs. Anti-roll bar fitted
Anti-roll bar diameter	16 mm to 20 mm (depending on model)
Rear coil springs:	
Total coils:	
R45	8.301
MG ZS	10.5
Active coils	8.97
Nominal height to wheel arch from hub centre – at unladen weight:	
R45	373 mm ± 15 mm
MG ZS	353 mm ± 15 mm

Steering

Type	Power-assisted rack and pinion, linear ratio system. Collapsible steering column with height adjustment
Turns lock to lock	3.48
Turning circle:	
Rover 45 models	10.3 m
MG ZS	11.2 m

Wheel alignment and steering angles – unladen condition

Front:

R45:

Camber angle	0° ± 0.45'
Castor angle	1° 38' ± 1°
King pin inclination	10° 42' ± 1°
Wheel alignment – toe-out	0° ± 0°.15' (0.0 mm ± 1.710 mm)

MG ZS:

Camber angle	-0°.20' ± 0.45'
Castor angle	4° 15' ± 1°
King pin inclination	12° 26' ± 1°
Wheel alignment – toe-out	0° ± 0°.15' (0.0 mm ± 1.710 mm)

Rear (all models):

Camber angle:

R45	-1° 3' ± 0°.45'
MG ZS	-0° 30' ± 0° 45'
Thrust angle	0° ± 0° 6'
Wheel alignment – toe-in	0° 22' ± 0° 15' (2.440 mm ± 1.710 mm)

Roadwheels

Steel	5.5J x 14 or 6.0J x 15
Alloy	5.5J x 14, 6.0J x 15, 6.5J x 16 or 7.0J x 17

Spare:

Full size (steel)	5.5J x 14 or 6.0J x R15
Space saver (steel)	3.5J x 15

Caution: The space saver spare wheel is for temporary use only. When in use, maximum roadspeed is 50 mph. Only one space saver wheel may be fitted at any one time.

Tyres

Type	Tubeless, steel braced radial

Wheel size:

5.5J x 14 steel and alloy wheels	185/65 R14 86T/H
6.0J x 15 steel and alloy wheels	195/55 R15 82H
6.5J x 16 alloy wheels	205/50 R16 87H
7.0J x 17 alloy wheels	205/45 R17 95M
3.5J x 15 spare wheel (space saver)	T125/80 R15 95M
Tyre pressures	See end of *Weekly checks* on page 0•18

Torque wrench settings

	Nm	lbf ft
Front suspension		
Anti-roll bar clamp bolts	22	16
Anti-roll bar link nuts	22	16
Shock absorber fork-to-shock absorber pinch-bolt nut	43	32
Shock absorber fork-to-lower control arm bolt **	64	47
Shock absorber upper mounting nuts **	38	28
Shock absorber damper rod/upper mounting centre nut	30	22
Lower control arm balljoint nut:		
1st stage	49	36
2nd stage	Tighten to align next split pin hole	
Lower control arm pivot bolts: **		
Front	64	47
Rear	83	61
Upper control arm balljoint nut:		
1st stage	39	29
2nd stage	Tighten to align next split pin hole	
Upper control arm pivot bracket-to-body nuts	64	47
Upper control arm pivot bolt nuts	Not available	
Rear suspension		
Anti-roll bar clamp bolts	14	10
Anti-roll bar-to-link bolt	14	10
Anti-roll bar link-to-lower arm bolt	45	33
Front (compensator) lateral link-to-body pivot bolt	45	33
Front (compensator) lateral link-to-trailing arm pivot bolt	45	33
Trailing arm compliance bush-to-body mounting bolts	78	58
Rear upper lateral link compliance bush-to-body mounting bolts	30	22
Rear upper lateral link-to-trailing arm pivot bolt **	47	35
Rear lower lateral link-to-crossmember pivot bolt **	47	35
Rear lower lateral link-to-trailing arm pivot bolt **	47	35
Shock absorber upper mounting nuts **	38	28
Shock absorber damper rod/upper mounting centre nut	30	22

Shock absorber-to-lower control arm bolt **	47	35
Hub nut *	180	133
Steering		
Steering wheel nut *	49	36
Steering column upper mounting nuts...........................	16	12
Steering column lower mounting clamp bolts	22	16
Steering column universal joint clamp bolts	28	21
Steering gear mountings:		
Flange mounting bolts	58	43
Clamp mounting bolts	38	28
Track rod end balljoint nut:		
1st stage	39	29
2nd stage	Tighten to align next split pin hole	
Track rod end locknut **	45	33
Steering gear feed pipe union	37	27
Steering gear return pipe union	28	21
Power steering pipe clips......................................	9	7
Power steering fluid reservoir mounting bolts	9	7
Four-cylinder petrol engines:		
Power steering pump mounting bracket bolts.................	45	33
Power steering pump-to-mounting bracket bolts	25	18
Power steering pump outlet pipe banjo union bolt	20	15
Power steering pump pulley bolts	9	7
V6 petrol engines:		
Power steering pump-to-mounting bracket bolts	25	18
Power steering pump outlet pipe union	28	21
Power steering pump pulley bolts	10	7
Diesel engines:		
Power steering pump outlet pipe banjo union bolt	37	27
Power steering pump pulley bolts	9	7
Power steering pump-to-coolant pump bolts	25	18
Roadwheels		
Roadwheel nuts	Refer to Chapter 1A or 1B	

* *Fit new nuts/bolts*
** *Tighten with vehicle weight on suspension*

1 General information and precautions

General information

The front suspension is of fully independent design with upper and lower control arms, shock absorber/coil spring assemblies and an anti-roll bar **(see illustration)**.

The fully independent rear suspension is of double wishbone type, utilising pressed steel trailing arms which have the roadwheel stub axles bolted into their rear ends **(see illustration)**. These are located longitudinally on the vehicle underbody via a large rubber bush, which is situated towards the centre of each arm. Each trailing arm assembly is located transversely by three lateral links, which utilise rubber mounting bushes at both their inner and outer ends. The rear suspension units incorporate coil springs and integral telescopic shock absorbers and are mounted onto the rear lower lateral link via a rubber mounting bush.

All models are fitted with a power-assisted rack-and-pinion steering gear. The hydraulic system is powered by a belt-driven pump, which is driven from the crankshaft pulley. The hydraulic fluid is cooled by passing it through a single bore cooling tube, located behind the front bumper. The power steering is speed-sensitive with more assistance at low speeds, and reduced assistance at higher speeds to

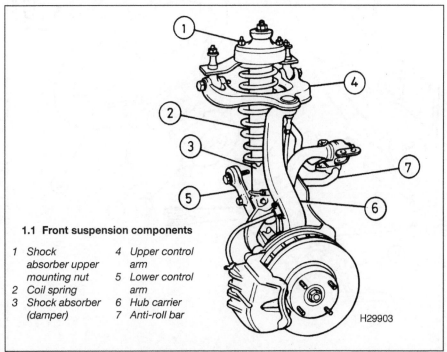

1.1 Front suspension components

1 Shock absorber upper mounting nut
2 Coil spring
3 Shock absorber (damper)
4 Upper control arm
5 Lower control arm
6 Hub carrier
7 Anti-roll bar

H29903

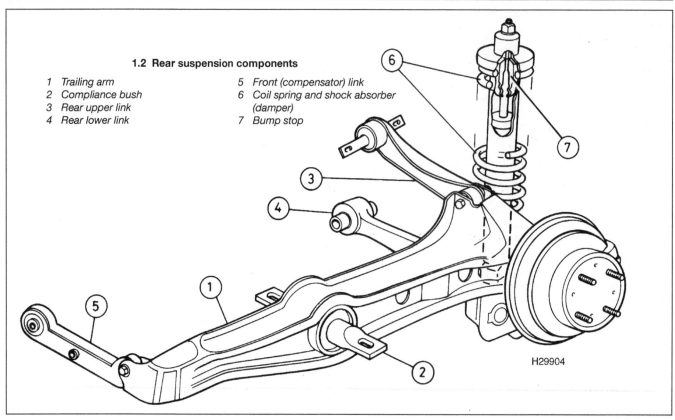

1.2 Rear suspension components

1 Trailing arm
2 Compliance bush
3 Rear upper link
4 Rear lower link
5 Front (compensator) link
6 Coil spring and shock absorber (damper)
7 Bump stop

H29904

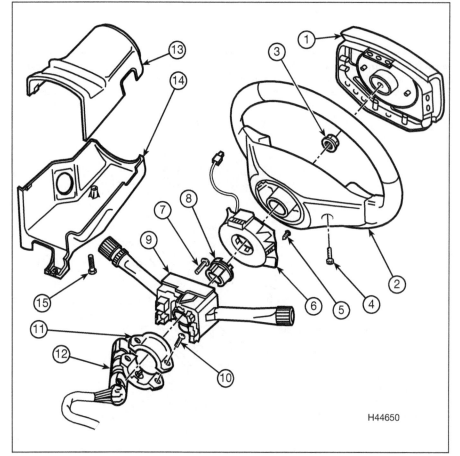

H44650

give a positive feel for cruising. This system uses a hydraulic control valve incorporated in the vehicle speed sensor on the transmission.

To provide driver protection in a frontal collision, the steering wheel is an energy-absorbing design, and an airbag is installed behind the padded centre cover **(see illustration)**. See Chapter 12 for full details.

The steering column has a two-piece collapsible upper section, and a solid lower shaft, with a universal joint at each end. The lower joint is attached to the steering rack input shaft **(see illustration)**. In an impact, the column mountings are deigned to absorb energy by deforming and/or moving. The steering column rake/wheel height is adjustable.

1.4 Steering wheel components

1 Airbag module
2 Steering wheel
3 Self locking nut
4 Torx bolt
5 Screw – self-tapping
6 Rotary coupler
7 Screw
8 Cancel cam – indicator switch
9 Lighting, indicators and wiper switch
10 Shear bolt
11 Bracket – steering lock/starter switch assembly
12 Steering lock assembly
13 Shroud – upper
14 Shroud – lower
15 Screw

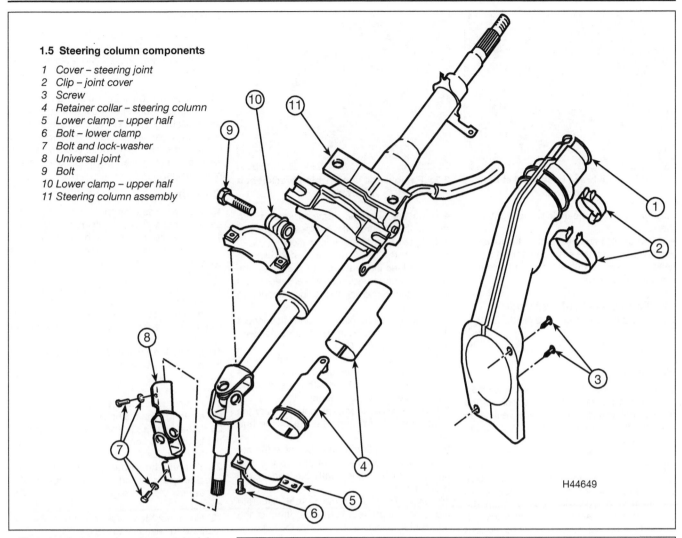

1.5 Steering column components

1 Cover – steering joint
2 Clip – joint cover
3 Screw
4 Retainer collar – steering column
5 Lower clamp – upper half
6 Bolt – lower clamp
7 Bolt and lock-washer
8 Universal joint
9 Bolt
10 Lower clamp – upper half
11 Steering column assembly

H44649

The steering gear is a rack and pinion design, with integral power assistance **(see illustration)**. The steering gear is attached to the front suspension crossmember. Steering effort is transmitted to the steering arms via track rods with adjustable balljoints at the steering arms.

Precautions

• The driveshaft hub and stub axle nuts are very tight – ensure the car is securely

1.6 Steering rack components

Note: On some models the pipe connections are on the upper part of the rack

1 Track rod end balljoint	6 Mounting rubber
2 Grommet – pinion shaft-to-body	7 Mounting bracket clamp
3 Grommet – pinion housing	8 Left-hand mounting bolt
4 Steering gear assembly	9 Right-hand mounting bolt
5 Fluid pipes	10 Washer
	11 Bush

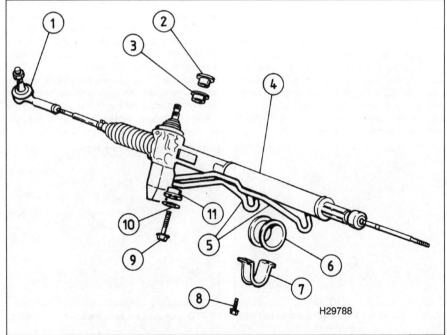

H29788

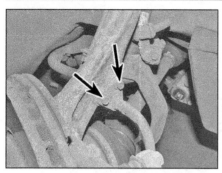

2.3 Undo the brake hose bracket bolts – arrowed

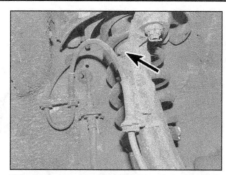

2.5a Remove the upper wiring bracket bolt (arrowed) . . .

Overhaul

13 Check the lower balljoint for excessive wear. If evident, it can be renewed, however special tools are required and a Rover dealer or suitably-equipped garage should carry out the work.
14 Check the balljoint rubber dust cover for damage and splits. If evident, check for the availability of parts, so the cover can be renewed separately. Prise off the circlips and remove the old dust cover, then clean the seating and fit the new cover. Secure with the new circlips.

Refitting

15 Before reassembly, clean all the components and examine them for damage.
16 Locate the splash guard on the hub carrier making sure that the location peg engages with the hole, then tighten the screws securely.
17 Refit the hub with reference to Section 3.
18 Apply a little grease to the splines on the driveshaft, and then locate the hub carrier together with the hub on the driveshaft splines.
19 Locate the lower end of the hub carrier on the balljoint stud on the lower arm and screw on the nut. Tighten the nut to the specified torque then align the split pin holes and fit a new split pin. If necessary the nut may be tightened to align the holes.
20 Locate the upper end of the hub carrier on the balljoint stud on the upper arm and screw on the nut loosely.
21 Tighten the upper balljoint nut to the specified torque and fit a new split pin. If necessary, the nut may be tightened to align the holes.
22 Reconnect the track rod end to the hub carrier with reference to Section 21.
23 Refit the ABS sensor and wiring and tighten the Torx screw to the specified torque (see Chapter 9 Specifications). Make sure the wiring is not twisted.
24 Refit the brake disc, pads, caliper and bracket with reference to Chapter 9.
25 Refit the brake hose bracket and tighten the bolts securely.
26 While an assistant depresses the footbrake, fit and tighten the new driveshaft nut to the specified torque (see Chapter 8 Specifications). Stake the nut collar into the groove in the driveshaft.
27 Refit the roadwheel, lower the vehicle to the ground then tighten the nuts to the specified torque.

supported when loosening and tightening them.
• A number of precautions must be observed when working on the steering components of vehicles equipped with airbags, and these are listed in Chapter 12.

2 Front swivel hub assembly – removal, overhaul and refitting

Removal

1 Apply the handbrake, then loosen the wheel nuts on the relevant wheel and jack up the front of the vehicle. Support the vehicle on axle stands (see *Jacking and vehicle support*). Remove the roadwheel.
2 Using a hammer and chisel-nosed tool tap up the staking securing the driveshaft nut to the groove in the CV joint stub. Have an assistant apply the footbrake and using a socket and extension bar, slacken the driveshaft nut. Unscrew and remove the nut. Discard the nut, as a new one will be required for refitting.
Caution: Be careful, as the nut is very tight.
3 Unbolt the brake hose bracket from the hub carrier **(see illustration)**, then unbolt the brake caliper bracket from the hub carrier and suspend the caliper (with pads) and bracket to one side with a length of wire attached to the coil spring. If preferred, the caliper and pads can be removed as described in Chapter 9, and then the caliper bracket unbolted.

4 Undo the two disc retaining screws and remove the disc from the hub assembly, Refer to Chapter 9, for further information.
5 Unbolt the ABS wheel sensor wiring supports **(see illustrations)**, then unscrew the Torx screw and remove the wheel sensor from the hub carrier leaving the wiring attached to the sensor.
6 Slacken the retaining nut and disconnect the track rod end from the hub carrier with reference to Section 21.
7 Extract the split pin, then unscrew the nut securing the upper control arm balljoint to the hub carrier until it is flush with the end of the balljoint stud **(see illustration)**.
8 Using a balljoint removal tool, separate the upper control arm from the top of the hub carrier.
9 Extract the split pin, then unscrew the nut securing the lower control arm to the hub carrier until it is flush with the end of the balljoint stud.
10 Using a balljoint removal tool, separate the lower control arm from the bottom of the hub carrier. Unscrew and remove the nut.
11 Support the hub carrier, then carefully pull it together with the hub from the end of the driveshaft, while tapping the end of the driveshaft with a soft-faced mallet. Support the driveshaft with a length of wire to prevent damage to the inner CV joint.
12 With the hub carrier assembly on the bench, remove the hub with reference to Section 3 then undo the screws and withdraw the splash guard. **Note:** *Removal of the hub will necessitate renewal of the bearings.*

3 Front hub bearings – checking and renewal

Checking

1 Apply the handbrake, then jack up the front of the vehicle and support it on axle stands (see *Jacking and vehicle support*).

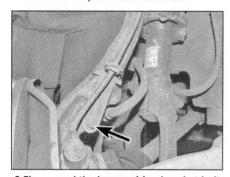

2.5b . . . and the lower wiring bracket bolt – arrowed

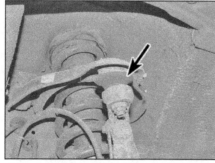

2.7 Upper control arm balljoint – arrowed

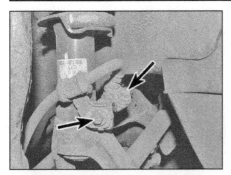

4.2 Undo the brake hose mounting bracket bolts – arrowed

2 Spin the wheel by hand and check for noise and roughness in the wheel bearings indicating excessive wear.

3 For a more thorough check, remove the brake disc as described in Chapter 9, then measure the amount of side play in the bearing. To do this, a dial gauge should be fixed so that its probe is in contact with the wheel contact face of the hub. Attempt to move the hub in and out, and check the movement in the bearing. Excessive play indicates wear in the bearing, and it must be renewed.

Renewal

Note: *Removal of the bearing renders it unserviceable for further use.*

4 Remove the front swivel hub assembly as described in Section 2.

5 Using a screwdriver, prise out the protector ring from the rear of the hub carrier.

6 The hub must now be pressed from the hub carrier before pressing out the bearing. To successfully carry out this work it will be necessary to support the bearing housing while the hub and bearing are being removed. If the necessary equipment is not available, have the work carried out by a Rover dealer or engineering works. Note also that the outer bearing race will have to be removed from the hub before fitting the hub to the new bearings.

7 With the hub removed, undo the screws and remove the splash shield from the hub carrier.

8 Using circlip pliers, extract the circlip from the groove in the hub carrier.

9 Support the hub and press out the bearing. **Note:** *The bearing will be damaged during this process and must not be re-used.*

10 Before installing the new bearing, thoroughly clean the hub and hub carrier.

11 Support the hub carrier with the circlip groove uppermost, then press the new bearing fully into position using a metal tube or adapter on the outer race. Fit the circlip making sure that it is fully engaged with the groove.

12 Fit the splash shield and tighten the screws.

13 Support the hub with the wheel studs facing downwards, then locate the new bearing and hub carrier on the hub making sure it is the correct way round.

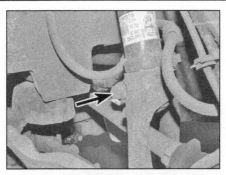

4.5 Pinch-bolt (arrowed) securing the bottom of the shock absorber

14 Using a suitable metal tube located only on the inner race, press the bearing housing fully onto the hub.

15 Press the protector ring into the rear of the hub carrier.

16 Refit the swivel hub assembly as described in Section 2.

---

4 Front shock absorber/ coil spring assembly – removal, overhaul and refitting

---

Caution: If renewing the shock absorber or spring during overhaul, both the left- and right-hand should be renewed as a pair, to preserve the handling characteristics of the vehicle.

Note: *Before attempting to dismantle the front suspension unit, a suitable tool to hold the coil spring in compression must be obtained. Adjustable coil spring compressors are readily available and are recommended for this operation. Any attempt to dismantle the unit without such a tool is likely to result in damage or personal injury.*

Removal

1 Apply the handbrake, then loosen the wheel nuts on the relevant wheel and jack up the front of the vehicle. Support the vehicle on axle stands (see *Jacking and vehicle support*). Remove the roadwheel.

2 Unbolt the brake hose brackets from the base of the shock absorber **(see illustration)**.

3 Disconnect the front anti-roll bar from the lower control arm with reference to Section 6.

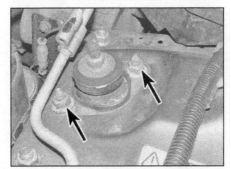

4.7a Unscrew the upper mounting nuts (arrowed) . . .

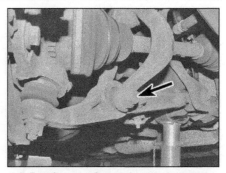

4.6 Bolt (arrowed) securing the fork to the lower arm

4 Position a trolley jack under the lower control arm to support it when the shock absorber assembly is removed.

5 Unscrew and remove the pinch-bolt securing the fork to the bottom of the shock absorber assembly **(see illustration)**.

6 Unscrew and remove the bolt securing the fork to the lower control arm noting which way round it is fitted, then withdraw the fork **(see illustration)**. If the fork is tight on the shock absorber, tap it free with a hammer. **Note:** *The forks are 'handed' on each side of the vehicle. The left-hand fork is marked VL and the right-hand fork is marked VR.*

7 Open the bonnet. Support the shock absorber assembly from under the front wheel arch, then unscrew the upper mounting nuts from inside the engine compartment and withdraw the unit from under the wheel arch **(see illustrations)**.

⚠ **Warning: Do not unscrew the centre nut from the top of the shock absorber during the removal procedure.**

Overhaul

Note: *Suitable coil spring compressor tools will be required for this operation.*

8 With the assembly on the bench, check the shock absorber for leaking fluid, dents, cracks or other obvious damage. Check the coil spring for chips or cracks, which could cause premature failure, and inspect the spring seats for hardness or general deterioration.

9 Clamp the lower end of the shock absorber assembly in a vice fitted with jaw protectors.

10 Fit spring compressors to the spring, and

4.7b . . . and withdraw the shock absorber/spring assembly from under the wheel arch

4.11 Mark the spring and mounting for refitting

4.12a Holding the shaft still using a ratchet and Allen key . . .

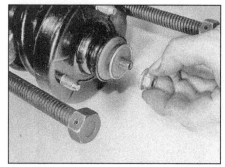

4.12b . . . and remove the centre nut

4.13a Remove the washer . . .

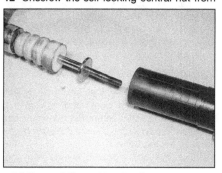

4.13b . . . and upper mounting

compress the spring until there is no pressure on the upper mounting and the central nut is raised from the washer.

> ⚠ **Warning: Use only purpose made spring compressor tools and follow the manufacturer's instructions.**

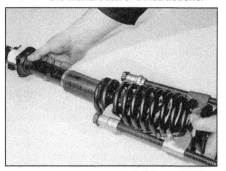

4.14a Remove the coil spring complete with compressor . . .

11 Mark the relationship of the shock absorber assembly components to ensure correct reassembly. As the components are removed, lay them out in order to ensure correct refitting **(see illustration)**.
12 Unscrew the self-locking central nut from

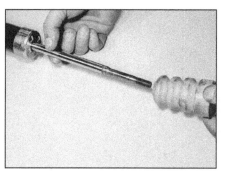

4.14b . . . followed by the dust cover . . .

the top of the shock absorber assembly while holding the shaft stationary with a 5.0 mm Allen key **(see illustrations)**.
13 Remove the washer, upper mounting, collar, mounting plate, lower mounting rubber and upper spring seat **(see illustrations)**.
14 Remove the coil spring (with compressors fitted), followed by the dust cover, stop plate and bump stop (note which way round it is fitted) **(see illustrations)**. If the compressors are to be left in position on the coil spring, put the spring in a safe place away from the work area as a precaution.
15 With the shock absorber assembly now dismantled, examine all the components for wear and damage. Check the rubber components for deterioration. Examine the shock absorber for damage and signs of fluid leakage, and check the piston rod for pitting along its entire length. While holding it in an upright position, test the operation of the shock absorber by moving the rod through a full stroke, and then through short strokes of 50 to 100 mm. In both cases, the resistance felt should be smooth and continuous. If the resistance is jerky, or uneven, or if there is any visible sign of wear or damage to the shock absorber, renewal is necessary.
16 Renew the coil spring if it is damaged or distorted.
17 To reassemble the shock absorber, first extend the piston rod as far as it will go.
18 Fit the bump stop, stop plate and dust cover onto the piston rod, making sure that the bump stop is the correct way round (ie, largest diameter uppermost).
19 Ensure that the coil spring is compressed

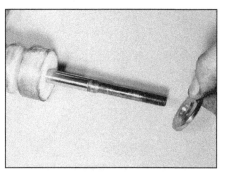

4.14c . . . then the stop plate . . .

4.14d . . . and finally the bump stop

4.19 Ensure that the lower end of the spring is located in the lower spring seat – arrowed

sufficiently to enable the upper mounting components to be fitted, then fit the spring over the piston rod, ensuring that the lower end of the spring is correctly located on the lower spring seat **(see illustration)**.

20 Locate the upper spring seat on the coil spring, followed by the lower mounting rubber, mounting plate, collar, upper mounting rubber, washer and nut. Before tightening the nut, position the components with the previously-made marks aligned. Where new components are being fitted, transfer the marks from the old components.

21 Tighten the self-locking nut to the specified torque while holding the piston rod with an Allen key.

22 Release the compressors while guiding the spring ends onto the seats.

23 Remove the assembly from the vice.

Refitting

24 Manoeuvre the shock absorber assembly into position under the wheel arch, passing the mounting studs through the holes in the body turret. Refit the upper mounting nuts loosely, but do not fully tighten them at this stage.

25 Fit the fork to the bottom of the shock absorber, making sure that the alignment tab enters the slot in the fork. Insert the pinch-bolt and screw on the nut loosely. **Note:** *The forks are 'handed' on each side of the vehicle. The left-hand fork is marked VL and the right-hand fork is marked VR.*

26 Locate the fork on the lower control arm, and insert the bolt with its head facing forwards. Screw on the nut loosely.

27 Using a trolley jack under the lower control arm, raise the front suspension until the weight of the vehicle is just supported.

28 Tighten the fork-to-shock absorber pinch-bolt, upper mounting nuts and fork-to-lower control arm bolt to the specified torques.

29 Reconnect the front anti-roll bar to the lower control arm with reference to Section 6.

30 Refit the brake hose bracket to the base of the shock absorber and tighten the bolts.

31 Refit the roadwheel, lower the vehicle to the ground and tighten the bolts to the specified torque setting.

5 Front suspension upper and lower control arms – removal, overhaul and refitting

Upper control arm

Removal

1 Remove the relevant front shock absorber/coil spring assembly as described in Section 4.

2 Position a trolley jack under the lower control arm to support the hub carrier when it is disconnected from the upper control arm.

3 Extract the split pin, and then unscrew the nut securing the upper control arm to the hub carrier until it is flush with the end of the balljoint stud **(see illustration)**.

4 Using a balljoint removal tool, separate the

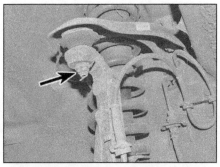

5.3 Remove split pin and upper balljoint nut – arrowed

upper control arm from the top of the hub carrier. Support the hub carrier, then unscrew and remove the nut.

5 From the top of the suspension turret inside the engine compartment **(see illustration)**, unscrew the upper control arm anchor nuts and withdraw the upper control arm and anchor assembly from under the wheel arch. Unscrew the nuts and remove the inner pivot bolts from the upper control arm. Note which way round the bolts are fitted; the head of the front bolt faces to the front and the head of the rear bolt faces to the rear.

Overhaul

6 If the inner pivot bushes are worn, remove the anchor from the body by unscrewing the nuts located in the engine compartment. Press the old bushes from the anchor, then press in the new bushes.

7 Check the upper balljoint for excessive wear. If evident, the complete upper control arm must be renewed.

8 Check the rubber dust cover for damage and splits. If evident, the cover can be renewed separately. Prise off the circlip and remove the old dust cover, then clean the seating and fit the new cover. Secure with the new circlip.

Refitting

9 Refitting is a reversal of removal, but tighten the nuts and bolts to the specified torque and delay fully tightening the fork-to-lower arm bolt and the upper arm inner pivot bolts until the weight of the vehicle is on the front suspension. Make sure that the pivot bolts are located with their heads facing away from each other. Fit a new split pin to the

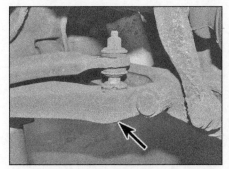

5.11 Anti-roll bar link to lower control arm – arrowed

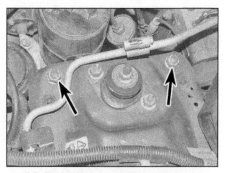

5.5 Undo the two upper control arm mounting nuts – arrowed

balljoint nut. Where necessary, tighten the nut further until the split pin hole is aligned with the serrations on the nut. **Note:** *The left- and right-hand upper control arms are different and must not be interchanged.* Have the front wheel alignment checked and adjusted at the earliest opportunity.

Lower control arm

Removal

10 Apply the handbrake, then loosen the wheel nuts on the relevant wheel and jack up the front of the vehicle. Support the vehicle on axle stands (see *Jacking and vehicle support*). Remove the roadwheel.

11 Unscrew the nut and disconnect the front anti-roll bar link from the lower control arm. Recover the rubber bush and washer **(see illustration)**.

12 Unscrew and remove the bolt securing the shock absorber lower fork to the lower control arm, noting that its head is facing the front of the vehicle **(see illustration)**.

13 Extract the split pin, then unscrew the nut securing the lower control arm to the hub carrier until it is flush with the end of the balljoint stud.

14 Using a balljoint removal tool, separate the lower control arm from the bottom of the hub carrier. Unscrew and remove the nut.

15 Unscrew and remove the two bolts securing the anti-roll bar mounting to the suspension crossmember.

16 Unscrew the nut and remove the washer from the lower arm rear pivot. Discard the nut and obtain a new one **(see illustration)**.

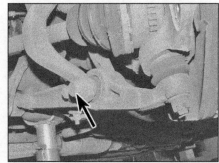

5.12 Fork lower mounting bolt – arrowed

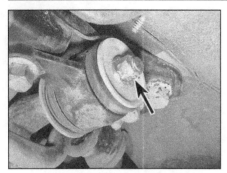

5.16 Lower arm rear pivot nut

17 Unscrew and remove the front pivot bolt, then slacken the rear pivot bush mounting bracket bolts sufficiently to allow the front bush to clear the suspension crossmember **(see illustration)**.

18 Withdraw the lower control arm from under the wheel arch and recover the washer from the rear pivot. Note that the front face of the washer is marked FR.

Caution: The lower control arm is in two sections bolted together. DO NOT attempt to separate the two sections.

Overhaul

19 Check the inner pivot and shock absorber fork rubber bushes for excessive wear including the bush in the rear bracket. The bushes may be renewed separately, however a press is required and a Rover dealer or suitably-equipped garage should carry out the work. After installation in the lower arm, the edges of the bush outer casing must be flush with the arm.

Refitting

20 Refitting is a reversal of the removal procedure but renew the inner pivot nut and make sure that the rear pivot washer is positioned with the face marked FR facing the front. Tighten all nuts and bolts to the specified torque, however delay fully tightening the inner front and rear pivot bolts and nuts, and the fork-to-lower arm bolt until the weight of the vehicle is on the suspension. Smear rubber grease to the face of the anti-roll bar washer before refitting it. Have the front wheel alignment checked and adjusted at the earliest opportunity.

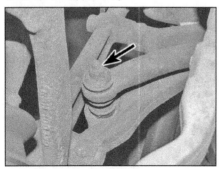

6.3 Anti-roll bar drop link upper nut – arrowed

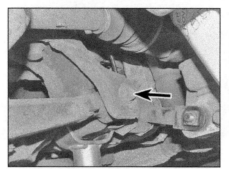

5.17a Remove the front pivot bolt (arrowed) . . .

6 Front suspension anti-roll bar – removal and refitting

Removal

1 Apply the handbrake, then loosen the wheel nuts on both front wheels and jack up the front of the vehicle. Support the vehicle on axle stands (see *Jacking and vehicle support*). Remove both front roadwheels.

2 Mark the anti-roll bar for position as an aid to refitting it.

3 Working on each side at a time, unscrew the nut from the top of the links on the lower arms while holding the links stationary with a spanner on the flats provided. Remove the nuts, cupped washers and rubber bushes noting that the cupped washers are located with their convex sides in contact with the bushes **(see illustration)**.

4 Raise the anti-roll bar from the links, then unscrew the lower nuts and remove the links from the lower arms. Recover the cupped washers and rubber bushes.

5 Detach the exhaust front downpipe from the exhaust manifold with reference to the relevant part of Chapter 4.

6 Beneath the vehicle, unhook the rubber mounting then lower the downpipe to the ground.

7 Prise the gearchange linkage balljoints from the levers on the transmission with reference to the relevant part of Chapter 7.

8 Unbolt the gearchange linkage bracket and lower it onto the exhaust downpipe.

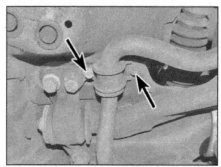

6.9a Anti roll bar mounting bracket bolts (arrowed) . . .

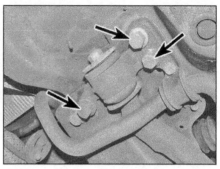

5.17b . . . and slacken the rear mounting bracket bolts – arrowed

9 Unscrew the bolts from the anti-roll bar mounting clamps on the suspension crossmember and remove the clamps. Note that the clamps are marked with an arrow facing the front of the vehicle **(see illustrations)**.

10 Manoeuvre the anti-roll bar over the gearchange linkage and withdraw from the vehicle.

11 Note the positions of the mounting rubbers then pull them from the anti-roll bar.

12 Check the anti-roll bar and mounting components for damage and wear and renew as necessary.

Refitting

13 Smear the bores of the mounting rubbers with rubber grease or similar lubricant, then fit them in their previously-noted positions on the anti-roll bar. Make sure that the split ends of the rubbers will face the front of the vehicle when the anti-roll bar is fitted.

14 Refit the links to the lower arms together with the rubber bushes and cupped washers, making sure that the convex side of the washers contact the bushes. Tighten the lower nuts to the specified torque. Refit the lower washers and rubber bushes to the links.

15 Manoeuvre the anti-roll bar in position and engage it with the links, then refit the upper washers and rubber bushes. Refit the nuts and tighten to the specified torque.

16 Refit the clamps on the anti-roll bar making sure the arrows point to the front of the vehicle. Insert the bolts and tighten to the specified torque.

17 Refit the gearchange linkage bracket and tighten the mounting bolts to the specified torque (see Chapter 7A Specifications).

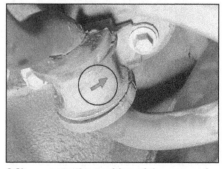

6.9b . . . note the position of the arrows for refitting

18 Lightly grease the gearchange balljoints then press them onto the transmission levers.
19 Refit the exhaust downpipe to the manifold with reference to the relevant part of Chapter 4, and reconnect the rubber mounting.
20 Refit the wheels and lower the vehicle; tighten the nuts to the specified torque.

7 Rear hub and bearings – checking, removal and refitting

Note: *The bearing is a sealed, pre-adjusted and prelubricated, double-row tapered-roller type and is intended to last the vehicle's entire service life without maintenance or attention. The bearing is an integral part of the hub and cannot be purchased separately. If renewal of the bearing is necessary, the complete hub assembly must be renewed as a unit.*

Checking

1 Chock the front wheels, then jack up the rear of the vehicle and support on axle stands (see *Jacking and vehicle support*). Release the handbrake.
2 Spin the wheel by hand and check for noise and roughness in the wheel bearings indicating excessive wear.
3 For a more thorough check, remove the brake drum or disc (as applicable) as described in Chapter 9, then measure the amount of side play in the bearing. To do this, a dial gauge should be fixed so that its probe is in contact with the wheel contact face of the hub. Attempt to move the hub in and out, and check the movement in the bearing. Excessive play indicates wear in the bearing, and the rear hub must be renewed complete.

Removal

4 Chock the front wheels, then jack up the rear of the vehicle and support it on axle stands. Remove the appropriate rear roadwheel.
5 Remove the rear brake drum or disc (as applicable) with reference to Chapter 9.
6 Prise out the cap from the centre of the hub assembly, then tap up the staking securing the hub-retaining nut to the groove in the stub axle using a screwdriver or small cold chisel.
7 Unscrew and remove the hub nut. Note that the nut is tightened to a high torque; make sure the vehicle is adequately supported while loosening the nut.
8 Pull the hub assembly from the stub axle and recover the washer **(see illustrations)**. Discard the hub nut and obtain a new one.

Refitting

9 Prior to refitting the hub, inspect the stub axle for signs of wear or scoring and, if necessary, renew it.
10 Apply a thin smear of grease to the hub bearing seal and refit the hub assembly. Refit the toothed washer, ensuring that its tooth locates with the groove in the stub axle.
11 Screw on the new hub nut and tighten it

7.8a Remove the hub and bearing assembly

to the specified torque, then stake the nut into the stub axle groove.
12 Tap the hub centre cap into the hub.
13 Refit the brake drum or disc (as applicable) with reference to Chapter 9.
14 Refit the roadwheel, then lower the vehicle to the ground and tighten the roadwheel nuts to the specified torque.
15 Apply the footbrake firmly several times, and then check the handbrake operation and adjustment with reference to Chapter 9.

8 Rear stub axle – removal and refitting

Note: *On later models, the stub axle is a complete assembly with the trailing arm and cannot be removed separately.*

Removal

1 Remove the rear hub assembly (Section 7).
2 On models fitted with rear drum brakes remove the rear brake shoes and disconnect the handbrake cable from the trailing shoe with reference to Chapter 9. Undo the bolts securing the handbrake cable and brake hose brackets to the trailing arm, then use a 12 mm ring spanner to compress the handbrake cable retaining clip and withdraw the cable from the backplate. Remove the four bolts securing the backplate to the trailing arm and carefully ease the backplate assembly outwards and off the end of the stub axle. Position the backplate assembly out of the way of the stub axle and tie it to the rear suspension unit coil spring using a piece of wire. Place a strong elastic band over the wheel cylinder pistons to prevent them coming out.
3 On models fitted with rear disc brakes, undo the four disc shield retaining bolts and remove the shield from the trailing arm.
4 On all models, using a socket and extension bar, undo the large stub axle retaining nut from the rear of the trailing arm assembly.
5 Unscrew and remove the four Torx bolts securing the stub axle mounting plate to the trailing arm assembly, then withdraw the stub axle and remove it from the vehicle.
6 Examine the stub axle spindle and mounting plate for signs of wear or damage such as scoring or cracking. If damaged, the stub axle must be renewed.

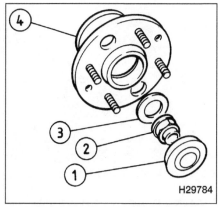

H29784

7.8b Rear hub and bearing components

1 Dust cap	*4 Hub and bearing*
2 Hub nut	*assembly*
3 Washer	

Refitting

7 Refitting is a reverse of the removal procedure, tightening all nuts and bolts to the specified torque settings.

9 Rear suspension shock absorber – removal, overhaul and refitting

Removal

1 Remove the rear seat backrest as described in Chapter 11.
2 On Hatchback models, open the tailgate, release the straps and lift out the parcel tray, then remove the parcel tray support panel from the relevant side by undoing the securing screws and releasing the retaining clips.
3 Remove the luggage compartment side trim with reference to Chapter 11, Section 28.
4 Chock the front wheels, then jack up the rear of the vehicle and support on axle stands (see *Jacking and vehicle support*). Remove the relevant rear wheel.
5 Support the weight of the rear lower lateral link and trailing arm with a trolley jack.
6 Inside the vehicle, remove the rubber cover (where applicable) from the top of the rear suspension unit, and then unscrew the two upper mounting nuts **(see illustration)**.

9.6 Undo the rear shock absorber upper mounting nuts

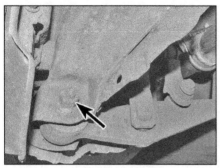

9.7 Lower lateral link-to-trailing arm pivot bolt

7 Unscrew the pivot bolt securing the rear lower lateral link to the trailing arm **(see illustration)**.

8 Unscrew the bolt securing the rear shock absorber to the rear lower lateral link, then release the unit from the link and manoeuvre it out from under the rear wheel arch **(see illustration)**.

Overhaul

Note: *Suitable coil spring compressor tools will be required for this operation. This procedure is similar to the front shock absorber overhaul, see Section 4 for further information.*

9 With the assembly on the bench, clean it thoroughly then check the shock absorber for leaking fluid, dents, cracks or other obvious damage. Check the coil spring and seats for damage or general deterioration.

10 Clamp the lower end of the shock absorber in a vice fitted with jaw protectors.

11 Fit spring compressors to the spring, and

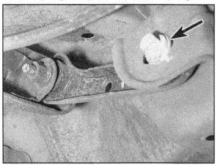

10.2a Front (compensator) link – elongated hole (arrowed) for adjustment

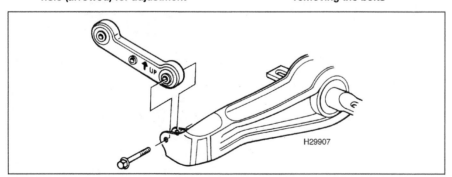

10.3 Link is marked with an arrow and the word UP for correct positioning – must face front of vehicle

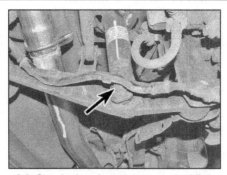

9.8 Shock absorber-to-lower lateral link bolt

compress the spring until there is no pressure on the upper mounting and the central nut is raised from the washer.

 Warning: Use only purpose made spring compressor tools and follow the manufacturer's instructions.

12 Note the relationship of the shock absorber assembly components to ensure correct reassembly. As the components are removed, lay them out in order to ensure correct refitting.

13 Unscrew the upper mounting retaining nut whilst retaining the damper piston with an Allen key.

14 Remove the nut and washer followed by the mounting plate assembly, noting the correct fitted positions of the mounting rubbers and spacer, and the upper spring rubber damper. Remove the coil spring then lift the dust seal and cover off the damper and slide the damper stop plate and rubber stop off the damper piston.

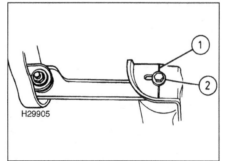

10.2b Mark a centre line (1) before removing the bolts

15 With the shock absorber assembly now dismantled, examine all the components for wear and damage. Check the rubber components for deterioration. Examine the shock absorber for damage and signs of fluid leakage, and check the piston rod for pitting along its entire length. While holding it in an upright position, test the operation of the shock absorber by moving the rod through a full stroke, and then through short strokes of 50 to 100 mm. In both cases, the resistance felt should be smooth and continuous. If the resistance is jerky, or uneven, or if there is any visible sign of wear or damage to the shock absorber, renewal is necessary.

16 Renew the coil spring if it is damaged or distorted.

17 Reassembly is a reversal of the removal procedure. Ensure that the spring ends are correctly located in the upper and lower seats and that the upper mounting plate retaining nut is tightened to the specified torque setting.

Refitting

18 Prior to refitting, examine the rear lower lateral link mounting bushes and renew any which are worn or damaged.

19 Ensure the rubber seal is in position on the upper mounting plate then refit the suspension unit, and screw on the upper mounting nuts hand-tight at this stage.

20 With the nut on the bottom of the unit facing forwards, offer up the lower lateral link and refit the shock absorber mounting bolt followed by the lower lateral link bolts. Tighten the bolts loosely at this stage.

21 Raise the trolley jack so that the rear suspension is supporting weight of the vehicle, then tighten the upper mounting nuts and lower bolts to the specified torque setting. Refit the rubber cover to the upper mounting and remove the trolley jack from under the trailing arm.

22 Refit the roadwheel, then lower the vehicle to the ground and tighten the roadwheel nuts to the specified torque.

23 Refit the luggage compartment side trim and rear seat backrest with reference to Chapter 11.

24 On Hatchback models, refit the parcel tray.

10 Rear suspension lateral links – removal, inspection and refitting

Removal

1 Chock the front wheels, then jack up the rear of the vehicle and support on axle stands (see *Jacking and vehicle support*). Remove the relevant rear roadwheel.

Front (compensator) link

2 Mark the position of the lateral link body pivot bolt in relation to the body. This mark can then be used as a guide on refitting and will ensure correct rear wheel alignment **(see illustrations)**.

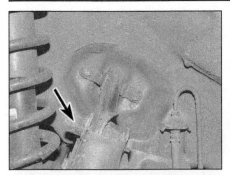

10.5 Bolt and nut (arrowed) securing the trailing arm to the upper link

3 Unscrew and remove both the pivot bolts securing the front lateral link to the body and trailing arm and remove the link from the vehicle. Note that the link has an arrow and the word UP marked on it **(see illustration)**.

Rear upper link

4 Use a trolley jack to support the weight of the trailing arm.
5 Unscrew and remove the pivot bolt securing the rear upper lateral link to the trailing arm assembly **(see illustration)**.
6 Undo the two bolts securing the inner mounting to the vehicle body and remove the link from the vehicle.

Rear lower link

7 Use a trolley jack to support the weight of the trailing arm.
8 On models equipped with ABS, undo the bolts securing the wheel sensor wiring lead bracket to the lower arm and release the wiring.
9 On models with a rear anti-roll bar, unscrew the bolt and disconnect the anti-roll bar.
10 Unscrew and remove the pivot bolts securing the lower rear lateral link to the crossmember, shock absorber and trailing arm **(see illustrations)**. Withdraw the link from under the vehicle. Note that the rear face of the link is marked with an L or R to indicate the left- or right-hand side.

Inspection

11 Examine the link and bushes for damage and wear and renew if necessary.
12 The bushes are a press-fit in the link and can be pressed out and in using a vice and

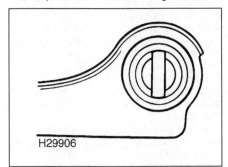

10.13 Upper link inner bush must be positioned as shown

two suitable-sized tubular drifts, such as sockets (one bearing on the hard outer edge of the bush and another bearing against the edge of the link).
13 When renewing the inner bush on the rear upper lateral link, mark the position of the bush mounting plate in relation to the lateral link before removing the worn bush. Fit the new bush so that the mounting plate is in the same position in relation to the lateral link **(see illustration)**.
14 When renewing the bushes of the rear lower link, make sure that the movement cut-outs are positioned as shown **(see illustration)**.

Refitting

15 Refitting is the reverse of removal, but delay fully tightening the pivot bolts until the weight of the vehicle is on the rear suspension. Have the rear wheel alignment checked and adjusted by a Rover dealer or tyre specialist.

11 Rear suspension trailing arm – removal and refitting

Removal

1 Chock the front wheels, then jack up the rear of the vehicle and support on axle stands (see *Jacking and vehicle support*). Remove the relevant rear wheel.
2 Remove the rear hub as described in Section 7.

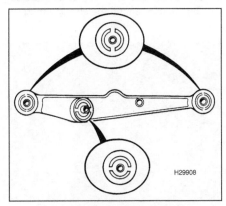

10.14 Lower link bushes must be positioned as shown

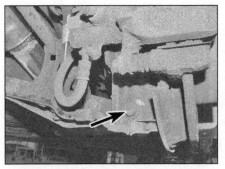

10.10a Lateral link to trailing arm pivot bolt

10.10b Lateral link to crossmember pivot bolt

Non-ABS models

3 Undo the bolts and remove the clips securing the handbrake cable and brake hose brackets to the trailing arm. Remove the four bolts securing the backplate to the trailing arm and carefully ease the backplate assembly outwards and off the end of the stub axle. Position the backplate out of the way of the stub axle and tie it to the rear suspension unit coil spring using a piece of wire.

ABS models

4 Remove the two brake caliper shield retaining screws and remove the shield from the caliper.
5 Slacken and remove the bolts securing the handbrake cable and brake hose retaining clamps to the trailing arm. Undo the two bolts securing the caliper mounting bracket to the trailing arm and slide the caliper off the disc. Tie the caliper to the rear suspension coil spring to avoid placing any strain on the hydraulic hose or handbrake cable.
6 Remove the ABS rear wheel sensor with reference to Chapter 9.

All models

7 Unscrew and remove the three pivot bolts securing the front (compensator) link, rear lower lateral link and rear upper lateral link to the trailing arm. See previous Section for further information on suspension links.
8 Remove the two bolts securing the trailing arm compliance bush to the vehicle body **(see illustration)**, and then manoeuvre the trailing arm assembly out of position and away from the vehicle.

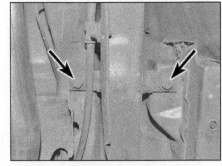

11.8 Trailing arm compliance bush mounting bolts

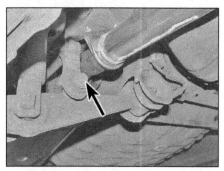

12.2 Anti-roll bar link mounting bolt

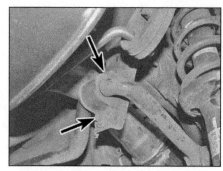

12.3 Anti-roll bar mounting clamp bolts

9 Inspect the trailing arm and compliance bush for wear and damage and renew as necessary. The bush is a press-fit in the arm and can be pressed out and in using a vice and two suitable-sized tubular drifts, such as sockets. The arm must be positioned with the outer face down when pressing out the old bush, and with the inner face down when pressing in the new bush. Make sure that the short mounting stub is located on the outside of the arm, and the arrow and LWR markings pointing downwards; the mounting stubs must be in line with the horizontal position of the arm.

Refitting

10 Refitting is the reverse of removal, but delay fully tightening the link pivot bolts until the weight of the vehicle is on the rear suspension. The trailing arm compliance bush mounting bolts can be fully tightened after locating the arm on the body. Refit the rear

hub with reference to Section 7. Have the rear wheel alignment checked and adjusted by a Rover dealer or tyre specialist.

12 Rear suspension anti-roll bar – removal and refitting

Removal

1 Chock the front wheels, then jack up the rear of the vehicle and support on axle stands (see *Jacking and vehicle support*). Remove both rear wheels.
2 Working on each side at a time, unscrew and remove the bolts securing the anti-roll bar links to the mountings on the rear lower lateral links **(see illustration)**.
3 Unscrew and remove the anti-roll bar mounting clamp bolts, then manoeuvre the bar from under the rear of the vehicle **(see illustration)**.

4 Unscrew the bolts at each end of the anti-roll bar and remove the side links and rubber bushes.
5 Note the positions of the mounting rubbers then pull them from the anti-roll bar.
6 Check the anti-roll bar and mounting components for damage and wear and renew as necessary.

Refitting

7 Smear the bores of the mounting rubbers with rubber grease or similar lubricant, then fit them in their previously-noted positions on the anti-roll bar. Make sure that the split ends of the rubbers will face the rear of the vehicle (ie, towards the mounting brackets) when the anti-roll bar is fitted.
8 Refit the side links and rubber bushes and tighten the bolts.
9 Refit the anti-roll bar to the underbody and locate the mounting rubbers in the brackets with their split ends facing rearwards.
10 Refit the side links to the rear lower lateral links, insert the bolts and tighten to the specified torque.
11 Refit the rear wheels, then lower the vehicle to the ground and tighten the roadwheel nuts to the specified torque setting.

13 Steering wheel – removal and refitting

Removal

⚠️ **Warning: Before starting this procedure, refer to the airbag precautions given in Chapter 12.**
1 Set the front wheels in the straight-ahead position. The steering wheel spokes should be horizontal.
2 Remove the ignition key then disconnect the negative (earth) lead from the battery followed by the positive lead. Wait ten minutes to allow the SRS system backup circuit to fully discharge.
3 Where applicable, remove the cruise control set/resume switch as described in Chapter 12.
4 Using a Torx key, unscrew the airbag module retaining screws from each side of the steering wheel **(see illustration)**.
5 Withdraw the airbag module from the steering wheel taking care not to allow it to hang on the wiring. Disconnect the wiring and remove the airbag from inside the vehicle **(see illustration)**. Store it in a safe place (see Precautions in Chapter 12).
6 Disconnect the horn wiring multiplug from the rotary coupler. The wire is located just above the steering wheel retaining nut **(see illustration)**.
7 Hold the steering wheel stationary, then loosen the retaining nut and unscrew two complete turns.
8 Mark the steering wheel and steering column in relation to each other, then rock the steering wheel from side-to-side until it

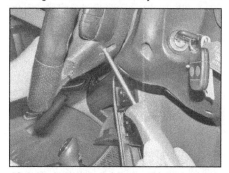

13.4 Undo the two airbag retaining screws

13.5 Disconnecting the airbag wiring connector

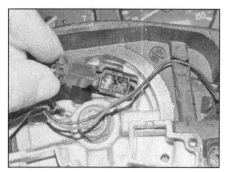

13.6 Disconnect the wiring inside the centre of the steering wheel

13.8 Withdraw the wiring as the wheel is removed

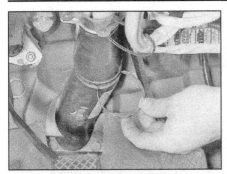

14.6a Remove the clips . . .

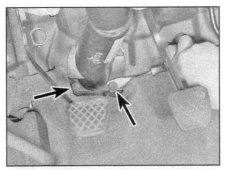

14.6b . . . and studs (arrowed) securing the cover around the steering column

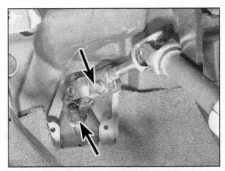

14.7 Universal joint clamp bolts

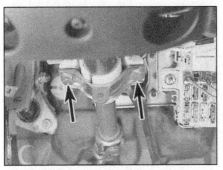

14.8a Unscrew the bolts (arrowed) . . .

14.8b . . . and remove the mounting clamp

14.9 Unscrew the steering column upper mounting nuts

is released from the splines. Remove the nut and withdraw the wiring through the steering wheel as it is removed (see illustration).

9 To prevent the rotary coupler from loosing its central setting, use adhesive tape to secure the upper part to the base.

Refitting

10 Refitting is a reversal of removal, but tighten the retaining nut to the specified torque and refer to Chapter 12 when refitting the airbag.

14 Steering column – removal and refitting

 Warning: Before starting this procedure, refer to the airbag precautions given in Chapter 12.

Removal

1 Remove the steering wheel as described in Section 13.

2 Remove the driver's pocket from the lower facia panel below the steering wheel, then undo the screws and remove the lower facia panel.

3 Undo the screws and remove the steering column upper and lower shrouds.

4 Disconnect the wiring multiplugs from the lighting and wiper switches.

5 Follow the wiring from the starter/ignition switch and disconnect the multiplug(s) from

the fusebox or main wiring harness located to the right-hand side of the facia panel.

6 Release the clips and studs securing the cover around the bottom of the steering column, and then withdraw the cover (see illustrations).

7 Unscrew and remove the clamp bolt securing the universal joint to the bottom of the steering column (see illustration).

8 Unscrew and remove the bolts from the column lower mounting clamp and remove the clamp (see illustrations).

9 At the upper end of the column, unscrew and remove the upper mounting nuts (see illustration).

10 Lower the steering column from its mounting bracket, release the column from the universal joint splines, and withdraw it from inside the vehicle.

11 Undo the retaining screws and remove the rotary coupler from the top of the column.

12 Remove the indicator cancellation cam.

13 Undo the retaining screws and withdraw the combined lighting and wiper switches.

14 If necessary, remove the steering lock/ignition switch as described in Section 15, but note that the shear bolts must be renewed. It is not possible to obtain individual components of the steering column; therefore if excessive wear is evident the column must be renewed complete.

Refitting

15 Refit the steering lock/ignition switch with

reference to Section 15 and tighten the shear bolts until their heads break off.

16 Refit the combined lighting and wiper switches and tighten the screws.

17 Refit the indicator cancellation cam, making sure that the engagement tangs are horizontal.

18 Refit the rotary coupler to the top of the column.

19 Engage the bottom of the column with the universal joint splines making sure that the bolt hole is aligned with the cut-out on the column. Insert the bolt but do not tighten it at this stage.

20 Locate the column on the upper mounting bracket and refit the nuts loosely.

21 Refit the lower clamp and tighten the bolts to the specified torque.

22 Tighten the upper mounting nuts to the specified torque.

23 Tighten the universal joint bolt to the specified torque.

24 Refit the cover to the bottom of the steering column, and secure with the clips and studs.

25 Reconnect the starter/ignition switch multi-plug(s) to the fusebox or main wiring loom.

26 Reconnect the wiring multiplugs to the lighting and wiper switches.

27 Refit the upper and lower column shrouds.

28 Refit the lower facia panel and the driver's pocket.

29 Refit the steering wheel with reference to Section 13.

15.10 Drill out the shear bolt heads (arrowed) using a 5 mm drill

15 Steering lock – removal and refitting

 Warning: Before starting this procedure, refer to the airbag precautions given in Chapter 12.

Removal

1 Set the front wheels in the straight-ahead position. The steering wheel spokes should be horizontal.
2 Remove the ignition key then disconnect the negative (earth) lead from the battery followed by the positive lead. Wait ten minutes to allow the SRS system backup circuit to fully discharge.
3 Remove the driver's pocket from the lower facia panel below the steering wheel, then undo the screws and remove the lower facia panel.
4 Undo the screws and remove the steering column upper and lower shrouds.
5 Follow the wiring from the starter/ignition switch and disconnect the multiplug(s) from the fusebox or main wiring harness located to the right-hand side of the facia panel.
6 Detach the ignition switch wiring from the supports by unscrewing the studs. Also release the cable tie.
7 Undo the screws and remove the ignition switch from the lock housing.
8 To remove the lock housing, unscrew and remove the bolts from the column lower mounting clamp and remove the clamp. At

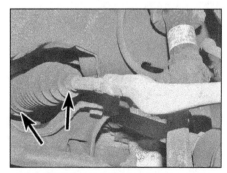

16.2 Clips (arrowed) securing the gaiter

the upper end of the column, unscrew and remove the upper mounting nuts.
9 Lower the steering column together with the steering wheel from its mounting bracket and rest it on the floor.
Caution: if the lock is to be re-used, take care not to cause any damage when drilling out the shear bolts
10 The steering lock housing is secured with shear bolts, which must be drilled out (see illustration). Centre punch the bolts and drill them out with a 5 mm drill bit then unscrew the remains of the shear bolts by using a self-locking wrench or similar on the exposed ends. Remove the lock from the steering column.

Refitting

11 Locate the lock housing on the steering column and hand-tighten the new bolts.
12 Insert the ignition key and check that the steering lock operates correctly. If all is well, tighten the shear bolts evenly until their heads shear off.
13 Locate the steering column on the upper mounting bracket and fit the nuts loosely.
14 Refit the lower clamp and tighten the bolts to the specified torque.
15 Tighten the upper mounting nuts to the specified torque.
16 Refit the switch to the housing and tighten the screws.
17 Reconnect the wiring and secure with the cable tie and supports.
18 Refit the steering column upper and lower shrouds.
19 Refit the lower facia panel and the driver's pocket.
20 Reconnect the battery positive then negative leads.

16 Steering gear rubber gaiters – renewal

1 Remove the track rod end as described in Section 21, then unscrew the locknut from the track rod. Note the number of turns necessary to remove the track rod end in order to maintain the toe-in setting.
2 Remove the clips then slide the gaiter off the end of the track rod arm (see illustration).
3 Thoroughly clean the track rod and the steering gear housing. Repair kits that consist of new gaiters and retaining clips are available from Rover dealers or motor factors.
4 Fit the new rubber gaiter and clips, ensuring that it is correctly seated in the grooves in the steering gear housing and track rod. Check that the gaiter is not twisted then tighten the clips.
5 Refit the locknut and track rod end with reference to Section 21.
6 Have the front wheel alignment checked and adjusted by a Rover dealer or suitably-equipped garage at the earliest opportunity.

17 Steering gear – removal, overhaul and refitting

Removal

1 Set the front wheels in the straight-ahead position and remove the ignition key to lock the steering. The steering wheel spokes should be horizontal.
2 Apply the handbrake, then jack up the front of the vehicle and support it on axle stands (see Jacking and vehicle support). Remove both front wheels.
3 Working inside the vehicle, pull back the driver's footwell carpet then release the clips and studs securing the cover around the bottom of the steering column (see illustrations 14.6a and 14.6b). Remove the cover.
4 Mark the relative positions of the steering gear pinion and joint to use as a guide when refitting, then unscrew and remove the two universal joint pinch-bolts (see illustration 14.7). Slide the universal joint up the steering column shaft splines until it is free from the steering gear pinion.
5 Working under the vehicle, remove the exhaust front pipe/catalytic converter as described in the relevant part of Chapter 4.
6 Unscrew the rear engine mounting through-bolt and remove the engine steady rod from the cylinder block. Push the rod to one side then unscrew the bolt from the power steering pipe clip. On V6 petrol engines, undo the retaining bolts and remove the upper engine steady rod.
7 Where applicable, undo the retaining bolts and remove the heat shield from the top of the steering rack hydraulic hose connections.
8 Position a suitable container beneath the steering gear, then unscrew the union nut and disconnect the feed pipe. Loosen the clip and disconnect the return hose from the steering gear housing. Where applicable, disconnect the fluid pipes from any retaining clips. Tape over or plug the pipe, hose and apertures in the housing to prevent dirt ingress.
9 Remove the track rod ends from each side of the steering gear as described in Section 21, noting the exact number of turns necessary to remove them.
10 Extend the steering rack fully to the passenger's side of the vehicle to enable the assembly to be removed. The pinion is already disconnected from the steering column, so if it is not possible to pull the track rod out, it will be necessary to turn the pinion.
11 Using a wide-bladed screwdriver, disconnect the gearchange balljoints from the levers on the transmission.
12 Unbolt the gearchange linkage from the suspension crossmember and lower it as far as possible.
13 Unscrew the bolts and remove the mounting clamp from the steering gear (see illustration).
14 Unscrew and remove the bolts and

washers securing the steering gear to the suspension crossmember **(see illustration)**. Where applicable, remove the mounting bracket for the hydraulic hose heat shield.

15 Carefully lower the steering gear until the pinion is free of the aperture in the underbody. Recover the pinion shaft seal.

16 Move the steering gear to the passenger's side of the vehicle, then lower the assembly and rotate it so that the pinion is facing the engine, and withdraw the steering gear from the driver's side.

17 If renewing the steering rack, remove the clamp rubber, the collars, and the mounting bushes from the old steering gear for fitting to the new unit.

Overhaul

18 Examine the steering gear assembly for signs of wear or damage and check that the rack moves freely throughout the full length of its travel with no signs of roughness or excessive free play between the steering gear pinion and rack. The steering gear is available only as a complete assembly with no individual components, the exception being the track rod ends and rubber gaiters. Therefore, if worn, the complete assembly must be renewed.

19 Inspect the steering gear mounting bushes and the pinion shaft seal for signs of damage or deterioration and renew as necessary.

Refitting

20 Extend the steering rack fully to the passenger's side of the housing, then position the steering gear in the vehicle and fit the pinion shaft seal. Make sure the seal slot is engaged with the tab on the pinion housing.

21 Lift the steering gear and locate the pinion in the aperture, then insert the bolts and washers loosely to secure the assembly on the crossmember. Where applicable refit the mounting bracket for the hydraulic hose heat shield.

22 Refit the clamp and rubber and tighten the bolts to the specified torque.

23 Fully tighten the mounting bolts to the specified torque.

24 Refit the gearchange linkage and tighten the bolts, then reconnect the balljoints to the levers.

25 Refit the track rod ends to the track rods with reference to Section 21.

26 Centralise the steering rack.

27 Reconnect the feed pipe and tighten the union nut to the specified torque.

28 Reconnect the return hose and tighten the clip, and where applicable refit the heat shield.

29 Refit and tighten the power steering pipe clip, then refit and tighten the engine steady rod to the cylinder block.

30 Refit the exhaust front pipe/catalytic converter together with a new gasket with reference to Chapter 4. Tighten the nuts to the specified torque. Refit the support bracket nuts and tighten to the specified torque.

17.13 Steering gear mounting clamp

31 Refit and tighten the rear engine mounting through-bolt.

32 Refit the roadwheels, tightening their nuts to the specified torque setting and position them straight-ahead.

33 Slide the universal joint on the steering gear pinion and refit the pinch-bolts. Make sure the bolts are located correctly then tighten them to the specified torque.

34 Refit the cover to the bottom of the steering column and secure with the clips and studs.

35 Lower the vehicle to the ground.

36 Bleed the power steering hydraulic system as described in Section 20.

37 Have the front wheel alignment checked and adjusted by a Rover dealer or suitably-equipped garage at the earliest opportunity.

18 Power steering pump
– removal and refitting

Petrol models

Removal

1 Apply the handbrake, then jack up the front of the vehicle and support it on axle stands (see *Jacking and vehicle support*).

2 Loosen only the power steering pump pulley bolts **(see illustration)**; this will prevent having to hold the pulley stationary later.

3 Remove the power steering pump drivebelt as described in Section 23.

4 Position a suitable container beneath the

18.2 Slackening the pump pulley retaining bolts – 6-cylinder engine shown

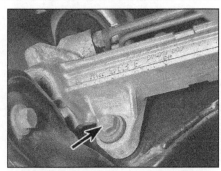

17.14 Steering gear mounting bolt

power steering pump to catch the spilled fluid.

5 Loosen the clip and disconnect the fluid inlet hose from the power steering pump **(see illustration)**. Tape over or plug the hose and aperture to prevent dirt ingress.

6 Unscrew the bolt securing the fluid outlet pipe clamp to the mounting bracket.

Caution: To prevent any damage to the components use two spanners; one to hold the adapter stationary while the other unscrews the union nut.

7 On 4-cylinder models, disconnect the outlet pipe from the power steering pump, noting the location of the O-ring. Tape over or plug the pipe and aperture to prevent dirt ingress.

8 On 6-cylinder models, undo the banjo bolt connection and disconnect the outlet pipe from the power steering pump **(see illustration 18.5)**, noting the location of the sealing washers. Tape over or plug the pipe and aperture to prevent dirt ingress.

9 Hold the drive pulley stationary and with the bolts already loosened (see paragraph 2), unscrew the bolts and remove the pulley from the drive flange.

10 Undo the mounting bolts, and then remove the power steering pump from its mounting bracket **(see illustration)**.

11 The power steering pump is a sealed unit and cannot be repaired. If faulty, the pump assembly must be renewed.

Refitting

12 Refitting is a reversal of removal, but tighten all nuts and bolts to the specified torques. Fit a new O-ring to the pump outlet

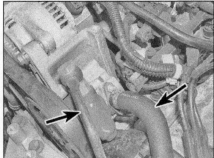

18.5 Outlet pipe and inlet hose (arrowed) – 6-cylinder engine shown

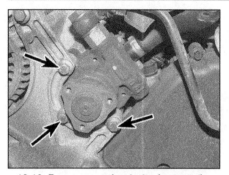

**18.10 Pump mounting bolts (arrowed) –
6-cylinder engine shown**

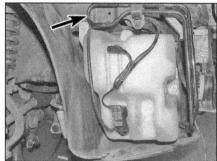

19.1 Oil cooler tube – V6 petrol models

pipe to the air conditioning compressor. Also refit the right-hand engine mounting with reference to Chapter 2C.
31 Refit the auxiliary drivebelt with reference to Chapter 5A.
32 Top up the hydraulic fluid reservoir and bleed the system as described in Section 20.

19 Power steering oil cooler
– removal and refitting

pipe union and lubricate it with hydraulic fluid before tightening the union nut. Refit the power steering drivebelt as described in Section 23. On completion bleed the hydraulic system as described in Section 20.

Diesel models

Removal

13 Loosen only the power steering pump pulley bolts using a Torx key; this will prevent having to hold the pulley stationary later when the drivebelt has been removed.
14 Remove the auxiliary drivebelt as described in Chapter 5A.
15 On models with air conditioning, remove the right-hand engine mounting as described in Chapter 2C, and unscrew the bolt securing the high-pressure pipe to the air conditioning compressor.
16 Fully unscrew the bolts and remove the pulley from the drive flange.
17 Position a suitable container beneath the power steering pump to catch the spilled fluid.
Caution: To prevent any damage to the components use two spanners; one to hold the adapter stationary while the other unscrews the union nut.
18 Using two spanners, one to hold the adapter stationary, unscrew the union nut and disconnect the outlet pipe from the power steering pump. Note the location of the O-ring.
19 Loosen the clip and disconnect the feed hose from the fluid reservoir. Tape over or plug the hose and apertures to prevent dirt ingress.
20 Unscrew the three short bolts securing the

support bracket to the power steering pump and coolant pump housing, then unscrew the two long bolts securing the power steering pump to the coolant pump.
21 Remove the power steering pump then loosen the clip and remove the hose.

Refitting

22 Clean the mating surfaces of the power steering pump and coolant pump.
23 Fit the hose to the new pump and tighten the clip.
24 Locate the power steering pump on the coolant pump making sure that the drive lugs are correctly aligned with each other. Insert the bolts together with their spacers and tighten to the specified torque.
25 Insert and hand-tighten the two long bolts securing the power steering pump to the coolant pump.
26 Insert the three short bolts, then progressively tighten all the bolts to the specified torque.
27 Fit a new O-ring to the outlet pipe union and lubricate it with a little hydraulic fluid. Reconnect the union to the power steering pump and tighten to the specified torque using two spanners, one to hold the adapter.
28 Reconnect the feed hose to the fluid reservoir and tighten the clip.
29 Refit the pulley to the drive flange and tighten the bolts to the specified torque. If preferred, hand-tighten the bolts at this stage and fully tighten them after the drivebelt has been refitted.
30 On models with air conditioning, refit and tighten the bolt securing the high-pressure

Removal

1 The oil cooler tube is located behind the front bumper below the right-hand side headlamp unit on V6 petrol models **(see illustration)**, and along the bottom of the radiator on diesel models. First apply the handbrake, and then jack up the front of the vehicle and support it on axle stands (see *Jacking and vehicle support*).
2 Remove the splash guard from under the radiator.
3 Remove the front bumper (see Chapter 11).
4 On V6 petrol models, unscrew the bolts securing the oil cooler retaining clips to the front inner wing panel/valance **(see illustration)**.
5 On diesel models, unscrew the mounting bolts securing the oil cooler to the front crossmember panel.
6 Remove the clamp plates and the rubber grommets.
7 Loosen the clip and disconnect the hydraulic fluid return hose from the top of the fluid reservoir. Tape over or plug the apertures.
8 Working beneath the vehicle, loosen the clips and disconnect the hoses from the oil cooler.
9 Remove the oil cooler from the vehicle.

Refitting

10 Refitting is the reverse of the removal procedure. On completion, bleed the system as described in Section 20.

20 Power steering system
– bleeding

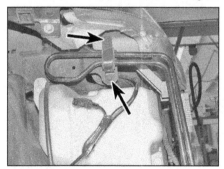

**19.4 Oil cooler upper mounting clamp
bolts**

**20.2 Power steering reservoir UPPER fluid
level mark**

Caution: Do not hold the steering at full lock for more than 10 seconds during the following procedure. Failure to do so could lead to overheating, and possible damage, of the power steering pump and steering gear.
1 Clean around the power steering fluid reservoir and check that the fluid level is between the upper and lower markings on the side of the reservoir.
2 Remove the cap from the power steering fluid reservoir and, if required, top-up the reservoir with the specified fluid (see *Lubricants and fluids*) until the level is at the upper mark on the outside of the reservoir **(see illustration)**.

3 Start the engine and allow it to run at idle for approximately 10 seconds, and then turn the engine off.

4 Check the level in the reservoir and top-up as necessary.

5 Start the engine once again and turn the steering to the full left-hand lock and then to the full right-hand lock. Then turn the engine off.

6 Again, check the level in the reservoir and top up as necessary.

7 Start the engine and allow it to run for 2 minutes.

8 With the engine idling, turn the steering to the full left-hand then full right-hand lock, noting the caution given at the beginning of this Section.

9 Stop the engine and top-up the fluid level to the upper mark on the reservoir. If any air bubbles are noticed in the fluid, wait until these have dispersed before topping-up the level.

10 Refit and tighten the cap to the reservoir. Recheck the level with the engine cold and top-up if necessary.

21 Track rod end – removal and refitting

Removal

1 Apply the handbrake, then jack up the front of the vehicle and support it on axle stands (see *Jacking and vehicle support*). Remove the relevant roadwheel.

2 Loosen the track rod end locknut by one quarter of a turn only **(see illustration)**. The track rod end will rotate to the end of the balljoint movement, so reposition it to the centre of its movement arc again.

3 Extract the split pin (where applicable), and undo the nut securing the track rod end balljoint to the arm on the hub carrier **(see illustration)**. Release the balljoint shank by using a suitable balljoint separator tool whilst taking care not to damage the balljoint rubber boot.

4 Unscrew the track rod end from the track rod, counting the exact number of turns necessary to do so. If the locknut is to be removed, mark its position on the track rod

and count the number of turns required to remove it so that it can be returned exactly to its original position on reassembly.

5 Clean the track rod end and the threads. Renew it if the balljoint movement is sloppy or too stiff, or if it is damaged in any way. Check the stud taper and threads and the rubber boot.

Refitting

6 If necessary, screw the locknut onto the track rod by the number of turns noted on removal.

7 Screw the track rod end onto the track rod by the number of turns noted on removal. This should bring it to within a quarter of a turn from the locknut, with the balljoint stud facing downwards.

8 Refit the balljoint stud to the hub carrier arm and tighten the retaining nut to the specified torque setting. Where applicable, use a new split pin to secure the retaining nut, if necessary tightening it as necessary to align the split pin holes.

9 Hold the track rod end horizontal at the mid point of its movement arc, then tighten the locknut.

10 Refit the roadwheel, then lower the vehicle to the ground and tighten the roadwheel nuts to the specified torque setting.

11 Check and, if necessary, adjust front wheel alignment.

22 Wheel alignment and steering angles

1 A vehicle's steering and suspension geometry is defined in five basic settings. All angles are expressed in degrees and the steering axis is defined as an imaginary line drawn through the centres of the front suspension upper and lower balljoints, extended where necessary to contact the ground **(see illustration)**.

Camber

2 Camber is the angle between each roadwheel and a vertical line drawn through its centre and tyre contact patch when viewed from the front or rear of the vehicle. Positive camber is when the roadwheels are

tilted outwards from the vertical at the top. Negative camber is when they are tilted inwards.

3 Camber is not adjustable and given for reference only. While it can be checked using a camber checking gauge, if the figure obtained is significantly different from that specified, then the vehicle must be taken for careful checking by a professional, as the fault can only be caused by wear or damage to the body or suspension components.

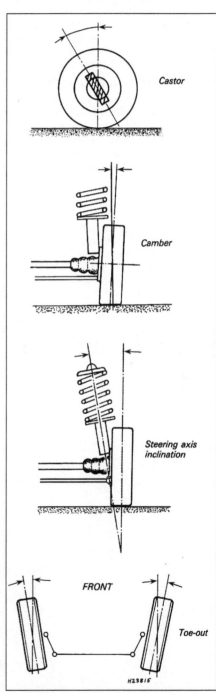

22.1 Wheel alignments and steering angles

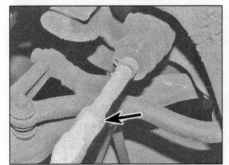

21.2 Track rod end adjustment locking nut – arrowed

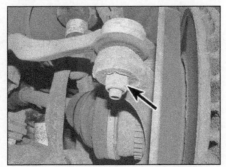

21.3 Undo the track rod end balljoint retaining nut – arrowed

Castor

4 Castor is the angle between the steering axis and a vertical line drawn through each roadwheel's centre and tyre contact patch when viewed from the side of the vehicle. Positive castor is when the steering axis is tilted so that it contacts the ground ahead of the vertical.

5 Castor is not adjustable and is given for reference only. While it can be checked using a castor checking gauge, if the figure obtained is significantly different from that specified, then the vehicle must be taken for careful checking by a professional, as the fault can only be caused by wear or damage to the body or suspension components.

Steering axis inclination (SAI)

6 Also known as kingpin inclination/KPI, this is the angle between the steering axis and a vertical line drawn through each roadwheel's centre and tyre contact patch when viewed from the front or rear of the vehicle.

7 SAI/KPI is not adjustable and is given for reference only.

Toe

8 Toe is the difference, viewed from above, between lines drawn through the roadwheel centres and the vehicle's centre-line. Toe-in is when the roadwheels point inwards, towards each other at the front. Toe-out is when they splay outwards from each other at the front.

9 At the front, toe setting is adjusted by screwing the track rods in or out of the track rod ends to alter the effective length of the track rod assemblies.

10 At the rear of the vehicle, toe setting is adjusted by slackening the front lateral link-to-body pivot bolt and repositioning the bolt in its mounting slot, thereby altering the position of the trailing arm assembly.

Toe-out on turns

11 Also known as turning angles, this is the difference, viewed from above, between the angles of rotation of the inside and outside front roadwheels when they have been turned through a given angle.

12 Toe-out on turns is set in production and is not adjustable, as such, but can be disturbed by altering the length of the track rods unequally. It is essential, therefore, to ensure that the track rod lengths are exactly the same on each side and that they are turned by the same amount whenever the toe setting is altered.

Checking and adjustment

13 Due to the special measuring equipment necessary to check wheel alignment and the skill required to use it properly, checking and adjustment of the settings is best left to a Rover dealer or similar expert. Note that most tyre-fitting shops now possess sophisticated checking equipment.

23 Power steering drivebelt – removal and refitting

1 Disconnect the battery negative terminal (refer to *Disconnecting the battery* in the Reference Section of this manual).

2 Where fitted remove the screws securing the engine acoustic cover, and remove it from the top of the engine.

3 Chock the rear wheels and apply the handbrake. Jack up the front of the vehicle, and support securely on axle stands (see *Jacking and vehicle support*). Remove the right-hand front roadwheel and, where applicable, remove the wheel arch liner.

4 Where fitted, undo the retaining screws and remove the splash shield from under the engine.

Removal

5 Fit a 13 mm spanner to the hexagon on the belt tensioner, and rotate fully clockwise to release belt tension.

6 Lock the tensioner in this position by fitting a 3 mm diameter locking pin, through a hole in the tensioner backplate.

7 Release the belt from the pulleys and tensioner, and remove the belt.

Refitting

8 Make sure that all pulleys are clean and check for any damage, then fit the new belt around the pulleys.

9 Use the 13 mm spanner to relieve tension on the locking pin, and remove the pin. Release the spanner, and allow the tension pulley to rest on the belt.

10 Ensure that the indicator marking on the tensioner falls within the 'gauge' recessed into the tensioner backplate (see illustration 6.19 in Chapter 5A). Check and adjust the tension of the drivebelt as described in Chapter 1A or 1B, Section 12.

11 Fit the roadwheel, engine undertray, engine cover and wheel arch liner, as required. Remove the stands, and lower the vehicle to the ground.

12 Use a torque wrench to tighten the roadwheel nuts to the specified torque.

13 Reconnect the battery earth lead.

Chapter 11
Bodywork and fittings

Contents

	Section number
Body exterior fittings – removal and refitting	25
Bonnet and hinges – removal, refitting and adjustment	8
Bonnet lock – removal and refitting	10
Bonnet release cable – removal and refitting	9
Boot lid – removal, refitting and adjustment	15
Boot lid lock and lock cylinder – removal and refitting	16
Boot lid/tailgate and fuel filler flap release cables – removal and refitting	17
Bumpers – removal and refitting	6
Central locking components – general information	20
Centre and rear consoles – removal and refitting	29
Door – removal, refitting and adjustment	11
Door handles and lock components – removal and refitting	13
Door inner trim panel – removal and refitting	12
Door window regulator and glass – removal and refitting	14
Electric window components – removal and refitting	21
Exterior mirror and glass – removal and refitting	22
Facia panel – removal and refitting	31
General information	1
Glovebox – removal and refitting	30
Interior trim panels – general information	28
Maintenance – bodywork and underframe	2
Maintenance – upholstery and carpets	3
Major body damage – repair	5
Minor body damage – repair	4
Radiator grille – removal and refitting	7
Seat belt components – removal and refitting	27
Seats – removal and refitting	26
Sunroof components – general information	24
Tailgate and support struts – removal, refitting and adjustment	18
Tailgate lock – removal, refitting and adjustment	19
Windscreen and rear window glass – general information	23

Degrees of difficulty

Easy, suitable for novice with little experience		Fairly easy, suitable for beginner with some experience		Fairly difficult, suitable for competent DIY mechanic		Difficult, suitable for experienced DIY mechanic		Very difficult, suitable for expert DIY or professional	

Specifications

Torque wrench settings	Nm	lbf ft
Bonnet hinge bolt	9	7
Boot lid hinge bolts	22	16
Boot lid lock	6	4
Boot lid striker	9	7
Door glass regulator:		
To door	9	7
To motor	7	5
Roller guide	8	6
Door lock	6	4
Door lock striker	18	13
Exterior handle	9	7
Exterior mirror	4	3
Facia	9	7
Front bumper to valance	9	7
Front door glass rear channel bolt	8	6
Front seat runner to floor	34	25
Rear door glass rear channel nut	4	3
Rear door glass rear channel bolt	8	6
Rear door lock and cover	7	5
Rear seat hinge	10	7
Seat belt anchor bolt	32	24
Seat belt reel	9	7
Seat belt stalk	35	26
Tailgate hinges	22	16
Tailgate lock striker	9	7

1 General information

The bodyshell is made of pressed-steel sections, and is available as a four-door Saloon or five-door Hatchback. Most components are welded together, but some use is made of structural adhesives. The front wings are bolted to the main body.

The front and rear body sections incorporate crumple zones and the doors are fitted with side bars. The lower areas of the body and doors are coated with an anti-stone chipping protective material.

Extensive use is made of plastic materials, mainly in the interior, but also in exterior components. Plastic components such as wheel arch liners and splash guards are fitted to the underside of the vehicle, to improve the body's resistance to corrosion.

2 Maintenance – bodywork and underframe

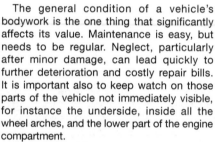

The general condition of a vehicle's bodywork is the one thing that significantly affects its value. Maintenance is easy, but needs to be regular. Neglect, particularly after minor damage, can lead quickly to further deterioration and costly repair bills. It is important also to keep watch on those parts of the vehicle not immediately visible, for instance the underside, inside all the wheel arches, and the lower part of the engine compartment.

The basic maintenance routine for the bodywork is washing – preferably with a lot of water, from a hose. This will remove all the loose solids, which may have stuck to the vehicle. It is important to flush these off in such a way as to prevent grit from scratching the finish. The wheel arches and underframe need washing in the same way, to remove any accumulated mud, which will retain moisture and tend to encourage rust. Paradoxically enough, the best time to clean the underframe and wheel arches is in wet weather, when the mud is thoroughly wet and soft. In very wet weather, the underframe is usually cleaned of large accumulations automatically, and this is a good time for inspection.

Periodically, except on vehicles with a wax-based underbody protective coating, it is a good idea to have the whole of the underframe of the vehicle steam-cleaned, engine compartment included, so that a thorough inspection can be carried out to see what minor repairs and renovations are necessary. Steam-cleaning is available at many garages, and is necessary for the removal of the accumulation of oily grime, which sometimes is allowed to become thick in certain areas. If steam-cleaning facilities are not available, there are some excellent

grease solvents available which can be brush-applied; the dirt can then be simply hosed off. Note that these methods should not be used on vehicles with wax-based underbody protective coating, or the coating will be removed. Such vehicles should be inspected annually, preferably just prior to Winter, when the underbody should be washed down, and any damage to the wax coating repaired. Ideally, a completely fresh coat should be applied. It would also be worth considering the use of such wax-based protection for injection into door panels, sills, box sections, etc, as an additional safeguard against rust damage, where such protection is not provided by the vehicle manufacturer.

After washing paintwork, wipe off with a chamois leather to give an unspotted clear finish. A coat of clear protective wax polish will give added protection against chemical pollutants in the air. If the paintwork sheen has dulled or oxidised, use a cleaner/polisher combination to restore the brilliance of the shine. This requires a little effort, but such dulling is usually caused because regular washing has been neglected. Care needs to be taken with metallic paintwork, as special non-abrasive cleaner/polisher is required to avoid damage to the finish. Always check that the door and ventilator opening drain holes and pipes are completely clear, so that water can be drained out. Brightwork should be treated in the same way as paintwork. Windscreens and windows can be kept clear of the smeary film, which often appears, by the use of proprietary glass cleaner. Never use any form of wax or other body or chromium polish on glass.

3 Maintenance – upholstery and carpets

Mats and carpets should be brushed or vacuum-cleaned regularly, to keep them free of grit. If they are badly stained, remove them from the vehicle for scrubbing or sponging, and make quite sure they are dry before refitting. Seats and interior trim panels can be kept clean by wiping with a damp cloth. If they do become stained (which can be more apparent on light-coloured upholstery), use a little liquid detergent and a soft nail brush to scour the grime out of the grain of the material. Do not forget to keep the headlining clean in the same way as the upholstery. When using liquid cleaners inside the vehicle, do not over-wet the surfaces being cleaned. Excessive damp could get into the seams and padded interior, causing stains, offensive odours or even rot.

Caution: If the inside of the vehicle gets wet accidentally, it is worthwhile taking some trouble to dry it out properly, particularly where carpets are involved. Do not leave oil or electric heaters inside the vehicle for this purpose.

4 Minor body damage – repair

Minor scratches

If the scratch is very superficial, and does not penetrate to the metal of the bodywork, repair is very simple. Lightly rub the area of the scratch with a paintwork renovator, or a very fine cutting paste, to remove loose paint from the scratch, and to clear the surrounding bodywork of wax polish. Rinse the area with clean water.

Apply touch-up paint to the scratch using a fine paint brush; continue to apply fine layers of paint until the surface of the paint in the scratch is level with the surrounding paintwork. Allow the new paint at least two weeks to harden, and then blend it into the surrounding paintwork by rubbing the scratch area with a paintwork renovator or a very fine cutting paste. Finally, apply wax polish.

Where the scratch has penetrated right through to the metal of the bodywork, causing the metal to rust, a different repair technique is required. Remove any loose rust from the bottom of the scratch with a penknife, and then apply rust-inhibiting paint to prevent the formation of rust in the future. Using a rubber or nylon applicator, fill the scratch with bodystopper paste. If required, this paste can be mixed with cellulose thinners to provide a very thin paste, which is ideal for filling narrow scratches. Before the stopper-paste in the scratch hardens, wrap a piece of smooth cotton rag around the top of a finger. Dip the finger in cellulose thinners, and quickly sweep it across the surface of the stopper-paste in the scratch; this will ensure that the surface of the stopper-paste is slightly hollowed. The scratch can now be painted over as described earlier in this Section.

Dents

When deep denting of the vehicle's bodywork has taken place, the first task is to pull the dent out, until the affected bodywork almost attains its original shape. There is little point in trying to restore the original shape completely, as the metal in the damaged area will have stretched on impact, and cannot be reshaped fully to its original contour. It is better to bring the level of the dent up to a point that is about 3 mm below the level of the surrounding bodywork. In cases where the dent is very shallow anyway, it is not worth trying to pull it out at all. If the underside of the dent is accessible, it can be hammered out gently from behind, using a mallet with a wooden or plastic head. Whilst doing this, hold a suitable block of wood firmly against the outside of the panel, to absorb the impact from the hammer blows and thus prevent a large area of the bodywork from being 'belled-out'.

Should the dent be in a section of the

bodywork, which has a double skin, or some other factor making it inaccessible from behind, a different technique is called for. Drill several small holes through the metal inside the area – particularly in the deeper section. Then screw long self-tapping screws into the holes, just sufficiently for them to gain a good purchase in the metal. Now the dent can be pulled out by pulling on the protruding heads of the screws with a pair of pliers.

The next stage of the repair is the removal of the paint from the damaged area, and from an inch or so of the surrounding 'sound' bodywork. This is accomplished most easily by using a wire brush or abrasive pad on a power drill, although it can be done just as effectively by hand, using sheets of abrasive paper. To complete the preparation for filling, score the surface of the bare metal with a screwdriver or the tang of a file, or alternatively, drill small holes in the affected area. This will provide a really good 'key' for the filler paste.

To complete the repair, see the Section on filling and respraying.

Rust holes or gashes

Remove all paint from the affected area, and from an inch or so of the surrounding 'sound' bodywork, using an abrasive pad or a wire brush on a power drill. If these are not available, a few sheets of abrasive paper will do the job most effectively. With the paint removed, you will be able to judge the severity of the corrosion, and therefore decide whether to renew the whole panel (if this is possible) or to repair the affected area. New body panels are not as expensive as most people think, and it is often quicker and more satisfactory to fit a new panel than to attempt to repair large areas of corrosion.

Remove all fittings from the affected area, except those that will act as a guide to the original shape of the damaged bodywork (eg headlight shells etc). Then, using tin snips or a hacksaw blade, remove all loose metal and any other metal badly affected by corrosion. Hammer the edges of the hole inwards, in order to create a slight depression for the filler paste.

Wire-brush the affected area to remove the powdery rust from the surface of the remaining metal. Paint the affected area with rust-inhibiting paint, if the back of the rusted area is accessible, treat this also.

Before filling can take place, it will be necessary to block the hole in some way. This can be achieved by the use of aluminium or plastic mesh, or aluminium tape.

Aluminium or plastic mesh, or glass-fibre matting, is probably the best material to use for a large hole. Cut a piece to the approximate size and shape of the hole to be filled, then position it in the hole so that its edges are below the level of the surrounding bodywork. It can be retained in position by several blobs of filler paste around its periphery.

Aluminium tape should be used for small or very narrow holes. Pull a piece off the roll, trim it to the approximate size and shape required, then pull off the backing paper (if used) and stick the tape over the hole; it can be overlapped if the thickness of one piece is insufficient. Burnish down the edges of the tape with the handle of a screwdriver or similar, to ensure that the tape is securely attached to the metal underneath.

Filling and respraying

Before using this Section, see the Sections on dent, deep scratch, rust holes and gash repairs.

Many types of bodyfiller are available, but generally speaking, those proprietary kits that contain a tin of filler paste and a tube of resin hardener are best for this type of repair. A wide, flexible plastic or nylon applicator will be found invaluable for imparting a smooth and well-contoured finish to the surface of the filler.

Mix up a little filler on a clean piece of card or board – measure the hardener carefully (follow the maker's instructions on the pack), otherwise the filler will set too rapidly or too slowly. Using the applicator, apply the filler paste to the prepared area; draw the applicator across the surface of the filler to achieve the correct contour and to level the surface. As soon as a contour that approximates to the correct one is achieved, stop working the paste – if you carry on too long, the paste will become sticky and begin to 'pick-up' on the applicator. Continue to add thin layers of filler paste at 20-minute intervals, until the level of the filler is just proud of the surrounding bodywork.

Once the filler has hardened, the excess can be removed using a metal plane or file. From then on, progressively-finer grades of abrasive paper should be used, starting with a 40-grade production paper, and finishing with a 400-grade wet-and-dry paper. Always wrap the abrasive paper around a flat rubber, cork, or wooden block – otherwise the surface of the filler will not be completely flat. During the smoothing of the filler surface, the wet-and-dry paper should be periodically rinsed in water. This will ensure that a very smooth finish is imparted to the filler at the final stage.

At this stage, the 'dent' should be surrounded by a ring of bare metal, which in turn should be encircled by the finely 'feathered' edge of the good paintwork. Rinse the repair area with clean water, until all of the dust produced by the rubbing-down operation has gone.

Spray the whole area with a light coat of primer – this will show up any imperfections in the surface of the filler. Repair these imperfections with fresh filler paste or bodystopper, and once more smooth the surface with abrasive paper. Repeat this spray-and-repair procedure until you are satisfied that the surface of the filler, and the feathered edge of the paintwork, are perfect. Clean the repair area with clean water, and allow drying fully.

HAYNES HiNT *If bodystopper is used, it can be mixed with cellulose thinners to form a really thin paste, which is ideal for filling small holes.*

The repair area is now ready for final spraying. Paint spraying must be carried out in a warm, dry, windless and dust-free atmosphere. This condition can be created artificially if you have access to a large indoor working area, but if you are forced to work in the open, you will have to pick your day very carefully. If you are working indoors, dousing the floor in the work area with water will help to settle the dust that would otherwise be in the atmosphere. If the repair area is confined to one body panel, mask off the surrounding panels; this will help to minimise the effects of a slight mis-match in paint colours. Bodywork fittings (eg chrome strips, door handles etc) will also need to be masked off. Use genuine masking tape, and several thicknesses of newspaper, for the masking operations.

Before commencing to spray, agitate the aerosol can thoroughly, and then spray a test area (an old tin, or similar) until the technique is mastered. Cover the repair area with a thick coat of primer; the thickness should be built up using several thin layers of paint, rather than one thick one. Using 400-grade wet-and-dry paper, rub down the surface of the primer until it is really smooth. While doing this, the work area should be thoroughly doused with water, and the wet-and-dry paper periodically rinsed in water. Allow to dry before spraying on more paint.

Spray on the top coat, again building up the thickness by using several thin layers of paint. Start spraying at one edge of the repair area, and then, using a side-to-side motion, work until the whole repair area and about 2 inches of the surrounding original paintwork is covered. Remove all masking material 10 to 15 minutes after spraying on the final coat of paint.

Allow the new paint at least two weeks to harden, then, using a paintwork renovator, or a very fine cutting paste, blend the edges of the paint into the existing paintwork. Finally, apply wax polish.

Plastic components

With the use of more and more plastic body components by the vehicle manufacturers (eg bumpers. spoilers, and in some cases major body panels), rectification of more serious damage to such items has become a matter of either entrusting repair work to a specialist in this field, or renewing complete components. Repair of such damage by the DIY owner is not really feasible, owing to the cost of the equipment and materials required for effecting such repairs. The basic technique involves making a groove along the line of the crack in the plastic, using a rotary burr in a power drill. The damaged part is then welded

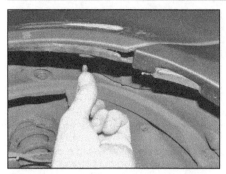

6.2a Remove the liner securing screws . . .

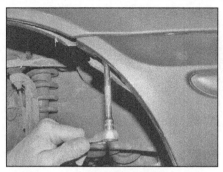

6.2b . . . and remove the bumper side retaining bolt

6.4a Front bumper outer mounting screw (RH side shown) . . .

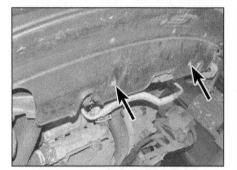

6.4b . . . and inner mounting bolts – arrowed

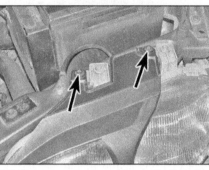

6.5 Bumper upper mounting bolts (LH side shown)

5 Major body damage – repair

Where serious damage has occurred, or large areas need renewal due to neglect, it means that complete new panels will need welding-in, and this is best left to professionals. If the damage is due to impact, it will also be necessary to check completely the alignment of the bodyshell, and this can only be carried out accurately by a Rover dealer using special jigs. If the body is left misaligned, it is primarily dangerous, as the car will not handle properly, and secondly, uneven stresses will be imposed on the steering, suspension and possibly transmission, causing abnormal wear, or complete failure, particularly to such items as the tyres.

6 Bumpers – removal and refitting

back together, using a hot-air gun to heat up and fuse a plastic filler rod into the groove. Any excess plastic is then removed, and the area rubbed down to a smooth finish. It is important that a filler rod of the correct plastic is used, as body components can be made of a variety of different types (eg polycarbonate, ABS, polypropylene).

Damage of a less serious nature (abrasions, minor cracks etc) can be repaired by the DIY owner using a two-part epoxy filler repair material. Once mixed in equal proportions, this is used in similar fashion to the bodywork filler used on metal panels. The filler is usually cured in twenty to thirty minutes, ready for sanding and painting.

If the owner is renewing a complete component himself, or if he has repaired it with epoxy filler, he will be left with the problem of finding a suitable paint for finishing

which is compatible with the type of plastic used. At one time, the use of a universal paint was not possible, owing to the complex range of plastics encountered in body component applications. Standard paints, generally speaking, will not bond to plastic or rubber satisfactorily. However, it is now possible to obtain a plastic body parts finishing kit that consists of a pre-primer treatment, a primer and coloured top coat. Full instructions are normally supplied with a kit, but basically, the method of use is to first apply the pre-primer to the component concerned, and allow it to dry for up to 30 minutes. Then the primer is applied, and left to dry for about an hour before finally applying the special-coloured top coat. The result is a correctly coloured component, where the paint will flex with the plastic or rubber, a property that standard paint does not normally possess.

Front bumper

Removal

1 Apply the handbrake, then jack up the front of the vehicle and support it on axle stands (see *Jacking and vehicle support*).
2 Working beneath the front wheel arches, unscrew and remove the fasteners securing the bottom front of each wheel arch liner to the front wings for access to the bumper upper mounting bolts. Pull back the liners and unscrew the bolts **(see illustrations)**.
3 Undo the screws securing the front of the wheel arch liners to the bottom of the front bumper.
4 Undo the mounting screws from the bottom of the front bumper **(see illustrations)**.
5 Undo the screws securing the top of the bumper to the front upper crossmember **(see illustration)**.
6 With the help of an assistant, withdraw the bumper from the front of the vehicle, releasing the securing clips at both sides of the bumper. Disconnect the wiring for the front foglights as the bumper is removed **(see illustrations)**.
7 If necessary, remove the radiator grille with

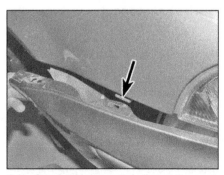

6.6a Carefully release the clips at the each side of the bumper

6.6b Disconnecting the wiring from the foglights when removing the front bumper

6.8 Locate peg into slot arrowed

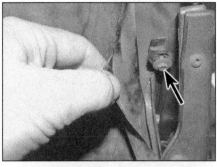

6.10 Unscrew the rear bumper side mounting bolt – arrowed

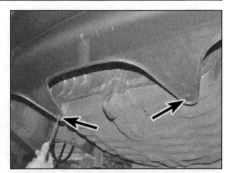

6.11 Remove the two lower bumper bolts – arrowed

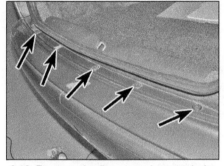

6.12 Remove the five upper bumper bolts – arrowed

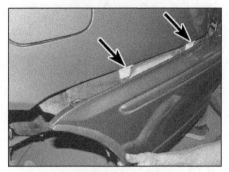

6.13 Carefully release the clips (arrowed) at the each side of the bumper

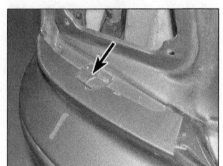

6.14 Bumper locating clip – rear light removed for clarity

reference to Section 7. The lower intake grille can also be removed by first undoing the retaining screws, and the foglights can be removed with reference to Chapter 12.

Refitting

8 Refitting is a reversal of removal, but make sure that the bumper engages correctly with the side clips and front locating pegs **(see illustration)**. Tighten all fasteners and screws and make sure that the clips are fully engaged.

Rear bumper

Removal

9 Open the tailgate or boot lid.
10 Working under each rear wheel arch, pull back the liner and undo the bolts securing the rear bumper to the body panel **(see illustration)**.
11 Under the rear of the bumper, unscrew and remove the fasteners securing the bumper to the underbody **(see illustration)**.
12 Undo and remove the fasteners along the top edge of the rear bumper **(see illustration)**.
13 With the help of an assistant, withdraw the rear bumper from the vehicle, releasing the securing clips at both sides of the bumper **(see illustration)**.

Refitting

14 Refitting is a reversal of removal, but make sure that the bumper engages correctly with the side securing clips and locating pegs below the rear lights **(see illustration)**. Tighten all fasteners and screws and make sure that the clips are fully engaged.

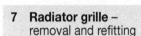

7 Radiator grille – removal and refitting

Removal

1 Open the bonnet.
2 Working your way around the inside of the grille, undo the retaining nuts and then withdraw the radiator grille from the bonnet **(see illustrations)**.

Refitting

3 Refitting is a reversal of removal. Note the nuts are made of pressed-out metal and the pegs on the back of the grille are plastic. Do not overtighten, as the plastic pegs will break.

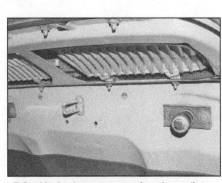

7.2a Undo the nuts securing the radiator grille to the bonnet . . .

8 Bonnet and hinges – removal, refitting and adjustment

Removal

1 Open the bonnet and have an assistant support it. Using a pencil or felt tip pen, mark the outline of each bonnet hinge relative to the bonnet, to use as a guide on refitting.
2 Disconnect the windscreen washer fluid supply hose from the connector under the bonnet **(see illustration)**.
3 Unscrew the bolts securing the bonnet to the hinges and, with the help of an assistant, carefully lift the bonnet clear. Store the bonnet out of the way in a safe place **(see illustration)**.
4 Inspect the bonnet hinges for signs of wear

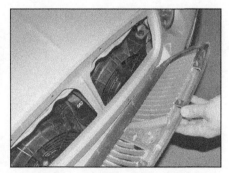

7.2b . . . and remove the grille

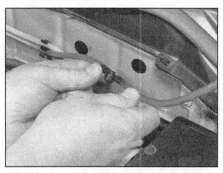

8.2 Disconnecting the windscreen washer fluid supply hose

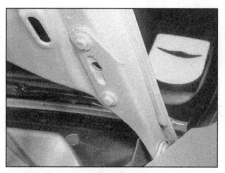

8.3 Bolts securing the hinges to the bonnet

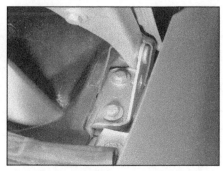

8.4 The bonnet hinges are bolted to the inner wing panel

and free play at the pivots, and if necessary renew them by unscrewing the bolts on the inner wing panel **(see illustration)**. Mark the positions of the hinges before removing them to ensure correct refitting.

Refitting

5 With the aid of an assistant, offer up the bonnet, and loosely fit the retaining bolts. Align the hinges with the marks made on removal, then tighten the retaining bolts securely.
6 Reconnect the windscreen washer fluid supply hose.
7 Adjust the alignment of the bonnet as follows.

Adjustment

8 Close the bonnet, and check for alignment with the adjacent panels. If necessary, slacken the hinge bolts and re-align the bonnet to suit. Once the bonnet is correctly aligned, tighten the hinge bolts to the specified torque setting.
9 Once the bonnet is correctly aligned,

check that the bonnet fastens and releases in a satisfactory manner. If adjustment is necessary, slacken the bonnet striker bolts and adjust the position to suit. Once the lock is operating correctly, securely tighten all the retaining bolts. Make sure that the bonnet striker enters the lock centrally.
10 If necessary, align the front edge of the bonnet with the wing panels by turning the support rubbers screwed into the body front panel, to raise or lower the front edge as required.

9 Bonnet release cable – removal and refitting

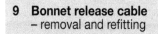

Removal

1 Open and support the bonnet.
2 Remove the bonnet locks from the engine

compartment front crossmember as described in Section 10.
3 Apply the handbrake, then jack up the front of the vehicle and support it on axle stands (see *Jacking and vehicle support*). Remove the right-hand front roadwheel.
4 Remove the right-hand front wheel arch liner as described in Section 25.
5 Working under the front wing, release the cable from the clips, and then pull the cable through from the crossmember.
6 Open the driver's door then undo the screws and remove the sill finisher from the door aperture.
7 Remove the trim panel from the right-hand side of the driver's footwell. To do this, remove the fastener and unclip the panel.
8 Unhook the inner cable end fitting from the release lever, then carefully push out the rubber grommet from the panel beneath the front wing and pull the cable through into the passenger compartment.
9 If necessary the lever can be unbolted from the side panel.

Refitting

10 Refitting is a reversal of removal, but refer to Sections 25 and 10 when refitting the wheel arch liner and bonnet lock, and check the bonnet release mechanism for correct operation on completion.

10 Bonnet lock – removal and refitting

10.2 Bonnet lock mounting bolts – LH side shown

10.3a Unclip the outer cable . . .

Removal

1 Open and support the bonnet. Note there are two bonnet locks, one at each side of the crossmember.
2 Unscrew the securing bolts, and remove the lock assembly from the cross panel **(see illustration)**.
3 Unclip the outer cable from the lock assembly and then release the inner cable **(see illustrations)**.
4 Withdraw the assembly from the vehicle and then, if required, follow the same procedure to remove the lock from the other side of the crossmember.
5 To remove the bonnet striker/catch from

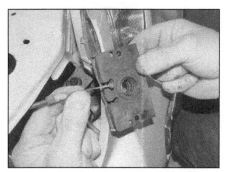

10.3b . . . and release the inner cable

10.5 Bonnet striker/catch mounting bolts

10.6 Bonnet safety catch mounting bolts

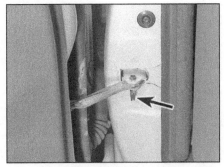

11.2 Door check arm roll pin

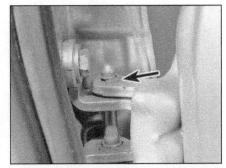

11.4 E-clip securing the door hinge pin

the bonnet, undo the two retaining bolts **(see illustration)**. The catch can be adjusted by turning the centre post with a screwdriver which will adjust the tension on the spring.

6 To remove the bonnet safety catch from the crossmember, undo the two retaining bolts **(see illustration)**.

Refitting

7 Refitting is a reversal of removal but check that the bonnet is correctly aligned with the front wings. If adjustment is necessary, refer to Section 8.

11 Door –
removal, refitting and adjustment

Removal

1 Disconnect the battery negative (earth) lead (see *Disconnecting the battery*).
2 Drive out the roll-pin securing the door check arm to its body bracket **(see illustration)**.
3 Pull back the rubber boot then disconnect the wiring multiplug between the door and A-pillar.
4 Extract the E-clip from the top of each door hinge pin **(see illustration)**.
5 Support the door on blocks of wood or alternatively have an assistant support the door.
6 Using a soft-metal drift, carefully drive out the hinge pins. Withdraw the door from the body.
7 If necessary, the hinge sections may be unbolted from the A- or B-pillars and doors, however mark their positions before removing them as an aid to refitting **(see illustration)**.

Refitting

8 Refitting is a reversal of removal, but lightly grease the hinge pins before inserting them and make sure that the door fits correctly in its aperture with equal gaps at all points between it and the surrounding bodywork. The door must also be flush with the surrounding bodywork. If necessary, position the vehicle on a firm level surface and adjust the door as follows.

Adjustment

9 To adjust the front edge of the door so that

11.7 The door hinges are bolted to the A- and B-pillars

it is flush with the surrounding bodywork, loosen the hinge bolts on the door itself. Move the door in or out, and then tighten the bolts. Check that the bottom edge of the door is parallel with the sill, and that the waistline is aligned with the wing and other door. If necessary, a shim may be located between one of the hinges and the door.
10 To adjust the door backwards or forwards, or up and down within the body aperture, loosen the hinge bolts on the body. Move the door as necessary then tighten the bolts.
11 The striker alignment should be checked after either the door or the lock has been disturbed. To adjust a striker, slacken its screws, reposition it then securely tighten the screws **(see illustration)**.

12 Door inner trim panel
– removal and refitting

Front door
Removal

1 Ensure the ignition and all accessories are switched off.
2 On models equipped with manually-operated windows, remove the window regulator handle spring clip by hooking it out with a screwdriver or bent piece of wire, then pull the handle off the spindle and remove the escutcheon.
3 Undo the screw securing the interior door handle to the door inner panel **(see illustration)**.

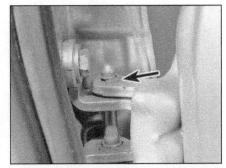

11.11 Door striker

4 Slide the interior door handle forwards and pull it outwards until the operating rod can be disconnected by releasing the plastic clip. Remove the interior door handle **(see illustration)**.
5 Unscrew and remove the screw from the

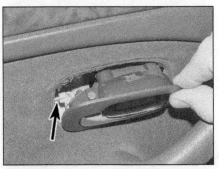

12.3 Undo the screw securing the interior door handle to the door inner panel . . .

12.4 Slide the door handle forwards, then disconnect the operating rod – arrowed

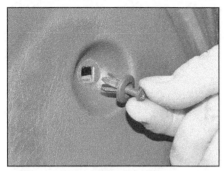

12.5 Inner trim panel, front upper corner screw

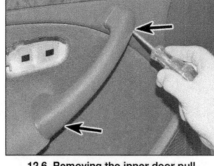

12.6 Removing the inner door pull retaining screws

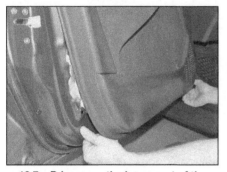

12.7a Prise away the lower part of the inner trim panel . . .

front upper corner of the inner trim panel **(see illustration)**.

6 Undo the two screws from the door pull handle **(see illustration)**.

7 Using a wide-blade screwdriver, carefully prise out the trim panel clips, starting from

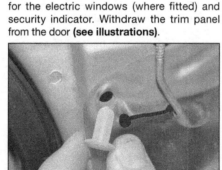

12.7b . . . and lift the trim panel over the locking button

the lower edge, and then lift the panel from the upper shoulder and locking knob. As the panel is being removed, disconnect the wiring for the electric windows (where fitted) and security indicator. Withdraw the trim panel from the door **(see illustrations)**.

8 If necessary the door pocket, grab handle, window lift switch (where fitted), and lock indicator may be removed from the panel by undoing the screws.

9 To remove the plastic membrane, remove the wiring connector multiplugs. Extract the plastic dowels and remove the membrane while feeding the wiring through the hole **(see illustrations)**.

Refitting

10 Refitting is a reversal of removal.

Rear door

Removal

11 On models equipped with manually-operated windows, remove the window regulator handle spring clip by hooking it out with a screwdriver or bent piece of wire, then pull the handle off the spindle and remove the escutcheon **(see illustration)**.

12 Undo the screw securing the interior door handle to the door inner panel **(see illustration)**.

13 Slide the interior door handle forwards and pull it outwards until the operating rod can be disconnected by prising up the plastic clip **(see illustration)**.

14 Where necessary, disconnect the wiring from the electric window lift switch. Withdraw the interior door handle **(see illustration)**.

15 Undo the screws from the door pull handle **(see illustration)**.

16 Using a wide-blade screwdriver, carefully prise out the trim panel clips and lift the panel from the upper shoulder and locking knob.

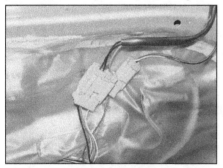

12.9a Release the wiring block connectors from the door panel . . .

12.9b . . . remove the plastic locating dowels . . .

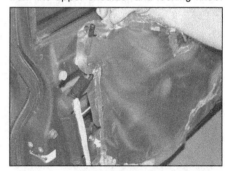

12.9c . . . and peel the plastic membrane from the door panel

12.11 Using a piece of wire to hook out the securing clip

12.12 Removing the screw from the rear door interior door handle

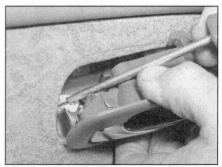

12.13 Slide the interior door handle forwards and disconnect the operating rod

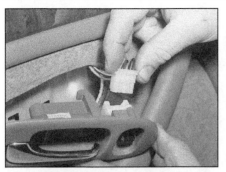

12.14 Disconnecting the wiring from the electric window lift switch

12.15 Door pull handle lower retaining screw

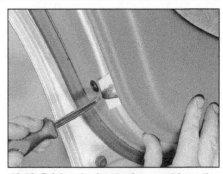

12.16 Prising the inner trim panel from the rear door

Withdraw the trim panel from the door **(see illustration)**.
17 If necessary, the door protector, door grip, and locking knob guide may be removed from the trim panel by undoing the screws.
18 To remove the plastic membrane, extract the plastic dowels and detach the wiring harness clips **(see illustrations)**.

Refitting

19 Refitting is a reversal of removal.

13 Door handles and lock components
– removal and refitting

Interior handles

Removal

1 Undo the screw securing the interior door handle to the door inner panel.
2 Slide the interior door handle forwards and pull it outwards until the operating rod can be disconnected by prising out the plastic clip.
3 On the rear door, disconnect the wiring from the electric window lift switch.
4 Remove the interior door handle.

Refitting

5 Refitting is a reversal of removal.

Front exterior handles

Removal

6 As a precaution, protect the paintwork around the exterior handle using adhesive tape.
7 Fully raise the window glass, then remove the door inner trim panel and membrane as described in Section 12.
8 Disconnect the private lock wiring multiplug and release the wiring from the support clips. Alternatively the wiring and microswitch can be disconnected from the exterior door handle as it is being removed.
9 Unscrew the bolts securing the exterior door handle to the door. Access to the bolts is gained through the apertures in the door inner panel **(see illustration)**.
10 Carefully withdraw the handle from the outside of the door, then disconnect the operating rod and private lock rod using a

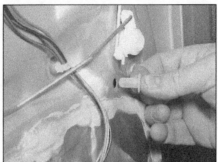

12.18a Remove the plastic dowels . . .

screwdriver. Do not disturb the setting of the threaded operating rod. Where applicable, detach the clip and disconnect the microswitch from the handle **(see illustrations)**.
11 If necessary, the private lock may be

13.9 Unscrew the mounting bolts . . .

13.10b Detach the securing clip . . .

12.18b . . . and carefully peel away the membrane

removed from the handle assembly by pulling out the retaining clip.

Refitting

12 Refitting is a reversal of removal, but check the operation of the exterior handle before

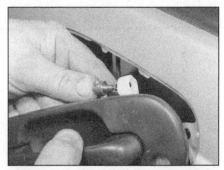

13.10a . . . then disconnect the operating rod and private lock rod from the door handle

13.10c . . . and disconnect the microswitch from the handle

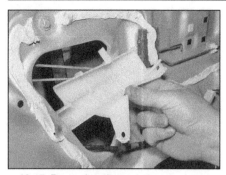

13.15 Removing the rear door lock rod guide and protector

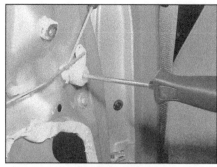

13.16 Removing the locking knob crank from the door

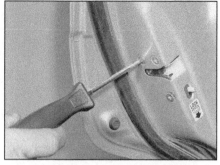

13.17 Undoing the screws securing the lock to the rear edge of the rear door

13.18a Unscrew the bolts . . .

13.18b . . . withdraw the exterior handle from the door . . .

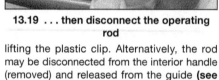

13.19 . . . then disconnect the operating rod

refitting the door inner trim panel. Remove the protective tape on completion.

Rear exterior handles

Removal

13 Protect the paintwork around the exterior handle using adhesive tape.
14 Fully raise the window glass, then remove the door inner trim panel and membrane as described in Section 12.
15 Undo the screws and remove the lock rod guide and protector **(see illustration)**.
16 Undo the screw and remove the locking knob crank from the door **(see illustration)**.
17 Release the lock control rods from the guides on the inner door panel. Undo the screws securing the lock to the rear edge of the door, and then lower the lock inside the door to allow access to the exterior door handle mounting bolts **(see illustration)**.
18 Unscrew the bolts securing the exterior

door handle to the door and carefully withdraw the handle from the outside as far as possible to reveal the operating rods **(see illustrations)**.
19 Disconnect the operating rod using a screwdriver and carefully withdraw the handle from the door **(see illustration)**. Do not disturb the setting of the threaded operating rod.

Refitting

20 Refitting is a reversal of removal, but check the operation of the exterior handle before refitting the door inner trim panel. Remove the protective tape on completion.

Front lock

Removal

21 Remove the exterior door handle as described previously in this Section.
22 Reach inside the door and disconnect the interior handle operating rod from the lock by

lifting the plastic clip. Alternatively, the rod may be disconnected from the interior handle (removed) and released from the guide **(see illustration)**.
23 Disconnect the central locking wiring at the connector and release the wiring from the clips.
24 Unscrew the bolt securing the bottom of the rear window guide channel to the door.
25 Unscrew the door lock mounting screws on the rear edge of the door **(see illustration)**.
26 Move the rear window guide channel forwards and withdraw the lock from inside the door. At the same time, release the operating rod from the felt **(see illustration)**.
27 Undo the screws and remove the cover from the lock.
28 If necessary, separate the mechanism from the lock by undoing the screws. Do not disturb the setting of the threaded operating rod.

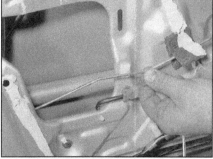

13.22 Releasing the front door lock operating rod from the guide

13.25 Unscrewing the front door lock mounting screws

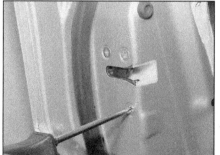

13.26 Removing the front door lock from the door

Refitting

29 Refitting is a reversal of removal, but check the operation of the door lock before refitting the door inner trim panel.

Rear lock

Removal

30 Remove the exterior door handle as described previously in this Section.

31 Reach inside the door and disconnect the inner handle and locking knob operating rods from the lock by lifting the plastic clips. Do not disturb the setting of the threaded operating rod.

32 Disconnect the central locking wiring at the connector and release the wiring from the clips **(see illustration)**.

33 Withdraw the lock from inside the door **(see illustration)**.

34 If necessary, separate the mechanism from the lock by undoing the screws.

Refitting

35 Refitting is a reversal of removal, but check the operation of the door lock before refitting the door inner trim panel.

Front lock switch

Removal

36 Remove the front door inner trim panel and plastic membrane as described in Section 12.

37 Reach through the aperture and disconnect the wiring leading to the lock switch. Also release the wiring from the clips.

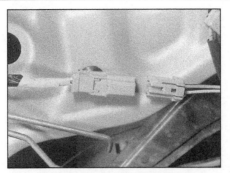

13.32 Disconnecting the wiring connectors

38 Using a suitable instrument, hook out the retaining spring clip from the private lock and withdraw the switch.

Refitting

39 Refitting is a reversal of removal.

---

14 Door window regulator and glass – removal and refitting

Front door

Removal

1 Remove the door inner trim panel and membrane as described in Section 12.

2 Move the window so that the bolts securing the glass to the regulator are visible through the holes in the inner door panel. To do this on manually-operated windows, temporarily refit the

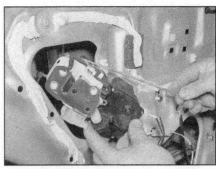

13.33 Removing the rear door lock from the door

handle to the regulator. On electrically-operated windows, temporarily switch on the ignition and operate the switch on the centre console.

3 Loosen the bolts (do not completely remove them), then position the large holes in the regulator over the bolt heads and release the regulator from the glass **(see illustrations)**.

4 Tilt the glass forwards then withdraw it from the top of the door **(see illustration)**.

5 To remove the regulator, where applicable disconnect the wiring multiplug from the motor and release the wiring from the clip. Mark the position of the regulator mounting bolts using a marker pen or pencil **(see illustrations)**.

6 Unscrew and remove the bolts and withdraw the regulator through the aperture in the door inner panel **(see illustrations)**.

7 To remove the motor (where fitted) from the regulator, first mark the position of the sector gear with a marker pen. Using a Torx key, unscrew the bolts and remove the motor.

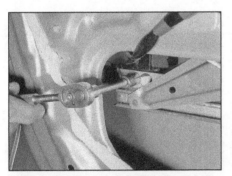

14.3a Loosening the rear bolt securing the window glass to the regulator

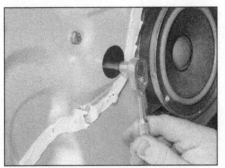

14.3b Loosening the front bolt securing the window glass to the regulator

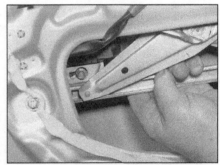

14.3c Releasing the window glass from the regulator

14.4 Removing the window glass from the front door

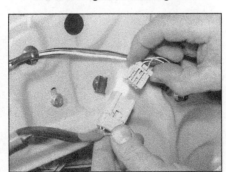

14.5a Disconnect the wiring . . .

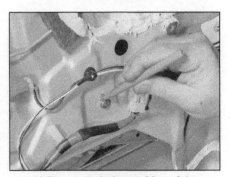

14.5b . . . mark the position of the mounting bolts . . .

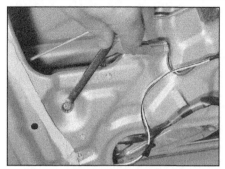

14.6a . . . then unscrew the bolts . . .

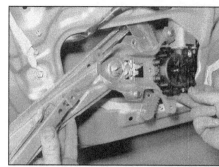

14.6b . . . and withdraw the regulator

14.11 Unscrewing the bolts securing the rear window glass to the regulator

Refitting

8 Refitting is a reversal of removal, but apply a little grease to the sliding surfaces of the regulator. Tighten the mounting bolts to the specified torque. Check the operation of the

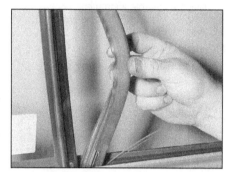

14.12 Removing the rubber weatherstrip from the rear glass channel

window before refitting the door inner trim panel. When fully raised, the upper edge of the glass must be aligned with the upper channel in the door. If necessary, adjust the window regulator position then tighten the bolts.

Rear door

Removal

9 Remove the door inner trim panel and membrane as described in Section 12.
10 Move the window so that the bolts securing the glass to the regulator are visible through the holes in the inner door panel. To do this on manually-operated windows, temporarily refit the handle to the regulator. On electrically-operated windows, temporarily reconnect the wiring to the electric window operating switch.
11 Unscrew and remove the bolts securing the glass to the regulator, and lower the glass to the bottom of the door (see illustration).
12 Pull the rubber weatherstrip upwards from the rear glass channel (see illustration). Leave the remaining weatherstrip in position.
13 Remove the rear glass channel as follows. Unscrew the upper mounting nut and the two lower mounting bolts, then twist the channel clockwise through 90° while carefully lifting the channel from the door. It will be necessary to carefully pull the top opening slightly apart when easing out the channel bracket (see illustrations).
14 Withdraw the glass from the top of the door without tilting it (see illustration).
15 To remove the regulator, where applicable disconnect the wiring multiplug from the motor and release the wiring from the clip. Mark the position of the regulator mounting bolts using a marker pen or pencil (see illustrations).
16 Unscrew and remove the bolts and withdraw the regulator through the aperture in the door inner panel (see illustrations).

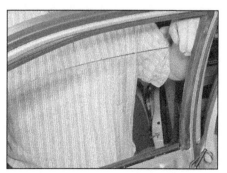

14.13a Rear glass channel upper mounting nut

14.13b Remove the rear glass channel from the slotted upper mounting . . .

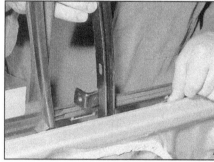

14.13c . . . then twist the channel through 90° and lift from the door

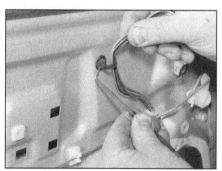

14.14 Removing the rear door glass

14.15a Releasing the wiring from the clip

14.15b Marking the position of the regulator mounting bolts

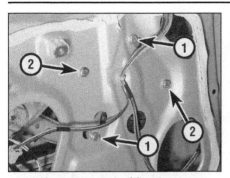

14.16a Loosen bolts (1) and unscrew completely bolts (2)

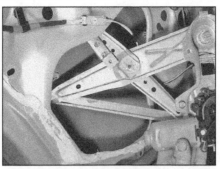

14.16b Removing the regulator from the rear door

14.17 Regulator motor mounting screws – arrowed

17 To remove the motor (where fitted) from the regulator, first mark the position of the sector gear with a marker pen. Using a Torx key, unscrew the bolts and remove the motor **(see illustration)**.

Refitting

18 Refitting is a reversal of removal, but apply a little grease to the sliding surfaces of the regulator. Delay tightening the rear glass channel mounting bolts and nut to the specified torque until the glass has been wound up and down several times to align the channel. Check the operation of the window before refitting the door inner trim panel. When fully raised, the upper edge of the glass must be aligned with the upper channel in the door. If necessary, adjust the window regulator position then tighten the bolts to the specified torque setting.

15 Boot lid – removal, refitting and adjustment

Removal

1 Remove the boot lid lock as described in Section 16.
2 Release the boot lid release cable from the clips on the right-hand hinge arm.
3 Withdraw the release cable from the boot lid. As an aid to refitting the cable, tie a length of string to it before removing it and leave the string in position in the boot lid.

4 Where applicable, remove both number plate lights from the boot lid as described in Chapter 12, Section 7.
5 Remove the private lock access cover from inside the boot lid **(see illustration)**.
6 Disconnect the wiring multiplug leading to the private lock and release the wiring from the clip.
7 Release the wiring harness from the clips on the boot lid and right-hand hinge arm **(see illustration)**, then withdraw the harness from the boot lid. As an aid to refitting the wiring, tie a length of string to it before removing it and leave the string in position in the boot lid.
8 Mark the positions of the hinge mounting bolts on the boot lid.
9 With the help of an assistant, unscrew the four hinge retaining bolts and lift the boot lid away from the vehicle **(see illustration)**.

Refitting and adjustment

10 Offer up the boot lid, and fit the hinge bolts loosely. Align the bolts with the marks made on dismantling, and tighten them securely.
11 Tie the string to the number plate light connectors on the wiring harness, then carefully draw the wiring into the boot lid and secure with the clips in the boot lid and right-hand hinge arm. Untie the string.
12 Refit both number plate lights with reference to Chapter 12.
13 Reconnect the wiring to the private lock and secure in the clip. Refit the access cover.
14 Tie the string to the release cable and draw it into position and secure in the clips on the right-hand hinge arm. Untie the string.

15 Refit the boot lid lock with reference to Section 16.
16 Close the boot lid and check that it is correctly aligned with all surrounding bodywork, with an equal clearance all around. If necessary, adjustment can be made by slackening the hinge bolts and repositioning the boot lid. Once correctly positioned, tighten the hinge bolts to the specified torque. Check that the boot lid closes correctly and that the lock engages centrally with the striker. If not, loosen the striker retaining bolts and reposition the striker. Tighten the striker retaining bolts securely on completion.

16 Boot lid lock and lock cylinder – removal and refitting

Boot lid lock

Removal

1 Open the boot lid and unclip the cover from the lock on the bottom edge of the boot lid.
2 Release the clip and disconnect the operating rod from the lock.
3 Unscrew the two bolts and release the lock from the boot lid **(see illustration)**.
4 Disconnect the wiring, then unhook the release cable and withdraw the lock from the vehicle.

Refitting

5 Refitting is a reversal of removal. Tighten the lock retaining bolts to the specified torque.

15.5 Unclip the access cover

15.7 Unclip the wiring from the hinge arm

15.9 Boot lid hinge retaining bolts – RH side shown

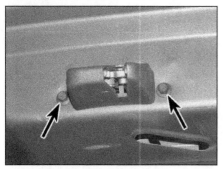

16.3 Boot lock retaining bolts – arrowed

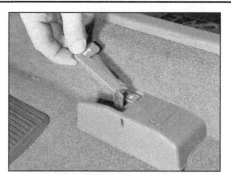

17.3 Pull off the control knobs . . .

On completion, check that the boot lid closes correctly and that the striker enters the lock centrally. If necessary, adjust the position of the striker by loosening the retaining bolts. Retighten the bolts on completion.

Boot lid lock cylinder

Removal

6 Open the boot lid and remove the lock cylinder access cover.
7 Disconnect the wiring plug and release the wiring from the clip.
8 Lift the plastic clip and disconnect the operating rod from the lock cylinder.
9 Undo the single retaining screw and withdraw the lock cylinder from the boot lid. Recover the chrome ring.

Refitting

10 Refitting is a reversal of removal.

17 Boot lid/tailgate and fuel filler flap release cables – removal and refitting

Removal

1 Remove the rear seat as described in Section 26. Also remove the luggage compartment left-hand side trim panels and rear valance panel with reference to Section 28.
2 Remove the door sill finishers from the rear door apertures and front driver's door aperture.
3 Carefully pull the control knobs from the front cable levers **(see illustration)**.
4 Prise out the cover and remove the screw, then prise out the stud. Undo the screw, and remove the control knob cover **(see illustrations)**.

5 Unscrew the lower anchor bolt for the driver's seat belt.
6 Prise out the studs securing the rear edge of the carpet to the floor, release it from the driver's side and fold it forwards for access to the release cables.
7 At the rear of the vehicle, unclip the cable and disconnect it from the boot lid/tailgate lock **(see illustration)**.
8 Release the cable from the clips in the luggage compartment and pull the rear section through the body.
9 Fold back the carpet from the inner sill and release the cable from the sill clips.
10 Unscrew the front cable control bracket bolts and disconnect the cables.
11 Disconnect the cable from the fuel flap and release it from the clips.
12 Withdraw both cables from inside the car.

Refitting

13 Refitting is a reversal of removal but tighten the seat belt anchor bolt to the specified torque.

18 Tailgate and support struts – removal, refitting and adjustment

Tailgate

Removal

1 Remove the rear seat as described in Section 26. Also remove the luggage compartment side trim panels with reference to Section 28.

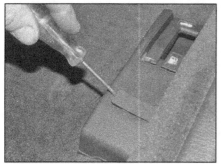

17.4a . . . then prise out the cover . . .

17.4b . . . remove the screw . . .

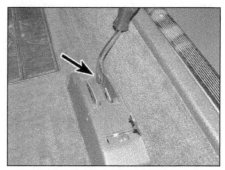

17.4c . . . prise out the stud . . .

17.4d . . . and remove the cover

17.4e Lever assembly on the floor bracket

17.7 Tailgate lock release cable

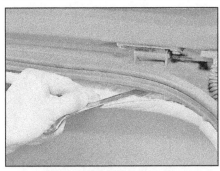

18.10 Slackening the tailgate hinge securing nuts

2 Working on each side at a time, carefully pull the weatherstrip from the D-pillar. Unscrew the rear seat belt lower anchor bolt, then unclip the D-pillar trim panel and feed the seat belt through it.

3 Unclip and remove the side finishers from each side of the tailgate window.

4 Undo the screw and remove the grip from the tailgate.

5 Unscrew the centre pins from the retaining clips, then use a wide-bladed screwdriver to prise off the trim panel.

6 Release the wiring harness from the clips on the rear of the body and disconnect the multiplugs located on the right-hand side of the luggage compartment.

7 Remove the wiring harness rubber boot from the top right-hand corner of the tailgate, and then pull the harness through onto the tailgate.

8 Have an assistant support the tailgate then disconnect the support struts from the

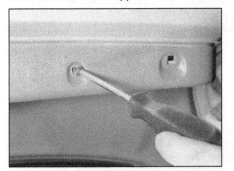

19.1a Undo the screw . . .

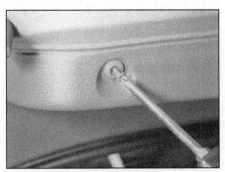

19.2a Loosen the screws . . .

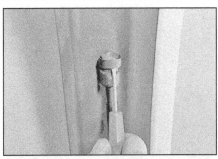

18.18 Using a screwdriver to prise out the upper retaining spring clip from the tailgate strut

balljoints by carefully prising out the spring clips with a screwdriver. Carefully lower the struts onto the body.

9 Remove the trim from the headlining and carefully pull down the rear edge for access to the tailgate hinges.

10 Unscrew the hinge nuts and lift the tailgate from the rear of the vehicle **(see illustration)**.

11 Clean away the sealant from the hinges and roof.

Refitting and adjustment

12 Apply suitable sealant to the faces of the hinges which contact the roof, then with the help of an assistant offer the tailgate onto the body and locate the hinge studs in their holes. Screw on the retaining nuts hand-tight at this stage.

13 Locate the support struts onto the balljoints and press in the spring clips.

14 Carefully close the tailgate and check that it is aligned with the surrounding bodywork.

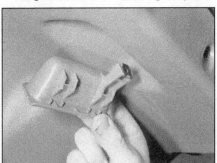

19.1b . . . and remove the hand grip from the tailgate trim

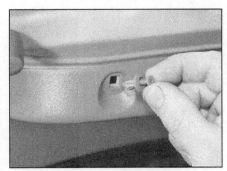

19.2b . . . and remove the clips from the lower edge of the tailgate trim panel

Reposition as necessary then tighten the hinge nuts to the specified torque.

15 Check that the tailgate is flush with the surrounding bodywork, and if necessary screw the support rubbers on each side in or out as required.

16 The remaining procedure is a reversal of removal, but if necessary adjust the tailgate striker as described in Section 19.

Support struts

Removal

17 Support the tailgate in the open position by using a stout piece of wood, or with the help of an assistant.

18 Carefully prise out the upper retaining spring clip from the strut using a screwdriver, and disconnect the strut from the tailgate **(see illustration)**.

19 Repeat the procedure for the strut-to-body mounting and remove the strut from the vehicle. Note that the cylinder end of the strut is located on the body.

20 If necessary the ball-studs can be unscrewed for renewal.

Refitting

21 Refitting is a reversal of removal, but ensure that the strut is pressed firmly onto each of its balljoints.

19	Tailgate lock – removal, refitting and adjustment	

Tailgate lock

Removal

1 Open the tailgate then undo the single screw and remove the hand grip from the trim **(see illustrations)**.

2 Loosen the screws and remove the special clips from the lower edge of the trim panel **(see illustrations)**.

3 Using a wide-bladed screwdriver, carefully prise off the upper trim strips from each side of the tailgate window **(see illustrations)**.

4 Prise off the trim panel.

5 Unscrew the lock mounting bolts **(see illustration)**.

6 Withdraw the lock then release the plastic

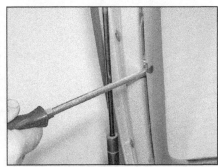

19.3a Carefully prise away the upper trim strips . . .

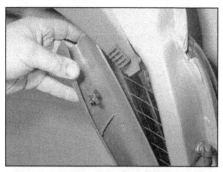

19.3b . . . and release them from their clips

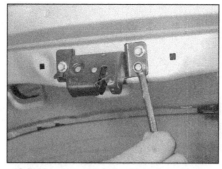

19.5 Unscrew the tailgate lock mounting bolts . . .

19.6a . . . then release the clip . . .

19.6b . . . and disconnect the operating rod

19.6c Disconnecting the central locking wiring from the tailgate lock

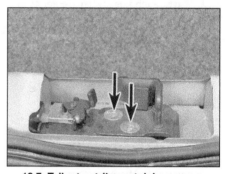

19.7 Tailgate striker retaining screws

clip and disconnect the operating rod and central locking wiring **(see illustrations)**.

Refitting

7 Refitting is a reversal of removal. On completion, check that the tailgate closes

19.12 Tailgate lock cylinder accessible through the aperture in the tailgate inner panel

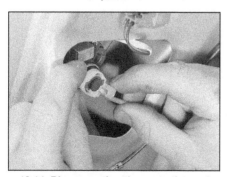

19.14 Disconnecting the operating rod from the lock cylinder

easily and does not rattle when closed. If adjustment is necessary, slacken the tailgate striker retaining screws and reposition the striker as necessary **(see illustration)**. Once the tailgate operation is satisfactory, tighten the striker retaining bolts to the specified torque.

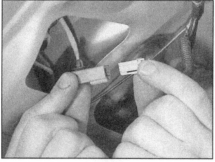

19.13 Disconnecting the wiring plug from the tailgate lock cylinder

19.15 Removing the tailgate lock cylinder

Tailgate lock cylinder

Removal

8 Open the tailgate then undo the single screw and remove the handle grip from the trim panel.
9 Loosen the screws and remove the special clips from the lower edge of the trim panel.
10 Using a wide-bladed screwdriver, carefully prise off the upper trim strips from each side of the tailgate window.
11 Prise off the trim panel.
12 The tailgate lock cylinder is accessible through the aperture in the tailgate inner panel **(see illustration)**.
13 Disconnect the wiring plug **(see illustration)**.
14 Prise up the plastic clip and disconnect the operating rod from the lock cylinder **(see illustration)**.
15 Unscrew the mounting bolt and remove the lock cylinder from the tailgate **(see illustration)**.

Refitting

16 Refitting is a reversal of removal.

20 Central locking components – general information

The central locking system is controlled by an ECU located beneath the centre of the facia. The system automatically locks all doors, with the exception of the tailgate, when the driver's door is locked.

The driver's door lock incorporates a micro switch, which completes an earth circuit in

22.4a Use a screwdriver and cloth . . .

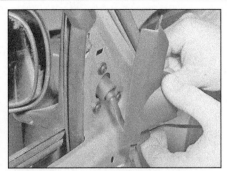

22.4b . . . to prise away the triangular panel . . .

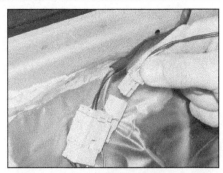

22.4c . . . and disconnecting the electric mirror wiring

the ECU that then operates the door lock motors on the doors. When the driver's door is unlocked, the earth circuit is completed again and the ECU then unlocks the doors.

The door lock motors are removed when removing the door locks as described in Section 13.

The ECU is removed by first removing the centre console as described in Section 29. Undo the screws securing the ashtray assembly to the facia, then disconnect the wiring for the cigar lighter and withdraw the ashtray assembly. The ECU can now be removed by undoing the screws, and then disconnecting the wiring multiplugs. Refitting is a reversal of removal.

21 Electric window components – removal and refitting

Window master switch

Removal

1 Remove the rear console as described in Section 29.
2 Invert the rear console, then undo the screws and remove the master switch and housing from the console.
3 Release the cable strap then undo the screws and remove the switches from the housing.

Refitting

4 Refitting is a reversal of removal.

Driver's window switch

Removal

5 Remove the driver's door inner trim panel as described in Section 12.
6 Detach the wiring multiplug from the bracket and disconnect.
7 Undo the screws and withdraw the switch.

Refitting

8 Refitting is a reversal of removal.

Passenger's window switch

9 The procedure is the same as that described in paragraphs 1 to 4.

Window regulator motor

10 The procedure is described in Section 14.

Electronic control unit

Removal

11 Remove the front door inner trim panel as described in Section 12.
12 Pull back the upper corner of the plastic membrane for access to the control unit.
13 Undo the screws and withdraw the unit from the door, then disconnect the two multiplugs.

Refitting

14 Refitting is a reversal of removal.

Electric window relay

Removal

15 The electric window relay is located on the fusebox beneath the facia on the driver's side. To gain access to the relay, remove the driver's pocket from the lower facia panel below the steering wheel, then undo the screws and remove the lower facia panel. Pull the relay out from its socket.

Refitting

16 Refitting is a reversal of removal.

22 Exterior mirror and glass – removal and refitting

Mirror glass

⚠ Warning: It is recommended that gloves are worn during the following procedure.

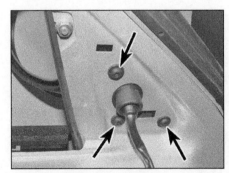

22.5a Undo the Torx screws (arrowed) . . .

Removal

1 Adjust the mirror glass, so that the inside edge is pressed in as far as it will go. With the mirror glass held pressed in on the inside (nearest the vehicle), slide the mirror glass outwards away from the vehicle and disengage it from the damper blade. With the mirror released (on electric mirror models), disconnect the wiring from the two terminals on the rear of the mirror glass.

Refitting

2 On models equipped with electrically-operated mirrors, connect the wiring connectors to the heating element terminals then locate the mirror, making sure the damper blade in the mirror housing locates in the slot and secures correctly.

Mirror assembly

Removal

3 Remove the door inner trim panel as described in Section 12.
4 Carefully prise off the triangular panel at the front of the window aperture, then disconnect the mirror and tweeter wiring at the plug and release the wiring from the clips (see illustrations).
5 Support the mirror, then undo the Torx screws and withdraw the mirror from the outside of the door (see illustrations).

Refitting

6 Refitting is a reversal of removal.

22.5b . . . and withdraw the mirror from the outside of the door

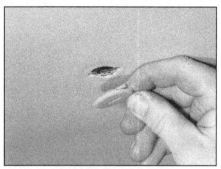

24.2a In an emergency, remove the round plug from the headlining . . .

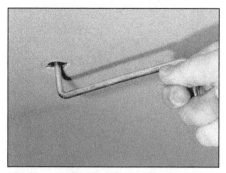

24.2b . . . then use the cranked key from the tool kit to close the roof

23 Windscreen and rear window glass – general information

The windscreen and rear window are bonded in position with special adhesive. Renewal of these windows is a difficult, messy and time-consuming task, which is beyond the scope of the home mechanic. It is difficult, unless one has plenty of practice, to obtain a secure, waterproof fit. Furthermore, the task carries a high risk of breakage. In view of this, owners are strongly advised to have this work carried out by one of the many specialist windscreen fitters.

24 Sunroof components – general information

1 A sunroof is available on all models, depending on model this may be electrically-operated or manually-operated. Due to the complexity of the sunroof mechanism, considerable expertise is needed to repair or renew sunroof components successfully. Removal of the sunroof requires the headlining to be removed, which is a complex and tedious operation and not a task to be undertaken lightly. Any problems with the sunroof should therefore be referred to a Rover dealer.
2 On models equipped with an electrically-operated sunroof, if the sunroof motor fails to operate, first check the relevant fuse. If the

fault cannot be traced and rectified, then the sunroof can be opened and closed manually by using the cranked key in the vehicle tool kit or a suitable Torx key. Use a screwdriver or coin to remove the round plug in the centre of the headlining, then insert the cranked key and turn it until the roof is fully closed (**see illustrations**).

25 Body exterior fittings – removal and refitting

Wheel arch liner

Removal

1 Jack up the front or rear of the vehicle and support on axle stands (see *Jacking and vehicle support*). Remove the roadwheel.
2 The wheel arch liner is retained by screws and bolts together with some fasteners, and with these removed the liner can be withdrawn from under the wheel arch (**see illustrations**).

Refitting

3 Refitting is a reversal of removal.

Boot lid motif

Removal

4 Open the boot lid then remove the rear number plate.
5 Working through the apertures in the inner panel, unscrew the nuts and screws then remove the motif from the outside of the boot lid.

Refitting

6 Refitting is a reversal of removal.

Engine front splash guard

Removal

7 Apply the handbrake, then jack up the front of the vehicle and support it on axle stands (see *Jacking and vehicle support*).
8 The guard is retained with bolts and fasteners, and with these removed the guard can be lowered from the front of the vehicle (**see illustration**).

Refitting

9 Refitting is a reversal of removal.

Engine main splash guard (diesel engine models)

Removal

10 Apply the handbrake, then jack up the front of the vehicle and support it on axle stands (see *Jacking and vehicle support*).
11 Unscrew the bolts and fasteners and lower the guard from under the engine compartment.
12 If necessary, the access panel can be removed by turning the fasteners.

Refitting

13 Refitting is a reversal of removal.

26 Seats – removal and refitting

Front seat

Removal

1 Slide the seat fully forwards then unclip the cover (where fitted) from the rear of the inner seat runner.
2 Unscrew and remove the bolts from the rear of both seat runners (**see illustration**).
3 Slide the seat fully rearwards and unscrew the bolts from the front of the seat runners (**see illustration**).
4 Tilt the seat backwards and disconnect the wiring connectors from under the seat (**see illustration**), then remove the seat from inside the vehicle.

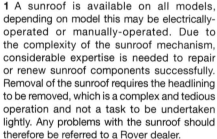

25.2a Removing a front wheel arch liner

25.2b Removing a rear wheel arch liner

25.8 On MG models, there is a splash shield across the front of the vehicle

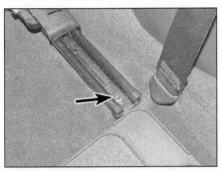

26.2 Unscrew the rear mounting bolts

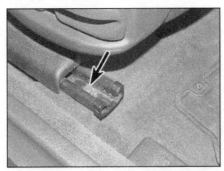

26.3 Unscrew the front mounting bolts

26.4 Disconnect the wiring connectors
– arrowed

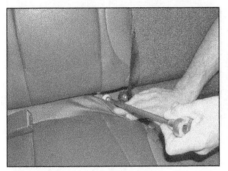

26.6 Remove the seat cushion mounting
bolt

26.7 Carefully guide the seat belt buckles
past the seat cushion

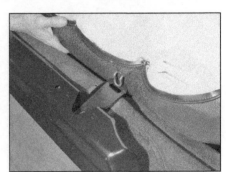

26.8 Unhook the seat cushion from the
bracket

Refitting

5 Refitting is a reversal of removal, making sure the wiring connectors are secure and tightening the seat runner bolts to the specified torque.

26.10 Unclip the cover from the hinge

26.13 Where fitted, remove the cover from
the centre hinge

Rear seat cushion (Saloon)

Removal

6 Pull back the corner of the rear part of the seat cushion, next to the seat belt stalk

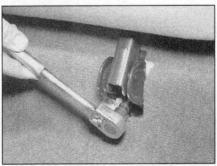

26.11 Unscrew the bolts from the rear seat
cushion hinges

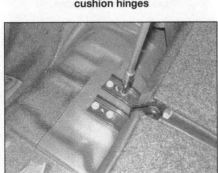

26.14 Unscrew the mounting bolts

anchorage point, and then using a socket, unscrew and remove the mounting bolt **(see illustration)**.
7 Lift the rear of the cushion from beneath the backrest taking care to guide the seat belt buckles through the holes in the cushion **(see illustration)**.
8 Unhook the front part of the cushion from the brackets **(see illustration)**.

Refitting

9 Refitting is a reversal of removal.

Rear seat cushion (Hatchback)

Removal

10 Unclip the cover from the hinge on the front of the rear seat cushion **(see illustration)**.
11 Unscrew the bolts from the front hinges and then lift the cushion out from inside the car **(see illustration)**.

Refitting

12 Refitting is a reversal of removal.

Rear seat backrest

Removal

13 Fold the backrest forwards then, where fitted, unclip the cover from the centre hinge **(see illustration)**.
14 Pull the boot carpet back and unscrew and remove the bolts securing the centre hinge to the floor **(see illustration)**.
15 Move the backrest inwards from the hinge pin and remove it from inside the vehicle **(see illustration)**.

26.15a Lift out the seat backrest . . .

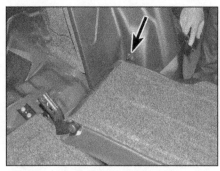

26.15b . . . disengaging it from the outer hinge pin – arrowed

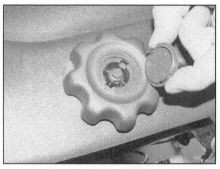

26.21a Unclip the cover . . .

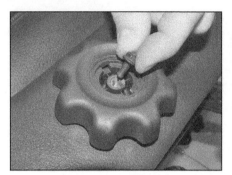

26.21b . . . undo the bolt . . .

26.21c . . . and remove the control wheel

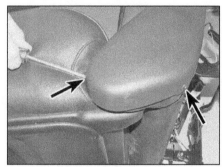

26.22 Undo the two retaining screw – arrowed

Refitting

16 Refitting is a reversal of removal.

Rear seat armrest

Removal

17 Lower the rear seat armrest, then slide out the backing panel.
18 Undo the crosshead screws securing the armrest to the seat base, then withdraw the armrest.

Refitting

19 Refitting is a reversal of removal.

Front seat adjustment belt

Removal

20 Remove the front seat as described in paragraphs 1 to 4 at the beginning of this Section.
21 Unclip the cover, undo the retaining bolt and remove the control wheel (see illustrations).
22 Undo the two retaining screws at the rear of the trim panel (see illustration).
23 Undo the retaining screw at the front inside edge of the seat and release the panel from the side of the seat (see illustration)
24 Slide the belt and drive gears from the seat mechanism (see illustration).

Refitting

25 Refitting is a reversal of removal.

Front seat support cable

Removal

26 To make access easier, remove the front

seat as described in paragraphs 1 to 4 at the beginning of this Section.
27 Unclip the rear plastic panel from the rear of the seat at the bottom and pull it down to release the upper clips. Take care when

26.23 Undo the screw (arrowed) on the inside of the seat frame

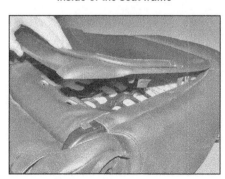

26.27a Unclip the panel . . .

releasing the panel as the securing clips are plastic and can break easily (see illustrations).
28 Release the outer cable from the plastic seat support and then disconnect the inner cable (see illustrations).

26.24 Withdrawing the belt and gears from the seat mechanism

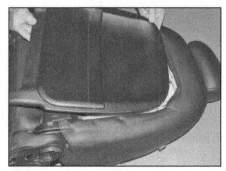

26.27b . . . and remove the panel from the seat

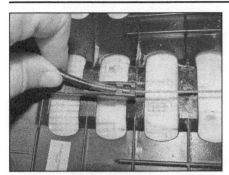

26.28a Release the outer cable . . .

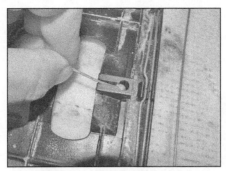

26.28b . . . and the inner cable

26.29 Undo the two retaining screws
– arrowed

29 Undo the retaining screws at the front edge of the seat and release the control wheel and bracket, withdraw the cable from the seat (see illustration).

Refitting

30 Refitting is a reversal of removal.

27 Seat belt components
– removal and refitting

Note: *Note the positions of any washers and spacers on the seat belt anchors, and ensure that they are refitted in their original positions.*

Front seat belt and stalk

Warning: The front seat belt reel incorporates a pretensioner, which is activated together with the airbag. Observe the safety

precautions given in Chapter 12. When handling the pretensioner reel, do not knock or tap it.

Removal

1 Disconnect the battery negative then positive leads, and **wait 10 minutes** (this is a safety requirement of the airbag/SRS system).
2 Remove the lower trim panel from the B-pillar with reference to Section 28.
3 The SRS sensor must now be set to its locked position. To do this, swivel out the sensor and turn it clockwise 90°.
4 Prise the cover from the belt upper mounting, and unscrew the bolt (see illustrations).
5 Remove the clip which secures the upper trim panel to the B-pillar, and release the seat belt from the trim.
6 Prise the cover from the belt lower mounting, and unscrew the bolt (see illustration).
7 Unscrew the bolts and remove the reel from the bottom of the B-pillar (see illustrations).

8 Remove the seat belt from inside the car.
9 To remove the stalk, first remove the seat as described in Section 26.
10 Unscrew the bolt and remove the stalk from the seat.

Refitting

11 Refitting is a reversal of removal, but tighten the mounting bolts to the specified torque. Set the SRS sensor to its unlocked position by turning it anti-clockwise 90° and swivelling it inward. After resetting the sensor, **do not** knock or tap the reel.

Centre rear seat belt (Hatchback)

Removal

12 Fold the rear seat cushion forwards and remove the belt and buckles from the clips in the backrest.
13 Unscrew the mounting bolts and remove the buckles and belt (see illustration).

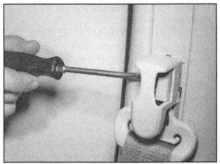

27.4a Carefully prise away the cover . . .

27.4b . . . for access to the front seat belt
upper mounting bolt

27.6 Front seat belt lower mounting bolt
on the inner sill panel

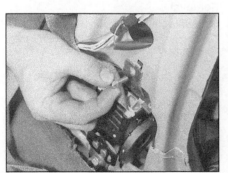

27.7a Unscrewing the front seat belt reel
upper mounting bolt . . .

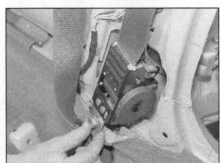

27.7b . . . and lower mounting bolt

27.13 Centre rear seat belt mounting bolt

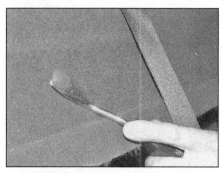

27.19 Release the retaining clips

27.20 Prise out the belt guide

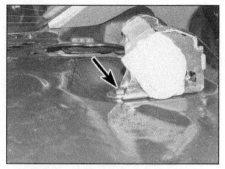

27.22 Undo the reel mounting bolt – arrowed

27.24a Removing the rear door sill panel . . .

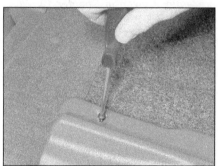

27.24b . . . and side trim panel . . .

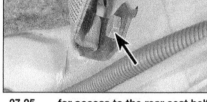

27.25 . . . for access to the rear seat belt lower mounting bolt – arrowed

Refitting

14 Refitting is a reversal of removal, but tighten the mounting bolts to the specified torque.

Centre rear seat belt (Saloon)

Removal

15 Remove both rear loudspeakers as described in Chapter 12.

16 Remove the rear seat cushion as described in Section 26.

17 Remove the upper trim panels from the D-pillars with reference to Section 28.

18 Note the fitted position of the centre seat belt. Unscrew the bolts securing the centre seat belt and buckle to the floor.

19 Release the retaining clips securing the rear parcel shelf to the body (see illustration).

20 Prise out the centre seat belt guide from the trim panel and remove it from the belt (see illustration).

21 Remove the parcel shelf for access to the seat belt reel.

22 Unscrew the mounting bolt and remove the reel from the body panel (see illustration).

Refitting

23 Refitting is a reversal of removal, but tighten the mounting bolts to the specified torque.

Side rear seat belt (Hatchback)

Removal

24 Remove the lower trim panel from the D-pillar, and then pull out the weatherstrip from the front of the upper trim panel. Open tailgate and pull out the weatherstrip from the rear of the upper trim panel, also remove the rear door sill panel and side trim panel (see illustrations).

25 Unscrew and remove the seat belt lower mounting bolt (see illustration).

26 Using a wide-bladed screwdriver, prise out the upper trim panel and feed the seat belt through the hole.

27 Remove the side trim/carpet by undoing the screws and depressing the centre pins of the fasteners.

28 Unscrew and remove the seat belt upper mounting bolt (see illustration).

29 Unscrew and remove the mounting bolts and remove the reel from the body (see illustration).

30 Unscrew and remove the mounting bolt and remove the seat belt buckle from the floor.

Refitting

31 Refitting is a reversal of removal, but tighten the mounting bolts to the specified torque.

Side rear seat belt (Saloon)

Removal

32 Remove the upper and lower trim panels from the D-pillar (see Section 28), then remove the rear loudspeakers as described in Chapter 12.

33 Note the fitted position of the seat belt buckle then unbolt it.

34 Undo the screws securing the rear parcel shelf to the body and move the shelf for access to the seat belt reel.

35 Unscrew the bolt and remove the reel.

Refitting

36 Refitting is a reversal of removal, but tighten the mounting bolts to the specified torque.

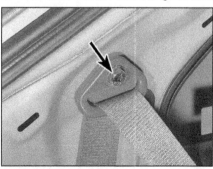

27.28 Rear seat belt upper mounting bolt – arrowed

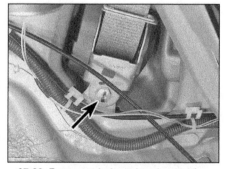

27.29 Rear seat belt reel and mounting bolt – arrowed

28 Interior trim panels – general information

Interior trim panels

1 The interior trim panels are secured either by screws or by various types of trim fasteners, usually studs or clips (see illustrations).

2 Check that there are no other panels overlapping the one to be removed. Usually there is a sequence that has to be followed that will become obvious on close inspection.

3 Remove all obvious fasteners, such as screws. If the panel will not come free then it is held by hidden clips or fasteners. These are usually situated around the edge of the panel and can be prised up to release them. Note, however, that they can break quite easily so new ones should be available. The best way of releasing such clips, in the absence of the correct type of tool, is to use a large flat-bladed screwdriver positioned directly beneath the clip. Note that in many cases the adjacent sealing strip must be prised back to release a panel.

4 When removing a panel, never use excessive force or the panel may be damaged. Always check carefully that all fasteners have been removed or released before attempting to withdraw a panel.

5 Refitting is the reverse of the removal procedure. Secure the fasteners by pressing them firmly into place and ensure that all disturbed components are correctly secured to prevent rattles. Use a suitable trim adhesive (a Rover dealer should be able to recommend a proprietary product) on reassembly.

 HAYNES HINT *If adhesives were found at any point on removal, use white spirit to remove all traces of old adhesive, then wash off all traces of spirit using soapy water.*

Carpets

6 The passenger compartment floor carpet is in one piece and is secured at its edges by screws or clips, usually the same fasteners used to secure the various adjoining trim panels.

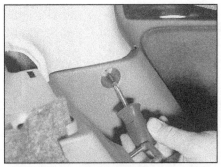
28.1a Screw fixing of a side trim panel

28.1b Removing a stud fixing

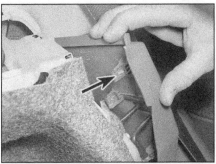
28.1c The clip fixings are very tight and require careful removal to avoid breakage

7 Carpet removal and refitting is reasonably straightforward but very time-consuming due to the fact that all adjoining trim panels must be removed first, as must components such as the seats, the centre console and seat belt lower anchorages.

Headlining

8 The headlining is clipped to the roof and can be withdrawn once all fittings such as the grab handles, sun visors, sunroof (if fitted), windscreen and related trim panels have been removed and the door, tailgate and sunroof aperture sealing strips have been pulled clear.

9 Note that headlining removal requires considerable skill and experience if it is to be carried out without damage and is therefore best entrusted to an expert. In particular the headlining must not be bent otherwise it will be permanently creased.

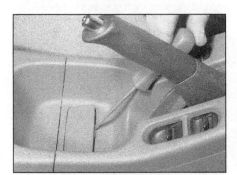
29.2 Prise out the cover . . .

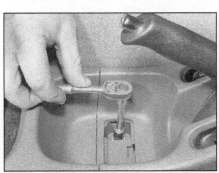
29.3 . . . and unscrew the rear console front mounting screws

28.1d Removing a side trim panel from the luggage compartment

29 Centre and rear consoles – removal and refitting

Rear console

Removal

1 Adjust both front seats to the fully forward position.

2 Using a screwdriver carefully prise the cover from the front end of the rear console (see illustration).

3 Unscrew the two retaining screws securing the front of the console to the floor (see illustration).

4 At the rear lower corners of the console, unscrew and remove the retaining screws. Do not remove the screws from the sides of the console (see illustration).

29.4 Remove the console rear mounting screws – arrowed

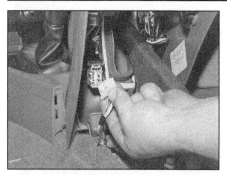

29.5 Disconnecting the electric window wiring multiplugs

29.11 Removing the gear knob

29.13a Prise up the retaining tabs . . .

29.13b . . . and remove the radio mounting box

29.13c Push out the hazard switch . . .

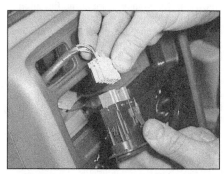

29.13d . . . and disconnect the wiring

5 Lift the console slightly and disconnect the wiring multiplugs for the electric windows. Withdraw the console from inside the vehicle (see illustration).

6 If necessary, the console components may be dismantled by undoing the screws/nuts. Remove the ashtray lid first.

Refitting

7 Refitting is a reversal of removal. When

reconnecting the electric window wiring multiplugs, connect the brown multiplug to the right-hand side.

Centre console

Removal

8 Remove the rear console as described earlier in this Section, paragraphs 1 to 5.
9 Adjust both front seats to the fully back position.
10 Remove the radio as described in Chapter 12.
11 On manual models, carefully prise the gear selector surround panel from the console. If preferred, unscrew the gear knob and leave the surround panel in the console (see illustration).
12 On automatic models, carefully prise the gear selector surround panel from the console and pull the gear knob upwards to release.
13 Use a screwdriver to prise out the plastic retaining tabs, then remove the radio mounting box and push out the hazard and heated rear window switches from the console. Disconnect the wiring and remove the switches (see illustrations).
14 Undo the five screws securing the front of the console to the facia panel (see illustrations).
15 Withdraw the console from inside the vehicle and disconnect the wiring from the digital clock (see illustration).

Refitting

16 Refitting is a reversal of removal.

29.13e Disconnecting the wiring from the heated rear window switch

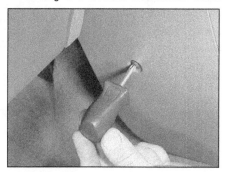

29.14a Unscrew the side screws . . .

29.14b . . . centre screw . . .

29.14c . . . and two upper screws

30 Glovebox –
removal and refitting

Removal

1 Unscrew the mounting screws from the bottom of the glovebox **(see illustration)**.
2 Withdraw the glovebox from inside the car **(see illustration)**.

Refitting

3 Refitting is a reversal of removal.

31 Facia panel –
removal and refitting

> ⚠ *Warning: Make sure that the safety recommendations given in Chapter 12 are followed, particularly where a passenger airbag is fitted, in order to prevent personal injury. Refer also to Chapter 10 when working on the steering column.*

Removal

1 Switch off the ignition and remove the ignition key, then disconnect the battery negative then positive leads, and **wait 10 minutes** (this is a safety requirement of the airbag system).
2 Remove the centre console as described in Section 29.
3 Remove the passenger side airbag module as described in Chapter 12.

31.5a Undo the outer screw . . .

31.6a Undo the outer screws . . .

29.15 . . . then withdraw the console and disconnect the wiring from the digital clock

30.2 . . . and withdraw the glovebox from the facia

4 Remove the driver's storage compartment from the lower trim panel beneath the steering column. To do this lift out the bottom edge and unhook the top **(see illustration)**.
5 Undo the screws and remove the lower and

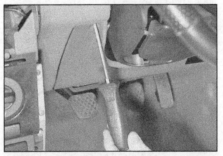

31.5b . . . and inner screw, and remove the lower trim panel from under the steering column

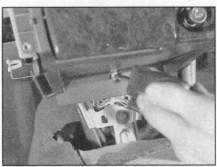

31.6b . . . and lower screw . . .

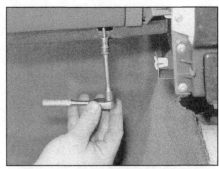

30.1 Unscrew the bottom mounting screws . . .

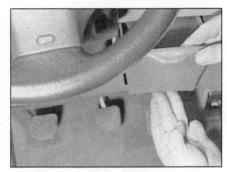

31.4 Removing the driver's storage compartment

bottom trim panels from under the steering column and facia **(see illustrations)**.
6 Undo the screws securing the ashtray assembly to the facia, then disconnect the wiring for the cigar lighter and withdraw the ashtray assembly **(see illustrations)**.

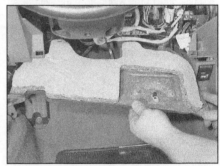

31.5c Removing the bottom trim panel from under the facia

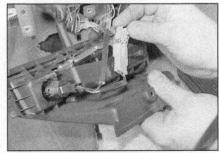

31.6c . . . then remove the ashtray assembly and disconnect the wiring for the cigar lighter

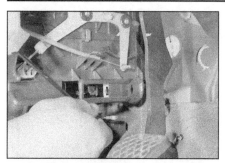

31.7 Disconnecting the heater control cables from the right-hand side of the heater assembly

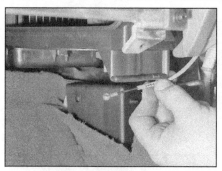

31.9 Disconnecting the facia centre vent cable from the heater assembly

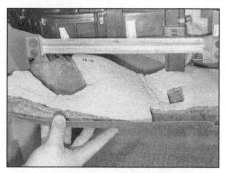

31.10 Removing the lower cover from under the passenger side of the facia

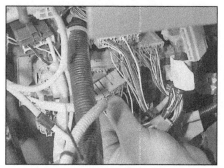

31.16 Disconnecting the facia wiring multiplugs from the fusebox

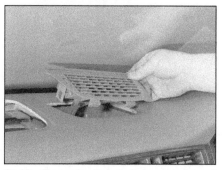

31.18a Removing the centre upper air vent

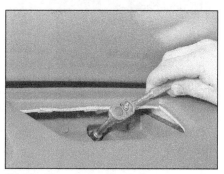

31.18b Unscrewing the facia upper centre mounting bolt

7 Unhook the heater control cables from the levers on the right-hand side of the heater assembly (see illustration).
8 Undo the screws securing the heater control panel to the facia, then withdraw the panel and disconnect the wiring from the switches.
9 Disconnect the facia centre vent cable from the heater assembly. It is located beneath the centre of the facia (see illustration).
10 Remove the glovebox and the lower cover from the passenger side of the facia (see illustration).
11 Disconnect the alarm ECU wiring multiplugs and, where applicable, the multiplug for the starter relay. Note on some models the starter relay is located in the engine compartment.
12 Unclip the wiring from the facia support panel.
13 Remove the steering column lower cover by releasing the clips and extracting the studs.

14 At the top of the steering column, remove the wiring harness clip from the stud.
15 Unscrew and remove the steering column upper mounting nuts and lower mounting bolts, then lower the steering column to the floor. There is no need to remove the steering wheel or to disconnect the steering column from the steering gear. Release the clamps as necessary to prevent straining the wiring harness.
16 Disconnect the multiplugs connecting the facia wiring to the body loom and fusebox. Note carefully the positions of the multiplugs as two of them are of identical type and can be refitted in the wrong positions (see illustration).
17 Disconnect the earth wire from the terminal beneath the instrument panel. Also detach the radio aerial lead from the clips on the facia.
18 Carefully prise up the rear edge of the centre upper air vent using a screwdriver and

cloth to prevent damage to the facia. Remove the vent and unscrew the facia mounting bolt (see illustrations).
19 Prise out the side access covers for access to the facia side mounting bolts. Unscrew and remove the bolts (see illustration).
20 Unscrew and remove the remaining bolts securing the facia to the bulkhead. They are located at the centre bottom and in the glovebox aperture (see illustrations).
21 Cover the gear lever with a cloth or card to prevent damage to the facia. Alternatively, temporarily refit the gear knob.
22 With the help of an assistant, withdraw the facia from the bulkhead

Refitting

23 Refitting is a reversal of removal, tightening the facia mounting bolts to the specified torque setting.

31.19 Carefully prise out the side covers for access to the facia side mounting bolts

31.20a Unscrewing the facia lower centre mounting bolt

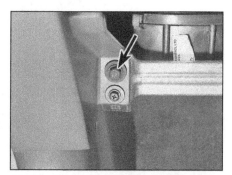

31.20b The facia mounting bolt located in the glovebox aperture

Chapter 12
Body electrical systems

Contents

Section number

Audio unit – removal and refitting. 23
Battery – check and maintenance . See *Weekly checks* and Chapter 5A
Battery – removal and refitting .See Chapter 5A
Bulbs (exterior lamps) – renewal 5
Bulbs (interior lamps) – renewal 6
Cigar lighter – removal and refitting 13
Clock – removal and refitting 14
Cruise control system – general. 26
Dim-dip headlamp system – operation 9
Electrical fault finding – general information 2
Exterior lamp units – removal and refitting. 7
Fuses, fusible links and relays – location and renewal. 3
General information and precautions. 1
Headlamp beams – alignment 8
Horn – removal and refitting. 18
Instrument panel – removal and refitting 11

Section number

Instrument panel components – removal and refitting. 12
Integrated (Multi Function) control unit – removal and refitting 10
Radio aerial – removal and refitting 25
Speakers – removal and refitting 24
Supplementary Restraint System (SRS) – component removal and
    refitting 16
Supplementary Restraint System (SRS) – operation 15
Switches – removal and refitting 4
Tailgate wiper motor – removal and refitting 22
Vehicle speed sensor – removal and refitting. 17
Washer fluid level check. . . . . .See *Weekly checks*
Windscreen wiper motor and linkage – removal and refitting 20
Windscreen/tailgate washer system components – removal and
    refitting 21
Wiper arm – removal and refitting 19
Wiper blades check . . . . .See *Weekly checks*

Degrees of difficulty

Easy, suitable for novice with little experience	**Fairly easy,** suitable for beginner with some experience	**Fairly difficult,** suitable for competent DIY mechanic	**Difficult,** suitable for experienced DIY mechanic	**Very difficult,** suitable for expert DIY or professional

Specifications

System

Type . . . .   12 volt, negative earth

Bulbs

	Wattage
Direction indicator	21
Front foglight	H1 – 55
Glovebox light	5
Headlamps:	
Dipped beam	H7 – 55
Main beam	H1 – 55
Interior light	5
Luggage compartment light.	5
Number plate light	5
Rear foglight.	21
Reversing light	21
Sidelight	5
Side repeater	5
Stop-light	21
Tail light.	5

Torque wrench settings

	Nm	lbf ft
Airbag diagnostic and control unit	9	7
Airbag harness earth wire Torx screw	10	7
Driver's airbag module Torx screws	9	7
Horn	22	16
Passenger's airbag module lower nuts	9	7
Passenger's airbag module upper nuts	6	4
SRS impact sensor to inside of sill.	6	4
Tailgate wiper arm	14	10
Tailgate wiper motor.	8	6
Tailgate wiper spindle.	2	1
Windscreen wiper arm	18	13
Windscreen wiper motor linkage	8	6
Windscreen wiper motor	9	7

1 General information and precautions

General information

The electrical system is of the 12 volt negative earth type and comprises a 12 volt battery, an alternator with integral voltage regulator, a starter motor and related electrical accessories, components and wiring. The battery is of the maintenance-free type and is charged by the alternator, which is belt-driven from a crankshaft-mounted pulley.

While some repair procedures are given, the usual course of action is to renew a defective component. The owner whose interest extends beyond mere component renewal should obtain a copy of the *Automotive Electrical & Electronic Systems Manual*, available from the publishers of this Manual.

Precautions

It is necessary to take extra care when working on the electrical system to avoid damage to semi-conductor devices (diodes and transistors) and to avoid the risk of personal injury. Certain procedures must be followed when removing the SRS components. In addition to the precautions given in *Safety first!* at the beginning of this Manual, observe the following when working on the system:

a) *Always remove rings, watches, etc, before working on the electrical system. Even with the battery disconnected, capacitive discharge could occur if a component's live terminal is earthed through a metal object. This could cause a shock or nasty burn.*

b) *Do not reverse the battery connections. Components such as the alternator, fuel injection/ignition system ECU, or any other having semi-conductor circuitry could be irreparably damaged.*

c) *If the engine is being started using jump leads and a slave battery, connect the batteries positive-to-positive and negative-to-negative.*

d) *Never disconnect the battery terminals, the alternator, any electrical wiring or any test instruments when the engine is running.*

e) *Do not allow the engine to turn the alternator when the alternator is not connected.*

f) *Always ensure that the battery negative lead is disconnected when working on the electrical system.*

g) *Before using electric-arc welding equipment on the vehicle, disconnect the battery, alternator and components such as the fuel injection/ignition system ECU to protect them.*

A number of additional precautions must be observed when working on vehicles equipped with airbags (SRS), they are as follows:

a) *Before working on any part of the SRS system, switch off the ignition and disconnect the negative then positive battery leads, then **wait at least ten minutes** to allow the system backup circuit to fully discharge.*

b) *Do not use ohmmeters or any other device capable of supplying current on any of the SRS components, as this may cause accidental detonation.*

c) *Always use new parts. Never fit parts that are from another vehicle or show signs of damage through being dropped or improperly handled.*

d) *Airbags are classed as pyrotechnical devices and must be stored and handled according to the relevant laws in the country concerned. Place a disconnected airbag unit with the pad surface facing upwards and never rest anything on the pad. Store it on a secure flat surface, away from flammable materials, high heat sources, oils, grease, detergents or water, and never leave it unattended.*

e) *The SRS indicator light should extinguish 3 seconds after the ignition switch is turned to position II. If this is not the case, have the system checked by a Rover dealer.*

f) *No attempt should be made to carry out repairs to the airbag components.*

g) *Renew the airbag unit and-slip ring every ten years, regardless of condition.*

h) *Return an unwanted airbag unit to your dealer for safe disposal. Do not endanger others by careless disposal of a unit.*

2 Electrical fault finding – general information

A typical electrical circuit consists of an electrical component, any switches, relays, motors, fuses, fusible links or circuit breakers related to that component and the wiring and connectors that link the component to both the battery and the chassis. To help you pinpoint an electrical circuit problem, wiring diagrams are included at the end of this Chapter.

Before tackling any troublesome electrical circuit, first study the appropriate wiring diagrams to get a complete understanding of what components are included in that individual circuit. Trouble spots, for instance, can be narrowed down by noting if other components related to the circuit are operating properly. If several components or circuits fail at one time, then the problem is probably in a fuse or earth connection, because several circuits are often routed through the same fuse and earth connections.

Electrical problems usually stem from simple causes, such as loose or corroded connections, a blown fuse, a melted fusible link or a faulty relay. Inspect the condition of all fuses, wires and connections in a problem circuit before testing the components. Use the diagrams to note which terminal connections will need to be checked in order to pinpoint the trouble spot.

The basic tools needed for electrical fault finding include a circuit tester or voltmeter (a 12 volt bulb with a set of test leads can also be used), a continuity tester, a battery and set of test leads, and a jumper wire, preferably with a circuit breaker incorporated, which can be used to bypass electrical components. Before attempting to locate a problem with test instruments, use the wiring diagram to decide where to make the connections.

Voltage checks

Voltage checks should be performed if a circuit is not functioning properly. Connect one lead of a circuit tester to either the negative battery terminal or a known good earth. Connect the other lead to a connector in the circuit being tested, preferably nearest to the battery or fuse. If the bulb of the tester lights then voltage is present, which means that the part of the circuit between the connector and the battery is problem-free. Continue checking the rest of the circuit in the same fashion. When you reach a point at which no voltage is present, the problem lies between that point and the last test point with voltage. Most problems can be traced to a loose connection. Bear in mind that some circuits are only live when the ignition switch is switched to a particular position.

Finding a short circuit

One method of finding a short circuit is to remove the fuse and connect a test light or voltmeter to the fuse terminals with all the relevant electrical components switched off. There should be no voltage present in the circuit. Move the wiring from side-to-side while watching the test light. If the bulb lights up, there is a short to earth somewhere in that area, probably where the insulation has rubbed through. The same test can be performed on each component in the circuit, even a switch.

Earth check

Perform an earth test to check whether a component is properly earthed. Disconnect the battery and connect one lead of a self-powered test light, known as a continuity tester, to a known good earth point. Connect the other lead to the wire or earth connection being tested. If the bulb lights up, the earth is good. If not, the earth is faulty.

If an earth connection is thought to be faulty, dismantle the connection and clean back to bare metal both the bodyshell and the wire terminal or the component's earth connection mating surface. Be careful to remove all traces of dirt and corrosion, and then use a knife to trim away any paint, so that a clean metal-to-metal joint is made. On reassembly, tighten the joint fasteners securely; if a wire terminal is being refitted, use serrated washers between the terminal and the bodyshell to ensure a clean and secure connection. When the connection is remade, prevent the onset of corrosion in the future by applying a coat of petroleum jelly or silicone-based grease, or by spraying on a proprietary ignition sealer or a water dispersant lubricant at regular intervals.

The vehicle's wiring harness has several multiple-earth connections; refer to the wiring diagrams for further information.

Continuity check

A continuity check is necessary to determine if there are any breaks in a circuit. With the circuit off (ie: no power in the circuit), a self-powered continuity tester can be used to check the circuit. Connect the test leads to both ends of the circuit, or to the positive end and a good earth. If the test light comes on, the circuit is passing current properly. If the light does not come on, there is a break somewhere in the circuit. The same procedure can be used to test a switch, by connecting the continuity tester to the switch terminals. With the switch turned on, the test light should come on.

Finding an open circuit

When checking for possible open circuits, it is often difficult to locate them by sight because oxidation or terminal misalignment are hidden by the connectors. Merely moving a connector on a sensor or in the wiring harness may correct the open circuit condition. Remember this when an open circuit is indicated when fault finding in a circuit. Intermittent problems may also be caused by oxidised or loose connections.

General

Electrical fault finding is simple if you keep in mind that all electrical circuits are basically electricity flowing from the battery, through the wires, switches, relays, fuses and fusible links to each electrical component (light bulb, motor, etc) and to earth, from which it is passed back to the battery. Any electrical problem is an interruption in the flow of electricity from the battery.

3 Fuses, fusible links and relays – location and renewal

Fuses

1 The main fusebox is located behind the driver's storage compartment located in the facia beneath the steering wheel. A further fusebox is located in the rear left-hand corner of the engine compartment for engine-related fuses.
2 To access the fusebox located beneath the steering wheel, first open the storage compartment then push it upwards against the spring tension and release it from the lower pivots. Pull the compartment outwards away from the facia; the fusebox can then be viewed behind the facia.
3 To access the engine compartment fusebox,

open the bonnet then depress the catch and unhook the lid **(see illustration)**.
4 To remove a fuse, first switch off the circuit concerned (or the ignition), then fit the tweezers and pull the fuse out of its terminals. Slide the fuse sideways from the tweezers. The wire within the fuse is clearly visible. If the fuse is blown, the wire will be broken or melted.
5 Always renew a fuse with one of an identical rating. Never use a fuse with a different rating from the original or substitute anything else. The fuse rating is stamped on top of the fuse. Fuses are also colour-coded for easy recognition.
6 If a new fuse blows immediately, find the cause before renewing it again. A short to earth as a result of faulty insulation is the most likely cause. Where a fuse protects more than one circuit, try to isolate the defect by switching on each circuit in turn (if possible) until the fuse blows again.
7 If any of the spare fuses are used, always renew them so that a spare of each rating is available.

Fusible links

8 The fusible links are located in the engine compartment fusebox, situated on the left-hand rear side of the engine compartment. Unclip the lid to gain access to them.
9 All links are numbered on the rear of the fusebox lid.
10 To remove a fusible link, first ensure that the circuit concerned is switched off then prise off the plastic cover. Slacken the two link retaining screws then lift the fusible link out of the fusebox. The wire within the fusible link is clearly visible. If the fuse is blown, it will be broken or melted. A blown fusible link indicates a serious wiring or system fault, which must be diagnosed before the link is renewed.
11 Always renew a fusible link with one of an identical rating. Never use a link with a different rating from the original or substitute anything else. On refitting, tighten the link retaining screws securely and refit the link cover.

Relays

12 Refer to the relevant wiring diagram for the details of the various relays. The main

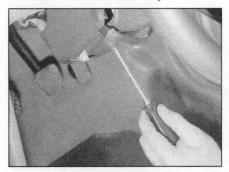

4.2a Undo the screws . . .

3.3 Engine compartment fusebox

relays are located in the engine compartment fusebox.
13 If a circuit or system controlled by a relay develops a fault and the relay is suspect, operate the system. If the relay is functioning, it should be possible to hear it click as it is energised. If this is the case, the fault lies with the components or wiring of the system. If the relay is not being energised, then either the relay is not receiving a main supply or a switching voltage, or the relay itself is faulty. Testing is by the substitution of a known good unit but be careful as some relays are identical in appearance, but perform different functions.
14 To renew a relay, ensure that the ignition switch is off, then simply pull direct from the socket and press in the new relay.

4 Switches – removal and refitting

1 Disconnect the battery negative lead before removing any switch and after refitting the switch, reconnect the lead.

Switches on steering column

Removal

2 Undo the screws and remove the steering column upper and lower shrouds **(see illustrations)**.
3 Disconnect the wiring multiplugs from the lighting and wiper switches **(see illustration)**.
4 With the ignition key inserted, turn the steering wheel to give access to the switch

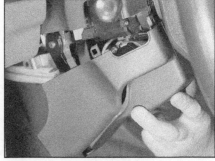

4.2b . . . and remove the steering column lower . . .

4.2c ... and upper shrouds

4.3 Disconnecting the wiring multiplugs from the wiper/lighting switches

4.4a Undo the switch mounting screws ...

4.4b ... then depress the tab ...

4.4c ... and withdraw the switch from the base

Refitting

6 Refitting is a reversal of removal.

Facia switches

Removal

7 Check that the relevant switch is in the off position, then taking care not to scratch or damage the switch or its surround, prise it out using a suitable flat-bladed screwdriver. Withdraw the switch until the connector plug appears then disconnect the wiring connector and remove the switch **(see illustrations)**. Where applicable, tie a piece of string to the wiring connector to prevent it from falling behind the facia panel.

Refitting

8 On refitting, connect the wiring connector to the switch and press the switch into position until the retaining clips click into place.

retaining screws. Undo the screws then depress the tab and slide the switch from the base **(see illustrations)**.

5 If it is required to remove the switch base, remove the steering wheel as described in Chapter 10 then undo the screws and remove the rotary coupler from the top of the column. Remove the indicator cancellation cam, then undo the screws and withdraw the base **(see illustrations)**.

4.5a Removing the indicator cancellation cam ...

4.5b ... and switch base

4.7a Using a screwdriver, prise out the hazard switch ...

4.7b ... then disconnect the wiring multiplug

4.7c Using a screwdriver, prise out the foglight switch ...

4.7d ... then disconnect the wiring multiplug

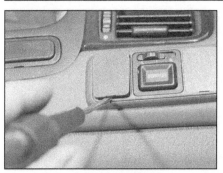

4.9a Use a screwdriver . . .

4.9b . . . to prise out the blank . . .

4.9c . . . then push out the exterior mirror switch . . .

Exterior mirror switch

Removal

9 Where blanks are fitted next to the switch, prise out one of them and press out the switch from behind **(see illustrations)**.

10 Where there are no blanks, remove the driver's storage compartment from the lower trim panel beneath the steering column then undo the screws and remove the lower trim panel from the facia. Reach up behind the facia and press out the exterior mirror switch.

11 Disconnect the wiring multiplug from the rear of the switch **(see illustration)**.

Refitting

12 Refitting is a reversal of removal.

Horn push switch

Removal

13 Remove the driver's airbag as described in Section 16.

14 Disconnect the earth wiring from the base of the steering wheel.

15 Disconnect the wiring leading to the rotary coupler.

16 Using a screwdriver, carefully prise the switch from the steering wheel taking care not to damage the covering.

17 Disconnect the spade connectors and remove the switch.

Refitting

18 Refitting is a reversal of removal.

Courtesy lamp switches

Removal

19 With the door open, undo the screw securing the courtesy lamp to the body. Pull out the switch and tie a piece of string to the wiring to prevent it dropping into the body **(see illustration)**.

20 Disconnect the wiring and remove the switch from the vehicle.

Refitting

21 Refitting is a reverse of removal.

Handbrake warning lamp switch

Removal

22 Remove the rear console as described in Chapter 11.

23 Disconnect the wiring from the switch located on the left-hand side of the handbrake lever **(see illustration)**.

24 Undo the screw and remove the switch.

Refitting

25 Refitting is a reversal of removal.

Glovebox illumination switch

Removal

26 Remove the glovebox (see Chapter 11).

27 Reach up behind the upper lip of the facia and disconnect the wiring from the switch **(see illustration)**.

28 Undo the screws and remove the switch.

Refitting

29 Refitting is a reversal of removal.

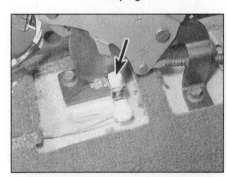

4.11 . . . and disconnect the wiring multiplug

4.23 Handbrake warning lamp switch

Ignition switch

Removal

30 Remove the ignition key then disconnect the negative (earth) lead from the battery followed by the positive lead. Wait ten minutes to allow the SRS system backup circuit to fully discharge.

31 Remove the driver's pocket from the lower facia panel below the steering wheel, then undo the screws and remove the lower facia panel.

32 Undo the screws and remove the steering column upper and lower shrouds.

33 Disconnect the two starter switch multiplugs from the fusebox located to the right-hand side of the steering wheel.

34 Detach the ignition switch wiring from the supports by unscrewing the studs. Also release the cable tie.

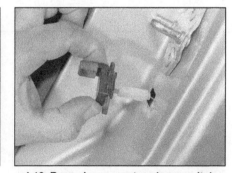

4.19 Removing a courtesy lamp switch

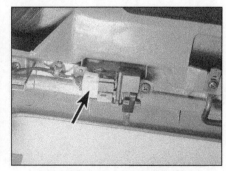

4.27 Wiring plug on the glovebox illumination switch

4.35a Undo the screws . . .

4.35b . . . and remove the ignition switch from the lock housing

4.42a Undo the screws . . .

4.42b . . . and withdraw the interior light assembly

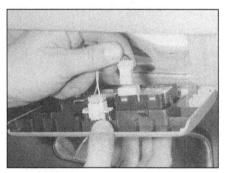

4.43a Disconnect the wiring . . .

4.43b . . . and remove the sunroof control switch from the light assembly

35 Undo the screws and remove the ignition switch from the lock housing **(see illustrations)**.

Refitting

36 Refit the switch and tighten the screws.
37 Reconnect the wiring and secure with the cable tie and supports.
38 Refit the steering column upper and lower shrouds.
39 Refit the lower facia panel and the driver's pocket.
40 Reconnect the battery positive then negative leads.

Sunroof control switch

Removal

41 Prise the lens from the interior light located at the front of the headlining.
42 Unscrew and remove the screws and with-draw the light assembly **(see illustrations)**.

43 Disconnect the wiring from the rear of the switch and press the switch from the housing **(see illustrations)**.

Refitting

44 Refitting is a reversal of removal.

5 Bulbs (exterior lamps) – renewal

General

1 Whenever a bulb is renewed, note the following:
 a) *Remember that if the lamp has just been in use, the bulb may be extremely hot.*
 b) *Always check the bulb contacts and holder, ensuring that there is clean metal-to-metal contact between the bulb and*

its live contacts and earth. Clean off any corrosion or dirt before fitting a new bulb.
 c) *Always ensure that the new bulb is of the correct rating and that the glass envelope is completely clean before fitting. This applies particularly to headlamp bulbs. If necessary, use methylated spirit to clean the glass.*

Outer (main and dip) headlamp

2 Working in the engine compartment, unclip the plastic cover from the rear of the headlamp unit **(see illustration)**.
3 Unplug the wiring connector, then unhook the ears of the bulb retaining clips and swivel them away from the bulb **(see illustrations)**.
4 Withdraw the bulb **(see illustration)**.
5 When handling a new bulb, use a tissue or clean cloth to avoid touching the glass with the fingers. Moisture and grease from the skin

5.2 Unclip the cover . . .

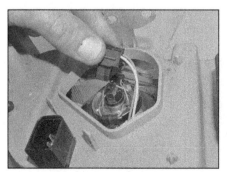

5.3a . . . unplug the wiring connector . . .

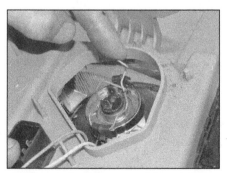

5.3b . . . unhook the ears of the retaining clips . . .

5.4 . . . then remove the outer headlamp bulb

5.7 Remove the cover . . .

5.12 Removing the front sidelight bulbholder

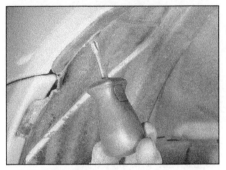

5.16 Undo the screw and pull back the wheel arch liner . . .

5.17 . . . then withdraw the bulbholder . . .

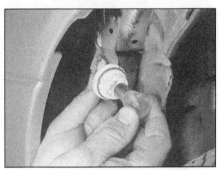

5.18 . . . and remove the front direction indicator bulb

can cause blackening and rapid failure of this type of bulb.

> **HAYNES HINT**
> *If the glass of a headlamp bulb is accidentally touched, wipe it clean using methylated spirit.*

6 Refitting is the reverse of the removal procedure. Ensure that the metal tab on the bulb base is located in the cut-out at the top of the headlamp.

Inner (main) headlamp

7 Working in the engine compartment, remove the rubber cover from the rear of the headlamp unit **(see illustration)**.
8 Unplug the wiring connector, then unhook the ears of the bulb retaining clips and swivel them away from the bulb **(see illustrations 5.3a and 5.3b)**.

9 Withdraw the bulb, observing the precautions given in paragraph 5.
10 Refitting is the reverse of the removal procedure. Ensure that the metal base of the bulb is located correctly in the rear of the headlamp.

Front sidelight

11 Working in the engine compartment, remove the rubber cover from the rear of the headlamp unit.
12 Pull the bulbholder from the headlamp reflector **(see illustration)**.
13 Pull the capless (push-fit) bulb out of its socket to remove.
14 Refitting is the reverse of the removal procedure.

Front direction indicator

15 If working on the right-hand indicator turn the front wheels on full left lock, and *vice versa*.
16 Undo the screw from the fastener securing

the wheel arch liner to the front wing behind the front direction indicator, then fold back the liner along its crease line for access to the rear of the light **(see illustration)**.
17 Twist the front direction indicator bulbholder anti-clockwise and remove it from the rear of the indicator light **(see illustration)**. There is no need to disconnect the wiring.
18 Depress and twist the bulb to remove it from the bulbholder **(see illustration)**.
19 Refitting is a reversal of removal.

Direction indicator side repeater

20 Carefully press the side repeater light towards the front of the vehicle and withdraw it from the wing **(see illustration)**.
21 Twist the bulbholder anti-clockwise and remove it from the light, then pull the capless (push-fit) bulb out of its socket **(see illustrations)**.
22 Refitting is a reversal of removal.

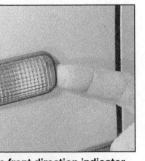

5.20 Press the front direction indicator side repeater light forwards to remove it from the wing

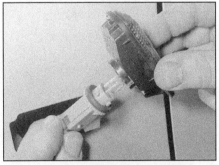

5.21a Twist the bulbholder from the light . . .

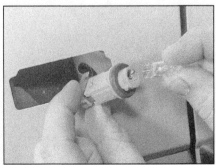

5.21b . . . and pull out the capless bulb

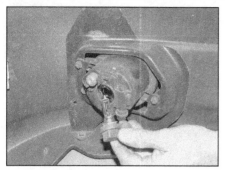

5.25 Twist the bulbholder to remove

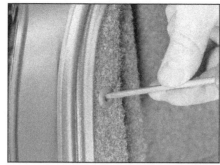

5.27a Slightly depress the clip centre pin . . .

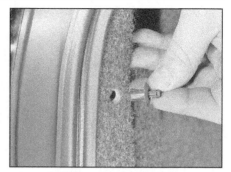

5.27b . . . then remove it

Front fog/driving lamp

23 Undo the fastener securing the wheel arch liner to the lower edge of the front bumper and pull it to one side.

24 Reach up behind the bumper and disconnect the wiring connector from the fog/ driving lamp.

25 Twist the bulb holder anti-clockwise from the rear of the light, and then withdraw the bulb (see illustration).

26 Refitting is a reversal of removal.

Rear light cluster

27 Open the tailgate or boot lid and unclip the covering from the rear of the luggage compartment for access to the rear light. To release the clip, depress its centre pin slightly using a screwdriver (see illustrations).

28 Depress the clip and disconnect the wiring

multiplug from the rear of the light unit (see illustration).

29 On Hatchback models, squeeze together the two tabs then withdraw the bulbholder (see illustration).

30 On Saloon models, move the lever inwards while supporting the rear of the light cluster, then withdraw the unit from the rear.

31 Depress and twist the bulb to remove it from the bulbholder (see illustration). If a bulb has blown, it will be blackened. If necessary, temporarily reconnect the wiring to the cluster and compare the functions of each bulb with its counterpart on the other side of the vehicle.

32 Refitting is a reversal of removal. To refit the luggage compartment covering clips, push the centre pins out before refitting them, then press in the pins flush (see illustration).

Number plate lamps

Note: On later 2005 facelift models, the number plate lights are in the rear bumper and are clipped in position (see illustration).

33 Open the tailgate/boot lid for access to the number plate lamps.

34 Undo the screws and withdraw the light unit.

35 On Hatchback models, depress the tab and unclip the lens. Recover the gasket. The bulb is of the capless (push-fit) type and can be pulled out of the lamp unit.

36 On Saloon models, remove the festoon-type bulb from the spring contacts (see illustration).

37 Refitting is a reverse of the removal procedure. On Saloon models, check the tension of the spring contacts and, if necessary, bend them so that they firmly contact the bulb end caps.

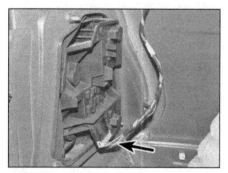

5.28 Disconnecting the wiring connector

5.29 Releasing the clip to remove the bulbholder

5.31 Removing a bulb from the rear light cluster

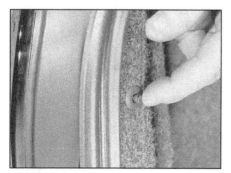

5.32 Press in the clip pins until flush

5.33 Release light unit using a small screwdriver

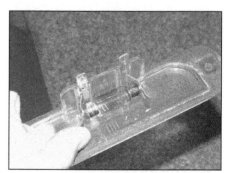

5.36 Removing the festoon bulb

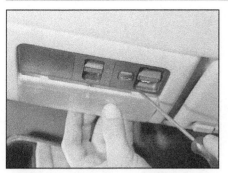

6.2a Use a screwdriver to prise off the interior light lens . . .

6.2b . . . then remove the festoon bulb from its spring contacts

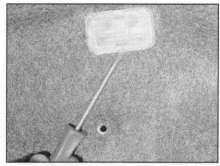

6.4a Prise off the lens . . .

6 Bulbs (interior lamps) – renewal

General

1 Refer to Section 5.

Interior lamps

2 Using a small screwdriver, carefully prise the lens off the lamp unit then remove the festoon bulb from its spring contacts **(see illustrations)**.

3 Fit the new bulb using a reversal of the removal procedure. Check the tension of the spring contacts and, if necessary, bend them so that they firmly contact the bulb end caps.

Luggage compartment lamp

Hatchback

4 Using a small screwdriver, carefully prise the lens off the lamp unit then remove the festoon bulb from its spring contacts **(see illustrations)**.

5 Fit the new bulb using a reversal of the removal procedure. Check the tension of the spring contacts and, if necessary, bend them so that they firmly contact the bulb end caps.

Saloon

6 Reach inside the access hole along side the light unit and press the retaining clip to release it from the rear shelf panel **(see illustration)**.

7 Depress and twist the bulb to remove it **(see illustration)**.

8 Fit the new bulb using a reversal of the removal procedure.

Instrument panel illumination and warning lamps

9 Remove the instrument panel as described in Section 11.

10 Twist the relevant bulbholder anti-clockwise and withdraw it from the rear of the panel.

11 Most of the main panel illumination bulbs are integral with their holders, however the main panel illumination bulbs (with a red envelope over the glass) and some lower warning bulbs are of the capless (push-fit) type **(see illustrations)**.

12 Fit the new bulb/bulbholder using a reversal of the removal procedure.

Digital clock illumination

13 Remove the centre console as described in Chapter 11.

6.4b . . . then remove the festoon bulb from the luggage compartment lamp

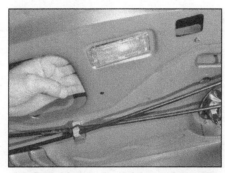

6.6 Releasing the boot light retaining clip

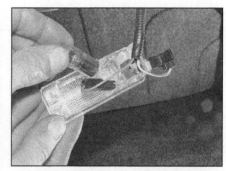

6.7 Removing the bayonet type bulb

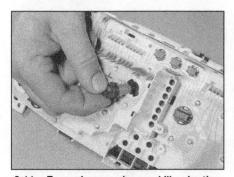

6.11a Removing a main panel illumination bulbholder . . .

6.11b . . . and bulb

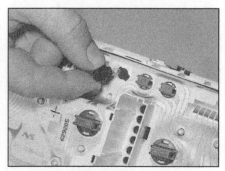

6.11c Removing a warning lamp bulbholder . . .

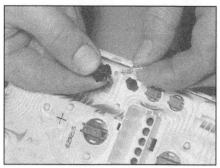

6.11d . . . and bulb

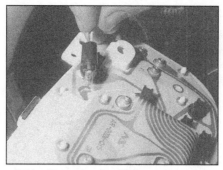

6.11e Removing the SRS warning lamp bulbholder and wiring . . .

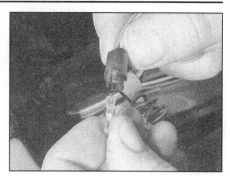

6.11f . . . and bulb

6.14a Remove the bulbholder . . .

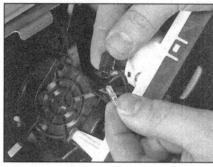

6.14b . . . and pull out the digital clock illumination bulb

14 Unscrew and remove the bulbholder, then pull out the wedge-type bulb **(see illustrations)**.

15 Fit the new bulb/bulbholder using a reversal of the removal procedure.

7 Exterior lamp units – removal and refitting

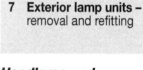

Headlamp and direction indicator

1 Remove the front bumper as described in Chapter 11.
2 Unscrew the bolts securing the crossmember to the front valance just below the headlamps, and remove it **(see illustrations)**.
3 Unscrew the headlamp mounting bolts **(see illustrations)**.
4 Twist the indicator bulbholder anti-clockwise and remove from the rear of the indicator light.
5 Disconnect the headlamp wiring multiplug **(see illustration)**. On later models also dis-

7.2a Unscrew the bolts (arrowed) . . .

7.2b . . . and remove the crossmember from the front valance

7.3a Headlamp lower mounting bolt . . .

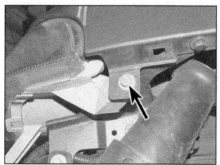

7.3b . . . side bolt . . .

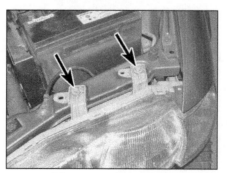

7.3c . . . and upper bolts

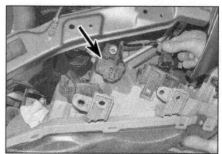

7.5 Disconnecting the headlamp wiring multiplugs – headlight levelling motor arrowed

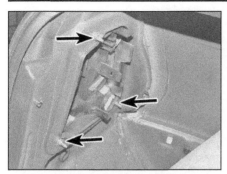

7.13a Undo the mounting nuts (arrowed) . . .

7.13b . . . and withdraw the rear light unit

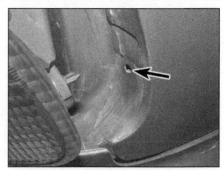

7.15 Align locating peg with hole in rear panel – arrowed

connect the wiring from the headlamp levelling motor.

6 Withdraw the headlamp from the front of the vehicle.

7 Refitting is a reversal of removal, but tighten the bracket bolts securely and on completion check and if necessary adjust the headlamp beam setting (see Section 8).

Direction indicator side repeater

8 Carefully press the side repeater light towards the front of the vehicle and withdraw it from the wing **(see illustration 5.20)**.

9 Twist the bulbholder anti-clockwise and remove it from the light, then withdraw the side repeater **(see illustrations 5.21)**.

10 Refitting is a reversal of removal.

Rear lamp cluster

11 Open the tailgate or boot lid and unclip the covering from the rear of the luggage

compartment for access to the rear light. To release the clip, depress its centre pin slightly using a screwdriver **(see illustrations 5.27)**.

12 Depress the clip and disconnect the wiring multiplug from the rear of the light unit.

13 Unscrew the mounting nuts and withdraw the unit from the rear panel **(see illustrations)**.

14 Check the rubber seal around the outside edge of the light unit.

15 Refitting is a reversal of removal. The rubber seal must be renewed if damaged and make sure the locating peg on the rear of the light unit locates correctly **(see illustration)**.

Number plate lamps

Note: *On later 2005 facelift models, the number plate lights are in the rear bumper and are clipped in position.*

16 Open the tailgate/boot lid for access to the number plate lamps.

17 Undo the screws and withdraw the light unit **(see illustrations)**.

18 Disconnect the wiring connector(s).

19 Refitting is a reverse of the removal procedure.

High-level stop-lamp

20 Using a Torx key undo the screws and remove the trim from the high-level stop-lamp.

21 Unscrew the mounting nuts **(see illustration)**, withdraw the stop-lamp, and disconnect the wiring.

22 Refitting is a reversal of removal.

Front foglamp/driving lamp

23 Remove the front bumper as described in Chapter 11.

24 Undo the three mounting bolts and withdraw the lamp from the rear of the bumper **(see illustration)**.

25 Refitting is a reversal of removal. If necessary, the foglight beam may be adjusted by using a screwdriver to turn the knob on the rear of the lamp **(see illustration)**.

> **8 Headlamp beams – alignment**

If the headlamps are thought to be out of alignment, then accurate adjustment of their beams is only possible using optical beam setting equipment, and this work should therefore be carried out by a Rover dealer or workshop with the necessary facilities.

7.17a Undo the two retaining screws (arrowed) . . .

7.17b . . . and withdraw the light unit

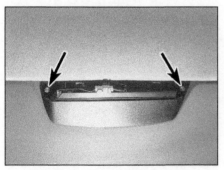

7.21 Undo the two mounting nuts – arrowed

7.24 Undo the foglight mounting bolts – arrowed

7.25 Insert screwdriver in position shown (arrowed) to adjust foglamp

8.2a Adjusting outer adjuster . . .

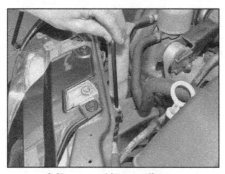

8.2b . . . and inner adjuster

For reference, the headlamps can be adjusted by using a suitably-sized crosshead screwdriver to rotate the two adjuster assemblies fitted to the rear of each lamp. The outer adjuster controls the horizontal setting and the inner adjuster controls the vertical setting (see illustrations).

9 Dim-dip headlamp system – operation

This system comprises the dim-dip resistor, which is riveted to the underside of the battery tray. The air cleaner and battery tray must be removed for access to the resistor.

The dim-dip unit is supplied with current from the sidelamp circuit and energised by a feed from the ignition switch. When energised, the unit allows battery voltage to pass through

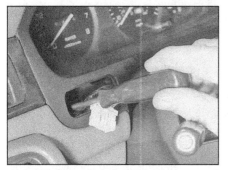

11.4a Undo the instrument panel surround lower mounting screws . . .

11.4c . . . and remove the surround

the resistor to the headlamp dipped-beam circuits. This energises the headlamps with approximately one-sixth of their normal power so that the vehicle cannot be driven using sidelights alone.

The system is controlled by the multi-function unit, which is located inside the vehicle behind the lower facia panel on the driver's side of the vehicle. See Section 10 for the removal and refitting procedure.

10 Integrated (Multi Function) control unit – removal and refitting

Removal

1 The multi function unit (MFU) is a central control for the following circuits:
a) Front and rear wipers.
b) Courtesy lamp delay.

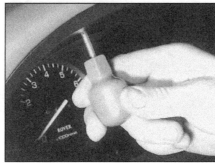

11.5a Removing the instrument panel lower mounting screws . . .

c) Heated rear window.
d) Horn.
e) Lights-on alarm.
f) Dim-dip.
g) Rear foglights.
h) Engine immobiliser.
i) Catalyst overheat warning.
j) Seat belt warning.

2 Disconnect the battery negative lead followed by the positive lead.
3 Remove the driver's storage compartment from the lower trim panel beneath the steering column.
4 Undo the screws and remove the lower trim panel from the facia.
5 Disconnect the two multiplugs from the top of the fusebox.
6 Unscrew the fusebox mounting bolts and detach it from the studs.
7 Disconnect the wiring multiplugs from the MFU integrated control unit, and release the unit from the back of the fusebox.
8 Withdraw the unit from inside the vehicle.

Refitting

9 Refitting is a reversal of removal.

11 Instrument panel – removal and refitting

Removal

1 Adjust the steering column to its lowest position.
2 Using a screwdriver, carefully prise out the foglight switch from the instrument panel surround and disconnect the wiring multiplug.
3 Similarly, prise out the blank from the other side of the surround.
4 Using a cross-head screwdriver, undo the screws and withdraw the surround. The retaining screws are located at the lower corners and under the upper edge of the surround (see illustrations).
5 Undo the instrument panel retaining screws and withdraw the panel for access to the wiring. The upper edge of the panel should be tilted down (see illustrations).
6 Disconnect the wiring, where necessary remove the SRS warning bulbholder,

11.5b . . . and upper mounting screws

11.4b . . . and upper mounting screws . . .

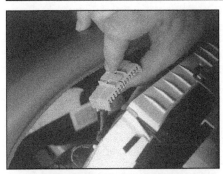

11.6 Disconnecting the wiring from the rear of the instrument panel

and release the wiring from the clip **(see illustration)**.

7 Withdraw the instrument panel from behind the steering wheel.

Refitting

8 Refitting is a reversal of removal. On completion, check the operation of all panel warning lamps and instrument surround switches to ensure that they are functioning correctly.

12 Instrument panel components – removal and refitting

Removal

1 The procedure for removing the following instruments is identical.
   a) Speedometer.
   b) Tachometer.
   c) Coolant temperature gauge.
   d) Fuel gauge.

2 Remove the instrument panel as described in Section 11.

3 Disconnect the illumination bulb and wiring lead from the rear of the instrument housing.

4 Undo the screw and remove the support bracket from the top of the instrument housing.

5 Working your way around the instrument housing, carefully release the retaining clips and remove the front cover from the housing.

6 Depending on which instrument gauge requires removing, undo the relevant retaining screws and remove the appropriate instrument gauge.

Refitting

7 Refitting is a reversal of removal.

13 Cigar lighter – removal and refitting

Removal

1 Remove the centre console as described in Chapter 11.

2 Undo the screws securing the ashtray assembly to the facia, then disconnect the

wiring for the cigar lighter and withdraw the ashtray assembly.

3 Remove the cigar lighter element, then unscrew the central screw and remove the cigar lighter components from the assembly.

Refitting

4 Refitting is a reversal of removal.

14 Clock – removal and refitting

Removal

1 Remove the centre console as described in Chapter 11.

2 Undo the retaining screws and remove the clock from the console.

Refitting

3 Refitting is a reversal of removal.

15 Supplementary Restraint System (SRS) – operation

At vehicle start-up, a warning light located in the steering wheel centre pad (single airbag system) or instrument panel (twin airbag system) will illuminate when the system electrical circuits are activated by turning the ignition switch to position II and will stay illuminated for 3 seconds whilst the system performs a self-diagnosis test. If this test is satisfactory, the light will extinguish. If the test is unsatisfactory, the light will remain on or fail to illuminate at all, denoting that the system must be serviced as soon as possible. System operation is as follows:

Upon the vehicle suffering a frontal impact over a specified force, a sensor inside the airbag control unit, which is located on the steering wheel (single driver's airbag system) or beneath the front centre console (twin airbag system), activates the system. A sensor (fitted to discriminate between actual impact and driving on rough road surfaces, etc) is also activated and power is supplied to the airbag ignitor from the battery or a backup circuit, causing the airbag to inflate within 30 milliseconds.

As the driver of the vehicle is thrown forward into the inflated airbag it immediately discharges its contents through a vent, thereby providing a progressive deceleration and reducing the risk of injury from contact with the steering wheel, facia or windscreen. The total time taken from the start of airbag inflation to its complete deflation is approximately 0.1 seconds.

A severe frontal impact will also activate the front seat belt pretensioners in order to take up any slack.

16 Supplementary Restraint System (SRS) – component removal and refitting

 Warning: Under no circumstances attempt to diagnose problems with SRS components using standard workshop equipment.

Note: All SRS system wiring can be identified by its yellow protective covering. The information in this Section is limited to those components which must be removed to gain access to other components on the vehicle. Read carefully the precautions given in Section 1 of this Chapter before commencing work on any part of the system.

Driver's airbag module

Removal

1 With the ignition switched off, disconnect the battery negative then positive leads and **wait at least 10 minutes** to allow the SRS backup system to completely discharge. With the front wheels in the straight-ahead position, remove the ignition key.

2 Using a Torx screwdriver, undo the retaining screws from each side of the steering wheel and release the airbag module from the steering wheel. Do not allow the airbag module to hang on its wiring **(see illustration)**.

3 Disconnect the wiring from the centre rear of the module **(see illustration)**.

4 Remove the module from the steering wheel and place it in safe storage.

5 If the module is to be renewed, record its bar code and obtain the new unit from a Rover dealer.

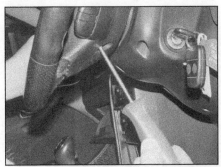

16.2 Removing the screws securing the airbag module to the steering wheel

16.3 Disconnecting the wiring from the airbag module

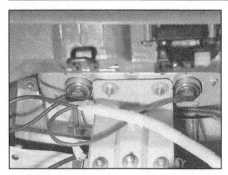

16.9 Passenger airbag module viewed from under the facia

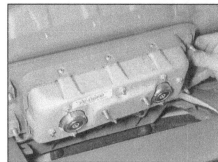

16.10 Removing the passenger airbag module from the facia

16.19a Removing the steering column lower shroud . . .

16.19b . . . and upper shroud

Refitting

6 Refit the airbag module by reversing the removal procedure, noting the following:
a) *The cable wiring connector must face upwards when refitted to the rear of the module.*
b) *Observe the specified torque wrench setting when tightening the airbag module retaining screws (TX30 Torx type) and take care not to cross-thread them.*
c) *Reconnect both battery leads; negative lead last, and turn the ignition switch to the II position. Check the condition of the system by observing the SRS warning light located in the steering wheel centre pad. The light should stay illuminated for 3 seconds whilst the system performs a self-diagnosis test. If the test is satisfactory, the light will extinguish. If the test is unsatisfactory, the light will remain on or fail to illuminate at all,*

denoting that the system must be serviced as soon as possible.

Passenger airbag module

Removal

7 With the ignition switched off, disconnect the battery negative then positive leads and **wait at least 10 minutes** to allow the SRS backup system to completely discharge.
8 Remove the glovebox as described in Chapter 11.
9 Working from under the facia, identify the wiring on the airbag module for position, and then disconnect them **(see illustration)**. **Note**: *On later models, there is only one wiring connector on the airbag unit.*
10 Unscrew and remove the retaining nuts securing the airbag module and mounting bracket to the facia, then remove the module and place it in safe storage **(see illustration)**.

11 If the module is to be renewed, record its bar code and obtain the new unit from a Rover dealer.

Refitting

12 Refit the airbag module by reversing the removal procedure, noting the following:
a) *The module lower retaining nuts **must** be renewed. Tighten the nuts progressively to the specified torque noting that the upper nuts and the lower nuts are tightened to different torques.*
b) *Reconnect both battery leads; negative lead last, and turn the ignition switch to the II position. Check the condition of the system by observing the SRS warning light located in the steering wheel centre pad. The light should stay illuminated for 3 seconds whilst the system performs a self-diagnosis test. If the test is satisfactory, the light will extinguish. If the test is unsatisfactory, the light will remain on or fail to illuminate at all, denoting that the system must be serviced as soon as possible.*

Airbag diagnostic and control unit

Removal

13 With the ignition key removed, disconnect the battery negative then positive leads, then **wait at least 10 minutes** to allow the SRS backup system to completely discharge.
14 Remove the rear section of centre console as described in Chapter 11.
15 Pull back the carpet (where applicable), and then unscrew the three retaining bolts from the control unit.
16 Disconnect the wiring multiplug and withdraw the control unit from inside the vehicle.

Refitting

17 Refitting is a reversal of removal, noting the following:
a) *Make sure the mating faces of the control unit and floor panel are clean and free from any burrs.*
b) *Take care to ensure that wiring is not trapped.*
c) *On completion, carry out a system check as described in paragraph 6.*

Rotary coupler

Removal

18 Remove the steering wheel as described in Chapter 10. To prevent the rotary coupler from losing its central setting, use adhesive tape to secure the upper part to the base.
19 Undo the screws and remove the steering column lower and upper shrouds **(see illustrations)**.
20 Disconnect the wiring multiplugs from the rotary coupler **(see illustrations)**.
21 Undo the screws and remove the rotary coupler from the wiper/lighting switch base **(see illustrations)**.

16.20a Disconnecting the SRS multiplug . . .

16.20b . . . and horn multiplug from the rear of the rotary coupler

Refitting

22 Offer up the rotary coupler to the switch base and align the slots with the projections on the cancelling sleeve. Insert the screws and tighten securely.
23 Remove the adhesive tape from the rotary coupler and reconnect the wiring multiplugs.
24 Refit the steering column upper and lower shrouds.
25 Refit the steering wheel as described in Chapter 10.

Front seat belt pretensioners

26 Seat belt pretensioners are built into the front seat belt reels, remove the front seat belts as described in Chapter 11.

Seat airbag module

27 Seat airbag modules are built into the front seats (depending on model), remove the front seats as described in Chapter 11. Take the seat to a Rover specialist to have the airbag module replaced.

Side impact sensors

Note: *There are two side impact sensors (one at each side of the vehicle), bolted to the inside of the sill, under the carpet.*
28 With the ignition key removed, disconnect the battery negative then positive leads, then **wait at least 10 minutes** to allow the SRS backup system to completely discharge.
29 Remove the front seat as described in Chapter 11, Section 26.
30 Undo the retaining screws and remove the tread plate from along the bottom of the door aperture.
31 Pull back the carpet then unscrew the retaining screws from the sensor on the inside of the sill panel.
32 Disconnect the wiring multiplug and withdraw the sensor from inside the vehicle.

Refitting

33 Refitting is a reversal of removal, noting the following:
a) *Make sure the mating faces of the control unit and floor panel are clean and free from any burrs.*
b) *Take care to ensure that wiring is not trapped.*
c) *On completion, carry out a system check as described in paragraph 6.*

18.3a Disconnect the wiring connector . . .

16.21a Undo the screws . . .

17 Vehicle speed sensor
– removal and refitting

Refer to Chapter 7A, Section 6.

18 Horn –
removal and refitting

Removal

Note: *On some models there are two horns (one at each side), bolted to the front valance behind the bumper.*
1 Disconnect the battery negative terminal.
2 Remove the front bumper as described in Chapter 11.
3 Disconnect the wiring multiplug and unbolt the horn from the bracket **(see illustrations)**.

Refitting

4 Refitting is a reversal of the removal procedure.

19 Wiper arm –
removal and refitting

Windscreen wiper arm
Removal
1 Operate the wiper motor, then switch it off

18.3b . . . and undo the mounting bolt – arrowed

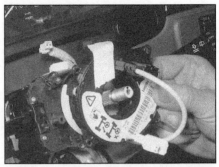
16.21b . . . and remove the rotary coupler from the wiper/lighting switch base

so that the wiper arm returns to the 'parked' position.
2 Stick a piece of tape on the windscreen, along the edge of the wiper blade, to use as an alignment aid on refitting.
3 Unscrew and remove the spindle nut, then lift the blade off the glass and pull the wiper arm off its spindle **(see illustration)**. If necessary, the arm can be levered off the spindle using a suitable flat-bladed screwdriver. If both windscreen wiper arms are removed, note their locations, as different arms are fitted to the driver's and passenger's sides.

Refitting
4 Refitting is a reversal of removal, but ensure that the wiper arm and spindle splines are clean and dry and align the blades with the tape fitted before tightening the spindle nut.

Tailgate wiper arm
Removal
5 Operate the tailgate wiper motor, and then switch it off so that the wiper arm returns to the 'parked' position.
6 Stick a piece of tape on the windscreen, along the edge of the wiper blade, to use as an alignment aid on refitting.
7 Lift and unclip the plastic cover, then unscrew the spindle nut **(see illustration)**.
8 Lift the blade off the glass and pull the wiper arm off its spindle **(see illustration)**. If necessary, the arm can be levered off the spindle using a suitable flat-bladed screwdriver.

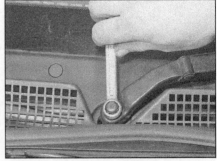
19.3 Unscrewing the spindle nut from the windscreen wiper arm

Refitting

9 Refitting is a reversal of removal, but ensure that the wiper arm and spindle splines are clean and dry and align the blade with the tape fitted before tightening the spindle nut to the specified torque.

20 Windscreen wiper motor and linkage – removal and refitting

Removal

1 Remove both wiper arms as described in Section 19. For improved access, temporarily unbolt the cooling system expansion tank and position it away from the bulkhead – **do not** disconnect the hoses from it **(see illustration)**.

2 With the bonnet open, remove the fasteners

19.7 Undo the spindle nut . . .

19.8 . . . and remove the tailgate wiper arm

securing the scuttle cover in front of the windscreen. The rear fasteners are removed by prising up their centre discs then lifting them out. To remove the front fasteners use a pair of pliers to squeeze the bottom tabs, then

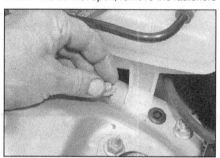

20.1 Temporarily unbolt the cooling system expansion tank and position it away from the bulkhead

20.2a Removing the scuttle cover rear fasteners

push them up through the holes. If necessary, release the weatherstrip from the fasteners **(see illustrations)**.

3 Release the outer ends of the scuttle cover from the bonnet hinges on each side, and withdraw it from the car **(see illustration)**. To aid releasing the scuttle cover end rubbers, have an assistant temporarily hold the bonnet semi-closed.

4 Disconnect the wiring multiplug from the wiper motor **(see illustration)**.

5 Unscrew the mounting bolts and withdraw the wiper motor and linkage from the bulkhead **(see illustrations)**.

6 Release the multiplug from the linkage, then unbolt and remove the motor **(see illustration)**.

Refitting

7 Refitting is a reversal of removal, but tighten the mounting bolts to the specified torque.

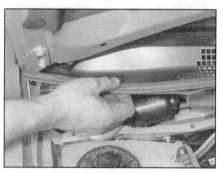

20.2b The scuttle cover front fasteners are removed by squeezing the bottom tabs

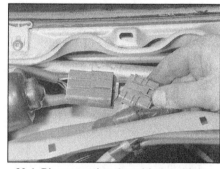

20.3 Removing the scuttle cover

20.5a Unscrew the mounting bolts . . .

20.5b . . . and remove the wiper motor and linkage from the bulkhead

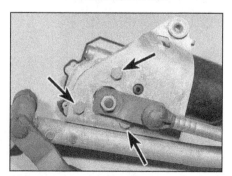

20.6 Bolts securing the motor to the wiper linkage

20.4 Disconnecting the wiring multiplug from the wiper motor

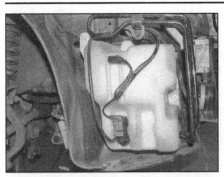

21.1 Washer reservoir location – bumper removed

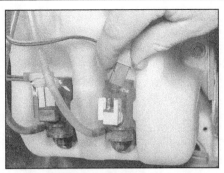

21.3a Disconnecting the windscreen washer pump wiring . . .

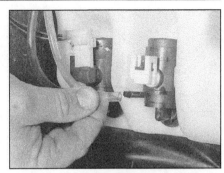

21.3b . . . and tubing from the pump

21 Windscreen/tailgate washer system components – removal and refitting

1 The windscreen washer reservoir is situated beneath the right-hand (RHD) or left-hand (LHD) wheel arch (see illustration) with its filler neck protruding into the engine compartment. The washer system pump is mounted on the side of the reservoir. On Hatchback models, the reservoir is also used to supply the tailgate washer system via a second pump.

Windscreen washer reservoir

Removal

2 Remove the appropriate headlamp as described in Section 7. This procedure includes the removal of the front bumper.
3 Disconnect the wiring connector(s) and plastic tubing from the pump(s) (see illustrations).
4 Unscrew the mounting bolts and withdraw the reservoir from the front valance (see illustration).
5 Empty the washer fluid from the reservoir.
6 Remove the pumps as described later in this Section.

Refitting

7 Refitting is a reversal of removal. Ensure that the washer tubes are not trapped when refitting the reservoir and note that the connectors for the pumps are colour-coded to aid correct reconnection on reassembly. Refill

the reservoir with the correct washer solution on completion.

Pump

Removal

8 Carry out the procedure given in paragraphs 2 and 3 earlier in this Section.
9 Carefully ease the pump from the rubber grommet using a twisting action (see illustration).
10 Use a screwdriver to prise the grommet from the reservoir (see illustration).

Refitting

11 Refitting is a reversal of removal.

 HAYNES HiNT *Apply a little lubricant (such as washing-up liquid) to the rubber grommet to help it locate in the reservoir.*

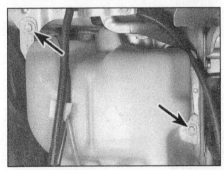

21.4 Windscreen washer reservoir mounting bolts

Windscreen washer jet

Removal

12 Open the bonnet and disconnect the plastic tube from the bottom of the jet.
13 Using pliers, squeeze together the tabs and release the jet from the bonnet. Recover the gasket (see illustrations).

Refitting

14 Refitting is a reversal of removal. On completion operate the washers and check that the jet is directed to the top of the screen. If necessary, use a pin or suitable instrument to adjust the jet.

Tailgate washer jet

Removal

15 The washer jet is located at the top of the tailgate, and is retained with a tab located

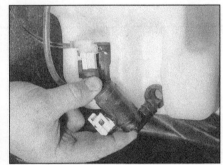

21.9 Removing the pump . . .

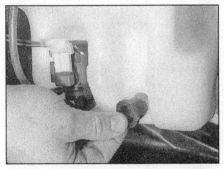

21.10 . . . and grommet from the washer reservoir

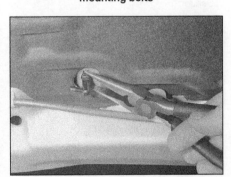

21.13a Squeeze together the tabs . . .

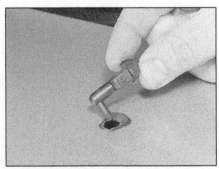

21.13b . . . and remove the windscreen washer jet from the bonnet

22.2 Removing the rubber cap from the tailgate wiper motor drive spindle

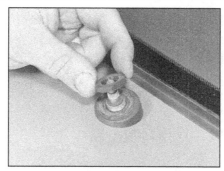

22.4a Unscrew the spindle nut . . .

22.4b . . . and remove the flat washer and rubber seal

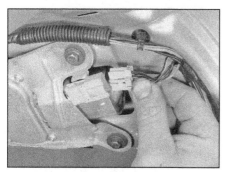

22.5 Disconnect the wiring . . .

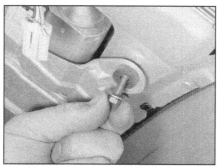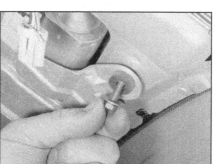

22.6a . . . then unscrew the mounting bolts . . .

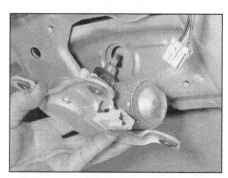

22.6b . . . and remove the tailgate wiper motor

directly below the jet position (ie, the bottom rear face).

16 Taking care not to damage the paintwork, use a thin screwdriver or similar tool to depress the tab, and then release the jet from the tailgate.

23.2a Withdraw the audio unit from the facia . . .

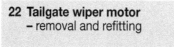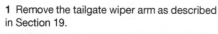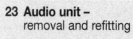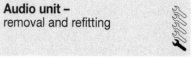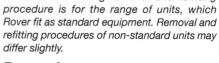

23.2b . . . then disconnect the wiring plugs . . .

23.2c . . . and aerial lead

17 Pull out the plastic tubing only far enough to disconnect it from the jet. **Do not** pull it out further otherwise the tubing may be damaged. If necessary, use a clip to prevent the tubing falling back into the tailgate.

Refitting

18 Refitting is a reversal of removal. On completion, operate the washers and check that the jet is directed to the top of the screen. If necessary, use a pin or suitable instrument to adjust the jet.

22 Tailgate wiper motor – removal and refitting

Removal

1 Remove the tailgate wiper arm as described in Section 19.

2 Remove the rubber spindle cap **(see illustration)**.

3 Remove the interior trim from the tailgate with reference to Chapter 11, Section 28.

4 Unscrew the spindle nut and remove the flat washer and rubber seal **(see illustrations)**.

5 Disconnect the wiring multiplug from the wiper motor **(see illustration)**.

6 Unscrew the mounting bolts and withdraw the wiper motor from the tailgate **(see illustrations)**.

Refitting

7 Refitting is a reversal of removal, but tighten all nuts and bolts to the specified torque.

23 Audio unit – removal and refitting

Note: *The following removal and refitting procedure is for the range of units, which Rover fit as standard equipment. Removal and refitting procedures of non-standard units may differ slightly.*

Removal

1 Disconnect the battery negative (earth) lead (see *Disconnecting the battery*). Switch off the ignition and remove the ignition key.

2 To remove the unit, two standard DIN extraction tools are required. These are two U-shaped rods, which are inserted into the four small holes in the front of the unit to release the unit retaining clips. The tools may be obtained from a Rover dealer or any audio accessory

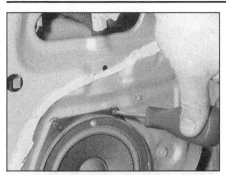

24.1a Undo the front speaker retaining screws . . .

24.1b . . . withdraw the speaker . . .

24.1c . . . and disconnect the wiring

24.5 Remove the parcel tray support . . .

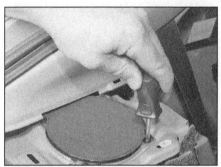

24.6a . . . then undo the screws . . .

24.6b . . . and disconnect the wiring from the rear speaker

outlet, or can be made out of 3.0 mm wire rod, such as welding rod. Using the tools, push back the clamps on the left and right-hand sides of the audio unit, then withdraw the unit and disconnect the wiring plugs and aerial **(see illustrations)**.

Refitting

3 Refitting is the reverse of the removal procedure. On completion, connect the battery negative lead and reactivate the security code.

24 Speakers –
removal and refitting

Front speaker

Removal

1 To remove a main speaker, remove the front door inner trim panel as described in Chapter 11, then undo the speaker retaining screws. Disconnect the speaker wiring connectors and remove the speaker from the door **(see illustrations)**.

2 To remove a tweeter, remove the door inner trim panel as described in Chapter 11, then carefully prise off the triangular panel at the front of the window aperture. Disconnect the wiring at the plug and release the wiring from the clips.

Refitting

3 Refitting is a reversal of removal.

Rear speaker (Hatchback)

Removal

4 Open the tailgate then unhook the straps and remove the rear parcel shelf.
5 Undo the screws then unclip the parcel tray support from the side of the luggage compartment **(see illustration)**.
6 Undo the screws and withdraw the speaker from its mounting, then disconnect the wiring **(see illustrations)**.

Refitting

7 Refitting is a reversal of removal.

Rear speaker (Saloon)

Removal

8 Open the boot lid. Reach under the rear shelf and disconnect the wiring from the rear speaker.
9 Unscrew the nuts securing the speaker to the rear shelf.
10 Inside the passenger compartment, withdraw the speaker.

Refitting

11 Refitting is a reversal of removal.

25 Radio aerial –
removal and refitting

Removal

1 Prise the lens from the interior light located at the front of the headlining.

2 Unscrew and remove the screws and withdraw the light assembly.
3 Unscrew the nut and disconnect the lead from the aerial **(see illustration)**.
4 Unscrew the mounting nuts and remove the aerial from the roof.
5 Removal of the aerial lead involves removal of the audio unit as described in Section 23, together with removal of interior trim.

Refitting

6 Refitting is a reversal of removal.

26 Cruise control system
– general

1 The cruise control system is a vacuum-operated system; the main components being a vacuum actuator unit mounted near

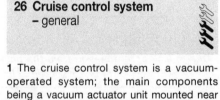

25.3 Aerial lead (arrowed) and aerial mounting nuts (shown with interior light removed)

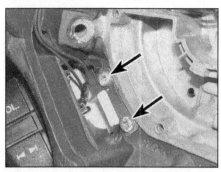

26.12 Remove the two screws (arrowed)

26.23 Removing the air intake hose

the throttle housing, a vacuum control unit located under the battery mounting bracket, a control relay and ECU located on the side of the passenger footwell, a main switch located on the instrument panel surround, and a set/resume switch located on the steering wheel.

Interface ECU

Removal

2 Disconnect the battery negative (earth) lead (see *Disconnecting the battery*).
3 Inside the car remove the side trim panel from the passenger's (left-hand) footwell.
4 Unscrew the ECU mounting nuts, then disconnect the wiring multiplug and remove the ECU.

Refitting

5 Refitting is a reversal of removal.

Cruise control ECU

Removal

6 Disconnect the battery negative (earth) lead (see *Disconnecting the battery*).
7 Working inside the passenger's footwell, disconnect the wiring connector from the ECU

on the left-hand side of the heater unit housing (to the left-hand side of the centre console).
8 Undo the two retaining bolts and remove the ECU from the passenger's side foowell.

Refitting

9 Refitting is a reversal of removal.

Steering wheel switches

Removal

10 Remove the airbag module from the steering wheel as described in Section 16.
11 Remove the horn push switches from the steering wheel.
12 Undo the screws and disconnect the wiring then remove the set/resume switch **(see illustration)**.

Refitting

13 Refitting is a reversal of removal.

Cruise control main switch

Removal

14 Carefully prise the switch from the instrument surround using a small screwdriver.

15 Disconnect the wiring multiplug and remove the switch.

Refitting

16 Refitting is a reversal of removal.

Vacuum control unit

Removal

17 Remove the battery as described in Chapter 5A.
18 Disconnect the multiplug from the cruise control vacuum control unit.
19 Disconnect the vacuum hose and release the control unit from the three rubber mountings on the battery tray mounting bracket.
20 If necessary, remove the rubber mountings from the mounting bracket and refit them to the control unit. Apply a soapy solution to help the fitment of the rubber mountings to the control unit.

Refitting

21 Refitting is a reversal of removal.

Cruise control actuator unit

Removal

22 Disconnect the battery negative (earth) lead (see *Disconnecting the battery*).
23 Slacken the securing clips and remove the air intake hose from the air filter housing and the throttle housing **(see illustration)**.
24 Disconnect the actuator pullrod from the lever on the throttle housing.
25 Disconnect the vacuum hose from the actuator unit.
26 Unscrew the mounting nut and remove the actuator unit from the engine compartment.

Refitting

27 Refitting is a reversal of removal.

Wiring diagrams

Due to lack of information from the manufacturer, wiring diagrams are not available to cover the modified electrical systems introduced with the April 2004 facelift. The following diagrams cover only 1999 to early 2004 models.

Rover 45/MG ZS wiring diagrams

Diagram 1

Key to symbols

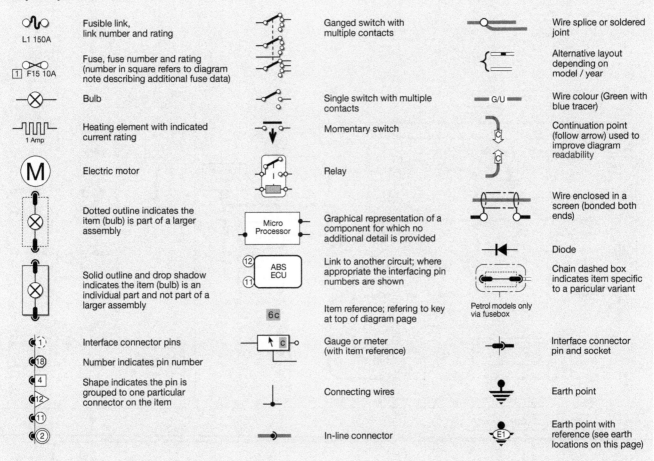

L1 150A	Fusible link, link number and rating
☐1 F15 10A	Fuse, fuse number and rating (number in square refers to diagram note describing additional fuse data)
—⊗—	Bulb
⊓⊔⊓⊔ 1 Amp	Heating element with indicated current rating
(M)	Electric motor
⊗	Dotted outline indicates the item (bulb) is part of a larger assembly
⊗	Solid outline and drop shadow indicates the item (bulb) is an individual part and not part of a larger assembly
①	Interface connector pins
⑱	Number indicates pin number
④	Shape indicates the pin is grouped to one particular connector on the item
⑫	
⑪	
②	

	Ganged switch with multiple contacts
	Single switch with multiple contacts
	Momentary switch
	Relay
Micro Processor	Graphical representation of a component for which no additional detail is provided
12 ABS ECU 11	Link to another circuit; where appropriate the interfacing pin numbers are shown
6c	Item reference; refering to key at top of diagram page
↖ c	Gauge or meter (with item reference)
	Connecting wires
	In-line connector

	Wire splice or soldered joint
	Alternative layout depending on model / year
— G/U —	Wire colour (Green with blue tracer)
C	Continuation point (follow arrow) used to improve diagram readability
	Wire enclosed in a screen (bonded both ends)
⊢◁—	Diode
Petrol models only via fusebox	Chain dashed box indicates item specific to a pariular variant
	Interface connector pin and socket
	Earth point
E1	Earth point with reference (see earth locations on this page)

Key to circuits

Diagram 1	Information on wiring diagrams.	Diagram 8	Fuel pump and gauge, supplementary restraint system.
Diagram 2	Starting and charging, cigar lighter.	Diagram 9	Anti-lock braking system (ABS), powered sunroof.
Diagram 3	Cooling fan, horns, clock, head, side, tail and number plate lights.	Diagram 10	Electric windows, folding electric door mirrors.
Diagram 4	Stop and reversing lights, fog lamps.	Diagram 11	Parking distance control (PDC), centralised door locking.
Diagram 5	Headlight levelling, directional indicators, lights on alarm.	Diagram 12	Audio system (in car entertainment ICE).
Diagram 6	Heater blower, interior illumination, heated rear screen.	Diagram 13	Instrumentation
Diagram 7	Headlight power wash, front / rear wash wipe, diagnostic socket.	Diagram 14	Engine and passenger fuse box details

Earth locations

E2	LH front of engine compartment.		E5	RH front of engine compartment.
E3	LH front of engine compartment.		E9	Top of engine, centre rear.
E10	Under engine compartment fusebox.		E12	RH rear of engine compartment under coolant expansion tank.
E14	Beneath LH seat.		E1	Base of RH 'A' post inside passenger compartment.
E11	Rear of headlining.		E13	Beneath RH seat.
E7	Behind LH rear trim panel.		E6	Behind RH rear trim panel.
E8	RH side of tail door behind trim panel.		E4	Behind luggage compartment carpet on RH side.

H33418

Wire colours

B	Black	P	Purple
G	Green	R	Red
K	Pink	S	Grey
Lg	Light green	U	Blue
N	Brown	W	White
O	Orange	Y	Yellow

Key to items

1 Battery
2 Ignition switch
3 Starter motor
4 Alternator
5 Passenger compartment fusebox
6 Engine compartment fusebox
  a = R100 main relay
7 R102 starter relay
8 R114 glow plug relay

9 Cigar lighter

Diagram 2

H33419

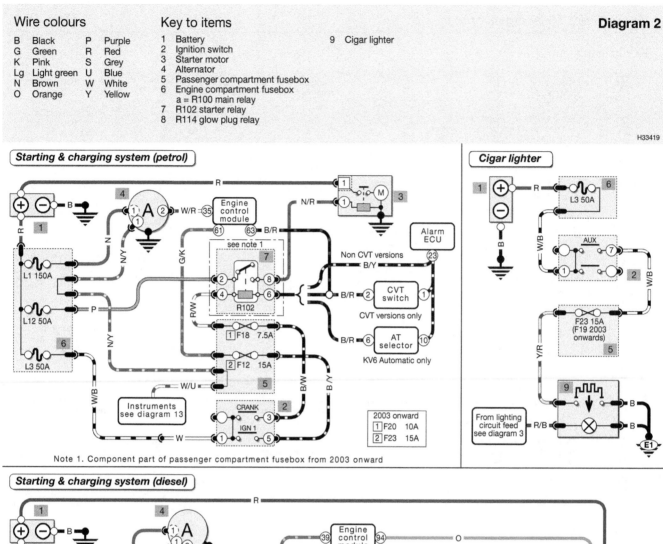

Note 1. Component part of passenger compartment fusebox from 2003 onward

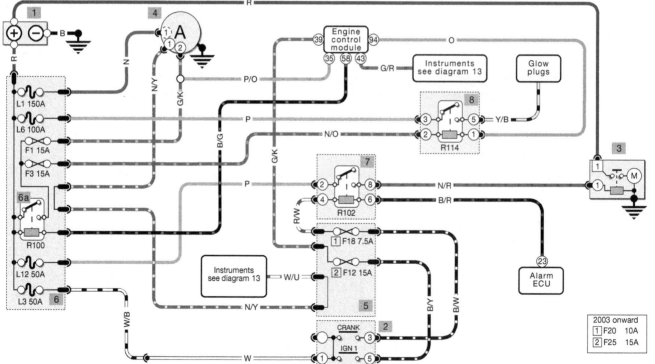

Wire colours

B	Black	P	Purple
G	Green	R	Red
K	Pink	S	Grey
Lg	Light green	U	Blue
N	Brown	W	White
O	Orange	Y	Yellow

Key to items

1 Battery
2 Ignition switch
5 Passenger compartment fuse box
6 Engine compartment fuse box
   a = R100 main relay
5 Horn switch (LH)
10 R133 horn relay
11 Horn switch
12 Rotary coupler
13 Horn
14 Cooling fan motor

15 R117 cooling fan relay
16 Clock module
17 Light switch
18 RH headlamp
   a = main
   b = dip
   c = side
19 LH headlamp
   a = main
   b = dip
   c = side

20 RH tail lamp cluster
   a = tail lamp
21 LH tail lamp cluster
   a = tail lamp
22 RH numberplate light
23 LH numberplate light

Diagram 3

H33420

Cooling fans

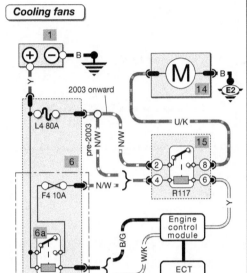

Horns

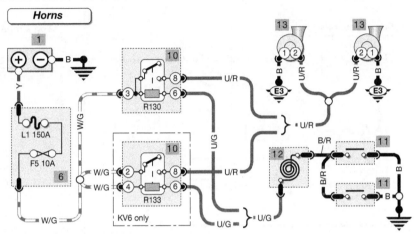

Head, side, tail & number plate lights

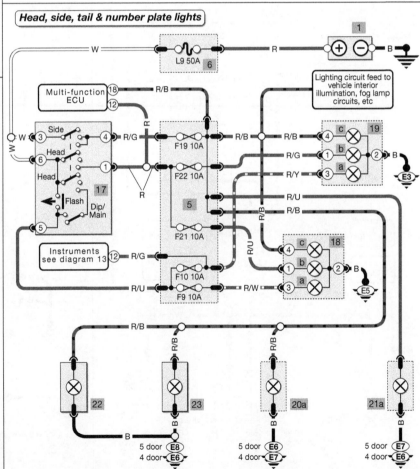

Clock

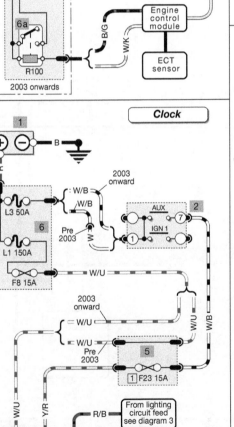

Wire colours

B	Black	P	Purple
G	Green	R	Red
K	Pink	S	Grey
Lg	Light green	U	Blue
N	Brown	W	White
O	Orange	Y	Yellow

Key to items

1 Battery
2 Ignition switch
5 Passenger compartment fuse box
  a = R217 reversing relay
6 Engine compartment fuse box
  e = R130 fog light relay
20 RH Tail lamp cluster
  b = brake light
  c = fog light
  e = reversing light

21 LH Tail lamp cluster
  b = brake light
  c = fog light
  e = reversing light
28 Brake pedal switch
29 High level brake light
30 RH front fog lamp
31 LH front fog lamp
32 Fog lamp switch
33 Reversing lamp switch
34 R217 reversing lamp relay

Diagram 4

H33421

Stop & reversing lights

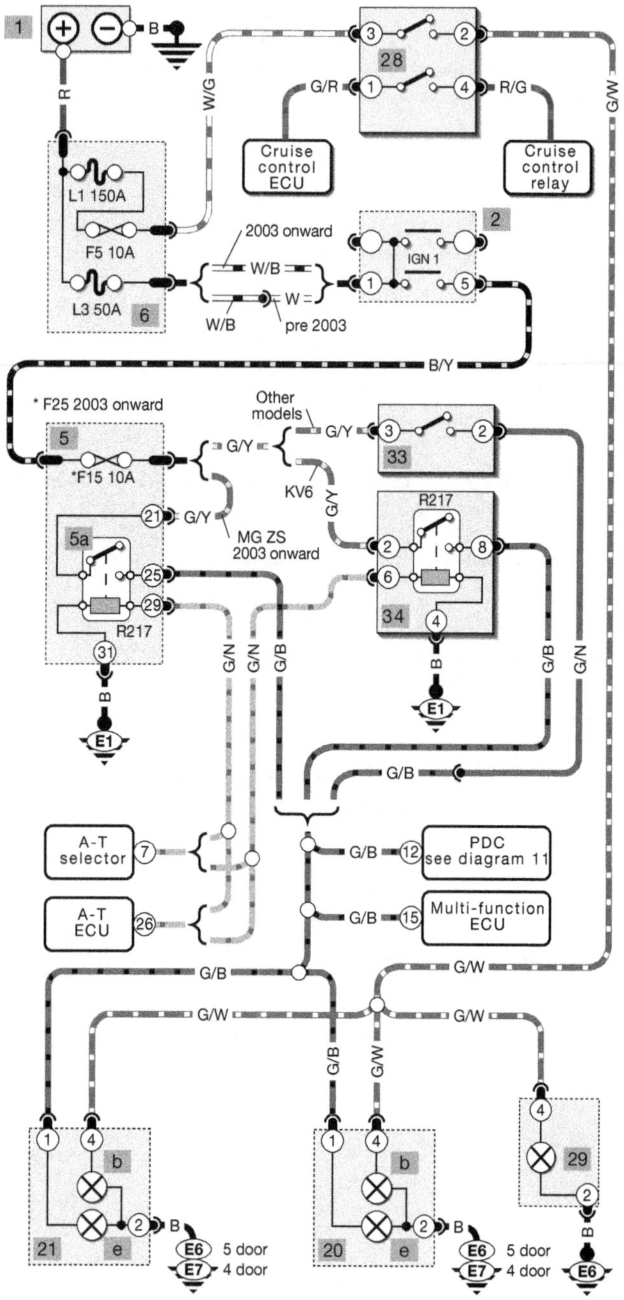

Fog lamps

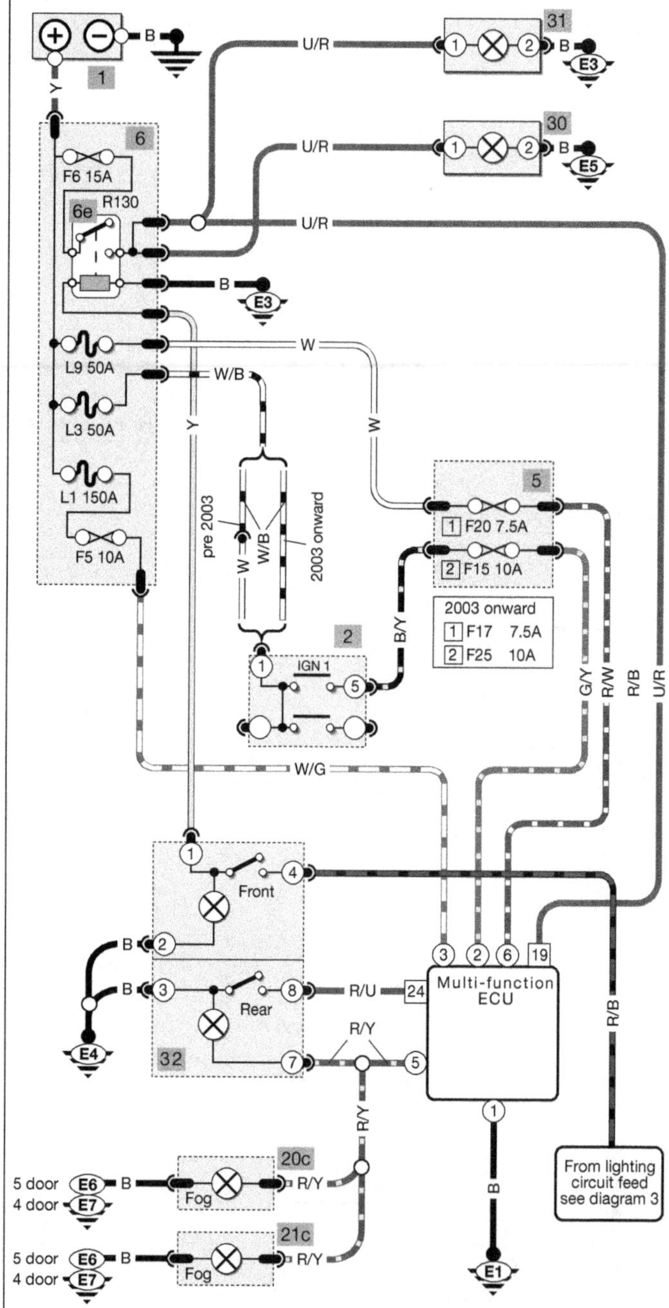

Wire colours

B	Black	P	Purple
G	Green	R	Red
K	Pink	S	Grey
Lg	Light green	U	Blue
N	Brown	W	White
O	Orange	Y	Yellow

Key to items

1 Battery
2 Ignition switch
5 Passenger compartment fuse box
   b = R141 hazard warning relay
6 Engine compartment fuse box
18 RH headlamp cluster
   d = RH front indicator
19 LH headlamp cluster
   d = LH front indicator

20 RH tail lamp cluster
   d = RH rear indicator
21 LH tail lamp cluster
   d = LH rear indicator
24 RH direction indicator
   repeater
25 LH direction indicator
   repeater
36 Inline fuse (F15)

37 Headlamp leveling switch
38 RH headlamp leveling motor
39 LH headlamp leveling motor
42 R141 hazard warning relay
44 Direction indicator switch
50 RH front door switch

Diagram 5

H33422

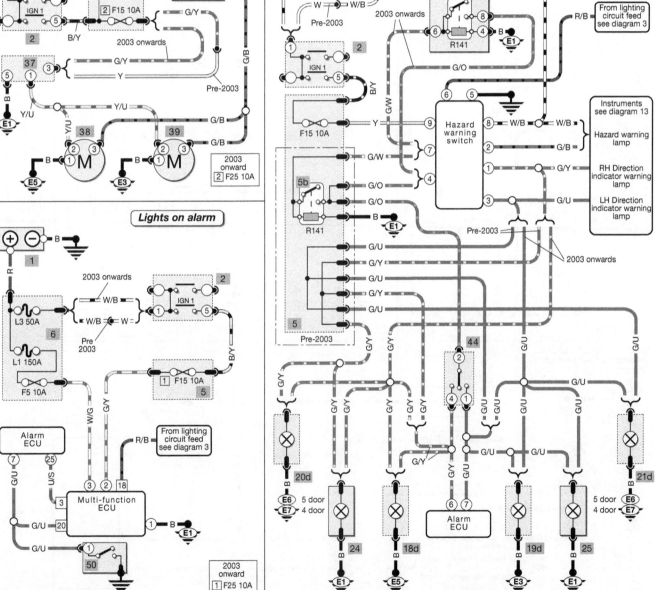

Headlight leveling

Lights on alarm

Directional indicators and hazard warning lights

Wire colours

B	Black	P	Purple
G	Green	R	Red
K	Pink	S	Grey
Lg	Light green	U	Blue
N	Brown	W	White
O	Orange	Y	Yellow

Key to items

1 Battery
2 Ignition switch
5 Passenger compartment fuse box
6 Engine compartment fuse box
   b = R176 blower relay
   c = R136 heated rear window relay
45 Glove box light
46 Interior light
47 Luggage compartment light
48 Boot / tailgate light switch
49 Inline diode
50 Door switch RH front
51 Door switch LH front
52 Door switch RH rear
53 Door switch LH rear
55 Fresh / recirculated air switch
56 Air mode motor (fresh/recirculate)
57 Inline diode
58 Blower motor switch
59 Resistor pack
60 Blower motor
62 Rear screen heater switch
63 Rear screen heater element

Diagram 6

H33423

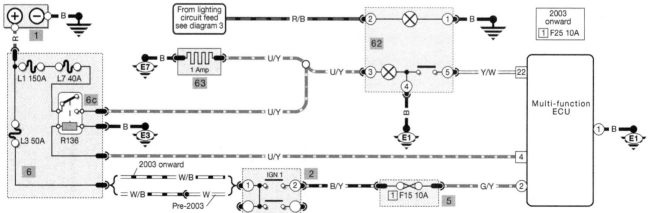

Wire colours

B	Black	P	Purple
G	Green	R	Red
K	Pink	S	Grey
Lg	Light green	U	Blue
N	Brown	W	White
O	Orange	Y	Yellow

Key to items

1 Battery
2 Ignition switch
5 Passenger compartmant fuse box
   c = R137 rear wiper relay
   d = R139 power wash relay
6 Passenger compartment fuse box
33 Reversing lamp switch
65 R137 rear wiper relay
66 Rear screen wiper motor
67 Rear screen wash / wipe switch

68 Rear screen washer pump
69 Windscreen washer pump
70 Windscreen wiper motor
71 Windscreen wash / wipe switch
72 Inline fuse (F27)
74 R139 headlight power wash relay
75 Inline fuse (F26)
76 Power wash pump
78 Diagnostic socket

Diagram 7

H33424

Headlight power wash

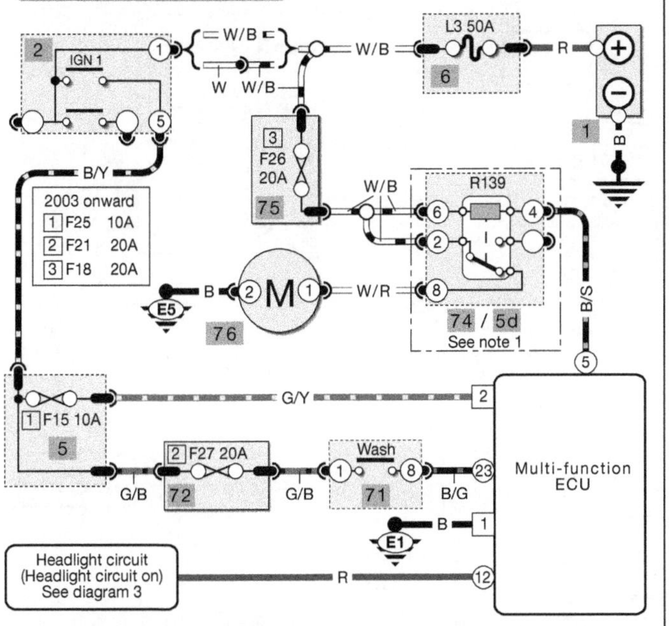

2003 onward
1 F25 10A
2 F21 20A
3 F18 20A

1 F15 10A

2 F27 20A

Headlight circuit
(Headlight circuit on)
See diagram 3

Multi-function ECU

Note 1. Component part of passenger compartment fusebox from 2003 onward

Front / rear wash wipe

2003 onward
1 F13 10A
2 F17 7.5A
3 F21 20A

1 F15 10A
2 F13 15A

3 F27 20A

Reverse relay (R217)
See note 1

Multi-function ECU

5 door
4 door

Note 1. Component part of passenger compartment fusebox from 2003 onward

Diagnostic socket

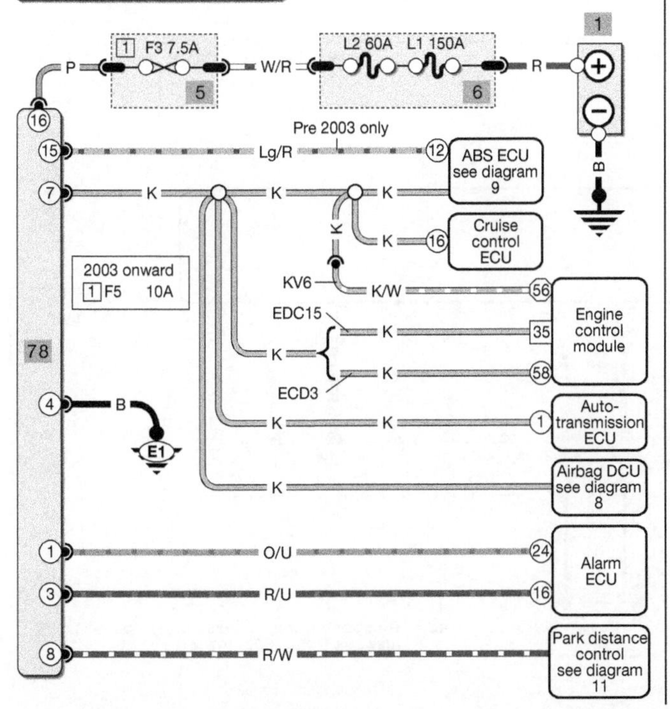

1 F3 7.5A

2003 onward
1 F5 10A

Pre 2003 only

ABS ECU
see diagram 9

Cruise control ECU

Engine control module

Auto-transmission ECU

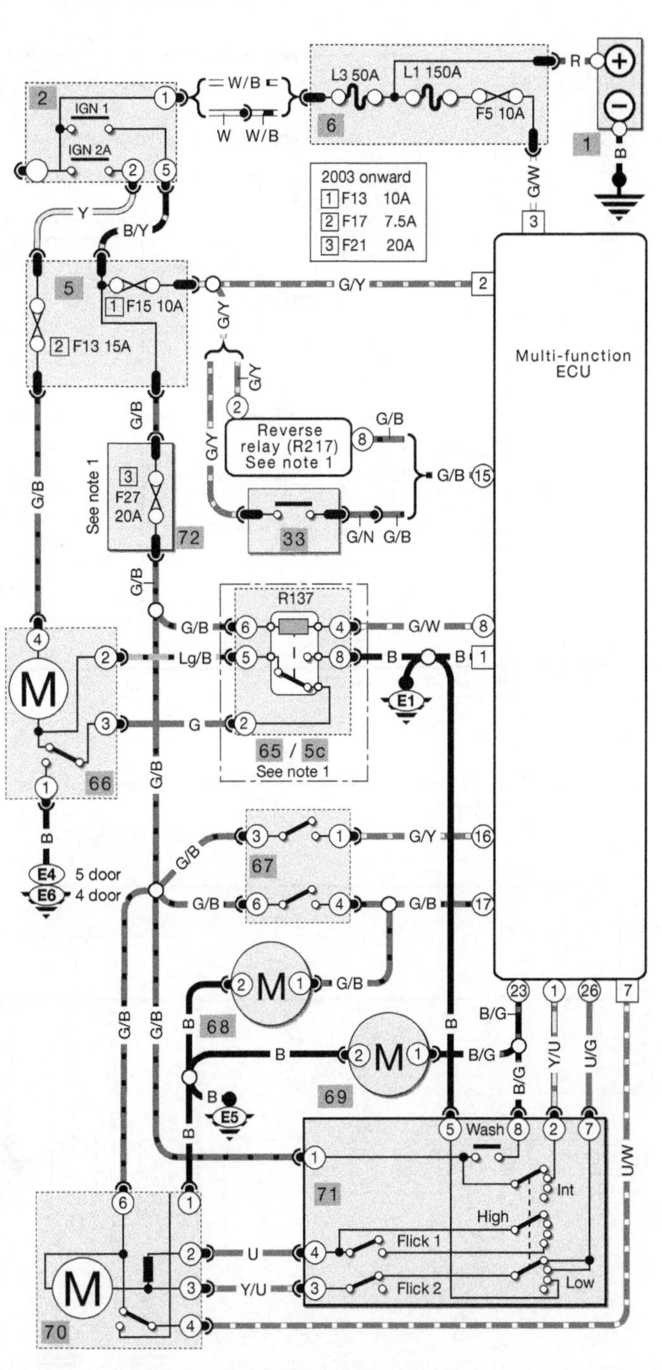

Airbag DCU
see diagram 8

Alarm ECU

Park distance control
see diagram 11

Wash
Int
High
Flick 1
Flick 2
Low

Wire colours

B	Black	P	Purple
G	Green	R	Red
K	Pink	S	Grey
Lg	Light green	U	Blue
N	Brown	W	White
O	Orange	Y	Yellow

Key to items

1 Battery
2 Ignition switch
5 Passenger compartmant fuse box
6 Engine compartment fuse box
  a = R100 main relay
  d = R103 fuel pump relay
12 Rotary coupler
80 Collision cutout switch
81 Fuel pump (diesel)
82 Fuel tank unit

84 Inline fuse (F25)
85 Drivers side airbag sensor
86 Passenger side airbag sensor
87 Drivers airbag
88 Passenger airbag
89 Side airbag RH
90 Side airbag LH
91 RH seatbelt pre-tensioner
92 LH seatbelt pre-tensioner

Diagram 8

H33425

Fuel pump and gauge

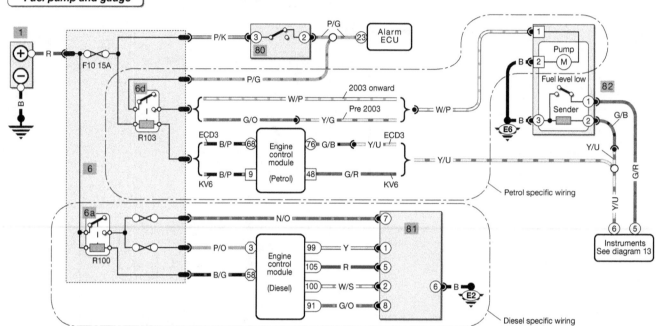

Supplementary restraint system

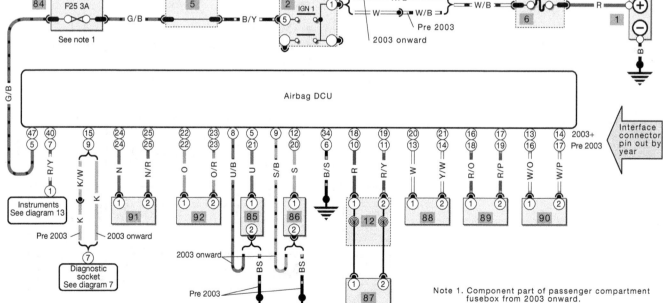

Note 1. Component part of passenger compartment fusebox from 2003 onward.

Wire colours

B Black
G Green
K Pink
Lg Light green
N Brown
O Orange
P Purple
R Red
S Grey
U Blue
W White
Y Yellow

Key to items

1   Battery
2   Ignition switch
5   Passenger compartment fuse box
    e = R143 window lift relay
6   Engine compartment fuse box
28 Brake pedal switch
94 ABS ECU
95 RH front ABS sensor
96 LH front ABS sensor
97 RH rear ABS sensor
98 LH rear ABS sensor
100 Sunroof motor
101 Sunroof switch
102 R164 sunroof open relay
103 R165 sunroof close relay

Diagram 9

H33426

Anti-lock braking system

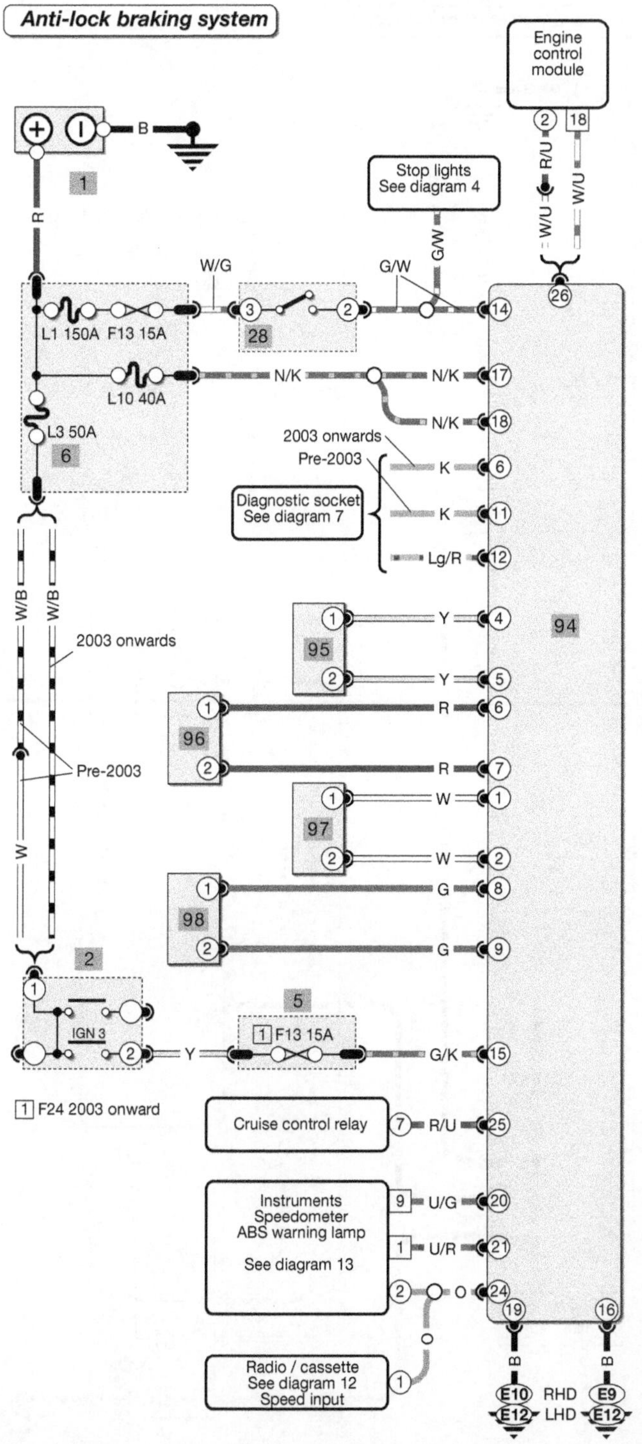

Engine control module

Stop lights
See diagram 4

L1 150A F13 15A
28
L10 40A N/K
L3 50A
6

2003 onwards
Pre-2003

Diagnostic socket
See diagram 7

95
96
97
98

2
1 F24 2003 onward
IGN 3
5
1 F13 15A

Cruise control relay

Instruments
Speedometer
ABS warning lamp
See diagram 13

Radio / cassette
See diagram 12
Speed input

94

E10 RHD E9
E12 LHD E12

Powered sunroof

2003 onward
1 F7 30A
2 F4 20A
3 F17 10A

L1 150A
L2 60A
L9 50A
6

1 F1 30A
2 F7 20A
5e
R143
5
3 F20 7.5A

Multi-function ECU

CLOSE
OPEN
TILT
101

Tlit1
Tlit2
100
M

R165
103
R164
102

E11

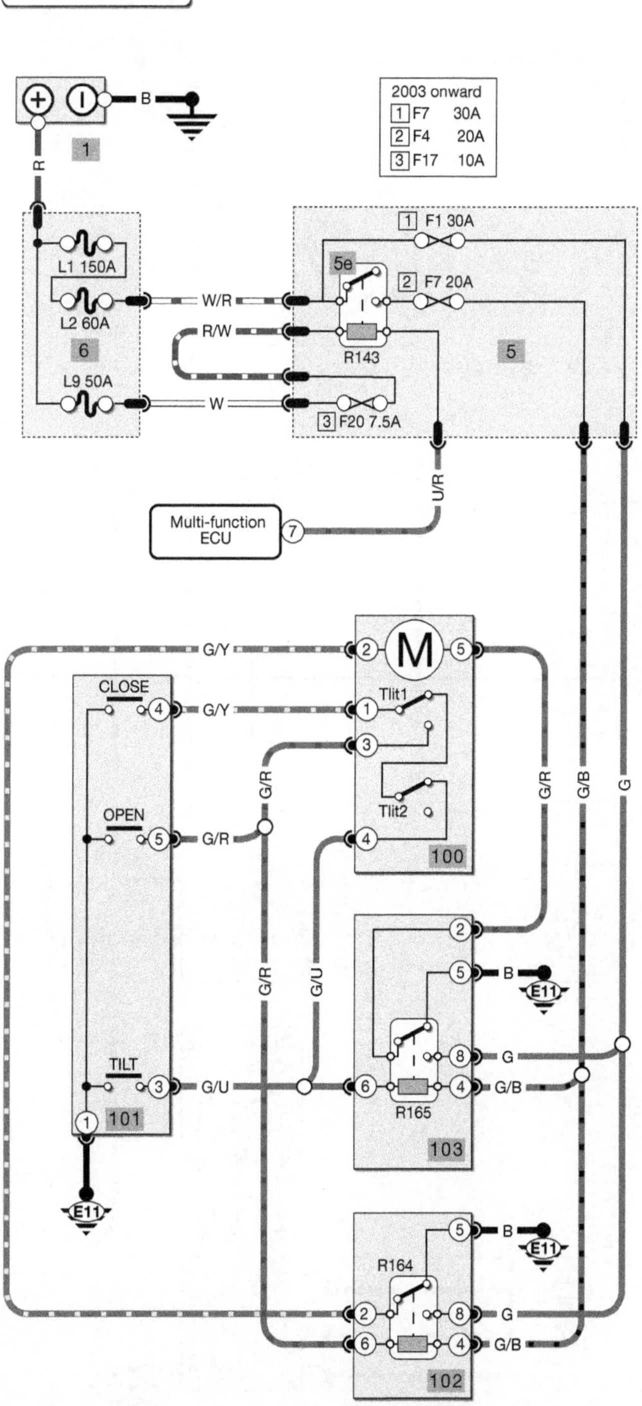

Wire colours

B	Black	P	Purple
G	Green	R	Red
K	Pink	S	Grey
Lg	Light green	U	Blue
N	Brown	W	White
O	Orange	Y	Yellow

Key to items

1   Battery
2   Ignition switch
5   Passenger compartmant fuse box
    e = R143 window lift relay
6   Engine compartment fuse box
105 Window lift ECU
106 RH front window switch
107 LH front window switch
108 RH front window motor
109 LH front window motor
111 RH door mirror folding motor
112 LH door mirror folding motor
113 RH door mirror (position motor & heater)
114 LH door mirror (position motor & heater)
115 Folding mirror ECU
116 Mirror switch

Diagram 10

H33427

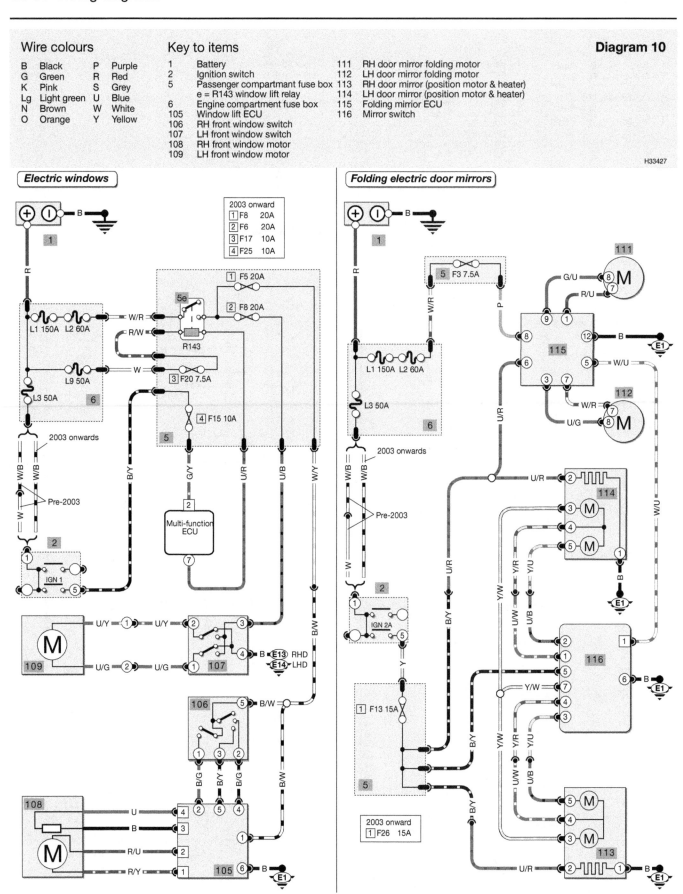

Electric windows

Folding electric door mirrors

Wire colours

B	Black	P	Purple
G	Green	R	Red
K	Pink	S	Grey
Lg	Light green	U	Blue
N	Brown	W	White
O	Orange	Y	Yellow

Key to items

1   Battery
2   Ignition switch
5   Passenger compartmant fuse box
6   Engine compartment fuse box
118   Park distance controller
119   LH outer ultrasonic transducer
120   LH inner ultrasonic transducer
121   RH inner ultrasonic transducer
122   RH outer ultrasonic transducer

125   RH barrel lock
126   RH front door motorised lock
127   RH rear door motorised lock
128   LH front door motorised lock
129   LH rear door motorised lock

Diagram 11

H33428

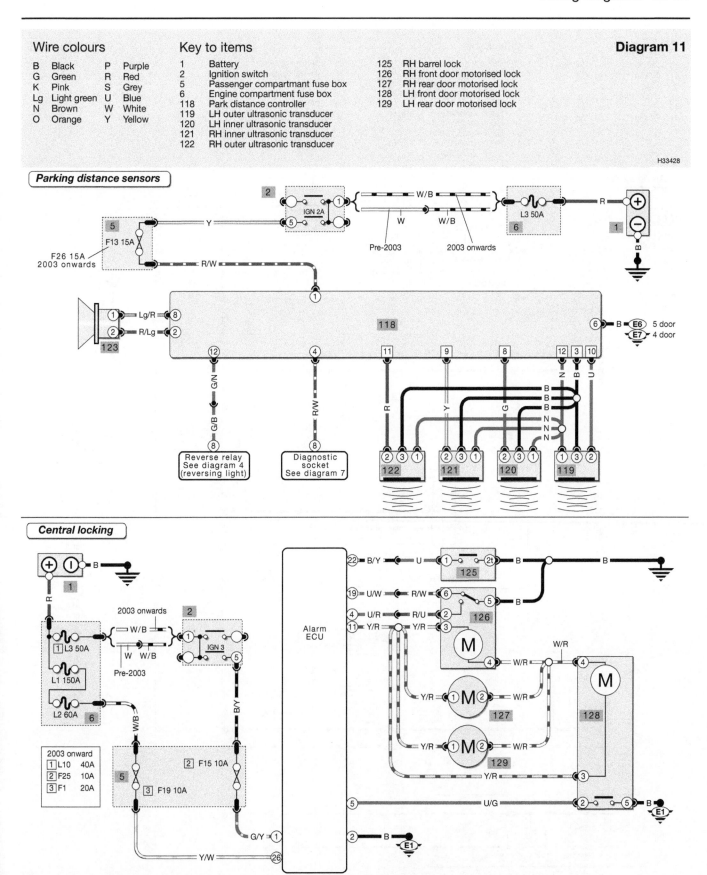

Parking distance sensors

Central locking

Wire colours

B	Black	P	Purple
G	Green	R	Red
K	Pink	S	Grey
Lg	Light green	U	Blue
N	Brown	W	White
O	Orange	Y	Yellow

Key to items

1	Battery
2	Ignition switch
5	Passenger compartment fuse box
6	Engine compartment fuse box
12	Rotary coupler
131	Radio / cassette / CD player
132	CD auto-changer
133	ICE remote switch
134	RH front speaker
135	LH front speaker
136	RH rear speaker
137	LH rear speaker
138	RH front tweeter
139	LH front tweeter

Diagram 12

H33429

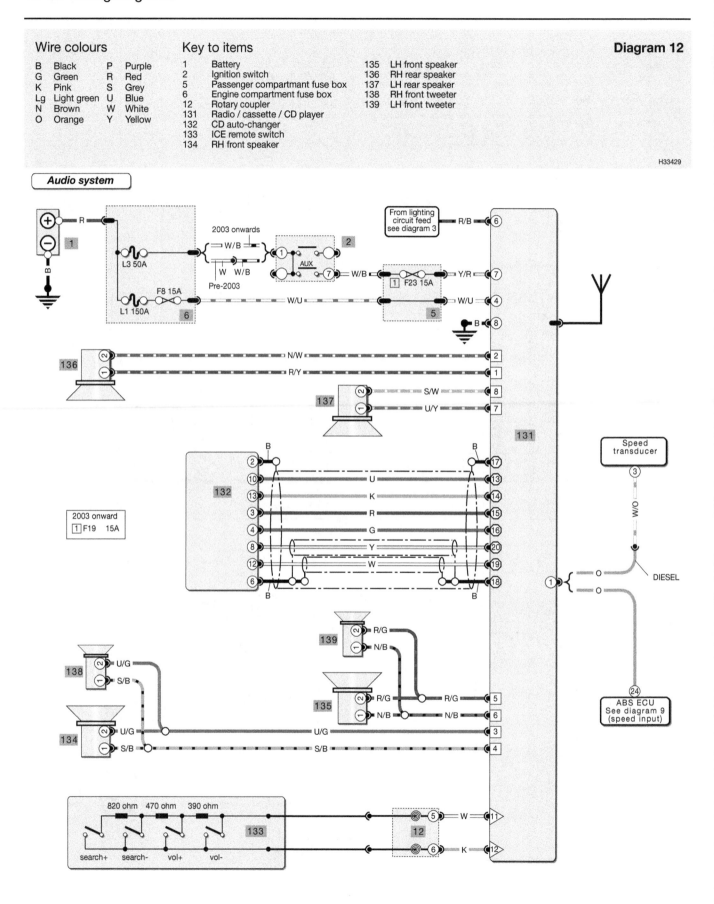

Audio system

Wire colours

B	Black	P	Purple
G	Green	R	Red
K	Pink	S	Grey
Lg	Light green	U	Blue
N	Brown	W	White
O	Orange	Y	Yellow

Key to items

1 Battery
2 Ignition switch
5 Passenger compartmant fuse box
6 Engine compartment fuse box
141 Handbrake switch
142 Brake fluid level switch
143 Instrument cluster
  a fuel gauge
  b speedometer
  c coolant temperature gauge
  d tachometer
e low fuel warning lamp

f oil pressure warning lamp
g main beam warning lamp
h anti-theft alarm LED
i engine management warning lamp
j ignition / no charge warning lamp
k LH direction indicator warning lamp
l RH direction indicator warning lamp
m hazard warning lamp
n cruise control warning lamp
p glow plug warning lamp

q handbrake / low brake fluid warning lamp
r door open warning lamp
s luggage compartment warning lamp
t SRS warning lamp
u engine management warning lamp
v ABS warning lamp
w transmission oil warning lamp
x sport mode warning lamp
z instrument illumination

Diagram 13

H33430

Instrumentation

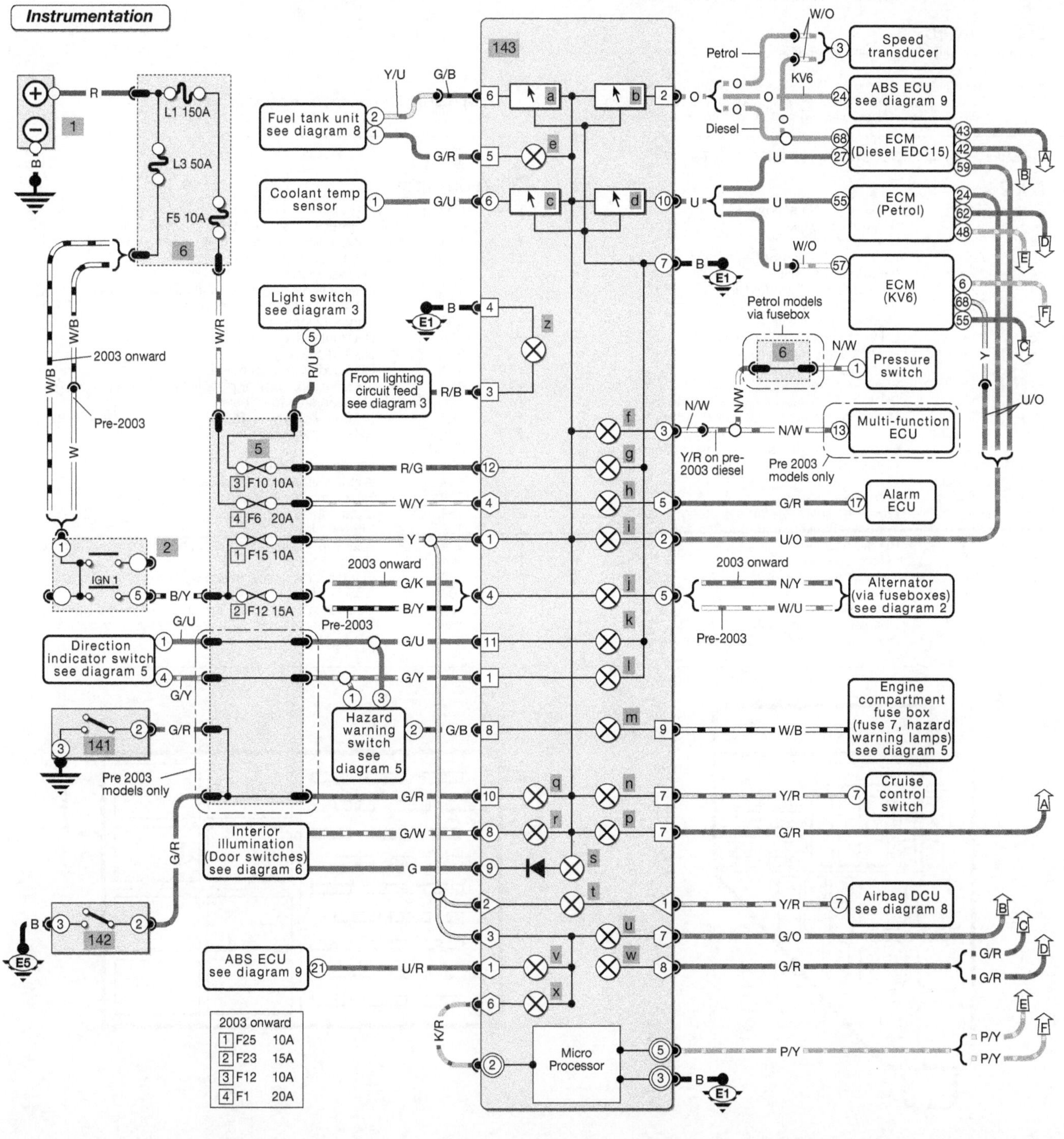

Engine compartment fuse box data ⑥

Diagram 14

2002

Fuse	Rating	Function
F1	15A	Alternator / generator, speed transducer, gearbox secondary speed sensor
F2	20A	Gearbox interface unit, auto transmission selector, auto transmission ECU, fuel injection, engine control module, ignition coil
F3	15A	Glow plug relay, fuel pump, MAF sensor, ERG solenoid, heated 0₂ sensor (HO2S)
F4	10A	Cooling fan, air conditioning compressor clutch relay
F5	10A	Horn, brake pedal switch, multi-function ECU
F6	15A	Front fog lamps, multi-function ECU
F7	15A	Hazard warning switch, instruments (hazard warning lamp)
F8	15A	Radio / cassette / CD, clock
F9	10A	Air conditioning clutch motor
F10	20A	Collision cutout switch, fuel pump

2003 onward

As above but with the following amendments:

Fuse	Rating	Function
F1	15A	Cam shaft position sensor, purge control valve, ECM, HO2S, clutch pedal position sensor, butterfly valve, balance valve
F7	30A	Hazard warning switch, instruments (hazard warning lamp)

Passenger compartment fuse box data ⑤

2002

Fuse	Rating	Function
F1	30A	Sunroof close relay
F2	20A	Heated seats
F3	7.5A	Interior lights and boot light, diagnostic socket
F4	20A	RH rear window lift
F5	20A	RH front (driver) window lift
F6	20A	Alarm ECU, anti-theft LED
F7	20A	LH rear window lift
F8	20A	LH front (passenger) window lift
F9	10A	RH headlamp main beam
F10	10A	LH headlamp main beam
F11	15A	Engine control module
F12	15A	ECM, instruments (ignition warning), cruise control
F13	15A	Rear wiper, mirrors, seat heater relays, blower, A/C
F14	Not used	
F15	10A	Headlamp levelling sw, instruments (hazard warning light)
F16	10A	ABS ECU
F17	Not used	
F18	7.5A	Starter relay
F19	10A	Front side lights, tail lamps, interior illumination
F20	7.5A	Window lift relay, sunroof relays, MF ECU
F21	10A	RH dip headlamp
F22	10A	LH dip headlamp
F23	15A	Cigar lighter, clock, radio
F24	Not used	
F25	3A	Airbag DCU
F26	20A	Headlamp power wash
F27	20A	Rear wiper relay, front & rear wash / wipe

2003 onwards

Fuse	Rating	Function
F1	20A	AlarmECU, anti-theft LED, alarm sounder
F2	20A	RH rear window lift
F3	15A	Engine control module
F4	20A	LH rear window lift
F5	10A	Interior lights and boot light, diagnostic socket
F6	20A	LH front (passenger) window lift
F7	30A	Sunroof close relay
F8	20A	RH front (driver) window lift
F9	20A	Heated seats
F10	10A	RH headlamp main beam
F11	10A	LH tail lamp, number plate lights, RH front side light
F12	10A	LH headlamp main beam
F13	10A	LH front side lights, RH tail lamp, interior illumination
F14	10A	RH dip headlamp
F15	Not used	
F16	10A	LH dip headlamp
F17	10A	Window lift relay, multi-function ECU
F18	20A	Headlamp power wash
F19	15A	Cigar lighter, clock, radio
F20	10A	Starter relay
F21	20A	Rear wiper relay, wash/wipe, headlight levelling motors
F22	Not used	
F23	15A	ECM, instruments (ignition warning), cruise control
F24	10A	ABS ECU
F25	10A	Headlamp levelling sw, instruments (hazard warning light)
F26	15A	Rear wiper, mirrors, seat heater relays, blower, A/C
F27	5A	Airbag DCU

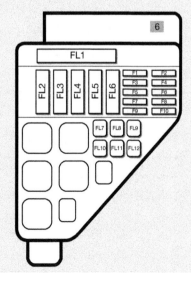

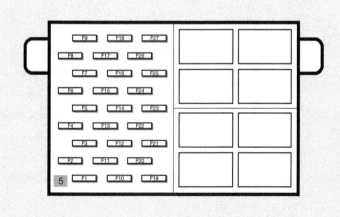

H33431

Dimensions and weights . . . . **REF•1**
Conversion factors . . . . **REF•2**
Buying spare parts . . . . **REF•3**
Vehicle identification . . . . **REF•4**
General repair procedures . . . . **REF•5**
Jacking and vehicle support . . . . **REF•6**
Disconnecting the battery . . . . **REF•7**
Tools and working facilities . . . . **REF•8**
MOT test checks . . . . **REF•10**
Fault finding . . . . **REF•14**
Glossary of technical terms . . . . **REF•22**
Index . . . . **REF•27**

Dimensions and weights

Dimensions

Rover 45

Overall length:
- 4-door . . . . 4517 mm
- 5-door . . . . 4362 mm

Overall width – including mirrors . . . . 1923 mm
Overall height – at unladen weight . . . . 1394 mm
Ground clearance – at unladen weight . . . . 135 mm
Wheelbase . . . . 2620 mm
Turning circle . . . . 10.3 m
Front overhang . . . . 850 mm
Rear overhang:
- 4-door . . . . 1047 mm
- 5-door . . . . 892 mm

MG ZS

Overall length:
- 4-door . . . . 4532 mm
- 5-door . . . . 4377 mm

Overall width – including mirrors . . . . 1923 mm
Overall height – at unladen weight . . . . 1386 mm
Ground clearance – at unladen weight . . . . 127 mm
Wheelbase . . . . 2620 mm
Turning circle . . . . 11.2 m
Front overhang . . . . 865 mm
Rear overhang:
- 4-door . . . . 1047 mm
- 5-door . . . . 892 mm

Weights

Unladen (fuel tank 90% full):
- 1.4 and 1.6 litre petrol models . . . . 1105 to 1205 kg
- 1.8 litre petrol model:
  - Manual transmission . . . . 1125 to 1215 kg
  - Automatic transmission . . . . 1150 to 1240 kg
- 2.0 litre petrol model . . . . 1265 to 1320 kg
- 2.5 litre petrol model . . . . 1235 to 1285 kg
- Diesel model . . . . 1230 to 1325 kg

Maximum gross vehicle weight:
- 1.4, 1.6 and 1.8 litre petrol models . . . . 1640 kg
- 2.0 litre and 2.5 petrol models . . . . 1720 kg
- Diesel model (manual transmission) . . . . 1720 kg

Maximum front axle load:
- 1.4, 1.6 and 1.8 litre petrol models . . . . 845 kg
- 2.0 and 2.5 litre petrol models . . . . 940 kg
- Diesel model . . . . 940 kg

Maximum rear axle load (must not be exceeded) . . . . 840 kg

Towing weights:
- Maximum towing weight – braked trailer* . . . . . . 1000 kg
- Maximum towing weight – unbraked trailer* . . . . 500 kg
- Maximum towing hitch downward load . . . . 70 kg

Maximum roof rack load – including weight of rack . . . . 65 kg

Allows restart on 12 % (1 in 8) gradient with two occupants

Conversion factors

Length (distance)

Inches (in)	x 25.4	= Millimetres (mm)	x 0.0394	= Inches (in)
Feet (ft)	x 0.305	= Metres (m)	x 3.281	= Feet (ft)
Miles	x 1.609	= Kilometres (km)	x 0.621	= Miles

Volume (capacity)

Cubic inches (cu in; in³)	x 16.387	= Cubic centimetres (cc; cm³)	x 0.061	= Cubic inches (cu in; in³)
Imperial pints (Imp pt)	x 0.568	= Litres (l)	x 1.76	= Imperial pints (Imp pt)
Imperial quarts (Imp qt)	x 1.137	= Litres (l)	x 0.88	= Imperial quarts (Imp qt)
Imperial quarts (Imp qt)	x 1.201	= US quarts (US qt)	x 0.833	= Imperial quarts (Imp qt)
US quarts (US qt)	x 0.946	= Litres (l)	x 1.057	= US quarts (US qt)
Imperial gallons (Imp gal)	x 4.546	= Litres (l)	x 0.22	= Imperial gallons (Imp gal)
Imperial gallons (Imp gal)	x 1.201	= US gallons (US gal)	x 0.833	= Imperial gallons (Imp gal)
US gallons (US gal)	x 3.785	= Litres (l)	x 0.264	= US gallons (US gal)

Mass (weight)

Ounces (oz)	x 28.35	= Grams (g)	x 0.035	= Ounces (oz)
Pounds (lb)	x 0.454	= Kilograms (kg)	x 2.205	= Pounds (lb)

Force

Ounces-force (ozf; oz)	x 0.278	= Newtons (N)	x 3.6	= Ounces-force (ozf; oz)
Pounds-force (lbf; lb)	x 4.448	= Newtons (N)	x 0.225	= Pounds-force (lbf; lb)
Newtons (N)	x 0.1	= Kilograms-force (kgf; kg)	x 9.81	= Newtons (N)

Pressure

Pounds-force per square inch (psi; lbf/in²; lb/in²)	x 0.070	= Kilograms-force per square centimetre (kgf/cm²; kg/cm²)	x 14.223	= Pounds-force per square inch (psi; lbf/in²; lb/in²)
Pounds-force per square inch (psi; lbf/in²; lb/in²)	x 0.068	= Atmospheres (atm)	x 14.696	= Pounds-force per square inch (psi; lbf/in²; lb/in²)
Pounds-force per square inch (psi; lbf/in²; lb/in²)	x 0.069	= Bars	x 14.5	= Pounds-force per square inch (psi; lbf/in²; lb/in²)
Pounds-force per square inch (psi; lbf/in²; lb/in²)	x 6.895	= Kilopascals (kPa)	x 0.145	= Pounds-force per square inch (psi; lbf/in²; lb/in²)
Kilopascals (kPa)	x 0.01	= Kilograms-force per square centimetre (kgf/cm²; kg/cm²)	x 98.1	= Kilopascals (kPa)
Millibar (mbar)	x 100	= Pascals (Pa)	x 0.01	= Millibar (mbar)
Millibar (mbar)	x 0.0145	= Pounds-force per square inch (psi; lbf/in²; lb/in²)	x 68.947	= Millibar (mbar)
Millibar (mbar)	x 0.75	= Millimetres of mercury (mmHg)	x 1.333	= Millibar (mbar)
Millibar (mbar)	x 0.401	= Inches of water (inH$_2$O)	x 2.491	= Millibar (mbar)
Millimetres of mercury (mmHg)	x 0.535	= Inches of water (inH$_2$O)	x 1.868	= Millimetres of mercury (mmHg)
Inches of water (inH$_2$O)	x 0.036	= Pounds-force per square inch (psi; lbf/in²; lb/in²)	x 27.68	= Inches of water (inH$_2$O)

Torque (moment of force)

Pounds-force inches (lbf in; lb in)	x 1.152	= Kilograms-force centimetre (kgf cm; kg cm)	x 0.868	= Pounds-force inches (lbf in; lb in)
Pounds-force inches (lbf in; lb in)	x 0.113	= Newton metres (Nm)	x 8.85	= Pounds-force inches (lbf in; lb in)
Pounds-force inches (lbf in; lb in)	x 0.083	= Pounds-force feet (lbf ft; lb ft)	x 12	= Pounds-force inches (lbf in; lb in)
Pounds-force feet (lbf ft; lb ft)	x 0.138	= Kilograms-force metres (kgf m; kg m)	x 7.233	= Pounds-force feet (lbf ft; lb ft)
Pounds-force feet (lbf ft; lb ft)	x 1.356	= Newton metres (Nm)	x 0.738	= Pounds-force feet (lbf ft; lb ft)
Newton metres (Nm)	x 0.102	= Kilograms-force metres (kgf m; kg m)	x 9.804	= Newton metres (Nm)

Power

Horsepower (hp)	x 745.7	= Watts (W)	x 0.0013	= Horsepower (hp)

Velocity (speed)

Miles per hour (miles/hr; mph)	x 1.609	= Kilometres per hour (km/hr; kph)	x 0.621	= Miles per hour (miles/hr; mph)

Fuel consumption*

Miles per gallon, Imperial (mpg)	x 0.354	= Kilometres per litre (km/l)	x 2.825	= Miles per gallon, Imperial (mpg)
Miles per gallon, US (mpg)	x 0.425	= Kilometres per litre (km/l)	x 2.352	= Miles per gallon, US (mpg)

Temperature

Degrees Fahrenheit = (°C x 1.8) + 32   Degrees Celsius (Degrees Centigrade; °C) = (°F - 32) x 0.56

It is common practice to convert from miles per gallon (mpg) to litres/100 kilometres (l/100km), where mpg x l/100 km = 282

Spare parts are available from many sources, including makers appointed garages, accessory shops, and motor factors. To be sure of obtaining the correct parts, it will sometimes be necessary to quote the vehicle identification number. If possible, it can also be useful to take the old parts along for positive identification. Items such as starter motors and alternators may be available under a service exchange scheme – any parts returned should be clean.

Our advice regarding spare parts is as follows.

Officially appointed garages

This is the best source of parts which are peculiar to your car, and which are not otherwise generally available (eg, badges, interior trim, certain body panels, etc). It is also the only place at which you should buy parts if the vehicle is still under warranty.

Accessory shops

These are very good places to buy materials and components needed for the maintenance of your car (oil, air and fuel filters, light bulbs, drivebelts, greases, brake pads, tough-up paint, etc). Components of this nature sold by a reputable shop are of the same standard as those used by the car manufacturer.

Besides components, these shops also sell tools and general accessories, usually have convenient opening hours, charge lower prices, and can often be found close to home. Some accessory shops have parts counters where components needed for almost any repair job can be purchased or ordered.

Motor factors

Good factors will stock all the more important components, which wear out comparatively quickly, and can sometimes supply individual components needed for the overhaul of a larger assembly (e.g. brake seals and hydraulic parts, bearing shells, pistons, valves). They may also handle work such as cylinder block reboring, crankshaft regrinding, etc.

Tyre and exhaust specialists

These outlets may be independent, or members of a local or national chain. They frequently offer competitive prices when compared with a main dealer or local garage, but it will pay to obtain several quotes before making a decision. When researching prices, also ask what extras may be added – for instance fitting a new valve and balancing the wheel are both commonly charged on top of the price of a new tyre.

Other sources

Beware of parts or materials obtained from market stalls, car boot sales or similar outlets. Such items are not invariably sub-standard, but there is little chance of compensation if they do prove unsatisfactory. In the case of safety-critical components such as brake pads, there is the risk not only of financial loss, but also of an accident causing injury or death.

Second-hand components or assemblies obtained from a car breaker or scrapyard can be a good buy in some circumstances, but this sort of purchase is best made by the experienced DIY mechanic.

Modifications are a continuing and unpublicised process in vehicle manufacture, quite apart from major model changes. Spare parts manuals and lists are compiled upon a numerical basis, the individual vehicle identification numbers being essential to correct identification of the component concerned.

When ordering spare parts, always give as much information as possible. Quote the vehicle model; year of manufacture, body and engine numbers as appropriate.

The *vehicle identification plate* is situated on the bottom of the passenger (left-hand) door pillar (see illustration). It gives the VIN (vehicle identification number), vehicle weight information and paint and trim colour codes.

The *vehicle identification number* is repeated in the form of stamped numbers on the centre of the engine compartment bulkhead (see illustration), and also on a plate visible through the lower left-hand corner of the windscreen.

The *body number* is stamped into a plate fixed to the side of the spare wheel well, in the luggage compartment (see illustration).

The *engine number* on 1.4, 1.6 and 1.8 litre petrol engines is stamped on the front face of the cylinder block at the transmission end.

On 2.0 and 2.5 litre V6 petrol engines it is stamped on the left hand end of the cylinder block just above the transmission casing (see illustration). On diesel engines, the engine number is stamped on the upper front face of the cylinder block, at the centre.

The *Manual Transmission number* is stamped on label attached to the upper part of the transmission housing. On 1.4, 1.6 and 1.8 litre petrol engines the label is near the rear of the transmission. On 2.0 and 2.5 litre V6 petrol engines the label is near the front of the transmission. On diesel engines, the label is near the top (centre) of the transmission.

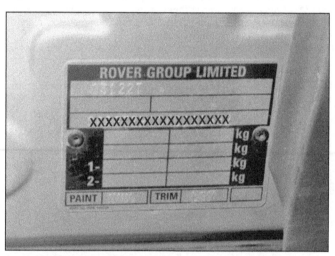

Vehicle identification plate on passenger door pillar

Vehicle identification number on engine compartment bulkhead

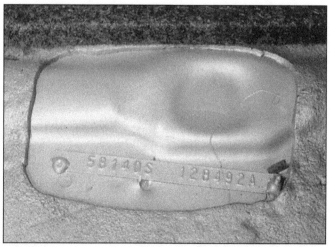

Vehicle body number is stamped onto a plate fixed to the side of the spare wheel well

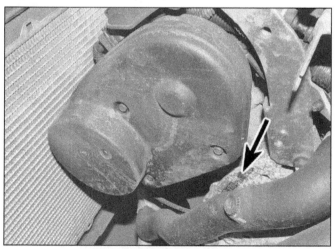

Location of engine number –
V6 petrol engines

Whenever servicing, repair or overhaul work is carried out on the car or its components, observe the following procedures and instructions. This will assist in carrying out the operation efficiently and to a professional standard of workmanship.

Joint mating faces and gaskets

When separating components at their mating faces, never insert screwdrivers or similar implements into the joint between the faces in order to prise them apart. This can cause severe damage which results in oil leaks, coolant leaks, etc upon reassembly. Separation is usually achieved by tapping along the joint with a soft-faced hammer in order to break the seal. However, note that this method may not be suitable where dowels are used for component location.

Where a gasket is used between the mating faces of two components, a new one must be fitted on reassembly; fit it dry unless otherwise stated in the repair procedure. Make sure that the mating faces are clean and dry, with all traces of old gasket removed. When cleaning a joint face, use a tool which is unlikely to score or damage the face, and remove any burrs or nicks with an oilstone or fine file.

Make sure that tapped holes are cleaned with a pipe cleaner, and keep them free of jointing compound, if this is being used, unless specifically instructed otherwise.

Ensure that all orifices, channels or pipes are clear, and blow through them, preferably using compressed air.

Oil seals

Oil seals can be removed by levering them out with a wide flat-bladed screwdriver or similar implement. Alternatively, a number of self-tapping screws may be screwed into the seal, and these used as a purchase for pliers or some similar device in order to pull the seal free.

Whenever an oil seal is removed from its working location, either individually or as part of an assembly, it should be renewed.

The very fine sealing lip of the seal is easily damaged, and will not seal if the surface it contacts is not completely clean and free from scratches, nicks or grooves. If the original sealing surface of the component cannot be restored, and the manufacturer has not made provision for slight relocation of the seal relative to the sealing surface, the component should be renewed.

Protect the lips of the seal from any surface which may damage them in the course of fitting. Use tape or a conical sleeve where possible. Lubricate the seal lips with oil before fitting and, on dual-lipped seals, fill the space between the lips with grease.

Unless otherwise stated, oil seals must be fitted with their sealing lips toward the lubricant to be sealed.

Use a tubular drift or block of wood of the appropriate size to install the seal and, if the seal housing is shouldered, drive the seal down to the shoulder. If the seal housing is unshouldered, the seal should be fitted with its face flush with the housing top face (unless otherwise instructed).

Screw threads and fastenings

Seized nuts, bolts and screws are quite a common occurrence where corrosion has set in, and the use of penetrating oil or releasing fluid will often overcome this problem if the offending item is soaked for a while before attempting to release it. The use of an impact driver may also provide a means of releasing such stubborn fastening devices, when used in conjunction with the appropriate screwdriver bit or socket. If none of these methods works, it may be necessary to resort to the careful application of heat, or the use of a hacksaw or nut splitter device.

Studs are usually removed by locking two nuts together on the threaded part, and then using a spanner on the lower nut to unscrew the stud. Studs or bolts which have broken off below the surface of the component in which they are mounted can sometimes be removed using a stud extractor. Always ensure that a blind tapped hole is completely free from oil, grease, water or other fluid before installing the bolt or stud. Failure to do this could cause the housing to crack due to the hydraulic action of the bolt or stud as it is screwed in.

When tightening a castellated nut to accept a split pin, tighten the nut to the specified torque, where applicable, and then tighten further to the next split pin hole. Never slacken the nut to align the split pin hole, unless stated in the repair procedure.

When checking or retightening a nut or bolt to a specified torque setting, slacken the nut or bolt by a quarter of a turn, and then retighten to the specified setting. However, this should not be attempted where angular tightening has been used.

For some screw fastenings, notably cylinder head bolts or nuts, torque wrench settings are no longer specified for the latter stages of tightening, "angle-tightening" being called up instead. Typically, a fairly low torque wrench setting will be applied to the bolts/nuts in the correct sequence, followed by one or more stages of tightening through specified angles.

Locknuts, locktabs and washers

Any fastening which will rotate against a component or housing during tightening should always have a washer between it and the relevant component or housing.

Spring or split washers should always be renewed when they are used to lock a critical component such as a big-end bearing retaining bolt or nut. Locktabs which are folded over to retain a nut or bolt should always be renewed.

Self-locking nuts can be re-used in non-critical areas, providing resistance can be felt when the locking portion passes over the bolt or stud thread. However, it should be noted that self-locking stiffnuts tend to lose their effectiveness after long periods of use, and should then be renewed as a matter of course.

Split pins must always be replaced with new ones of the correct size for the hole.

When thread-locking compound is found on the threads of a fastener which is to be re-used, it should be cleaned off with a wire brush and solvent, and fresh compound applied on reassembly.

Special tools

Some repair procedures in this manual entail the use of special tools such as a press, two or three-legged pullers, spring compressors, etc. Wherever possible, suitable readily-available alternatives to the manufacturer's special tools are described, and are shown in use. In some instances, where no alternative is possible, it has been necessary to resort to the use of a manufacturer's tool, and this has been done for reasons of safety as well as the efficient completion of the repair operation. Unless you are highly-skilled and have a thorough understanding of the procedures described, never attempt to bypass the use of any special tool when the procedure described specifies its use. Not only is there a very great risk of personal injury, but expensive damage could be caused to the components involved.

Environmental considerations

When disposing of used engine oil, brake fluid, antifreeze, etc, give due consideration to any detrimental environmental effects. Do not, for instance, pour any of the above liquids down drains into the general sewage system, or onto the ground to soak away. Many local council refuse tips provide a facility for waste oil disposal, as do some garages. If none of these facilities are available, consult your local Environmental Health Department, or the National Rivers Authority, for further advice.

With the universal tightening-up of legislation regarding the emission of environmentally-harmful substances from motor vehicles, most vehicles have tamperproof devices fitted to the main adjustment points of the fuel system. These devices are primarily designed to prevent unqualified persons from adjusting the fuel/air mixture, with the chance of a consequent increase in toxic emissions. If such devices are found during servicing or overhaul, they should, wherever possible, be renewed or refitted in accordance with the manufacturer's requirements or current legislation.

Note: It is antisocial and illegal to dump oil down the drain. To find the location of your local oil recycling bank, call this number free.

OIL CARE

FOLLOW THE CODE

OIL BANK LINE
0800 66 33 66
www.oilbankline.org.uk

The jack supplied with the vehicle tool kit should only be used for changing the roadwheels – see *Wheel changing* at the front of this Manual.

When using the jack supplied with the vehicle, position it on firm ground and locate its head in the relevant vehicle jacking point **(see illustration)**.

On models fitted with side skirt/sill extension trim panels; the access panel must first be removed from the trim panel to gain access to jacking points 2, 3, 4 and 5.

When carrying out any other kind of work, raise the vehicle using a hydraulic (or trolley) jack, and always supplement this jack with

axle stands positioned under the indicated points. Always use the recommended jacking and support points, and refer to the following instructions:

If the front of the vehicle is to be raised, firmly apply the handbrake and place the jack head under point 1. Jack the vehicle up and position the axle stands either on the sills at points 2 and 3, or the underbody longitudinal supports at points 7.

To raise the rear of the vehicle, chock the front wheels and place the jack head under point 6, the reinforced location pad immediately in front of the rear towing eye. The axle stands should be placed either on

the sills at points 4 and 5 or the underbody longitudinal supports at points 8.

To raise the side of the vehicle, place the jack head under the sill at point 2 or 3 (as applicable) at the front, then jack up the vehicle and position an axle stand under the longitudinal support at point 7. Remove the jack and position it under point 4 or 5 (as applicable) then jack up the rear of the vehicle and position an axle stand under the longitudinal support at point 8.

Never work under, around or near a raised vehicle unless it is adequately supported in at least two places.

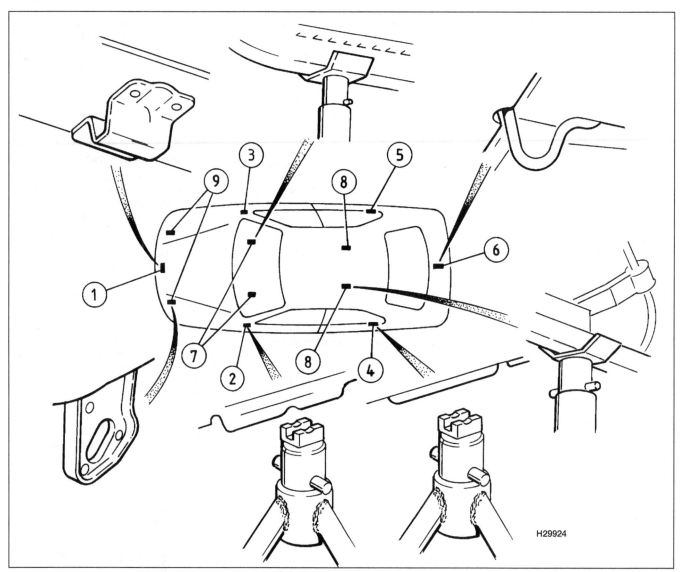

Jacking and support points

1 Front central jacking point
2 Left-hand front jacking/support point
3 Right-hand front jacking/support point
4 Left-hand rear jacking/support point
5 Right-hand rear jacking/support point
6 Rear central jacking and lashing point
7 Front body jacking/support point
8 Rear body jacking/support point
9 Front lashing eyes

Several systems fitted to the car require battery power to be available at all times, either to ensure that their continued operation (such as the clock) or to maintain control unit memories (such as that in the engine management system's control module) which would be wiped if the battery were to be disconnected. Whenever the battery is to be disconnected therefore, first note the following, to ensure that there are no unforeseen consequences of this action:

a) *First, on any vehicle with central locking, it is a wise precaution to remove the ignition key, and to keep it with you, so that it does not get locked in, if the central locking should engage accidentally when the battery is reconnected.*

b) *The car's engine control module (ECM) will lose the information stored in its memory when the battery is disconnected. This includes idling and operating values, and any fault codes detected – in the case of the fault codes, if it is thought likely that the system has developed a fault for which the corresponding code has been logged, the car must be taken to a suitably-equipped garage for the codes to be read, using the special diagnostic equipment necessary for this. Whenever the battery is disconnected, the information relating to idle speed control and other operating values will have to be re-programmed into the unit's memory. The ECM does this by*

itself, but until then, there may be surging, hesitation, erratic idle and a generally inferior level of performance. To allow the ECM to relearn these values, start the engine and let it run as close to idle speed as possible until it reaches its normal operating temperature, then run it for approximately two minutes at 1200 rpm. Next, drive the car as far as necessary – approximately 5 miles of varied driving conditions is usually sufficient – to complete the relearning process.

c) *If the battery is disconnected while the alarm system is armed or activated, the alarm will remain in the same state when the battery is reconnected. The same applies to the engine immobiliser system.*

d) *If a standard audio unit is fitted, and the unit and/or the battery is disconnected, the unit will not function again on reconnection until the correct security code is entered. Details of this procedure, which varies according to the unit and model year, are given in the audio operating guide supplied with the car when new. Ensure you have the correct code before you disconnect the battery. For obvious security reasons, the procedure is not given in this manual. If you do not have the code or details of the correct procedure, but can supply proof of ownership and a legitimate reason for wanting this information, an MG Rover specialist or car audio dealer may be able to help.*

e) *Where electric windows with 'one-touch' operation are fitted, this function may not work correctly until each window has been reset. This is done by fully opening the window with the button pressed, then keeping the button pressed for a few seconds after opening, so the system can 'learn' the fully-open position. Close the window, and again keep the button pressed for a few seconds after closing.*

Devices known as 'memory-savers' (or 'code-savers') can be used to avoid some of the above problems. Precise details vary according to the device used. Typically, it is plugged into the cigarette lighter, and is connected by its own wires to a spare battery; the car's own battery is then disconnected from the electrical system, leaving the 'memory-saver' to pass sufficient current to maintain audio unit security codes and ECU memory values, and also to run permanently-live circuits such as the clock, all the while isolating the battery in the event of a short-circuit occurring while work is carried out.

⚠️ **Warning: Some of these devices allow a considerable amount of current to pass, which can mean that many of the car's systems are still operational when the main battery is disconnected. If a 'memory-saver' is used, ensure that the circuit concerned is actually 'dead' before carrying out any work on it!**

Introduction

A selection of good tools is a fundamental requirement for anyone contemplating the maintenance and repair of a motor vehicle. For the owner who does not possess any, their purchase will prove a considerable expense, offsetting some of the savings made by doing-it-yourself. However, provided that the tools purchased meet the relevant national safety standards and are of good quality, they will last for many years and prove an extremely worthwhile investment.

To help the average owner to decide which tools are needed to carry out the various tasks detailed in this manual, we have compiled three lists of tools under the following headings: *Maintenance and minor repair, Repair and overhaul*, and *Special*. Newcomers to practical mechanics should start off with the *Maintenance and minor repair* tool kit, and confine themselves to the simpler jobs around the vehicle. Then, as confidence and experience grow, more difficult tasks can be undertaken, with extra tools being purchased as, and when, they are needed. In this way, a *Maintenance and minor repair* tool kit can be built up into a *Repair and overhaul* tool kit over a considerable period of time, without any major cash outlays. The experienced do-it-yourselfer will have a tool kit good enough for most repair and overhaul procedures, and will add tools from the *Special* category when it is felt that the expense is justified by the amount of use to which these tools will be put.

Maintenance and minor repair tool kit

The tools given in this list should be considered as a minimum requirement if routine maintenance, servicing and minor repair operations are to be undertaken. We recommend the purchase of combination spanners (ring one end, open-ended the other); although more expensive than open-ended ones, they do give the advantages of both types of spanner.

☐ *Combination spanners:*
Metric - 8 to 19 mm inclusive
☐ *Adjustable spanner - 35 mm jaw (approx.)*
☐ *Spark plug spanner (with rubber insert) - petrol models*
☐ *Spark plug gap adjustment tool - petrol models*
☐ *Set of feeler gauges*
☐ *Brake bleed nipple spanner*
☐ *Screwdrivers:*
Flat blade - 100 mm long x 6 mm dia
Cross blade - 100 mm long x 6 mm dia
Torx - various sizes (not all vehicles)
☐ *Combination pliers*
☐ *Hacksaw (junior)*
☐ *Tyre pump*
☐ *Tyre pressure gauge*
☐ *Oil can*
☐ *Oil filter removal tool*
☐ *Fine emery cloth*
☐ *Wire brush (small)*
☐ *Funnel (medium size)*
☐ *Sump drain plug key (not all vehicles)*

Repair and overhaul tool kit

These tools are virtually essential for anyone undertaking any major repairs to a motor vehicle, and are additional to those given in the *Maintenance and minor repair* list. Included in this list is a comprehensive set of sockets. Although these are expensive, they will be found invaluable as they are so versatile - particularly if various drives are included in the set. We recommend the half-inch square-drive type, as this can be used with most proprietary torque wrenches.

The tools in this list will sometimes need to be supplemented by tools from the *Special* list:

☐ *Sockets (or box spanners) to cover range in previous list (including Torx sockets)*
☐ *Reversible ratchet drive (for use with sockets)*
☐ *Extension piece, 250 mm (for use with sockets)*
☐ *Universal joint (for use with sockets)*
☐ *Flexible handle or sliding T "breaker bar" (for use with sockets)*
☐ *Torque wrench (for use with sockets)*
☐ *Self-locking grips*
☐ *Ball pein hammer*
☐ *Soft-faced mallet (plastic or rubber)*
☐ *Screwdrivers:*
Flat blade - long & sturdy, short (chubby), and narrow (electrician's) types
Cross blade - long & sturdy, and short (chubby) types
☐ *Pliers:*
Long-nosed
Side cutters (electrician's)
Circlip (internal and external)
☐ *Cold chisel - 25 mm*
☐ *Scriber*
☐ *Scraper*
☐ *Centre-punch*
☐ *Pin punch*
☐ *Hacksaw*
☐ *Brake hose clamp*
☐ *Brake/clutch bleeding kit*
☐ *Selection of twist drills*
☐ *Steel rule/straight-edge*
☐ *Allen keys (inc. splined/Torx type)*
☐ *Selection of files*
☐ *Wire brush*
☐ *Axle stands*
☐ *Jack (strong trolley or hydraulic type)*
☐ *Light with extension lead*
☐ *Universal electrical multi-meter*

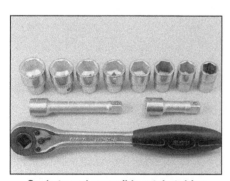

Sockets and reversible ratchet drive

Brake bleeding kit

Torx key, socket and bit

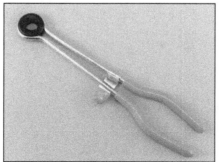

Hose clamp

Angular-tightening gauge

Special tools

The tools in this list are those which are not used regularly, are expensive to buy, or which need to be used in accordance with their manufacturers' instructions. Unless relatively difficult mechanical jobs are undertaken frequently, it will not be economic to buy many of these tools. Where this is the case, you could consider clubbing together with friends (or joining a motorists' club) to make a joint purchase, or borrowing the tools against a deposit from a local garage or tool hire specialist. It is worth noting that many of the larger DIY superstores now carry a large range of special tools for hire at modest rates.

The following list contains only those tools and instruments freely available to the public, and not those special tools produced by the vehicle manufacturer specifically for its dealer network. You will find occasional references to these manufacturers' special tools in the text of this manual. Generally, an alternative method of doing the job without the vehicle manufacturers' special tool is given. However, sometimes there is no alternative to using them. Where this is the case and the relevant tool cannot be bought or borrowed, you will have to entrust the work to a dealer.

- ☐ Angular-tightening gauge
- ☐ Valve spring compressor
- ☐ Valve grinding tool
- ☐ Piston ring compressor
- ☐ Piston ring removal/installation tool
- ☐ Cylinder bore hone
- ☐ Balljoint separator
- ☐ Coil spring compressors (where applicable)
- ☐ Two/three-legged hub and bearing puller
- ☐ Impact screwdriver
- ☐ Micrometer and/or vernier calipers
- ☐ Dial gauge
- ☐ Stroboscopic timing light
- ☐ Dwell angle meter/tachometer
- ☐ Fault code reader
- ☐ Cylinder compression gauge
- ☐ Hand-operated vacuum pump and gauge
- ☐ Clutch plate alignment set
- ☐ Brake shoe steady spring cup removal tool
- ☐ Bush and bearing removal/installation set
- ☐ Stud extractors
- ☐ Tap and die set
- ☐ Lifting tackle
- ☐ Trolley jack

Buying tools

Reputable motor accessory shops and superstores often offer excellent quality tools at discount prices, so it pays to shop around.

Remember, you don't have to buy the most expensive items on the shelf, but it is always advisable to steer clear of the very cheap tools. Beware of 'bargains' offered on market stalls or at car boot sales. There are plenty of good tools around at reasonable prices, but always aim to purchase items which meet the relevant national safety standards. If in doubt, ask the proprietor or manager of the shop for advice before making a purchase.

Care and maintenance of tools

Having purchased a reasonable tool kit, it is necessary to keep the tools in a clean and serviceable condition. After use, always wipe off any dirt, grease and metal particles using a clean, dry cloth, before putting the tools away. Never leave them lying around after they have been used. A simple tool rack on the garage or workshop wall for items such as screwdrivers and pliers is a good idea. Store all normal spanners and sockets in a metal box. Any measuring instruments, gauges, meters, etc, must be carefully stored where they cannot be damaged or become rusty.

Take a little care when tools are used. Hammer heads inevitably become marked, and screwdrivers lose the keen edge on their blades from time to time. A little timely attention with emery cloth or a file will soon restore items like this to a good finish.

Working facilities

Not to be forgotten when discussing tools is the workshop itself. If anything more than routine maintenance is to be carried out, a suitable working area becomes essential.

It is appreciated that many an owner-mechanic is forced by circumstances to remove an engine or similar item without the benefit of a garage or workshop. Having done this, any repairs should always be done under the cover of a roof.

Wherever possible, any dismantling should be done on a clean, flat workbench or table at a suitable working height.

Any workbench needs a vice; one with a jaw opening of 100 mm is suitable for most jobs. As mentioned previously, some clean dry storage space is also required for tools, as well as for any lubricants, cleaning fluids, touch-up paints etc, which become necessary.

Another item which may be required, and which has a much more general usage, is an electric drill with a chuck capacity of at least 8 mm. This, together with a good range of twist drills, is virtually essential for fitting accessories.

Last, but not least, always keep a supply of old newspapers and clean, lint-free rags available, and try to keep any working area as clean as possible.

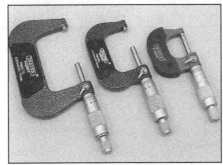

Micrometers

Dial test indicator ("dial gauge")

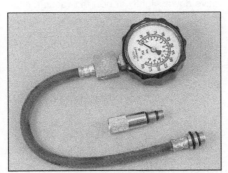

Strap wrench

Compression tester

Fault code reader

This is a guide to getting your vehicle through the MOT test. Obviously it will not be possible to examine the vehicle to the same standard as the professional MOT tester. However, working through the following checks will enable you to identify any problem areas before submitting the vehicle for the test.

It has only been possible to summarise the test requirements here, based on the regulations in force at the time of printing. Test standards are becoming increasingly stringent, although there are some exemptions for older vehicles.

An assistant will be needed to help carry out some of these checks.

The checks have been sub-divided into four categories, as follows:

1 Checks carried out **FROM THE DRIVER'S SEAT**

2 Checks carried out **WITH THE VEHICLE ON THE GROUND**

3 Checks carried out **WITH THE VEHICLE RAISED AND THE WHEELS FREE TO TURN**

4 Checks carried out on **YOUR VEHICLE'S EXHAUST EMISSION SYSTEM**

---

1 Checks carried out **FROM THE DRIVER'S SEAT**

Handbrake

☐ Test the operation of the handbrake. Excessive travel (too many clicks) indicates incorrect brake or cable adjustment.
☐ Check that the handbrake cannot be released by tapping the lever sideways. Check the security of the lever mountings.

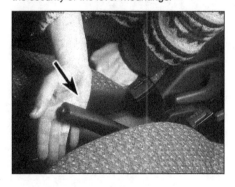

Footbrake

☐ Depress the brake pedal and check that it does not creep down to the floor, indicating a master cylinder fault. Release the pedal, wait a few seconds, then depress it again. If the pedal travels nearly to the floor before firm resistance is felt, brake adjustment or repair is necessary. If the pedal feels spongy, there is air in the hydraulic system which must be removed by bleeding.

☐ Check that the brake pedal is secure and in good condition. Check also for signs of fluid leaks on the pedal, floor or carpets, which would indicate failed seals in the brake master cylinder.
☐ Check the servo unit (when applicable) by operating the brake pedal several times, then keeping the pedal depressed and starting the engine. As the engine starts, the pedal will move down slightly. If not, the vacuum hose or the servo itself may be faulty.

Steering wheel and column

☐ Examine the steering wheel for fractures or looseness of the hub, spokes or rim.
☐ Move the steering wheel from side to side and then up and down. Check that the steering wheel is not loose on the column, indicating wear or a loose retaining nut. Continue moving the steering wheel as before, but also turn it slightly from left to right.
☐ Check that the steering wheel is not loose on the column, and that there is no abnormal

movement of the steering wheel, indicating wear in the column support bearings or couplings.

Windscreen, mirrors and sunvisor

☐ The windscreen must be free of cracks or other significant damage within the driver's field of view. (Small stone chips are acceptable.) Rear view mirrors must be secure, intact, and capable of being adjusted.

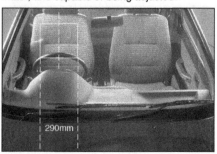

☐ The driver's sunvisor must be capable of being stored in the "up" position.

Seat belts and seats

Note: *The following checks are applicable to all seat belts, front and rear.*

☐ Examine the webbing of all the belts (including rear belts if fitted) for cuts, serious fraying or deterioration. Fasten and unfasten each belt to check the buckles. If applicable, check the retracting mechanism. Check the security of all seat belt mountings accessible from inside the vehicle.

☐ Seat belts with pre-tensioners, once activated, have a "flag" or similar showing on the seat belt stalk. This, in itself, is not a reason for test failure.

☐ The front seats themselves must be securely attached and the backrests must lock in the upright position.

Doors

☐ Both front doors must be able to be opened and closed from outside and inside, and must latch securely when closed.

2 Checks carried out WITH THE VEHICLE ON THE GROUND

Vehicle identification

☐ Number plates must be in good condition, secure and legible, with letters and numbers correctly spaced – spacing at (A) should be at least twice that at (B).

☐ The VIN plate and/or homologation plate must be legible.

Electrical equipment

☐ Switch on the ignition and check the operation of the horn.

☐ Check the windscreen washers and wipers, examining the wiper blades; renew damaged or perished blades. Also check the operation of the stop-lights.

☐ Check the operation of the sidelights and number plate lights. The lenses and reflectors must be secure, clean and undamaged.

☐ Check the operation and alignment of the headlights. The headlight reflectors must not be tarnished and the lenses must be undamaged.

☐ Switch on the ignition and check the operation of the direction indicators (including the instrument panel tell-tale) and the hazard warning lights. Operation of the sidelights and stop-lights must not affect the indicators - if it does, the cause is usually a bad earth at the rear light cluster.

☐ Check the operation of the rear foglight(s), including the warning light on the instrument panel or in the switch.

☐ The ABS warning light must illuminate in accordance with the manufacturers' design. For most vehicles, the ABS warning light should illuminate when the ignition is switched on, and (if the system is operating properly) extinguish after a few seconds. Refer to the owner's handbook.

Footbrake

☐ Examine the master cylinder, brake pipes and servo unit for leaks, loose mountings, corrosion or other damage.

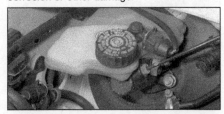

☐ The fluid reservoir must be secure and the fluid level must be between the upper (**A**) and lower (**B**) markings.

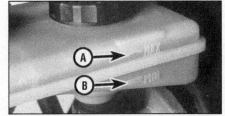

☐ Inspect both front brake flexible hoses for cracks or deterioration of the rubber. Turn the steering from lock to lock, and ensure that the hoses do not contact the wheel, tyre, or any part of the steering or suspension mechanism. With the brake pedal firmly depressed, check the hoses for bulges or leaks under pressure.

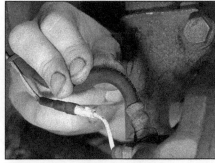

Steering and suspension

☐ Have your assistant turn the steering wheel from side to side slightly, up to the point where the steering gear just begins to transmit this movement to the roadwheels. Check for excessive free play between the steering wheel and the steering gear, indicating wear or insecurity of the steering column joints, the column-to-steering gear coupling, or the steering gear itself.

☐ Have your assistant turn the steering wheel more vigorously in each direction, so that the roadwheels just begin to turn. As this is done, examine all the steering joints, linkages, fittings and attachments. Renew any component that shows signs of wear or damage. On vehicles with power steering, check the security and condition of the steering pump, drivebelt and hoses.

☐ Check that the vehicle is standing level, and at approximately the correct ride height.

Shock absorbers

☐ Depress each corner of the vehicle in turn, then release it. The vehicle should rise and then settle in its normal position. If the vehicle continues to rise and fall, the shock absorber is defective. A shock absorber which has seized will also cause the vehicle to fail.

Exhaust system

☐ Start the engine. With your assistant holding a rag over the tailpipe, check the entire system for leaks. Repair or renew leaking sections.

3 Checks carried out
WITH THE VEHICLE RAISED AND THE WHEELS FREE TO TURN

Jack up the front and rear of the vehicle, and securely support it on axle stands. Position the stands clear of the suspension assemblies. Ensure that the wheels are clear of the ground and that the steering can be turned from lock to lock.

Steering mechanism

☐ Have your assistant turn the steering from lock to lock. Check that the steering turns smoothly, and that no part of the steering mechanism, including a wheel or tyre, fouls any brake hose or pipe or any part of the body structure.
☐ Examine the steering rack rubber gaiters for damage or insecurity of the retaining clips. If power steering is fitted, check for signs of damage or leakage of the fluid hoses, pipes or connections. Also check for excessive stiffness or binding of the steering, a missing split pin or locking device, or severe corrosion of the body structure within 30 cm of any steering component attachment point.

Front and rear suspension and wheel bearings

☐ Starting at the front right-hand side, grasp the roadwheel at the 3 o'clock and 9 o'clock positions and rock gently but firmly. Check for free play or insecurity at the wheel bearings, suspension balljoints, or suspension mountings, pivots and attachments.
☐ Now grasp the wheel at the 12 o'clock and 6 o'clock positions and repeat the previous inspection. Spin the wheel, and check for roughness or tightness of the front wheel bearing.

☐ If excess free play is suspected at a component pivot point, this can be confirmed by using a large screwdriver or similar tool and levering between the mounting and the component attachment. This will confirm whether the wear is in the pivot bush, its retaining bolt, or in the mounting itself (the bolt holes can often become elongated).

☐ Carry out all the above checks at the other front wheel, and then at both rear wheels.

Springs and shock absorbers

☐ Examine the suspension struts (when applicable) for serious fluid leakage, corrosion, or damage to the casing. Also check the security of the mounting points.
☐ If coil springs are fitted, check that the spring ends locate in their seats, and that the spring is not corroded, cracked or broken.
☐ If leaf springs are fitted, check that all leaves are intact, that the axle is securely attached to each spring, and that there is no deterioration of the spring eye mountings, bushes, and shackles.

☐ The same general checks apply to vehicles fitted with other suspension types, such as torsion bars, hydraulic displacer units, etc. Ensure that all mountings and attachments are secure, that there are no signs of excessive wear, corrosion or damage, and (on hydraulic types) that there are no fluid leaks or damaged pipes.
☐ Inspect the shock absorbers for signs of serious fluid leakage. Check for wear of the mounting bushes or attachments, or damage to the body of the unit.

Driveshafts (fwd vehicles only)

☐ Rotate each front wheel in turn and inspect the constant velocity joint gaiters for splits or damage. Also check that each driveshaft is straight and undamaged.

Braking system

☐ If possible without dismantling, check brake pad wear and disc condition. Ensure that the friction lining material has not worn excessively, (A) and that the discs are not fractured, pitted, scored or badly worn (B).

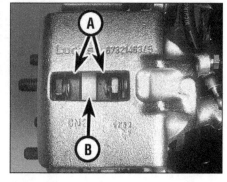

☐ Examine all the rigid brake pipes underneath the vehicle, and the flexible hose(s) at the rear. Look for corrosion, chafing or insecurity of the pipes, and for signs of bulging under pressure, chafing, splits or deterioration of the flexible hoses.
☐ Look for signs of fluid leaks at the brake calipers or on the brake backplates. Repair or renew leaking components.
☐ Slowly spin each wheel, while your assistant depresses and releases the footbrake. Ensure that each brake is operating and does not bind when the pedal is released.

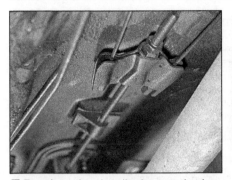

CO emissions (mixture)

☐ The MOT tester has access to the CO limits for all vehicles. The CO level is measured at idle speed, and at 'fast idle' (2500 to 3000 rpm). The following limits are given as a general guide:

At idle speed – Less than 0.5% CO
At 'fast idle' – Less than 0.3% CO
Lambda reading – 0.97 to 1.03

☐ If the CO level is too high, this may point to poor maintenance, a fuel injection system problem, faulty lambda (oxygen) sensor or catalytic converter. Try an injector cleaning treatment, and check the vehicle's ECU for fault codes.

HC emissions

☐ The MOT tester has access to HC limits for all vehicles. The HC level is measured at 'fast idle' (2500 to 3000 rpm). The following limits are given as a general guide:

At 'fast idle' – Less then 200 ppm

☐ Excessive HC emissions are typically caused by oil being burnt (worn engine), or by a blocked crankcase ventilation system ('breather'). If the engine oil is old and thin, an oil change may help. If the engine is running badly, check the vehicle's ECU for fault codes.

Diesel models

☐ The only emission test for diesel engines is measuring exhaust smoke density, using a calibrated smoke meter. The test involves accelerating the engine at least 3 times to its maximum unloaded speed.

Note: *On engines with a timing belt, it is VITAL that the belt is in good condition before the test is carried out.*

☐ With the engine warmed up, it is first purged by running at around 2500 rpm for 20 seconds. A governor check is then carried out, by slowly accelerating the engine to its maximum speed. After this, the smoke meter is connected, and the engine is accelerated quickly to maximum speed three times. If the smoke density is less than the limits given below, the vehicle will pass:

Non-turbo vehicles: 2.5m-1
Turbocharged vehicles: 3.0m-1

☐ If excess smoke is produced, try fitting a new air cleaner element, or using an injector cleaning treatment. If the engine is running badly, where applicable, check the vehicle's ECU for fault codes. Also check the vehicle's EGR system, where applicable. At high mileages, the injectors may require professional attention.

☐ Examine the handbrake mechanism, checking for frayed or broken cables, excessive corrosion, or wear or insecurity of the linkage. Check that the mechanism works on each relevant wheel, and releases fully, without binding.

☐ It is not possible to test brake efficiency without special equipment, but a road test can be carried out later to check that the vehicle pulls up in a straight line.

Fuel and exhaust systems

☐ Inspect the fuel tank (including the filler cap), fuel pipes, hoses and unions. All components must be secure and free from leaks.

☐ Examine the exhaust system over its entire length, checking for any damaged, broken or missing mountings, security of the retaining clamps and rust or corrosion.

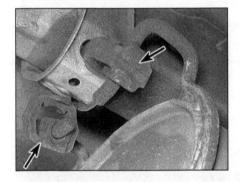

Wheels and tyres

☐ Examine the sidewalls and tread area of each tyre in turn. Check for cuts, tears, lumps, bulges, separation of the tread, and exposure of the ply or cord due to wear or damage. Check that the tyre bead is correctly seated on the wheel rim, that the valve is sound and properly seated, and that the wheel is not distorted or damaged.

☐ Check that the tyres are of the correct size for the vehicle, that they are of the same size

and type on each axle, and that the pressures are correct.

☐ Check the tyre tread depth. The legal minimum at the time of writing is 1.6 mm over at least three-quarters of the tread width. Abnormal tread wear may indicate incorrect front wheel alignment.

Body corrosion

☐ Check the condition of the entire vehicle structure for signs of corrosion in load-bearing areas. (These include chassis box sections, side sills, cross-members, pillars, and all suspension, steering, braking system and seat belt mountings and anchorages.) Any corrosion which has seriously reduced the thickness of a load-bearing area is likely to cause the vehicle to fail. In this case professional repairs are likely to be needed.

☐ Damage or corrosion which causes sharp or otherwise dangerous edges to be exposed will also cause the vehicle to fail.

---

4 Checks carried out on **YOUR VEHICLE'S EXHAUST EMISSION SYSTEM**

Petrol models

☐ The engine should be warmed up, and running well (ignition system in good order, air filter element clean, etc).

☐ Before testing, run the engine at around 2500 rpm for 20 seconds. Let the engine drop to idle, and watch for smoke from the exhaust. If the idle speed is too high, or if dense blue or black smoke emerges for more than 5 seconds, the vehicle will fail. Typically, blue smoke signifies oil burning (engine wear); black smoke means unburnt fuel (dirty air cleaner element, or other fuel system fault).

☐ An exhaust gas analyser for measuring carbon monoxide (CO) and hydrocarbons (HC) is now needed. If one cannot be hired or borrowed, have a local garage perform the check.

Engine

- ☐ Engine fails to rotate when attempting to start
- ☐ Engine rotates, but will not start
- ☐ Engine difficult to start when cold
- ☐ Engine difficult to start when hot
- ☐ Starter motor noisy or excessively-rough in engagement
- ☐ Engine starts, but stops immediately
- ☐ Engine idles erratically
- ☐ Engine misfires at idle speed
- ☐ Engine misfires throughout the driving speed range
- ☐ Engine hesitates on acceleration
- ☐ Engine stalls
- ☐ Engine lacks power
- ☐ Engine backfires
- ☐ Oil pressure warning light illuminated with engine running
- ☐ Engine runs-on after switching off
- ☐ Engine noises

Cooling system

- ☐ Overheating
- ☐ Overcooling
- ☐ Internal coolant leakage
- ☐ External coolant leakage
- ☐ Corrosion

Fuel and exhaust systems

- ☐ Excessive fuel consumption
- ☐ Fuel leakage and/or fuel odour
- ☐ Excessive noise or fumes from the exhaust system

Clutch

- ☐ Pedal travels to floor – no pressure or very little resistance
- ☐ Clutch fails to disengage (unable to select gears)
- ☐ Clutch slips (engine speed increases, with no increase in vehicle speed)
- ☐ Judder as clutch is engaged
- ☐ Noise when depressing or releasing clutch pedal

Manual transmission

- ☐ Noisy in neutral with engine running
- ☐ Noisy in one particular gear
- ☐ Difficulty engaging gears
- ☐ Jumps out of gear
- ☐ Vibration
- ☐ Lubricant leaks

Automatic transmission

- ☐ Fluid leakage
- ☐ Transmission fluid brown, or has burned smell
- ☐ Engine will not start in any gear, or starts in gears other than Park or Neutral
- ☐ General gear selection problems
- ☐ Transmission will not down shift (kickdown) with accelerator pedal fully depressed
- ☐ Transmission slips, shifts roughly, is noisy, or has no drive in forward or reverse gears

Driveshafts

- ☐ Vibration when accelerating or decelerating
- ☐ Clicking or knocking noise on turns (at slow speed on full-lock)

Braking system

- ☐ Vehicle pulls to one side under braking
- ☐ Noise (grinding or high-pitched squeal) when brakes applied
- ☐ Excessive brake pedal travel
- ☐ Brake pedal feels spongy when depressed
- ☐ Excessive brake pedal effort required to stop vehicle
- ☐ Judder felt through brake pedal or steering wheel when braking
- ☐ Pedal pulsates when braking hard
- ☐ Brakes binding
- ☐ Rear wheels locking under normal braking

Steering and suspension

- ☐ Vehicle pulls to one side
- ☐ Wheel wobble and vibration
- ☐ Excessive pitching and/or rolling around corners, or during braking
- ☐ Wandering or general instability
- ☐ Excessively-stiff steering
- ☐ Excessive play in steering
- ☐ Lack of power assistance
- ☐ Tyre wear excessive

Electrical system

- ☐ Battery will not hold a charge for more than a few days
- ☐ Ignition/no-charge warning light remains illuminated with engine running
- ☐ Ignition/no-charge warning light fails to come on
- ☐ Lights inoperative
- ☐ Instrument readings inaccurate or erratic
- ☐ Horn inoperative, or unsatisfactory in operation
- ☐ Windscreen/tailgate wipers inoperative, or unsatisfactory in operation
- ☐ Windscreen/tailgate washers inoperative, or unsatisfactory in operation
- ☐ Electric windows inoperative, or unsatisfactory in operation
- ☐ Central locking system inoperative, or unsatisfactory in operation

Introduction

The vehicle owner who does his or her own maintenance according to the recommended service schedules should not have to use this section of the manual very often. Modern component reliability is such that, provided those items subject to wear or deterioration are inspected or renewed at the specified intervals, sudden failure is comparatively rare. Faults do not usually just happen as a result of sudden failure, but develop over a period of time. Major mechanical failures in particular are usually preceded by characteristic symptoms over hundreds or even thousands of miles. Those components which do occasionally fail without warning are often small and easily carried in the vehicle.

With any fault-finding, the first step is to decide where to begin investigations. This may be obvious, but some detective work may be necessary. The owner who makes half a dozen haphazard adjustments or replacements may be successful in curing a fault (or its symptoms), but will be none the wiser if the fault recurs, and ultimately may have spent more time and money than was necessary. A calm and logical approach will be found to be more satisfactory in the long run. Always take into account any warning signs that may have been noticed in the period preceding the fault – power loss, high or low gauge readings, unusual smells, etc – and remember – failure of components such as fuses or spark plugs may only be pointers to some underlying fault.

The pages which follow provide an easy-reference guide to the more common problems which may occur during the operation of the vehicle. These problems and their possible causes are grouped under headings denoting various components or systems, such as Engine, Cooling system, etc. The general Chapter which deals with the problem is also shown in brackets; refer to the relevant part of that Chapter for system-specific information. Whatever the fault, certain basic principles apply. These are as follows:

Verify the fault. This is simply a matter of being sure that you know what the symptoms are before starting work. This is particularly important if you are investigating a fault for someone else, who may not have described it very accurately.

Don't overlook the obvious. For example, if the vehicle won't start, is there fuel in the tank? (Don't take anyone else's word on this particular point, and don't trust the fuel gauge either!) If an electrical fault is indicated, look for loose or broken wires before digging out the test gear.

Cure the disease, not the symptom. Substituting a flat battery with a fully charged one will get you off the hard shoulder, but if the underlying cause is not attended to, the new battery will go the same way. Similarly, changing oil-fouled spark plugs for a new set will get you moving again, but remember that the reason for the fouling (if it wasn't simply an incorrect grade of plug) will have to be established and corrected.

Don't take anything for granted. Particularly, don't forget that a 'new' component may itself be defective (especially if it's been rattling around in the boot for months), and don't leave components out of a fault diagnosis sequence just because they are new or recently fitted. When you do finally diagnose a difficult fault, you'll probably realise that all the evidence was there from the start.

Engine

Engine fails to rotate when attempting to start

- [ ] Battery terminal connections loose or corroded (see *Weekly checks*).
- [ ] Battery discharged or faulty (Chapter 5A).
- [ ] Broken, loose or disconnected wiring in the starting circuit (Chapter 5A).
- [ ] Defective starter solenoid or switch (Chapter 5A).
- [ ] Defective starter motor (Chapter 5A).
- [ ] Starter pinion or flywheel ring gear teeth loose or broken (Chapters 2 and 5A).
- [ ] Engine earth strap broken or disconnected (Chapter 5A).

Engine rotates, but will not start

- [ ] Fuel tank empty.
- [ ] Battery discharged (engine rotates slowly) (Chapter 5A).
- [ ] Battery terminal connections loose or corroded (see *Weekly checks*).
- [ ] Ignition components damp or damaged – petrol models (Chapters 1A and 5B).
- [ ] Broken, loose or disconnected wiring in the ignition circuit – petrol models (Chapters 1A and 5B).
- [ ] Worn, faulty or incorrectly-gapped spark plugs – petrol models (Chapter 1A).
- [ ] Preheating system faulty – diesel models (Chapter 5C).
- [ ] Fuel injection system faulty – petrol models (Chapter 4A).
- [ ] Stop solenoid faulty – diesel models (Chapter 4B).
- [ ] Air in fuel system – diesel models (Chapter 4B).
- [ ] Major mechanical failure (e.g. camshaft drive) (Chapter 2).

Engine difficult to start when cold

- [ ] Battery discharged (Chapter 5A).
- [ ] Battery terminal connections loose or corroded (see *Weekly checks*).
- [ ] Worn, faulty or incorrectly-gapped spark plugs – petrol models (Chapter 1A).
- [ ] Preheating system faulty – diesel models (Chapter 5C).
- [ ] Fuel injection system faulty – petrol models (Chapter 4A).
- [ ] Other ignition system fault – petrol models (Chapters 1A and 5B).
- [ ] Low cylinder compressions (Chapter 2).

Engine difficult to start when hot

- [ ] Air filter element dirty or clogged (Chapter 1).
- [ ] Fuel injection system faulty – petrol models (Chapter 4A).
- [ ] Low cylinder compressions (Chapter 2).

Starter motor noisy or excessively rough in engagement

- [ ] Starter pinion or flywheel ring gear teeth loose or broken (Chapters 2 and 5A).
- [ ] Starter motor mounting bolts loose or missing (Chapter 5A).
- [ ] Starter motor internal components worn or damaged (Chapter 5A).

Engine starts, but stops immediately

- [ ] Loose or faulty electrical connections in the ignition circuit – petrol models (Chapters 1A and 5B).
- [ ] Vacuum leak at the throttle body or inlet manifold – petrol models (Chapter 4A).
- [ ] Blocked injector/fuel injection system fault – petrol models (Chapter 4A).

Engine idles erratically

- [ ] Air filter element clogged (Chapter 1).
- [ ] Vacuum leak at the throttle body, inlet manifold or associated hoses – petrol models (Chapter 4A).
- [ ] Worn, faulty or incorrectly-gapped spark plugs – petrol models (Chapter 1A).
- [ ] Uneven or low cylinder compressions (Chapter 2).
- [ ] Camshaft lobes worn (Chapter 2).
- [ ] Timing belt/chain incorrectly fitted (Chapter 2).
- [ ] Blocked injector/fuel injection system fault – petrol models (Chapter 4A).
- [ ] Faulty injector(s) – diesel models (Chapter 4B).

Engine misfires at idle speed

- [ ] Worn, faulty or incorrectly-gapped spark plugs – petrol models (Chapter 1A).
- [ ] Faulty coil or spark plug HT leads – petrol models (Chapter 1A).
- [ ] Vacuum leak at the throttle body, inlet manifold or associated hoses – petrol models (Chapter 4A).
- [ ] Blocked injector/fuel injection system fault – petrol models (Chapter 4A).
- [ ] Faulty injector(s) – diesel models (Chapter 4B).
- [ ] Uneven or low cylinder compressions (Chapter 2).
- [ ] Disconnected, leaking, or perished crankcase ventilation hoses (Chapter 4C).

Engine misfires throughout the driving speed range

- [ ] Fuel filter choked (Chapter 1).
- [ ] Fuel pump faulty, or delivery pressure low – petrol models (Chapter 4A).
- [ ] Fuel tank vent blocked, or fuel pipes restricted (Chapter 4).
- [ ] Vacuum leak at the throttle body, inlet manifold or associated hoses – petrol models (Chapter 4A).
- [ ] Worn, faulty or incorrectly-gapped spark plugs – petrol models (Chapter 1A).
- [ ] Faulty spark plug HT leads – petrol models (Chapter 1A).
- [ ] Faulty injector(s) – diesel models (Chapter 4B).
- [ ] Faulty ignition coil – petrol models (Chapter 5B).
- [ ] Uneven or low cylinder compressions (Chapter 2).
- [ ] Blocked injector/fuel injection system fault – petrol models (Chapter 4A).

Engine (continued)

Engine hesitates on acceleration

☐ Worn, faulty or incorrectly-gapped spark plugs – petrol models (Chapter 1A).
☐ Vacuum leak at the throttle body, inlet manifold or associated hoses – petrol models (Chapter 4A).
☐ Blocked injector/fuel injection system fault – petrol models (Chapter 4A).
☐ Faulty injector(s) – diesel models (Chapter 4B).

Engine stalls

☐ Vacuum leak at the throttle body, inlet manifold or associated hoses – petrol models (Chapter 4A).
☐ Fuel filter choked (Chapter 1).
☐ Fuel pump faulty, or delivery pressure low – petrol models (Chapter 4A).
☐ Fuel tank vent blocked, or fuel pipes restricted (Chapter 4).
☐ Blocked injector/fuel injection system fault – petrol models (Chapter 4A).
☐ Faulty injector(s) – diesel models (Chapter 4B).

Engine lacks power

☐ Timing belt/chain incorrectly fitted or tensioned (Chapter 2).
☐ Fuel filter choked (Chapter 1).
☐ Fuel pump faulty, or delivery pressure low – petrol models (Chapter 4A).
☐ Uneven or low cylinder compressions (Chapter 2).
☐ Worn, faulty or incorrectly-gapped spark plugs – petrol models (Chapter 1A).
☐ Vacuum leak at the throttle body, inlet manifold or associated hoses – petrol models (Chapter 4A).
☐ Blocked injector/fuel injection system fault – petrol models (Chapter 4A).
☐ Faulty injector(s) – diesel models (Chapter 4B).
☐ Injection pump timing incorrect – diesel models (Chapter 4B).
☐ Air trapped in fuel system – diesel models (Chapter 4B).
☐ Brakes binding (Chapters 1 and 9).
☐ Clutch slipping (Chapter 6).

Engine backfires

☐ Timing belt/chain incorrectly fitted or tensioned (Chapter 2).
☐ Vacuum leak at the throttle body, inlet manifold or associated hoses – petrol models (Chapter 4A).
☐ Blocked injector/fuel injection system fault – petrol models (Chapter 4A).

Oil pressure warning light illuminated with engine running

☐ Low oil level, or incorrect oil grade (see *Weekly checks*).
☐ Faulty oil pressure sensor (Chapter 5A).
☐ Worn engine bearings and/or oil pump (Chapter 2).
☐ High engine operating temperature (Chapter 3).
☐ Oil pressure relief valve defective (Chapter 2).
☐ Oil pick-up strainer clogged (Chapter 2).

Engine runs-on after switching off

☐ Excessive carbon build-up in engine (Chapter 2).
☐ High engine operating temperature (Chapter 3).
☐ Fuel injection system faulty – petrol models (Chapter 4A).
☐ Faulty stop solenoid – diesel models (Chapter 4B).

Engine noises

Pre-ignition (pinking) or knocking during acceleration or under load

☐ Ignition timing incorrect/ignition system fault – petrol models (Chapters 1A and 5B).
☐ Incorrect grade of spark plug – petrol models (Chapter 1A).
☐ Incorrect grade of fuel (Chapter 4).
☐ Vacuum leak at the throttle body, inlet manifold or associated hoses – petrol models (Chapter 4A).
☐ Excessive carbon build-up in engine (Chapter 2).
☐ Blocked injector/injection system fault – petrol models (Chapter 4A).

Whistling or wheezing noises

☐ Leaking inlet manifold or throttle body gasket – petrol models (Chapter 4A).
☐ Leaking exhaust manifold gasket or pipe-to-manifold joint (Chapter 4).
☐ Leaking vacuum hose (Chapters 4, 5 and 9).
☐ Blowing cylinder head gasket (Chapter 2).

Tapping or rattling noises

☐ Worn valve gear or camshaft (Chapter 2).
☐ Ancillary component fault (coolant pump, alternator, etc) (Chapters 3, 5, etc).

Knocking or thumping noises

☐ Worn big-end bearings (regular heavy knocking, perhaps less under load) (Chapter 2).
☐ Worn main bearings (rumbling and knocking, perhaps worsening under load) (Chapter 2).
☐ Piston slap (most noticeable when cold) (Chapter 2).
☐ Ancillary component fault (coolant pump, alternator, etc) (Chapters 3, 5, etc).

Cooling system

Overheating

☐ Insufficient coolant in system (see *Weekly checks*).
☐ Thermostat faulty (Chapter 3).
☐ Radiator core blocked, or grille restricted (Chapter 3).
☐ Electric cooling fan or thermostatic switch faulty (Chapter 3).
☐ Inaccurate temperature gauge sender unit (Chapter 3).
☐ Airlock in cooling system (Chapter 3).
☐ Expansion tank pressure cap faulty (Chapter 3).

Overcooling

☐ Thermostat faulty (Chapter 3).
☐ Inaccurate temperature gauge sender unit (Chapter 3).

Internal coolant leakage

☐ Leaking cylinder head gasket (Chapter 2).
☐ Cracked cylinder head or cylinder block (Chapter 2).

External coolant leakage

☐ Deteriorated or damaged hoses or hose clips (Chapter 1).
☐ Radiator core or heater matrix leaking (Chapter 3).
☐ Pressure cap faulty (Chapter 3).
☐ Coolant pump internal seal leaking (Chapter 3).
☐ Coolant pump-to-block seal leaking (Chapter 3).
☐ Boiling due to overheating (Chapter 3).
☐ Core plug leaking (Chapter 2).

Corrosion

☐ Infrequent draining and flushing (Chapter 1).
☐ Incorrect coolant mixture or inappropriate coolant type (see *Weekly checks*).

Fuel and exhaust systems

Excessive fuel consumption

- [ ] Air filter element dirty or clogged (Chapter 1).
- [ ] Fuel injection system faulty – petrol models (Chapter 4A).
- [ ] Faulty injector(s) – diesel models (Chapter 4B).
- [ ] Ignition timing incorrect/ignition system faulty – petrol models (Chapters 1A and 5B).
- [ ] Tyres under-inflated (see *Weekly checks*).

Fuel leakage and/or fuel odour

- [ ] Damaged or corroded fuel tank, pipes or connections (Chapter 4).

Excessive noise or fumes from the exhaust system

- [ ] Leaking exhaust system or manifold joints (Chapters 1 and 4).
- [ ] Leaking, corroded or damaged silencers or pipe (Chapters 1 and 4).
- [ ] Broken mountings causing body or suspension contact (Chapter 1).

Clutch

Pedal travels to floor – no pressure or very little resistance

- [ ] Broken clutch cable (Chapter 6).
- [ ] Broken clutch release bearing or arm (Chapter 6).
- [ ] Broken diaphragm spring in clutch pressure plate (Chapter 6).

Clutch fails to disengage (unable to select gears)

- [ ] Faulty clutch cable (Chapter 6).
- [ ] Clutch disc sticking on gearbox input shaft splines (Chapter 6).
- [ ] Clutch disc sticking to flywheel or pressure plate (Chapter 6).
- [ ] Faulty pressure plate assembly (Chapter 6).
- [ ] Clutch release mechanism worn or incorrectly assembled (Chapter 6).

Clutch slips (engine speed increases, with no increase in vehicle speed)

- [ ] Worn clutch cable (Chapter 6).
- [ ] Clutch disc linings excessively worn (Chapter 6).
- [ ] Clutch disc linings contaminated with oil or grease (Chapter 6).
- [ ] Faulty pressure plate or weak diaphragm spring (Chapter 6).

Judder as clutch is engaged

- [ ] Clutch disc linings contaminated with oil or grease (Chapter 6).
- [ ] Clutch disc linings excessively worn (Chapter 6).
- [ ] Faulty or distorted pressure plate or diaphragm spring (Chapter 6).
- [ ] Worn or loose engine or gearbox mountings (Chapter 2).
- [ ] Clutch disc hub or gearbox input shaft splines worn (Chapter 6).

Noise when depressing or releasing clutch pedal

- [ ] Worn clutch release bearing (Chapter 6).
- [ ] Worn clutch cable (Chapter 6)
- [ ] Worn or dry clutch pedal pivot (Chapter 6).
- [ ] Faulty pressure plate assembly (Chapter 6).
- [ ] Pressure plate diaphragm spring broken (Chapter 6).
- [ ] Broken clutch friction plate cushioning springs (Chapter 6).

Manual transmission

Noisy in neutral with engine running

- [ ] Input shaft bearings worn (noise apparent with clutch pedal released, but not when depressed) (Chapter 7).*
- [ ] Clutch release bearing worn (noise apparent with clutch pedal depressed, possibly less when released) (Chapter 6).

Noisy in one particular gear

- [ ] Worn, damaged or chipped gear teeth (Chapter 7).*

Difficulty engaging gears

- [ ] Clutch faulty (Chapter 6).
- [ ] Worn or damaged gear linkage (Chapter 7).
- [ ] Worn synchroniser units (Chapter 7).*

Jumps out of gear

- [ ] Worn or damaged gear linkage (Chapter 7).
- [ ] Worn synchroniser units (Chapter 7).*
- [ ] Worn selector forks (Chapter 7).*

Vibration

- [ ] Lack of oil (Chapter 1).
- [ ] Worn bearings (Chapter 7).*

Lubricant leaks

- [ ] Leaking oil seal (Chapter 7).
- [ ] Leaking housing joint (Chapter 7).*
- [ ] Leaking input shaft oil seal (Chapter 7).*

*Although the corrective action necessary to remedy the symptoms described is beyond the scope of the home mechanic, the above information should be helpful in isolating the cause of the condition, so that the owner can communicate clearly with a professional mechanic.

Automatic transmission

Note: *Due to the complexity of the automatic transmission, it is difficult for the home mechanic to properly diagnose and service this unit. For problems other than the following, the vehicle should be taken to a dealer service department or automatic transmission specialist. Do not be too hasty in removing the transmission if a fault is suspected, as most of the testing is carried out with the unit still fitted.*

Fluid leakage

☐ Automatic transmission fluid is usually dark in colour. Fluid leaks should not be confused with engine oil, which can easily be blown onto the transmission by airflow.
☐ To determine the source of a leak, first remove all built-up dirt and grime from the transmission housing and surrounding areas using a degreasing agent, or by steam-cleaning. Drive the vehicle at low speed, so airflow will not blow the leak far from its source. Raise and support the vehicle, and determine where the leak is coming from. The following are common areas of leakage:
a) *Oil pan – where applicable.*
b) *Dipstick tube – where applicable.*
c) *Transmission-to-fluid cooler pipes/unions.*

Transmission fluid brown, or has burned smell

☐ Transmission fluid level low, or fluid in need of renewal.

General gear selection problems

☐ Chapter 7B deals with checking and adjusting the selector cable on automatic transmissions. The following are common problems, which may be caused by a poorly adjusted cable:

a) *Engine starting in gears other than Park or Neutral.*
b) *Indicator panel indicating a gear other than the one actually being used.*
c) *Vehicle moves when in Park or Neutral.*
d) *Poor gearshift quality or erratic gearchanges*
☐ Refer to Chapter 7B for the selector cable adjustment procedure.

Transmission will not downshift (kickdown) with accelerator pedal fully depressed

☐ Low transmission fluid level.
☐ Incorrect selector cable adjustment (Chapter 7B).
☐ Incorrect kickdown cable adjustment (Chapter 7B).
☐ Electronic control system fault (Chapter 7B).

Engine will not start in any gear, or starts in gears other than Park or Neutral

☐ Incorrect selector cable adjustment (Chapter 7B).
☐ Incorrect multi-function switch adjustment (Chapter 7B).

Transmission slips, is noisy, or has no drive in forward or reverse gears

☐ There are many probable causes for the above problems, but the home mechanic should be concerned with only one possibility – fluid level. Before taking the vehicle to a dealer or transmission specialist, check the fluid level and condition of the fluid as described in Chapter 1. Correct the fluid level as necessary, or change the fluid and filter if needed. If the problem persists, professional help will be necessary.

Driveshafts

Vibration when accelerating or decelerating

☐ Worn inner constant velocity joint (Chapter 8).
☐ Bent or distorted driveshaft (Chapter 8).
☐ Worn intermediate bearing (Chapter 8).

Clicking or knocking noise on turns (at slow speed on full-lock)

☐ Worn outer constant velocity joint (Chapter 8).
☐ Lack of constant velocity joint lubricant, possibly due to damaged gaiter (Chapter 8).

Braking system

Note: *Before assuming that a brake problem exists, make sure that the tyres are in good condition and correctly inflated, that the front wheel alignment is correct, and that the vehicle is not loaded with weight in an unequal manner. Apart from checking the condition of all pipe and hose connections, any faults occurring on the anti-lock braking system should be referred to a Renault dealer for diagnosis.*

Vehicle pulls to one side under braking

☐ Worn, defective, damaged or contaminated front or rear brake pads/shoes on one side (Chapters 1 and 9).
☐ Seized or partially-seized front or rear brake caliper/wheel cylinder piston (Chapter 9).
☐ A mixture of brake pad/shoe lining materials fitted between sides (Chapter 9).
☐ Brake caliper or rear brake backplate mounting bolts loose (Chapter 9).
☐ Worn or damaged steering or suspension components (Chapters 1 and 10).

Noise (grinding or high-pitched squeal) when brakes applied

☐ Brake pad/shoe friction lining material worn down to metal backing (Chapters 1 and 9).
☐ Excessive corrosion of brake disc or drum – may be apparent after the vehicle has been standing for some time (Chapters 1 and 9).
☐ Foreign object (stone chipping, etc) trapped between brake disc and shield (Chapters 1 and 9).

Excessive brake pedal travel

☐ Faulty rear drum brake self-adjust mechanism (Chapter 9).
☐ Faulty master cylinder (Chapter 9).
☐ Air in hydraulic system (Chapter 9).
☐ Faulty vacuum servo unit (Chapter 9).
☐ Faulty vacuum pump – diesel models (Chapter 9).

Brake pedal feels spongy when depressed

☐ Air in hydraulic system (Chapter 9).
☐ Deteriorated flexible rubber brake hoses (Chapters 1 and 9).
☐ Master cylinder mountings loose (Chapter 9).
☐ Faulty master cylinder (Chapter 9).

Excessive brake pedal effort required to stop vehicle

☐ Faulty vacuum servo unit (Chapter 9).
☐ Disconnected, damaged or insecure brake servo vacuum hose (Chapters 1 and 9).
☐ Faulty vacuum pump – diesel models (Chapter 9).
☐ Primary or secondary hydraulic circuit failure (Chapter 9).
☐ Seized brake caliper or wheel cylinder piston(s) (Chapter 9).
☐ Brake pads/shoes incorrectly fitted (Chapter 9).
☐ Incorrect grade of brake pads/shoes fitted (Chapter 9).
☐ Brake pads/shoe linings contaminated (Chapter 9).

Judder felt through brake pedal or steering wheel when braking

☐ Excessive run-out or distortion of brake disc(s) or drum(s) (Chapter 9).
☐ Brake pad/shoe linings worn (Chapters 1 and 9).
☐ Brake caliper or rear brake backplate mounting bolts loose (Chapter 9).
☐ Wear in suspension or steering components or mountings (Chapters 1 and 10).

Pedal pulsates when braking hard

☐ Normal feature of ABS – no fault

Brakes binding

☐ Seized brake caliper/wheel cylinder piston(s) (Chapter 9).
☐ Incorrectly-adjusted handbrake mechanism (Chapter 9).
☐ Faulty master cylinder (Chapter 9).

Rear wheels locking under normal braking

☐ Rear brake pad/shoe linings contaminated (Chapters 1 and 9).
☐ Rear brake discs/drums warped (Chapters 1 and 9).

Steering and suspension

Note: *Before diagnosing suspension or steering faults, be sure that the trouble is not due to incorrect tyre pressures, mixtures of tyre types, or binding brakes.*

Vehicle pulls to one side

☐ Defective tyre (see *Weekly checks*).
☐ Excessive wear in suspension or steering components (Chapters 1 and 10).
☐ Incorrect front wheel alignment (Chapter 10).
☐ Accident damage to steering or suspension components (Chapters 1 and 10).

Wheel wobble and vibration

☐ Front roadwheels out of balance (vibration felt mainly through the steering wheel) (Chapter 10).
☐ Rear roadwheels out of balance (vibration felt throughout the vehicle) (Chapter 10).
☐ Roadwheels damaged or distorted (Chapter 10).
☐ Faulty or damaged tyre (see *Weekly checks*).
☐ Worn steering or suspension joints, bushes or components (Chapters 1 and 10).
☐ Wheel bolts loose (Chapter 1 and 10).

Excessive pitching and/or rolling around corners, or during braking

☐ Defective shock absorbers (Chapters 1 and 10).
☐ Broken or weak coil spring and/or suspension component (Chapters 1 and 10).
☐ Worn or damaged anti-roll bar or mountings (Chapter 10).

Wandering or general instability

☐ Incorrect front wheel alignment (Chapter 10).
☐ Worn steering or suspension joints, bushes or components (Chapters 1 and 10).
☐ Roadwheels out of balance (Chapter 10).
☐ Faulty or damaged tyre (see *Weekly checks*).
☐ Wheel bolts loose (Chapter 10).
☐ Defective shock absorbers (Chapters 1 and 10).

Excessively-stiff steering

☐ Seized track rod end balljoint or suspension balljoint (Chapters 1 and 10).
☐ Broken or incorrectly adjusted auxiliary drivebelt (Chapter 1).
☐ Incorrect front wheel alignment (Chapter 10).
☐ Steering gear damaged (Chapter 10).

Excessive play in steering

☐ Worn steering column universal joint(s) (Chapter 10).
☐ Worn steering track rod end balljoints (Chapters 1 and 10).
☐ Worn steering gear (Chapter 10).
☐ Worn steering or suspension joints, bushes or components (Chapters 1 and 10).

Lack of power assistance

☐ Broken or incorrectly-adjusted auxiliary drivebelt (Chapter 1).
☐ Incorrect power steering fluid level (see *Weekly checks*).
☐ Restriction in power steering fluid hoses (Chapter 10).
☐ Faulty power steering pump (Chapter 10).
☐ Faulty steering gear (Chapter 10).

Tyre wear excessive

Tyres worn on inside or outside edges

☐ Tyres under-inflated (wear on both edges) (see *Weekly checks*).
☐ Incorrect camber or castor angles (wear on one edge only) (Chapter 10).
☐ Worn steering or suspension joints, bushes or components (Chapters 1 and 10).
☐ Excessively-hard cornering.
☐ Accident damage.

Tyre treads exhibit feathered edges

☐ Incorrect toe setting (Chapter 10).

Tyres worn in centre of tread

☐ Tyres over-inflated (see *Weekly checks*).

Tyres worn on inside and outside edges

☐ Tyres under-inflated (see *Weekly checks*).
☐ Worn shock absorbers (Chapter 10).

Tyres worn unevenly

☐ Tyres/wheels out of balance (see *Weekly checks*).
☐ Excessive wheel or tyre run-out (Chapter 10).
☐ Worn shock absorbers (Chapters 1 and 10).
☐ Faulty tyre (see *Weekly checks*).

Electrical system

Note: *For problems associated with the starting system, refer to the faults listed under 'Engine' earlier in this Section.*

Battery will not hold a charge more than a few days

☐ Battery defective internally (Chapter 5A).
☐ Battery electrolyte level low – where applicable (see *Weekly checks*).
☐ Battery terminal connections loose or corroded (see *Weekly checks*).
☐ Auxiliary drivebelt worn – or incorrectly adjusted, where applicable (Chapter 1).
☐ Alternator not charging at correct output (Chapter 5A).
☐ Alternator or voltage regulator faulty (Chapter 5A).
☐ Short-circuit causing continual battery drain (Chapters 5 and 12).

Ignition/no-charge warning light remains illuminated with engine running

☐ Auxiliary drivebelt broken, worn, or incorrectly adjusted (Chapter 1).
☐ Internal fault in alternator or voltage regulator (Chapter 5A).
☐ Broken, disconnected, or loose wiring in charging circuit (Chapter 5A).

Ignition/no-charge warning light fails to come on

☐ Warning light bulb blown (Chapter 12).
☐ Broken, disconnected, or loose wiring in warning light circuit (Chapter 12).
☐ Alternator faulty (Chapter 5A).

Electrical system (continued)

Lights inoperative

- [ ] Bulb blown (Chapter 12).
- [ ] Corrosion of bulb or bulb holder contacts (Chapter 12).
- [ ] Blown fuse (Chapter 12).
- [ ] Faulty relay (Chapter 12).
- [ ] Broken, loose, or disconnected wiring (Chapter 12).
- [ ] Faulty switch (Chapter 12).

Instrument readings inaccurate or erratic

Instrument readings increase with engine speed

- [ ] Faulty voltage regulator (Chapter 12).

Fuel or temperature gauges give no reading

- [ ] Faulty gauge sender unit (Chapters 3 and 4).
- [ ] Wiring open-circuit (Chapter 12).
- [ ] Faulty gauge (Chapter 12).

Fuel or temperature gauges give continuous maximum reading

- [ ] Faulty gauge sender unit (Chapters 3 and 4).
- [ ] Wiring short-circuit (Chapter 12).
- [ ] Faulty gauge (Chapter 12).

Horn inoperative, or unsatisfactory in operation

Horn operates all the time

- [ ] Horn contacts permanently bridged or horn push stuck down (Chapter 12).

Horn fails to operate

- [ ] Blown fuse (Chapter 12).
- [ ] Cable or connections loose, broken or disconnected (Chapter 12).
- [ ] Faulty horn (Chapter 12).

Horn emits intermittent or unsatisfactory sound

- [ ] Cable connections loose (Chapter 12).
- [ ] Horn mountings loose (Chapter 12).
- [ ] Faulty horn (Chapter 12).

Windscreen/tailgate wipers inoperative, or unsatisfactory in operation

Wipers fail to operate, or operate very slowly

- [ ] Wiper blades stuck to screen, or linkage seized or binding (see Weekly checks and Chapter 12).
- [ ] Blown fuse (Chapter 12).
- [ ] Cable or connections loose, broken or disconnected (Chapter 12).
- [ ] Faulty relay (Chapter 12).
- [ ] Faulty wiper motor (Chapter 12).

Wiper blades sweep over too large or too small an area of the glass

- [ ] Wiper arms incorrectly positioned on spindles (Chapter 12).
- [ ] Excessive wear of wiper linkage (Chapter 12).
- [ ] Wiper motor or linkage mountings loose or insecure (Chapter 12).

Wiper blades fail to clean the glass effectively

- [ ] Wiper blade rubbers worn or perished (see Weekly checks).
- [ ] Wiper arm tension springs broken, or arm pivots seized (Chapter 12).
- [ ] Insufficient windscreen washer additive to adequately remove road film (see Weekly checks).

Windscreen/tailgate washers inoperative, or unsatisfactory in operation

One or more washer jets inoperative

- [ ] Blocked washer jet (Chapter 12).
- [ ] Disconnected, kinked or restricted fluid hose (Chapter 12).
- [ ] Insufficient fluid in washer reservoir (see Weekly checks).

Washer pump fails to operate

- [ ] Broken or disconnected wiring or connections (Chapter 12).
- [ ] Blown fuse (Chapter 12).
- [ ] Faulty washer switch (Chapter 12).
- [ ] Faulty washer pump (Chapter 12).

Washer pump runs for some time before fluid is emitted from jets

- [ ] Faulty one-way valve in fluid supply hose (Chapter 12).

Electric windows inoperative, or unsatisfactory in operation

Window glass will only move in one direction

- [ ] Faulty switch (Chapter 12).

Window glass slow to move

- [ ] Regulator seized or damaged, or in need of lubrication (Chapter 11).
- [ ] Door internal components or trim fouling regulator (Chapter 11).
- [ ] Faulty motor (Chapter 11).

Window glass fails to move

- [ ] Blown fuse (Chapter 12).
- [ ] Faulty relay (Chapter 12).
- [ ] Broken or disconnected wiring or connections (Chapter 12).
- [ ] Faulty motor (Chapter 12).

Central locking system inoperative, or unsatisfactory in operation

Complete system failure

- [ ] Blown fuse (Chapter 12).
- [ ] Faulty relay (Chapter 12).
- [ ] Broken or disconnected wiring or connections (Chapter 12).
- [ ] Faulty motor (Chapter 11).

Latch locks but will not unlock, or unlocks but will not lock

- [ ] Faulty switch (Chapter 12).
- [ ] Broken or disconnected latch operating rods or levers (Chapter 11).
- [ ] Faulty relay (Chapter 12).
- [ ] Faulty motor (Chapter 11).

One solenoid/motor fails to operate

- [ ] Broken or disconnected wiring or connections (Chapter 12).
- [ ] Faulty motor (Chapter 11).
- [ ] Broken, binding or disconnected lock operating rods or levers (Chapter 11).
- [ ] Fault in door lock (Chapter 11).

A

ABS (Anti-lock brake system) A system, usually electronically controlled, that senses incipient wheel lockup during braking and relieves hydraulic pressure at wheels that are about to skid.

Air bag An inflatable bag hidden in the steering wheel (driver's side) or the dash or glovebox (passenger side). In a head-on collision, the bags inflate, preventing the driver and front passenger from being thrown forward into the steering wheel or windscreen.

Air cleaner A metal or plastic housing, containing a filter element, which removes dust and dirt from the air being drawn into the engine.

Air filter element The actual filter in an air cleaner system, usually manufactured from pleated paper and requiring renewal at regular intervals.

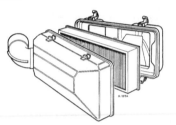

Air filter

Allen key A hexagonal wrench which fits into a recessed hexagonal hole.

Alligator clip A long-nosed spring-loaded metal clip with meshing teeth. Used to make temporary electrical connections.

Alternator A component in the electrical system which converts mechanical energy from a drivebelt into electrical energy to charge the battery and to operate the starting system, ignition system and electrical accessories.

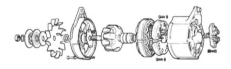

Alternator (exploded view)

Ampere (amp) A unit of measurement for the flow of electric current. One amp is the amount of current produced by one volt acting through a resistance of one ohm.

Anaerobic sealer A substance used to prevent bolts and screws from loosening. Anaerobic means that it does not require oxygen for activation. The Loctite brand is widely used.

Antifreeze A substance (usually ethylene glycol) mixed with water, and added to a vehicle's cooling system, to prevent freezing of the coolant in winter. Antifreeze also contains chemicals to inhibit corrosion and the formation of rust and other deposits that would tend to clog the radiator and coolant passages and reduce cooling efficiency.

Anti-seize compound A coating that reduces the risk of seizing on fasteners that are subjected to high temperatures, such as exhaust manifold bolts and nuts.

Anti-seize compound

Asbestos A natural fibrous mineral with great heat resistance, commonly used in the composition of brake friction materials. Asbestos is a health hazard and the dust created by brake systems should never be inhaled or ingested.

Axle A shaft on which a wheel revolves, or which revolves with a wheel. Also, a solid beam that connects the two wheels at one end of the vehicle. An axle which also transmits power to the wheels is known as a live axle.

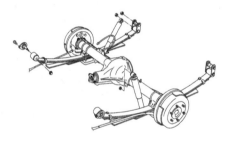

Axle assembly

Axleshaft A single rotating shaft, on either side of the differential, which delivers power from the final drive assembly to the drive wheels. Also called a driveshaft or a halfshaft.

B

Ball bearing An anti-friction bearing consisting of a hardened inner and outer race with hardened steel balls between two races.

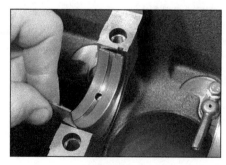

Bearing

Bearing The curved surface on a shaft or in a bore, or the part assembled into either, that permits relative motion between them with minimum wear and friction.

Big-end bearing The bearing in the end of the connecting rod that's attached to the crankshaft.

Bleed nipple A valve on a brake wheel cylinder, caliper or other hydraulic component that is opened to purge the hydraulic system of air. Also called a bleed screw.

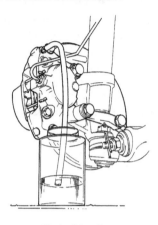

Brake bleeding

Brake bleeding Procedure for removing air from lines of a hydraulic brake system.

Brake disc The component of a disc brake that rotates with the wheels.

Brake drum The component of a drum brake that rotates with the wheels.

Brake linings The friction material which contacts the brake disc or drum to retard the vehicle's speed. The linings are bonded or riveted to the brake pads or shoes.

Brake pads The replaceable friction pads that pinch the brake disc when the brakes are applied. Brake pads consist of a friction material bonded or riveted to a rigid backing plate.

Brake shoe The crescent-shaped carrier to which the brake linings are mounted and which forces the lining against the rotating drum during braking.

Braking systems For more information on braking systems, consult the *Haynes Automotive Brake Manual*.

Breaker bar A long socket wrench handle providing greater leverage.

Bulkhead The insulated partition between the engine and the passenger compartment.

C

Caliper The non-rotating part of a disc-brake assembly that straddles the disc and carries the brake pads. The caliper also contains the hydraulic components that cause the pads to pinch the disc when the brakes are applied. A caliper is also a measuring tool that can be set to measure inside or outside dimensions of an object.

Camshaft A rotating shaft on which a series of cam lobes operate the valve mechanisms. The camshaft may be driven by gears, by sprockets and chain or by sprockets and a belt.

Canister A container in an evaporative emission control system; contains activated charcoal granules to trap vapours from the fuel system.

Canister

Carburettor A device which mixes fuel with air in the proper proportions to provide a desired power output from a spark ignition internal combustion engine.

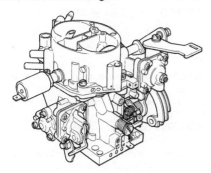

Carburettor

Castellated Resembling the parapets along the top of a castle wall. For example, a castellated balljoint stud nut.

Castellated nut

Castor In wheel alignment, the backward or forward tilt of the steering axis. Castor is positive when the steering axis is inclined rearward at the top.

Catalytic converter A silencer-like device in the exhaust system which converts certain pollutants in the exhaust gases into less harmful substances.

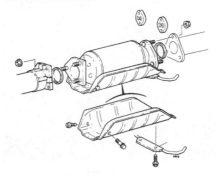

Catalytic converter

Circlip A ring-shaped clip used to prevent endwise movement of cylindrical parts and shafts. An internal circlip is installed in a groove in a housing; an external circlip fits into a groove on the outside of a cylindrical piece such as a shaft.

Clearance The amount of space between two parts. For example, between a piston and a cylinder, between a bearing and a journal, etc.

Coil spring A spiral of elastic steel found in various sizes throughout a vehicle, for example as a springing medium in the suspension and in the valve train.

Compression Reduction in volume, and increase in pressure and temperature, of a gas, caused by squeezing it into a smaller space.

Compression ratio The relationship between cylinder volume when the piston is at top dead centre and cylinder volume when the piston is at bottom dead centre.

Constant velocity (CV) joint A type of universal joint that cancels out vibrations caused by driving power being transmitted through an angle.

Core plug A disc or cup-shaped metal device inserted in a hole in a casting through which core was removed when the casting was formed. Also known as a freeze plug or expansion plug.

Crankcase The lower part of the engine block in which the crankshaft rotates.

Crankshaft The main rotating member, or shaft, running the length of the crankcase, with offset "throws" to which the connecting rods are attached.

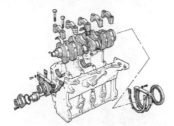

Crankshaft assembly

Crocodile clip See Alligator clip

D

Diagnostic code Code numbers obtained by accessing the diagnostic mode of an engine management computer. This code can be used to determine the area in the system where a malfunction may be located.

Disc brake A brake design incorporating a rotating disc onto which brake pads are squeezed. The resulting friction converts the energy of a moving vehicle into heat.

Double-overhead cam (DOHC) An engine that uses two overhead camshafts, usually one for the intake valves and one for the exhaust valves.

Drivebelt(s) The belt(s) used to drive accessories such as the alternator, water pump, power steering pump, air conditioning compressor, etc. off the crankshaft pulley.

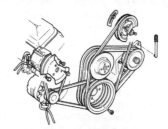

Accessory drivebelts

Driveshaft Any shaft used to transmit motion. Commonly used when referring to the axleshafts on a front wheel drive vehicle.

Driveshaft

Drum brake A type of brake using a drum-shaped metal cylinder attached to the inner surface of the wheel. When the brake pedal is pressed, curved brake shoes with friction linings press against the inside of the drum to slow or stop the vehicle.

Drum brake assembly

E

EGR valve A valve used to introduce exhaust gases into the intake air stream.

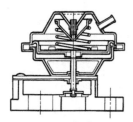

EGR valve

Electronic control unit (ECU) A computer which controls (for instance) ignition and fuel injection systems, or an anti-lock braking system. For more information refer to the *Haynes Automotive Electrical and Electronic Systems Manual.*

Electronic Fuel Injection (EFI) A computer controlled fuel system that distributes fuel through an injector located in each intake port of the engine.

Emergency brake A braking system, independent of the main hydraulic system, that can be used to slow or stop the vehicle if the primary brakes fail, or to hold the vehicle stationary even though the brake pedal isn't depressed. It usually consists of a hand lever that actuates either front or rear brakes mechanically through a series of cables and linkages. Also known as a handbrake or parking brake.

Endfloat The amount of lengthwise movement between two parts. As applied to a crankshaft, the distance that the crankshaft can move forward and back in the cylinder block.

Engine management system (EMS) A computer controlled system which manages the fuel injection and the ignition systems in an integrated fashion.

Exhaust manifold A part with several passages through which exhaust gases leave the engine combustion chambers and enter the exhaust pipe.

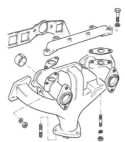

Exhaust manifold

F

Fan clutch A viscous (fluid) drive coupling device which permits variable engine fan speeds in relation to engine speeds.

Feeler blade A thin strip or blade of hardened steel, ground to an exact thickness, used to check or measure clearances between parts.

Feeler blade

Firing order The order in which the engine cylinders fire, or deliver their power strokes, beginning with the number one cylinder.

Flywheel A heavy spinning wheel in which energy is absorbed and stored by means of momentum. On cars, the flywheel is attached to the crankshaft to smooth out firing impulses.

Free play The amount of travel before any action takes place. The "looseness" in a linkage, or an assembly of parts, between the initial application of force and actual movement. For example, the distance the brake pedal moves before the pistons in the master cylinder are actuated.

Fuse An electrical device which protects a circuit against accidental overload. The typical fuse contains a soft piece of metal which is calibrated to melt at a predetermined current flow (expressed as amps) and break the circuit.

Fusible link A circuit protection device consisting of a conductor surrounded by heat-resistant insulation. The conductor is smaller than the wire it protects, so it acts as the weakest link in the circuit. Unlike a blown fuse, a failed fusible link must frequently be cut from the wire for replacement.

G

Gap The distance the spark must travel in jumping from the centre electrode to the side

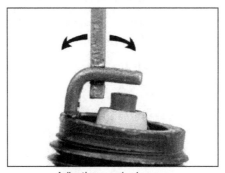

Adjusting spark plug gap

electrode in a spark plug. Also refers to the spacing between the points in a contact breaker assembly in a conventional points-type ignition, or to the distance between the reluctor or rotor and the pickup coil in an electronic ignition.

Gasket Any thin, soft material - usually cork, cardboard, asbestos or soft metal - installed between two metal surfaces to ensure a good seal. For instance, the cylinder head gasket seals the joint between the block and the cylinder head.

Gasket

Gauge An instrument panel display used to monitor engine conditions. A gauge with a movable pointer on a dial or a fixed scale is an analogue gauge. A gauge with a numerical readout is called a digital gauge.

H

Halfshaft A rotating shaft that transmits power from the final drive unit to a drive wheel, usually when referring to a live rear axle.

Harmonic balancer A device designed to reduce torsion or twisting vibration in the crankshaft. May be incorporated in the crankshaft pulley. Also known as a vibration damper.

Hone An abrasive tool for correcting small irregularities or differences in diameter in an engine cylinder, brake cylinder, etc.

Hydraulic tappet A tappet that utilises hydraulic pressure from the engine's lubrication system to maintain zero clearance (constant contact with both camshaft and valve stem). Automatically adjusts to variation in valve stem length. Hydraulic tappets also reduce valve noise.

I

Ignition timing The moment at which the spark plug fires, usually expressed in the number of crankshaft degrees before the piston reaches the top of its stroke.

Inlet manifold A tube or housing with passages through which flows the air-fuel mixture (carburettor vehicles and vehicles with throttle body injection) or air only (port fuel-injected vehicles) to the port openings in the cylinder head.

J

Jump start Starting the engine of a vehicle with a discharged or weak battery by attaching jump leads from the weak battery to a charged or helper battery.

L

Load Sensing Proportioning Valve (LSPV) A brake hydraulic system control valve that works like a proportioning valve, but also takes into consideration the amount of weight carried by the rear axle.

Locknut A nut used to lock an adjustment nut, or other threaded component, in place. For example, a locknut is employed to keep the adjusting nut on the rocker arm in position.

Lockwasher A form of washer designed to prevent an attaching nut from working loose.

M

MacPherson strut A type of front suspension system devised by Earle MacPherson at Ford of England. In its original form, a simple lateral link with the anti-roll bar creates the lower control arm. A long strut - an integral coil spring and shock absorber - is mounted between the body and the steering knuckle. Many modern so-called MacPherson strut systems use a conventional lower A-arm and don't rely on the anti-roll bar for location.

Multimeter An electrical test instrument with the capability to measure voltage, current and resistance.

N

NOx Oxides of Nitrogen. A common toxic pollutant emitted by petrol and diesel engines at higher temperatures.

O

Ohm The unit of electrical resistance. One volt applied to a resistance of one ohm will produce a current of one amp.

Ohmmeter An instrument for measuring electrical resistance.

O-ring A type of sealing ring made of a special rubber-like material; in use, the O-ring is compressed into a groove to provide the sealing action.

O-ring

Overhead cam (ohc) engine An engine with the camshaft(s) located on top of the cylinder head(s).

Overhead valve (ohv) engine An engine with the valves located in the cylinder head, but with the camshaft located in the engine block.

Oxygen sensor A device installed in the engine exhaust manifold, which senses the oxygen content in the exhaust and converts this information into an electric current. Also called a Lambda sensor.

P

Phillips screw A type of screw head having a cross instead of a slot for a corresponding type of screwdriver.

Plastigage A thin strip of plastic thread, available in different sizes, used for measuring clearances. For example, a strip of Plastigage is laid across a bearing journal. The parts are assembled and dismantled; the width of the crushed strip indicates the clearance between journal and bearing.

Plastigage

Propeller shaft The long hollow tube with universal joints at both ends that carries power from the transmission to the differential on front-engined rear wheel drive vehicles.

Proportioning valve A hydraulic control valve which limits the amount of pressure to the rear brakes during panic stops to prevent wheel lock-up.

R

Rack-and-pinion steering A steering system with a pinion gear on the end of the steering shaft that mates with a rack (think of a geared wheel opened up and laid flat). When the steering wheel is turned, the pinion turns, moving the rack to the left or right. This movement is transmitted through the track rods to the steering arms at the wheels.

Radiator A liquid-to-air heat transfer device designed to reduce the temperature of the coolant in an internal combustion engine cooling system.

Refrigerant Any substance used as a heat transfer agent in an air-conditioning system. R-12 has been the principle refrigerant for many years; recently, however, manufacturers have begun using R-134a, a non-CFC substance that is considered less harmful to the ozone in the upper atmosphere.

Rocker arm A lever arm that rocks on a shaft or pivots on a stud. In an overhead valve engine, the rocker arm converts the upward movement of the pushrod into a downward movement to open a valve.

Rotor In a distributor, the rotating device inside the cap that connects the centre electrode and the outer terminals as it turns, distributing the high voltage from the coil secondary winding to the proper spark plug. Also, that part of an alternator which rotates inside the stator. Also, the rotating assembly of a turbocharger, including the compressor wheel, shaft and turbine wheel.

Runout The amount of wobble (in-and-out movement) of a gear or wheel as it's rotated. The amount a shaft rotates "out-of-true." The out-of-round condition of a rotating part.

S

Sealant A liquid or paste used to prevent leakage at a joint. Sometimes used in conjunction with a gasket.

Sealed beam lamp An older headlight design which integrates the reflector, lens and filaments into a hermetically-sealed one-piece unit. When a filament burns out or the lens cracks, the entire unit is simply replaced.

Serpentine drivebelt A single, long, wide accessory drivebelt that's used on some newer vehicles to drive all the accessories, instead of a series of smaller, shorter belts. Serpentine drivebelts are usually tensioned by an automatic tensioner.

Serpentine drivebelt

Shim Thin spacer, commonly used to adjust the clearance or relative positions between two parts. For example, shims inserted into or under bucket tappets control valve clearances. Clearance is adjusted by changing the thickness of the shim.

Slide hammer A special puller that screws into or hooks onto a component such as a shaft or bearing; a heavy sliding handle on the shaft bottoms against the end of the shaft to knock the component free.

Sprocket A tooth or projection on the periphery of a wheel, shaped to engage with a chain or drivebelt. Commonly used to refer to the sprocket wheel itself.

Starter inhibitor switch On vehicles with an automatic transmission, a switch that prevents starting if the vehicle is not in Neutral or Park.

Strut See MacPherson strut.

T

Tappet A cylindrical component which transmits motion from the cam to the valve stem, either directly or via a pushrod and rocker arm. Also called a cam follower.

Thermostat A heat-controlled valve that regulates the flow of coolant between the cylinder block and the radiator, so maintaining optimum engine operating temperature. A thermostat is also used in some air cleaners in which the temperature is regulated.

Thrust bearing The bearing in the clutch assembly that is moved in to the release levers by clutch pedal action to disengage the clutch. Also referred to as a release bearing.

Timing belt A toothed belt which drives the camshaft. Serious engine damage may result if it breaks in service.

Timing chain A chain which drives the camshaft.

Toe-in The amount the front wheels are closer together at the front than at the rear. On rear wheel drive vehicles, a slight amount of toe-in is usually specified to keep the front wheels running parallel on the road by offsetting other forces that tend to spread the wheels apart.

Toe-out The amount the front wheels are closer together at the rear than at the front. On front wheel drive vehicles, a slight amount of toe-out is usually specified.

Tools For full information on choosing and using tools, refer to the *Haynes Automotive Tools Manual*.

Tracer A stripe of a second colour applied to a wire insulator to distinguish that wire from another one with the same colour insulator.

Tune-up A process of accurate and careful adjustments and parts replacement to obtain the best possible engine performance.

Turbocharger A centrifugal device, driven by exhaust gases, that pressurises the intake air. Normally used to increase the power output from a given engine displacement, but can also be used primarily to reduce exhaust emissions (as on VW's "Umwelt" Diesel engine).

U

Universal joint or U-joint A double-pivoted connection for transmitting power from a driving to a driven shaft through an angle. A U-joint consists of two Y-shaped yokes and a cross-shaped member called the spider.

V

Valve A device through which the flow of liquid, gas, vacuum, or loose material in bulk may be started, stopped, or regulated by a movable part that opens, shuts, or partially obstructs one or more ports or passageways. A valve is also the movable part of such a device.

Valve clearance The clearance between the valve tip (the end of the valve stem) and the rocker arm or tappet. The valve clearance is measured when the valve is closed.

Vernier caliper A precision measuring instrument that measures inside and outside dimensions. Not quite as accurate as a micrometer, but more convenient.

Viscosity The thickness of a liquid or its resistance to flow.

Volt A unit for expressing electrical "pressure" in a circuit. One volt that will produce a current of one ampere through a resistance of one ohm.

W

Welding Various processes used to join metal items by heating the areas to be joined to a molten state and fusing them together. For more information refer to the *Haynes Automotive Welding Manual*.

Wiring diagram A drawing portraying the components and wires in a vehicle's electrical system, using standardised symbols. For more information refer to the *Haynes Automotive Electrical and Electronic Systems Manual*.

Note: *References throughout this index are in the form "**Chapter number**" • "**Page number**". So, for example, 2C•15 refers to page 15 of Chapter 2C.*

A

Accelerator cable – 4A•4, 4B•3, 4C•3
  traction control system – 4B•14
Accelerator pedal – 4A•5, 4B•4, 4C•4
Accessory shops – REF•3
Actuator unit cruise control – 12•20
Aerial – 12•19
Air conditioning system – 1A•11, 1B•10,
  3•4, 3•13, 3•14
  compressor drivebelt – 3•13
  refrigerant leaks – 1A•10, 1B•9
Air control valve – 4A•7, 4B•7
Air filter – 1A•15, 1B•14, 4A•3, 4B•3, 4C•3
Air temperature sensor – 4A•8, 4C•7
Airbags – 0•5
  diagnostic and control unit – 12•14
  module – 12•13, 12•14, 12•15
Airflow sensor – 4C•7
Alarm remote keypad battery – 1A•8, 1B•7
Alternator – 5A•4
Antifreeze – 0•13, 0•18, 1A•8, 1A•17, 1B•7,
  1B•14
  leaks – 1B•9
Anti-lock Braking System – 9•2, 9•17
Anti-roll bar – 10•10, 10•14
Armrest – 11•20
Audio unit – 12•18
Automatic transmission – 7B•1 *et seq*, 2D•4,
  2D•6, 2E•3, 2E•4
  automatic transmission fluid – 0•18, 1A•9,
  1B•8, 7B•5
  fault finding – REF•18
Auxiliary drivebelt – 1A•11, 1B•10, 5A•6
  tensioner – 2C•23

B

Battery – 0•5, 0•16, 5A•3, REF•7
  alarm remote keypad – 1A•8, 1B•7
Big-end bearings – 2D•14, 2E•12
Bleeding
  brakes – 9•5
  clutch hydraulic system – 6•6
  fuel system – 4C•5
  power steering system – 10•18
Blower motor – 3•12
Body electrical systems – 12•1 *et seq*
Bodywork and fittings – 11•1 *et seq*
Bodywork corrosion – 1A•8, 1B•6, REF•13
Bonnet – 11•5, 11•6
Boot lid – 11•13, 11•14
  motif – 11•18
Brake fluid – 0•13, 0•18, 1A•15, 1B•14
Brake fluid leaks – 1A•10, 1B•10
Brake pedal – 9•3
  switch – 4C•8
Braking system – 1A•12, 1A•14, 1B•11,
  1B•13, 9•1 *et seq*, REF•10, REF•11, REF•12
  fault finding – REF•19
Bulbs – 12•6, 12•9
Bumpers – 11•4
Buying spare parts – REF•3

C

Cables
  accelerator – 4A•4, 4B•3, 4B•14, 4C•3
  automatic transmission selector – 7B•2

bonnet release – 11•6
boot lid – 11•14
filler flap release – 4B•3, 11•14
handbrake – 9•16
tailgate – 11•14
Calipers – 9•8, 9•14
Camber – 10•19
Camshafts – 2A•10, 2B•16, 2C•12
  cover – 2A•4, 2B•4, 2C•4
  oil seals – 2A•9, 2B•15, 2C•11
  position sensor – 4A•9, 4B•8
  sprockets – 2B•14, 2C•8, 2C•11
Carpets – 11•23
Castor – 10•20
Catalytic converter – 4C•12, 4D•5
Central locking – 11•16
Centre console – 11•23
Charcoal canister – 4D•3
Charging – 5A•3, 5A•4
Cigar lighter – 12•13
Clock – 12•9, 12•13
Clutch – 6•1 *et seq*
  fault finding – REF•17
  switch (cruise control) – 4B•14
Coil spring – 10•7
Coils – 5B•2, 5B•3
Compensator link – 10•12
Compression test – 2A•3, 2B•3, 2C•3
Compressor – 3•14, 3•15
Condenser – 3•15
Connecting rods – 2D•9, 2D•13, 2D•18,
  2E•8, 2E•10, 2E•14
Console – 11•23
Continuity check – 12•3
Conversion factors – REF•2
Coolant – 0•13, 0•18
Coolant – 1A•8, 1A•17, 1B•7, 1B•14
  leaks – 1A•9, 1B•9
Coolant pump – 3•7
  housing (diesel engines) – 3•8
Coolant temperature sensor – 3•10, 4A•8,
  4B•8, 4C•7
Cooling, heating and ventilation systems –
  3•1 *et seq*
  fault finding – REF•16
Courtesy lamps – 12•9
  switches – 12•5
Crankcase – 2D•12, 2E•9
Crankcase emission control – 4D•1, 4D•3,
  4D•4
Crankcase pressure limiting valve – 4D•4
Crankshaft – 2D•11, 2D•14, 2D•16, 2E•8,
  2E•12, 2E•13
  oil seals – 2A•15, 2B•26, 2C•21
  position sensor – 4A•10, 4B•8, 4C•7
  pulley – 2A•5, 2B•6, 2C•5
  sprocket – 2B•15, 2C•8
Cruise control – 4B•13, 12•19
  actuator unit – 12•20
  main switch – 12•20
Cut-off switch – 4A•10, 4B•9
Cylinder block/crankcase – 2D•12, 2E•9
Cylinder head – 2A•11, 2B•18, 2C•14, 2D•7,
  2D•8, 2D•9, 2E•6, 2E•7
Cylinder liners – 2D•12
Cylinder numbering (V6 engine) – 2B•3

D

Depressurising fuel injection system –
  4A•6, 4B•4
Diesel engine in-car repair procedures –
  2C•1 *et seq*
***Diesel engine removal and general
  overhaul procedures*** – 2E•1 *et seq*
Dim-dip headlamp system – 12•12
Dimensions – REF•1
Direction indicator – 12•7, 12•10, 12•11
Disconnecting the battery – REF•7
Discs – 9•9, 9•15
Doors – 11•7, 11•9, 11•11, REF•11
Drivebelt – 1A•11, 1B•10, 5A•6
  air conditioning compressor – 3•13
  power steering – 10•20
  tensioner – 2C•23
Driveplate – 2A•16, 2B•27, 2C•22
Driveshafts – 1A•12, 1B•11, 8•1 *et seq*,
  REF•12
  fault finding – REF•18
  oil seals – 7A•5, 7B•5
Drivetrain – 1A•14, 1B•13
Driving lamp – 12•8, 12•11
Drums – 9•12

E

Electric windows – 11•17
Electrical systems – 0•17, 1A•14, 1B•13,
  REF•11
  fault finding – 12•2, REF•20, REF•21
Electronic Control Unit
  automatic transmission – 7B•5
  cruise control – 4B•14, 12•20
  electric windows – 11•17
Electronic Diesel Control (EDC) system –
  4C•7
Emission control systems – 4D•1 *et seq*,
  REF•13
Engine control module (ECM) – 4A•9, 4B•9,
  4C•8
Engine coolant temperature sensor – 3•10
Engine fault finding – REF•15, REF•16
Engine oil – 0•12, 0•18, 1A•6, 1B•6
  leaks – 1A•10, 1B•9
Engine splash guards – 11•18
Environmental considerations – REF•5
Evaporative emissions (EVAP) control –
  4D•2, 4D•3
Evaporator – 3•16
Exhaust emission control – 4D•4
Earth check – 12•2
Exhaust Gas Recirculation (EGR) – 4D•3,
  4D•4
  EGR cooler – 4D•4
  EGR solenoid valve – 4D•4
  EGR valve – 4D•4
Exhaust manifold – 4A•11, 4B•12
  heat shield – 4A•11
Exhaust system – 1A•12, 1B•10, 4A•12,
  4B•15, 4C•12, REF•12, REF•13
Expansion tank – 3•4
Expansion valve – 3•16

F

Facia panel – 11•25
  switches – 12•4

Note: *References throughout this index are in the form "Chapter number"* • *"Page number". So, for example, 2C•15 refers to page 15 of Chapter 2C.*

Fan – 3•4, 3•9, 3•10
Fault finding – REF•14 et seq
   automatic transmission – REF•18
   braking system – REF•19
   clutch – REF•17
   cooling system – REF•16
   driveshafts – REF•18
   electrical system – 12•2, REF•20, REF•21
   engine – REF•15, REF•16
   fuel and exhaust systems – REF•17
   manual transmission – REF•17
   steering and suspension – REF•20
Filler flap release cable – 4B•3, 11•14
Filler neck – 4A•3, 4B•3
Filter
   air – 1A•15, 1B•14, 4A•3, 4B•3, 4C•3
   fuel – 1A•18, 1B•7
   heater/ventilation air intake – 1A•7, 1B•13, 3•12
   oil – 1A•6, 1B•6
Fluid cooler – 7B•4
Fluid leaks – 1A•11, 1B•10
Fluid seals – 7B•4
Fluids – 0•18
Flywheel – 2A•16, 2B•26, 2C•21
Foglamp – 12•8, 12•11
Fuel and exhaust systems –
   4-cylinder petrol engines – 4A•1 et seq
Fuel and exhaust systems –
   diesel engines – 4C•1 et seq
Fuel and exhaust systems –
   V6 engines – 4B•1 et seq
Fuel filler flap release cable – 4A•3, 11•14
Fuel filler neck – 4C•3
Fuel filter – 1A•18, 1B•7
Fuel gauge sender unit – 4A•6, 4B•5, 4C•5
Fuel inertia cut-off switch – 4A•10, 4B•9
Fuel injection pump – 4C•5
   drivebelt – 2C•9
   drivebelt cover – 2C•9
   drivebelt sprockets and tensioner – 2C•11
Fuel injection system – 4A•5, 4A•6, 4A•7, 4B•5, 4B•6, 4C•4, 4C•5, REF•13
Fuel injector needle lift sensor – 4C•8
Fuel injectors – 4A•7, 4B•6, 4C•6
Fuel leaks – 1A•10, 1B•9
Fuel pressure damper – 4B•7
Fuel pressure regulator – 4A•7
Fuel pump – 4A•6, 4B•5
   temperature sensor – 4C•7
Fuel rail – 4A•7, 4B•6
Fuel tank – 4A•3, 4B•3, 4C•3
Fume or gas intoxication – 0•5
Fuses – 12•3
Fusible links – 12•3

G

Gaiters
   driveshaft – 1A•12, 8•4
   steering gear – 10•16
Gear selector shaft oil seal – 7A•5
Gearchange linkage – 7A•3
General repair procedures – REF•5
Glass – 11•11, 11•18
Glossary of technical terms – REF•22 et seq
Glovebox – 11•25
   illumination switch – 12•5

Glow plugs – 5C•2
Grille – 11•5

H

Handbrake – 1A•13, 1B•12, 9•15, 9•16, REF•10
   warning lamp switch – 12•5
Handles – 11•9
Headlamp – 12•6, 12•7, 12•10, 12•12
   beams alignment – 12•11
Headlining – 11•23
Heated oxygen sensor – 4A•9
Heater – 3•10
   air intake filter – 1A•7, 1B•13, 3•12
   blower motor – 3•12
   controls – 3•12
   matrix – 3•11
   valve – 3•12
High-level stop-lamp – 12•11
Hinges – 1A•14, 1B•12, 11•5
Horn – 12•15
   switch – 12•5
Hoses – 1A•9, 1B•8, 1B•9, 3•4, 9•6
HT coils – 5B•2, 5B•3
Hub – 10•6, 10•11
Hydraulic modulator (ABS) – 9•17
Hydraulic tappets – 2A•10, 2B•16, 2C•12

I

Identifying leaks – 0•10
Idle air control valve – 4A•7, 4B•7
Ignition switch – 5A•9, 12•5
Ignition system – petrol engines – 5B•1 et seq
Indicators – 12•7, 12•10, 12•11
Inertia cut-off switch – 4A•10, 4B•9
Inhibitor switch – 7B•3
Injection pump – 4C•5
   drivebelt – 2C•9
   drivebelt sprockets and tensioner – 2C•11
Injector needle lift sensor – 4C•8
Injectors – 4A•7, 4B•6, 4C•6
Inlet manifold – 4A•10, 4B•10, 4B•12
Input shaft oil seal – 7A•5
Instruments – 1A•14, 1B•13, 12•12, 12•13
   illumination – 12•9
Intake air temperature sensor – 4A•8, 4C•7
Integrated (Multi Function) control unit – 12•12
Intercooler – 4C•9, 4C•10
Interior lamps – 12•9
   switches – 12•5

J

Jacking and vehicle support – REF•6
Jump starting – 0•8

L

Lateral links – 10•12
Leakdown test – 2C•3
Leaks – 0•10
Locks – 1A•14, 1B•12
   bonnet – 11•6
   boot lid – 11•13
   central locking – 11•16
   door – 11•9
   tailgate – 11•15
Lower control arm – 10•9
Lubricants and fluids – 0•18
Luggage compartment lamp – 12•9

M

Main bearings – 2D•14, 2E•12
Manifold absolute pressure sensor – 4A•9, 4B•9, 4C•8
Manifolds – 4A•10, 4B•10, 4C•10
Manual transmission – 2D•4, 2D•6, 2E•3, 2E•4, 7A•1 et seq
   oil – 0•18, 1A•8, 1B•8, 7A•2
Mass airflow sensor – 4C•7
Master cylinder
   brake – 9•6
   clutch – 6•3
Mirrors – 11•17, REF•10
   switch – 12•5
MOT test checks – REF•10 et seq
Mountings – 2A•16, 2B•27, 2C•22
Multi Function control unit – 12•12

N

Number plate – 1A•14, 1B•12
Number plate lamps – 12•8, 12•11

O

Oil
   engine – 0•12, 0•18, 1A•6, 1A•10, 1B•6, leaks – 1B•9
   manual transmission – 0•18, 1A•8, 7A•2
Oil cooler – 2B•25, 2C•23
Oil filter – 1A•6, 1B•6
Oil pressure switch – 2B•25, 5A•10
Oil pump – 2A•14, 2A•15, 2B•22, 2B•24, 2C•18, 2C•19
Oil seals – 7A•5, 7B•5, REF•5
   camshaft – 2A•9, 2B•15, 2C•11
   crankshaft – 2A•15, 2B•26, 2C•21
Open circuit – 12•3
Oxygen sensors – 4A•9, 4B•9

P

Pads – 9•7, 9•13
Pedals
   accelerator – 4A•5, 4B•4, 4C•4
   brake – 9•3
   clutch – 6•3
Petrol engine in-car repair procedures
   4-cylinder – 2A•1 et seq
   V6 – 2B•1 et seq
Petrol engine removal and overhaul
   procedures – 2D•1 et seq
Pipes – 1A•9, 1B•9, 9•6
Piston rings – 2D•15, 2E•13
Pistons – 2D•9, 2D•13, 2D•18, 2E•8, 2E•10, 2E•14
Power steering
   drivebelt – 101A•12, 0•20
   fluid – 0•12, 0•18
   fluid leaks – 1A•10, 1B•9
   oil cooler – 10•18
   pressure switch – 4B•9
   pump – 10•17
Preheating system – diesel engines – 5C•1 et seq
Pressure relief valve – 2A•15, 2B•22
Priming fuel injection system – 4A•6, 4C•5
Proportioning valve – 9•10
Puncture repair – 0•9
Purge valve – 4D•3

Note: *References throughout this index are in the form "Chapter number" • "Page number". So, for example, 2C•15 refers to page 15 of Chapter 2C.*

R

Radiator – 3•4
 cooling fan relay – 3•9, 3•10
 grille – 11•5
Radio aerial – 12•19
Rear light cluster – 12•8, 12•11
Rear window glass – 11•18
Receiver/drier unit – 3•15
Refrigerant leaks – 1A•10, 1B•9
Regulator (window) – 11•11, 11•17
Relays – 12•3
 electric windows – 11•17
 glow plug – 5C•2
 radiator cooling fan – 3•9, 3•10
Release bearing – 6•5
Release fork and lever – 6•5
Reluctor rings (ABS) – 9•18
Remote keypad battery – 1A•8, 1B•7
Reversing light switch – 7A•7
Road test – 1A•14, 1B•13
Roadside repairs – 0•7 *et seq*
Rotary coupler (airbag) – 12•14
Routine maintenance and servicing –
 diesel models – 1B•1 *et seq*
 petrol models – 1A•1 *et seq*
 bodywork and underframe – 11•2
 upholstery and carpets – 11•2

S

Safety first! – 0•5, 0•12, 0•13
Scratches – 11•2
Seat belt – 1A•14, 1B•12, 11•21
 pretensioners – 12•15
Seats – 11•18
 airbag module – 12•15
Secondary accelerator cable (Traction control system) – 4B•14
Secondary throttle actuator (Traction control system) – 4B•15
Secondary throttle position sensor (Traction control system) – 4B•14
Selector (automatic transmission)
 cable – 7B•2
 indicator – 7B•2
 mechanism – 7B•2
Servo unit – 9•4
 vacuum pump – 9•18
Shock absorber – 1A•13, 1B•12, 10•7, REF•11, REF•12
Shoes – 9•10
Side impact sensors – 12•15
Sidelight – 12•7
Slave cylinder clutch – 6•3
Spark plugs – 1A•16
Speakers – 12•19
Speed sensor – 4C•8, 7A•7
Splash guards – 11•18
Springs – 10•7, REF•12
SRS system – 1A•14, 1A•19, 1B•13, 1B•16, 12•13
Starter motor – 5A•8, 5A•9
 inhibitor switch – 7B•3
Starting and charging systems – 5A•1 *et seq*
Start-up after overhaul – 2D•20, 2E•15

Steady bar – 2A•17, 2C•22
Steering – 1A•13, 1A•14, 1B•11, 1B•13, REF•11, REF•12
Steering angles – 10•19
Steering column – 10•15, REF•10
 switches – 12•3
Steering gear – 10•16
Steering lock – 10•16
Steering wheel – 10•14, REF•10
 switches – 12•20
Stop-lamp – 12•11
 switch – 9•17
Struts
 suspension – 10•11
 tailgate support – 11•14, 11•15
Stub axle – 10•11
Sump – 2A•13, 2B•21, 2C•17
Sunroof – 11•18
 switch – 12•6
Supplementary Restraint system (SRS) – 12•13
Suspension and steering – 1A•13, 1A•14, 1B•11, 1B•12, 10•1 *et seq*, REF•11, REF•12
 fault finding – REF•20
Switches – 12•3
 brake pedal – 4C•8
 clutch – 4B•14
 cooling system – 3•9
 cruise control – 4B•14, 12•20
 door lock – 11•11
 ignition – 5A•9
 oil pressure – 2B•25
 oil pressure warning light – 5A•10
 power steering pressure – 4B•9
 reversing light – 7A•7
 starter inhibitor – 7B•3
 stop-lamp – 9•17
 trinary pressure – 3•16
 window – 11•17
Swivel hub – 10•6

T

Tailgate – 11•14, 11•15
 washer jet – 12•17
 washer system – 12•17
 wiper arm – 12•15
 wiper motor – 12•18
Tappets – 2A•10, 2B•16, 2C•12
Technical terms – REF•22 *et seq*
Temperature sensor – 3•10, 4A•8, 4B•8, 4C•7
 probe – 3•16
Tensioner – 2A•6, 2A•8, 2B•15, 2C•9, 2C•11, 2C•23
Thermostat – 3•5
Throttle actuator (Traction control system) – 4B•15
Throttle body – 4A•7, 4B•5
Throttle position sensor – 4A•8, 4B•8, 4C•8
 Traction control system – 4B•14
Timing belt – 2A•6, 2A•8, 2B•8, 2C•6
 covers – 2A•5, 2B•7, 2C•5
 tensioner and sprockets – 2B•14, 2C•8
Timing (ignition) – 5B•2, 5B•3
Timing marks – 2A•4, 2B•4, 2C•4
Tools and working facilities – REF•8 *et seq*

Torque converter fluid seal – 7B•4
Towing – 0•10
Track rod end – 10•19
Traction control system – 4B•14
Trailing arm – 10•13
Transmission mountings – 2A•16, 2B•27, 2C•22
Trim panels – 11•7, 11•18, 11•23
Trinary pressure switch – 3•16
Turbocharger – 4C•8, 4C•9, 4C•10
Tyres – REF•13
 condition and pressure – 0•14
 pressures – 0•18

U

Underbonnet hoses and pipes – 1A•9, 1B•9
Underbonnet check points – 0•11
Upper control arm – 10•9

V

Vacuum actuator (cruise control) – 4B•14
Vacuum control unit cruise control – 12•20
Vacuum hoses – 1A•9, 1B•8
Vacuum pump
 braking system – 9•18
 cruise control – 4B•14
Vacuum servo unit – 9•4
Valve timing marks – 2B•4
Valves – 2D•8, 2D•9, 2E•6, 2E•7
Variable induction system – 4B•13
Vehicle identification – REF•4, REF•11
Vehicle speed sensor – 4C•8, 7A•7
Vehicle support – REF•6
Ventilation air intake filter – 1A•7, 1B•13, 3•12
Voltage checks – 12•2

W

Warning lamps – 12•9
Washer system – 12•17
 fluid – 0•15
 jet – 12•17
 pump – 12•17
 reservoir – 12•17
Weekly checks – 0•11 *et seq*
Weights – REF•1
Wheels – REF•13
 alignment – 10•19
 bearings – 10•6, 10•11, REF•12
 changing – 0•9
Wheel arch liner – 11•18
Wheel cylinders – 9•13
Wheel sensor (ABS) – 9•17, 9•18
Window regulator and glass – 11•11, 11•17, 11•18
Windscreen – 1A•14, 1B•12, 11•18, REF•10
 washer jet – 12•17
 washer reservoir – 12•17
 wiper arm – 12•15
 wiper motor and linkage – 12•16
Wiper arm – 12•15
Wiper blades – 0•15
Wiper motor – 12•16, 12•18
Wiring diagrams – 12•21 *et seq*
Working facilities – REF•9

Left blank for Manual listings

Left blank for Manual listings

Preserving Our Motoring Heritage

<
The Model J Duesenberg
Derham Tourster.
Only eight of these
magnificent cars were
ever built – this is the
only example to be found
outside the United States
of America

Almost every car you've ever loved, loathed or desired is gathered under one roof at the Haynes Motor Museum. Over 300 immaculately presented cars and motorbikes represent every aspect of our motoring heritage, from elegant reminders of bygone days, such as the superb Model J Duesenberg to curiosities like the bug-eyed BMW Isetta. There are also many old friends and flames. Perhaps you remember the 1959 Ford Popular that you did your courting in? The magnificent 'Red Collection' is a spectacle of classic sports cars including AC, Alfa Romeo, Austin Healey, Ferrari, Lamborghini, Maserati, MG, Riley, Porsche and Triumph.

A Perfect Day Out

Each and every vehicle at the Haynes Motor Museum has played its part in the history and culture of Motoring. Today, they make a wonderful spectacle and a great day out for all the family. Bring the kids, bring Mum and Dad, but above all bring your camera to capture those golden memories for ever. You will also find an impressive array of motoring memorabilia, a comfortable 70 seat video cinema and one of the most extensive transport book shops in Britain. The Pit Stop Cafe serves everything from a cup of tea to wholesome, home-made meals or, if you prefer, you can enjoy the large picnic area nestled in the beautiful rural surroundings of Somerset.

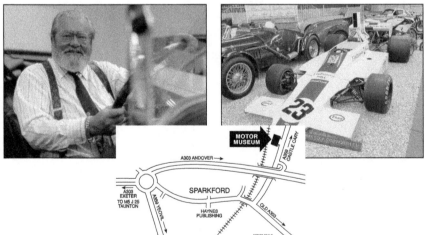

>
John Haynes O.B.E.,
Founder and
Chairman of the
museum at the wheel
of a Haynes Light 12.

<
Graham Hill's Lola
Cosworth Formula 1
car next to a 1934
Riley Sports.

The Museum is situated on the A359 Yeovil to Frome road at Sparkford, just off the A303 in Somerset. It is about 40 miles south of Bristol, and 25 minutes drive from the M5 intersection at Taunton.
Open 9.30am - 5.30pm (10.00am - 4.00pm Winter) 7 days a week, *except Christmas Day, Boxing Day and New Years Day*
Special rates available for schools, coach parties and outings Charitable Trust No. 292048